CO-CBU-928

To Miriam Astour

We who stand on the shoulders of Michael C. Astour
salute you, Miriam.

You are the solid rock of Michael's foundation.
Thank you.

MICHAEL C. ASTOUR

Crossing Boundaries and Linking Horizons

Studies in Honor of Michael C. Astour on His 80th Birthday

edited by

Gordon D. Young

Mark W. Chavalas

Richard E. Averbeck

with the assistance of

Kevin L. Danti

CDL Press

Bethesda, Maryland

Library of Congress Cataloging-in-Publication

Crossing boundaries and linking horizons : studies in honor of Michael C. Astour on his 80th birthday / edited by Gordon D. Young, Mark W. Chavalas, Richard E. Averbeck ; with the assistance of Kevin L. Danti.

p. cm.

Includes bibliographical references.

ISBN 1-883053-32-3

1. Religion 2. Middle-East—Civilization I. Astour, Michael C. II. Young, Gordon Douglas. III. Chavalas, Mark W. (Mark William), 1954– IV. Averbeck, Richard E. V. Danti, Kevin L.

BL27.C76 1997

939′.4—dc21 97-35047

CIP

Preface

The present volume began as papers delivered at special sessions in honor of the life and work of Michael C. Astour at his 80th birthday held during the joint annual meetings of the Middle West Branch of the American Oriental Society, the Midwest Region of the Society of Biblical Literature, and the Midwest members of the American Schools of Oriental Research. To these were added papers by scholars unable to attend the conference, but who wished to participate in this volume in his honor. The sessions were held on February 11 and 12, 1996, in the conference facilities of the First United Methodist Church of La Grange, Illinois. Thus, special thanks go first to the Reverend Robert Atkins, its pastor, who provided the excellent facilities, and to members of his congregation who provided much cordial assistance at the very beginning of this project.

The editors also wish to thank the office personnel of their respective departments for valuable assistance: the Departments of History of Purdue University (Young) and the University of Wisconsin at La Crosse (Chavalas), and the Department of Old Testament and Semitic Languages of Trinity Evangelical Divinity School (Averbeck). The Jewish Studies Program at Purdue University must also be thanked for the various services it rendered and for some expenses it absorbed during the editorial process.

A special thanks also goes to Kevin L. Danti, who while carrying a full load of classes as a Purdue University undergraduate History major, nonetheless devoted many hours and much assistance over the months since the conference.

Table of Contents

Introduction

dub-sar eme-gi$_7$ nu-mu-(un)-zu-a
a-na-àm dub-sar e-ne[1]

A scribe who does not know Sumerian,
what (kind of) a scribe is he?

In such a fashion did Old Babylonian scribes taunt their poorly educated colleagues—and in Sumerian, of course! In this volume we honor a man for whom we may borrow the sentiment and rephrase, "Scholars of Mediterranean, Biblical and Near Eastern Studies who do not know the work of Michael Astour, what kind of scholars are they?" Or, "what does their scholarship amount to?"

Weaving a path across the Aegean, Anatolia and the East Mediterranean, through the Bible Lands and Egypt to the south, across Syria to the lands beyond, north, east and south—with important stops at Ugarit, Ebla and Mari on the way—Michael Astour's work has touched upon nearly all the lands, peoples and cultures we study so diligently in this region. From *Hellenosemitica*, to numerous works charting the geography of Syria and other regions, Michael's work has defined the discipline of Historical Geography.[2] He has incorporated the study of the land—in both its physical and human dimensions—with the study of all the available written sources from the pre-Sargonic Sumerian and Old Kingdom Egyptian, through the Greco-Roman, Byzantine and Arabic geographers—with all the intermediate stops (and languages) in between. To these he has added observations

1 A variant reads: a-na-àm nam-dub-sar-ra-ni, "what does his scribeship (amount to)?"

2 See the list of his publications on pp. xv-xxiii, below.

derived from his travels, and from rational deductions prompted by all of the above. In the process, he has filled numerous blank spots on our regional maps of the Ancient Near East—most notably the scarcely known region of the Ṭūr ᶜAbdīn.[3] To all of the foregoing, he has applied the critical methods and standards of both historian and geographer, as well as those of the philologist. Along the way he has addressed problems of the chronology of the Ancient Near Eastern and Egyptian worlds, and such enigmatic topics as mythology, pastoralists and pastoralism, the ᶜApiru, religious imagery and literary motifs. His learning is simply astonishing, and is not solely concerned with the ancient Near East and East Mediterranean. He is a scholar of Yiddish and of the Bible, as well as a teacher of modern European History. His references to, and analogies from, later European and World History have frequently made difficult or obscure matters much easier for us to understand. In short, as Cyrus Gordon noted in a congratulatory message read to the audience at our conference, Michael Astour is one of the last of the polymaths in our fields. That he has been able to accomplish so much, given the unlikely prospects of his life—both physical and scholarly—from 1939 to the mid-1950's makes his achievements all the more remarkable.

Among my earliest memories of Michael is sitting in his class at Brandeis University as he was discussing the characteristics of epic poetry in its various manifestations when the topic of Minnehaha and Lake Gitcheegumee came up. Fresh from Minnesota, I volunteered a local tradition that Lake Minnetonka (just outside of Minneapolis) and not Lake Superior was Longfellow's Lake Gitcheegumee. Wrong (as would come to be a habit with me!), and for the next several minutes our class was told why it was Lake Superior, and with no details omitted! I learned quickly that here was a scholar to be reckoned with. Where in the world did this man newly arrived from Poland and France, fresh from years of restricted life in the Soviet

---

3 Astour, M. C., "The North Mesopotamian Kingdom of Ilānṣūra," in G. D. Young, ed. *Mari in Retrospect: Fifty Years of Mari and Mari Studies* (Eisenbrauns: Winona Lake, Ind., 1992) 1-33.

Union, who was perfecting his spoken English by watching children's cartoons on Saturday mornings, learn about Minnehaha and Lake Gitcheegumee? Well, we've all been reckoning with Michael for the past 40+ years.

Several in Michael's classes have gone on to become scholars and teachers of our respective fields, and it is clear that many of our accomplishments derive from listening to, reading and absorbing what Michael has written and said—both as regards the factual as well as the methodological fundamentals—and especially the methodological. The same goes for many who were not privileged to sit in those classrooms, but have read and listened to his numerous publications and conference papers. This is especially so by those who regularly attend the joint annual meetings of the Middle West Branch of the American Oriental Society, which he has served as president, and the Midwest Region of the Society of Biblical Literature. So it especially appropriate that our tribute began as a plenary session of the 1996 conference of these organizations. That the several papers read at that conference have been augmented by the numerous papers added by scholars who could not attend, but wished to join in this tribute, speaks volumes about the respect for Michael and his scholarship which is worldwide, and has both multi- and interdisciplinary influences. Some sense of his work—his influences, perspectives, and methodology—can be gained from the transcripts of two sessions of interview transcribed in the pages which follow.

In this volume, we honor Michael Astour by demonstrating the extraordinary dimensions of his influence. Little that is written herein does not touch upon subjects on which he has already spoken or written in a long and productive scholarly life. The various contributions on the pages which follow have been written in the spirit of Michael's method, vision and overarching impact on our several fields Thus, *Crossing Boundaries and Linking Horizons* seems a most fitting characterization of the life and work of Michael C. Astour, and it is a great pleasure to offer this collection of essays to a valued teacher, respected colleague and lifelong friend.

One last point: I should like to acknowledge and commend the work of Mark Chavalas and Richard Averbeck who did so much to arrange the jubilee, in editing this volume, and handling the numerous, often tiresome, problems such an activity entails—and with such grace. Most especially, I want to thank them for allowing me the privilege to preside at the jubilee, and to participate in the editing of this volume.

Michael, we hope that in what follows, we have done you justice.

Gordon D. Young
Department of History
Purdue University

Publications of Michael C. Astour

BOOKS

A History of Jews in Ancient Times. Yiddish Bukh. Warsaw. 1958. 100 pp. Yiddish.

Hellenosemitica: An Ethnic and Cultural Study in West Semitic Impact on Mycenaean Greece. E. J. Brill. Leiden. 1965. xix + 415 pp. 2nd edition with additions and corrections, 1967.

History of the Freeland League and of the Territorialist Idea. Freeland League. Buenos Aires and New York. xx + 932 pp. Yiddish.

Hittite History and Absolute Chronology of the Bronze Age. Studies in Mediterranean Archaeology, Pocketbook 73. Paul Åströms förlag. Partille, Sweden. iv + 152 pp.

BOOK EDITED

Editor. Israel Zinberg, *Di geshikte fun der literatur bay yidn*, IX (History of Jewish Literature). Prepared for print from a microfilm of the newly found manuscript. Brandeis University and CYCO Publishing House. New York. 1966. 336 pp. Yiddish.

WORK IN PROGRESS

Assyria and Her Neighbors: Historical and Geographical Studies.

Articles and Review Articles on Ancient Near Eastern and East Mediterranean Subjects

The Primitive Notion of Yahweh. *YIVO-Bleter* 13 (1938): 477-504, 1 map. Yiddish.

Biblical Tradition as a Source of Hebrew Prehistory. *Bulletin of the Institute for Jewish History*. No. 22 (1957): 1-25. Polish.

The Ḫabiru Problem and the Conquest of Canaan. *Bleter far Geshikhte* 11 (1958): 59-90. Yiddish.

Benê-Iamina et Jéricho. *Semitica*, No. 9 (1959): 5-20.

Les étrangers à Ugarit et le statut juridique des Ḫabiru. *Revue d'Assyriologie et d'Archéologie Orientale* 53 (1959): 70-76.

Metamorphose de Baal. Les rivalités commerciales du IXe siècle. *Evidences*, No. 75 (January-February, 1959): 34-40; No. 77 (May-June, 1959): 54-58.

Review article of E. Orbach (Auerbach). *Hamidbar ve'ereṣ habḥirah*, I. *Di Goldene Keyt* 32 (1959): 236-45. Yiddish.

History and Legend: The Conquest of Canaan at the Light of Archaeology. *The Zukunft* 65 (1960): 109-14.

Review article of A. Dupont-Sommer. *Les écrits esséniens, découverts près de la Mer Morts. Di Goldene Keyt* 35 (1960): 150-59. Yiddish.

Place Names from the Kingdom of Alalaḫ in the North Syrian List of Thutmose III: A Study in Historical Topography. *Journal of Near Eastern Studies* 22 (1963): 220-41, 1 map.

Un texte d'Ugarit récemment découvert et ses rapports avec l'origine des cultes bachiques Grecs. *Revue de l'Histoire des Religions* 164 (1963): 1-15.

Greek Names in the Semitic World and Semitic Names in the Greek World. *Journal of Near Eastern Studies* 23 (1964): 193-201.

Religion of Ancient Jews. In Zygmunt Poniatowski, ed. *Zarys dziejów religii* (An Outline of the History of Religion). Warsaw: Iskry. 1964: 301-29.

Second Millennium B.C. Cypriot and Cretan Onomastica Reconsidered. *Journal of the American Oriental Society* 84 (1964): 240-54.

The Amarna Age Forerunners of Biblical Anti-Royalism. In *For Max Weinreich on His Seventieth Birthday: Studies in Jewish Languages, Literature, and Society*. Mouton. The Hague. 1964: 6-17.

New Evidence on the Last Days of Ugarit. *American Journal of Archaeology* 69 (1965): 253-58.

Sabtah and Sabteca: Ethiopian Pharaoh Names in Genesis 10. *Journal of Biblical Literature* 84 (1965): 422-25.

The Origin of the Terms 'Canaan,' 'Phoenician,' and 'Purple'. *Journal of Near Eastern Studies* 24 (1965): 346-50.

Aegean Place-Names in an Egyptian Inscription. *American Journal of Archaeology* 70 (1966): 313-17.

Political and Cosmic Symbolism in Genesis 14 and in Its Babylonian Sources. In *Biblical Motifs: Origins and Transformations.* Philip W. Lown Institute, Brandeis University: *Study and Texts* III. Harvard University Press. Cambridge, Mass. 1966: 65-112.

Some New Divine Names from Ugarit. *Journal of the American Oriental Society* 86 (1966): 277-84.

Tamar the Hierodule: An Essay in the Method of Vestigial Motifs. *Journal of Biblical Literature* 85 (1966): 185-96.

The Problem of Semitic in Ancient Crete. *Journal of the American Oriental Society* 87 (1967): 290-95.

Mesopotamian and Transtigridian Place Names in the Medinet Habu Lists of Ramses III. *Journal of the American Oriental Society* 88 (1968): 733-52.

Semitic Elements in the Kumarbi Myth: An Onomastic Inquiry. *Journal of Near Eastern Studies* 27 (1968): 172-77.

Two Ugaritic Serpent Charms. *Journal of Near Eastern Studies* 27 (1968): 13-36.

La triade de déesses de fertilité à Ugarit et en Grèce. In C. F. A. Schaeffer, ed. *Ugaritica* VI. Mission de Ras Shamra XVII. Bibliothèque Archéologique et Historique 81. Institut Français d'Archéologie de Beyrouth. Paris. 1969: 9-23.

The Partition of the Confederacy of Mukiš-Nuhašše-Nii by Šuppiluliuma: A Study in Political Geography of the Amarna Age. *Orientalia* 38 (1969): 381-414.

Ma'ḫadu, the Harbor of Ugarit. *Journal of the Economic and Social History of the Orient* 13 (1970): 113-27.

Toponyms in the Hurrian Alphabetic Tablet RS 24.285. *Ugarit-Forschungen* 2 (1970): 1-6.

841 B.C.: The First Assyrian Invasion of Israel. *Journal of the American Oriental Society* 91 (1971): 383-89.

A Letter and Two Economic Texts. Chapter 2 in L. R. Fisher, ed. *The Claremont Ras Shamra Tablets.* Analecta Orientalia 48. Pontifical Biblical Institute. Rome. 1971: 24-29 and pls. III-VI.

Tell Mardiḫ and Ebla. *Ugarit-Forschungen* 3 (1971): 9-19.

Ḫattušilis, Ḫalab, and Ḫanigalbat. *Journal of Near Eastern Studies* 31 (1972): 102-9.

Some Recent Works on Ancient Syria and the Sea People. *Journal of the American Oriental Society* 92 (1972): 447-59.

The Merchant Class of Ugarit. In D. O. Edzard, ed. *Gesellschaftsklassen in Alten Zweistromland und in den angrenzenden Gebieten.* XVIII. Rencontre Assyriologique Internationale, München, 29. Juni bis 3. Juli 1970. Bayerisch Academie der Wissenschaften. Munich. 1972: 11-26.

A North Mesopotamian Locale of the Keret Epic? *Ugarit-Forschungen* 5 (1973): 29-39.

Note toponymique à la tablette A. 1270 de Mari. *Revue d'assyriologie et d'archéologie orientale* 67 (1973): 73-75.

Ugarit and the Aegean: A Brief Summary of Archaeological and Epigraphic Evidence. In H. A. Hoffner, Jr., ed. *Orient and Occident: Essays Presented to Cyrus H. Gordon on the Occasion of His Sixty-fifth Birthday.* Alter Orient und altes Testament 22. Verlag Butzon & Bercker Kevelaer. Neukirchener-Vluyn. 1973: 17-27.

Place Names. Chapter 8 in L. R. Fisher, ed. *Ras Shamra Parallels,* II. Analecta Orientalia 51. Pontifical Biblical Institute. Rome. 1974: 249-369.

26 articles in K. Crim, ed. *The Interpreter's Dictionary of the Bible.* Supplementary Volume. Abingdon. Nashville. 1976. ("Amphictyony." "Androgyny." "Arpad." "Calneh." "Canneh." "Carmel, Mount." "Chilmad." "Dedan." "Eden." "Habiru." "Hadrach." "Hittites." "Japheth." "Joash." "Kir." "Kue." "La^{c}ir." "Mitanni." "Sepharad." "Sepharvaim." "Shalman." "Sinites." "Succoth-Benoth." "Tel-assar." "Yahwe." "Ya'udi.")

Ezekiel's Prophesy of Gog and the Cuthean Legend of Naram-Sin. *Journal of Biblical Literature* 95 (1976): 567-79.

Review article of L. W. Stefaniak, ed. *Archeologia Palestyny: praca zbiorowa. Archeologia* 27 (1976): 201-6. Translated into Polish by A Pasicki.

Continuité et changement dans la toponymie de la Syrie du Nord. In *La Toponymie Antique: Actes du Colloque de Strasbourg, 12-14 juin 1975.* Université des Sciences Humaines de Strasbourg. Travaux du Centre de Recherche sur le Proche-Orient et la Grèce Antique 4. E. J. Brill. Leiden. 1977: 117-41 and folding map.

Review article of I. E. S. Edwards, *et al.*, eds. *Cambridge Ancient History,* Volume 2. Part 2. 3rd edition. *Bulletin of the American Schools of Oriental Research* 227 (October, 1977): 66-69.

Tunip-Hamath and Its Region: A Contribution to the Historical Geography of Central Syria. *Orientalia* 46 (1977): 51-64.

Les Hourrites en Syrie du Nord: Rapport Sommaire. *Revue Hittite et Asianique* 36 (1978): 1-22.

The Rabbeans: A Tribal Society on the Euphrates from Yahdun-Lim to Julius Caesar. Syro-Mesopotamian Studies 2/1. Malibu, Calif. 12 pp. January, 1978.

The Arena of Tiglath-pileser III's Campaign Against Sarduri III (743 B.C.). Assur 2/3. Malibu, Calif. 23 pp. October, 1979.

The Kingdom of Siyannu-Ušnatu. *Ugarit-Forschungen* 11 (1979): 13-28.

Yahweh in Egyptian Topographic Lists. In M. Görg and E. Pusch, eds. *Festschrift Elmar Edel.* Studien zu Geschichte, Kultur und Religion Ägyptens und des alten Testament 1. Bamberg. 1979: 17-34.

King Ammurapi and the Hittite Princess. *Ugarit-Forschungen* 12 (1980): 103-8.

North Syrian Toponyms Derived from Plant Names. In G. Rendsburg, R. Adler, M. Arla and N. Winter, eds. *The Bible World: Essays in Honor of Cyrus H. Gordon.* KTAV Publishing House and the Institute of Hebrew Culture and Education of New York University. New York. 1980: 3-8.

The Nether World and Its Denizens at Ugarit. *Mesopotamia: Copenhagen Studies in Assyriology* 8 (1980): 227-38.

Les frontières et les districts du royaume d'Ugarit (Éléments de topographie historique régionale). *Ugarit-Forschungen* 13 (1981): 1-12.

Toponymic Parallels Between the Nuzi Area and North Syria, with an appendix: Nuzi Place Names in Egyptian Topographic Lists. In M. A. Morrison and D. I. Owen, eds. *Studies on the Civilization and Culture of Nuzi and the Hurrians in Honor of Ernest R.Lacheman.* Studies on the Civilization and Culture of Nuzi and the Hurrians 1. Eisenbrauns. Winona Lake, Ind. 1981: 11-26.

Ugarit and the Great Powers. In G. D. Young, ed. *Ugarit in Retrospect: Fifty Years of Ugarit and Ugaritic.* Eisenbrauns. Winona Lake, Ind. 1981: 3-29 and folding map.

Ancient Greek Civilization in Southern Italy. *The Journal of Aesthetic Education* 19 (1985): 23-37.

The Name of the Ninth Kassite Ruler. *Journal of the American Oriental Society* 106 (1986): 327-31.

Semites and Hurrians in Northern Transtigris. In M. A. Morrison and D. I. Owen, eds. *Studies on the Civilization and Culture of Nuzi and the Hurrians* 2. Eisenbrauns. Winona Lake, Ind. 1987: 3-68.

Remarks on KTU 1.96. *Studi epigrapfici e linguistici* 5 (1988): 13-24.

The Geographical and Political Structure of the Ebla Empire. In H. Hauptman and H. Waetzoldt, eds. *Wirtschaft und Gesellschaft von Ebla: Akten der Internationalen Tagung, Heidelberg 4.-7. November 1986.* Heidelberger Studien zum Alten Orient 2. Heidelberger Orientverlag. Heidelberg. 1988: 139-58.

The Origin of the Samaritans: Critical Examination of the Evidence. In S. Shaath. ed. *Studies in the History and Archaeology of Palestine. Proceedings of the First International Symposium on Palestine Antiquities,* III. Aleppo University Press. Aleppo. 1988: 9-53.

Toponymy of Ebla and Ethnohistory of Northern Syria: A Preliminary Survey. *Journal of the American Oriental Society* 108 (1988): 545-55.

The Location of Ḫaṣurā of the Mari Texts. *Maarav* 7 (1991): 51-65.

An Outline of the History of Ebla (Part I). *Eblaitica* 3 (1992): 3-82.

Sparagmos, Omophagia, and Ecstatic Prophesy at Mari. *Ugarit Forschungen* 24 (1992): 1-2.

The Date of the Destruction of Palace G at Ebla. In M. W. Chavalas and J. L. Hayes, eds. *New Horizons in the Study of Ancient Syria.* Bibliotheca Mesopotamica 25. Undena Publications. Malibu, Calif. 1992: 23-39.

The North Mesopotamian Kingdom of Ilānṣurā. In G. D. Young, ed. *Mari in Retrospect: Fifty Years of Mari and Mari Studies.* Eisenbrauns. Winona Lake, Ind. 1992: 1-33.

Twenty-five articles in D. N. Freedman, ed. *The Anchor Bible Dictionary.* Doubleday. New York. 1992. ("Alalakh." "Amraphel." "Aner." "Arioch." "Ashteroth-Karnaim." "Bera." "Birsha." "Chedorlaomer." "Ellasar." "El-Paran." "Eshcol." "Goiim." "Ham." "Hazazon-Tamar." "Melchizedek." "Salem." "Salt Sea." "Shaveh, Valley of." "Shaveh-Kiriathaim." "Shemeber." "Shinab." "Siddim, Valley of." "Tidal." "Zoar." "Zuzim.")

La Topographie du royaume d'Ougarit. In M. Yon, M. Sznycer and P.Bordreuil, eds. *Le pays d'Ougarit autour de 1200 av. J.-C.* Ras Shamra-Ougarit XI. Actes du Colloque International, Paris, 28 juin - 1[er] juillet 1993. Editions Recherche sur les Civilisations. Paris. 1995: 55-69.

Overland Trade Routes in Ancient Western Asia. In J. M. Sasson, ed. *Civilizations of the Ancient Near East.* Charles Scribner's Sons. New York. 1995: 1401-20.

Some Unrecognized North Syrian Toponyms in Egyptian Sources. In J. Coleson and V. Mathews, eds. *Go to the Land I Will Show You: Studies in Honor of Dwight W. Young.* Eisenbrauns. Winona Lake, Ind. 1996: 213-41.

Who Was the King of the Hurrian Troops at the Siege of Emar? In M. W. Chavalas, ed. *Emar: The History, Religion, and Culture of a Bronze Age Town in Syria.* CDL Press. Bethesda, Md. 1996: 25-56.

Review article of A. Archi, P. Piacentini and F. Pomponio. *I nomi di luogo dei testi di Ebla* (*ARES* 2). *Journal of the American Oriental Society* 116 (1997): 332-38.

The Toponyms of Ebla. Journal of the American Oriental Society 117/2 (1997): 332-38.

The Hapiru in the Amarna Texts. To appear in B. J. Beitzel and G. D. Young, eds. *Tell El-Amarna in Retrospect.* Eisenbrauns. Winona Lake, Ind., (forthcoming).

Book Reviews

C. H. Gordon, *Ugarit and Minoan Crete. Journal of Near Eastern Studies* 26 (1967): 131-33.

H. H. B. Huffmon, *Amorite Personal Names in the Mari Texts. Journal of Near Eastern Studies* 26 (1967): 225-29.

W. Stevenson Smith, *Interconnections in the Ancient Near East. Journal of Near Eastern Studies* 27 (1968): 150-52.

G. Buccellati, *The Amorites of the Ur III Period. Journal of Near Eastern Studies* 28 (1969): 220-24.

F. Imparati, *I Hurriti. Journal of Near Eastern Studies* 28 (1969): 63.

M. Mayrhofer. *Die Indo-Arier im alten Vorderasien. Journal of Near Eastern Studies* 28 (1969): 63-65.

N. Avigad *et al.*, eds., *E. L. Sukenik Memorial Volume. Journal of Near Eastern Studies* 29 (1970): 207.

G. Buccellati, *Cities and Nations of Ancient Syria. Journal of Near Eastern Studies* 29 (1970): 294-96.

R. Labat, A. Caquot, M. Sznycer, and M. Viera, *Les religions du Proche-Orient asiatique. Journal of Near Eastern Studies* 31 (1972): 112-19.

R. du Mesnil du Buisson, *Études sur les dieux phéniciens hérités par l'Empire romain. Journal of Near Eastern Studies* 32 (1973): 265-66.

A. Haldar, *Who Were the Amorites? Journal of Near Eastern Studies* 34 (1975): 217-19.

H. Ringgren, *Religions of the Ancient Near East. Journal of Near Eastern Studies* 34 (1975): 215-17.

L. W. Stefaniak, ed. *Archeologia Palestyny: praca zbiorowa* (Archaeology of Palestine: A Collective Work). *Journal of the American Oriental Society* 98 (1978): 152-53.

M. Heltzer, *The Rural Community of Ancient Ugarit. Journal of Near Eastern Studies* 39 (1980): 163-67.

J. H. Hayes and J. M. Miller, eds. *Israelite and Judean History. Journal of the American Oriental Society* 102 (1982): 192-95.

J. Strange, *Caphtor-Keftiu: A New Investigation. Journal of the American Oriental Society* 102 (1982): 395-96.

N. Groom, *A Dictionary of Arabic Toponymy and Placesnames. Journal of the American Oriental Society* 107 (1987): 339-40.

S. Eichler, *et al.*, eds. *Tall al-Ḥamīdiya 1: Vorbericht 1984. Journal of the American Oriental Society* 108 (1988): 304-6.

Sh. Aḥituv, *Canaanite Toponyms in Ancient Egyptian Documents. Journal of Near Eastern Studies* 48 (1989): 35-38.

D. J. W. Meijer, *A Survey in Northeastern Syria. Journal of the American Oriental Society* 109 (1989): 506-8.

Kh. Nashef, *Rekonstruktion der Reiserouten zur Zeit der altassyrischen Handels-Niederlassungen. Journal of the American Oriental Society* 109 (1989): 686-88.

S. Eichler, *et. al.*, eds. *Tall al-Ḥamīdiya II: Symposium on Recent Excavations in the Upper Khabur Region; Vorbericht 1985-1987. Journal of the American Oriental Society* 113 (1993): 112-15.

J. D. Granger, *The Cities of Seleucid Syria. Journal of the American Oriental Society* 114 (1994): 267-70.

G. Wilhelm, *The Hurrians. Journal of Near Eastern Studies* 58 (1994): 225-30.

Principal Articles in Yiddish on Literary and Cultural Topics

Isak Babel (1894–1941). In L. Domankiewicz, L. Leneman, L. Kurland, A. Shulman and M. Kutcher, eds. *Almanac*, Published by the Union of Yiddish Writers and Journalists in France. Paris. 1960: 199-202.

Notes on Boris Pasternak's Poetry. *Frailand* No. 3 (30), February, 1959: 14-16.

Morals to Be Drawn from the Case of Boris Pasternak. *Oifn Shvel* No. 3 (139). May-June, 1959: 9-12.

Leyzer Volf: the Man, the Poet, the Territorialist. *Oifn Shvel* No. 5 (143). October-November, 1959: 6-10.

Morris Rosenfeld: The Poet and Fighter of His Generation. *The Zukunft*, 67 (1962): 162-68

Osip Mandelshtam. *Di Goldene Keyt* 43 (1962): 197-206.

Jews in the Soviet *World History. Oifn Shvel* No. 4 (155). May-June (1963): 1-4.

Sutzkever's Poetical Beginning. In *The Jubilee Book in Honor of the Fiftieth Birthday of Avrom Sutzkever.* Tel Aviv. 1963: 22-42.

The Newly Found Volume of Dr. Israel Zinberg's *History of Jewish Literature. Di Goldene Keyt* 49 (1964): 14-21.

Hundred Years of the New Yiddish Literature. *Di Goldene Keyt* 51 (1965): 1-19.

The Fiftieth Anniversary of Sholem-Aleichem's Death. *Oifn Shvel* No. 5 (177). May-June, 1966: 1-5.

Dr. Israel Zinberg on the Beginning of the New Yiddish Literature. In *The Fourth World Conference of Jewish Studies*, II. Jerusalem. 1968: 151-55.

Dr. Max Weinreich. *Oifn Shvel* No. 1 (188). January-February,1969: 1-3.

A. I. Solzhenitsyn and His Creations. *Oifn Shvel* No. 4 (191). July-August, 1969: 6-9. No. 5 (192). September-October, 1969: 2-5.

The Secular Jewish Vilna. In M. Ḥazqoni-Shtarkman ed. *Chesed le-Avrohom: Jubilee Book in Honor of the Eightieth Birthday of Avrom Golomb.* Los Angeles. 1970: 319-32.

Joseph Czernichow-Danieli. *Oifn Shvel* No. 2-3 (200-1). March-June, 1971: 3-9.

Zalman Reizen: Lines of Remembrance. *Oifn Shvel* No. 200. October-November, 1985: 1-5.

An Interview with Michael Astour

on the Occasion of His Being Honored by the Middle West Branch of the American Oriental Society, February 11 and 12, 1996

David. I. Owen and Gordon D. Young

David I. Owen: It is difficult to find a subject in which Michael Astour has at one time or another not worked. It is perhaps more difficult to contribute something original to those areas in which he has already researched. Tonight I have taken the easy route by avoiding scholarly minutiae in order to probe into Michael's past with questions about himself and his long and distinguished career. Since his early years, Michael has been an inveterate traveler. His infinite curiosity of the world at large and especially of Europe and the Near East took him to Paris for his higher education, and then even to Palestine and Egypt in the late thirties of this century when he was a young man. The horrors of the rise of Communism, Nazism and World War destroyed his family and the world he had known. He was dislocated to central Asia where fate would have it his life was spared, and he found his partner and wife Miriam, with whom he has shared a subsequently full, and not uninteresting, life of scholarship, teaching, and travel. Fate, chance and choice have all conspired to shape their destiny. That he and Miriam would eventually enjoy long and productive careers in the United States, they could never have foretold. That we, his students, friends [and] colleagues would be gathered here tonight to honor Michael's forthcoming eightieth birthday is, no doubt, from the perspective of his life, nothing short of miraculous. Although I have known Michael for thirty-four years—first as a fellow student, then as a teacher, and as a dear friend—tonight I wish to begin long before that

* This interview was transcribed and slightly edited by Gordon D. Young and Kevin L. Danti. The interview occurred during the evening of February 11th with David I. Owen and continued on the morning of February 12th with Gordon D. Young.

time [going back] to his own university years in Paris, and to start by asking him to share with us some of his recollections, albeit in brief, of those years that he studied in Paris with some of the great scholars of this century.

David I. Owen: *Michael, let's begin with your university years at the Sorbonne, and those teachers who you think provided you with the influence and the inspiration that led you to a scholarly career.*

Michael Astour: Actually, my career had already been determined before I came to the Sorbonne. I arrived there with a plan [in mind]—with certain intentions of what to study, and so on. I became very much interested in—maybe it is symbolic—two events that happened in 1929: first of all, Ras Shamra was discovered, and I was immediately interested by it. I cut out the information in the press, the photographs, and so on. At the same time, I became very much interested in pre-Hellenic Greece. I wanted to know what Greece was like before the arrival of the classical Greeks. So, again, I found an interesting article about the Minoan civilization, and that, as you can see, is a kind of a forerunner to *Hellenosemitica,*[1] even though I had not thought about it at all up to that time. Well, in 1931—it was my only trip abroad with my parents—we stayed in Paris for a while. I visited other things, but in Paris, of course, I was much impressed by the Near Eastern and Egyptian collection in the Louvre. It was decided then, since my mother had a brother in Paris—a lawyer—that I would go to Paris and study at the Sorbonne. He wanted me to stay right there in 1931 when I was fourteen years old, but I wisely refused (and I believe I was right because the following years, from '31 to '34 formed me; they gave me my identity, my attitude—my world outlook). But anyway, in 1934, I came to Paris for the Fall semester. My French was very poor at that time—I later improved it—and looked around to see what I could study. One of the things I saw was a series of lectures given by Charles Virolleaud—I hadn't heard of his name before—on two topics: the legend of Ba^{c}al, and the legends of Etana and Adapa. I knew of the latter topic because, with the help of my parents, I had bought

[1] Astour (1965).

many important books in previous years, among them the book by Gressmann[2]—something similar to Pritchard's ANET.[3] One course was given at the École des Hautes Études at the Sorbonne, and the other in the Palais Rouge, that was the Institute of Art near the Luxembourg Garden. Both of them actually concerned the newly discovered Ugaritic texts, the publication of which had been conferred to him. He had a small group of students—very small! (Here in America it wouldn't have been supported by universities because the expenses per student would be too high, but in France they allowed it.) The core of the group, with my arrival, consisted of four people. There was Andrée Herdner, who, as you know, published the cuneiform texts discovered by Virolleaud.[4] Then there was a refugee from Germany. He was the oldest of us—Dr. Arnold Wadler, who had published a book (he had the time to publish only half of it) called *Der Turm von Babel*,[5] The Tower of Babel. He had an obsession that all languages of the world derived from one single language, and he attended the courses of Virolleaud in Ugaritic precisely with this goal: to find out what were the elements that came from the original pre-language. Then there was Zacharia Mayani (who later published a book about the Hyksos and some other works[6]) and myself, the youngest and probably the last surviving of his students. From time to time others would come, but we four stayed for this entire time.

So I believe that Virolleaud's influence on me was very great because he introduced me to the Ugaritic language still very poorly known at that time. We were groping together with him with this unknown language trying to find Hebrew and other parallels, but it was very instructive—very important—and I learned a great deal of the texts before they were published.

---

2 Gressmann (1926).

3 Pritchard (1969).

4 Herdner (1963).

5 Wadler (1935).

6 Mayani (1956).

Owen: *What was your relationship with Virolleaud?*

Astour: I would say that he was first of all a very pleasant, gentle person. He took an interest in me—especially in the later years [of the 1930's] when I came to Paris again to study something very different from ancient studies. He gave me all kinds of support. He gave me a card to work in the library of the École des Hautes Études and in the Bibliothéque Nationale, and I remember that he gave me as a gift the newly published volume, *La déesse Anat*[7] (a very great honor for me!). I thought that he was only lending it to me, but he said, "No. I give it to you. It is good to encourage young scholars."

Then, after the war—after I returned to the civilized world, if I may say so—I got in contact with him again and it turned out that he had kept the typescripts of two of my early studies. He returned them to me, but I was able to use very little of them because everything had changed in Ugaritic studies—and everything else!—but some of the ideas I later used in some articles. He also did his best to get for me a fellowship in the Centre Nationale de Recherche Scientifique so that I could write a thesis. (At that time I thought about writing a more general study of the Amarna letters. Later, of course, I had to deal only with particular questions.) He was very disappointed when I didn't receive it. The first time [I applied] there were only ten fellowships [to be awarded] in the non-classical civilizations, which included everything that our [American] Oriental Society covers. When we applied, we were supported by Professors Dupont-Sommer and Nougayrol, but it was a Japanese who won it. The second time it was me, but only eight were admitted [that year]. The Minister of Education said that one of eight is more than ten percent, and foreigners have the right to only ten percent of the awards. By then, thanks to my friends in America, I had already received an entrance visa to the United States (which was helped by the fact that I was born in Russia, and the Russian quota at that time was practically not used). So I decided that I would go and try my luck in the United States. Virolleaud asked, "What can I do?" "Well," I said, "you can write me recommendations." One of them was to Professor Cyrus Gordon who, when I

---

7 Virolleaud (1938).

visited him for the first time, already knew something about me. (I had already published six articles in Poland and in Paris.) Well, that is what he did for me.

Owen: *So you consider him the most influential of the scholars in the late thirties that you studied with?*

Astour: I would say yes, but I had others. I'll speak very briefly about them. I followed not only Semitic studies, but also, in general, the entire ancient history—Roman and Greek, and, of course, the Ancient Near East—and then the History of Religions, and Russian Literature. (I took Russian Literature because it gave me a credit and freed me from a special test in a foreign language, and because it was my first year in Paris and I simply couldn't write the written test in French. The next year I could, and I received quite a good grade on my written paper—but that's a different story.) So let me say who else influenced me.

The professor of Egyptology (but he also taught the Asiatic Ancient Near East in another year) was Raymond Weill. What do I owe to him? First of all, he was a very good Egyptologist, so whatever I knew and learned in Egyptian history came first of all from him. Second, he also gave special seminars in the École des Hautes Études where he introduced me to some of the finesses of Egyptology: for instance, the origins of Egyptian religion, the integration of the gods—their linking together in families—the origin of the Ennead, of the Osirian divinities. That was his method for studying and it was very important. Then I owe to him his introduction into the astronomical basis of the Egyptian chronology. And then a third thing: he wrote an article—quite a long study—about the origin of the Egyptian bondage story. He believed that it came from the Hyksos. The Hyksos who were expelled from Egypt came to Canaan and told the story about their old days of domination in Egypt, and then the Hebrews, the Israelites, took it over from the Canaanites. For a long time I believed in it, but later, as I explained in my presidential address in 1989,[8] I understood that if the story

---

8 "The Birth and Growth of the Egyptian Bondage Story," Presidential address delivered

was that early, we should have found it in the earliest parts of the Old Testament. In the Hebrew Bible, however, we find it for the first time in Deuteronomy. In Hebrew and Biblical Studies, I had Professor Adolphe Lods who wrote several books about that time, including *Israël des origines au milieu du VIIIe siécle* and *Les prophètes d'Israël et les débuts du judaïsme*[9]—and then a very fine posthumous *History of Ancient Hebrew Literature.*[10] I gained a much better knowledge from him about Hebrew philology, Hebrew linguistics, and the critical separation of sources (in, for example, the book of Samuel). He was a very strict scholar who liked all kinds of precision in the parsing of such texts as the Hebrew version of Ben Sira.

In other fields, André Piganiol, a Roman historian, didn't influence me so much personally (he had at that time a rather dull course in Roman Egypt which had a great deal to do with statistics, with land, and so on), but his books on Roman history[11] are very good because of his critical analyses of early Roman history—how it was falsified because the Romans knew practically nothing about it, how they pushed into their past practices of later times and created mythical ancestors for themselves in the time of the monarchy and revolution.

Then Professor Charles Picard: I took the course in Greek archaeology with him. It was extremely interesting. We had molds of ancient statues, metopes and other things housed in the Institute of Art. From then on I could understand Greek art a lot better than I did before. When I asked him (in connection with my course in the History of Religion) about the Eleusinian Mysteries, he recommended some very good books. I believe that I owe to him my interest in this part of Greek religion. Well, [in answer to your question], these were the most important ones.

---

at the annual joint meeting of the Middle West Branch of the American Oriental Society, the Midwest Region of the Society of Biblical Literature, and Midwest Members of the American Schools of Oriental Research at Evanston, Illinois, on January 30, 1989.

9 Lods (1935).

10 Lods (1950).

11 See, for example, Piganiol (1917, 1926, 1930 and 1939).

Owen: *It's obvious that you had such a tremendous range of education at that period that had a profound influence on the direction of your scholarship in later life.*

Astour: Yes. Absolutely.

Owen: *Thirty years ago you published Hellenosemitica, a ground-breaking, controversial, and remarkably well-sold book considering the difficulty when it came out, but give us some insight into how this volume evolved in your own mind.*

Astour: Well, I wrote about it very briefly in the preface to [*Hellenosemitica*], but I will repeat it now. First of all, as I told you before, I was interested both in ancient Greece and the Near East. In my late teens, I was very fascinated by Greek literature and Greek mythology—especially in Greek mythology, *Iliad* and *Odyssey*, and the surviving tragedies—and I had a very good collection of Greek myths beautifully narrated by the Russian-Polish Hellenist, Tadeusz Zieliński.[12] So, from the very beginning, I was well versed in Greek mythology. Later I studied Ugaritic, Babylonian, and other myths, but I was reluctant to associate them. One remark said in passing by Virolleaud about the poem of Aqhat, where we have the mother of the eagles spelled *tsade mem lamed*—Semel, Simel or whatever—was that it was the same name as that of Dionysos' mother, Semele. That struck me because I had never made these kinds of parallels before.

In addition, our professor in Greek history, Pierre Roussel, whom I didn't mention before, gave us a very fine course in Greek colonization—a subject that fascinated me. He said that Herodotus and Thucydides used to speak about Phoenician settlement in the islands in Greece, but that their statements were now completely rejected and obsolete. (Well, Martin Bernal here can explain much better about this attitude!) Just before the war, I happened quite accidently to open a book by Victor Bérard, *De l'origine des cultes arcadiens: essai de méthode en mythologie grecque.*[13] I leafed

12 Zieliński (1930).

13 Bérard (1894).

through it to where he made a comparison between Semitic and Greek religion. At that time, little was known about Phoenician religion because, except for a few inscriptions, our knowledge came completely from secondary sources. Since I had already a background in Semitic languages and religion, I was struck by the closeness of the parallels he drew, but I had no time to follow it up. Later, as you know, I found myself in the Soviet Union—in part in prison and in part in Central Asia. I started thinking about it again there, and then when I heard about the inscription of Kara Tepe and about the mention of Danunim, the Danaans (that was just when I left the camp), I began to think seriously that maybe, despite all of the denial of Phoenician/West Semitic influence on the Greeks, there was something to be learned. Little by little, the more I read Herodotus and others, the more I found that their claims were well founded. It [the Phoenician/West Semitic influence on Greece] was not stupid invention; it had a philological and a religious basis. So I started writing notes for myself. (I wrote them in very small script with green, alizarin ink which later paled, and which now I have great trouble reading!) But, what was important, and, I would say, current and actual, I used as a part of *Hellenosemitica.*

When I came to New York, and, with the help of Professor Cyrus Gordon, I received a fellowship at Brandeis University in the Graduate School, and a job as assistant professor of Yiddish Literature for two thirds of my time and one third in Russian, I had to have a topic for my dissertation. At that time, Professor Max Weinreich, who was the Director of the YIVO Institute of Jewish Studies, and who knew me as a young man from Wilna, asked me what I had prepared for a dissertation—for what did I have the greatest material. I said, "*Hellenosemitica.*" All he said was, "Work on it." So that is how it happened.

Owen: *A number of people have asked why you never completed the second volume that you spoke about in your Hellenosemitica.*

Astour: Well, I'll tell you. First of all, it took me time to finish the first one. I wrote it first as a dissertation. Then, when it was accepted by Brill, I had to rework it—to edit it, to shorten it, to add things. That took me a lot of time. Meanwhile, I read an article by the late Ignace Gelb about Semites in

Syria,[14] where he wrote that in all of the Alalakh place-names there are only four that are Semitic; the rest are pre-Semitic. My work on the Alalakh texts and Ugarit suggested something different. That work, you know, spread like an oil stain from Ugarit to Alalakh, from Alalakh later to Ebla, to Mari, to Emar, and so on.

From childhood on—maybe from twelve years old—I was always fascinated with geography. I was drawing maps. I was enlarging maps from smaller maps and atlases. So I've always had a certain inclination. I never thought about it later, until I got completely engaged in the study of the toponymy and topography of Ugarit, on which I published several articles, but not the complete corpus of place-names. So I became completely absorbed by a different topic—a more realistic one, I would say, more down to earth. I had to deal with actual settlements, with villages and towns, with mountains and so on, so I simply didn't have time to write about *Hellenosemitica*, or to prepare the second volume. But I published a few things about the subject later; for instance, "La triade de déesses de fertilité à Ugarit et en Gréce,"[15] and, *i.a.*, two articles on the Ugaritic text RS 22.225 (KTU 1.96) dealing with eating a god's flesh and drinking his blood, suggesting similarities with the Bacchic rituals.[16] Even the cautious Johannes de Moor noted that "Similarities between the cult of Baᶜlu and that of Dionysos have been indicated by Gaster [1939: 112s.], Astour [1963: 1-15; 1965: 176ss.] and Albright [1968: 114s]. Though not all of the material adduced by these scholars is really convincing, at least the relation between RS 22.225 and the Dionysiac rites seems undeniable."[17] And perhaps you saw my short note in one of the recent volumes of *Ugarit-Forschungen.*[18] I found that there is a Mari text which has not been approached from the Hellenosemitic point of view: how an ecstatic prophet in Saggaratum came to the governor and

---

14 Gelb (1961).

15 Astour (1969).

16 Astour (1963 and 1988c).

17 de Moor (1971) 78 n. 18.

18 Astour (1992b).

said, "Give me something of the property of Zimri-Lim. I gave him a lamb. He ate the lamb alive" before delivering his prophecy. In other words, he did not kill the lamb, but rent it apart and swallowed its hot blood and quivering flesh, exactly as it is told about the Bacchic revelers—how they would rend apart an animal or a human being and eat it raw. These articles belong to the field of *Hellenosemitica*, and I gave lectures about other aspects of that field. If I had time and a publisher, I could collect all of them and produce a second, smaller volume.

Owen: *Speaking of time, we are rapidly running out. I wanted to ask you one last thing this evening—on your work, which, as you just explained, took you into the area of toponymy and geography. Would you say a few words about the importance of the study of geographical history?*

Astour: History doesn't happen in empty space, nor in heaven, or wherever. It happens on earth, in concrete places—very, I would say, *precise* places. There was a time when historical geography was studied with great interest. For instance, until now, and for hundreds of years, scholars have been disputing which Alpine pass Hannibal used when he invaded Italy. Well, I think that that is important not only for Hannibal, but also for Hattushilish, for Shalmaneser and for Tukulti-Ninurta I (who made invasions of Armenia). We want to know how these armies marched, where they stopped, where they fought, and where all the places were located.

Right now, interest in historical geography is very low—extremely low! When we compare modern maps with those in old nineteenth or turn of the century historical books, we see that the earlier maps were large scale, on two leaves at least, and were beautifully engraved. Every place-name that could be identified was put on them. Now, compare the first and second editions of the *Cambridge Ancient History*.[19] The old maps may have been imprecise because the compilers didn't know much, but they were very clear, made with black lines, and all the towns that could be identified or located were put on them. Now when I look at the second edition of the

19 See Bury, *et al.* (1927) and Edwards, *et al.* (1975).

CAH vol. III, they are made in pale gray so that one can't distinguish where there is a river, or where the coast, and so on, and towns are placed haphazardly. For instance, did they put in Syria all the royal cities that they knew? No, they put in just one or two, and the rest they ignore. If there are too many cities in one place, the name of the country is put off to the side. (Let's say that Massachusetts has a lot of settlements, so let's put the name in the Adirondacks where there is a lot of space!) That procedure, I believe, is completely incorrect, and even detrimental to the study of history.

I have also found almost no maps of ancient Syria or northern Mesopotamia where there are no mistakes. For instance, Hama is usually put on the other side of the Orontes even though the excavated part of Hama, the tell (the citadel), is on the left bank. Tuttul, in Soviet editions, is put on the other side of the Balikh. Even in such important editions as the *Répertoire géographique des textes cunéiformes*, in the sixth volume by del Monte and Tischler,[20] Diyarbakir is put on the opposite side of the Tigris. Why? Why not put the geographical names where they belong? Why not take a Turkish (or Syrian) map and check where a site is located? Halab, for example, is displaced by 50 or 60 miles to the east on some maps. I believe that geographical sites should be shown in their real places, and that one should follow a certain methodology about how one can find out about the places, their names, their locations, and so on. I seem to recall that one of the team working on the Mari texts complained somewhere that some scholars try to locate towns mentioned in those texts on the basis of extra-Mariote evidence. But of course such scholars are right in their approach. We should use all the sources we can find—not only Mariote, but also Old, Middle and Neo-Assyrian, Hittite, Babylonian, Egyptian, even Greek and Roman, and for some areas, medieval and modern toponyms, and especially such that occur in itineraries. One should also use administrative lists of settlements by districts, correlate them with other documents, and try to find patterns. This is the method.

---

20 del Monte and Tischler (1978).

There are two things that are vital for history: geography and chronology, because everything happens in space and time. I did some work in chronology as well,[21] because we have to make precise determinations.

Owen: *Well, thank you. Unfortunately tonight we have plenty of space, but we have run out of time. Tomorrow Gordon Young will continue with this interview, and I'm sure a great many more interesting thoughts from Michael will be forthcoming.*

> **Gordon D. Young:** Good morning ladies and gentlemen. We are here to continue from last night's interview and session of personal reminiscences with Michael Astour, whom we are honoring as we celebrate the approach of his eightieth birthday. Last evening, David Owen gave a series of excellent questions to Michael making it much more difficult for me this morning. Since David was unable to be here this morning, I have been asked to continue the interview. For those of you sitting here, I would like you to be thinking of questions of your own, because when I am through, I am sure you will have numerous questions David and I have not thought to ask.

Gordon D. Young: *Michael, welcome again and congratulations! Your's has been an extraordinary career, and I am honored to be sitting here next to you, if only to ask questions. One thing that I noticed last night was that you have taken a great deal of pleasure in all the work you have done, but I was wondering if you would comment on what work has given you the most pleasure.*

Michael C. Astour: I am basically an historian, and an historian in modern times, especially one of antiquity, has to do a lot of detective work; finding the clues—the evidence—piecing them together, and coming to some conclusion. This is what is called heuristic. The field of finding and verifying is probably the most exciting. You feel that you are approaching some kind of a mystery or enigma which has not been solved, or solved sufficiently.

---

21 See, *i.a.*, Astour, (1989).

Then you feel the solution getting warmer and warmer, and that is what gives the greatest satisfaction. For instance, there are some topics on which I worked intermittently for many years, such as chapter fourteen of Genesis. I started it as a student and went the completely wrong way. At that time, I was under the influence of Hugo Winckler and his astral theories.[22] So I tried to find some kind of an astral or solar pattern. There was nothing. Then, little by little, when I came to the original documents, I came closer and closer to finding out what the answer was. That gave me a lot of satisfaction, even though if I were to publish it now, I would have to change a lot. My contribution in this field, in the *Anchor Bible Dictionary*,[23] already shows several differences and exceptions following what other scholars, for instance Tadmor,[24] put into it. Another example, mentioned in my presidential address in 1989 in Evanston, concerns the birth and growth of the tale, or story, of Egyptian bondage.[25] This, too, interested me from my earliest student years, and coming to it again later gave me a great deal of satisfaction. In other words, it is not so much the descriptive little things that I did, which were about certain place-names, certain dates, etc., as it was the larger essays in which a lot of material had to be put together, interpreted and then described.

Young: *Would you say that your training in France led toward the broad appreciation that you have for Mediterranean and Near Eastern studies, or did you achieve your own focus independently?*

Astour: Well I have always had my own focus, and you know I didn't ask my professors, "Will it be on the test?" I did a great deal of, as the French say, *bouquiner*: browsing in books on my own. In the Sorbonne, there were

---

22 These ideas are expounded in several of his works, most systematically in Winckler (1907; 2nd ed., 1919).

23 See the several articles in the *Anchor Bible Dictionary* listed in the "Bibliography of Michael C. Astour" in this volume, most dealing with Genesis 14.

24 Tadmor (1982).

25 See n. 8 above.

two windows where you asked for books. The attendants at the windows would then order them, and bring them downstairs by a kind of elevator. One of the elevators was then broken—they had not fixed it for a year or so—and so you had to put in your application and wait to receive the book in the next day or two. The man who was servicing the elevator knew me and said, "Look, if nobody's watching, go and look for yourself." This is something we can do now thanks to open stacks policies, but it was not possible at that time in the Sorbonne. (I don't know if the Sorbonne is still that way—probably not.) So, I went around to the books in the speciality I was looking for, and I found some new things which I would take out and read. In this way, I had my own, if not an approach, at least my own way of working.

What my study in France gave me was, first of all, the methodology. They had good instruction on how to write dissertations, theses, etc. Second was the very spirit of the lectures. France is famous for its *clarté latine*—the very clear, explicit definitions. That made a lasting impression on me. Whether that is good or bad I don't know. I sent a copy of my article about the Benê-Iamina[26] to Goetze when I came here [to the U.S.A.], and when we met he said, "your article is very French." Well, what did he expect? It was written in French, and it was written by a disciple of French scholars! So how could it not be? Of course it wouldn't be German, even though, I had already read a great deal of German literature.

I believe that most of the French scholars are more objective than several others. In other words, they are not apologetic. They don't try very much to glorify the past of France. They have a certain doctrine, or a certain approach. That is also how I was educated back in Wilna in our Jewish milieu. The people whom I knew—teachers, authors, and my own father, who was an historian in his own way—were very much against apologetics in the writing of history. Write it as it was. Try to find out the real causes. Even if the approach to anti-Semitism was not forgotten, to say that perhaps Jews themselves provoked it, in some cases, could be the objective response.

---

26 Astour (1959).

As for my interest in the Mediterranean Basin, I already spoke about that yesterday. I was always very fascinated and impressed by the Greek civilization. On the other hand, I also studied ancient Semitic languages and Near Eastern history with great interest.

Young: *Were you encouraged to take this broad look?*

Astour: No. Absolutely not. I didn't have it yet. I wasn't quite conscious of it. It developed by itself.

Young: *Well, following on the lines of that, there are in this room, and on many college campuses, young scholars who will be coming to pick up the reins and follow you. What advice do you have for young scholars who are interested in pursuing your kind of pursuits?*

Astour: Well, perhaps you remember when I taught in the graduate school of Mediterranean Studies at Brandeis that I told you, "don't come to your research with some pre-conceived notions and try to prove them. Just go along and see how the evidence fits. Modify your notions if you need to, and don't look for a special defense or apologetic, or aggrandize something that is dear to you. Simply go ahead and study, and to whichever conclusions you logically come, publish them."

Young: *What about preparation for work in historical geography?*

Astour: First of all, you have to have good topographic maps, not the ones that are printed in textbooks, articles and so on—mere sketches. When I was in Paris in 1970 (at that time my interests grew more and more in historical topography and toponymy), I went to an office of the French cartographical institute on Rue de la Boëtie and bought a big set of 1:50,000 maps made by the French general staff at the time they ruled Syria. That was extremely important. 1:50,000 is a big scale—going 5 centimeters to the kilometer. These maps have the elevations, contours, place-names, etc. (Of course, the place-names were written for French soldiers, so it was Frenchified with *ch* for *sh*, with *nn* to show that it wasn't nasal *n*, and so on.) This was very worthwhile, as I mentioned in my 1993 paper at the colloquium about Ugarit around 1200. I was there assigned the topic of the topography of the kingdom of Ugarit.[27] When I first came to the area of the ancient kingdom of Ugarit from the north, it seemed to me that the country was *déja vu;* that I had seen it already. I had already pored over the maps of that area.

Second, and very important, are the descriptions of travelers—the older the better, because they found the country less changed, and the old roads still open. That is very important.

Third, of course, are modern statistics and the descriptions of the terrain—about the cultural areas, of the produce they cultivate, the location of the vineyards, the olive groves, and cereals, and so on. These are the modern sources, and the more you use them the better.

Then, of course, there are the ancient sources. You have to make all the lists—whether it is on cards, as I did, or on a computer—all the citations of place-names in ancient sources, and group them by area and by period. For example, the Alalakh texts belong to two different periods: (1) the Late Old Babylonian (as they used to be called, even though the texts never belonged to Babylonia, and are better described as Late Middle Bronze Age) from level VII, the seventeenth century, and (2) the Late Bronze Age (which is level IV, separated from level VII by an archival gap in the fifteenth century). What I did was to put them on the same cards. If the place-name occurred in level VII, as most of them did, I would put in front of the number of the corresponding tablet a little elevated circle, so that I knew exactly whether it belonged to level VII, level IV, or both. It is very important not to confuse the different periods. The same also goes for Ugaritic texts, even though they all belong unfortunately to the Late Bronze Age only. We don't have any texts from the Middle Bronze Age. Even though we have the palace, it is completely empty. Unfortunately, as I mentioned about Ebla, if the place where the archives are kept is not burned down and collapsed, then we have no chance to find the tablets, because they would be dumped after a while and we don't know where they would have dumped

---

27 Astour (1995).

them.[28] Sometimes we find them, as in Abu Salabikh, [Young interjects, "and Amarna." Astour responds, "Amarna, yes."] but otherwise no.

Then, you must have cross references to the mentions of the same places in other sources. For instance, if I wrote a list of all the place-names belonging to Northern Syria (which I had planned to write a long time ago) this would not quite have been historical research, but it would have been a very useful thing. The definition of Northern Syria is approximately up to Homs. In other words, as far as Hittite domination ever reached, or, let us say, of Ebla. Originally I was sticking to Syria as the Romans defined it (only west of the Euphrates), but in several periods (in the Ebla Period, in the Yamhad Period and then later in the kingdom of Bît Adini), the same state extended on both sides of the Euphrates. So I believe that we should stick to a meridian passing a little bit east of Haran, and also include it in our study of Syria. I didn't begin that way, but experience led me to include this area too, what we call Osrhoene, or at least the western part of it. So we have to have cross-references. I would not have assembled the data by provenience as they do in the *Répertoire Géographique* published in Germany,[29] but by country. In other words, we should put together the cuneiform sources from Alalakh and Ugarit. Ebla probably would go separately because that is third millennium, but in the second millennium we have Alalakh and Ugarit in which a great deal overlaps and gives us very valuable historical information about the extension of the Kingdom of Ugarit under the Hittites. Then, of course, we have the Hittite texts—both Old Kingdom and New Kingdom.

The Egyptian texts are also an extremely important source which was misunderstood in the earlier usage of these sources. People didn't have any comparable evidence, so they found many endings like *-še*, which they later discovered to be Hurrian, attached to Semitic names. Well anyway, Egyptian sources must also be included. As for the cuneiform sources, I didn't

---

28 Astour (1989) 91 n. 127; (1992a) 23.

29 The *Répertoire Géographique des Textes Cunéiformes*, in several volumes, is Beihefte zum Tübinger Atlas des vorderen Orients, Reihe B (Geisteswissenschaften) Nr. 7, published by D. Ludwig Reichert Verlag, Wiesbaden, under the general editorship of W. Röllig, J.-R. Kupper, W. F. Leemans, and J. Nougayrol.

mention Emar, which is quite important, and Mari, which does not have many place-names from western Syria, the other side of the Euphrates, but they all are very important. Sometimes they are live itineraries.

We have to study ancient itineraries. Grayson, in his chapter on the Neo-Assyrian period,[30] where he examined the sources, said that scholars put too great a value on the itineraries, and he doesn't believe that they are really so reliable because some have noted that the itineraries omitted stations. Yes, but there was a pattern in the omission of the stations. For instance, Aššurbanipal, when he (or his scribe) described his itinerary along the Jagh-Jagh and Ḫabur, listed just one in two for some reason. That is, he omitted every station in between the ones he mentioned. Once we understand that, we can then compare it to other itineraries and learn the location. In general, itineraries are extremely reliable. They tell us the geographical relationship among the different points, how they were located, and also what were their approximate distances. We have to know how much a soldier could travel, probably bearing a lot of things such as a weapon, a shield, and a food supply. (I myself was once a scoutmaster and went on excursions. I knew how much distance the scouts could go. Once, we went thirty-six kilometers one way, and then returned the same thirty-six the next day, but this was exceptional.) Usually we find from Greek, Assyrian, and the Old Babylonian Urbana and Yale itineraries[31] what was the average stage. It was about twenty-five to thirty kilometers—sometimes one or two more if it was necessary to reach safety or a water source, but no more. So when you find in some explanations of itineraries that some troop marched eighteen kilometers in one day and then forty-two the next, it cannot be so. You have to total the two together to equal sixty kilometers. That was the maximum. In other words, they made it in about two days at thirty kilometers a day. This would be the case especially in Syria and Mesopotamia in the summer, with all of the heat and dust in that region. So, these sorts of things must always be taken into account when evaluating the itineraries.

---

30 Grayson (1982) 247.

31 See Goetze (1953) and Hallo (1964).

Now we come to the post-cuneiform sources. We have alphabetic sources in Aramaic and some in Hebrew from the Bible referring to northern Syria, but very little. We have Greek information and Roman. We have very little, practically nothing, from the Hellenistic period. Absolutely nothing is known about Syria from local Hellenistic sources—inscriptions, etc.—but we have references in Polybius who lived in Hellenistic times. Much of the Hellenistic evidence was later transmitted to Ptolemy in the Roman era. So, that is very important, even though people have said, as Na'aman wrote, that there were so many invasions in northern Syria that very few place-names could survive.[32] Yes, it is true for the northern part which now belongs to Turkey. Here the Turks settled for good, and they changed practically all the place-names little by little. Now, they have even taken Haran off the map, and replaced it with some very banal Turkish name. Originally many place-names survived even in the Turkish part, especially in the mountains of Ṭūr ᶜAbdīn—in remote settled areas like this they had more of a chance to survive.

The most important thing is that those who came to Syria, such as the Hurrians, left their trace in the toponymics—quite a strong one. The Hittites left one or two names from the Neo-Hittite period like Hattarikka, and maybe another name, Ta-mar-[ma?]-ri which I thought was Hittite, but which Tadmor, in his new edition, found so badly damaged that it is impossible to restore.[33] The people who came next and remained were Aramean Semitic-speakers, and therefore the transmission of the place-names from one Semitic language to another was very easy. There are a lot of Aramaic place-names and most of them were new, but the Arameans also took over some of the old names, and didn't change them very much. For instance, we would expect that the Ugaritic signs which we are still transliterating by the Arabic *tha*, the *ṯ*, would change in Aramaic to *tau*, but in most cases they did not. For instance, when there was a name such as ᶜAštar or ᶜAštart, it remained a *shin*, which, by the way, tells something about how the Ugaritians pronounced it.

---

32 Na'aman (1974) 268 and n. 17. Refutation in Astour (1989) 60 and n. 391.

33 Tadmor (1994) 148 *ad* l. 8.

Finally, we come to the Arabic and modern names. These should be taken with great caution because if they are just banal topographic names, they could appear anywhere. Do you see what I mean? For instance, if the place is named a forest, an olive grove, a spring or whatever, if the name—despite it's banality—corresponds well to the location of a similar name from antiquity, then you can assume that the names are the same. In other words, a toponymist and a topographist has to use a great deal of material which spans 4000 years or more.

Young: *And keep a level head.*

Astour: Yes. And keep a level head. There is another, different requirement. One should have a basic knowledge of Arabic and Turkish topographic terminology. Then, of course, you have to collate the data—to put it all together with the cross-references. Sometimes the card on which you made notes will be very long because you have to quote all of the references, and typing all of the topographic evidence for the preparation for a book is a most tedious thing. It is much more interesting to study the material and to find some new conclusions than to take the ready results and transfer them mechanically. You have to do it yourself and cannot entrust it to anyone who is not in the field. They will make horrible mistakes and confuse things, and then you have to edit it.

Is that a direct enough answer?

Young: *It is a direct enough answer.*

Astour: And now a few words about toponymy. Toponymy means the study of place-names, and this is now very much neglected. I believe that a very nice man and a good friend of mine, Jean Bottéro, told me that in some of my articles I devote too much space to etymologies. However, that is precisely one of the objectives of toponymy. F. T. Wainwright, a specialist in toponymy, has written, "since the place-name scholar's material is linguistic, his approach must be linguistic."[34] So it is very interesting to

---

[34] Wainwright (1962) 42.

know how people named their settlements: for gods, for natural characteristics, for a place's defensibility, for names of plants, names of animals, names of kings, or just for mere mortals, as we do in America. That is very interesting because it tells us about the ethno-history of that area. The toponymy of the United States is a famous example. Here we find Indian names, Spanish names, French names, English names, classical names and so on. The place-name tells us something about the history of an area—what populations came to the area, what they were interested in, which periods influenced them, and the like. For instance, there are many classical and biblical place-names in upper New York state. So one needs to determine the origin of the names, their meanings, and what meaning they had for these people. For that kind of knowledge, you have to know some Semitic languages: Akkadian by all means, Hebrew, Aramaic, what we know about Amorite, and now the Eblaic language which is neither Amorite nor Akkadian, but has elements of both, and all West Semitic languages. So, I believe that studying the meaning of the place-names is very important. For the Ugaritic and Alalakhian names, I gave whatever were the most plausible etymologies—sometimes two or three versions.

Young: *I have a few more questions Michael, but I believe there might be some questions in the crowd. so why don't we ask if someone has a question? Jack Sasson.*

Sasson: *Yes. Actually, I have a question that deals with the whole nature of history and history writing. As you know, there was a period of time—perhaps in America it came in the '70's—when people had very strong doubts about the reliability of history writing as we do it: not so much the reliability of history, but the fact that* we *are writing history. The point being that if we think of it as a huge puzzle, where we look for the evidence to place the facts, the evidence becomes the pieces of the puzzle. The question becomes then one of not only our own reliability—that is whether we are really right and asking the correct questions—but whether the evidence itself was in anyway a fixed amount of information, or was it always constantly changing depending on whether someone is using it, reading it, and all of these shades. So the question becomes where are we with history? How can we deal with history when we can question even* *the reliability of our evidence, and the reliability of the people who are writing it? One more little point here: people have pointed out recently that women were completely taken out from history writing, and suddenly right now we have a huge amount of scholarship being done by people who are resurrecting it. So how can we be reliable when our evidence itself may have been perhaps seen from peculiar angles, and we ourselves have specific points that we want to bring out?*

Astour: Yes, I understand, but this is a part of a much broader philosophical question about the theory of knowledge. How can we know about the thing in itself, and not as it appears to us? Well, we have to work with our senses and with such abilities as we possess. We cannot have the absolute truth. What we have is sufficient. For instance, take a look at the development of astronomy. It developed little by little with the improvement of our instruments and our mathematical abilities and so on. Now, of course, we have the satellites and all of these missions such as the Viking, Explorer and so on. In other words, our historical knowledge improves all the time. It is not absolute, but it should be the best that we can reach.

With regard to your point about evidence, if we have royal inscriptions, be they Assyrian, Hittite or even Roman, we have to understand who wrote them and why. They were written for self-praise. They will probably never admit to any kind of defeat. I am now writing an article about Ḫaššum and what Ḫattušiliš I wrote about it, "I defeated them at Mount Atalur." But he didn't take Ḫaššum initially, and to do so he had to go by a different itinerary. In other words, as I said, you should believe not what the king said, but what he did after the battle, and the same is true for Shalmaneser III. What he did at Qarqar! He killed in the first edition of the annals 14,000, then 21,000, then 28,000, and he filled the Orontes with their bodies. But what was the goal of his expedition? Probably to take Hamath. At Qarqar, he made a complete turn about and went to a country which was loyal to him, Unqi-Patina, and then back home. In other words, that was a defeat, and for several years he did not try to repeat this expedition.

What Ḫattušiliš says is that he defeated his enemies at the Mount Atalur, but he didn't go down Atalur. He went somewhere north, to the river Puruna, and attacked Ḫaššum from the north where they didn't expect him. That kind of analysis is our business. Practically everybody writes that he defeated the enemy at Atalur and then took Ḫaššum, but it was done in *two* stages, and, as he said, "only a few days later." That means that there was a gap between the two expeditions. Well, you have to evaluate the information, and you must understand who wrote it and for what reasons.

Take Herodotus, whom I love very much (I fell in love with Herodotus when I was fourteen years old and read him in Russian translation); such a fine writer, such a fine observer and psychologist and so on, but he was very biased—extremely biased—pro-Athenian, pro-Delphic and so on. These are the things we have to find out.

Another writer whom the later Greek authorities regarded as more truthful than Herodotus, but who was a liar, was Ctesias. Even though we know very little about him, we know he was a liar. I am absolutely sure that he was never actually a court physician for Artaxerxes II. He invented it all. He knew nothing. His list of the kings of Assyria is totally invented: names taken, as they say in Yiddish, "*nemen fun der Hagode*" (literally, "names taken from the Haggadah," *i.e.*, irrelevant). If you find references, or probable quotations from Ctesias in Diodorus about the expedition of Cyrus the Younger, you see that he was terribly pro-Spartan, as we know he actually was. So you see we have to validate things. We have to know who wrote and what for—what was the goal—and make the corrections.

Sasson: *But do you not foresee a day in which Ctesias will be believed more and Herodotus less. I mean these things keep on changing—revisionism and what have you.*

Astour: It is not a question of revisionism. The Hellenistic Greek authors believed that Ctesias was more trustworthy, and that belief lasted until the Behistun inscription of Darius the Great was deciphered and published in the nineteenth century C.E. Then we found out that Herodotus was completely right about this story·[35] He repeated the whole official story of

---

35 For more on the question of Herodotus' honesty, see Edwin Yamauchi's contribution to this volume, "Herodotus—Historian or Liar?"

Darius, and listed his accomplices in the assassination of Smerdis—or the alleged Smerdis—with one single mistake. In other words, he had very good references. Probably one of the refugees who fled from Persia told him all of the story. You see, then we started to believe Herodotus a lot more.

Sasson: *But, may I just add one more coda; that people who are studying the Behistun rock now question completely what is said? They think the writer there was completely fanciful.*

Astour: Absolutely! Absolutely! Darius was a usurper without any claim to the throne. He invented the stories that Cyrus and Cambyses were Achaemenids. They were not. The story about the Pseudo-Smerdis the Mede—the *magus*—is also completely invented as we can see because of what happened. This man, who claimed to be Bardia (and certainly was), the son of Cyrus, was accepted by the entire empire, but for two years thereafter there were insurrections against Darius—even in Persia itself. So, of course, that is the obligation of the historian—to evaluate the evidence and who wrote it. Of course, the usurper wouldn't write he was a usurper and that he seized the throne by sheer force.

Young: *Jack, were you using the terms revision or revisionism as naughty words?*

Sasson: *No.*

Young: *Historians make revisions all the time. That's our business.*

Astour: You see, we can never be sure that what we wrote will be true after us, or even in our own time. We have to make changes. May I say something about myself—about Ebla? I made the mistake to publish in 1971 a little article called "Tell Mardikh and Ebla" in which I denied, or said that there was only a 50% chance, that Tell Mardikh was Ebla; that the Ibbit-Lim statue (which contained the first hint that Tell Mardikh might be Ebla) was not made at Tell Mardikh,[36] and Pettinato later gloated about it.[37] But

---

36 Astour (1971).

37 Pettinato (1976) 12 n. 2; (1979) 27.

Matthiae himself wrote that there is a 50% chance that the statue was made in Ebla, or 50% that it was brought as a votive gift from somewhere else. Why did I think that Tell Mardikh couldn't be Ebla? I relied on Gudea. Gudea wrote that he brought his timber from Uršu in the mountains of Ebla,[38] and nobody at the time I was writing could even dream that Ebla was such a huge empire. Do you understand? I wrote at that time that unless we find texts in Tell Mardikh that shows it was Ebla, we must hold the identification in suspension. Subsequently, they found the texts and I believed. That was normal method. That was already a proof. It was not one stray tablet that was found, but an entire archive. It was quite clear. I sat down and wrote it all down. (You know, when you write it down you see things more clearly.) I wrote down all the proofs and, yes, I had made a mistake, but I made it on the basis of the then available evidence, and I wouldn't be stubborn and say, "No! No! It is not so," as some scholars might. No, I recognized I was wrong, but I would say, in the right ways.

Young: *For all the right reasons.*

Astour: I didn't invent it. I relied on what there was available. Now, there is a lot more available. That is what every historian has to do. When new evidence appears, or when some colleague makes a better proposal, one has to revise.

Mrs. Miriam Astour: *What about women in ancient history?*

Astour: First of all, some women do appear in ancient history very prominently—especially in Herodotus. He was very much interested in women and their influence, as was also the author of the history of King David. Therein appeared a lot of women—influential women—who played a great role like Bathsheba and Abigail. Even if the women didn't play an active role, they still contributed, as in the story of Tamar. This author was very much

---

38 Gudea's Statue B inscription, col. V:53-VI:58. See Thureau-Dangin (1907) 68. English translation by A. L. Oppenheim in Pritchard (1969) 268-69. See also Steible (1991) 1.164-65.

interested in women. He believed that women are wise. (For example, the wise women of Tekoa who influenced King David).

The same is true about Herodotus. Even in Roman times—especially in the Empire, but even in the Republic—we hear about many outstanding women. Quite a few. We can mention Cornelia, the mother of the Gracchi, and, of course, Cleopatra (there were several Cleopatras in the history of the Ptolemies), and Queen Sammuramat (Semiramis) in Assyria. But these were only very outstanding women, and, by the way, the same is true for men as well. We hear very little about plebeians. They were not politicians and so on. So, of course, we know little about women, but we know quite a bit about their juridical situation from the laws and the business documents. We understand that in Babylonia women had a very high status. They were almost equal juridically to men, but in Assyria, absolutely not. If there is not information about women, what can we do? How can we increase the number of pages devoted to women at that time? Until recently, women couldn't vote in the U.S.A., so they didn't take part in politics. Now they do take quite a big part in politics. So things change.

Mark Chavalas: *Let me ask a question about the future. What type of unfinished business do you have? In other words, what is your future scholarship?*

Young: *Mark that was one of my last questions.*

Chavalas: *I am sorry to do that. In other words, what types of things would you leave unfinished that you would almost make a plea for scholars to continue?*

Astour: I would like that some young scholar, or a graduate student, who is preparing his or her thesis, or whatever, and who is interested in the field, should contact me. Better now than later. Not posthumously! [Much laughter!] I propose that such a volunteer edit my materials on Syrian topography and toponymy and publish it under our joint names. He or she can even put my name on the lower line—something like "prepared by xyz from the posthumous papers of Dr. Astour," in smaller type or whatever. What I want is to save my work from oblivion because I put a great deal of effort into it, and I think it may be useful as a reference work. That is the most important thing.

Besides that, I have a great deal of preliminary notes in many fields, including Ebla, but here comes the catch. Unfortunately, when I write my first impressions, I do it in Russian. That is an old habit of mine, to write for myself not in French, Yiddish, or English, but in Russian. Of course, when I work on it, I write in English and also keep my card file in English. So, it would be extremely useful if this co-author, or at least his or her spouse, could know Russian well enough to use my notes. But this is more difficult because the notes are chaotic. In other words, they reflect the progress in my research in all stages—my original opinion, my later opinion, my final opinion (if it could be final), and so on. So, the completion of this project would bring me a great deal of satisfaction. If you know somebody who would like to do this kind of work, I would be very happy to meet him or her, to give him or her a place to work, and to introduce him or her to my materials.

Michael Fox: *I'm very interested in your work on Eastern European Jewish social movements. Besides the staggering breadth, is there any kind of integral connection between your work in modern European Jewish History and your ancient historiography?*

Astour: No. Absolutely not. As they used to say at the beginning of the century about political problems, my work is on two planes, two different planes. It has to do with me as a Jew from Wilna—a secular Jew of the twentieth century—and the rest is completely unconnected to it. What connection could there be? The only connection could be the methodology. That is all. In my book on the Freeland League and the Territorialist idea, I wrote in the preface that no historian could be absolutely objective.[39] Even when we write about ancient Greece, each author has his own approach. Let me add parenthetically that if you read works by British or German authors about the Macedonian conquest of Greece, they tend to sympathize with Philip and Alexander. If the works were written by French authors, someone such as Clemenceau, they would sympathize with the Greek republicans. But what a historian should do—be he or she British, German, Jewish,

---

39 Astour (1966a).

French or whatever—is to tell the facts as they were. You will find commentaries which imply, "Ah, the naive Greeks who believed that they could keep their freedom and fought in such a futile way. Why didn't they surrender to Alexander voluntarily?" Well, because they were republican Greeks who cherished enormously their freedom and their autonomy. They killed each other for many decades for just that freedom. So, when Philip and Alexander came, not all of the Greeks wanted to surrender to them. But, as I have said, in giving the facts, I have to be completely true to those facts, and not have any kind of bias. That is the thing that connects the two fields—which is easier for ancient history than for modern.

Ronald Veenker: *I have imagined you through the years, Michael, as your students have gone on to become fine scholars, and have heard so many fine things about you. I have always been fascinated with your location in Edwardsville. I have often thought of the aphorism from the Bible, "A prophet is not without honor save in his own home town." I have imagined you teaching history. What courses did you teach? Did you teach freshmen in the large survey courses of civilization?*

Astour: Yes. That was the obligation of all—even the most senior members of the department. Now I must tell you that I was very happy that I landed at Southern Illinois University at Edwardsville. I spent twenty-two years there in full-time teaching and several years in part-time after my retirement, with great satisfaction. The one exception to that statement is that I didn't have a doctoral program in ancient Near Eastern History. Nor did Edwardsville's bigger sister, Southern Illinois University at Carbondale which is older, has more students and a doctoral program. At Edwardsville, we could only offer the Master's. So, for me it would make no difference at all. I directed four theses in ancient history; a fifth one, was supposed to be in Assyrian history. That girl, however, married and moved away to Albuquerque, and that was that. The rest were men.

One of them wanted to write about Roman history, so I gave him a topic about Aurelian during the troubled time in Roman history. He wrote quite a fine work. Another was a Saudi Arab who wrote about the Nabateans and had great trouble with English, so it was revised several times by the committee who asked him to improve it and finally found somebody to help him with his English. A third student was a Zionist Jew from Los Angeles who wrote about Jewish tribes in Arabia—that was also my proposal. The fourth one, which was the best, was written by a veteran of the Vietnam war, James Jackson. He was really fascinated with the Amarna Age and his thesis was entitled, "The Life and Times of Tushratta." David Owen saw it and liked it very much, but probably as the result of Agent Orange, he contracted cancer, first in the jaw, which forced him to interrupt his studies in the graduate school. He later returned with a large hole caused by the cancer treatment. For his dissertation, I taught him Hebrew in his free time, privately, and tried to introduce him to cuneiform. He was a very promising young man, but he died when the cancer recurred in his heart. Before he died, he received some extra money from the Veterans Administration and went to Egypt to see Luxor, Karnak, Amarna and so on. He came back very happy and died a month later.

I was regarded with respect at Southern Illinois University at Edwardsville. They promoted me earlier than many of my colleagues who had had longer service than I had. They gave me travel money (even for Europe) and money also for research. There was absolutely no envy or quarrels, at least in our department. (I don't know much about the other departments in our school.) So, I was completely satisfied. Unfortunately, one ages.

As for teaching, my curriculum was the standard one. First of all, we had several courses for the upper-classmen in Ancient History. At that time we had the quarter system, but now we have changed to the semester system. The change was one reason I declined to teach anymore. There is just too much time in a semester.

I taught two quarter segments on the Ancient Near East, two on Greece, and three on Rome, including Byzantine History. This was the cycle. Beside that, once I was promoted to full professor, I had one third of the time released for research so I had to teach only two courses. Then, of course, I had to teach General Studies. For a time I taught a very brief survey of Ancient History, but later mostly twentieth century which I liked more, being an eyewitness to much of it [general laughter]. Beside that, from time to time I had graduate seminars in Ancient History in which we studied different questions from the Ancient Near East and the Aegean world, later Greece and so on, and the students wrote term papers. Also, I taught historiography and thesis writing from time to time. The teaching was quite satisfactory. I gave mini-courses that lasted only one quarter and had fewer credits—about the First World War, Europe between the two wars, about the collapse and resurrection of France, etc. These were things that were close to me. Once I was invited by the Department of Art to give a course on ancient Near Eastern art. That subject was new for me, but I liked it very much. The only difficult thing was selecting the slides from our collection, and writing a list of them so I would know what I was showing. [General laughter.] That was quite interesting. Then, I participated several times in an interdepartmental course on war and peace; with the Department of Philosophy, while I was from History. I remember that I was talking about the origins of great wars; how they came to be—making a comparison of the Peloponnesian War and the First World War. There was a great similarity.

Sasson: *I have a parting question if possible. Is it too late?*

Young: *No. Go ahead.*

Sasson: *We had some sessions this morning, Anson Rainey and others, and some of them really dealt with the issue of biblical historiography. How seriously do you take the text—how do you use it, etc.? If you're talking about revisionism—if you're talking about how scholars actually wear different glasses when viewing a document—the most powerful example you can use is biblical historiography. What kind of reflections do you have over the number of years in which you wrote about biblical history? Where are we going now? Are we ever going to solve these questions, do you think?*

Astour: I used to be a member of the Society of Biblical Literature, but when I noticed that I was no longer publishing in this field, I resigned. Why should I be a member of a society to which I am not contributing? I published three articles in the *Journal of Biblical Literature*,[40] but later became engaged in other fields. On the other hand, I continued to make quite a few notes in

---

40 Astour (1965b, 1966b, and 1976).

Russian about problems of biblical literature, but they will probably never be published. One of them that I would like to finish is the Presidential address about Egyptian bondage.[41] I didn't have the time to finish all of it; so some is already typed, and some is written in long hand because I had very little time when I wrote it.

What my approach was, I really can't tell you. I spoke once at one of our regional meetings with the late Gösta Ahlström and Diana Edelman. They asked me why I was no longer writing on biblical topics. I said because there is only one biblical text with very few variants or changes (in the Qumran documents or the versions), and all we do is tread the same water trying to explain the same verses. I told them the cuneiform field is always full of news; new texts are discovered, new interpretations are given and so on. That appeals to me more. Then, when I looked back on all of the things that I published that have connections to biblical studies, I recognized that they all were comparative. For instance, Gordon Young earlier in the conference mentioned my article about the forerunners of biblical anti-royalism in the Amarna Age.[42] This dealt mainly with the Amarna, and not biblical, material. Then I published a little known article in the Edel *Festschrift*, "Yahweh in Egyptian Topographic Texts."[43] There again I utilized the Egyptian evidence.

Here is another example. Once, while teaching a course in the history of ancient Western Asia at the graduate school of Brandeis University, I touched, for some reason, upon chapter 38 of Genesis—about Tamar, her two husbands, and her father-in-law Judah—and I said that in ancient Babylonia the priestesses could be married, but didn't have the right to have children. For childbearing, they had to bring another woman—a substitute wife. So I said, perhaps in the beginning the story was not that her husband didn't want to have a son, but that *she* couldn't have a child. When she pretended to be a *qedeshah* or a *zonah*, she actually was one, a hierodule. We should understand that she was supposed to be burned for being preg-

41 See n. 8 above.

42 Astour (1964).

43 Astour (1979).

nant. That is what they did with priestesses in Babylonia who violated some taboos. Then David Owen said, "That's interesting. You must publish it." So, I did. I typed it up and I read it at the meeting of the Society of Biblical Literature at Nashville before the new year of 1966. Then it was published.[44] All of my biblical articles are based on extra biblical material, and even the Presidential address about the Egyptian bondage story was largely based on Assyrian and Egyptian material, but with a lot more biblical analysis.[45]

Young: *Michael, we have been at it for a little over an hour. Are you getting tired?*

Astour: I am not, but how about you? [General laughter.]

Young: *Let me ask you one final question, which Jack was starting to get to, about your reaction to the various papers that have been delivered in your honor so far.*

Astour: First of all, I thank the authors of the papers for coming to this meeting and dedicating them to me. I had the opportunity of talking to some of them and frankly telling them my opinion. The time does not allow me to repeat here my remarks. I shall dwell only on a couple of them which raise particularly important methodological and historical questions in my own field of research.

Now about the paper on Ashshuwa and the Mycenaean sword: all of this neo-analysis about pre-Homeric, pre-Mycenaean remains and vestiges in the *Iliad* is not very new in my opinion. When the ancients described the shield of Ajax, which covered him from head to feet, they already knew what such a shield looked like. By the way, in a later addition to the *Iliad*, the *Dolonia* (Book X), he wore a helmet made of boar tusks. Aha! This boar's tusk helmet was only used in the sixteenth century, but not in the thirteenth, say the neo-analysts. As I wrote in my review of the corresponding volume of the *Cambridge Ancient History* in the *Bulletin of the American Schools of Oriental Research*[46]—why should we think that it had to survive in oral

---

44 Astour (1966b).

45 See n. 8 above.

46 Astour (1977b).

transmission through six or seven hundred years, when the Greeks already knew about Mycenaean weapons and metals from opening graves? We know from Plutarch[47]—that at the behest of the Spartan king Agesilaus (fourth century B.C.E.) the alleged tomb of Alcmene was opened, and that a bronze tablet was found there with a long inscription in an unknown script, which they thought resembled Egyptian signs (it was probably written in Linear B). The tombs for them were holy places of heroes. They would steal the bones of the alleged heroes who were buried there from one place to another as the Spartans did with those of Orestes from Tegea.[48] Of course, in so doing, they would find weapons, the helmet, the shield. If the shields were made of good strong leather, they could survive a long time in a closed place, together with the swords and everything else. They knew that the swords were made of bronze and not iron. That is where their knowledge came from, not oral transmission.

As for Rainey, I can't agree with his definition of Canaan.[49] I learned a very fascinating thing about the new references in Ramessid and Hittite documents—about the Danuna as a synonym of Kizzuwadna.[50] Well, that is something I wrote about in *Hellenosemitica*,[51] and later almost abandoned, because there was no evidence that the Late Bronze Age land of Danuna was located in eastern Cilicia. Now it turns out that I was not wrong after all. Of course, I don't agree with Rainey—and he doesn't agree with me—about the definition of who were the ᶜApiru/Hapiru. I believe they were tribesmen who lived among the settled population and sold their services. He quoted that the king of Hazor ran away from his city, and was conquering land for the Hapiru—not the Hapiru conquering for the king

47 Plutarch, *de daemonio Socrates* 5. (*Plutarch's Moralia in fifteen volumes.* Loeb Classical Library. Cambridge and London [1959]: vol. VII: 576-78.)

48 Herodotus I: 67-68. Similarly, Cimon, in 475 B.C.E., brought to Athens from the island of Scyrus the bones ascribed to the Athenian hero Theseus (Plutarch, *Theseus,* 7).

49 Subsequently published as Rainey (1996).

50 See Edel (1994) I: 50-91 (texts 20-38); II: 94.

51 Astour (1965a) 1-9.

of Hazor, but the king of Hazor for the Hapiru. In other words, the Hapiru themselves had claim to the land.

It is very difficult to know what is meant by Canaan. In some cases, both in Alalakh and Ugarit, they would define the provenience, the origin, of the foreigner who came to them, not as usual by his city. We find, for instance, in Alalakh a man from Ammiya—which was quite normal because Idrimi went there, and probably brought back with him some people.[52] We also find Sidonians, Tyrians, people from Akko, people from Beirut, people from Sarepta (probably), and certainly people from Simyra. Then suddenly it is just Canaanite. It is strange. Let us imagine that we have to deal with Germany before Bismarck. Then people identified themselves as from Hesse, Bavaria, Saxon-Coburg-Gotha, which is very comparable to the city states of ancient times. Then, suddenly, somebody is German. That would be not admissible. You would have to show it was political. So, if Canaan was at that time, as I believe, designated in the broader sense as the Egyptian possessions in Asia, why would they define him in such a broad allegiance? That is a little strange and I don't have an explanation for it.

Young: *Well Michael, thank you very much.* [*Applause.*] *As I said last night, your influence is very long-lasting.*

Astour: I don't know how broad it is.

Young: *I would say it is pretty broad, as reflected by some of the tribute that came in from around the world which I read last night. Thanks again.*

Bibliography

Albright, W. F. (1968) *Yahweh and the Gods of Canaan: A Historical Analysis of Two Contrasting Faiths.* London. **Astour, M. C.** (1959) Bené-Iamina et Jericho. *Semitica* 9: 5-20. (1963) Un texte d'Ugarit récemment découvert et ses rapports avec l'origine des cultes

52 See Dietrich and Loretz (1981) 204, ll. 18-20. "... I went to the land of Canaan (*ki-in-a-nim*^{ki}). In the land of Canaan lies the city of Ammiya."

bachiques grecs. *Revue de l'Histoire des Religions* 164: 1-15. (1964) The Amarna Age Forerunners of Biblical Anti-Royalism. In *For Max Weinreich on His Seventieth Birthday: Studies in Jewish Languages, Literature, and Society.* The Hague: 6-17. (1965a) *Hellenosemitica: An Ethnic and Cultural Study in West Semitic Impact on Mycenaean Greece.* Leiden. 2nd edition with additions and corrections, 1967. (1965b) Sabtah and Sabteca: Ethiopian Pharaoh Names in Genesis 10. *Journal of Biblical Literature* 84: 422-25. (1966a) *History of the Freeland League and of the Territorialist Idea.* Buenos Aires and New York. Yiddish. (1966b) Tamar the Hierodule: an Essay in the Method of Vestigial Motifs. *Journal of Biblical Literature* 85: 185-96. (1969) La triade de déesses de fertilité à Ugarit et en Gréce. In Schaeffer 1969: 9-23. (1971) Tell Mardikh and Ebla. *Ugarit-Forschungen* 3: 9-19. (1976) Ezekiel's Prophesy of Gog and the Cuthean Legend of Naram-Sin. *Journal of Biblical Literature* 95: 567-79. (1977a) Continuité et changement dans la toponymie de la Syrie du Nord. In *La Toponymie Antique: Actes du Colloque de Strasbourg. 12-14 juin 1975.* Université des Sciences Humaines de Strasbourg. Travaux du Centre de Recherche sur le Proche-Orient et la Grèce Antique 4. Leiden: 117-41 and folding map. (1977b) Review article of I. E. S. Edwards, *et al.*, eds. *Cambridge Ancient History,* Volume 2. Part 2. 3 ed. *Bulletin of the American Schools of Oriental Research* 227: 66-69. (1979) Yahweh in Egyptian Topographic Lists. In Görg and Puesch 1979: 17-34. (1980) North Syrian Toponyms Derived from Plant Names. In Rendsburg, Adler, Arla and Winter 1980: 3-8. (1988a) Toponymy of Ebla and Ethnohistory of Northern Syria: A Preliminary Survey. *Journal of the American Oriental Society* 108: 545-55. (1988b) The Geographical and Political Structure of the Ebla Empire. In Hauptman and Waetzoldt 1988: 139-58. (1988c) Remarks on KTU 1.96. *Studi epigrafici e linguistici* 5: 13-24. (1989) *Hittite History and Absolute Chronology of the Bronze Age.* Partille. (1992a) The Date of the Destruction of Palace G at Ebla. In Chavalas and Hayes 1992: 23-39. (1992b) Sparagmos, Omophagia, and Ecstatic Prophesy at Mari. *Ugarit Forschungen* 24: 1-2. (1995) La Topographie du royaume d'Ougarit. In Yon, Sznycer and Bordreuil 1995: 55-69. **Bérard, V.** (1894) *De l'origine des cultes arcadiens: essai de methode en mythologie grecque.* Bibliothéque des écoles françaises d'Athenes et de Rome 67. Paris. **Bury, J. B., *et al.*** (1927) *The Cambridge Ancient History.* 1st ed. Cambridge. **Chavalas, M. W., and J. L. Hayes**, eds. (1992) *New Horizons in the Study of Ancient Syria.* Bibliotheca Mesopotamica 25. Malibu, Calif. **del Monte, G. F., and J. Tischler** (1978) *Die Orts- und Gewassernamen der hethitischen Texte.* Répertoire géographique des textes cunéiformes 6. Tübinger Atlas der Vorderen Orients, Reihe B (Geisteswissenschaften) 7/6. Wiesbaden. **de Moor, J. C.** (1971) *The Seasonal Pattern in the Ugaritic Myth of Ba^{c}lu According to the Version of Of Ilimilku.* Alter Orient und altes Testament 16. Neukirchen-Vluyn. **Dietrich, M., and O. Loretz** (1981) Die Inschrift der Statue des Königs Idrimi von Alalah. *Ugarit Forschungen* 13: 201-69. **Edel, E.** (1994) *Die Ägyptisch-hethitische Korrespondenz in babylonischer und hethitischer Sprache.* 2 vols. Opladen. **Edwards, I. E. S., *et al.*** (1975) *The Cambridge Ancient History.* 3rd ed. Cambridge. **Gaster, T. H.** (1939) Baal is Risen . . . An Ancient Hebrew Passion Play from Ras-Shamra-Ugarit. *Iraq* 6: 109-43. **Gelb, I. J.** (1961) The Early History of the West Semitic Peoples. *Journal of Cuneiform Studies* 15: 27-47.

Goetze, A. (1953) An Old Babylonian Itinerary. *Journal of Cuneiform Studies* 7: 51-72. **Görg, M., and E. Puesch**, eds. (1979) *Festschrift Elmar Edel. Studien zu Geschichte, Kultur und Religion Ägyptens und des alten Testament,* I. Bamberg. **Grayson, A. K.** (1982) Assyria: Ashur-dan II to Ashur-nirari V (934-745 B.C.). *Cambridge Ancient History,* 2 ed. Vol. III/1. **Gressman, H., *et al.*** (1926) *Altorientalische Texte und Bilder zum alten Testament.* 2nd ed. Berlin. **Hallo, W. W.** (1964) The Road to Emar. *Journal of Cuneiform Studies* 18: 57-88. **Hauptman, H., and H. Waetzoldt**, eds. (1988) *Wirtschaft und Gesellschaft von Ebla: Akten der Internationalen Tagung, Heidelberg 4.-7. November 1986.* Heidelberger Studien zum Alten Orient 2. Heidelberg. **Herdner, A.** (1963) *Corpus de tablettes en cunéiformes alphabétiques découvertes à Ras Shamra-Ugarit à 1939.* Mission de Ras Shamra 10. Paris. **Lods, A.** (1930) *Israël des origines au milieu du VIIIe siécle.* L'evolution de l'humanité, synthese collective 27. Paris. (1935) *Les Prophètes d'Israël et le débuts du judaïsme.* L'evolution de l'humanité, synthese collective 28, part 1. Paris. (1950) *Histoire de la literature hébraïque et juive depuis les origines jusqu'à la ruine de l'État juif.* Paris. **Mayani, Z.** (1956) *Les Hyksos et le monde de la Bible.* Bibliothéque historique. Paris. **Na'aman, N.** (1974) Syria at the Transition from the Old Babylonian Period to the Middle Babylonian Period. *Ugarit Forschungen* 6: 265-74. **Pettinato, G.** (1976) Carchemis – Kar-Kamis: Le prime attestazioni del III millennio. *Oriens Antiquus* 15: 12-15. (1979) *Ebla: Un impero inciso nell'argilla.* Milan. **Piganiol, A.** (1917) *Essai sur les origines romaines.* Bibliothéque des Écoles françaises d'Athenes et de Rome 110. Paris. (1926) *Histoire romaine.* Paris. (1930) *La conquète romaine.* Peuples et civilisations 3. Paris. (1939) *Histoire de Rome.* Clio 3. Paris. **Pritchard, J. B.** (1969) *Ancient Near Eastern Texts Relating to the Old Testament.* 3 ed. with supplement. Princeton. **Rainey A. F.** (1996) "Who Is a Canaanite? A Review of the Textual Evidence." *Bulletin of the American Schools of Oriental Research* 304: 1-5. **Rendsburg, G., R. Adler, M. Arla, and N. Winters**, eds. (1980) *The Bible World: Essays in Honor of Cyrus H. Gordon.* New York. **Schaeffer, C. F. A.** (1969) *Ugaritica* 6. Mission de Ras Shamra 17. Bibliothéque Archéologique et Historique 81. Paris. **Steible, H.** (1991) *Die Neusumerischen Bau- und Weihinschriften.* Freiburger Altorientalische Studien 9. 2 vols, Stuttgart. **Tadmor, H.** (1982) Tid^c al. *Ensiglopediah Miqra'it* 8: 435-36. Jerusalem. (1994) *The Inscriptions of Tiglath-Pileser III, King of Assyria.* Jerusalem. **Thureau-Dangin, F.** (1907) *Die sumerischen und akkadischen Königsinschriften.* Leipzig. **Virolleaud, C.** (1938) *La déesse Anat: poéme de Ras Shamra.* Mission de Ras Shamra 4. Bibliothéque archéologique et historique 28. Paris. **Wadler, A.** (1935) *Der Turm von Babel:* Urgemeinschaft der Sprachen. Basel. **Wainwright, F. T.** (1962) *Archaeology and Place-Names and History: An Essay on Problems of Coordination.* London. **Winckler, H.** (1907) *Die babylonische Geisteskultur in ihrer Beziehung zur Kulturentwicklung der Menschheit.* Leipzig. (2 ed., 1919) **Yon, M., M. Sznycer, and P. Bordreuil**, eds. (1995) *Ras Shamra-Ougarit XI. Le pays d'Ougarit autour de 1200 av. J.-C.* Actes du Colloque International de Paris, 28 juin – 1er juillet 1993. **Zieliński, T.** (1930) *Starożytność bajeczna* (Fabled Antiquity). Warsaw.

Ritual Formula, Textual Frame, and Thematic Echo in the Cylinders of Gudea*

Richard E. Averbeck
Trinity Evangelical Divinity School, Deerfield, Ill.

Michael Astour is well known for his practice of collecting the plain details of texts and discerning within them patterns that form the basis of sound scholarly hypotheses or conclusions. He insists upon a good rigorous method that allows the ancient text(s) to take scholars to their natural destinations (geographical or otherwise). The goal of this article is to apply this kind of rigorous method and mentality to the analysis of the literary structure of the Gudea Cylinders.

The hymnic temple building composition recorded on Gudea Cylinders A and B is renowned as one of the lengthiest and most skillful masterpieces in the corpus of extant Sumerian literature.[1] Its poetic pattern of line

* I owe a special debt of thanks to both Åke Sjöberg and Jacob Klein for openly discussing with me some of the questions raised here. I also thank the former for access to the resources of the Babylonian section of the University Museum of the University of Pennsylvania, and the latter for reading an earlier draft of this paper and making many valuable suggestions for its improvement. The views expressed here and any remaining errors are, of course, my responsibility.

Additional abbreviations for this article are AnOr = Analecta Orientalia (28 = Falkenstein [1949], 29 = Falkenstein [1950], 30 = Falkenstein [1966], 52 = Cooper [1978]); PSD = *The Sumerian Dictionary of the University Museum of the University of Pennsylvania*, Sjöberg, ed. (1984-); SAHG = *Sumerische und Akkadische Hymnen und Gebete*, Falkenstein and von Soden (1953); SAKI = *Die sumerischen und akkadischen Königsinschriften*, Thureau-Dangin (1907); TCL = Textes cunéiformes. Musée du Louvre – Départment des Antiquités Orientales (8 = Thureau-Dangin [1925]).

1 The primary source for the cuneiform text of the Gudea Cylinders is the very good

formation, parallel lines, strophic arrangement, and motif development is classic and has been the subject of some brief studies.[2] A great deal more needs to be done on these and other features of the text, including the broad range of religious notions expressed in the composition.[3] None of these subjects, however, are the primary focus of the present article.

Instead, this essay is concerned primarily with the large scale literary structure (*i.e.*, macrostructure) and overall interpretation of the Gudea Cylinders. The goal is to provide a badly needed framework and contextual guide for examining the distinct sections and ultimately the individual lines or groups of lines of this text. The difficulty of understanding the Gudea

---

hand copy by Thureau Dangin in TCL 8 (1925). The same author also produced a transliteration with German translation and a few notes in SAKI (1907) 88-141 (*cf.* also his French edition [1905] 135-99). There was also a French edition by Lambert and Tournay (1948a, 1948b) with later revisions for Cylinder A (1950). The earlier English translations by Barton (1929) and Price (1927) are not reliable. For a recent "working edition" including transliteration, translation, and limited commentary, see Averbeck (1987) 582-712. T. Jacobsen's translation with a few notes ([1987] 386-444) is innovative and wonderfully fluent. See now also the very important work of Edzard (1997) and major selections from the Gudea Cylinders with notes and biblical parallels by Averbeck in Hallo and Younger (forthcoming). The very recent transliteration and English translation of the Gudea Cylinders with a few notes by Wilson (1996) is useful for its index of Sumerian word occurrences, and as a collation of translations and grammatical remarks from various secondary sources, especially those of Falkenstein (1949, 1950, and 1966), Thomsen (1984), and Jacobsen (1987). Surprisingly, however, it contains no references to and shows no awareness of some of the more recent studies of the Gudea Cylinders or even the most important *Pennsylvania Sumerian Dictionary* (PSD), the first volume of which appeared in 1984.

Thureau-Dangin's translation in SAKI is still valuable today, but the standard German translation is that of A. Falkenstein in SAHG (1953) 137-82. Falkenstein never produced an actual edition of the Cylinders, but his grammatical, historical, cultural, and literary analysis in AnOr 28-30 is still held in high regard. Averbeck (1987) focuses on the religious rituals and ideas as well as the overall structure of the composition. Suter (1995) compares the pictorial representations of the temple building project with the written account in the Cylinders.

2 See, *e.g.*, Falkenstein (1966) 181-87; Heimpel (1970) 492-95 (esp. regarding Gudea Cyl. A i 11-16 and xxi 1-12); and Suter (1995) 153-65.

3 For now, see the preliminary discussion of some of these matters in Averbeck (1987) chapters 3 (temple and ruler), 8 (prayers), and 9 (dreams and dream incubation).

Cylinders makes this framework especially desirable and, in fact, indispensable. Perhaps some of the difficulties can at least be reduced to manageable proportions by working from the top down as well as the bottom up. That is, the word by word and line by line (*i.e.*, bottom up) focus of the standard philological method is absolutely necessary. One must of course start there. But, at the same time, while staying fully engaged with the text on that level, it is important that we take a serious look at the composition *as a whole* from a literary and structural point of view (*i.e.*, the top down).[4]

Preliminary Questions

The issue of the literary macrostructure of the Gudea Cylinders is closely related to two other questions. First, how many Cylinders were there originally? Two or three? Second, what is the literary genre of the composition inscribed on the Cylinders? Is it a royal dedicatory inscription, a temple hymn, a building dedication hymn, some combination of these, or something else? The answers to these two questions will, of course, have important implications for the literary structure of the composition as a whole which, in turn, will contribute much to the solutions to these two questions. Unfortunately, we cannot deal with all the details in the present article. Each of these two preliminary questions requires a separate full-scale article. I offer here only a brief summary of the main factors involved, and some tentative conclusions. This will be sufficient as background to our more complete discussion of the literary macrostructure of the composition preserved on Gudea Cylinders A and B.

---

4 See the similar point made elsewhere, for example, in Vanstiphout (1986) 2.

Was There a Third Cylinder?

The scholarly disagreement over whether or not there was originally another Cylinder has not been resolved. Falkenstein,[5] Wilcke,[6] Sauren,[7] Klein,[8] and Suter[9] either explicitly or implicitly argue that there was no third Cylinder. Oppenheim,[10] Kramer,[11] Baer,[12] van Dijk,[13] Jacobsen,[14] and Hurowitz[15] say, yes, there was a third Cylinder, and that it originally constituted the first part of the trilogy. Thus, there would have been Cyl. A (not extant, except perhaps a few fragments; see below), Cyl. B (extant "Cyl. A"), and Cyl. C (extant "Cyl. B").

If there was originally a third Cylinder, it must have stood before the current Cyl. A. It could hardly be placed anywhere else since, based on content analysis, Cyl. B obviously connects to the end of Cyl. A, and the end of Cyl. B is undoubtedly the end of the composition. Presumably, the supposed third Cylinder would have contained "hymns with general praise of the temple and of Ningirsu," as well as descriptions of:

> events leading up to the decision to build, explaining why a fairly recent existing structure built by Gudea's father-in-law, Ur-Baba, was deemed

5 (1966) 178-79.

6 (1975) 241. First, Wilcke assumes that Cyl. A i 1-16 comprises the prologue to the composition as a whole and, therefore, treats Cyls. A and B as a complete composition. Second, he points to Cyl. A i 17-18 as the beginning of the narration and especially emphasizes a supposed similarity between these lines and the standard u_4-ba ("in that day") formula which begins other narratives after prologue introductions.

7 (1975) 96-97 n. 5.

8 (1989a) 58 n. 14.

9 (1995) 77.

10 (1956) 211.

11 (1969) 141-42 n. 5 and (1988) 2.

12 (1971) 3.

13 (1983) 11 n. 25.

14 (1987) 386.

15 (1992) 33-38.

insufficient. It may also have told of the election of Gudea as ruler by the city god, Ningirsu.[16]

Those who argue for the existence of a third Cylinder usually do so primarily on the basis of: (1) certain unplaced fragments, the contents of which do not seem to fit in the (badly broken) final columns of Cyl. B, (2) the closing lines of Cyls. A and B, which they understand to designate Cyl. A as the "middle hymn" and Cyl. B as the "final hymn" in a trilogy, and (3) the opening line(s) of Cyl. A, with which one might compare the u_4-ba ("in that day") formula structure found in the epics and royal hymns, and which was often preceded by a hymnic or mythological and sometimes a rather lengthy introduction, followed by a description of past events.[17] We shall deal with each of these points only briefly here.

The Unplaced Fragments. First, Thureau-Dangin published eleven fragments along with Cyls. A and B.[18] Except for Cyl. B xviii-xxiv where there are some major breaks, there are only a few chips here and there yielding small lacunae in the composition (see esp. Cyl. A xv 1-5, xvi 1-5, and xvii 1-6). Baer later published a twelfth fragment and used some of them to suggest restorations of portions of the broken sections in Cyl. B xviii-xxiv. The leftover fragments he assigned to the supposed third Cylinder because they did not fit either physically or in terms of content into the lacunae at the end of Cyl. B.[19]

---

16 Jacobsen (1987) 386. For the Eninnu built by Urbaba, see Steible (1991) 1: 134-40 and the treatment of ii 6 - iii 7 in Averbeck (1987) 315-17. Based on Gudea Cyl. A xxx 15 (see also Gudea Cyl. B xxiv 16), and according to a suggestion which he credits to A. Shaffer, Jacobsen ([1987] 386 n. 1) takes the title of the composition to be: é-[d]nin-gír-su-ka dù-a "The House of Ningirsu having been built." See the review of literature and opinions in Hurowitz (1992) 35-38.

17 See the summary in Hurowitz (1992) 33-35.

18 Thureau-Dangin (1925) plates LIII and LIV.

19 Baer (1971). More recently, van Dijk ([1983] 11 n. 25) suggested that, although we cannot preclude the possibility that these latter fragments belong to Cyl. B, their style and content is different from Cyls. A and B. He suspected that especially fragment 1 reflects the mythological content of the third Cylinder. It is interesting, however, that he also refers to fragment 5 in this regard, the same fragment from which Falkenstein

Even before Baer's publication, however, Falkenstein felt it was sufficient to simply point out that one of the fragments reads: [gù]-dé-a [é]-mu ma-[d]ù-e (5 i 3) which could be translated either "Gudea shall build my house for me" or "Gudea, my house you shall build for me." According to his understanding, this could only fit into a report *parallel* to Gudea Cyl. A because such a statement would be understandable neither at the end of Cyl. B, which is still fragmentary, nor in a preceding third Cylinder.[20] Therefore, he assigned such fragments to a similar but separate composition, not a supposed third Cylinder.[21] To be sure, it is strange that so little of the supposed third Cylinder was preserved, especially since Cyls. A and B were found together, albeit in broken condition. Most recently, Edzard has collated the fragments and established, at least to his own satisfaction, that Baer's joins are in error and that none of the fragments can be shown to belong to the end of Cyl. B. He therefore treats the fragments separately.[22]

The Closing Lines of Cylinders A and B. The second factor that contributes to the question of whether or not there was a third Cylinder is the closing lines of both Cyls. A and B. They read:

Gudea Cyl. A xxx 15-16	Gudea Cyl. B xxiv 16-17
(15) é-^{d}nin-gír-su-ka dù-a The house of Ningirsu having been built,	(16) é-^{d}nin-gír-su-[k]a dù-a The house of Ningirsu having been built,
(16) zà-mí mu-ru-bi-im the hymn, it is its *middle* (or *middle part*)	(17) zà-mí egir-bi<-im>[23] the hymn, it is its *end* (or *end part*).

concludes that it is not likely that the fragments witness to the first Cylinder in a supposed trilogy (see presently).

20 Falkenstein (1966) 179 n. 1.

21 *Ibid.*, 171 and 187 n. 2. See similarly Sauren (1975) 96-97 n. 5.

22 Personal communication. I would like to express my sincere thanks to Professor Edzard for giving me advanced access to the results of his collation work. See now Edzard (1997) 88-89, 101-6.

23 One should either restore the -im at the end of Cyl. B xxiv 17 or, as Falkenstein does, assume an -m grammatically ([1950] 76; *cf.* the corresponding line in Cyl. A). Based

The rendering one chooses for murub and egir in the last lines of Cyls. A and B, respectively, reflects whether one holds to the two or three Cylinder theory. If one accepts the three Cylinder theory he translates the last line of Gudea Cyl. A as "the hymn, it is its *middle part*,"[24] (not "it is its *middle*"),[25] thus identifying Cyl. A as the middle hymn and Cyl. B as the final hymn in a trilogy. The last line of Cyl. B would be treated similarly ("it is its *end part*"; not "it is its *end*").

In the lexical texts mu-ru(-b) often serves as a syllabic writing of $murub_4$, which is translated by Akkadian *qablītu* "middle part, inner part" or *qablu* "middle, center, middle part."[26] In Sumerian literature the term is relatively infrequent and normally written syllabically (a few times $murub_2$). Seemingly, it can refer to either the middle portion or being in the middle (or midst) of something. For example, in Gudea Cyl. A xxvi 17 we find the expression: mu-ru-dingir-re-ne-ka "in the midst of the gods."[27]

---

on a close examination of a very useful photograph of the Cylinders in the Museum Tablet Room of the University of Pennsylvania, it is likely that -im should be restored at the end of this line in Cyl. B. There was no room for the scribe to write it on the Cylinder although he probably intended to do so. In fact, even the -bi is written off the edge of the column into Cyl. B column i.

Grammatically, according to Falkenstein, in these last lines of Cyls. A and B the impersonal third person pronoun -bi "its" is followed by the short form of the enclitic copula (-àm > -m) used predicatively ([1949] 147-48 and [1950] 76 and n. 2).

24 See, *e.g.*, Jacobsen (1987) 425. Jacob Klein pointed out to me in personal communication that, normally, when such expressions as a-da-ab, tigi, and zà-mí occur in the middle or at the end of a composition they refer to the previous section as a whole, not the point at which they occur in the composition. This might suggest that zà-mí mu-ru-bi(-im) refers to the entirety of Gudea Cyl. A, not the "middle" of the hymn. However, the situation here in the Gudea Cylinders is unusual (see presently).

25 See, *e.g.*, the remarks in Falkenstein (1966) 178 and his translation in SAHG (166, "Mitte des Priesliedes für den Bau des Hauses Ningirsus") where he sets it off in parentheses and italics as if it were a colophon (*cf.* also Gudea Cyl. B xxiv 16-17, SAHG 182).

26 CAD Q 3 and 6, respectively.

27 Klein ([1989a] 58 n. 14) argues that in similar syntactical contexts $murub_2$ means "middle-point," "center," not "middle-part." He cites as examples Lugalbanda Epic II line 223 (lugal-bàn-da KA-kešda-gar-ra-šeš-a-ne-ne-ka $murub_4$?-ba ba-an-gub "did

The normal Akkadian lexical equivalents for egir include *(w)arka* (adv.) "afterward, behind, to the rear"; *(w)arkānu* (adv.) "afterward"; *(w)arkatu* "rear side (of a building), rear area, rear part, etc.,"[28] plus other words from the root **(w)ark-*. It often serves in prepositional or adverbial expressions (see, *e.g.*, Gudea Cyl. B ii 10 and xv 13), but it can refer to the rear part or rear end of something, sometimes in opposition to the front part or front end (sag "head, front").[29] In the OB royal inscriptions we commonly find the expression "in (or to) the end of the day(s or time)" (*i.e.*, "in/for the future").[30] At least sometimes, however, it may be taken to mean simply "in the future (*i.e.*, after, behind) days (or time)" as a period of time.

Unfortunately, to this writer's knowledge, we have no parallels where murub$_4$ or egir is used to enumerate tablets or sections of long composi-

---

Lugalbanda step into the midst of his brothers' formed phalanx"; the text is from Wilcke [1969] 112, and the translation from Jacobsen [1987] 335) and the Ḫendur-sanga Hymn lines 211′ and 222′ where we find the repeated expression murub$_4$-ukkin-na-ka "in the midst (middle) of the assembly" (Edzard and Wilcke [1976] 154-55).

28 CAD A 2: 271, 273, and 274, respectively.

29 See, *e.g.*, Nanna's Journey to Nippur line 198, where the text reads: nidba-a sag-bi ennegi^{ki}-a egir-b[i urí^{ki}-ma] "The offering's front is in Ennegi, i[ts] rear [is in Ur]" (Ferrara [1973] 58 and 91). Here the text seems to refer to the front (sag) and back (egir) "ends" of a procession of offerings. One should compare lines 307-8 of the same composition: nì-sag-^{giš}má ní-sag ga-ra-ni-ib-sum nì-egir-^{giš}má nì-egir ga-ra-ni-ib-sum "That which is in the prow of the boat I would give to you (as) a 'first offering,' (and) that which is in the stern of the boat I would give to you (as) a 'last offering'" (Ferrara [1973] 73 and 102). Here the idea is more that of front and back "portions," "parts." See Ferrara (1973) 121 for comments and further parallels.

Klein ([1989a] 58 n. 14) concludes that "... egir (= *warkatum*) is ambiguous, and could mean either 'end-part' or 'end-point'."

30 It is written in various ways. See, **e.g.**: u$_4$-da egir-ra (Frayne [1990] 300, Rimsin 20, 39; same as Kärki [1980] 150-52, Rimsin 8, 39); egir-u$_4$-da-aš (Frayne [1990] 245, Waradsin 22, 27; same as Kärki [1980] 89-91, Waradsin 7, 27); and in the combination u$_4$-me-da u$_4$-da egir-bi-šè "from our days until the end of days" (*i.e.*, "any day in the future"; Frayne [1990] 303, Rimsin 23, 40; same as Kärki [1980] 165-67, Rimsin 18, 40). Compare also Shulgi E 231: ki-tukun-šè egir-u$_4$-da mu-e-z[i (?)] "Henceforth(?), to the end of time, it [will] not rise(?)" (cited from a manuscript of Jacob Klein in the files of the PSD, used with his kind permission).

tions. Because of this, and because of the semantic ambiguity of these terms, they by themselves cannot provide a definitive answer to the question of whether or not there was a third Cylinder. Sumerian mu-ru(-b) could indicate either the middle point or the middle portion, and egir either the end point or the end portion.

The Opening Lines of Cylinder A. Third, since the supposed third Cylinder would necessarily stand at the front of the trilogy, Falkenstein and others have often based their scepticism about a third Cylinder on the similarity between the beginning of Gudea Cyl. A and the initial lines of certain mythological texts, which refer to a *day* (u_4) when *destiny* (nam–tar) was determined.[31] The first three lines of Cyl. A read as follows:

---

31 See Falkenstein (1966) 178-79, where he refers to van Dijk (1953) 39. One should consult van Dijk (1964-65) 16-34, where he has pointed out that the expression in line 1 (in many of its occurrences) and other very similar expressions may hearken back to primeval days. It is especially used this way in some of the myths and epics. Krispijn ([1982] 84-85) concurs and applies it to the present context, suggesting that the primeval time was repeated on a yearly holiday (probably New Year's day). He assigns Gudea's experience of the dream (Cyl. A i 12ff.) to just such a day. Krispijn's view may be supported by comparing Gudea Cyl. A i 1ff. with Inanna and Iddindagan lines 25-27 and 171-75, where destiny is said to have been determined on particularly auspicious days, either monthly at the new moon or yearly on New Year's day (Römer [1965] 129 and 133 and Reisman [1973] 186 and 190). Perhaps compare also the Nanshe Hymn lines 5 and 94-96 (Heimpel [1981] 82-83 and 88-89) and Heimpel's explanation of the importance of the New Year's day in that composition (Heimpel [1981] 66-68).

Another interpretation, suggested to me in a personal communication by Sol Cohen, is that Gudea Cyl. A i 1-9 serves as an overall pre-summary of what will be described in the composition as a whole. Thus interpreted, the purpose of the first few lines would be to refer to the period of time (some time ago) when destiny was determined for heaven and earth, and Lagash received a favorable destiny (Cyl. A i 2). The following lines and columns go on to describe what happened during that time.

Perhaps line 1 has the same basic intent as Cyl. B v 16 where, in the context of describing the special day on which Ningirsu and Baba took up residence in the new Eninnu, the text says: u_4 è-àm nam tar-ra-àm "the day was coming forth, the destiny was being determined." That particular day was not the New Year's day (*cf.* Cyl. B iii 5-8), although it was apparently closely associated with the New Year festival or period of time. This intertextual parallel may suggest that Cyl. A i 1 designates a day that, *in retrospect*, was a particularly significant day in the religious scheme of things. In that case, the narrator referred back to it as "a day when destiny was being determined in heaven and earth." Significantly, it was apparently also an èš-èš festival

u_4 a[n-k]i-a nam tar-[re-d]a

On a day when destiny was being determined in heaven and earth,

laga[š^{ki}]-e me-gal-la [sag] an-šè mi-ni-íb-íl

Lagash, in great office,[32] lifted (its) head toward heaven,

^{d}en-líl-e en-^{d}nin-gír-sú-šè igi-zi mu-ši-bar

(and) Enlil looked at prince Ningirsu with favor.

One might compare line 1 with the opening lines of Enki's Journey to Nippur where the text reads: u_4-ri-a nam ba-tar-ra-ba "In those remote days, when destiny was determined,"[33] and Enki and Ninmaḫ which begins: u_4-ri-a-ta u_4 an-ki-bi-ta ba-an-[dím?] gi_6-ri-a-ta gi_6 an-ki-bi-ta b[a-an-dím?] [mu-ri]-a-[ta] mu nam b[a-tar-ra-ba], which Jacobsen translates: "In the days of yore, the days when heaven and earth had been [fashioned?], in the nights of yore, the nights when heaven and earth had been [fashioned?], in the years of yore, the years when the modes of be[ing were determined]."[34]

There are, however, certain problems with comparing the beginning of Gudea Cyl. A with the beginning of these mythological texts. For one thing, although they begin with a mythological prologue, it may be argued that

---

day, which provided the occasion for Gudea to be performing prayers and offerings on the evening when the "day" began (Cyl. A i 12-14; see Neugebauer [1957] 106 for the fact that they conceived of the day as beginning in the evening). Before the next evening arrived Gudea had traveled to Urukug and celebrated the same festival there (Cyl. A ii 23). If this interpretation is correct, one cannot use the mythological texts or the epics as the key to interpreting line 1 of Gudea Cyl. A (contra Falkenstein, van Dijk, and Krispijn above).

32 Regarding the Sumerian term *me*, here rendered "office," see footnote 98 below and Averbeck (1987) 590 n. 6 for a summary of the translation difficulties and proposals. Here in Cyl. A i 2 I have followed Jacobsen (1987) 388.

33 See Al-Fouadi (1969) 57-59 for comments. According to Al-Fouadi, this composition is a mythologically based temple building text. That is, "in the days of yore" (as Jacobsen would translate the expression) Enki built a temple and then went to report its completion to Enlil in Nippur. Thus, there are some significant content parallels between this composition and the Gudea Cylinders.

34 Jacobsen (1987) 153. For the Sumerian text see Benito (1969), and for a discussion of these lines, pp. 45-46.

the Cylinders as a whole do not purport to be mythological, but, instead, present themselves as an account of the piety and diligence of Gudea in the project to which he was called by the god Ningirsu. More importantly, the expression at the beginning of Cyl. A is not u_4-ri-a "in days of yore." Although the association with determining destiny suggests that this distinction might not be weighty, it may be proposed that the true parallel is not with the mythological texts but, rather, with the royal hymns.

For example, the first 29 lines of Shulgi F comprise the prologue to the hymn, explaining the purpose for which Shulgi was born. After this introduction the combination u_4-ba ... nam–tar occurs:

> *u_4-ba* an-né ki-en-gi-ra *nam* bí-in-*tar* kalam-e gù ba-an-dè ᵈdil-ím-babbar-re unken-né ḫúl-la ba-ta-an-è
>
> At that time, An determined the fate in Sumer, (and) called to the Land; Dilimbabbar brought out (the word) to the (divine?) assembly in joy.[35]

Immediately after this the text is broken. After the break, the subject is the establishing and lauding of Shulgi's kingship. Shulgi D is another example where, again, the first 56 lines or so serve as an opening praise of Shulgi. Although line 57 is partially broken, certain parts of it can be restored and lines 58-59 carry its theme forward in such a way that the same essential structure as Shulgi F can be discerned:

> *u_4-ba* [ ] an-né? x x [ ] dub mu-ù-ši-[íb-sar] *nam* mu-ù-ši-[íb-*tar*] ᵈnin-líl-lá sizkur-a-ra-[zu-a] šà im-ma-an-š[ed$_x$?] an ki-nam-tar-tar-[ra] na-nam na-nam [dingir-an-na?] ba-su$_8$-su$_8$-ge-[eš]
>
> On that day, An? . . . . [. . . . .], a tablet he? [wrote] for you?, the fate he? [decreed] for you?, Ninlil's heart was soothed? with prayers and supplications; to heaven, the place where fate is decreed, came [the gods of heaven?] with (their) ready approval.[36]

---

35 According to the text, Shulgi was born to fill the granaries and treasuries of the land, ensure abundant fertility of produce animals, see that their firstlings were brought to the Ekur in Nippur, and ensure justice in the land. I thank Jacob Klein for his special kindness in permitting these lines to be cited directly from his unpublished manuscript of Shulgi F in the Museum Tablet Room at the University of Pennsylvania.

36 See Klein (1981) 72-75.

Thus, in these royal hymns, as well as in epics, u_4-ba is often used to begin a new section describing previous events, especially at the outset of a poetic narrative.[37] Its occurrence within a context of destiny determination is what makes these passages particularly relevant to the discussion of the first lines of Gudea Cyl. A, suggesting that in this literary composition something has come before the u_4 and nam-tar combination in the first line of Cyl. A. But this argument from context applies just as well to the mythological texts cited above. That is, nam–tar occurs in the mythological texts as well, but at the very *beginning* of the composition as a whole, while u_4-ba (the key term in the royal hymns cited above; see both Shulgi D and F), in point of fact, occurs in the opening lines of neither the mythological texts nor the Gudea Cylinders.

Therefore, on the one hand, a superficial comparison of Cyl. A i 1 with the mythological texts would suggest that line 1 is the opening line of the composition. On the other hand, the comparison with royal hymns would leave room for proposing that a third Cylinder originally stood before that which is currently referred to as Cyl. A. Its content would likely be very much like that suggested by Jacobsen (cited above).

Unfortunately, in this case, one comparison seems as reasonable as the other. Neither one is exact enough to demand that any comparison be made whatsoever. Among other things, the first line of Cyl. A has neither u_4-ri-a (*cf.* the mythological texts) nor u_4-ba (*cf.* the royal hymns and epics). So then, the use of u_4 and nam–tar in the first line of Gudea Cyl. A does not provide conclusive evidence for either the two or the three Cylinder view. Hurowitz favors the three cylinder theory, and supports it primarily by reference to parallel compositions in which hymnic prologues introduce construction accounts. Once again, however, the wording of the parallel texts does not correspond precisely to that of the first line of Gudea Cyl. A.[38]In this writer's opinion, the strongest argument for only two original

---

37 See the remarks and literature cited in Berlin (1979) 64 comment on line 14, and Wilcke (1975) 239-45.

38 Hurowitz (1992) 36-37. The prayer to Numušda and the Hymn to the city of Nippur are only very general parallels (*e.g.*, prayer to Numušda has no u_4 "day"), and the

Cylinders (the favored view) arises from the overall "shape" of the two Cylinder composition as it stands (see below). Moreover, even if there was a third Cylinder, as its content has been outlined above it would have stood outside of the temple construction and consecration narrative framework of the two that we have (see the remarks on "genre" presently). Hurowitz agrees on this point.[39] As it stands, therefore, the composition is a coherent whole and should be treated as such in the analysis of its macrostructure.

What is the Genre of the Composition?

In discussing the "literary genre" of the Gudea Cylinders, definition of terms is all-important. As the term is used here, "genre" (from French *genre* meaning "kind, sort; fashion, mode") refers to a substantial set of features that a group of texts has in common which causes them to be labeled as a group.[40] By way of contrast, the "form" or "literary (macro)structure" of the composition (the main subject of this essay as regards the Gudea Cylinders, see below) refers to the large-scale literary and especially structural features of a text that make it unique as a piece of literature.[41] Of course,

---

relevant line in Enmerkar and the Lord of Aratta begins u_4-ri-a, not u_4 a[n-k]i-a as in the Gudea Cyl. A i 1 (*cf.* the remarks above).

Hurowitz ([1992] 37 n. 3) also refers to evidence for a common pattern of hymnic prologues in Sumerian literary compositions, but, once again, the terminology is not precisely the same as in the Gudea Cylinders (his citation of Enmerkar and Ensuḫ-keshdanna for an u_4-ba parallel should be to line 14, not 24).

39 *Ibid.*, 37-38.

40 According to Holman and Harmon (1986) 220: "*Genre* classification implies that there are groups of formal or technical characteristics existing among works of the same generic 'kind' regardless of time or place of composition, author, subject matter; and that these characteristics, when they define a particular group of works, are of basic significance in talking about literary art."

41 In their article entitled "Structure," Holman and Harmon (1986) 486 write that structure refers to: "The planned framework of a piece of literature....the term usually is applied to the general plan or outline." The problem is that, at this level, "structure" could easily be subordinated to "genre" since one feature of most so-called genres is an abstract structure held in common.

one of the features that a group of texts can have in common is a set of structural characteristics. The point is that here I am using the term "literary (macro)structure" to refer to that which is unique to the literary shape of the Gudea Cylinders and makes it distinct as a text even if it does share some level of formal and structural similarity to a group of texts that make up a specific discernible genre category.

The Gudea Cylinders can legitimately be compared to at least three different groups of Sumerian texts; (1) temple hymns, (2) royal dedicatory inscriptions, and (3) royal (building and dedication) hymns, respectively (see below). Each of these three groups of texts has potential for misapplication to the analysis of the Gudea Cylinders because every literary composition is unique in its own right, and we shall argue here that this is especially true of the Cylinders of Gudea. At least on some points that are pivotal to genre classification, the Cylinders are unique.[42] Moreover, the native Mesopotamian classifications or, better, characterizations of their own literary compositions do not necessarily help us here because they do not seem to serve as indicators of "genre," which is a literary concept that apparently did not rise to the conscious level in ancient Mesopotamian literary practice.[43]

I am qualifying the term "structure" with the term "literary" in order to refer to what has sometimes been called "form," defined as "the structure, tight or loose, supple or flaccid, of the whole composition." More specifically, it refers to "the actual welding of all parts into a whole, the individual organization of a work so that all its constituents however defined...cohere and harmonize. *In this sense form is often called organic form and sharply distinguished from abstract structure, especially as determined by genre.* The external and preconceived structure depending on genre is correspondingly named mechanical or abstract form in contrast with organic" (Orsini [1965] 286b, emphasis mine).

42 This point will be developed further in the following discussion. For the time being it is important to recognize that even modern theoreticians, if they allow genre criticism at all, must deal with such things as "mixed genres." Thus, literary compositions sometimes defy simple wholistic classifications (Ducrot and Todorov [1979] 151).

43 See the general remarks on this point in Grayson (1975) 4-5.

Temple Hymns and the Gudea Cylinders. First, Falkenstein referred to the Gudea Cylinders as "Die Bauhymne."[44] The composition does indeed manifest hymnic features as it recounts the process of building and dedicating the new Eninnu temple for Ningirsu, the chief deity of Lagash. In fact, the final line of each of the Cylinders serves as something of a colophon and refers to the composition as a "hymn of praise" (see zà-mí in Gudea Cyl. A xxx 16 and Cyl. B xxiv 17, cited above).[45] Moreover, the last sections of both Cyl. A and Cyl. B (except for the last three lines of each) are remarkably similar to the Temple Hymns in terms of both content (consisting of epithetical descriptions of beauty and numinous power) and structure (made up of an almost uninterrupted series of participial clauses; see the underlined /a/ throughout): [46]

---

44 Falkenstein (1966) 178.

45 See Wilcke (1975) 246-48 for a discussion of zà-mí. There has been some discussion of whether or not this is a genre term. Cooper ([1978] 4 n. 5) argues that it does not occur as a subscript and, therefore, one should not take it as a native genre classification. Hallo ([1981] 256) cites occasions where it in fact serves as a subscript and therefore argues that it is indeed a native genre indicator.

Whether or not one takes this term to be a genre classifier in Sumerian depends to some extent on how one defines "genre." If one takes into consideration that there are a few cases in which zà-mí serves as a subscript, then it will be hard to deny that in those cases at least it indicates something about the inherent nature of the composition. However, the broad use of the term in Sumerian texts suggests that it describes the genre of the literary text only in very broad terms (*i.e.*, the hymnic intent of the composer).

46 There are, of course, short hymnic passages of this type elsewhere in the Cylinders as well. See, for example, Gudea Cyl. A ix 11-12 in Ningirsu's description of the Eninnu during Gudea's second dream, and Gudea Cyl. B i 1-5, where this hymnic pattern is also used to laud the completed temple in order to set the scene for its dedication in the remainder of Cyl. B.

Regarding the Sumerian temple hymns in general, see Sjöberg and Bergmann (1969), Biggs (1976) 45-56, (1971) 193-207, and the proposal in Hruška (1976) 353-60. The collection of Sumerian temple hymns made by Enḫeduanna, the daughter of Sargon of Agade, reconstructed from tablets of the Ur III and (primarily) Old Babylonian periods (Sjöberg and Bergmann [1969] 5-6), and now known to have forerunners in the pre-Sargonic period (see Biggs [1976] 45-46 and Hruška's [1976]), establishes that this genre was already present in Sumerian literary tradition before the days of Gudea. This tradition seems to have contributed directly to the character

Gudea Cyl. A xxx 6-12

(6) é ^{d}utu-gim kalam-ma è-a̱
The temple which goes forth in the land like Utu,

(7) gu$_4$-gal-gim Iš-bar-ra gub-ba̱
which stands in the ISHbar like a great ox,

(8) ì-ti giri$_{17}$-zal-gim
which like moonlight and splendor

(9) unkin-né si-a̱
fills the assembly,

(10) ḫur-sag-sig$_7$-ga-gim
which like a green mountain

(11) ḫi-li gùr-a̱
is full of luxuriance,

(12) u$_6$-di-dè gub-ba̱
which stands out magnificently;

Gudea Cyl. B xxiv 9-14

(9) é kur-gal-gim an-né ús-sa̱
The temple which reaches unto heaven like a great mountain,

(10) ní-me-lám-bi kalam-ma šub-a̱
which has its radiant fearsomeness cast over the land,

(11) an-né ^{d}en-líl-e nam-lagaš^{ki}-tar-ra̱
(through) which the destiny of Lagash is determined by An and Enlil,

(12) ^{d}nin-gír-su-ka nam-nir-gál-ni
(through) which the prominence of Ningirsu

(13) kur-kur-re zu-a̱
is known by all the lands,

(14) é-ninnu an-ki-da mú-a̱
the Eninnu, which grows together with heaven and earth;

One may compare the canonical collection of Sumerian Temple Hymns for a similar relatively consistent manner of expression. See, for example, lines 1-5: [47]

(1) é-u$_6$-nir an-ki-da mú-a̱
Eunir, which has grown high, (uniting) heaven and earth,

(2) temen-an-ki unú-gal eridu^{ki}
foundation of heaven and earth, “Holy of Holies”, Eridu,

(3) abzu èš nun-bi-ir àm-gub
Abzu shrine, erected for its prince,

---

and phraseology of the Gudea Cylinders as did that of the royal hymns and inscriptions (for the latter see below).

47 Text and translation from Sjöberg and Bergmann (1969) 17.

(4) é du_6-kù ú-sikil-la rig_7-ga
House, holy mound, where pure food is eaten,

(5) pa_5-sikil-nun-na-ka a nag-gá
watered by the prince's pure canal,

Furthermore, both of the Gudea Cyls. end with the expression "Ningirsu, praise!" (^{d}nin-gír-su zà-mí; Cyl. A xxx 14 and B xxiv 15) followed only by the colophon (lines 15-16 and 16-17 respectively, cited above). One should compare this with line 542 of the temple hymn collection which stands just before the colophon in lines 543-49 and reads: ^{d}nisaba zà-mí "Nisaba, praise!"[48]

Nevertheless, since the Gudea Cyls. do more than simply describe and laud the temple, they do not fit comfortably within the specific Sumerian genre of hymns to temples as exemplified in the canonical collection of Sumerian Temple Hymns.[49] The Gudea Cyls., therefore, have affinities with the Sumerian Temple Hymns—a genre that we know was already active in the Old Sumerian literary tradition, long before the time of Gudea[50]—but

---

48 Text and translation from Sjöberg and Bergmann (1969) 49. Klein ([1981] 57 n. 138) has pointed out that the royal *hymns* of the Ur III and Isin periods have two different types of formulaic endings. Type A ends with a native generic subscript including a term such as tigi or a-da-ab. Type B ends, instead, with an expression which includes the term zà-mí "praise" or "be praised." The Shulgi Hymns manifest two different subtypes in the type B category: (1) hymns lauding the king in the first person (*i.e.*, self-laudatory hymns) or in the second person ending with "my (or 'your') praise is sweet" (see, *e.g.*, Shulgi B line 384: zà-má-mu dùg-ga-àm), and (2) hymns which refer to Shulgi in the third person and end by lauding the god (*e.g.*, "the lord Dilimbabbar, may (he) be praised," Shulgi X line 159, en ^{d}dil-ím-$babbar_x$ zà!-mí).

The doxology ^{d}nin-gír-su zà-mí "(To) Ningirsu (be) praise" in Gudea Cyl. A xxx 14 and B xxiv 15 belongs to his type B subtype 2, which is the simpler. However, in contrast to the Shulgi hymns, as Wilcke observes ([1975] 246-48), these lines in Cyls. A and B are bound with the hymnic epilogue that precedes them.

49 The contrast between the Eninnu hymn in the collection of Sumerian Temple Hymns (Sjöberg and Bergmann [1969] 31-32 lines 240-62) and the overall literary style and content of the Gudea Cyls. as they recount the building of the very same Eninnu (see below) illustrates this point well.

50 See Biggs (1971) and (1976) 45-56, where the Abu Salabikh texts are dated to about 2600 B.C. (*ibid.*, 26), about half a millennium earlier than Gudea. As Sjöberg argues,

should *not* be subsumed under that genre category. Rather, they recount, albeit in poetic style and with some hymnic interludes, the construction and consecration of the temple with special emphasis upon the ritual nature of the temple building process.

Unlike the Gudea Cylinders, the Temple Hymns emphasize neither the importance of the ruler who built the temple nor the temple construction and dedication procedures. Falkenstein was right. This is not just a Temple Hymn, but a "Bauhymne." Moreover, it is not just a temple "building hymn," but it is a temple building hymn with the ruler, Gudea, at the center of the project. On this level, the Gudea Cylinders show affinity with the Sumerian Royal Inscriptions (see presently) or, more specifically, the Royal Hymns (see below).

Royal Inscriptions and the Gudea Cylinders. While the preoccupation with the temple construction and consecration process lends to the composition its generally (poetic) "narrative" character, the emphasis upon the pious cooperation and initiative of the ruler, Gudea, adds a royal "dedicatory" effect. Gudea dedicated his own person and office, and the resources of Lagash which were therefore under his control, to the building of the new temple (the construction process, Cyl. A). He did all this specifically for the purpose of pleasing Ningirsu by providing a new home for him and his consort, Baba (the dedication process, Cyl. B). In fact, the prologues of both Cyl. A and Cyl. B (*i.e.*, Cyl. A i 1-11 and Cyl. B i 1-11) are followed by the introduction of Gudea as the wise and pious ruler who would carry out the will of the god(s):

> ensi$_2$ lú-geštu$_3$-dagal-kam geštu$_3$ ì-gá-gá nì-gal-gal-la šu mi-ni-mú-mú
>
> The ruler, being a wise and observant man, having paid attention, prayed, extolling (Ningirsu's) greatness (Gudea Cyl. A i 12-13; sacrificial activity follows).

"The Gudea Cylinders...may, when considered in relation to the short temple hymns among the texts from Abu Salabikh, be the climax of a long tradition of 'Old Sumerian' literature" (Sjöberg and Bergmann [1969] 6-7; *cf.* also the literature cited there), but the Gudea Cylinders do not actually fit into the genre category of "Temple Hymns." One might say that they are an extension or variation of the Temple Hymn literary genre.

ensi$_2$ kù-zu-àm inim-zu-àm nam-dingir-re kiri$_4$ ki im-mi-zu-zu

The ruler, being wise and one who knows the command, was bowing before the deities (Gudea Cyl. B i 12-13; prayer follows).

This dedicatory quality of the text is, of course, a well-known characteristic of the so-called "royal dedicatory inscriptions," of which Gudea Statue B is a good example.[51] In fact, since neither the Gudea Cylinders nor his Statues incorporate standard cultic rubrics into their compositions it is possible to argue that they both belong to the same general category known as "royal votive (*i.e.*, dedicatory) inscriptions."[52] However, there are also major differences between the Cylinders and the Statues. Since the bulk of Gudea Stat. B describes the construction of the same temple as the Gudea Cylinders, the comparisons and especially the contrasts between the two compositions are germane to the question of genre and structure in the Gudea Cylinders.

In general, both compositions recount the construction of the temple, but the narrative framework and focus is different. Roughly speaking, Gudea Stat. B has the following overall structure:

---

51 G. van Driel has argued convincingly that building inscriptions of the earliest periods, including those of Gudea, are "dedicatory" and are not basically different from other sorts of votive inscriptions; see van Driel (1973a and 1973b). More specifically, temple building texts characteristically emphasize that the temple was built for the god(s) and reflect, therefore, the ruler's motive for building the temple in the first place. The primary motive was to petition the god(s) for a long and prosperous life (van Driel [1973b] 68).

Specifically with regard to the Gudea Statues, van Driel writes that the statues themselves "are dedicatory objects, intended to remind the gods for whom they were meant of the pious deeds of the ensi." Correspondingly, the inscriptions almost always make known the name of the statue, which contains "some pious wish connected with the welfare of the prince" (van Driel [1973b] 102). Gudea Stat. B is no exception. Its name is lugal-mu é-a-ni mu-na-dù nam-ti ní-ba-mu "For my king I built his temple—life is my reward" (Gudea Stat. B vii 14-17; see Averbeck [1987] 713-36 for a working edition of Gudea Stat. B and now esp. Steible [1991] 1.155-79 and 2.6-38).

52 See Klein (1989a) 36 and the remarks on the *sagidda* to the *sagarra* rubrics in the royal hymns below (footnote 63).

I. *Provisions for the cult of the Statue i 1-20*

(ending with a curse against any ruler who does not perpetuate the regular cult provisions for the Statue, i 13-20)

II. *Description of the construction of the Eninnu ii 1-vii 9*

(beginning with a series of epithets concerning Ningirsu's calling and Gudea's piety regarding the building of the temple, ii 1-iii 11; and ending with a summary statement of the ruler's piety in building and the magnificence of the new temple, vi 77-vii 9)

III. *Fashioning, inscribing, dedicating, and maintaining the Statue vii 10-ix 30*

(concluding with a curse formula against anyone who would dare to remove, efface, demolish, etc., the Statue, vii 60-ix 30).[53]

---

53 Klein (1989b) 294 breaks the third section down further so that he ends up with five sections, but the point I am making here is that the whole third and last section is about the statue, not the temple. The same is true for the first section, resulting in an envelope around the middle portion which alone concentrates on the construction of the Eninnu, the same subject as Gudea Cyl. A.

Klein's proposal that Gudea Stat. B viii 21-26 is a warning against the neglect of Gudea's collection of songs in the cult is especially interesting (Klein [1989b] 296-98 and 300-1). It depends, however, on a certain interpretation of the relationship between lines 21-23 and 24-26, a relationship that is not recognized in previous, as well as more recent, treatments of Gudea Stat. B (see Klein [1989b] 297 n. 51; Steible [1991] 1.174-75 and 2.34; and the literature cited there). The passage reads (following Steible): (21) èn-du-KA-kéš-DU-mu (22) mu-mu ù-ta-gar (23) mu-ni ba-gá-gá (24) kisal-^{d}nin-gír-su-lugal-gá-ka (25) èš-gar-ra-bi bí-bí-TAG$_4$-TAG$_4$-a (26) igi-ni-šè nu-tuku-a "(21-22) who (when) he has removed my name from my collection of songs (23) and his name put (there), (24) who in the courtyard of Ningirsu, my lord, (25) its … (?) has removed from there (26) (and) does not celebrate before his eyes" (translation mine, but generally following Steible). Klein argues that these lines are a single unit and that the reference to the song collection continues into lines 24-26. He therefore renders the passage: "and after having removed my name from the collection of my songs, placing there (instead) his name, he neglects them in the regularly established ešeš-festivals of the courtyard of Ningirsu, my lord, and does not perform them in front of him" (Klein [1989b] 297).

He cites a parallel passage in Shulgi E, but in that composition the broader context refers only to Shulgi's collection of hymns. This is not the case in Gudea Stat. B. The parallel is nevertheless strong and Klein's rendering may be correct. Even if his rendering is not correct, the larger point that Klein makes regarding Shulgi's concern that his songs be recited not only in the cult but also throughout the whole realm stands. There is no indication that Gudea intended such wide distribution of his

This is not the place to undertake a full analysis of Gudea Stat. B. Here I offer only a few pertinent remarks regarding some of the major differences between Gudea Stat. B and Cyls. A and B. First, unlike the concern for the cult of the Statue in the first section of Gudea Stat. B, the Gudea Cylinders themselves record no explicit provision for the maintenance of the Cylinders, or even the cultic recitation of the composition recorded on the Cylinders.[54] Second, in Gudea Stat. B we find an extended summary of the

---

songs. Thus, with only one exception, the only copies we have of Gudea's songs are those on the original Gudea Cylinders and Statues, while Shulgi's Royal Hymns are know from numerous copies.

54 For the possibility that Gudea Stat. B makes reference to such perpetuation of Gudea's "collection of songs," perhaps including the Cylinders, see below.

Since the structural arrangement and content of a composition are normally functions of the purpose(s) or occasion(s) for which it was composed, one might venture to propose that Gudea Cyls. A and B may have been commissioned for a (yearly) temple (re)dedication festival (Hallo [1970] 119-20, 134; see also Hallo [1983] 9-20, esp. pp. 19-20, and Heimpel [1981] 101-2). If so, then the seven successive sections of Cyls. A and B which I will delineated below may have formed the libretto of a drama performed through the seven days. That reconstruction may coincide especially well with the last three days which would consist of: (1) the request to the Anunna gods to assist in bringing Ningirsu and Baba into the new Eninnu (Cyl. B i 1-ii 6, day five), (2) the entrance of Ningirsu and Baba into the new Eninnu and the arrival of the Anunna gods for the dedication banquet (Cyl. B ii 7-xiii 10, day six), and (3) the presentation of housewarming gifts, setting of a divine banquet, and determination of a good destiny by the Anunna gods for Lagash, the new Eninnu, and Gudea (Cyl. B xiii 11- xxiv 17, day seven; xxiv 9-17 may be considered a hymnic epilogue, *cf.* Cyl. A xxx 6-16 and the discussion above).

H. Sauren (1975) has proposed that the Gudea Cylinders constitute a "mystery play" composed on the occasion of the temple consecration and performed yearly at the temple dedication festival. The yearly festival lasted for seven days, the composition itself was written with the seven-day temple dedication feast in view, the successive and parallel sections of both Cylinders narrate the events of that festival, some of the construction and (original) dedication procedures were reenacted ritually year after year (*e.g.*, the fabrication and presentation of the first brick, the banquet for the gods, etc.), and the content of Cylinders A and B would have been read on days six and seven respectively (with regard to the latter point see esp. *ibid.*, 95 and 103 n. 41).

As fascinating as it is, Sauren's proposal is not particularly convincing for several reasons. First, the seven day sequence is essentially imposed upon the text and does not fit with certain statements in the text itself. For example, Cyl. B xvii 18ff. suggests that the divine banquet (referred to in xviii 18ff.) alone lasted for seven days. Second,

construction of the Eninnu (*i.e.*, Cyl. A type material),[55] but consecration and dedication procedures for the temple (*i.e.*, Gudea Cyl. B type material) are very abbreviated. This is probably due to that fact that in Stat. B the immediate concern was for the dedication and maintenance of the Statue, not the temple.[56] Third, Gudea Stat. B ends with a fully developed curse formula which is common in standard royal inscriptions but absent from the Gudea Cylinders.[57]

---

the proposed seven-fold parallels between the two Cylinders are artificial. It is natural that both the construction process (*i.e.*, Cyl. A) and the consecration process (*i.e.*, Cyl. B) be regulated by ritual procedures and other more pragmatic realities. Sauren has assumed that because such action sequences occur in both Cylinders they must be parallel to each other both individually and as a group. This is not the case. Certainly purification procedures would have been required before ritually or pragmatically important steps were taken in both processes. It is not feasible to suggest that Cylinders A and B recount parallel ritual procedures when it is clear that Cyl. A deals with building the Eninnu and Cyl. B deals with dedicating it. The divisions suggested by the present writer are seven in number, but they are based on the occurrences of a formulaic statement at transition points running successively through Cylinders A and B (see below for further details). They are not reconstructed from an unverifiable performance theory.

Whether or not the ritual drama and cultic recitation theory is correct at all is open to serious question. Klein objects to the notion that the Cylinders were "ever recited in the temple, during a cultic ceremony" ([1989a] 33-36, esp. p. 36). It is clear, however, that Cyl. B describes consecration and dedication procedures in contrast to Cyl. A which describes preliminary and construction procedures. The two Cylinders describe parallel activities neither practically nor ritually. Earlier theories that, in one way or another, connected the Gudea Cylinders with the celebration of sacred marriage at the New Year festival are even less credible than what Sauren has proposed (see, *e.g.*, Van Buren [1944] 35-46 and Frankfort [1948] 313-53, esp. pp. 317-18).

55 The construction (and dedication) accounts in both compositions (Stat. B ii 1-vii 9 and Cyl. A xii 21-Cyl. B xvii 16) are surrounded by materials pertinent to the peculiarities of the respective compositions. In Stat. B the focus at the beginning (i 1-20) and end (vii 10-ix 30) is upon the cult and maintenance of the Statue itself (see presently). As for the Cylinders, generally speaking, the first twelve columns of Cyl. A narrate Gudea's reception and clarification of Ningirsu's commission to build a new Eninnu, and the last seven columns of Cyl. B (*i.e.*, cols. xviii-xxiv) describe the divine banquet, festivities, and blessings resulting from the completion of the project.

56 In fact, the only substantial parallel to Cyl. B is embedded within the account of the *Statue's* entry into the new Eninnu (Stat. B vii 19-46, *cf.* Cyl. B xvii 17-xviii 9).

57 See Klein (1985) 8 nn. 8-9 and the literature cited there for this distinctive feature of royal inscriptions as opposed to royal hymns.

In general, the concern for the Statue itself on which the inscription was inscribed is a common feature of dedicatory inscriptions. In spite of some significant similarities and parallels, it distinguishes dedicatory inscriptions like Gudea Stat. B from the composition on Gudea Cyls. A and B.

Royal Hymns and the Gudea Cylinders. We have already observed that the Gudea Cylinders have some affinities to both temple hymns and royal dedicatory inscriptions, but we have also seen that there are also significant differences. Recently, Klein has proposed that the Gudea Cylinders actually belong to a "subgenre" of royal "hymns"—namely, "building and dedication hymns,"[58] a "literary form of limited distribution."[59] Gudea Cyls. A and B, in fact, may be the literary prototype of such compositions.[60]

Based upon a pattern established by Hurowitz in his very useful comparative treatment of (temple) building texts in the ancient Near East, Klein discerns a five point sequence of themes in all four of the texts he assigns to the category of building and dedication hymns (the Gudea Cylinders, Shulgi R, Ishme-Dagan I [or "Enlil's Chariot"], and Ur-Nammu B).[61] Although the proportions of the various sections often differ considerably from one composition to the next,[62] the comparison appears to be valid in

---

58 Klein (1989a).

59 Klein (1989a) 36. He concludes his remarks with the following evaluation of the labels genre and subgenre for royal hymns: "The above preliminary observations as to this literary form of limited distribution, which we have labeled as 'building and dedication' hymns, clearly demonstrates how inept and inadequate, from the literary point of view, [it] is when we speak of a genre of 'royal hymns.' The hymnal corpus, which we usually label as 'royal hymns,' cannot really be considered a distinct genre or subgenre of literature. The only feature, which is common to all these hymns is that they center around the king's personality."

60 Klein (1989a) 28.

61 See Klein (1989a) 27-28, 35-36, and the table on p. 63. *Cf.* Hurowitz (1985) and (1992) esp. the summary on p. 311.

For a full edition of Shulgi R, see now Klein (1990) 80-136. For revised editions of Ishme-Dagan I (originally edited by Civil [1968]) and Ur-Nammu B (originally edited by Castellino [1959] 106-18) see now Klein (1989a) 36-44 and 44-56, respectively.

62 For example, in Gudea Cyl. A the "praise of the Eninnu" is disproportionately small especially when compared to the much larger number of lines given over to it in the

a general sort of way (*i.e.*, from an overall structural point of view). As for the Gudea Cylinders, the five part sequence is as follows:

I. Commissioning of the building of the Eninnu (A i 1-xii 20)
II. Preparations and building the temple (A xii 21-xxix 12)
III. Praise of the Eninnu (A xxix 13-xxx 14)
IV. Dedication of the Eninnu (B i 1-xx 12)
V. Blessing of the Eninnu and Gudea (B xx 13-xxiv 8)

The same general pattern is found in Shulgi R (the building and dedicating of a boat) and Ishme-Dagan I (the building and dedicating of a chariot). I might add that, according to his structural analysis the division between Gudea Cyl. A and Cyl. B comes at a point in the structure of the composition that corresponds to the shift from the *sagidda* to the *sagarra* sections in Shulgi R and Ishme-Dagan I.[63] The same is not true, however, for the shift from the *sagidda* to the *sagarra* in Ur-Nammu B (the only other text out of the four that describes the building and dedication of a temple), but the latter also has a sixth and rather extended part to the sequence called "the realization of the blessing" (20 lines at the end of the composition). Klein himself admits that Ur-Nammu B has a much looser structural correspondence to the group as a whole.[64]

Without denying the general structural similarity between the Gudea Cylinders and these other "building and dedication hymns," one can legitimately question whether they actually constitute a distinct "subgenre" on that basis, or at least whether the Gudea Cylinders truly belong to that subgenre. After all, Hurowitz has shown that the fivefold pattern outlined above stretches across the boundaries of all sorts of literary genres in which we find commemorative building accounts in the ANE.

---

much smaller compositions of Shulgi R and Ishme-Dagan I. Similarly, the commissioning and preparation/building sections of Cyl. A are proportionately much larger than in Shulgi R and Ishme-Dagan I.

63 The terms *sagidda* and *sagarra* are rubrics that come at the end of the sections to which they refer. They seem to indicate the kind of music or, more specifically, the kind of musical instruments used in the accompaniment of that section of the song (see, *e.g.*, the brief remarks in Klein [1981] 26 and Wilcke [1975] 259-60).

64 Klein (1989a) 34-35.

Furthermore, Klein himself has argued convincingly that the Gudea Cylinders actually fall into the category of "royal votive inscriptions" because, among other things, they have no cultic rubrics (contrast the *sagidda* and *sagarra* sections of the other three compositions). Therefore, unlike the other three compositions, it is highly questionable whether the Gudea Cylinders would have ever been recited in the cult. Instead, they were supposedly "deposited in the temple before the gods, in order to constantly remind them of Gudea's pious act of restoring the Eninnu."[65] Thus, although it is true that, like the other three compositions, the Gudea Cylinders are hymnic (see "Temple Hymns and the Gudea Cylinders" above) and the topic is the royal piety of building and consecration (see "Royal Inscriptions and the Gudea Cylinders" above), nevertheless, these other major distinctions would seem to suggest that the Gudea Cylinders fall into a different (sub)genre category. In fact, maybe they are truly unique in the history and repertoire of (extant) ancient Sumerian hymnology and simply will not fit well into any of the (sub)genre categories of that literature.

Finally, in accordance with the view that this composition is genuinely unique, the analysis of the literary macrostructure of the Gudea Cylinders must take more into consideration than the fivefold pattern of ancient Near Eastern building accounts isolated by Hurowitz (see above). He is absolutely correct when he argues that "the five- or six-stage pattern ... is not a trivial one, reflecting simply the natural course of building, as if any building project anywhere and from any time would necessarily be described in this fashion."[66] This pattern is essentially Syro-Mesopotamian and should be taken as the standard pattern that they, in that place and time in particular, would naturally use to describe the process of temple building. It should be remembered, however, that Hurowitz did not separate temple building accounts from the accounts of other large building projects (*e.g.*, palaces). Moreover, he was fully aware that the accounts within which he was able to isolate the five (or six) stage pattern fall into various genres,[67]

---

65 Klein (1989a) 36.

66 Hurowitz (1992) 126.

67 Hurowitz (1992) 27-28.

which means that the existence of the pattern does not imply or delimit a literary genre. This, in turn, suggests that a careful analysis of the literary macrostructure native to the Gudea Cylinders may well isolate something other than the five (or six) stage temple building pattern so common in the ancient Near East. The remainder of this article is devoted to the isolation of that literary structure.

Literary Macrostructure in the Cylinders of Gudea

Whatever else one might say about the Gudea Cylinders, they constitute one of the most impressive extant temple building compositions from the ancient Near East. In fact, one cannot deal with the topic of temple building in the ancient Near East without taking a serious look at this text. Toward the end of his volume on Gudea's inscriptions, Falkenstein presents an outline of the composition with the major sections delineated as follows: [68]

Zylinder A

I. Einleitung I 1-9
II. Auftrag zum Bau des Eninnu I 10-VII 8
III. Vorbereitung vor dem Baubeginn VII 9-XII 20
IV. Vorbereitung des Baus XII 21-XVII 1?
V. Bau des Eninnu XVII 2?-XXIX 12
VI. Pries des Eninnu XXIX 13-XXX 14

Zylinder B

I. Preis des Eninnu I 1-11
II. Vorbereitung der Inthronisation Ningirsus und Babas im neuen Eninnu I 12-IV 24
III. Einzug Ningirsus und Babas V 1-VI 10
IV. Ausstattung des Eninnu VI 11-XVII 16
V. Feiern bei der Einweihung des neuen Eninnu XVII 17-XXIV 8
VI. Schlusspreis des neuen Eninnu XXIV 9-15.

68 Falkenstein (1966) 180-81. In the same place he also gives additional subdivisions under most of these main headings.

Thus, he divides Cyls. A and B each into six sections, four of them being major divisions, not including the introduction and hymnic epilogue in each Cylinder. His is a useful structural analysis, but it does not reflect the literary structure inherent to the text itself. Instead, he follows the general framework of the building process and, therefore, identifies the literary structure of the composition with the practical stages in the process of building the Eninnu. Others have taken a similar approach yielding varying results.[69] Unlike Falkenstein, some of these have come to the text with comparative purposes uppermost in their mind.[70]

---

69 See most recently Hurowitz (1992) 51-57 and Suter (1995) 80-82. From an archaeological point of view see Heinrich (1982) 1.137-42.

For example, in her dissertation, Suter, like Falkenstein, outlines the Cylinders based "primarily on plot units" (Suter 78), and isolates ten major units, five each in Cyls. A and B. They are: (1) The Project Cyl. A i 1-21; (2) Verification of the Revelation Cyl. A i 22-vii 8; (3) Verification of the Commission Cyl. A vii 9-xii 19; (4) Construction Preparations Cyl. A xii 20-xx 12; (5) Construction Cyl. A xx 13-xxx 16; (6) Inauguration Preparations Cyl. B i 1-19; (7) Induction of Ningirsu and Baba Cyl. B i 20-vi 3; (8) Induction of the Divine Staff Cyl. B vi 4-xiii 10; (9) Inauguration Presents Cyl. B xiii 11-xvi 2; and (10) Inauguration Banquet Cyl. B xvi 3-xxiv 17 (see Suter 80-82, with further breakdown of each section there and discussion on the following pages). Although I disagree with her literary structural analysis (see n. 71 below), her dissertation offers some helpful suggestions for the interpretation of certain sections of the composition. For example, she revives the possible interpretation once proposed by Lambert and Tournay that the so-called "seven blessings" in Cyl. A xx 24-xxi 12 actually refer to the marking off of the seven steps of a ziggurat (*ibid.*, 100-2).

Overall, Suter's goal was to examine "Gudea's temple building, integrating both written and pictorial sources, in an attempt to recreate a comprehensive image of this Sumerian ruler the way he chose to be remembered" (*ibid.*, vi). It is a fine dissertation, but it must be used with caution, not because the writer's work is unsatisfactory, but because the Stela Fragments that constitute her "pictorial sources" are so fragmentary that she is forced to speculate about their compatibility and about what the scenes might have looked like (*ibid.*, 264-65). Thus, she herself is forced to admit that her reconstructions are "hypothetical" (*ibid.*, 265), although she goes on to argue that, in the end, "it is possible to determine with more or less precision which events were likely to have been visualized on the stelae and which not" (*ibid.*, 341).

70 See, *e.g.*, Kapelrud (1963) 57-58 and the critique of Kapelrud's analysis by Rummel (1981) 277-84; Weinfeld (1972) 248-49; and then also Hurowitz (1992) 56-57.

My thesis is that *the native primary literary macrostructure of the composition recorded on the Gudea Cylinders surfaces in the form of an all-encompassing structural arrangement which is made explicit by the occurrence of a relatively frozen formula at the boundaries between the major sections of the composition.* In addition, a secondary substructural formula guides the careful reader through the most complicated section of the composition. Both formulas reflect the ritual nature of the textual account as a literary composition which, in turn, reflects the ritual nature of the temple building process itself as it is conceived in the Gudea Cylinders.[71] Furthermore, in addition to these formulas, there are identifiable broad overlapping and

---

71 Suter observes (based on her reading of Averbeck [1987]) that "Averbeck's structural analysis of the text is a description of its contents rather than a literary analysis" (Suter [1995] 75 n. 41), and "Falkenstein's outline is based mainly on the development of the plot, Averbeck's on one recurrent statement" (Suter [1995] 78). In a sense, she is correct, but I argued in my dissertation and continue to argue here that, first, in the case of the Gudea Cylinders, it would be a mistake to distinguish too much between "a description of the contents" and a "literary analysis" of the macrostructure of the composition. After all, the document does purport to describe and laud the building of the new Eninnu temple in ancient Lagash. Where I disagree with her, as well as with others (including Falkenstein) who have attempted to outline the literary structure of the composition, is in their failure to recognize the ritualistic nature of this particular composition.

Second, we must not confuse the stages in the actual construction and dedication of the temple with the ritual patterns that control that process from the perspective of this text as it is written. Thus, as it turns out, the structure of the composition is a reflex of the ritual nature of the composer's (and probably also Gudea's) historical conception (and experience) of the temple building and dedication processes (see Ellis [1968] 5-34 for an archaeological perspective on such rituals). The "recurring statement" (*i.e.*, ritual formula) which moves the story-line along is both a ritual and literary formula and should be taken seriously by those who are willing to see the text for what it is: a hymnic and, at the same time, step-by-step ritualistic description of a ruler's pious involvement in the process of building a temple in ancient Sumer. The ritualistic nature of the historical process as the text recounts the process is a historical and a literary reality, respectively. In effect, if my analysis is correct, the formulas (not just one but at least two, see below) provide an important foundation for the ongoing work of structural and other levels of literary analysis of this apparently unique composition.

Third, there are, of course, other levels of literary patterning in the Cylinders, some of which I treated in my dissertation and will also outline below. However, my main

narrow subsidiary structural indicators within the composition that one can also identify. They are secondary to the overall textual framework as it is defined by the formulas, but they add what might be called recurrent thematic echoes to the text at a literary structural level.

Ritual Formula and Textual Frame

The poetic narrative composition inscribed on the Gudea Cylinders includes not only descriptions of the practical steps in the construction and dedication of the temple (Cyl., A xii 21-B xvii 16), but also references to and, sometimes, portrayals of rituals performed before, during, and after the various steps in the construction and dedication procedures. This leaves its mark on all levels of the composition, including its literary macrostructure.

In very general terms, Gudea Cyl. A deals with the construction and Cyl. B the consecration and habitation of the temple. Both Cylinders end with a concluding hymn and colophon (Cyl. A xxx 6-16 and Cyl. B xxiv 9-17; see these lines cited above) which shows that, in one sense, they were conceived as the two main parts of a single composition. Each Cylinder also begins with a prologue. This also distinguishes between them as two relatively separable parts (Cyl. A i 1-11 and Cyl. B i 1-11), although the prologue in Cyl. B i 1-11 assumes the construction work in Cyl. A and, in fact, explicitly binds Cyl. B back to Cyl. A (see, *e.g.*, the comparison of Cyl. B i 11 with Cyl. A xx 23 below). Neither the concluding hymn/colophon sections nor the prologues can be treated in detail here. It is clear, however, that the division between Cyls. A and B should be considered the first level of macrostructure in the Cylinders.

---

concern here (as it was in my dissertation) is to establish a starting point for a more rigorous literary analysis at all levels of the text by uncovering the native overall literary structure of the composition as a whole (*i.e.*, the "outside boundaries" of the literary framework and major aspects of the basic literary infrastructure within which the remainder of the composition is enclosed, and by which it is carried along). The approach is "emic." The more "etic" modern approaches are useful in their own right, but they do not take into account some of the more native literary features of the composition, one of them being its literary *ritual* framework.

Many scholars assume the second level to be that of the stages in the construction process (see above). That structure is, of course, inherent to the subject of the poetic narrative. The question is whether or not it constitutes the main surface structure of the composition beyond the separation into two Cylinders. There is important evidence to the contrary.

The Main Structural Formula. On the one hand, the distinction between the literary structure of the composition and the stages and details of the building process reflected within it must be maintained. To identify or confuse these two levels of the text will result in an inadequate awareness of certain aspects of the composition. On the other hand, it is unrealistic to attempt to treat these levels of the text completely separately since the composer was the one who chose to recount the building process in this way.

In any case, it is important to recognize that the ritual performances as they are recounted in the Cylinders, some of which are described in relative detail and some of which are not, are often presented as if they either regulated, framed, or actually constituted part of the actual building work.[72] The main action sequence of building the temple, and the performance of rituals as an inherent part of that process, has left an indelible mark on the text. The literary structure follows the actions, but is indicated in a different and more explicit way than scholars have previously recognized. A relatively "frozen" formula marks the boundaries between what the composer presents as the major action complexes, some of those action complexes being focused especially on ritual actions.

This so-called "formula" stands out as a major division marker, occurring five times in essentially the same form in the Cylinders. It divides Cyl. A into four major sections and Cyl. B into three major sections, excluding the introductory prologues and concluding hymns/colophons (see above). The first occurrence is in Cyl. A vii 9-10, where the text reads:

---

72 The various ways in which rituals functioned in building the temple cannot be treated here. For now, see Averbeck (1987) 44-121 for a theoretical framework, 268-398 (*passim*) for the way the rituals contributed to regulating and framing the process, and 407-579 for in-depth analyses of the prayer and dream incubation scenes.

sipa-zi gù-dé-a gal mu-zu gal ì-ga-túm-mu

The devoted shepherd Gudea had come to know what was important, so he proceeded to carry out what was important.[73]

The others are found at Cyl. A xii 20, xxv 22-23, Cyl. B ii 7-8, and xiii 11-13 (the last is a slightly expanded version).[74] This formula was, in fact, used

---

73 The use of this (or a very similar) formula here and in other Sumerian compositions reaching back to Old Sumerian times has been observed by Falkenstein ([1966] 183 n. 5) and Alster ([1976] 110 n. 5, and [1992] 63, who translates line 10 "who is wise and also efficient"). As far as the present writer knows, however, its significance for the indigenous structure of the Gudea Cylinders has not been fully appreciated.

Falkenstein wrote: "Die einzelnen Abschnitte, die kleinen wie die grossen, folgen meist ohne Überleitung aufeinander. Diese Feststellung gilt aber für alle literarischen Erzeugnisse in sumerischer Sprache. Vereinzelt stellt die Wendung der gute Hirte Gudea ist weise und setzt Grosses in die Tat um zwar keine Verbindung zweier Abschnitte her, leitet aber auf eine neue Handlung des Stadtfürsten hin. Die Formel hat altsumerische Vorbilder" (Falkenstein [1966] 183; *cf.* also notes 4 and 5 there for references to the parallel passages to which he alluded). Therefore, according to his view, the formula does not make transitions from one section to the next, but, rather, simply leads into new actions by the ruler. Similarly, Jacobsen translates: "The able shepherd Gudea was greatly knowing, and great too at the carrying out" (*e.g.*, [1987] 396; Hurowitz follows Jacobsen's rendering [1992] 52-53).

According to the verb forms, the first part of the formula seems to refer to the previous section (*ḫamṭu*) while the second part seems to introduce what follows (*marû*). Thomsen ([1984] 118-22, esp. 120-22 and example 257 there) deals specifically with our passage and also gives other examples of such a shift from the so-called *ḫamṭu* to *marû* in the Gudea Cylinders and Gudea Stat. B. The translation endorsed here agrees with her that, basically, the shift indicates a change in viewpoint from the past action or condition to the future (or ingressive, or durative, etc.). Thus, wherever it occurs, the formula seems to introduce a shift from the previous section to a new action sequence on the part of Gudea. Specifically regarding the verb túm-mu, see now Yoshikawa (1993) and the literature cited there. The verbal preformative ì-ga- basically implies sequence, and in translation could be rendered "also," "and then," or "and now" in many contexts (see Thomsen [1984] 169-71).

74 The last passage reads: agrig-kala-[ga-]^{d}nanše-[k]e$_4$ sipa-gú-tuku-^{d}nin-gír-su-ka-ke$_4$ gal m[u]-zu gal ì-g[a]-túm-[m]u "The powerful steward of Nanshe, the obedient shepherd of Ningirsu, had come to know what was important, so he proceeded to carry out what was important."

Also, because it would be redundant in the context, sipa-zi gù-dé-a is left out of Cyl. A xii 20.

elsewhere in Sumerian literature to introduce action sequences, whether the sequence comprised the performance of a ritual or some other activity.

For example, Lugalbanda Epic II line 50 reads: lugal-bàn-da gal in-zu gal in-ga-an-túm-ma "Lugalbanda had come to know what was important, so he proceeded to carry out what was important."[75] In the context, Lugalbanda was aimlessly roaming the mountains seeking to rejoin the Urukian army, which had left him behind because of an illness that had befallen him. Coming across the nest of the Anzu-bird, and desiring to win its favor so that it might lend him aid in returning to the army, he proceeded to feed its young. Jacobsen, who gives the title "Lugalbanda and the Thunderbird" to the composition as a whole, entitles the section which line 50 introduces "Lugalbanda Regales Its Young," referring to the young of the Thunderbird (*i.e.*, the Anzu-bird).[76]

Similarly, in the myth known as "Inanna and Bilulu" lines 49-50 we read: (49) nin-mu gal mu-un-zu gal in-ga-an-túm-mu (50) kù ^{d}inanna-ke$_4$ gal mu-un-zu "Full knowledgeable My-lady was, and also she was full apt, full knowledgeable holy Inanna was, and also she was full apt."[77] The previous section of the myth recounts Inanna's longing for Dumuzi and her request of her mother, Ningal, that she be allowed to go to him at the sheepfold. In the following context, line 51 reads: kaš u$_4$-dal u$_4$-sù(?)-du(?) dúr-ru-na-bi-a "(Lager) beer laid up in remote days, in long (past) days." A large gap follows. Jacobsen assumes that the following lines "told of Inanna's preparations for the journey to the fold,"[78] where she would meet with

75 The transliteration is taken from Wilcke (1969) 96. Text "I" needs collation. It reads either tùm or tum$_4$.

76 Jacobsen ([1987] 324) translates the line "Lugalbanda was very knowing and great, too, at execution."

77 The translation and transliteration are that of Jacobsen (1953) 174-75 (except I read the sign túm rather than tù). He translates as if gal in-ga-an-túm-mu is to be assumed at the end of line 50, just as in line 49. Plate LXVII shows that it is not found on the tablet. It may have been left out in order to identify the gal in-ga-an-túm-mu of line 49 with the action taken in lines 51ff., see presently.

78 Jacobsen (1953) 175.

Dumuzi, the shepherd. Her preparations reflected her knowledge and aptness (*cf.* the formula in lines 49-50).

I know of no other clear parallels to this formula. Alster has argued that an Early Dynastic Lugalbanda composition from Abu Salabikh contains forerunners to the later "updated" versions of this formula cited above.[79] For example, in one occurrence the line reads: lugal-bàn-da gal-zu "Lugalbanda, the very knowing."[80]This is no more than a stock adjectival expression meaning "learned, wise, all knowing."[81] It is not combined with gal ì-ga-túm-mu (or its equivalent) in these passages. Other instances of this expression in verbal rather than adjectival form are also found in the same Abu Salabikh text. For example, [d]lama nin-sún gal in-zu "Lama-Ninsun is wise."[82]

Alster also refers to the Stela of the Vultures and the so-called "Barton Cylinder." In the Stela of the Vultures we find the repeated expression é-an-ma-túm-me gal na-ga-mu-zu "Eannatum was very clever indeed." Throughout the composition it introduces a ritual action described in the following way: "He made up the eyes of two doves with kohl, and anointed

79 See Alster (1976) 110 n. 5 and for a full list of the references Alster (1992) 63.

80 Biggs (1966) 85. *Cf.* Biggs (1976) plate 146 text 327 obv. ii 1 for this particular passage. Alster (1992) 63 renders the expression "Lugalbanda, the wise one."

81 See, *e.g.*, Enmerkar and the Lord of Aratta line 72, inim-gal ^{d}inanna-gal-zu-inim-ma-ke$_4$ me-a ḫu-mu-na-am-tùm "Let him acquire the important message of eloquent Inanna in (its) *me* on her behalf" (Cohen [1973] 67 and 115; *cf.* also lines 107 and 163; Jacobsen [1987] 284 renders line 72 "whither should he take the great message for wordwise Inanna?"); Shulgi A 19, where king Shulgi refers to himself saying, dub-sar-gal-zu-^{d}nisaba-kam-me-en "I am a wise scribe of Nisaba" (Klein [1981] 188-89); an Ishme-Dagan statuette which reads, ^{d}nin-gal ... ad-gi$_4$-gi$_4$-gal-zu nam-nin-a túm-ma "For the goddess Ningal, ... wise counselor, the one suitable for ladyship" (Frayne [1990] 44, Ishme-Dagan 13 lines 1-5; same as Kärki [1980] 11, Ishme-Dagan 8 lines 1-5); and a Sin-iddinam inscription regarding the building of the Ebabbar temple, which says, ^{d}utu en di-ku$_5$-an-ki gal-zu-eš-bar nì-gi-e bar-tam-e lugal-é-babbar-ra "For the god Utu, lord, judge of heaven and earth, wise in decisions, who chooses righteousness, lord of Ebabbar" (Frayne [1990] 163, Sin-iddinam 5 lines 1-5; same as Kärki [1980] 60, Sin-iddinam 5 lines 1-5).

82 Biggs (1976) plate 146 text 327 obv. i 3 for this particular passage (*cf.* Alster [1992] 63 for this rendering; *cf.* also ii 6 and iv 1 of the same text for similar verbal expressions).

their heads with cedar (resin). He released them to DN (...) in GN ..."[83] The Barton Cylinder has a similar expression in two places: (1) xv 11 reads da-ba-la-e gal ì-ga-mu-zu "Dabala, who is equally wise" (lit. "Dabala also knew much"),[84] and (2) xix 3 gal ì-ga-mu-zu "who is equally wise" (lit. "[Ešpeš] also knew much").[85] In the context, the former may introduce the building of a temple by a "semi-mythological person" named Dabala, while the latter introduces the closing of a gate and door by the deity Ešpeš.

Even though these compositions do not combine gal–zu with gal–túm-mu, the portion of the expression that does occur repeatedly in the Stele of Vultures is certainly formulaic. In fact, it repeatedly introduces a recurring series of ritual actions. However, the Barton Cylinder is so fragmentary and difficult to interpret that the seeming parallels to the use of the formula in the Gudea Cylinders cannot be pressed at this time.

The Gudea Cylinders are, of course, especially action oriented because they recount the building of a temple. In the parallel passages cited above, the formula often introduces especially important actions (sometimes ritual actions) by the primary actor in the respective composition. The same is true in the Gudea Cylinders and, in fact, in every instance the story line can be understood to progress to a different stage at the point where the formula occurs. Therefore, it would appear that the composition as a whole, could and probably should, be analyzed according to the divisions provided by this formulaic indicator of episodes. The occurrences of this formula would seem to provide the most valid internal point of departure for following the movements in the composition. They are, therefore, basic to following the practical and ritual processes, especially amid the more literary hymnic and mythological portions of the narrative.

---

83 The translation given here is from Cooper (1986) 33-39 (esp. p. 39 n. 19). See Steible (1982) 120-45 for the text itself. On the stela the occurrences are at xvi 41-42 (?, restored), xvii 48- xviii 1 (partially restored), xix 8-9 (mostly restored), xxi 12-13, Rs. i 31-32, and Rs. v 17-18 (restored).

84 See Alster (1992) 63 and now esp. Alster and Westenholz (1994) 24 and 30.

85 See Alster (1992) 63 and now esp. Alster and Westenholz (1994) 25 and 31.

Based on this formula, the Gudea Cylinders can be divided into seven main sections:

(1) the initial dream and Gudea's pilgrimage to obtain its interpretation (Cyl. A i 12-vii 8; excluding the prologue in Cyl. A i 1-11);

(2) incubation of a message dream (Cyl. A vii 9-xii 19);

(3) construction of the new Eninnu (Cyl. A xii 20-xxv 21);

(4) furnishing the new Eninnu (Cyl. A xxv 22-xxx 5; excluding the final hymn and colophon in Cyl. A xxx 6-16);

(5) preparation for the induction of Ningirsu and Baba into their new Eninnu (Cyl. B i 12-ii 6; excluding the prologue in Cyl. B i 1-11);

(6) induction of Ningirsu and Baba into their new Eninnu (Cyl. B ii 7-xiii 10); and, finally,

(7) dedication of the new Eninnu (Cyl. B xiii 11-xxiv 8; excluding the final hymn and colophon in Cyl. B xxiv 9-17).

A Minor Structural Formula. The third major section of Cyl. A is the most complicated but, fortunately, it is subdivided by the four- or fivefold occurrence of another formula. The first instance of this minor formula is in Cyl. A xiv 5-6, which reads, sipa-zi gù-dé-a ḫúl-la-gim im-ma-na-ni-íb-gar (the other instances are in Cyl. A xvii 4 [possibly], xvii 28, xx 4, and xx 12.).[86] It could be rendered either "For the devoted shepherd, Gudea, it was cause for rejoicing"[87] or, possibly, "On that occasion, (a feeling) like (that experienced at) a joyous festival resulted for the devoted shepherd, Gudea."[88] In

86 sipa-zi gù-dé-a is included only in the first occurrence of the formula, but the ruler is the contextual subject in all cases. Also, although the text is somewhat broken, the -na- seems to be missing in Cyl. A xx 12.

87 Jacobsen (1987) 405 (*cf.* also line 163 of Enmerkar and Ensuḫkeshdanna in Berlin [1979] 50-51 line 163 as rendered by Berlin, cited and discussed below). In Cyl. A xx 4 Jacobsen (1987) 412 cleverly, but questionably, combines the formula with previous lines.

88 The confusion over the grammar, interpretation, and proper translation of this clause is well documented; see, *e.g.*, Kramer (1947) 37 and Falkenstein (1950) 152 and 192. The term ḫúl-la-gim may mean simply "like joy." But the bilingual Akkadian translation is *kīma ḫidûtim ittaškanšum* (N perfect of *šakānu*; see the treatment of the bilingual Samsuiluna B, Sumerian lines 27-28 and Akkadian lines 31-32 below). In

either case, the point is that the successful completion of the previous step in the construction process resulted in personal joy (and fulfillment) for Gudea. Whether or not he manifested this through public festive activity is not certain.

The text is broken at Cyl. A xvii 1-4, but there is reason to suppose that the formula might have occurred in Cyl. A xvii 2-3. First, a different subject seems to be under consideration when the text resumes in xvii 5ff., specifically, the revelation of the giš-ḫur "plan, design" of the temple (see esp. xvii 17 é-a ^{d}en-ki-ke$_4$ giš-ḫur-bé si mu-na-sá "Enki prepared a plan of the temple for him [Gudea]"; *cf.* Cyl. A v 4, vi 5, and finally vii 6 "he will reveal the plan of his temple to you"). Second, some of the sign remnants in the break correspond to the formula (*e.g.*, there is a visible gar in xvii 3, at least in Thureau-Dangin's copy). Like the main structural formula referred to above, this expression is a natural divider. But, in contrast to that formula, this one seems to record only a response and conclusion to the previously narrated events without looking forward to what follows.

---

turn, Akkadian *ḫidûta šakānu* (= ḫúl–gar ?) can be rendered either "to make merry" or "to hold a festival" (CAD Ḫ 183b meaning d) and, in fact, Von Soden's translation of Samsuiluna B (Akkadian version) 31-32 is "wie ein Freudenfest wurde es ihm" (AHw 1138b meaning 15d; contrast CAD Ḫ 183b, lexical text section, "(Shamash) has been established in joy").

In his grammar, Falkenstein translated the Sumerian clause in three different ways, depending to some degree on the point of grammar he was intending to emphasize: (1) "man hat ihm dort etwas wie Freude gesetzt" ([1949] 171 and 152; third person singular -b- infix indicating an undefined plurality); (2) "sie setzten ihm dort? etwas wie Freude" ([1950] 192; the locative -ma- and locative-terminative -ni- meaning "there"—note also the assumed plurality); and (3) "man setzte es ihm wie in Freude" ([1950] 96; dative verbal infix, but also "as in joy"?). The latter translation and Von Soden's rendering (see above) reflect the problem caused by the -gim (= Akk. *kīma*).

We may tentatively view the grammar as follows. First, the -b- infix refers to an indefinite subject "it" (probably the situation resulting from the previous actions of the ruler). Second, -ma- and -ni- together mean "there" in the sense of "on that occasion" or "at that time." Third, -na- is the dative infix referring back to Gudea (analyzing the grammar as gù-dé-a[-ra]; *cf.* en-ra "for the lord" in Enmerkar and Ensuḫkeshdanna 163 cited and discussed below, Berlin [1979] 50-51). A literal translation would be something on the order of: "It (*i.e.*, the previous accomplishment) established something like rejoicing (or a joyous festival) there for the devoted shepherd, Gudea."

In his work on Samsuiluna B, Thureau-Dangin remarked on the formulaic nature of this expression in Gudea Cyl. A.[89] The very same clause occurs in Samsuiluna B lines 27-28 where, at the end of the mythological prologue, Shamash is said to have ḫúl-la-gim im-ma-na-ni-íb-gar (Akk. version lines 31-32 *ki-ma ḫi-du-tim it-ta-aš-ka-an-šum*[90]). It is obvious that the point of these lines in Samsuiluna B was to describe the joy of Shamash over Enlil's good decree for Sippar, which had been recounted previously in the prologue. Similarly, in the epic Enmerkar and Ensuḫkeshdanna, this clause describes the delight that Ensuḫkeshdanna felt over the prospect that, by means of sorcery, he might cause Enmerkar and Uruk to submit (line 163 en-ra ḫúl-la-gim im-ma-na-ni-ib-gar).[91] Again, it stands at the junction between two parts (strophes?) of the composition.[92]

A third parallel passage is found in Gilgamesh and Huwawa A lines 46-47, where one should probably read: ^giš^erin-sìg-gi ḫúl-la-gim im-mu-na-ni-ib-gar en-^d^gilgameš-e ḫúl-la-gim im-mu-na-ni-ib-gar.[93] In this composition, as in the others cited above, this combination of words is used to express the joy that resulted from the previous action as Gilgamesh proceeded with his plan. That is, there is a shift in the story-line just at this

---

89 Thureau-Dangin (19420-44) 7 n. 4.

90 See the lineation and readings of the Akkadian version by Sollberger (1967) 41. Three main translations have been offered: (1) "avec joie se comporta" (Thureau-Dangin [1942-44] 12); (2) adverbially "comme pour une tâche joyeuse" (Sollberger and Kupper [1971] 222); and (3) "wie ein Freudenfest wurde es ihm (GN)" (Von Soden, AHw 1138b meaning 15 d).

91 Berlin translates the line "This made the lord extremely happy" (Berlin [1979] 50-51).

92 Berlin comments that "This line both sums up the impact of the preceding strophe, and introduces the subject of the actions in the following stanza" (Berlin [1979] 80).

93 See Kramer (1947) 10-11 translates: "Who felled the cedar, acted joyfully, The lord Gilgamesh, acted joyfully." Kramer himself suggests that im-mu-na- here is for im-ma-na- in Gudea Cyl. A xiv 6, etc., although he reads ḫúl-la-gim IM mu-na-ni-ib-gar in his text edition (Kramer [1947] 37 n. 218).

Concerning the context of these lines, Kramer wrote: "In attributing the epithet ^giš^erin-sìg-gi (line 46) to Gilgamesh, the poet is running ahead of the story since the event that gave currency to that particular epithet has still to be related in the poem" (Kramer [1947] 37).

point. Finally, one might also consider line 25 of the bilingual myth Elevation of Ishtar: an-na-ra inim-bal-bar-zé-eb-ba-ke$_4$ ḫúl-la-eš nam-mi-in-gar, which Hruška translates "Die Vermittlung der Herzensfeude kam dem An sehr gelegen."[94] Although the expression is not exactly the same here as in the other cases cited above, it is close. Again, it describes the response of the main subject (this time the deity An), and comprises part of the introduction to An's verbal response. It is part of the narrative framework, not the dialogue.

The five (or six?) subsections in Cyl. A xii 20-xxv 21 that result from this analysis are: (1) the special preparation and purification of the populace, sacred precinct, and brick mold (Cyl. A xii 21-xiv 6); [possibly (2) gathering of laborers and materials (Cyl. A xiv 7-xvii 4?)]; (3) surveying and laying out the sacred area (Cyl. A xvii 5-28); (4) making and presenting the first brick (Cyl. A xvii 29-xx 4); (5) oracular confirmation of the architectural plan (Cyl. A xx 5-12); and (6) construction of the new temple (Cyl. A xx 13-xxv 21).

The Literary-Ritual Framework of the Gudea Cylinders. Overall, the following pattern results from recognizing the importance of these two formulas in Gudea Cyls. A and B:

---

94 Hruška (1969) 483 and 491.

GUDEA CYLINDER A

Hymnic Prologue (Cyl. A i 1-11)

I. Gudea's initial dream and its interpretation (Cyl. A i 12-vii 8)
II. Gudea's incubation of a second dream (Cyl. A vii 9-xii 19)
III. Gudea's construction of the new Eninnu temple (Cyl. A xii 20-xxv 21)

A. Social liminality, purification, and brick mold preparation (xii 21-xiv 6)
[B. Gathering of raw materials and laborers (xiv 7-xvii 4?)]
C. Surveying and laying out the sacred area (xvii 5-28)
D. Fabricating and presenting the first brick (xvii 29-xx 4)
E. Oracular confirmation of the architectural plan (xx 5-12)
F. Construction of the temple (xx 13-xxv 21)

IV. Gudea's outfitting of the temple and its associated structures (Cyl. A xxv 22-xxx 5)

Hymnic Epilogue (Cyl. A xxx 6-14)

Colophon (Cyl. A xxx 15-16)

GUDEA CYLINDER B

Hymnic Prologue (Cyl. B i 1-11)

V. Gudea's preparation for the induction of Ningirsu and Baba into the new Eninnu (Cyl. B i 12-ii 6)
VI. Gudea's induction of Ningirsu and Baba into the new Eninnu (Cyl. B ii 7- xiii 10)
VII. Gudea's celebration of the induction of Ningirsu and Baba into the new Eninnu (Cyl. B xiii 11-xxiv 8)

Hymnic Epilogue (Cyl. B xxiv 9-15)

Colophon (Cyl. B xxiv 16-17)

The first occurrence of the major structural formula (Cyl. A vii 9-10) links Nanshe's interpretation of Gudea's first dream to his incubation of a second dream based on that interpretation. The major formula in Cyl. A xii 20 leads from the divinatory confirmation of the second dream into the actual construction of the Eninnu. In Cyl. A xxv 22-23 it makes the connection between the previous construction of the Eninnu and the following section about the furnishing of the temple. The two occurrences of the formula in Cyl. B ii 7-8 and xiii 11-13 link the preparations for the induction of Ningirsu and Baba into the new Eninnu with their induction, and their induction with the celebrations associated with it, respectively.

This is not the time or place to show how all the other sections could, like the third, also be broken down further.[95] To be sure, there are other structural features of the text that one should take into consideration. The ones isolated below overlap with and bind together certain of the sections isolated by the formulas discussed above. Some even bind the two Cylinders together. But, in terms of literary surface structure, these latter features of the composition are both complementary and subsidiary to the main literary surface structure outlined above.

Thematic Echo in the Gudea Cylinders

The composer of the Gudea Cylinders consciously chose to use the formulas discussed in the previous section of this paper as a means of marking off certain major movements in the narrative. The purpose of the last part of this essay is to isolate other kinds of literary features of the text, especially those that may display structurally important interrelationships between and within the various sections of the Gudea Cylinders as outlined above.

---

95 See, *e.g.*, the natural divisions in section VI where another formula (all including the expression me-ni-da "with his/her *me*'s") divides a major part of the section (*i.e.*, Cyl. B vi 11-xii 25) into subsections. Each occurrence of the formula concludes the introduction of one of the minor administrative deities into the new Eninnu in anticipation of its habitation by Ningirsu and Baba.

For full outlines of Gudea Cyls. A and B, see for now Averbeck (1987) 335-52 and 390-98, respectively.

Literary patterns, structure, and plot in this composition, as in many literary masterpieces, is multifaceted.

This enterprise can be relatively subjective. How can we be sure whether a certain discerned parallel or pattern and the supposed structural implications thereof was consciously intended by the author, latent in the subject matter, or simply a repeated literary motif? In the latter two cases it may be misleading to make much of the parallel in terms of literary structural impact on the Gudea Cylinders as a whole, at least at the level of compositional intentionality.

Literary Echoes. The Gudea Cylinders begin in Cyl. A i 1-3 (cited above) by recalling the day on which Enlil determined a good destiny for Lagash. Likewise, in the concluding epilogue hymn the author includes a reference to the new Eninnu as the temple where "the destiny of Lagash is determined by An and Enlil" (Cyl. B xxiv 11, also cited above). This may be an instance of literary *inclusio*, but the question is whether the seeming *inclusio* was purposeful on the part of the author or whether this is just an instance of the repetition of a common literary and religious motif. After all, nam-tar (as a verb and a noun) occurs numerous times throughout the Cylinders. More is needed, and it is forthcoming.

For instance, what should one make of the final description of the new Eninnu as "reaching unto heaven like a great mountain" and "growing together with heaven and earth" (Cyl. B xxiv 9 and 14, respectively; cited above) in relation to comparable and, sometimes, identical motifs in Cyl. A xx 10-xxiv 17? See for example: Cyl. A xx 10 ("the separation of the Eninnu from heaven and earth"); xxi 16 ("the exalted temple which embraces heaven"); xxi 19-20 ("they were making the temple grow like a mountain range; they were making it float in mid-heaven like a cloud"); xxii 9-10 ("the ruler built the temple; he made grow; he made it grow like a great mountain"); xxiv 9 ("the devoted shepherd, Gudea, made [the temple] grow together with heaven and earth"); xxiv 11-14 ("he made its name resplendent even to the midst of the mountains; Gudea caused the temple of Ningirsu to go forth from the clouds like Utu"), xxiv 15 ("he caused it to grow like a mountain range of lapis lazuli"); and xxiv 16-17 ("like a mountain of glistening alabaster he made it stand out as a marvel").

It seems clear that in Cyl. B i 1-9 the author intended to capture the awe inspiring impact that the new temple structure had on the people (Cyl. B i 10: un ba-gar-gar kalam ba-gub-gub "The people were set there, the land stood still [in awe before it]") as well as the Anunna gods (Cyl. B i 11: ^{d}a-nun-na u$_{6}$-di-dé im-ma-šu$_{4}$-šu$_{4}$-ge-éš "[even] the Anunna gods stood there in admiration"). In order to do so he pulled together some of the most important descriptive motifs from the construction section in Cyl. A xx-xxv. Cyl. B i 1-9 reads:

> (1) é dim-gal-kalam-ma (2) an-ki-da mú-a (3) é-ninnu sig$_{4}$-zi ^{d}en-líl-e nam-du$_{10}$-ga tar-ra (4) ḫur-sag-nisi-ga u$_{6}$-e gub-ba (5) kur-kur-ta è-a (6) é kur-gal-àm an-né im-ús (7) ^{d}utu-àm an-šà-ge im-si (8) é-ninnu anzu$_{2}^{mušen}$-babbar$_{2}$-ra-àm (9) kur-ra du$_{10}$ mi-ni-íb-bad
>
> (1) The temple, the pillar of the land, (2) which grows together with heaven and earth; (3) the Eninnu, the proper brickwork (for) which Enlil decreed a good destiny; (4) the beautiful mountain range which stands out as a marvel, (5) which goes forth from the mountains; (6) being a big mountain, the temple reached unto heaven; (7) being Utu, it filled the midst of heaven; (8) the Eninnu, being the shining Anzu bird, (9) it spread (its) talons over the mountain.

In light of all these literary echoes, one could say that, from an overall literary macrostructural point of view, the author intentionally shaped the composition so that the concluding hymnic epilogue of Cyl. B tied the composition together. First, he reached all the way back to the beginning of Cyl. A (see the parallel between Cyl. B xxiv 9-11 and Cyl. A i 1-3 referred to above). Second, he reached back to the beginning of Cyl. B (see the parallel between Cyl. B xxiv 9 and 14 and Cyl. B i 2-9), which had already been tied back to the main section of Cyl. A by the multiple repetitions of numerous descriptive motifs in Cyl. A xx-xxiv. These multiple similarities of expression spread wide through the composition from beginning to end serve as literary echoes. They tie the two Cylinders together as a single composition on the level of literary motifs.

Other such motifs may encompass less of the composition but, nevertheless, appear to bind together certain major sections, or, at least, reiterate important overall compositional dynamics at pivotal points. For example,

Cyl. A i 5-9 comprises part of the prologue and reports that the seasonal flood, and thus abundant blessing, was called for in the decree of Enlil concerning Lagash.

> (5) šà gú-bé nam-gi$_4$ (6) šà-^{d}en-líl-lá gú-bé nam-gi$_4$ (7) šà gú-bé nam-gi$_4$ (8) a-gi$_6$-uru$_{16}$ nam-mul ní íl-íl (9) šà-^{d}en-líl-lá-ke$_4$ ^{i7}idigna-àm a-du$_{10}$-ga nam-túm
>
> (5) Surely the heart did overflow, (6) surely the heart of Enlil did overflow, (7) surely the heart did overflow, (8) surely the flood water did shine brightly, rising fearfully, (9) surely the heart of Enlil, being the Tigris river, did bring sweet water.

Cyl. A xxv 20-21 forms the conclusion to the account of the actual physical construction of the temple:

> (20) mu-dù šu im-ta-gar-ra-ta (21) šà-dingir-re-ne gú-bé gi$_4$-a-àm
>
> (20) He (Gudea) had built (the temple); after he had finished it (21) the heart of the gods did overflow.

The furnishing of the Eninnu follows in Cyl. A xxv 22ff. (*cf.* the structural outline above). Both of these passages use the same motif to refer to the coming of the seasonal flood waters to produce fertility and prosperity in the land. The expression used to tell of the favor of the gods when the construction of the temple was complete (xxv 21, "the heart of the gods did overflow") is the same as that used to refer to Enlil's favor in i 5 and 7, at the very beginning of the composition ("surely the heart [of Enlil] did overflow").

This seems to be a conscious device by which the author intended to draw the reader's attention to a particular climax in the narrative (*i.e.*, the actual construction had been completed). It is true that in this context the gods were also responding to the delicious meal provided for them in the completed temple (Cyl. A xxv 14-19). Eventually, however, Gudea would regale them at a seven day dedication feast in the new Eninnu (Cyl. B xvii 18-xxiv 8) where they would again bestow their abundant favor on the ruler and people as well as Ningirsu, Baba, and the temple itself. It appears that the author consciously intended to link Cyls. A and B together with this series from Cyl. i 5 and 7 through Cyl. A xxv 21 to Cyl. B xvii ff. (*cf.* also the festive meal of the gods in Cyl. B v 20-vi 2?). If this is so, then this structural feature covers only slightly less of the composition than the parallels between Cyl. A i 1-3, Cyl. A xx-xxv, Cyl. B i 1-11, and Cyl. B xxiv 9-14 discussed above.

Another important example of literary echo that encompasses almost the whole composition is based on the first recorded prayer in the Cylinders (Cyl. A ii 10-19). In it Gudea approached Ningirsu with the *immediate* purpose of enlisting the deity's support in obtaining the goddess Nanshe's help with the initial dream (Cyl. A ii 16-19), she being the dream interpreter of the gods. But before making that specific request the ruler spoke the following to Ningirsu (ii 13-15):

(ii 13) ur-sag m[a]-a-du$_{11}$ šu-zi ga-mu-ra-ab-gar
O warrior, you have commanded me, (so) let me execute it well for you!

(14) ^{d}nin-gír-su é-zu ga-mu-ra-dù
O Ningirsu, let me build your temple for you;

(15) me šu ga-mu-ra-ab-du$_7$
let me perfect the *me* for you![96]

In these lines Gudea declared his general purpose or plan, which of course was based on the previous dream command of Ningirsu (ii 13; *cf.* the initial dream, i 19). He spoke in the form of a cohortative self adjuration, which provided the background of the request for assistance (ii 16-19).[97] Further-

---

96 The poetic parallelism between Cyl. A ii 14 and 15 is particularly important. "O Ningirsu" clearly functions as a vocative at the head of, and applying to, both lines, thus binding them together. Moreover, these two lines end with similar sounds (dù and du$_7$; *cf.* also Cyl. B xvii 13 and 14 below). Another obvious element of the parallelism is the pre-verbal chain ga-mu-ra(-ab)- in both lines (see also line 13).

It should be noted that the parallelism of these lines does not necessarily mean that both are saying exactly the same thing. Instead, in this case the building of the temple and the perfecting of its *me* are conceived as two of the main but separate parts of one overall process (*i.e.*, regarding the meaning *me* as "office[s]" or "form[s]" or "function[s]," etc., see footnote 98 below).

97 The need for Nanshe's assistance was the most immediate concern. The fact that Gudea brought this to Ningirsu as a petition binds this entire prayer to the immediate situation (*i.e.*, the pilgrimage to NINA to obtain Nanshe's interpretation of the initial dream).

more, in a general way, it set the agenda for Gudea's fulfillment of that which Ningirsu had (enigmatically, in a symbolic dream) requested of Gudea.

Certain parallel texts in Cyl. B show that the terminology in Cyl. A ii 13-15 applies to the two major separable parts of the activities recorded on the Cylinders; namely, the construction and the dedication of the Eninnu. On the one hand, Cyl. A ii 13-14 is repeated *mutatis mutandis* in Cyl. B ii 19b-21 as part of the prayer in which Gudea reported the completion of the temple to Ningirsu. Cyl. B ii 19b-22 reads:

(19b) ... ur-sag ma-a-du$_{11}$
O warrior, you commanded me;

(20) šu-zi ma-ra-a-gar
I have performed faithfully for you!

(21) ^{d}nin-gír-su é-zu mu-ra-dù
O Ningirsu, I have built your temple for you;

(22) ḫúl-l[a] ḫ[a]-n[i]-ku$_4$-ku$_4$
may you enter it joyfully!

On the other hand, the perfecting of the *me* which Cyl. A ii 15 looks forward to is stated as fulfilled in Cyl. B xvii 14. After the *me*'s of the Eninnu had been properly installed (see Cyl. B vi 11-xii 25; note esp. the so-called "me-ni-da" section where the various minor deities enter "with his/her *me*'s," passim), and the necessary provisions for maintenance of the cult had been made by Gudea (see the chariot, regular cult, and bed as gifts from the ruler in Cyl. B xiii 14-xvii 12), then and only then the actual perfection of the *me*'s was declared. As Cyl. B xvii 12-14 puts it:

(12) nì-ul-uru-na-ke$_4$ pa bí-è
He (Gudea) had made the long lasting thing of his city resplendent.

(13) gù-dé-a é-ninnu mu-dù
Gudea had built the Eninnu,

(14) me-bé šu bí-du$_7$
he had perfected its *me*.

In effect, one might say that the "building" of the temple was accomplished in Cyl. A (see Cyl. B ii 19b-21) and what might be referred to as its "*me*ing" (*i.e.*, its "activating," or the installation of its divine administrative "offices") was accomplished in Cyl. B (see Cyl. B xvii 13-14). Note also that Gudea's full completion of the building of the temple is reiterated in Cyl. B xvii 13, but the "*me*ing" (or "activating") of the temple is not mentioned at all in Cyl. B ii 19b-21. The latter still needed to be accomplished later in the recorded events of Cyl. B and, therefore, could not be reported to the god and goddess in Cyl. B ii. The former, however, had been accomplished already in Cyl. A, so it could be reported in Cyl. B ii, as well as reiterated in Cyl. B xvii. It seems, therefore, that the "*me*ing" of the temple reached beyond its construction to its various internal (and associated external) functions.[98]

---

98 Sometimes it is not certain whether we should render *me* as singular or plural (see Farber-Flügge [1973] 117). It is most certainly a plural term in Cyl. B vi-xii and in Cyl. A x 6 (me-ninnu "the fifty *me*'s"), but the point in some contexts seems to be their overall general and collective effect upon the temple structure.

Me has been rendered in several ways (for relatively recent bibliography, see Cooper [1978] 106, remark on line 9). For example, "divine powers" (Falkenstein), "divine attributes" (Hallo and van Dijk), "numinous efficacy" (Oberhuber), "mana" (MSL), "*modus operandi*" (Jacobsen), and "form, image, shape, figure, symbol, etc." (Cohen [1973] 164-65). Farber-Flügge provides an extended list of references and useful discussion of the matter in her edition of the myth Inanna and Enki (1973) 97-164. Gragg's tentative explanation of it as a nominal form of the copula *me* "to be" is especially interesting (see Gragg [1968] 102-3; *cf.* Jacobsen [1946] 139 n. 20).

We cannot provide a full account of the matter here, but suffice it to say that Gudea Cyl. B vi-xii has often played an important part in scholarly discussions about the *me*'s. For example, in personal communication Thorkild Jacobsen once wrote to me that his previous interpretation (*modus operandi*) is incomplete, though not wrong. He suggested that the term denotes "office" in an extended sense, including such things as trades and occupations (see the list of the *me*'s in Inanna and Enki). The office includes the powers that go with the office. For example, the *me* of Utu consists of the power(s) of his office of "judge" and the *me* of Ningirsu the power(s) appertaining to his office of "warrior," etc. All of this derives from the view of the ancients that their world was a polity managed by the gods. Specifically, with regard to the *me*'s in the Gudea Cylinders, Jacobsen wrote that the *me*'s of the Eninnu "are the offices and occupations specified in Cylinder B."

I had already, independently, arrived at a very similar conclusion based upon my own analysis of *me* in the Cylinders. If, for example, one chooses the translation

So then, on the one hand, Cyl. A ii 13-15 sets the agenda for the temple construction and consecration project as a whole. On the other hand, Cyl. B xvii 12-14 seals it off so that what follows (*i.e.*, Cyl. B xvii 18-xxiv 8) describes the response of the gods to the completed project. Cyl. B xvii 12-14 functions on the human level much like Cyl. B xiii 9-10 on the divine. The latter reads:

(9) dingir-numun-zi-zi-da-ke$_4$
The gods of all proper seed

(10) é [m]u-dù mu-[b]é pa b[í-]è
built the temple and caused its name to shine brightly.

These passages summarize the importance of the respective human and divine contributions to the construction, and they do so in the context of describing their involvement in the dedication of the temple. In this regard, the parallels between Cyl. B xvii 12-14 and Cyl. A i-ii are of the utmost significance: Cyl. B xvii 12 (nì-ul-uru-na-ke$_4$ pa bí-è "he [Gudea] had made the long lasting thing of his city resplendent") recalls Cyl. A i 4 (uru-me-a nì-ul pa nam-è "surely he [Enlil] saw fit to make the long lasting thing resplendent in our city"), while Cyl. B xvii 13-14 coincides with Cyl. A ii 14-15 (see above).

A similar literary echo that essentially binds the two Cylinders together also involves the distinctive divine and human levels of activity, but this one is more limited in scope. Cyl. A xx 23 and Cyl. B i 11 are identical, except for the graphic variant of ù for u$_6$ in Cyl. A xx 23: ^{d}a-nun-na ù-di-dè im-ma-šu$_4$-šu$_4$-ge-éš "the Anunna gods stood there in admiration." Cyl. A xx 13-23 gives a summary of the temple construction process from the viewpoint of the involvement of the gods, concluding with the remark in line 23 about the Anunna gods:

"form" or its variants (see Cohen's translations cited above), he must include the notion of "function" or "activity" in his understanding of that English word in order to avoid attributing an overly "Platonic" concept to the Sumerians. That is, the Sumerian term is clearly used to refer to those offices and activities which activated the newly constructed Eninnu (Cyl. B vi-xii), including also the symbols and accouterments provided by Gudea for the activities of the god and goddess in the new temple (Cyl. B xiii-xvii).

(xx 13) gu-mu-ba-ra me šu im-du_7-du_7 (14) us-ga-kù-ge èš mu-gá-gá (15) é-a ^{d}en-ki-ke_4 temen mu-si-ge (16) ^{d}nanše dumu-eridu^{ki}-ke_4 eš-bar-kin-gá mí ba-ni-du_{11} (17) ama-lagaš^{ki} kù-^{d}gá-tùm-du_{10}-gé (18) sig_4-bi kur-ku_4-a mu-ni-tu (19) ^{d}ba-ba_6 nin dumu-sag-an-na-ke_4 (20) ì šem-eren-na ba-ni-sù (21) é-e en ba-gub la-gal ba-gub (22) me-e šu si im-ma-sá (23) ^{d}a-nun-na ù-di-dé im-ma-$šu_4$-$šu_4$-ge-éš

(xx 13) The Gumubara was perfecting the *me*, (14) the holy Usga was maintaining the sanctuary.[99] (15) Enki was imbedding (or filling in) the foundation of the temple. (16) Nanshe, the daughter of Eridu, cared for the (divinatory building) oracles. (17) The mother of Lagash, the holy Gatumdu(g), (18) fashioned its brick(s) according to (her) desire.[100] (19) Baba, the lady, the foremost daughter of An, (20) sprinkled oil and essence of cedar all around; (21) she set up the *en*-priest (and) *lagal*-priest over the temple. (22) The *me* was made to flourish (23) while the Anunna gods stood there in admiration.

Immediately after this summary from the divine perspective, the text recounts Gudea's actual construction of the Eninnu. It begins:

(xx 24) gù-dé-a lú-é-dù-a-ke_4
Gudea, the temple builder,

(25) é-a dusu-bi men-kù sag-gá mu-ni-gál
put the carrying-basket of the temple on (his) head (like) a holy crown;

(26) uš mu-gar á-gar ki im-mi-tag
he laid the foundation, shaping the terrain with a spade.[101]

The account of the physical construction and outfitting of the temple continues on through the end of Cyl. A, except for the final hymnic epilogue and the colophon.

The prologue of Cyl. B (i 1-11, cited above) describes the magnificence of the completed structure as it stood perched atop the temple platform or

---

99 On lines 13-14 and this passage as a whole see the notes in Averbeck (1987) 657-58.

100 For kur-ku_4 = *nizmatu* "wish, desire," see, *e.g.*, Sjöberg and Bergmann (1969) 91-92 and 153.

101 á-gar means "(some kind of) spade" (*cf.* Römer [1965] 62 n. 151 and the literature cited there; reference courtesy of Å. Sjöberg).

ziggurat (i 1-9), and the paralyzing awe of the people (i 10) and Anunna-gods (i 11) as they stood gazing at it. The main structural effect of this parallel between Cyl. A xx 23 and Cyl. B i 11 is to bind Cyls. A and B together into one unit. Cyl. A xx 23 shows the Anunna gods' favor toward the project on the divine level. Cyl. B i 11, on the other hand, shows their favor toward Gudea's actual finished product. The first occurrence of the line stands immediately before Gudea actually began the work (*cf.* Cyl. A xx 24), and the second stands after he had completed it (*cf.* Cyl. B i 1-9).[102]

Conceptual Echoes. Other kinds of parallels or patterns may be sought primarily at the conceptual rather than the verbal literary level. Gudea presented two chariots to Ningirsu, one in Cyl. A vii 11-29 (*cf.* the advice of Nanshe in vi 14-vii 8), and one in Cyl. B xiii 18-xiv 12 (*cf.* xvi 15-18). Civil seems to have assumed that Cyl. A vii and B xiii-xiv refer to the same chariot.[103] This, however, is difficult to maintain since the chariot referred to in Cyl. A was, according to the text, presented to Ningirsu as a gift at the beginning of the process in order to obtain a dream that would enable the ruler to build the temple. On the other hand, Cyl. B refers to another chariot which was offered at the time of the consecration of the temple. Whether or not we should try to make something of this structurally is another matter altogether.

There is also a general correspondence between Cyl. A xxv 22-xxix 12 (*i.e.*, the furnishing and outfitting of the temple and its supplementary structures) and Cyl. B vi 11-xii 25 (*i.e.*, the entrance of the minor deities with their *me*'s into the new Eninnu). Cyl. B vi-xii describes the filling of the inner areas of the sanctuary first and then moves progressively outward. Likewise, Cyl. A xxv 22-xxviii 2 describes the outfitting of the main temple area atop the ziggurat and then Cyl. A xxviii 3-xxix 12 goes on with a focus mainly on the supplementary structures and enterprises. The major significance of these observations lies in the distinction between the human

---

102 The prayer involvement of the Anunna-gods in the construction (Cyl. A xiv 1-4) and dedication (Cyl. B i 20-ii 6) processes may also contribute to this structural investigation, but I cannot pursue this here.

103 Civil (1968) 3.

contribution to the ongoing functions of the Eninnu in Cyl. A (Cyl. A xxv-xxix) and the divine contribution in Cyl. B (Cyl. B vi-xii). Similarly, one might also make something of the comparison between Gudea's pilgrimage to NINA in Cyl. A ii-vii and Ningirsu's pilgrimage to Eridu in Cyl. B ii-vi (see esp. iii 5-12), once again distinguishing between the human point of view and the divine.

In some cases the rituals occur in a pattern which, in turn, reflects the stage in the process of constructing or dedicating the temple. Whether or not such patterns were intended by the author or simply resulted from the relative stage in the ritual process of building and consecrating the temple is not certain. For example, the prayers in the Cylinders of Gudea may be viewed as a distinct complex of rituals within the composition.[104] Certain features stand out.

First, the recorded spoken prayers are concentrated at the beginning of each Cylinder (Cyl. A ii 8-23, ii 24-iv 2, iv 5-v 10, and viii 13-ix 4; Cyl. B i 12-ii 6 and ii 9-iii 4). They are concerned with preparations for the work of constructing (Cyl. A) and consecrating (Cyl. B) the temple, respectively. Second, the "unrecorded" prayers (*i.e.*, their content is not recorded but the fact that a prayer was spoken is mentioned as part of the narrative frame) initiated the chief tasks or the achieving of major objectives of the respective Cylinder. Third, with regard to the same unrecorded prayers, they were all delivered at daybreak on the day when the particular task was accomplished, or at least begun. None of the others were.

The unrecorded prayer in Cyl. A xiii 28-29 introduces the marking off of the sacred area, etc. (*cf.* Cyl. A xvii 5-28), even though it is separated from it by a description of the ongoing gathering of laborers and raw materials in Cyl. A xiv 7-xvii 4. Cyl. A xvii 29-xviii 2 leads directly to the making of the first brick (xviii 8ff.). Similarly, Cyl. B iv 22-23 is followed immediately by the entrance of Ningirsu and Baba into the new Eninnu. Thus, in Cyl. A, the two unrecorded prayers are related to the initial stages of the construction of the temple, while in Cyl. B the single unrecorded prayer

104 These prayers have been analyzed extensively in Averbeck (1987) 407-505.

leads directly to the most important element in the activation of the new temple. Apparently, the start of such special tasks was necessarily connected with the start of a new and special day. This is especially clear in Cyl. B iv 13-24 (*cf.* iii 5-9 and v 19b).

Several other thematic conceptual macrostructures could be isolated in the Gudea Cylinders, but they cannot be treated in detail here. For example, in Cyl. A i-xx Ningirsu's "intended meaning" (lit. šà "heart, mind") was the focal point of all that Gudea did. As a pious ruler he was faithful in pursuing the precise and full details of his god's desires every step of the way. The final dream incubation and its associated divinatory rituals (Cyl. A xx 5-12) brought an end to the preliminary stages of the process and led to the initiation of the actual construction work (Cyl. A xx 24ff.). The actual construction, in turn, is "framed" by the references to the gods' favor, especially that of the Anunna-gods (Cyl. A xx 13-23 and Cyl. B i 11; see above). One might also consider the parallels between Cyl. A xii-xx, which describes the rituals used to regulate the preliminary stages of the construction process, and Cyl. B i-vi, which describes the rituals used to initiate the habitation of the temple by Ningirsu and Baba. There are several steps to the ritual process in both Cyl. A xii-xx and Cyl. B i-vi.

On a less comprehensive level, there are thematic patterns that one can discern within each of the major divisions of the composition as demarcated by the major structural formula (see above). We have already observed several of these. Probably the most significant example is the relatively minor subsection formula in Cyl. A xii 20-xxv 21 (see the full discussion of this above). Similarly, in Cyl. B vi-xii, the entrance of the various deities into the new Eninnu with their *me*'s is clearly patterned by the repeated me-ni-da–dib formula and other features of the same subdivisions (see only a basic introduction to this subsection above).

On this level, Cyl. B xiii 11-xxiv 17 is particularly interesting. The previous section (Cyl. B ii 7-xiii 10) ends by restating the fact that "*the gods* of all proper seed had built the house and had caused its name to shine brightly" (Cyl. B xiii 9-10). That section emphasized the activities of the gods in the process of activating the temple. By way of contrast, the last section of the Cylinders, especially Cyl. B xiii 11-xvii 17, concentrates on

Gudea's role as the human temple builder and activator (see *e.g.*, Cyl. B xiii 14, xiv 9, xv 23, and esp. xvii 12-14; the latter passage is dealt with above), and the benefits that would accrue to him and the populace because of that (see esp. Cyl. B xx 14ff.).

Two subsections can be isolated within this major division: (1) the presentation and acceptance of Gudea's housewarming gifts to Ningirsu and Baba (Cyl. B xiii 14-xvii 17) and (2) the banquet (*i.e.*, "house warming party") of the gods during which good destinies were determined for Lagash, the Eninnu, and Gudea (Cyl. B xvii 18-xxiv 8; xxiv 9-17 is the hymnic epilogue). The first subsection (Cyl. B xiii 14-xvii 17) again shows major correspondences between the human and divine levels. Gudea bestowed three gifts upon the divine couple: (1) a well-equipped war chariot, appropriate to Ningirsu's character as a war deity (Cyl. B xiii 18-xiv 12), (2) utensils for eating (Cyl. B xiv 13-18), and (3) a bed (Cyl. B 14: 21-22). Each was accepted by Ningirsu and Baba in Cyl. B xvi 15-18, xvii 4-17, and xvi 19-xvii 3, respectively. Note that the order of presentation and reception of the last two gifts is reversed. In the section in which Gudea presents the gifts, the bed is referred to last, apparently because of its connection with fertility and abundance, a connection which is expanded upon in the following lines (Cyl. B xiv 25-xvi 1). In the passage where Ningirsu and Baba accept gifts, the eating utensils may have been placed last because of the natural background this provided for the banquet scene which follows in Cyl. B xvii 18ff.

Similar subsections must have been clearly manifest in Cyl. B xix 18ff. where the gods sat down to the banquet and proceeded to pronounce blessings and a good destiny upon Lagash, Ningirsu, the Eninnu, and Gudea himself. Unfortunately, the text is broken at this point, and the remainder of Cyl. B suffers from some rather serious lacunae. In spite of that, however, from what is preserved it is apparent that several speeches were given by the gods. First, (after a break) Ningirsu blessed the temple and decreed a good destiny for it (Cyl. B xx 14-xxii 5?). Second, (after a second break) Enki spoke a complimentary blessing upon the temple (Cyl. B xxii 17-xxiii?). Finally, after still another break, Ningirsu blessed Gudea (Cyl. B xxiii 16?-xxiv 8). The banquet was the conclusion to the temple building process, the capstone of all of Gudea's efforts with regard to this project. Undertaking and completing the building of the temple led to a blessing of good fortune for Gudea and his realm.

Summary and Conclusion

The literary macrostructural features elucidated here do not exhaust the repertoire available in Cylinders A and B of Gudea. They are, however, at least some of the major ones, and they provide a more adequate framework for examining the details of the composition section by section and line by line than has previously been set forth.

Of course, if there was a third Cylinder it would have had significant impact on the overall structure of the composition, but we do not have it, and, for that matter, we cannot be sure that it ever existed. Moreover, there is plenty of data to show that the two extant Cylinders are intimately bound together and, overall, provide us with a relatively coherent composition.

The Gudea Cylinders are hymnic, inscriptional, and ritualistic, all at once. All three influences make their impact felt on the structure, style, and texture of the composition. As a hymn they especially manifest certain features of temple hymns. As a dedicatory royal building inscription they recount the Eninnu's construction (Cyl. A) and consecration (Cyl. B) according to a pattern common in ancient Near Eastern temple building texts. Finally, as a ritual text the Cylinders show how the temple construction and habitation activities were regulated by complexes of ritual procedures.

The latter point is especially important for discerning the literary surface structure of the Cylinders. One ritual leads to another and together they regulate the stages in the actual construction and dedication work. In fact, a standard formula recurs at particularly pivotal points in the poetic narrative, thus dividing the composition into seven main divisions. Within that framework there are other formulaic patterns and thematic echoes which bind several main divisions together. Moreover, within each of the major sections of the composition as demarcated by the literary ritual formulas one can discern several kinds of subdivisions, but we have not been able to treat the latter in any kind of balanced or comprehensive way here.

Bibliography

Al-Fouadi, A. (1969) Enki's Journey to Nippur: The Journeys of the Gods. Ph.D. dissertation, University of Pennsylvania. Philadelphia. University Microfilms International, Ann Arbor, Mich. **Alster, B.** (1976) On the Earliest Sumerian Literary Tradition. *Journal of Cuneiform Studies* 28: 109-26. (1992) Interaction of Oral and Written Poetry in Early Mesopotamian Literature. In Vogelzang and Vanstiphout 1992: 23-69. **Alster, B., and A. Westenholz** (1994) The Barton Cylinder. *Acta Sumerologica* 16: 15-46. **Averbeck, R. E.** (1987) A Preliminary Study of Ritual and Structure in the Cylinders of Gudea. Ph.D. dissertation, Annenberg Research Institute (formerly Dropsie College). Philadelphia. University Microfilms International, Ann Arbor, Michigan. **Baer, A.** (1971) Goudéa, Cylindre B, Colonnes XVIII à XXIV. *Revue d'Assyriologique et d'Archéologie Orientale* 65: 1-14. **Barton, G. A.** (1929) *The Royal Inscriptions of Sumer and Akkad.* New Haven, Conn. **Beek, M. A., *et al.*,** eds. (1973) *Symbolae Biblicae et Mesopotamicae Francisco Mario Theodoro de Liagre Böhl Dedicatae.* Leiden. **Behrens, H., D. Loding, and M. Roth**, eds. (1989) *DUMU-E$_2$-DUB-BA-A: Studies in Honor of Åke W. Sjöberg.* Occasional Publications of the Samuel Noah Kramer Fund 11. Philadelphia. **Benito, C.** (1969) "Enki and Ninmah" and "Enki and the World Order." Ph.D. dissertation, University of Pennsylvania. Philadelphia. University Microfilms International, Ann Arbor, Mich. **Berlin, A.** (1979) *Enmerkar and Ensuḫkeshdanna.* Occasional Publications of the Babylonian Fund 2. Philadelphia. **Biggs, R. D.** (1966) The Abu Salabikh Tablets. A Preliminary Survey. *Journal of Cuneiform Studies* 20: 73-88. (1971) An Archaic Sumerian Version of the Kesh Temple Hymn from Tell Abu Salabikh. *Zeitschrift für Assyriologie und vorderasiatische Archäologie* 61: 193-207. (1976) *Inscriptions from Tell Abu Salabikh.* Oriental Institute Publications 99. Chicago. **Castellino, G.** (1959) Urnammu, Three Religious Texts (continued). *Zeitschrift für Assyriologie und vorderasiatische Archäologie* 53: 106-32. **Civil, M.** (1968) Išmedagan and Enlil's Chariot. *Journal of the American Oriental Society* 53: 3-14. **Cohen, M. E., D. C. Snell, and D. B. Weisberg**, eds. (1993) *The Tablet and the Scroll: Near Eastern Studies in Honor of William W. Hallo.* Bethesda, Md. **Cohen, S.** (1973) Enmerkar and the Lord of Aratta. Ph.D. dissertation, University of Pennsylvania. Philadelphia. University Microfilms International, Ann Arbor, Mich. **Cooper, J.** (1978) *The Return of Ninurta to Nippur.* Analecta Orientalia 52. Rome. (1986) *Sumerian and Akkadian Royal Inscriptions: Vol. I, Presargonic Inscriptions.* New Haven. **Ducrot, O., and T. Todorov** (1979) *Encyclopedic Dictionary of the Sciences of Language.* Transl. by C. Porter. Baltimore and London. **Edzard, D. O.** (1997) *Gudea and His Dynasty.* The Royal Inscriptions of Mesopotamia 3/1. Toronto. **Edzard, D. O., and Cl. Wilcke** (1976) Die Hendursanga-Hymne. In Eichler 1976: 139-76. **Eichler, B. L.**, ed. (1976) *Kramer Anniversary Volume.* Alter Orient und Altes Testament 25. Neukirchen-Vluyn. **Ellis, R. S.** (1968) *Foundation Deposits in Ancient Mesopotamia.* Yale Near Eastern Researches 2. New Haven. **Falkenstein, A.** (1949) *Grammatik der Sprache Gudeas von Lagaš I: Schrift- und Formenlehre.* Analecta Orientalia 28. Rome. (1950) *Grammatik der Sprache Gudeas von Lagaš II: Syntax.* Analecta Orientalia 29. Rome. (1966) *Die Inschriften Gudeas von Lagaš:*

Einleitung. Analecta Orientalia 30. Rome. **Falkenstein, A., and W. von Soden**, (1953) *Sumerische und Akkadische Hymnen und Gebete.* Zurich and Stuttgart. **Farber-Flügge, G.** (1973) *Der Mythos "Inanna und Enki" unter besonderer Berücksichtigung der Liste der m e.* Studia Pohl 10. Rome. **Ferrara, A. J.** (1973) *Nanna-Suen's Journey to Nippur.* Studia Pohl: Series Maior 2. Rome. **Finet, A.**, ed. (1970) *Actes de la XVIIe Rencontre Assyriologique Internationale.* Brussels. **Fox, M. V.**, ed. (1988) *Temple in Society*, 1-16. Winona Lake, Ind. **Frankfort, H.** (1948) *Kingship and the Gods: A Study of Ancient Near Eastern Religion as the Integration of Society and Nature.* Chicago. **Frayne, D.** (1990) *Old Babylonian Period (2003-1595 BC).* The Royal Inscriptions of Mesopotamia, Early Period 4. Toronto. **Gragg, G.** (1968) The Syntax of the Copula in Sumerian. In Verhaar 1968: 86-109. **Grayson, A. K.** (1975) *Babylonian Historical-Literary Texts.* Toronto. **Hallo, W. W.** (1970) The Cultic Setting of Sumerian Poetry. In Finet 1970: 116-34. Brussels. (1981) Review of Jerrold S. Cooper. *The Return of Ninurta to Nippur. Journal of the American Oriental Society* 101: 253-57. (1983) Sumerian Historiography. In Tadmor and Weinfeld 1983: 9-20. **Hallo, W. W., and K. L. Younger, Jr.**, eds. forth., *The Context of Scripture.* Vol. 2. Leiden. **Heimpel, W.** (1970) Observations on Rhythmical Structure in Sumerian Literary Texts. *Orientalia* n.s. 39: 492-95. (1981) The Nanshe Hymn. *Journal of Cuneiform Studies* 33: 65-139. **Heinrich, E.** (1982) *Die Tempel und Heiligtümer im alten Mesopotamien: Typologie, Morphologie und Geschichte.* 2 vols. Berlin. **Holman, C. H., and W. Harmon** (1986) *A Handbook to Literature.* Fifth edition. New York. **Hruška, B.** (1969) Das spätbabylonische Lehrgedicht "Inannas Erhöhung." *Archiv Orientální* 37: 473-522. (1976) Die sumerischen Tempelhymnen und die Deutung von Urn. 49. *Archiv Orientální* 44: 353-60. **Hurowitz, A.** (1985) The Priestly Account of Building the Tabernacle. *Journal of the American Oriental Society* 105: 21-30. (1992) *I Have Built you an Exalted House: Temple Building in the Bible in the Light of Mesopotamian and Northwest Semitic Writings.* Journal for the Study of the Old Testament and American Schools of Oriental Research Monograph Series 5. Sheffield. **Jacobsen, T.** (1946) Sumerian Mythology: A Review Article. *Journal of Near Eastern Studies* 5: 128-52. (1953) The Myth of Inanna and Bilulu. *Journal of Near Eastern Studies* 12: 160-91. (1976) *The Treasures of Darkness: A History of Mesopotamian Religion.* New Haven and London. (1987) *The Harps that Once....: Sumerian Poetry in Translation.* New Haven. **Kapelrud, A. S.** (1963) Temple Building, a Task for Gods and Kings. *Orientalia* n.s. 32: 56-62. **Kärki, I.** (1980) *Die sumerischen und akkadischen Königsinschriften der altbabylonische Zeit, I: Isin, Larsa, Uruk.* Studia Orientalia 49. Helsinki. **Klein, J.** (1981) *Three Šulgi Hymns: Sumerian Hymns Glorifying King Šulgi of Ur.* Ramat-Gan, Israel. (1985) Shulgi and Ishmedagan: Runners in the Service of the Gods (SRT 13). *Beer-Sheva* 2: 7-37. (1989a) Building and Dedication Hymns in Sumerian Literature. *Acta Sumerologica* 11: 27-67. (1989b) From Gudea to Šulgi: Continuity and Change in Sumerian Literary Tradition. In Behrens, *et al.* 1989: 289-301. (1990) Šulgi and Išmedagan: Originality and Dependence in Sumerian Royal Hymnology. In Klein and Skaist 1990: 65-136. **Klein, J., and A. Skaist**, eds. (1990) *Bar-Ilan Studies in Assyriology.* Bar-Ilan, Israel. **Kramer, S. N.** (1947) Gilgamesh and the Land of the Living. *Journal of Cuneiform Studies* 1: 3-46. (1969) *The Sacred Marriage Rite: Aspects of*

Faith, Myth, and Ritual in Ancient Sumer. Bloomington, Ind. (1988) The Temple in Sumerian Literature. In Fox 1988: 1-16. **Krispijn, Th. J. H.** (1982) De Tempelbouw van Gudea van Lagash. *Oosters Genootschap in Nederland* 11: 81-103. **Lambert, M., and R. Tournay** (1948a) Le Cylindre A de Gudéa. *Revue biblique* 55: 403-37. (1948b) Le Cylindre B de Gudéa. *Revue biblique* 55: 520-43. (1950) Corrections au Cylindre A de Gudéa. *Archiv Orientální* 18: 304-20. **Lieberman, S. J.**, ed. (1975) *Sumerological Studies in Honor of Thorkild Jacobsen*, 205-316. Assyriological Studies 20. Chicago. **Neugebauer, O.** (1957) *The Exact Sciences in Antiquity*. 2nd edition. Providence, R.I. **Oppenheim, A. L.** (1956) *The Interpretation of Dreams in the Ancient Near East*. Transactions of the American Philosophical Society 46: 3. Philadelphia. **Orsini, G. N. G.** (1965) Form. In Preminger 1965: 286-88. **Preminger, A.**, ed. (1965) *Encyclopedia of Poetry and Poetics*. Princeton. **Price, I. M.** (1927) *The Great Cylinder Inscriptions A and B of Gudea*. 2 parts (1899 and 1927). Leipzig. **Reisman, D.** (1973) Iddin-Dagan's Sacred Marriage Hymn. *Journal of Cuneiform Studies* 25: 185-202. **Römer, W. H. Ph.** (1965) *Sumerische 'Königshymnen' der Isin-Zeit*. Leiden. **Rummel, S.** (1981) Narrative Structures in the Ugaritic Texts. In S. Rummel, ed., *Ras Shamra Parallels*, vol. 3, 221-332. Analecta Orientalia 51. Rome. **Sauren, H.** (1975) Die Einweihung des Eninnu. In *Le Temple et le Culte*, 95-103. Rencontre Assyriologique Internationale 20. Leiden. **Sjöberg, Å, W., and E. Bergmann** (1969) *The Collection of the Sumerian Temple Hymns*. Texts from Cuneifrom Sources 3. Locust Valley, N.Y. **Sollberger, E.** (1967) Samsu-iluna's Bilingual Inscription B Text of the Akkadian Version. *Revue d'Assyriologique et d'Archéologie Orientale* 61: 39-44. **Sollberger, E. and J.-R. Kupper** (1971) *Inscriptions Royales Sumériennes et Akkadiennes*. Paris. **Steible, H.** (1982) *Die Altsumerischen Bau- und Weihinschriften: Teil 1 Inschriften aus Lagaš*. Freiburger Altorientalische Studien 5, 2 volumes. Wiesbaden. (1991) *Die Neusumerischen Bau- und Weihinschriften: Teil 1 Inschriften der II. Dynastie von Lagaš*. Freiburger Altorientalische Studien 9, 2 volumes. Stuttgart. **Suter, C. E.** (1995) Gudea's Temple Building: A Comparison of Written and Pictorial Accounts. Ph.D. dissertation, University of Pennsylvania. Philadelphia. University Microfilms International, Ann Arbor, Mich. **Tadmor, H., and M. Weinfeld**, eds. (1983) *History, Historiography and Interpretation: Studies in Biblical and Cuneiform Literatures*. Jerusalem. **Thomsen, M.-L.** (1984) *The Sumerian Language: An Introduction to its History and Grammatical Structure*. Mesopotamia – Copenhagen Studies in Assyriology 10. Copenhagen. **Thureau-Dangin, F.** (1905) *Les inscriptions de Sumer et Akkad*. Paris. (1907) *Die sumerischen und akkadischen Königsinschriften*. Vorderasiatische Bibliothek 1. Leipzig. (1925) *Les Cylindres de Goudéa découverts par Ernest de Sarzec à Tello*. Musée du Louvre – Départment des Antiquités Orientales, Textes cunéiformes 8. Paris. (1942/44) L'inscription bilingue B de Samsu-iluna. *Revue d'Assyriologique et d'Archéologie Orientale* 39: 5-17. **Van Buren, E. D.** (1944) The Sacred Marriage in Early Times in Mesopotamia. *Orientalia* n.s. 13: 1-72. **van Dijk, J. J. A.** (1953) *La Sagesse Suméro-Accadienne*. Commentationes Orientales 1. Leiden. (1964-65) Le motif cosmique dans la pensée sumérienne. *Acta Orientalia* 28: 1-59 (1983) *LUGAL UD ME-LÁM-bi NIR-GÁL: Le récit épique et didactique des Travaux de Ninurta, du Déluge et de la Nouvelle Création*. Leiden. **van Driel, G.** (1973a)

On "Standard" and "Triumphal" Inscriptions. In Beek 1973: 99-106. (1973b) Review of *Foundation Deposits in Ancient Mesopotamia* by Richard Ellis. *Journal of the American Oriental Society* 93: 67-74. **Vanstiphout, H.** (1986) Some Thoughts on Genre in Mesopotamian Literature. In *Keilschrift Literaturen,* 1-11. Berliner Beitrage zum Vorderen Orient 6. Rencontre Assyriologique Internationale 32. Berlin. **Verhaar, J. W. M.**, ed. (1968) *The Verb "Be" and its Synonyms.* Philosophical and Grammatical Studies 3. Dordrecht, Holland. **Vogelzang, M. E., and H. L. J. Vanstiphout**, eds. (1992) *Mesopotamian Epic Literature: Oral or Aural?.* Lewiston, N.Y. **Weinfeld, M.** (1972) *Deuteronomy and the Deuteronomic School.* Oxford. **Wilcke, Cl.** (1969) *Das Lugalbandaepos.* Wiesbaden. (1975) Formale Gesichtspunkte in der sumerischen Literatur. In Lieberman 1975: 205-316. **Wilson, E. J.** (1996) *The Cylinders of Gudea: Transliteration, Translation and Index.* Alter Orient und Altes Testament 244. Neukirchen-Vluyn. **Yoshikawa, M.** (1993) On the Aspectual Difference between tùm and túm-mu. In Cohen, *et al.* 1993: 309-14.

Real Property Sales at Emar*[1]

Gary Beckman
University of Michigan

Cuneiform records recovered from the ruins of Meskene/Emar[2] on the middle course of the Euphrates have afforded a view of a type of society in Late Bronze Age Syria significantly different from that whose buildings and documents have been recovered at Ras Shamra/Ugarit[3] and Tell Açana/Alalakh[4] in the coastal region.[5] In contrast to the royal archives of the latter two sites, Emar has yielded prima-

* Special abbreviations employed in this essay for texts are: AS 14: Tsukimoto 1992b; AOV: Arnaud 1987b; E6: Arnaud 1986; 1987b; GsK: Sigrist 1993; Hi: Tsukimoto 1990; 1991; 1992a; *Iraq* 54: Dalley and Tessier 1992; RE: Beckman 1996c; SMEA: Arnaud 1992; TBR: Arnaud 1991.

1 I am pleased to have been invited to contribute to a volume in honor of Professor Michael Astour, from whose writings on ancient Syria I have learned so much.

2 Chavalas (1996) will serve as a general introduction to the archaeology and texts of this site. See especially pp. 165-72 for a select bibliography of Emar studies published through 1995.

3 Above all, the works of Heltzer (1976), (1978), (1979), (1982a), (1982b) should be consulted on the society and economy of Ugarit. See also Liverani (1982). Sanmartín (1995) has recently discussed the economic texts inscribed in Ugaritic alphabetic cuneiform.

4 No synthesis of the socio-economic data from Alalakh has yet been produced. See Klengel (1974), (1979); and Gaál (1988) for preliminary studies.

5 Although it lies some 45 km from the sea as the crow flies, Tell Atçana affords easy access to the coast down the valley of the Orontes (Woolley [1968] 165-81). Klengel (1979) 435 supposes that the economic situation evidenced by the Alalakh tablets

rily texts generated by private households in the course of their economic and social lives. So extensive is this private documentation that, for instance, far more testaments and adoptions are known from Emar than have been published from all other Syrian and Mesopotamian sites of this period combined.[6] So too, transfers of real property among private citizens are better attested at Emar[7] than at any roughly contemporary settlement except trans-Tigridian Nuzi.

I have collected 210 real estate transactions from Emar, inscribed on a total of 167 tablets.[8] Multiple conveyances may be documented in a single record only if all of the property involved is acquired by the same individual. In most such instances the parcels are also sold or exchanged by but one person.[9] The prices of the land sales and the sizes of the plots in question are listed by property type in ascending price order in Figures I-V. An asterisk indicates that the tablet lists only an aggregate price for two or more properties. For purposes of comparison, I have converted all prices to shekels (gín).

---

ought to be typical for all of interior northern Syria. But the Emar archives—which were, of course, not available to Klengel—paint a different picture for the Middle Euphrates region.

6 See Beckman (1996b).

7 For a list of real estate transactions other than those published in E6, see Beckman (1996a) 10-11.

8 For preliminary studies of the real estate market at Emar and its records, see Lipiński (1990), (1992); and Leemans (1988) 213-25.

9 Multiple purchases from the god "Ninurta" are recorded on E6 2, 3, 9, 139, 147, 149, 163; RE 29; TBR 5, 9, 11, 16, and 17. More than one parcel is sold by a single human to a single buyer in E6 8, 85, 115, 225 and TBR 31. In E6 137, 138, 207; Hi 7; RE 86, and 90, one person buys two or more properties from different vendors.

The only apparent exceptions to this pattern are posed by E6 80, 114 and Hi 11, in which the details of an earlier transaction involving the property are restated, and by the exchanges RE 4 and Hi 6, where both sides of the deal are recorded. RE 77 is unclear, but seems to deal with the division of communal property.

When multiple transactions are treated in a single document, I have differentiated them here as A, B, *etc.*

This study is based primarily on sales records, for they are by far the most numerous type of real estate document found at Emar. In addition, a few exchanges[10] and gifts[11] of property are attested, as well as two confirmations of ownership issued by the king of Carchemish.[12] Most striking is the virtual absence of rental[13] or share-cropping agreements from the archives. Since such arrangements undoubtedly existed at Emar, customarily they must have been concluded without written contracts. Less likely, texts of this sort might have been kept in the homes of the individuals involved, rather than deposited in the central record office from which the weight of our documentation has been drawn.

Measures of length used at Emar include the "dike" (Akk. *ikû*), which was made up of a number of "sides" (Akk. *šiddu*),[14] in turn subdivided into "cubits" (Akk. *ammatu*).[15] Other fractions of the *ikû* are the "reed" (Sum. gi) and the "foot" (Sum. gìr). Unfortunately, we do not know the precise relationships of these measurements to one another, and cannot convert any of them to meters.[16]

---

10 AOV 10; Hi 6; RE 4, all of houses.

11 Hi 47; TBR 29, 47 (houses); RE 22; TBR 31 (lots); RE 1 (vineyard).

12 RE 54, 55, edited in Beckman (1996c) 71-73.

13 I know only of RE 90, the rental of a vineyard, edited in Beckman (1996c) 113-14.

14 CAD Š/2 407.

15 Occasionally expressed as N *ina ammati.* Note also *ammati* libir-*ú-ti*, "old cubits," RE 33:2. In the Emar texts this measure is always spelled *am-ma-ti*, regardless of whether it is preceded by a preposition. It is not possible to determine whether this writing is singular or plural, since the Emar scribes were not always careful in usage of case, and a writing such as 2 *aš-lu* (TBR 62:2) shows that the singular of a measure might be employed with a plural numeral.

16 According to the standard Sumerian-Babylonian system, 6 *ammātu* = 1 gi, 20 gi = 1 *ašlu* ("rope"), and 6 *ašlātu* = 1 *šiddu* (Sum. uš) (Powell [1990] 459, Table II). In the south the *ikû* was employed only as a surface measure, but in Assyria and elsewhere in the north it could serve as a unit of length seemingly synonymous with *ašlu* (Powell [1990] 477). If this is also the case at Emar, the Babylonian relationship of the *ašlu*/*ikû* and *šiddu* has been inverted. The standard Old Babylonian cubit has been estimated at approximately 50 cm (Powell [1990] 462).

As may be seen from the list of 62 house sales in Figure I, amounts paid for such structures and their land range from 12 to 4200 shekels. Leaving aside this final price, which is so aberrant that it must be confirmed by collation,[17] both dimensions and individual prices are available for 18 of these transactions (whose references appear in bold type), allowing the computation of price per square cubit. This varies from 0.002 shekel (E6 122) to 1.38 shekels per cubit (E6 141), with an average price of 0.46 shekel per cubit. To facilitate comparison of larger agricultural properties, price can be recalculated as price per square *ikû*, assuming an *ikû* equals 120 cubits, as in Middle Assyrian texts.[18] Prices range from 0.24 to 165.6 shekels per *ikû*, the average being 55.68. Some, but by no means all, of the lower prices are recorded in instances where a lender accepts a house in lieu of an outstanding debt,[19] or when a property is sold to a third party so that the owner might satisfy his creditors.[20]

Also well documented at Emar is the sale of undeveloped city plots, referred to by the Sumerogram KI accompanied by the Semitic gloss *erṣetu*.[21] Thirty-seven transactions of this sort are known (see Figure II), with selling prices ranging from 4 to 240 shekels. Of these sales, 20 (again indicated in bold) allow the calculation of price per cubit (stretching from 0.01 shekel in RE 11 to 2.6 shekels in RE 33).[22] These figures yield an average of 0.3

Poorly-attested linear measures in the Emar texts are *sarma'u* (Hi 4:2), *matāḫu* (RE 64:3—or is this a gloss for gìr? *Cf.* TBR 58:3: 4 gìr.ḫi.a *ma-ta-ḫu rupšu*), and *ašlu ša* N *ikû* (TBR 62:2-3). Note also the surface measure *zizi* (RE 90:1).

17 See note 22 below.

18 Powell (1990) 477.

19 E6 123.

20 E6 85A, 109; TBR 33, 65, 82.

21 For a review of discussions of this term, see Beckman (1996c) 6.

22 The extraordinarily high price of 2400 gín (wr. 40 ma.na) in RE 38 (collated) is perhaps to be emended to 40 gín[!].na. I have not taken this price into account here. The price per cubit in RE 33 (2.6 shekels) is almost five times higher than that of the next most expensive lot, RE 14 (0.54 shekel per cubit). Since RE 33:2 specifies "old" cubits, perhaps this document employs a different and larger measure.

shekel, which converts to 36.6 shekels per *ikû*. The average price of an empty lot is thus 66% of that fetched by houses.

Our sources also include a dozen records describing the sale of other city structures. Since we have no idea what *tugguru*-,[23] *ḫiṭru*-,[24] or *ḫablu*-buildings[25] were, let alone what a "place of the gate" (KI.KÁ)[26] might be, these transactions are not included in this study.

The tremendous variation in the value of urban real estate is surely to be explained by what a modern real estate broker would call "location, location, location!" But our ignorance of the details of the ancient topography of Emar[27] prevents us from situating these houses, even in those few instances when a note like "(situated) on the alley of the Temple of Dagan of the Reeds"[28] is included in the sale record.

On a few occasions alienation of real estate within the city is accompanied by a peculiar ceremony[29] involving a meal and the payment of a symbolic sum to the extended family, known as "the brothers,"[30] *e.g.*, "The *ḫukku*-bread has been broken and the table anointed with oil. The 'brothers' have received 1 shekel (of silver) (each?) as the *kaburu*-payment for the house."[31] This custom, found elsewhere on the Late Bronze Age Middle

---

23 E6 82, 115A, 138C, 144; TBR 5A, 5B, 20, 67.

24 E6 139B.

25 E6 85B.

26 Hi 4; TBR 63.

27 Pending the appearance of the final report on the archaeology of the site, see Margueron (1982) on the urban layout of Emar. Since those tablets whose provenience is known do not come from individual houses, we cannot associate structures mentioned in them with particular building remains, as Stone (1987) has done for Old Babylonian Nippur. But once the documents have been better ordered chronologically it may be possible to determine the relative placement of at least some dwellings. *Cf.* Porten (1968) for a study of the Jewish colony at Elephantine, especially p. 112, figure 5.

28 RE 70:1.

29 Scurlock (1993).

30 Bellotto (1995).

31 RE 20:19-21.

Euphrates,[32] is apparently a relic from an earlier era in which land had been held communally.[33]

Among our texts are contracts for the purchase of agricultural holdings of the citizens of Emar. In Figure III I have gathered 56 instances in which fields change hands. Field prices range from 0.83 shekel to as much as 215 shekels.[34] (Unfortunately, two tablets[35] mention only a vague price of kù.babbar *īṣi u mādim*, "the full amount of silver.")[36] On the basis of 18 of these documents (once more indicated in bold) whose values per *ikû* vary from 1 (*e.g.*, TBR 38) to 100 shekels (*e.g.*, E6 146), I have calculated an average price of 25.6 shekels per *ikû*, or 46% of the value of developed land within the walls of Emar. A striking comparison may be drawn between this figure and the average price per *ikû* of a field in thirteenth-century Ugarit: 56.5 shekels,[37] which is more than twice as high. Because this latter figure is based on a very small text sample, too much weight should not be placed on it,[38] but it is surely significant that agricultural land on the coast was approximately equal in value to houses on the Middle Euphrates.

In addition to fields, Emariote productive land included vineyards, for which 11 sales[39] are known (see Figure IV), and vegetable gardens, sales of which number three (see Figure V). Metrological uncertainties prevent us from calculating average silver values for these holdings. It is interesting to

---

32 MBQ-T 65:30-31 from Tall Munbāqa/Ekalte some 20 km north of Emar on the east bank of the Euphrates. The text has been published in Mayer (1992).

33 *Cf.* Beckman (1996b) 59.

34 D. Arnaud reads TBR 68:2: 1 *me* a.šà.meš, which at a total price of 10 shekels would yield a price of 0.1 shekel per *ikû*. Since this is far out of line with the other attested values of fields, and "100" is usually written *me-at* (rarely *me-tì*) at Emar, I suggest a reading 2[!] <*ikû*> a.šà.meš. This would give a more normal value of 5 shekels per *ikû*, but because of the uncertainty, TBR 68 has been left out of my calculations.

35 TBR 16:27, 17:22.

36 CAD I 221-22.

37 Haase (1967) 205.

38 It is also uncertain whether the Ugaritic *ikû* was the same size as that in use at Emar.

39 Plus a rental (RE 90A), a seizure (RE 90B), and a gift (RE 1).

observe that most of the vineyards in question are located not in the immediate vicinity of Emar itself, but in satellite towns such as Rabban,[40] Rabi,[41] and Uri.[42]

The great majority of real estate sale contracts in both city and country are styled after a single basic pattern,[43] of which the following text will serve as an illustration:

> A house, to its full extent, 27 cubits in length, 23 cubits in breadth. On the right it is bordered by (the property of) Abdu, son of Daḫuru. On the left it is bordered by the livestock shed? of Luluḫi. In the rear it is bordered by (the property of) Ribiya, son of Ḫuraṣu. In front it is bordered by the Broad Street of the Threshers?. The house belongs to King Zū-Aštarti, son of Baʿal-kabar.
>
> Yaḫṣiya, son of Mattiya, has purchased the house from King Zū-Aštarti, owner of the house, for 100 shekels of refined silver, the full price. He has received the silver and is! satisfied. Whoever in the future should make a claim on the house shall pay 2000 (shekels) of silver to the palace. If another tablet should turn up, the old one will be broken.[44]

To summarize: First, the type of property is mentioned, followed optionally by its general location and other qualifications. Then neighboring landholders and topographical features are listed, usually for all four sides. These are designated as "right, left, front, and back" (zag / gùb / egir / *pānu*) for urban property, and as "upper, lower (short) side, first, and second (long) side" (ús.sa.du an.ta / ús.sa.du ki.ta / sag.ki.1.kam / sag.ki. 2.kam) for rural holdings. Purchaser, seller, and price follow, in hybrid Akkadian and Sumerian formulation. The seller is thereupon declared to be

---

40 E6 1?, 3A, 89?, 138B; Hi 16; RE 16; TBR 51. On this town, see Fleming (1992) 64.

41 E6 11. Durand (1989) 168 suggests that this is simply a variant writing of Rabban.

42 E6 90. On this town in the Tall Munbāqa texts, see Mayer (1988) 49.

43 Note, however, that there are a small number of sales which do not display this structure: E6 81, 113, 122; TBR 20, 33, 37, 53, 56. Is it accidental that all of these are inscribed on tablets of Syro-Hittite type? On the typology of the Emar tablets, see Arnaud (1991) 9-10.

44 RE 9:1-26, edited in Beckman (1996c) 15-16.

satisfied,[45] and, on occasion, provision is made for the possible redemption of the property. Here too it might be noted that the sale occurred under duress, perhaps "in a year of hostilities."[46] The text then concludes with a sanction against reneging on the agreement, and often includes an affirmation of the priority of the present record over all previous sale documents. A list of witnesses concludes the record.

This documentary form differs significantly from that in use in contemporary Ugarit,[47] Alalakh,[48] Assyria,[49] and Nuzi[50] (see Figure VI).[51] It also shows many divergences from the familiar Old Babylonian property sale, from which it must certainly has evolved.[52] The clearest analogues are earlier real estate transactions from the kingdoms of Mari[53] and Hana,[54] and roughly contemporary[55] records from nearby Tall Munbāqa/Ekalte.[56] That is, we are dealing with an administrative and scribal tradition at home on the Middle Euphrates.

---

45 See Westbrook (1991) for the expression "his/her/their heart is pleased" in legal contexts.

46 See the list of occurrences of this phrase at Emar in Tsukimoto (1988) 162.

47 Haase (1967); *cf.* also Boyer (1955).

48 No property transactions are known from the fourteenth-century Level IV at Alalakh, but a few were recovered from Old Babylonian Level VII (Kienast 1979).

49 Koschaker (1928) 27-52.

50 Steele (1943) and Koschaker (1928) 52ff.

51 I have simply listed the most common features characterizing the documentation from each site. For details, see the works listed in notes 47-50, 53, and 55. "Late OB" indicates records from the time of Samsuiluna and later.

52 San Nicolò (1922).

53 Boyer (1958) 183.

54 Podany (1988) 254-77.

55 Mayer (1990) 64-66 dates his material to the fifteenth century, but Wilcke (1992) 124-25 has shown that these texts are almost certainly to be placed two centuries later.

56 Around 30 real estate transactions from this site have been identified (Mayer [1986] 126-27; [1988] 48; [1990] 45-47; [1993] 103), but only a few have been published: Mayer (1990) 54-62; (1992); von Soden (1982).

A characteristic of the Syrian tradition of real property boilerplate in general is the threat of severe punishment upon any party who might back out of the agreement. In the Emar texts, this sanction is almost always a fine of 2000 shekels of silver,[57] payable to the palace alone (in 30 texts) or, more frequently, to be divided[58] between the city authorities[59] and the deity indicated by the Sumerogram ᵈNIN.URTA (in 61 texts).[60] Since this sum is so out of proportion to the selling price of land in most transactions, I doubt whether it was ever actually collected. That is, no rational Emariote would have incurred a loss of 2000 shekels to recover a parcel of much lesser value. In this regard we might compare the clause found in sales from Hana, according to which hot asphalt was to be poured upon the head of whoever repudiated an agreement,[61] or that in Alalakh texts calling for the drinking of boiling lead![62]

In contrast to the situation at Nuzi[63]—the only other Late Bronze Age site to yield large numbers of comparable transactions[64]—no real estate

---

Dorneman (1979) 146 lists six property sales among the 14 documents excavated at Tell Hadidi/Azû, but none of these are yet available.

57 Rarely attested are fines of 200 (RE 33, 64; TBR 58, 63), 400 (E6 109; Hi 12; RE 64; TBR 58), 500 (E6 150), 1000 (AOV 4; E6 3, 14, 125, 140, 141, 156, 159; RE 59, 77B; TBR 12), 3000 (TBR 14), and 4000 shekels (SMEA 30 2). A nearly complete list of penalties in sale documents is appended to Figures I-IV. Not included there, however, are the sanctions from the sales of miscellaneous types of real property cited in notes 23-26.

58 The close association between this deity and the urban administration is discussed by Yamada (1994). *Cf.* Beckman (1995) 30.

59 Expressed as "the city" (uru^{ki}) or "Emar" (only E6 1). Occasionally the "brothers" are involved—on their own or with "Ninurta" or the city—and once the seller (E6 156).

60 On the deity standing behind this writing, see Fleming (1993) 94-98. I cannot accept his suggestion that ᵈNIN.KALAM in E6 282:6 is to be understood as *bēl māti.* Read simply ᵈNIN.URTA$^{!}$.

61 Podany (1988) 257-59.

62 AT 8:31-32; 61:15-19$^{?}$. Note also AT 57:38-40, which threatens the contract breaker with the amputation of his right hand.

63 See Maidman (1976).

64 I know of no certain land sales from Kassite Babylonia. Oelsner (1982) 407, n. 33 claims

magnate is in evidence at Emar. In fact, no single individual is attested as making more than a dozen acquisitions,[65] and no one alienates more than four parcels of land.[66] Most of the 27 buyers who purchase more than one property buy only two or three properties. To a certain extent, this situation is a function of the nature of the groups of tablets uncovered at Emar. For the most part,[67] these do not constitute family archives, such as are frequently attested for the Old Assyrian period or at Nuzi.[68] Rather, the bulk of the economic material was found in a temple (M_1) which served as a sort of central records office, where transactions were filed under divine oversight.[69] Therefore we should not expect to find a concentration of records from a single person or family, but a cross section of the community's business documents. Nonetheless, had there been a real estate tycoon in Emar, he certainly would have left his mark in this collection of material.

The kings of Emar do not have a particularly high profile in the real estate market. Although they could assign property to favored subordinates,[70] impose a special assessment on landowners,[71] and compel others to exchange parcels with the palace,[72] they also appear as buyers and sellers just

---

that no such documents are attested, but Gurney (1983) 4, n. 8 reports that a possible field sale was excavated at Isin. In the preliminary report on the tablets, Walker and Wilcke (1981) 100 describe the record in question, IB 1018b, only as "fragment of a sale contract, date lost."

65 Iṣṣur-Dagan, son of Baʿal-kabar (E6 137A-E, 138A-C, 139A-D).

66 Agalli, son of Ḫinnu-Dagan (E6 8A-D).

67 E6 199-226, however, seem to be the personal records of the "diviner" of Temple M_1 and his close relatives. See Fleming forthcoming.

68 Veenhof (1986b) 9-10.

69 See Beckman (1996a) 9.

70 E6 361. It is actually the queen who makes the grant here.

71 See Yamada (1993), who gathers attestations of the (forced[?]) sale of property necessitated by the demand for 30,000 shekels of silver for the royal treasury. Perhaps this sum was required to meet a tribute payment due the Hittite overlords—*cf.* Beckman (1995) 27, n. 51. I will demonstrate elsewhere that Yamada's postulation of an Emariote king "Arana" cannot be correct.

72 E6 8A-D.

like ordinary citizens. But such attestations are not numerous: Zū-Aštarte sells one property,[73] while his brother and successor Pilsu-Dagan is involved in six transactions.[74] Elli of the following generation participates in but one uncertain field sale.[75]

In 45 of the 167 tablets, the local ruler is attested in the list of witnesses, always as the first witness. The fact that almost three-quarters of the records forego royal participation demonstrates that the king's assent was not necessary to validate a transaction. Rather, it seems to have been Emariote practice to secure the most prominent available persons to witness an agreement, and to record their presence in roughly hierarchical order. Thus a number of texts feature a member of the Hittite imperial bureaucracy as the initial witness.[76]

In contrast to the modest presence of the monarch, the role of the city god "Ninurta" is extremely prominent in the Emar real estate market. As I have already mentioned, he is—along with the city itself—the notional recipient of threatened fines, and the temple in which most of the sales records were stored was probably his home. "Ninurta" is also occasionally called upon to curse those who might break an agreement.[77]

More significantly, "Ninurta" and the city elders[78] are the sellers in 69 (=33%) of the documented transactions.[79] On the other hand, neither the god nor the elders are ever attested as purchasers. How did they acquire this real estate? An indication is given by a remark concerning the prior status

---

73 RE 9.

74 E6 8A-D, 10, 137B; Hi 7B.

75 RE 86B.

76 Beckman (1992) 49.

77 So in AS 14. In E6 125 "Ninurta" is invoked along with Dagan and Išḫara, and in TBR 9 with Dagan alone. Note also TBR 67, where the curse is the responsibility of "the (anonymous) gods (dingir.meš)."

78 Usually [lú.meš]*šībūt* [uru]*Emar*[ki], but simply [uru]*Emar*[ki] in TBR 14 and [lú.meš]gal.gal [uru]*Emar*[ki] in RE 34.

79 AOV 1, 2; E6 1, 2A-B, 3A-B, 4, 9A-C, 11, 12, 126, 139A-D, 144, 146, 147A-C, 148, 149A-B, 150, 152-53; GsK 7; Hi 2, 7A; *Iraq* 54 4; RE 2, 5, 16, 24, 29A-B, 34, 38, 49, 52, 81, 91; SMEA 30 3, 4; TBR 1-4, 5A-B, 6-8, 9A-B, 10, 11A-B, 13, 14, 16A-C, 17A-B, 18.

of one property disposed of by the deity. The property's previous owner "had committed an offense against his city and his lord. In accordance with the offense which he committed, 'Ninurta' has taken his house,"[80] which he is hereby selling. Several other like passages are known.[81] The nature of the crime in question is uncertain, as is the identity of the "lord" who is sometimes mentioned. But in any case, it was surely as the representative of the city as a corporation that "Ninurta" took possession of the parcels which he subsequently sold. That is, we are not dealing with the alienation of temple land in these transactions, but with the disposal of delinquent property by the municipal authorities.

The economic preeminence of city officials over the Crown, just demonstrated, is in harmony with observations concerning the "limited" nature of kingship in Emar.[82] On this stretch of the Euphrates, urban institutions of long standing were more important than the local monarchy, which, seemingly, had been installed by the Hittite overlords only recently.[83]

I wish to emphasize the contrast between the Emar real estate transactions and what is known of land sales and royal grants of real property on the Syrian coast in the Late Bronze Age. First, as we have seen, unit prices for land were significantly lower in the valley of the great river. Second, Emariote transactions always involved single houses, fields, lots, vineyards, or gardens. We find no transfers of entire communities along with their inhabitants,[84] such as are known from Ugarit[85] or from the texts of Level

---

80 RE 34:10-13, edited by Beckman (1996c) 54-56.

81 E6 1, 11, 144; Hi 7; TBR 13, 65.

82 Fleming (1992).

83 Beckman (1995) 29.

84 Agricultural settlements in the Ancient Near East, including their fields, pasturage, vineyards, and gardens, had value not for their land itself, but only as centers of production for vegetable foodstuffs, livestock and associated raw materials (leather, wool, *etc.*), and small crafts. A member of the elite who "owned" such a settlement in actuality possessed the right to collect tax payments and service obligations from the inhabitants, and not their persons, houses, and fields. See Heltzer (1976) 49, and *cf.* Riemschneider (1958) for land grants in Ḫatti.

85 Heltzer (1976) 48-51.

VII at Alalakh.[86] Third, there does not seem to have been an extensive system of land grants in return for service within the palace economy comparable to the Ugaritic *pilku* / *ubdy* regime.[87] Finally, the king of Emar and members of the royal family participated only minimally in transfers of property, while in Ugarit the monarch seems to have been heavily involved in such matters.[88]

These differences between Ugarit and Emar are in keeping with what we otherwise know of the character of the respective local societies: the coastal kingdom was a classic Ancient Near Eastern palace economy, in which a small elite was supported by a broad base of semi-free peasants,[89] but the Middle Euphrates was the home of a relatively egalitarian society of traders and small producers. In Emar, the farmer might purchase his own land. In Ugarit, the agriculturalist was likely to be traded himself, along with his home town and his neighbors.

---

86 AT 52-58.

87 See Heltzer (1982b) for Ugarit. Just what obligations were generally incumbent upon Emariote property holders remains unclear. The term *ilku* is not mentioned in any of the records studied here, for Durand (1989) 168 has shown that its ostensible presence in E6 1:1 and 10 is based on a misreading. On the other hand, seven texts of other types do deal with the assignment of ^giš^tukul-service: AOV 13:12 (testament); E6 18:19 (decree of the king of Carchemish), 33:26 (legal case), 112:16 (testament), 276:6, 8, 14 (list of persons); Hi 46:11 (decree by a Hittite prince), Hi 47:4 (= Tsukimoto [1984], gift of house by a Hittite prince); *Iraq* 54 1:8 (adoption). In the records of Ḫatti, whence the use of this Sumerogram as a technical term for a duty of service was certainly borrowed, ^giš^tukul indicates an obligation to the Crown (Beal [1988]). Since Hittite imperial officials are involved in several of the documents just listed, perhaps the ^giš^tukul-service was owed not to the local ruler of Emar, but to the authorities of the Hittite empire. This impression is strengthened by a letter from Emar written in Hittite (Hagenbuchner [1989] 40-41, Nr. 23) in which the Great King of Ḫatti personally frees a high priestly official of Emar from *šaḫḫan-* and *luzzi-* obligations—*cf.* Beckman (1995) 31.

88 See the transactions such as RS 16.248 (PRU 4, 48f.) in which the king confiscates (*našû*) real property from one or more persons and reallocates (*nadānu*) them to a third party. On the formulary employed here, see Greenfield (1977). Many purchases, including RS 16.261++ (PRU 3, 159f.), were executed in the presence of the ruler and bear his seal. Skaist (1988) convincingly argues that all conveyances involving the king concerned royal land whose usufruct alone changed hands.

89 Liverani (1988) 546-52.

FIGURE I – HOUSES

Text Reference	*Dimensions*	*Price*	*Penalty*
AOV 4	not given	12 gín	1000 (gín); recipient not given
Hi 12	12x12x7 *ammati*	15 gín (= ¼ ma.na)	200 (gín) each to city and brothers
E6 80B	20x10 *ammati*	18 gín	none
E6 113	not given	20 gín	none?
E6 122	23x22 *ammati*	20 gín	none
TBR 53	not given	20 gín	none
Hi 9	15x8 *ammati*	26 gín	none
E6 123	not given	30 gín	none
RE 20	25x8x6 *ammati*	30 gín (= ½ ma.na)	1000 (gín) each to brothers and city
TBR 82	25x15 *ammati*	30 gín	2000 (gín) to palace
RE 80	not given	30⅓ gín	none
TBR 33	25x23 *ammati*	31 gín	none
TBR 37	not given	33 gín	none
E6 80A	20x10 *ammati*	36? gín	none
TBR 66	not given	40 gín	none
Hi 11C	27x15 *ammati*	41 gín	none
AOV 9	15x15 *ammati*	44 gín	none
TBR 65	not given	45 gín	none
Hi 8	23x9½ *ammati*	50 gín	2000 (gín) to palace
Hi 11B	27x15 *ammati*	50 gín	none
RE 12	20+x20+ *ammati*	55 gín	none
RE 59	24x20x10 *ikû*	60 gín (= 1 ma.na)	1000 (gín) to palace
SMEA 30, 2	27½x10x9 *ammati*	70 gín	2000 (gín) to palace
E6 81	not given	71? (gín)	none
E6 125	19x18x13 *ammati*	100 (gín)	1000 (gín) to palace
E6 225A	not given	100 gín	none
RE 9	27x23 *ammati*	100 gín	2000 (gín) to palace
RE 79	22x15 *ammati*	100 (gín)	2000 (gín) to palace
RE 29A	not given	100 (gín)*	1000 (gín) each to Ninurta and city
RE 29B	not given	100 (gín)*	1000 (gín) each to Ninurta and city
SMEA 30, 4	not given	100 (gín)*	1000 (gín) each to [ ]
TBR 10	2+x5 *ammati*	100 (gín)	lost
TBR 8	31x10x9 *ammati*	100+? gín	1000 (gín) each to Ninurta [and city]
E6 225B	not given	115+ gín*	none

TBR 4	[NxN] *ammati*	120 gín (= 100 (gín) ⅓ ma.na)	1000 (gín) each to Ninurta and city
TBR 56	not given	160 (gín)	2000 (gín) to palace
E6 20	not given	170 gín	1000 (gín) each to city and brothers
E6 9A	[NxNxN] *ammati*	200 (gín)*	1000 (gín) each to Ninurta and city
E6 9B	21x9 *ammati*	200 (gín)*	1000 (gín) each to Ninurta and city
E6 9C	17x13 *ammati*	200 (gín)*	1000 (gín) each to Ninurta and city
TBR 57	not given	200 (gín)	1000 (gín) each to city and brothers
RE 70	20x6 *ammati*	250 gín (= 200 (gín) ⅚ ma.na)	1000 (gín) each to Ninurta and city
E6 111	20x20 *ammati*	300 (gín)	1000 (gín) each to city and brothers
E6 141	38x29x15 *ammati*	300 (gín)	1000 (gín) to palace
RE 34	NxN *ammati*	300 (gín)	1000 (gín) each to city and Ninurta
E6 85A	20x10+ *ammati*	310 gín*	none
E6 156	not given	600 (gín)	1000 (gín) each to city and buyer
Hi 7A	[NxN] *ammati*	600 (gín)	1000 (gín) each to Ninurta and city
E6 139A	23x24 *ikû*	800 (gín)*	1000 (gín) each to Ninurta and city
E6 139C	[NxN] *ammati*	800 (gín)*	1000 (gín) each to Ninurta and city
E6 139D	[NxN] *ammati*	800 (gín)*	1000 (gín) each to Ninurta and city
E6 126	not given	1000 (gín)	1000 (gín) each to Ninurta and city
E6 158	21x13 *ammati*	4200 gín (= 70 ma.na)	2000 (gín) to palace
Hi 10	22x12 *ammati*	[N] gín	2000 (gín) to palace
TBR 60	lost?	[N] gín	[2000?] (gín) to palace
E6 97	21x16 *ammati*	lost	2000 (gín) to palace
E6 157	14x10½ *ammati*	lost	lost
E6 161	22x14 *ammati*	lost	1000 (gín) each to l[ú] and [ ]
TBR 54	16x9 *ammati*	lost	1000 (gín) to palace
TBR 59	20x[N] *ammati*	lost	2000 (gín) to palace
TBR 61	26x18 *ammati*	lost	lost
Hi 11A	27x15 *ammati*	not given	none

FIGURE II – LOTS

Text Reference	*Dimensions*	*Price*	*Penalty*
GsK 4	12x13x10 *ammati*	4 gín	none
RE 11	18x18 *ammati*	4½ gín	none
RE 68	25x16 *ammati*	6 gín	none
E6 114B	not given	8 gín	none
RE 3	10x10x6 *ammati*	10 gín	1000 (gín) each to palace and city
E6 150	20x9 *ammati*	14 gín	500 (gín) each to Ninurta and city
Hi 2	20x14 *ammati*	15 gín (= ¼ ma.na)	1000 (gín) each to Ninurta and city
TBR 81	not given	15 gín	none
E6 114A	not given	20 gín	none
E6 137D	18x17x13 *ammati*	20 gín	[2000$^?$ (gín)] to palace
Hi 1	20x9 *ammati*	20 gín	1000 (gín) each to city and brothers
Hi 6	23x19 *ammati*	20 gín	none
RE 91	not given	20$^?$ gín (= ⅓$^?$ ma.na)	1000 (gín) each to Ninurta and city
E6 171	17x5 *ammati*	25 gín (= ⅓ ma.na 5 gín)	lost
E6 76	24x18 *ammati*	30 gín	none
RE 31	17x2+ *ammati*	30$^?$ gín (= ½ ma.na$^?$)	none
TBR 14	not given	30$^?$ gín (= ½$^?$ ma.na)	1000 (gín) each to Ninurta and city; 1000 (gín) to palace
TBR 24	20x8 *ammati*	33 gín	none
TBR 64	not given	35 gín	none
E6 137E	30x20 *ammati*	40 gín	[2000$^?$ (gín)] to palace
E6 153	[NxN] *ammati*	40 gín (= ⅔ ma.na)	[1000$^?$] (gín) each to Ninurta and [city]
E6 110	25<x N> *ammati*	50 gín (= ⅚ ma.na)	1000 (gín) each to Ninurta and brothers
TBR 13	20x17 *ammati*	51 gín	1000 (gín) each to Ninurta and city
E6 207A	22x18x15 *ammati*	60 gín (= 1 ma.na)	none
E6 207B	18x12 *ammati*	60 gín (= 1 ma.na)	none
E6 94	30x10 *ammati*	100 (gín)	2000 (gín) to palace
TBR 1	not given	100+ gín	lost

E6 148	[N *ina*] *ammati rupšu*	110 gín	1000 (gín) each to Ninurta and city
RE 33	10x9x25 *ammati šibuti*	120 gín (= 2 ma.na)	100 (gín) each to Ninurta and brothers
E6 109	22x18 *ammati*	130 gín (=100 (gín) ½ ma.na)	200 (gín) each to Ninurta and brothers
RE 14	20x13 *ammati*	140 gín (= 100 (gín) ⅔ ma.na)	1000 (gín) each to Ninurta and city
RE 81	27½x10x9 *ammati*	2400 gín (= 40 ma.na)	1000 (gín) each to Ninurta and city
RE 38	10[?]xNxN *ammati*	N gín	lost
RE 86A	22x12 *ammati*	[N] gín	2000 (gín) to palace
E6 152	18x20 *ammati*	lost	lost
RE 43	10+x30+x20 [*ammati*]	lost	lost[?]
E6 130	18 *ina ammati* gíd.da	not given	1000 (gín) each to Ninurta and brothers

FIGURE III – FIELDS

Text Reference	*Dimensions*	*Area*	*Price*	*Penalty*
AS 14	2 *ikû* x 1 *ikû* 4 gi *ša ikî*		5/6 gín	1000 (gín) each to Ninurta and city
RE 2	1½ *ikû* x 5 *šiddu*		1½ gín	1000 (gín) each to Ninurta and city
RE 64	2 *ikû* x 3 *matāḫu ša ikî*		3 gín	200 (gín) to brothers
TBR 58	2 *ikû* x 4 gìr.ḫi.a *matāḫu*		7 gín	200 (gín) to brothers
Hi 14	½ x ½ *ikû*		10 gín	1000 (gín) each to city and brothers
TBR 38		10 *ikû*	10 gín	none
TBR 68		2? (*ikû*?)	10 gín	none
Hi 13	1 x 1 *ikû*		10 gín u 1 giš*šipšetu*	none
AOV 2	not given		11 gín	lost?
TBR 18	2 *ikû* x 3 *šiddu* x 2 *šiddu* 4 gìr		11 gín	1000 (gín) each to Ninurta and city
E6 115B	not given		20 gín*	none
E6 138A		10 *ikû*	20 gín	2000 (gín) to palace
GsK 7	1 x 1 *ikû*		20 gín	1000 (gín) each to Ninurta and city
RE 5	N x N *ikû*		20 (gín)	1000 (gín) each to Ninurta and city
RE 49	2 x 1 *ikû*		20 gín (= ⅓ ma.na)	1000 (gín) each to Ninurta? and city?
TBR 7	1 x 1 *ikû*		20 gín	1000 (gín) each to Ninurta and city
TBR 62	2 *ašlu ša* 7 *ikî* x 1 *ašlu ša* 6 *ikî* x 4? *ikû*	20 *ikû*	20 gín	2000 (gín) to palace
E6 137C	10 x 3 *ikû*		30 gín	[2000? (gín)] to palace
E6 147A	6 *ikû* 2 *šiddu ša ikî* x 1+ *ikû* 2 *šiddu ša ikî* 8 gi		30 gín (= ½ ma.na)*	1000 (gín) each to Ninurta and city
E6 147B	6 *ikû* x ½ *ikû* 2 gi		30 gín (= ½ ma.na)*	1000 (gín) each to Ninurta and city
E6 147C		8 *ikû* 2 *šiddu ša ikî*	30 gín (= ½ ma.na)*	1000 (gín) each to Ninurta and city
RE 24		30 *ikû*	30 gín (= ½ ma.na)	1000 (gín) each to Ninurta and city
RE 35	not given		30 gín (= ½ ma.na)	1000 (gín) each to city and brothers
RE 77A		4 *ikû*	30 gín (= ½ ma.na)	none

RE 77B	not given	30 gín (= ½ ma.na)!	1000 (gín); recipient not given
TBR 12	1½ x 1 *ikû*	30 gín	1000 (gín) to palace
TBR 19	6 *ikû* x 1 *ikû*	60 gín (= 1 ma.na)	1000 (gín) each to Ninurta and city
TBR 55	10 x 1 *ikû*	60 gín	2000 (gín) to palace
AOV 1	11 *ikû* x 1 *ikû*	100 (gín)	lost?
E6 142	2? x 1? [*ikû*]	100 (gín)	2000 (gín) to palace
E6 146	1 x 1 *ikû*	100 (gín)	1000 (gín) each to Ninurta and [city]
E6 163A	1 *ikû* x 1 *ikû*	100 (gín)*	lost
E6 163B	1 *ikû* u [ ] x 1 *ikû* 3 gìr	100 (gín)*	lost
SMEA 30, 3	1 x 1 *ikû*	100 (gín)	1000 (gín) each to Ninurta and city
TBR 2	[1 x 1] *ikû*	100 (gín)	1000 (gín) each to Ninurta and city
TBR 3	4 x 2 *ikû*	100 (gín)	1000 (gín) each to Ninurta and city
TBR 11A	2 x 1 *ikû*	100 (gín)*	1000 (gín) each to [ ]
TBR 11B	1 x 1 *ikû*	100 (gín)*	1000 (gín) each to [ ]
RE 52	[N x N] *ikû*	100+? gín	1000 (gín) each to Ninurta and city
E6 2A	1½ *ikû* x 1½ *ikû*	150 gín (=100 (gín) ⅚ ma.na)*	1000 (gín) each to Ninurta and city
E6 2B	1 *ikû* x [N] *šiddu*	150 gín (=100 (gín) ⅚ ma.na)*	1000 (gín) each to Ninurta and city
E6 3B	1 x 1 *ikû*	150 gín (=100 (gín) ⅚ ma.na)*	1000 (gín); recipient not given
E6 4	not given	200 (gín)	1000 (gín) each to Ninurta and city
TBR 6	1½ x 1 *ikû*	150 gín (=100 (gín) ⅚ ma.na)*	1000 (gín) each to Ninurta and city
TBR 9A	not given	200 gín*	1000 (gín) each to Ninurta and city
TBR 9B	not given	200 gín*	1000 (gín) each to Ninurta and city
Hi 15	[N x N] *ikû*	215 gín (=200 *meat* (gín) ¼ ma.na)	1000 (gín) each to [ ]
TBR 16A	1 *ikû* x 30 *ammati* x 20 *ammati*	kù.babbar *īṣi u mādim*	1000 (gín) each to Ninurta and city

TBR 16B	1½ *ikû* x 70 *ammati* x 40 *ammati*	kù.babbar *īṣi u mādim*	1000 (gín) each to Ninurta and city
TBR 16C	2 *ikû* x 2 *šiddu* x 38 *ammati*	kù.babbar *īṣi u mādim*	1000 (gín) each to Ninurta and city
TBR 17A	1 *ikû* x 30 *ammati* x 20 *ammati*	kù.babbar *īṣi u mādim*	1000 (gín) each to Ninurta and city
TBR 17B	1 *ikû* 3 *šiddu* x 70 [*ammati*] x 113 *ammati* x 80 *ammati*	kù.babbar *īṣi u mādim*	1000 (gín) each to Ninurta and city
E6 12	N *ikû* 1+ *šiddu* x N *ikû* 2+ *šiddu*	lost	lost
E6 149A	½ *ikû* x 2 *šiddu* 6 gìr	lost	1000 (gín) each to [Ninurta] and city
E6 149B	4½ *ikû* x 3 *šiddu* 5 gìr	lost	1000 (gín) each to [Ninurta] and city
Iraq 54, 4	6 *ikû*	lost	1000 (gín) each to [ ]

FIGURE IV – VINEYARDS

Text Reference	*Dimensions*	*Price*	*Penalty*
RE 16	1 *ikû* x 3 šiddu 5 gìr.meš$^{?}$	2 gín	1000 (gín) each to Ninurta and city
E6 89	1$^{?}$ x 1$^{?}$ *šiddu*	15½ (gín) 20 ^{giš}*pa*[ ]	lost
TBR 51	not given	43 gín (= ⅔ ma.na 3 gín)	1000 (gín) each to city and brothers
E6 138B	1½ *ikû* x 1 *ikû* 5 gìr	50 gín	2000 (gín) to palace
E6 90	3 *šiddu ša ikî* x 2 *šiddu ša ikî*	60 gín	none
E6 140	3 *šiddu* 3 gi x 3 *šiddu* 3 gi x [N] *šiddu* 8 gi x 3 *šiddu* 5 gi	100 (gín)	1000 (gín) to palace
E6 11	1½ *ikû* x 2 *šiddu*	100+$^{?}$ gín	1000 (gín) each to city and palace
E6 3A	1 *ikû* u <1$^{?}$> *šiddu* x 1 *ikû*	150 gín (= 100 (gín) ⅚ ma.na)	1000 (gín); recipient not given
Hi 16	2 *ikû* x 2 *šiddu*	200 (gín)	1000 (gín) each to Ninurta and city
AOV 3	lost	kù.babbar *īṣi u mādim*	1000 gín each to Ninurta and city
E6 1	1 *ikû* 1 *šiddu* x 1 *šiddu*	not given$^{?}$	[N] *līm* (gín) each to Ninurta and Emar

FIGURE V – GARDENS

Text Reference	*Dimensions*	*Price*	*Penalty*
E6 137A	[N *šiddu*] 2 gi *ša ikî* x [N *šiddu*] 3 gi *ša ikî*	100+$^{?}$ gín	[2000$^{?}$ (gín)] to palace
E6 137B	1 *ikû* x [N] *šiddu* x 1 *šiddu ša ikî*	20 gín	[2000$^{?}$ (gín)] to palace
E6 206	3 *šiddu ša ikî* x 2 *šiddu* 7 gi.meš *ša ikî* x 1 *šiddu ša ikî*	100 (gín) for ½ share	none

FIGURE VI – FEATURES OF REAL PROPERTY SALE DOCUMENTS

Feature	*Emar*	*Ekalte*	*Ugarit*	*Alalakh VII*	*Middle Assyria*	*Nuzi*	*Hana*	*Mari*	*Late Old Babylonian*
Complete delineation of boundaries	yes	yes	no	no	no	optional	yes	optional	optional
Urban Property									
first side	zag	zag	—	*ite*	—	—	ús.sa.du an.ta	da	da
third side	egir	egir	—	—	—	—	sag.ki an.ta	—	sag.bi (.1.kam)
surface measures	—	—	—	—	—	—	sar	sar	sar
length measures	*ammatu*	*ammatu*	—	—	—	—	—	—	—
Agricultural property									
first side	ús.sa.du an.ta	ús.sa.du an.ta	—	—	—	*ina lēt, ina elēn*	ús.sa.du an.ta	da	da
third side	sag.ki .1.kam	egir	—	—	—	*ina iltān*	sag.ki an.ta	sag.1 (.1.kam)	sag.bi
surface measures	*ikû, zizi*	*ikû*	*imēru, ikû, kumānu, purīdu*	*imēru, ikû, kumānu, purīdu*	*imēru, ikû, kumānu, purīdu*	*imēru, awiḫaru, kumānu, ḫararnu*	*ikû*, sar	*ikû*, sar	*ikû*, sar
length measures	*ikû, šiddu,* gi, gìr	*mētequ*	*purīdu*	—	—	*ammatu, tayāru, mindatu*	—	—	—

Feature	*Emar*	*Ekalte*	*Ugarit*	*Alalakh VII*	*Middle Assyria*	*Nuzi*	*Hana*	*Mari*	*Late Old Babylonian*
Verb used of seller	—	—	*pašāru* + *ṣamātu*, *nadānu*	—	*nadānu* + *šubbû*	*kīma* ḫa.la *nadānu*	—	*naḫālu*	—
Verb used of buyer	*šâmu*	*šâmu*	*šâmu*, *leqû* + *ṣamātu*	*šâmu*	—	*kīma* níg.ba *nadānu*	in.ši.in. šám, *šâmu*	in.ši.šám	in.ši(.in). šám
Payment in	silver	silver	silver	misc. goods	tin	misc. goods	silver	silver	silver
Verb used of payment	*maḫāru*	*maḫāru*	—	*nadû*	*maḫāru*	—	in.na.lá	in.na.an.lá, *šaqālu*	in.na(.an). lá
Closing gesture or statement	*libbašu ṭâb*	*libbašu ṭâb*	—	—	*ṭuppa dannata šaṭāru*	—	^{giš}gan.na	—	^{giš}gan.na
Verb in irrevocability clause	*baqāru*, *ragāmu*	*baqāru*	*târu*	*nabalkutu*	*târu*, *dabābu*	*nabalkutu*	*baqāru*	*baqāru*	*ragāmu*, *târu*
Oath	no	no	no	no	no	no	yes	yes	yes
Sanction for reneging	large fine	large fine	large fine, forfeiture, hot lead	paymt. of entire sum, forfeiture	—	large fine	large fine hot asphalt	large fine	—
Witnesses	yes	yes	yes	yes	yes	yes	yes	yes	yes
Date	optional	optional	no	optional	yes	no	optional	yes	yes

Bibliography

Aerts, E., and H. Klengel, eds. (1990) *The Town as Regional Economic Centre in the Ancient Near East.* Leuven. **Arnaud, D.** (1986) *Recherches au pays d'Aštata. Emar VI.1-3.* Paris. (1987a) *Recherches au pays d'Aštata. Emar VI.4.* Paris. (1987b) La Syrie du moyen-Euphrate sous la protectorat hittite: contrats de droit privé. *Aula Orientalis* 5: 211-41. (1991) *Textes syriens de l'Âge du Bronze Récent.* Aula Orientalis-Supplementa 1. Barcelona. (1992) Tablettes de genres divers du Moyen-Euphrate. *Studi Micenei ed egeo-anatolici* 30: 195-245. **Beal, R.** (1988) The GIŠTUKUL-institution in Second Millennium Ḫatti. *Altorientalische Forschungen* 15: 269-305. **Beckman, G.** (1992) Hittite Administration in Syria in the Light of the Texts from Ḫattuša, Ugarit, and Emar. In Chavalas and Hayes 1992: 41-49. (1995) Hittite Provincial Administration in Anatolia and Syria: The View from Maşat and Emar. In Carruba, *et al.* 1995:19-37. (1996a) Emar and Its Archives. In Chavalas 1996:1-12. (1996b) Family Values on the Middle Euphrates in the Thirteenth Century B.C.E. In Chavalas 1966: 57-79. (1996c) *Texts from the Vicinity of Emar in the Collection of Jonathan Rosen.* Padua. **Bellotto, N.** (1993) Il LÚ.MEŠ.*aḫ-ḫi-a* a Emar. *Altorientalische Forschungen* 22: 210-28. **Beyer, D.**, ed. (1982) *Meskéné – Emar. Dix ans de travaux 1972-1982.* Paris. **Boyer, G.** (1955) La place des textes d'Ugarit dans l'histoire de l'ancien droit oriental. In Nougayrol 1955: 283-308. (1958) *Textes juridiques.* Archives royales de Mari Transcrites et Traduites 8. Paris. **Carruba, O., M. Giorgieri, and C. Mora**, eds., (1995) *Atti del II Congresso Internazionale di Hittitologia.* Studia Mediterranea 9. Pavia. **Chavalas, M. W.**, ed. (1996) *Emar: The History, Religion, and Culture of a Syrian Town in the Late Bronze Age.* Bethesda, Md. **Chavalas, M. W., and J. L. Hayes**, eds. (1992) *New Horizons in the Study of Ancient Syria.* Bibliotheca Mesopotamica 25. Malibu, Calif. **Dalley, S., and B. Tessier** (1992) Tablets from the Vicinity of Emar and Elsewhere. *Iraq* 54: 83-111. **Dandamayev, M., *et al.***, eds. (1982) *Societies and Languages of the Ancient Near East. Studies in Honour of I. M. Diakonoff.* Warminster. **Dietrich, M., and O. Loretz**, eds. (1995) *Ugarit. Ein ostmediterrannes Kulturzentrum im Alten Orient.* Band I. *Ugarit und seine altorientalisches Umwelt.* Abhandlungen zur Literatur Alt-Syrien-Palästinas 7. Münster. **Dornemann, R.** (1979) Tell Hadidi: A Millennium of City Occupation. In Freedman 1979: 113-51. **Durand, J.-M.** (1989) Review of Arnaud (1986). *Revue d'Assyriologie* 83: 163-91. **Ellis, M. DeJ.**, ed. (1977) *Essays on the Ancient Near East in Memory of Jacob Joel Finkelstein.* Memoires of the Connecticut Academy of Arts and Sciences 19. Hamden, Conn. **Fleming, D.** (1992) A Limited Kingship: Late Bronze Emar in Ancient Syria. *Ugarit-Forschungen* 24: 59-71. (1993) Baal and Dagan in Ancient Syria. *Zeitschrift für Assyriologie* 83: 88-98. (Forth.) *Time at Emar.* Mesopotamian Civilizations. Winona Lake, Ind. **Freedman, D. N.**, ed. (1979) *Archaeological Reports from the Tabqa Dam Project.* Annual of the American Schools of Oriental Research 44. Cambridge, Mass. **Gaál, E.** (1988) The Social Structure of Alalaḫ. In Heltzer and Lipiński 1988: 99-110. **Garelli, P.**, ed. (1974) *Le palais et la royauté.* Paris. Greenfield, J. (1977) *našû-nadānu* and Its Congeners. In Ellis 1977: 87-91. **Gurney, O. R.** (1983) *The Middle Babylonian Legal and Economic Texts from Ur.* London. **Haase, R.** (1967) Anmerkungen zum ugaritischen Immobilienkauf. *Zeitschrift für Assyriologie* 58: 196-210. **Hagenbuchner, A.** (1989) *Die Korrespondenz der Hethiter*, 2. Teil. Texte der Hethiter 16. Heidelberg. **Heltzer, M.** (1976) *The Rural Community in Ancient Ugarit.* Wiesbaden. (1978) *Goods, Prices and the Organization of Trade in Ugarit.* Wiesbaden. (1979) Royal Economy in Ancient Ugarit. In Lipiński 1979: 459-96. (1982a) *The Internal Organization of the Kingdom of Ugarit.* Wiesbaden. (1982b) Zum Steuersystem in Ugarit (*pilku-ubdy* und Ähnliches). In Hirsch 1982: 112-17. **Heltzer, M., and E. Lipiński**, eds. (1988) *Society and Economy in the Eastern Mediterranean (c. 1500-1000 B.C.).* Orientalia Lovaniensia Analecta 23. Leuven. **Hirsch, H.**, ed. (1982) *Vorträge gehalten auf der 28. Rencontre Assyriologique Internationale in Wien 6.-10. 1981.* Archiv für Orientforschung Beiheft 19. Vienna. **Hrouda, B., *et al.***, eds. (1981) *Isin-Išan Bahrīyāt II.* Abhandlungen der Bayrischen Akademie der Wissenschaften 87. Munich. **Kienast, B.** (1979) Die altbabylonischen Kaufurkunden aus Alalaḫ. *Welt des Orients* 11: 35-63. **Klengel, H.** (1974) Königtum und Palast nach den Alalaḫ-Texten. In Garelli 1974: 273-82. (1979) Die Palastwirtschaft in Alalaḫ. In Lipiński 1979: 435-57. **Koschaker, P.** (1928) *Neue keilschriftliche Rechtsurkunden aus der el-Amarna-Zeit.* Abhandlungen der Philologisch-historischen Klasse der Sächsischen Akademie der Wissenschaften 39/V. Leipzig. **Leemans, W. F.** (1988) Aperçu sur les textes juridiques d'Emar. *Journal of the Economic and Social History of the Orient* 31: 207-42. **Lipiński, E.** (1979) Ed. *State and Temple Economy in the Ancient Near East.* Orientalia Lovaniensia Analecta 6. Leuven. (1990) Le marché immobilier à Ugarit et à Emar au XIIIe siècle av. n. è. In Aerts and Klengel 1990: 25-58. (1992) Arcanes et conjonctures du marché immobilier à Ugarit et à Emar au XIIIe siècle av. n. è. *Altorientalische Forschungen* 19: 40-43. **Lipiński, E.**, ed. (1979) *State and Temple Economy in the Ancient Near East.* Orientalia Lovaniensia Analecta 6. Leuven. **Liverani, M.** (1982) Ville et campagne dans le royaume d'Ugarit. Essai d'analyse économique. In Dandamayev 1982: 250-58. (1988) *Antico Oriente: Storia, società, economia.* Rome. **Maidman, M.** (1976) *A Socio-Economic Analysis of a Nuzi Family Archive.* Dissertation, University of Pennsylvania. **Margueron, J.** (1982) Architecture et urbanisme. In Beyer (1982) 23-39. **Mayer, W.** (1986) Die Tontafelfunde von Tall Munbāqa 1984. *Mitteilungen der Deutschen Orient-Gesellschaft zu Berlin* 118: 126-31. (1988) Die Tontafelfunde von Tall Munbāqa 1986. *Mitteilungen der Deutschen Orient-Gesellschaft zu Berlin* 120: 48-50. (1990) Der antike Name von Tall Munbāqa, die Schreiber und die chronologische Einordnung der Tafelfunde: Die Tontafelfunde von Tall Munbāqa 1988. *Mitteilungen der Deutschen Orient-Gesellschaft zu Berlin* 122: 45-66. (1992) Eine Urkunde über Grundstückskäufe aus Ekalte/Tall Munbāqa. *Ugarit-Forschungen* 24: 263-74. (1993) Die Tontafelfunde von Tall Munbāqa/Ekalte 1989 und 1990. *Mitteilungen der Deutschen Orient-Gesellschaft zu Berlin* 125: 103-7. **Nougayrol, J.** (1955) *Le palais royal d'Ugarit, 3: Textes Accadiens des Archives Sud.* Mission de Ras Shamra 6. Paris. **Oelsner, J.** (1982) Zur Organisation des gesellschaftlichen Lebens im kassitischen und nachkassitischen Babylonien: Verwaltungsstruktur und Gemeinschaften. In Hirsch 1982: 403-10. **Podany, A.** (1988) *The Chronology and History of the Hana Period.* Ph.D. dissertation, University of California at Los Angeles. **Porten, B.** (1968) *Archives from Elephantine. The Life of an Ancient Jewish*

Military Colony. Berkeley. **Powell, M.** (1990) Masse und Gewichte. *Reallexikon der Assyriologie* 7: 457-517. **Rainey, A. F., *et al.***, eds. (1993) *Kinattūtu ša dārâti. Raphael Kutscher Memorial Volume*. Tel Aviv Occasional Publications. Tel Aviv. **Riemschneider, K.** (1958) Die hethitischen Landschenkungsurkunden. *Mitteilungen des Instituts für Orientforschung* 6: 321-81. **Sanmartín, J.** (1995) Wirtschaft und Handel in Ugarit: Kulturgrammatische Aspekte. In Dietrich and Loretz 1995: 131-58. **San Nicolò, M.** (1922) *Die Schlußklauseln der altbabylonischen Kauf- und Tauschverträge*. Münchener Beiträge zur Papyrusforschung und antiken Rechtsgeschichte 4. Munich. **Scurlock, J.** (1993) Once more *ku-bu-ru. Nouvelles Assyriologiques Brève et Utilitaires*. 1993/21. **Sigrist, R. M.** (1993) Seven Emar Tablets. In Rainey 1993: 165-84. **Skaist, A.** (1988) A Unique Closing Formula in the Contracts from Ugarit. In Heltzer and Lipiński 1988: 151-59. **von Soden, W.** (1982) Eine altbabylonische Urkunde (79 MQB 15) aus Tall Munbāqa. *Mitteilungen der Deutschen Orient-Gesellschaft zu Berlin* 114: 71-78. **Steele, F.** (1943) *Nuzi Real Estate Transactions*. American Oriental Series 25. New Haven. **Stone, E.** (1987) *Nippur Neighborhoods*. Studies in Ancient Oriental Civilization 44. Chicago. **Tsukimoto, A.** (1984) Eine neue Urkunde des Tili-šarruma, Sohn des Königs von Karkamiš. *Acta Sumerologica* 6: 65-74. (1988) Sieben spätbronzezeitliche Urkunden aus Syrien. *Acta Sumerologica* 10:153-89. (1990) Akkadian Tablets in the Hirayama Collection (I). *Acta Sumerologica* 12: 177-227. (1991) Akkadian Tablets in the Hirayama Collection (II). *Acta Sumerologica* 13: 275-333. (1992a) Akkadian Tablets in the Hirayama Collection (III). *Acta Sumerologica* 14: 289-310. (1992b) An Akkadian Field Sale Document Privately Held in Tokyo. *Acta Sumerologica* 14: 311-14. **Veenhof, K. R.** (1986a) Ed. *Cuneiform Archives and Libraries*. Publications de l'Institut historique-archéologique néerlandais de Stamboul 57. Leiden. (1986b) Cuneiform Archives. An Introduction. In Veenhof 1986a: 1-36. **Walker, C. B. F., and Cl. Wilcke** (1981) Preliminary Report on the Inscriptions. In Hrouda 1981: 91-102. **Westbrook, R.** (1991) The Phrase "His Heart is Satisfied" in Ancient Near Eastern Legal Sources. *Journal of the American Oriental Society* 111: 219-24. **Wilcke, Cl.** (1992) AḪ, die 'Brüder' von Emar. Untersuchungen zur Schreibertradition am Euphratknie. *Aula Orientalis* 10: 115-50. **Wooley, C. L.** (1968) *A Forgotten Kingdom*. New York. **Yamada, M.** (1993) "Arana-Documents" from Emar. *Orient* 29: 130-46. (1994) The Dynastic Seal and Ninurta's Seal: Preliminary Remarks on Sealing by the Local Authorities of Emar. *Iraq* 56: 59-62.

Did Zimri-Lim Play a Role in Developing the Use of Tin-Bronze in Palestine?*

Barry J. Beitzel
Trinity Evangelical Divinity School

The emergence and character of Palestine's MB IIA material culture has long been a subject which arouses controversy. Did this culture develop in an environment that was indigenously or externally based? If it was an indigenous culture, was it an appropriate response to more favorable climatic or economic conditions? If it was an externally based culture, on the other hand, should its origins be sought along the Levantine seacoast (*e.g.*, Byblos), somewhere within inland Syria (*e.g.*, Ebla, Qatna, Hama, Carchemish), or elsewhere? Is MB IIA culture an outgrowth of the preceding period, and does it exhibit features of continuity with MB IIB-C, or is it to be regarded as a discrete entity which should be divorced from either or both of those? If, as has recently been argued rather convincingly, the MB IIA period manifests a material culture that is markedly distinct from its predecessor, do these cultural innovations then come to

* I am very pleased to contribute to a volume designed to honor a scholar who has done so very much to advance our understanding of ancient Near Eastern history and to whom I am indebted for his personal friendship, amicable hospitality and professional generosity over the years.

Abbreviation list: ARMT: *Archives royales de Mari transcrites et traduites* (7 = Bottéro [1957]; 13 = Dossin [1964]; 23 = Bardet [1984]; 25 = Limet [1986]); ARM: *Archives royales de Mari* (10 = Dossin [1967] = TCL 31); CAD: *Chicago Assyrian Dictionary*; CT: *Cuneiform Texts from Babylonian Tablets…in the British Museum* (2 = Pinches [1896]); RLA: *Reallexikon der Assyriologie*, Ebeling and Meissner, *et al.* [1932–]); TCL: *Textes cuneiformes, Musée du Louvre.*

exist amidst static or changing social and political conditions? Does MB IIA Palestine display characteristics which are ascribable to mass movements of people(s), or can its salient features and innovations more effectively be attributed to other influences?[1]

It is one aspect of this last question towards which the present essay is aimed. Patty Gerstenblith (1980); (1983) published a challenge to a widely-accepted theory, conventionally called the "Amorite hypothesis." This theory proposes that a migration or migrations into Palestine of West Semitic-speaking peoples, discernible from Mesopotamian sources, best explains the cultural upheaval associated with the destruction of EB IV—MB I Palestine and subsequent introduction of the culturally-distinct MB IIA period (according to Gerstenblith MB I).[2]

Primarily taking into account some conspicuous factors of cultural innovation, association of certain ceramic assemblages which exhibit similarities with those of Syria and points beyond, and settlement patterns, Gerstenblith argues that the common denominator among all of these MB IIA material elements was their linkage to an overland trade network. As a consequence, she offers a bold counter-hypothesis, according to which the

---

1 I wish to acknowledge the immense benefit an earlier draft of my essay gained from the insightful comments of Professors William Dever, Abraham Malamat, James Muhly and Jack Sasson. Naturally, any remaining errors or misjudgments are my responsibility alone.

2 By "MB IIA," I mean to denote the system of classification developed by W. F. Albright and adopted, *inter alia*, by the *Encyclopedia of Archaeological Excavations in the Holy Land* (Avi-Yonah[1975]; Stern [1992]) and utilized very recently in the publication of A. Mazar [1990] 174-91 to refer to that stretch of time between c. 2000–1800/1750 in Palestinian history. This same period has been denominated as "MB I" by a number of scholars—including Kathleen Kenyon (1951); (1970); William Dever (*e.g.*, [1980]; [1985]; [1991]), and Patty Gerstenblith herself. Most recently, Israel Finkelstein (1996) has argued that this period should be designated as the "Late Urban Period I." Such difference in nomenclature is almost always a consequence of how individual scholars identify and assign a name to the *preceding* period; moreover, particular preferred nomenclature is generally adopted largely on pragmatic grounds. Whatever the case, these various terms are meant to identify the same time span, and therefore the terminology I have employed here in this essay is rather inconsequential to the central arguments presented. For the arbitrary nature of archaeological periodization, the reader is advised to consult Redford (1992) 64-69.

opening of trade between Palestine and Syria, and hence with the more distant and culturally sophisticated lands of Anatolia and Mesopotamia, must be considered as a possible mechanism to explain the introduction of those features that characterize MB IIA culture. Gerstenblith does not argue that her explanation is able to account fully for the massive institutional restructuring of Middle Bronze Age Palestine, (see, *e.g.*, [1983] 125), but her study surely demonstrates the ability to construct a somewhat comprehensive organizational model to explain MB IIA's cultural transformation that is not *necessarily* anchored to migratory or imperialistic patterns, or ethnic affiliations.

However, in a *BASOR* article, Kamp and Yoffee (1980) rightly criticize Gerstenblith's "trade model" in part because, while she posits a trade mechanism (the so-called "What?" question), her work searches out or specifies very little concerning how such a mechanism might have operated (the "How?" question). They conclude that "the onus of demonstrating both how trading organizations arose and how they effected growth of other sociocultural institutions remains with those who advance the proposition" (1980) 99.

Without seeking to defend a trade mechanism as an *exclusive* model, this essay nevertheless represents a provisional attempt to address this "How?" question, namely, to delineate what I perceive to have been *one of a constellation of processes* by which Palestine's MB IIA culture developed fully, at least in a metallurgical sense, and how this process might have impacted the technological and socio-economic innovations seen throughout MB II culture. Specifically, the essay will investigate the possibility that Zimri-Lim, the MB II sovereign from Mari (Tell Ḥarīri) who was contemporary with Ḫammurapi of Babylon and Išme-Dagan, son of Šamši-Addu of Assyria, took steps which brought under his control the flow of tin resources from Anšan and eastern Iran, and moved with insight and alacrity to expand newly-developing western markets in the Levantine and Mediterranean worlds, perhaps in Palestine in particular. Moreover, I will suggest the possibility that, as a consequence of Zimri-Lim's socio-political maneuvers, the *Bronze* Age—in an industrial and technological sense—arrived fully in Palestine.

I. *Role and Source(s) of Tin*

Some time during the first half of the Early Bronze period, Near Eastern smiths learned that adding a limited amount of tin to copper produces a superior grade of metal in terms of malleability, strength, and resilience. Hence tin became increasingly prized as an essential component in the casting of an alloy to become known as bronze. Tin normally occurs in nature as an oxide (stannic oxide = SnO_2), more commonly known since Greco-Roman times as "cassiterite." Cassiterite can be found in alluvial form in streams that flow out of tin-rich granite hills that are eroding. The nuggets of tin stone are relatively heavy; like gold, they are deposited in the bed of a stream and could be panned. It is necessary to smelt the oxide to produce metallic tin.

Mainly occurring in certain specific types of Pre-Cambrian, Tertiary and Quaternary geological sediments (de Jesus [1980] 51-52; Ajayi and Crowder [1985] sec. #3), tin was scarcely available to Near Eastern metallurgists. According to metallurgical investigation now spanning almost three decades, both Mesopotamia and Syro-Palestine were devoid of tin deposits, and the mineral had to be imported from more distant regions. Though fields in Egypt, along the Atlantic seacoast, and in central Europe appear to have been exploited to some limited degree during a portion of the Bronze Age (Waldbaum [1978] 65; de Jesus [1980]; Wagstaff [1985] 87-88; McGeehan-Liritzis [1996]), the vast majority of scholars today argue, with very good reason, that the tin[3] used in the Near East, at least during the Middle Bronze Age, was derived from the rich, abundant cassiterite deposit bands of western Afghanistan (*e.g.*, Muhly, [1973]; [1976]; [1978]; [1981]; [1983]; [1995]; [1997] 9; Muhly and Wertime [1973]; Cleuziou and Berthoud [1982]; Stech and Piggott [1986]; Moorey [1994] 299-300; *contra* Dayton [1973]). Near Eastern documentation from that era consistently indicates that tin was being imported from such eastern sources. Among

---

[3] For the equation *annaku* = "tin" (*i.e.*, not "lead," "arsenic," "copper," or even "ingot-torque"), see Landsberger (1965); Muhly and Wertime (1973) 115-19; de Jesus (1980) 57-58; Waetzoldt (1981); Limet (1985a); and *CAD* A/2: 127-30.

other eastern entrepôts mentioned in earlier texts, tin is sometimes said have been transported through Dilmun, Magan, or Meluhha *en route* to Mesopotamia (Leemans [1960] 35; Muhly [1973] 292-300; Cleuziou and Berthoud; Moorey [1982] 16; [1985] 128-29; [1994] 298 [with bibliography cited there]; Potts [1994] 148-65), and numerous textual references relate the transport of this metallurgic resource through Susa (*cf. infra*). At the same time, tin is known to have entered the Mesopotamian valley through Šušarrā (Tell Shemshara) and the Rania Plain (Laessøe [1959]; Muhly [1973] 302-3; Larsen [1976] 88-89).

Exploitation of cassiterite sources from Thailand or Malaysia during the Middle Bronze Age is now viewed with serious skepticism. Likewise, the recent theory of Yener ([1989]; [1995]; Yener and Ozbal [1987]; Yener and Vandiver [1993]; *cf.* Ünal [1989] 286; Piggott [1996] 158-60), that the tin sources supplying this metal to the Near East in antiquity are to be located in the central portion of the Taurus Range of south-central Anatolia, must still be considered speculative and highly unlikely, at least during the Middle Bronze Age (Malamat [1990] 67; Muhly [1993]; [1994] 16-17; [1995] 1507). In point of fact, during the MB IIA, literally tons of tin oxide from eastern landscapes were being imported *into* central Anatolia (*cf. infra*), carried there by hundreds of pack-asses over many hundreds of miles of absolutely rugged terrain, and sold at comparatively high prices in towns located no more than 75 miles from Kestel and Göltepe, the site of Yener's discovery. What is more, no documentary sources deriving from that era indicate that tin was available from Anatolia, nor from any other sources close at hand.

Near Eastern smiths, therefore, had access to distant eastern sources of the metallic asset, which begins to show up in the archaeological record of the EBA. In that period various tin-bronze objects make their appearance in Mesopotamia (Tepe Gawra, Tell Brak, Kish, Der, Ubaid, Ur; see Maxwell-Hyslop [1946]; [1949]; Stech and Pigott [1986]; Cleuziou and Berthoud [1982]; de Jesus [1980] 152-53; Muhly [1983] 353; [1995] 1506; [1997] 8; Moorey [1982] 13, 25-36; [1994] 301), and central and northwestern Anatolia (Troy, Poliochni, Thermi, Beşiktepe, Norşuntepe, Alişar; see de Jesus [1980] 33-34, 150-51; Muhly [1995] 1507). Towards the end of the

EBA, such objects begin to appear in somewhat significant quantity in Syria (Ebla, Amuq, Tell Sweihat, Tell Judeida, Byblos, Ras Shamra; see Gerstenblith [1980] 76; Muhly [1983] 354; Philip [1991]), and at the very end of this period tin-bronze makes its appearance in Egypt (Muhly [1978] 45). For Palestine, however, only a few isolated objects have been attested thus far (Bab edh-Dhra, Jericho, Gezer, Teleilāt Ghassul; see Maddin, Muhly and Stech-Wheeler [1980] 115-19; Moorey and Schweizer [1972] 192-93; Muhly [1973] 334-35; Philip [1991]), which has led Muhly (1973) 335 to conclude that Palestine did not use tin-bronze until the Middle Bronze Age.

II. *Tin and the Development of a Local Bronze Industry*

Metallurgic specialists have long differentiated between possessing such objects and producing such objects, which begs the questions: How soon were tin objects locally manufactured in various areas of the Near East? When did such an industrial craftsmanship become native to Palestine?

It cannot be overemphasized in responding to this query that our present understanding of nascent industrial ventures having to do with tin is based upon very limited analytical evidence. Moreover, the relevant issues are extremely protracted and complex, not allowing any simplistic or obvious solution. I suggest that in order to demonstrate that various objects have been produced by local artisans, and have not been imported from other regions, the scholar must give attention to at least two lines of inquiry.

Firstly, archaeological evidence uncovered from a particular site can provide testimony of an actual local industry. Whether it be in the form of metallurgic assemblages, the repertorial forms and stylistic features of which lack analogies from what is otherwise known across the Near East, or in the form of unambiguous signs of metalworking itself (*e.g.*, crucible fragments, molds, ingots, pot bellows, furnaces, *tuyères*, mortars, ore crushers, ladles, slag, ores, workshops, toolkits, and the like), it is clear that such evidence should be attributed to local production and craftsmanship, and not to trade or import. Secondly, documentary sources may describe smiths or artistic activities and/or objects, in terms of a certain type or quality of metallurgical craftsmanship, or these texts may make reference to such sheer quantities of metal being shipped to, registered at, or housed in a particular location that a local industry must be presupposed. In either event, while this evidence should not mitigate the fact that the raw material most likely had arrived at a particular site via the mechanism of trade, it does demonstrate that the material would have been transformed and crafted into cultural objects as a result of *local* expertise.

Based in large measure upon such criteria, scholars have identified a localized tin industry as early as the fourth millennium in Afghanistan (Piggott [1996] 159; Muhly [1997] 9-10), around 2700 B.C. (EB I) in Mesopotamia (de Jesus [1980] 35-44; 152; Muhly [1983]; Moorey [1994] 301), near 2400 (Troy II) in northwest Anatolia (Stech and Piggott [1986] 52-56; Muhly [1995] 1506), and approximately 2250 in Oman (Cleuziou and Berthoud [1982] 18) and Iran (Muhly [1995]; 1504; Piggott [1996] 145). Local industrial use of tin is attested in Syria around 2200 (Gerstenblith [1983] 89-100; Philip [1991]).

But what can be said of a local industrial use of bronze in Palestine during the Middle Bronze Age? A consensus of contemporary scholarship on this issue is surely reflected in the studied characterization by A. Mazar (1990) 175: "MB IIA is distinguished by an almost total revolution in all aspects of material culture: settlement pattern, urbanism, architecture, pottery, *metallurgy*, and burial customs" [emphasis mine] (*cf.* B. Mazar [1968]; Bunimovitz [1992]; Finkelstein [1992]; Joffe [1997]). The only caveat to Mazar's characterization is that tin-bronze metallurgy, as an attested MB IIA Palestinian phenomenon, is not nearly as precocious as Mazar's statement may imply. Moreover, I suggest that such metallurgy, as a function of a local craft tradition in Palestine (*vis-à-vis* imported objects of trade), is not indisputably attested until the very end of MB IIA or the very beginning of MB IIB.

Although a percentage of tin-bronze has been discovered in a dagger from a late EB III or early EB IV-MB I context at Bab edh-Dhra (Maddin, Muhly and Stech-Wheeler [1980] 115; Stech, Muhly and Maddin [1985] 79-80; Philip [1991] 93-94), and a number of objects consisting of a tin-bronze alloy have been discovered in MBA Palestine, at least in the central and northern sectors of the country, Moorey and Schweizer (1972) 193 have concluded that "tin by no means had superseded copper for the production of exactly comparable objects" (*cf.* Birmingham [1977] 119). Middle Bronze objects of tin-bronze so far known from Palestinian contexts (chisel-axes, "duckbill" axes, shaft-hold axes, battle axes, daggers, toggle pins, bits, nail fragments) have already been carefully scrutinized by a number of scholars (Moorey and Schweizer [1972] 192-95; Maddin and Stech-Wheeler [1976]; Branigan, McKerrel and Tylecote [1976]; Birmingham [1977]; Tubb [1983]; Gerstenblith [1980]; [1983]; Stech, Muhly and Maddin [1985]; Littauer and Crouwel [1986]; Philip [1991]) and need not detain us here. Suffice to say that the great majority of the pieces studied manifest a stylistic linkage to Syrian prototypes. This observation is consonant with what scholars have concluded after examining other aspects of MB Palestinian cultural patterns, whether it be various ceramic assemblages (Gerstenblith [1983] 59-87; Tubb [1983]; Joffe [1997] 214-15) or glyptic art (A. Mazar [1981] 136), where the evidence is also thought to be best understood in light of its affinities with Syrian analogues.

Even if the MB IIA culture arose around 2000 B.C. and was fully developed as an urban culture by 1900 (Dever [1976]; [1985]; [1991]) or just slightly thereafter (Tubb [1983] 57-59), and for a number of compelling reasons I'm not suggesting otherwise (*pace* Bietak [1991]), the total amount of tin found in objects exhumed from MB IIA Palestinian contexts represents less than the quantity of an average single caravan shipment of the mineral during the MBA (*cf.* Astour [1995] 1402-3), and it has been conjectured that all the pieces found could have emerged from one single smithing facility (Stech, Muhly and Maddin [1985] 81). Distinct archaeological remains of local metallurgy or tell-tale signs of the endeavor have not yet been clearly identified for that era. And, to my knowledge, there are no texts from the early part of MB IIA that would attest to a localized tin craft in Palestine. Thus, the current artifactual and documentary state of affairs hardly bespeaks a local industrial craftsmanship in tin for the MB IIA period, and no other evidence can be adduced—that is, until the time of Zimri-Lim.

III. *The Flow of Tin during the MBA and Zimri-Lim's Role*

What, then, might have been the role of Zimri-Lim of Mari in developing the local use of tin in Palestine? The scenario commences at the Anatolian site of Kaniš (Kültepe). Documentary evidence from Kaniš[4] discloses that near the end of the first quarter of the eighteenth century, as the political fortunes of the Lim dynasty began to revive at Mari under the genius of Zimri-Lim, certain Assyrian merchant families were engaged in an extensive commercial enterprise, shipping tin and textiles (mostly wools) to a number of markets across North Mesopotamia and Anatolia, including Kaniš itself. When they arrived at their destinations, these goods were sold (or traded) for silver or gold. It was a tightly organized trade in which a series of some 30 Assyrian commercial colonies, trading associations and interconnected caravanserais were spread across the 500 or so airline miles that separated the capital cities of Aššur and Kaniš. It was a very extensive and highly profitable trade. Larsen (1982a) 40 has calculated that some 13½ tons of tin and about 17,500 pieces of textile are actually documented in the available texts that describe this trading network, and he proposes that 100 tons of tin and at least 100,000 textiles would be a very conservative estimate of the total goods trafficked in Anatolia via this medium (*cf.* Veenhof [1972] 69-76, 79-80; Larsen [1982b] 230-31; Muhly [1995] 1508). The Assyrians sold the tin in Anatolia for twice what they had paid for it in Aššur (Muhly [1973] 292), and the textiles commanded a price in Anatolia five times greater than was paid in Aššur (Larsen [1982a] 41). These Assyrian merchants have been justifiably described as "millionaires" (Larsen [1982b] 232; [1977] 132-39).

Now the texts from Kaniš indicate that for about two generations (*kārum* Ib = Šamši-Addu, Išme-Dagan), northern Mesopotamia must have been a consolidated political entity, as the Assyrian merchants traveled with relative ease between stations on a route that was generally secure (*cf.* Polanyi [1975] 133-36, for the importance of peace during such commercial ventures; Yoffee [1981] 25-26, suggests how models of trade

---

4 Relevant texts also derive from other Anatolian sites, especially Hattuša Ib (Boghazköy).

can be constructed). At the same time, the distribution of "Ḫabur ware" throughout northern Mesopotamian localities and at Kaniš suggests that this entire region represented a homogeneous cultural entity. It is pertinent to note in this regard that Kaniš II exhibits Amuq/Cilician ceramics, whereas Ḫabur ware does not appear until Kaniš Ib (Orlin [1970] 171, 183; Hamlin [1971] 245-78, 291-95; RLA 4.30 [*s.v.* "Ḫābūr-Ware"]). It is plausible, then, as asserted by Hamlin (1971) 295, that both the trading enterprise and the ceramic assemblage are to be associated with the Assyrian government of Šamši-Addu. As a consequence, one might have surmised that this Assyrian dynasty was destined to enjoy a period of peace and great prosperity (for the extent of Šamši-Addu's domain, *cf.* Kupper [1985] 147; Charpin and Durand [1985] 300-2; see also Whiting [1990] 170-84). In point of fact, the dynasty does continue to exist for some time after the events described in this essay.

But suddenly and mysteriously, this profitable trade between Aššur and Kaniš came to a halt, after which a modest reoccupation of the *kārum* was soon aborted. Scholars of the Old Assyrian period date the destruction of *kārum* Ib between 1775–1750 (Özgüç [1963] 104; Orlin [1970] 246; *cf.* Veenhof [1995] 865; Muhly [1973] 326). Most attempts to explain this mystery have focused upon Anatolian politics, suggesting either a dynastic move from Kaniš to a more strategic location (Gurney [1973] 236, 240-41) or a total collapse of the local political system (Orlin [1970] 246; Muhly [1973] 326-27). Now while it is clear enough that Kaniš was visited by a destruction at the end of level Ib, if we assume with Orlin (1970) 56 that the chief aim of the trading colonies—in the first place—was to procure copper, or with Muhly (1973) 292 and Larsen (1977); (1982a) 42 that the chief aim was to make a profit, does it not follow that the Assyrians should have found it economically expedient to have established colonies with a new government, or to have relocated with the existing government, in an effort to satisfy their lucrative partisan objective? For the solution to this mystery, perhaps we need to examine the other end of the trade route, particulary since the military sovereignty along the route belonged to Aššur, not Kaniš; it was the Assyrian government which maintained extraterritorial authority over the colonies in Anatolia (Orlin [1970] 61-65; Larsen [1976] 119-20; [1977] 120).[5]

But it is precisely an inspection of the Assyrian side of the tin-trade ledger that leads us ultimately to the burgeoning kingdom of Zimri-Lim. Hence, we should examine the possible role this Mesopotamian monarch may have played in the cessation of Assyrian colonization and trade in Anatolia.

According to the story told by his date-formulae and correspondence, by recapturing his capital city, wrested from his father some 20 years earlier by means of a palace *coup* in which Šamši-Addu appears to have been implicated (*cf.* Villard [1995] 874), Zimri-Lim succeeded in carving out a modest niche in Assyria's empire, now inherited by Išme-Dagan.[6] Sensing that the Assyrian was kept occupied on other frontiers (*e.g.*, Ešnunna, Babylon), Zimri-Lim opportunistically seized the city-states of Terqa, Sagarātum and Tuttul, thus bringing under his control the middle-Euphrates and lower Ḫabur river valleys (Charpin and Durand [1985] 323, 332; *cf.* Finet [1985]).

But his efforts to enlarge this niche northward into the prized regions of the upper Ḫabur river and eastward across the Jezīrah, necessary as they were (Finet [1968-72] 226-27; Charpin and Durand [1985] 332; *cf.* Villard [1995] 874), brought him inevitably into military conflict with Išme-

---

5 Zimri-Lim himself must have maintained some limited relationship with Kaniš and Hattuša. This connection between Mari and Anatolian sites can be seen in just a few *ARM* tablets (*e.g.*, [1] 7.173 =ZL 6′, an economic dispatch of 5 shekels of silver to an Ašur-bani, the man of Kaniš [see also Finet (1985) 88]; and [2] Dossin (1939) 70-73 [unknown date, though Dossin argues that the text derives from the time of Zimri-Lim], a severely fragmented letter from an unidentified prince presumably in North Mesopotamia; the text appears to have nothing to do with tin).

6 Texts from *ARM* 10 indicate that there was extreme uncertainty at the beginning of Zimri-Lim's reign about what was to come (*cf.* Charpin and Durand [1985] 327). This article by Charpin and Durand is a landmark study of Zimri-Lim's rise to power, which cogently challenges some earlier assumptions. Their work is especially enlightening on Yahdun-Lim's loss of his throne at Mari, how discrete realms were created under Išme-Dagan and Yasmah-Addu, the time that lapsed between the end of the Assyrian period and the advent of Zimri-Lim, and some of the specifics having to do with Zimri-Lim's ascendancy to the Mari throne. Serious interaction with some aspects of this work has been undertaken by Whiting (1990).

Dagan[7] and, in this case, at the city of Razamā, a fortified city of commercial and strategic importance most likely located in the vicinity of Tell Ḥayal (Beitzel [1984] 34-36, and nn. 39-42; Astour [1995] 1409, suggests the nearby site of Tell Qsayba). Numerous texts reflect upon the logistics, outcome and consequences of this "First Battle of Razamā" (as it is known today in Mari studies), in which Zimri-Lim was victorious. This battle was clearly fought for control of land near the upper Ḫabur valley and within the Ḫabur triangle itself, as is subsequently indicated by the territories and kings numbered among Zimri-Lim's vassals. Among the 20 or so clients added at this time to Zimri-Lim's dominion were princes from every sector of the Ḫabur triangle. Cities which had explicitly served as stations along the Assyrian tin route—including Razamā, as well as Karanā, Andariq, Ašiḫum, Naḫur, Talḫāyum, Luḫšyum, Niḫriyā—were now wrested from Assyrian control, only to fall under Zimri-Lim's hegemony.

One effect of this battle was to give Zimri-Lim a virtual—if temporary—monopoly over much of the terrain which had been traversed by the Assyrian merchants. At the same time, it placed him in a commanding economic position with respect to western markets which, it seems, he wasted no time in exploiting (*cf. infra*). The research of Birot (1978) 185-86 has conclusively demonstrated that this "Battle of Razamā" must be dated between Ḫammurapi's 27th and 29th regnal years, or between 1766–1764 (Charpin and Durand [1985] 306; Charpin [1987] 130; Villard [1993]), a date to which I shall return. Of course, this date bears a striking correspondence to the moment when Assyrian tin trade with Kaniš was discontinued. It is difficult to avoid the conclusion, based on this geographic, chronological, and documentary evidence, that the kingdom of Zimri-Lim may have stood in the way and prevented a revival of Assyrian colonization in Anatolia.

---

7 Kupper (1985) 147 discusses the extent of Šamši-Addu's domain, from the Euphrates river basin as far east as the mountains of Kurdistan (*cf.* Charpin and Durand [1985] 300-2). According to Villard (1995) 874 Šamši-Addu had been *economically* motivated to extend his kingdom into the Ḫabur region, and even to the site of Mari by 1796.

My interpretation of these data seems to be borne out by other MB II evidence from Babylonia. First, the much-heralded Old Babylonian Itinerary texts describe a circuitous journey taken by a caravan or army between the cities of Larsa and Imār. Hallo (1964) 84-86 and Muhly (1973) 299-301 assume that this route did not follow the direct and natural course of the Euphrates between these cities because of the presence of a hostile power ensconced there, whom they identify as Zimri-Lim. To them the Itinerary texts therefore reflect a period during which the kingdoms of Larsa and Mari were antagonistic, or between the 31st-35th years of Ḫammurapi (=1762-1759). This appears to be a well-founded assessment of the situation, but it is beneficial to observe that if the itinerary had, indeed, been designed to avoid Zimri-Lim, the route actually taken should then tell us something about the extent of his domain. Given the route charted by a number of scholars who have studied the OB Itinerary, tracing it across the central stretches of the Ḫabur triangle (Goetze [1953]; Hallo [1964]; Beitzel [1978]; Haas and Wäfler [1985]; see now Weiss [1985], for the important equation Šubat-Enlil=T. Leilan; Haas and Wäfler [1985] 63, for the equation Šuna=T. Ḥamādīya; *cf.* Villard [1995] 875, for the likely equation Ašnakkum=Chāgar Bāzār), a geographical situation obtains which closely correlates with what has already been suggested concerning the location of the vassals and cities within Zimri-Lim's realm in the immediate aftermath of the Battle of Razamā.

I suggest that this hostility between Mari and Larsa was related to some degree to Zimri-Lim's victory at Razamā, which had occurred only four to five years earlier. It is instructive to observe that most of Ḫammurapi's year-dates after the year of the Battle of Razamā refer to hostilities specifically directly against cities which had played a prominent role in the supply of tin to Mari, and the first of these activities apparently transpired with the support of Zimri-Lim (Sasson [1995] 906). In point of fact, Zimri-Lim and Ḫammurapi maintained friendly relations as late as 1765 (Villard [1986] 408; *cf.* Limet [1985b] 44-46; Charpin [1987] 130, 137, for a decisive military victory by Ḫammurapi in the Ḫabur triangle in that same year). Whatever the case, year-dates 30 and 32 record measures taken by the Babylonian sovereign against the cities of Ešnunna and Elam, important suppliers of tin.

In year-formula 31, Ḫammurapi defeated Larsa, another city which played a substantial role in the flow of tin into Mesopotamia (*cf.* Limet [1985b] 46). And year-dates 33 and 35 record how Zimri-Lim's city itself was eliminated by Ḫammurapi's forces. All this enhances the supposition that economics played a crucial part in Ḫammurapi's actions over the past seven or so years of Mari's existence. It also suggests strongly that the Battle of Razamā, in point of fact, may have set into motion a chain of events which eventually brought the Babylonian hordes through the city-gates of Mari. In any event, a Babylonian text that dates to a period immediately following the collapse of Mari, the so-called "Dream-Book Itinerary," indicates that tin trade between Mesopotamia and western depots followed the course of the Euphrates, right past the site of Tell Ḥarīri, and on to the sites of Aleppo, Qatna and Ḥazor (Muhly [1973] 294-95; *cf.* text CT 2.20, and refer to Leemans [1960] 105-6; Muhly [1973] 300-1).

As a result of Zimri-Lim's political initiatives at Razamā and elsewhere, tin in substantial quantities came to be warehoused in and dispatched from Mari. It is clear that tin arrived in Zimri-Lim's capital city from eastern sources, via caravan trade, apparently by means of an established "tin route" (Villard [1986] 406). The metal arrived at Zimri-Lim's capital from Susa, where there is known to have existed a tin market, via Ešnunna and/or Larsa, and Sippar (Bottéro [1957] 293-94; Birot [1960] 314; Limet [1985a] 202; [1985b] 43-48; Villard [1986] 405; Moorey [1994] 298). Tin came to Mari in ready-to-be-used ingots (*lē'u*; *CAD* L 159) each weighing about 11 pounds (*ca.* 5 kilograms), which presupposes that Mari's artisans were also working with metals, not just with ores or minerals (Muhly [1995]1509). The caravaneers were regularly paid in gold (exchange rate of 1: 50) or silver (exchange rate of 1: 10-14; Limet [1985b] 48; Muhly [1995] 1509; *cf.* Veenhof [1995] 864), though several grades of tin are attested in the *ARM* (Limet [1985a] 202; [1986]).[8] On rare occasions they were reimbursed in lapis lazuli.

8 For comparative ratios at some other sites during the MB (and LB) periods, consult Heltzer (1977) and Vargyas (1986), though they arrive at differing conclusions.

IV. *The Flow of Tin into Palestine and Zimri-Lim's Role*

At this point, someone might well be saying, "This all seems quite reasonable, but what does it have to do with Palestine?" Birot conclusively dated the "First Battle of Razamā" between the years 1766-64, which corresponds to Zimri-Lim's years 8′-10′ (Charpin and Durand [1985] 306.[9] As a consequence of Zimri-Lim's victory at Razamā, he gained a momentary monopoly over the Old Assyrian route connecting Aššur and Kaniš, a route which I have elsewhere endeavored to trace out across the southern stretches of the Ḫabur triangle (Beitzel [1992]). In addition, Zimri-Lim's capital city already rested astride the commercial artery of the Euphrates and the considerable trade that was plied there.

It is precisely at this point in Zimri-Lim's reign that he seems actively to have moved his field of interest and commerce into the Mediterranean and Levantine worlds. According to a series of recently published texts (*ARMT* 23.535-548), Zimri-Lim departed from Mari on the twelfth month of year 8′ and undertook a commercially-motivated four-month journey to Ugarit (Villard [1986] 387-92).[10] He was accompanied on this trip by "elite troops" (*ṣābum beḫrum*) from Idamaraz, one of the most important districts within the Ḫabur triangle (Beitzel [1992] 50-53), comprised in part of several towns which had functioned as stations along the Assyrian tin route (*cf.* Bonechi [1992] 16). To solidify his position in that region, the Mari sovereign first traveled into the "Upper Country" (*mātum elîtum*, i.e., within or near the eastern sector of the Ḫabur triangle; Dossin [1938] 184 n.1; Finet [1968-72] 226; *CAD* E: 113) and exchanged valuable gifts with

---

9 Use of the prime sign with Zimri-Lim year dates refers to a series of years that are known to be consecutive. Unfortunately, the chronological relationship of this sequence to the precise time when Zimri-Lim mounted the Mari throne, or to the total length of his reign, is not yet certain (Anbar [1979]; Sasson [1980a] 1-10; Charpin and Durand [1985] 306; Whiting [1990]; *cf.* Villard [1993]).

10 Around the time Zimri-Lim went to Ugarit on this trip, relations between Mari and Elam went very sour, which must have had profound implications in terms of the flow of tin. Whether this was directly related to the Battle of Razamā, either as cause or consequence, cannot yet be determined. Limet (1985b) 44-45 holds that the actual rupture of relations occurred just after month four of year 9′, which would follow immediately on the heels of Zimri-Lim's return from Ugarit.

local monarchs from a number of towns there (again including at least one important town which had been part of the tin trade [Talḫāyum; *cf. ARMT* 13.144.53-54]), before proceeding on his journey to the Mediterranean. The year-name assigned by the Mari chancellery to year nine makes reference to Zimri-Lim's presentation of a great throne to the god of Maḫanum, a town which now can be located in *mātum elîtum* (Villard [1986] 407), and, plausibly, may have been involved in this series of events. At various locations along the journey, and during his stay at Ugarit, quantities of tin were dispatched to several locations, including Ḫazor (Villard [1986] 398; Muhly [1997] 11; other western emporia attested in Zimri-Lim texts at Mari include Byblos, Crete and Cyprus [*cf.* Muhly (1973) 258, 293; (1995) 1510; Limet (1985a) 202]).[11]

Yet another tablet, the "tin itinerary text" (Bonechi [1992] 21), which has been dated to Zimri-Lim year 9′, is related to these events. This document details the itinerary for a shipment of tin to various points across the Mediterranean and Levantine worlds, including Aleppo, Muzunnum, Layišum,[12] Ugarit, Crete, Qatna and Ḫazor (Dossin [1970] 97-106; see now *ARMT* 23.556; *cf. ARMT* 7.86-88 for other shipments of tin to the west). Of these sites, only Aleppo, Ḫazor and Qatna had been mentioned in the earlier Assyrian literature from Mari, but always in a context quite aside from that of tin, while the remaining towns are not cited at all in that previous literature. This raises the spectre that the "Itinerary" text is delineating a new or newly-developing avenue for tin in the west. Esse (1991) 14-19 illustrates how political events can affect trade routes. Whatever that case may be, Ḫazor figures quite prominently in this text, as the city received three sizable consignments of tin.

---

11 Another text dating from Zimri-Lim 9′ (month 8) indicates that some people from Crete came to visit Zimri-Lim at Mari (Villard [1986] 402 n. 106). Could this mission have been motivated by newly-developing economic considerations (*cf.* Muhly [1995] 1510)?

12 This site must be located somewhere in northern Syria, not in Palestine (so Sasson [1984] 249; Astour [1991] 54-55; Bonechi [1992] 19). Malamat (1989b) 117 n. 2; (1990) 67 suggests the possibility of two separate cities with the name, one in North Syria and the other in northern Palestine.

Another tablet dating from Zimri-Lim year 9′ (*ARMT* 7.236) details the shipment of a substantial amount of tin from Mari to Ḥazor. In all, some eighteen Zimri-Lim texts make explicit mention of Ḥazor (Bonechi [1992] 21; *cf.* Charpin and Durand [1994] 63), which is a remarkably high number of references to a site so far removed from Mari.[13] Almost all of these dispatches deal with diplomatic missions and the exchange of economic goods.

In point of fact, between years 6′ and 11′ of Zimri-Lim's reign, unusually friendly relations existed between Zimri-Lim and Ibni-Addu, king of Ḥazor. During those years, Zimri-Lim and Ibni-Addu exchanged, in addition to tin, a rather large number of luxury goods, including objects of gold and silver, lapis lazuli necklaces, pearl necklaces, wine, various woolen garments, and assorted chariot parts (Bonechi [1992] 9-16). Durand (*ARMT* 23: 475 n. 2) has suggested that Yatar-Aya, a secondary wife of Zimri-Lim who accompanied him on a portion of his trip to Ugarit, may have come originally from Ḥazor (see Sasson [1973] 60 n.2, for an earlier suggestion). It is difficult to escape the conclusion, therefore, that Ḥazor served as a strategic caravan center of the first order, according to the *ARM*, and that the city was linked in some manner with Aleppo and Qatna, as well as with various seacoast ports along the eastern Mediterranean (Bonechi, [1992] 17).

As for Ḥazor itself, it was precisely in this period that the city reached its maximum extent of some 200 acres, making it the largest MB II Palestinian site and rivaling those of Syria (Joffe [1997] 215). Middle Bronze cuneiform documents that reflect very close onomastic and orthographic ties to Mari have been discovered at Ḥazor in recent years (Horowitz and Shaffer [1992a]; especially [1992b]),[14] and, in the summer of 1996, the site

---

13 Many of these texts have been carefully studied by Malamat (1977); (1982);(1983); (1989a); (1989b); (1990); see Durand (1990) 63 n.129, for TH 72-16. Another town with the same name (= "enclosure") attested in the *ARM* must be located along the mid-Euphrates, near Sagarātum (Bonechi [1992] 19, 21).

14 For the cuneiform texts that have been exhumed at Ḥazor, see Artzi and Malamat (1960) 115-17; Landsberger and Tadmor (1964); Hallo and Tadmor (1977); Tadmor

yielded up a MB II letter sent from Mari to Ḥazor concerning commercial transactions, on which the city-name "Mari" now occurs.

Based solely on the quantity of tin shipped from Mari to Ḥazor, a local bronze industry must be presupposed (*cf.* Muhly [1995] 1511). The 50 minas known to be consigned there[15] in the Itinerary text alone would suffice for some 850-900 pounds of bronze alloy, and this was only one of numerous shipments to Ḥazor, which again plausibly bespeaks a local industrial use of the metal. Moreover, local craftsmanship is clearly reflected in *ARMT* 25.119 [Zimri-Lim 12′], which describes a "Ḥazorite"-ring, fashioned of gold, that was given by Zimri-Lim to the king of Karanā (Bonechi [1992] 17). This reference is understood to denote a ring that was made after the fashion of Ḥazor craftsmanship (Malamat [1989b] 118). Here then is clear and unambiguous evidence that at least one site within Palestine was involved in a local craft tradition having to do with metallurgy by the very end of MB IIA. This, I believe, is the earliest clearly demonstrable evidence of local smithing in that country.

How then shall we respond to the question under consideration? In the first place, one needs readily to acknowledge that particular, monocausal or single-factor explanations of ancient historical reality are notoriously tenuous, at times even woefully simplistic. So let me underscore that whatever is discussed here must be considered to be only one in a broad array of political, social and economic processes that contributed to what we refer to as Palestine's MB IIA culture. This essay seeks to address the coming of the Bronze Age to Palestine *only in the sense of the advent of a local metallurgical tradition.* Further, while it is the task of the scholar to attempt to paint as complete a picture of an ancient culture as possible, due care must be given not to "overuse" discrete—even multidisciplinary—bits of data, particularly when so much is still unknown about that culture.

(1977); Beck (1983); Horowitz and Shaffer (1992a); (1992b); and now, esp. Horowitz (1996).

15 The first two distributions to Ḥazor mentioned in this text total fifty minas of tin. The amount of the third consignment is regrettably lost at the bottom of the text. Malamat (1989a) 57 conjectures that perhaps another 20 minas are reflected in this distribution.

Having said that, it remains the hypothesis of this essay that, while many internal complexities yet require elucidation, Zimri-Lim appears to have succeeded in linking Palestine with the essential natural resource of tin, otherwise inaccessible in the volume that would have been required to initiate a local bronze industry there. For Zimri-Lim himself, this astute move may have contributed in a significant way to the opulent wealth that was transparently part of his short-lived kingdom. But for Palestine, Zimri-Lim's move very likely paved the way for the inauguration of the *Bronze* Age, in the sense of a local industrial technology.

Bibliography

Ajayi, J. F. A., and M. Crowder (1985) *Historical Atlas of Africa.* Essex, England. **Anbar, M.** (1979) La durée du règne de Zimri-Lim, roi de Mari. *Israel Oriental Studies* 9: 1-8. **Artzi, P., and A. Malamat** (1960) *Apud* Y. Yadin, Y. Aharoni, R. Amiran, T. Dothan, I. Dunayevsky, and J. Perrot (eds.), *Hazor II,* 115-17. Jerusalem. **Astour, M. C.** (1991) The Location of Ḫaṣurā of the Mari Texts. *MAARAV* 7: 51-65. (1995) Overland Trade Routes in Ancient Western Asia. In Sasson 1995b: 1401-20. **Avi-Yonah** (1975) *Encyclopedia of Archaeological Excavations in the Holy Land.* 4 vols. Englewood Cliffs, N.J. **Beck, P.** (1983) The Bronze Plaque from Hazor. *Israel Exploration Journal* 33: 78-80. **Beitzel, B. J.** (1978) From Ḫarran to Imar along the Old Babylonian Itinerary: The Evidence from the *Archives Royales de Mari.* In Tuttle 1978: 209-19. (1984) Išme-Dagan's Military Actions in the Jezīrah: A Geographical Study. *Iraq* 46: 29-42. (1992) The Old Assyrian Caravan Road in the Mari Royal Archives. In Young 1992: 35-57. **Ben-Tor, A.** (1986) The Trade Relations of Palestine in the Early Bronze Age. *Journal of the Economic and Social History of the Orient* 29: 1-27. **Bietak, M.** (1991) Egypt and Canaan During the Middle Bronze Age. *Bulletin of the American Schools of Oriental Research* 281: 27-72. **Biran, A., and J. Aviram**, eds. (1990) *Biblical Archaeology Today, 1990.* Jerusalem. **Birmingham, J.** (1977) Spectrographic Analyses of Some Middle Bronze Age Metal Objects. *Levant* 9: 115-20. **Birot, M.** (1960) *Textes administratifs de la salle 5 du Palais.* ARMT 9. Paris. (1978) Review of *The Old Babylonian Tablets from Tell al-Rimah,* by S. Dalley, C. B. F. Walker, and J. D. Hawkins. *Revue d'Assyriologie et d'Archéologie Orientale* 72: 181-90. **Bonechi, M.** (1992) Relations amicales syro-palestiniennes: Mari et Haṣor au XVIIIe siècle av. J.C. In Charpin 1992: 9-22. **Bottéro, J.** (1957) *Textes économiques et administratifs.* ARMT 7. Paris. **Branigan, K., H. McKerrel, and F. R. Tylecote** (1976) An Examination of Some Palestinian Bronzes. *Journal of the Historical Metallurgy Society* 10/1: 15-23. **Bunimovitz, S.** (1992) The Middle Bronze Age Fortifications in Palestine as a Social Phenomenon. *Tel Aviv* 19: 221-34. **Cagni, L.**, ed. (1981) *La Lingua di Ebla.* Naples. **Charpin, D.** (1987) Šubat-Enlil et le pays d'Apum. *MARI*

5: 129-40. (1992) ed., *Florilegium marianum: Recueil d'études en l'honneur de Michel Fleury.* Mémoires de N.A.B.U. 1. Paris. **Charpin, D., and J.-M. Durand** (1985) La prise du pouvoir par Zimri-Lim. *MARI* 4: 293-343. **Charpin, D., and J.-M. Durand**, eds. (1994) *Florilegium marianum: Recueil d'études à la mémoire de Maurice Birot.* Mémoires de N.A.B.U. 3. Paris. **Chebab, M.** (1939) Tombe phénicienne de Sin el-Fil. In [no editor listed] (ed.), *Mélanges syriens offerts à Monsieur René Dussaud* 2: 803-10. BAH 30. Paris. **Cleuziou, S., and T. Berthoud** (1982) Early Tin in The Near East: A Reassessment in the Light of New Evidence from Western Afghanistan. *Expedition* 25/1: 14-19. **Cooper, J. S., and G. M. Schwartz**, eds. (1996) T*he Study of the Ancient Near East in the Twenty-First Century.* W. F. Albright Centennial Conference. Winona Lake, Ind. **Cross, F. M., W. E. Lemke, and P. D. Miller, Jr.**, eds. (1976) *Magnalia Dei—The Mighty Acts of God: Essays on the Bible and Archaeology in Memory of G. Ernest Wright.* Garden City, N.Y. **Dayton, J. E.** (1973) The Problem of Tin in the Ancient World: A Reply to Dr Muhly and Dr Wertime. *World Archaeology* 5: 123-25. **Dever, W. G.** (1976) The Beginning of the Middle Bronze Age in Syria-Palestine. In Cross, *et al.* 1976: 3-38. (1980) New Vistas on the EB IV ('MB I') Horizon in Syria-Palestine. *Bulletin of the American Schools of Oriental Research* 237: 35-64. (1985) Relations between Syria-Palestine and Egypt in the 'Hyksos' Period. Tubb 1985: 69-87. (1991) Tell el-Dab'a and Levantine Middle Bronze Age Chronology: A Rejoinder to Manfred Bietak. *Bulletin of the American Schools of Oriental Research* 281: 73-79. **Dossin, G.** (1938) Signaux lumineux au pays de Mari. *Revue d'Assyriologie et d'Archéologie Orientale* 35: 174-86. (1939) Une mention de Ḫattuša dans une lettre de Mari. *Revue hittite et asianique* 5: 70-76. (1970) La route de l'étain en Mésopotamie au temps de Zimri-Lim. *Revue d'Assyriologie et d'Archéologie Orientale* 64: 97-106. **Dossin, G., *et al.***, eds. (1964) *Textes Divers.* ARMT 13. Paris. **Durand, J.-M.** (1990) La cité-état d'Imâr à l'époque des rois de Mari. *MARI* 6: 39-92. **Durand, J.-M., and J.-R. Kupper**, eds. (1985*) Miscellanea Babylonica: Mélanges offerts à Maurice Birot,* 147-51. **Edwards, I. E. S., C. J. Gadd, N. G. L. Hammond, and E. Sollberger**, eds. (1973) *Cambridge Ancient History* 2/1: 228-55. Cambridge. **Eichler, S., V. Haas, D. Steudler, M. Wäfler, and D. Warburton**, eds. (1985) *Tall al-Ḥamidīya 1 (Vorbericht 1984).* Orbis Biblicus et Orientalis, Series Archaeologica 4. Göttingen. **Eichler, S., M. Wäfler, and D. Warburton**, eds. (1990) *Tall al-Ḥamidīya 2 (Vorbericht 1985–1987).* Orbis Biblicus et Orientalis, Series Archaeologica 6. Göttingen. **Esse, D. L.** (1991) *Subsistence, Trade, and Social Change in Early Bronze Age Palestine.* SAOC 50. Chicago. **Finet, A.** (1968-) La politique d'expansion au temps de Hammurapi de Babylone. *Annuaire de 72l'Institut de Philologie et d'Histoire orientales et slaves* 20: 223-46. (1985) Une requête d'Išme-Dagan à Zimri-Lim. In Durand and Kupper 1985: 87-90. **Finkelstein, I.** (1992) Middle Bronze Age 'Fortifications': A Reflection of Social Organization and Political Formations. *Tel Aviv* 19: 201-20. (1996) Toward a New Periodization and Nomenclature of the Archaeology of the Southern Levant. In Cooper and Schwartz 1996: 103-23. **Franklin, A. D., J. S. Olin, and T. A. Wertime**, eds. (1978) *The Search for Ancient Tin.* Washington D.C. **Fugmann, E.** (1958) *Hama. Fouilles et Recherches 1931-1938.* Nationalmuseets Skrifter, Større Beretninger 4. Copenhagen. **Gautier, J.-E.** (1895) Note sur les fouilles entreprises dans la haute vallée de l'Oronte. *Comptes-rendus de l'Academie des Inscriptions et Belles-Lettres* 23: 441-64. **Gerstenblith, P.** (1980) Reassessment of the Beginning of the Middle Bronze Age in Syria-Palestine. *Bulletin of the American Schools of Oriental Research* 237: 65-84. (1983) *The Levant at the Beginning of the Middle Bronze Age.* ASOR Dissertation Series 5. Ann Arbor, Mich. **Goetze, A.** (1953) An Old Babylonian Itinerary. *Journal of Cuneiform Studies* 7: 51-72. **Guiges, P. E.** (1937) Lébéà, Kafer-Ğarra, Qrayé: Nécropoles de la région sidonienne. *Bulletin du Musée de Beyrouth* 1: 35-76. (1938) Lébéà, Kafer-Ğarra, Qrayé: Nécropoles de la région sidonienne (suite). *Bulletin du Musée de Beyrouth* 2: 27-72. **Gurney, O. R.** (1973) Anatolia *c.* 1750-1600 B.C. In Edwards, *et al.* 1973: 228-55. **Haas, V., and M. Wäfler** (1985) Möglichkeiten der Identifizierung des Tall al-Ḥamidīya. In Eichler, *et al.* 1985: 53-76. **Hallo, W. W.** (1964) The Road to Emar. *Journal of Cuneiform Studies* 18: 57-88. **Hallo, W. W., and H. Tadmor** (1977) A Lawsuit from Hazor. *Israel Exploration Journal* 27: 1-11. **Hamlin, C.** (1971) The Habur Ware Ceramic Assemblage of Northern Mesopotamia: An Analysis of Its Distribution. Ph.D. dissertation, University of Pennsylvania. **Hawkins, J. D.**, ed. (1977) *Trade in the Ancient Near East.* London. **Heltzer, M.** (1977) The Metal Trade of Ugarit and the Problem of Transportation of Commerical Goods. In Hawkins 1977: 203-22. **Horowitz, W.** (1996) The Cuneiform Tablets at Tel Hazor. *Israel Exploration Journal* 46/3-4: 268-69. **Horowitz, W., and A. Shaffer** (1992a) An Administrative Tablet from Hazor: A Preliminary Edition. *Israel Exploration Journal* 42: 21-33. (1992b) A Fragment of a Letter from Hazor. *Israel Exploration Journal* 42: 165-67. **Hrouda, B.** (1972-75) Ḫābūr-Ware. RLA 4. 29-31. **de Jesus, P. S.** (1980) *The Development of Prehistoric Mining and Metallurgy in Anatolia.* BAR International Series 74 (i, ii). Oxford. **Joffe, A. H.** (1997) Palestine in the Bronze Age. In Meyers 1997: 212-17. **Kamp, K. A., and N. Yoffee** (1980) Ethnicity in Ancient Western Asia during the Early Second Millennium B.C.: Archaeological Assessments and Ethnoarchaeological Prospectives. *Bulletin of the American Schools of Oriental Research* 237: 85-104. **Kenyon, K. M.** (1951) Some Notes on the History of Jericho in the Second Millennium B.C. *Palestine Exploration Quarterly* 83: 101-38. (1970) *Archaeology in the Holy Land.* New York/Washington. **Kupper, J.-R.** (1985) Šamši-Adad et l'Assyrie. In Durand and Kupper 1985: 147-51. **Laessøe, J.** (1959) *The Shemshāra Tablets; a Preliminary Report.* Copenhagen. **Landsberger, B.** (1965) Tin and Lead: the Adventures of Two Vocables. *Journal of Near Eastern Studies* 24: 285-96. **Landsberger, B., and H. Tadmor** (1964) Fragments of Clay Liver Models from Hazor. *Israel Exploration Journal* 14: 201-18. **Larsen, M. T.** (1976) *The Old Assyrian City-State and Its Colonies.* Mesopotamia 4. Copenhagen. (1977) Partnerships in the Old Assyrian Trade. In Hawkins 1977: 119-45. (1982a) Caravans and Trade in Ancient Mesopotamia and Asia Minor. *Bulletin of the Society for Mesopotamian Studies* 4: 33-45. (1982b) Your Money or Your Life! A Portrait of an Assyrian Businessman. In Postgate 1982: 214-45. **Lebeau , M., and P. Talon**, eds. (1989) *Reflets des deux fleuves: Volume de mélanges offerts à André Finet.* Akkadica Supplement 6. Leuven. **Leemans, W. F.** (1960) *Foreign Trade in the Old Babylonian Period.* Leiden. **Limet, H.** (1985a) La technique du Bronze dans les archives de Mari. In Durand and Kupper 1985: 201-10. (1985b) Les rapports entre Mari et l'Elam à l'époque de Zimri-Lim. *Studi epigrafici* *e linguistici* 2: 43-52. (1986) *Textes administratifs relatifs aux métaux.* ARMT 25. Paris. **Littauer, M. A., and J. Crouwel** (1986) A Near Eastern Bridle Bit of the Second Millennium B.C. in New York. *Levant* 18: 163-71. **Maddin, R., J. D. Muhly, and T. Stech-Wheeler** (1980) Research at the Center for Ancient Metallurgy. *Paléorient* 6: 111-19. **Maddin R., and T. Stech-Wheeler** (1976) Metallurgical Study of Seven Bar Ingots. *Israel Exploration Journal* 26: 170-73. **Maddin, R., T. Stech-Wheeler, and J. D. Muhly** (1980) Distinguishing Artifacts Made of Native Copper. *Journal of Archaeological Science* 7: 211-25. **Malamat, A.** (1977) *Mari and the Bible: A Collection of Studies.* Jerusalem. (1982) Silver, Gold and Precious Stones from Hazor: Trade and Trouble in a New Mari Document. *Journal of Jewish Studies* 33: 71-9 (Studies Yadin). (1983) "Silver, Gold, and Precious Stones from Hazor" in a New Mari Document. *Biblical Archaeologist* 46: 169-74. (1989a) *Mari and the Early Israelite Experience.* The Schweich Lectures 1984. Oxford. (1989b) Hazor Once Again in New Mari Documents. In Lebeau and Talon 1989: 117-18. (1990) Mari and Hazor – Trade Relations in the Old Babylonian Period. In Biran and Aviram 1990: 66-70. **Maxwell-Hyslop, R.** (1946) Daggers and Swords in Western Asia—A Study from Prehistoric Times to 600 B.C. *Iraq* 8: 1-65. (1949) Western Asiatic Shaft-Hole Axes. *Iraq* 11: 90-129. **Mazar, A.** (1981) Review of *The Seal Impressions from Tell Atchana/Alalakh,* by D. Collon. *Israel Exploration Journal* 31: 135-36. (1990) *Archaeology of the Land of the Bible 10,000-586 B.C.E.* New York. **Mazar, B.** (1968) The Middle Bronze Age in Palestine. *Israel Exploration Journal* 18: 65-97. **McGeehan-Liritzis, V.** (1996) *The Role and Development of Metallurgy in the Late Neolithic and Early Bronze Age of Greece.* Studies in Mediterranean Archaeology 122. Jonsered, Sweden. **Meyers, E. M.**, ed. (1997) *The Oxford Encyclopedia of Archaeology in the Near East.* 5 vols. New York/Oxford. **Moorey, P. R. S.** (1982) The Archaeological Evidence for Metallurgy and Related Technologies in Mesopotamia, *c.* 5500–2100 B.C. *Iraq* 44: 13-38. (1985) *Materials and Manufacture in Ancient Mesopotamia: The Evidence of Archaeology and Art.* BAR International Series 237. Oxford. (1994) *Ancient Mesopotamian Materials and Industries: The Archaeological Evidence.* Oxford. **Moorey, P. R. S., and F. Schweizer** (1972) Copper and Copper Alloys in Ancient Iraq, Syria and Palestine: Some New Analyses. *Archaeometry* 14/2: 177-98. **Muhly, J. D.** (1973) *Copper and Tin: The Distribution of Mineral Resources and the Nature of the Metals Trade in the Bronze Age.* Transactions of the Connecticut Academy of Arts and Sciences 43. Hamden, Conn. (1976) *Supplement to Copper and Tin.* Transactions of the Connecticut Academy of Arts and Sciences 46. Hamden, Conn. (1978) New Evidence for Sources of and Trade in Bronze Age Tin. In Franklin, *et al.* 1978: 43-48. (1981) The Origin of Agriculture and Technology—West or East Asia? *Technology and Culture* 22/1: 125-48. (1983) Kupfer. B. Archäologisch. RLA 6: 348-64. Berlin/New York. (1993) Early Bronze Age Tin and the Taurus. *American Journal of Archaeology* 97: 239-54. (1994) Bronze Age Source of Tin Found in Turkey? *Biblical Archaeology Review* 20/3: 16-17. (1995) Mining and Metalwork in Ancient Western Asia. In Sasson 1995b: 1501-19. (1997) Metals. In Meyers 1997: 1-15. **Muhly, J. D., and T. A. Wertime** (1973) Evidence for the Sources and Use of Tin during the Bronze Age of the Near East. *World Archaeology* 5: 111-22. **Orlin, L. L.** (1970) *Assyrian Colonies in Cappadocia.*

Studies in Ancient History 1. The Hague and Paris. **Özgüç, T.** (1963) An Assyrian Trading Outpost. *Scientific American* 208/2: 96-106. **Philip, G.** (1991) Tin, Arsenic, Lead: Alloying Practices in Syria-Palestine around 2000 B.C. *Levant* 23: 93-104. **Pigott, V. C.** (1996) Near Eastern Archaeometallurgy: Modern Research and Future Directions. In Cooper and Schwartz 1996: 139-76. **Polanyi, K.** (1975) Traders and Trade. In Sabloff and Lamberg-Karlovsky 1975: 133-54. **Postgate, J. N.**, ed. (1982) *Societies and Languages of the Ancient Near East: Studies in Honour of I. M. Diakonoff.* Warminster, England. **Potts, T.** (1994) *Mesopotamia and the East: An Archaeological and Historical Study of Foreign Relations, ca. 3400–2000 B.C.* Oxford University Committee for Archaeology Monograph 37. Oxford. **Redford, D. B.** (1981) The Acquisition of Foreign Goods and Services in the Old Kingdom. *Scripta Mediterranea* 2: 5-16. (1992) *Egypt, Canaan, and Israel in Ancient Times.* Princeton. **Sabloff, J. A., and C. C. Lamberg-Karlovsky**, ed. (1975) *Ancient Civilization and Trade.* School of American Research Advanced Seminar Series. Albuquerque. **Sasson, J. M.** (1973) Biographical Notices on Some Royal Ladies from Mari. *Journal of Cuneiform Studies* 25: 59-78. (1980a) *Dated Texts from Mari: A Tabulation.* ARTANES 4. Malibu. (1980b) Two Recent Works on Mari. *Archiv für Orientforschung* 27: 127-35. (1984) Zimri-Lim Takes the Grand Tour. *Biblical Archaeologist* 47: 246-51. (1995a) King Hammurabi of Babylon. In Sasson 1995b: 901-15. (1995b) Ed., *Civilizations of the Ancient Near East.* 4 vols. New York. **Stech, T., J. D. Muhly, and R. Maddin** (1985) Metallurgical Studies on Artifacts from the Tomb Near ʿEnan. *ʿAtiqot* 17: 76-82. **Stech, T., and V. C. Pigott** (1986) The Metals Trade in Southwest Asia in the Third Millennium B.C. *Iraq* 48: 39-64. **Stern, E.** (1993) *The New Encyclopedia of Archaeological Excavations in the Holy Land.* 4 vols. Jerusalem. **Tadmor, H.** (1977) A Lexicographical Text from Hazor. *Israel Exploration Journal* 27: 98-102. **Tubb, J. N.** (1983) The MBIIA Period in Palestine: Its Relationship with Syria and Its Origin. *Levant* 15: 49-62. (1985) Ed., *Palestine in the Bronze and Iron Ages: Papers in Honour of Olga Tufnell.* London. **Tuttle, G. A.**, ed. (1978) *Biblical and Near Eastern Studies: Essays in Honor of William Sanford LaSor.* Grand Rapids, Mich. **Ünal, A.** (1989) On the Writing of Hittite History. *Journal of the American Oriental Society* 109/2: 283-87. **Vargyas, P.** (1986) Trade and Prices in Ugarit. *Oikumene* 5: 103-16. **Veenhof, K. R.** (1972) *Aspects of Old Assyrian Trade and its Terminology.* Studia et Documenta ad iura orientis antiqui pertinentia 10. Leiden. (1995) Kanesh: An Assyrian Colony in Anatolia. In Sasson 1995b: 859-71. **Villard, P.** (1986) Un roi de Mari à Ugarit. *Ugarit-Forschungen* 18: 387-412. (1993) La place des années de "Kahat" et d'"Adad d'Alep" dans la chronologie du règne de Zimri-Lim. *MARI* 7: 315-28. (1995) Shamshi-Adad and Sons: The Rise and Fall of an Upper Mesopotamian Empire. In Sasson 1995b: 873-83. **Waetzoldt, H.** (1981) Zur Terminologie der Metalle in den Texten aus Ebla. In Cagni 1981: 363-78. **Wagstaff, J. M.** (1985) *The Evolution of Middle Eastern Landscapes: An Outline to A.D. 1840.* Totowa, N.J. **Waldbaum, J. C.** (1978) *From Bronze to Iron: The Transition from the Bronze Age to the Iron Age in the Eastern Mediterranean.* Studies in Mediterranean Archaeology 54. Göteburg. **Weiss, H.** (1985) Tell Leilan and Shubat Enlil. *MARI* 4: 269-92. **Whiting, R. M.** (1990) Tell Leilan/Šubat-Enlil: Chronological Problems and Perspectives. In Eichler, *et al.* 1990: 167-218. **Yener, K. A.**

(1989) Kestel: An Early Bronze Age Source of Tin Ore in the Taurus Mountains. *Science* 244: 117-264. (1995) Early Bronze Age Tin Processing at Göltepe and Kestel, Turkey. In Sasson 1995b: 1519-21. **Yener, K. A., and H. Ozbal** (1987) Tin in the Turkish Taurus Mountains. *Antiquity* 61: 220-26. **Yener, K. A., and P. B. Vandiver** (1993) Tin Processing at Göltepe, an Early Bronze Age Site in Anatolia. *American Journal of Archaeology* 97: 207-38. **Yoffee, N.** (1981) *Explaining Trade in Ancient Western Asia.* MANE 2/2. Malibu, Calif. **Young, G. D.**, ed. (1992) *Mari in Retrospect: Fifty Years of Mari and Mari Studies.* Winona Lake, Ind.

Black from the Oases*

Martin Bernal
Cornell University

The first draft of this paper was written some years ago, and in volume II of *Black Athena* I touched on some of the issues involved.[1] However, for a number of reasons, it seems appropriate to publish it now in a tribute to Michael Astour. In the first place, Professor Astour is a great authority on historical geography and toponymy with which much of this paper is concerned. Secondly, he has been an inspiration both as a student of the relations among many different civilizations and for his concern with the sociology of knowledge. Above all, we admire his combination of broadness of vision with a wonderful concreteness and specificity.

It is a strange coincidence that the Latin *niger,* from which we derive "negro" and "nigger," should be the same as the name of the major river of West Africa. If one should want to connect the two, the most likely explanation would be that the river name came from the Latin color because "black" people lived along its banks. There is in fact a neat parallel for this in the toponym "Sudan," which comes from the Arabic *Bilād as Sūdān,* "Land of the Blacks." The converse would appear much less likely. At first glance, both laymen and scholars would find it very improbable that a "good" Latin word like *niger* could come from Africa. This is precisely what

* I should like to thank many friends and colleagues for help with this paper, especially Professor Gordon Messing, who doesn't believe a word of it.

1 Bernal (1991) 96-98.

I want to propose; that is to say, I maintain that there is a connection between the color and the river name, but that the Latin word comes from the Sahara and not *vice versa.* I believe that *niger* comes from the skin color of the people of Niger rather than that the place-name originates from the color term.

Lexicography

In a moving image of mortality, the Old Woman of Tekoah warned King David: "We shall all die: we shall be like water that is spilt on the ground and lost."[2] The Hebrew for "like water that is spilt" is וְכַמַּיִם הַנִּגָּרִים *wəkammáyim hanniggårîm.* The root *(n)gr* has two semantic fields in West Semitic. One of these, which appears in Ugaritic and four times in Punic inscriptions, as well as in New Hebrew, is a loanword from the Sumerian na(n)gar and the Akkadian *naggâru,* "carpenter."[3] This is not, however, attested in the Bible. There, it is restricted to what appears to be a derivative of a Semitic root *grr,* single or doubled, found in גָּרוֹן *gårôn,* "throat," and גַּרְגָּרוֹת *gargårôt,* "neck," the Arabic *ğarāğir,* and Geʿez *gʷəre,* "throat," with connotations of "swallow."

The Arabic *ğarā* means "flow" or "stream" and this seems to have been the general meaning of *ngr* in the Bible. In the three examples in the *niphal,* the third-person feminine perfect, נִגְּרָה *niggərâh* in Ps. 70:3 and Lam. 3:49, as well as the plural participle נִגָּרִים *niggårîm,* the semantic field is of a liquid—usually water—that gushes out or falls down, usually onto the ground, and is lost. In Job 20:28, נִגָּרוֹת *niggårôt* is translated as "torrents" or "rushing waters." In Sabaean, however, *ngr* appears to have meant "cultivated land."[4] A reconciliation between the two semantic fields can be achieved through toponymy.

---

2 II. Sam 14:14. *The New English Bible* translation.

3 See Tomback (1978) 210.

4 For descriptions and wonderful illustrations of how torrents can lead to cultivated land, see Pietro Laureano (1995), esp. 55-59.

Geography

There are many place-names containing *gr(r)* or *ngr* both in the Arabian desert and the Sahara. These include: Gerar, Gerrha, Gir, Gira, Giratha, Gerasa, Garama, Nigrae, Nigeir, and Nigira. Gərâr (גְּרָר in the LXX Γεράρ), one of the places where Abraham pretended that Sarah was his sister, appears to have been the modern Wadi Jerash in the desert between Ashkelon and Beersheba.[5]

There are four recorded toponyms with the name Γέρρα: (1) a fort in Coele Syria, some 35 kilometers southeast of Damascus[6]; (2) a port apparently near Salwa on the Saudi frontier with Qatar[7]; (3) an alternative name for Djerba which is well known for its oases; and (4) on the coast of Sinai.

Γείρα was a city to the south of the river identified with the modern El Gerâra in the Algerian Sahara to the south of the river. Γείρα was located there by Ptolemy.[8]

Γέρρασσα was a city 50 kilometers east of the Sea of Galilee on the banks of a wadi that flowed towards the Yarmuk River.

Garama was the capital of the Garamantes, discussed below. It seems to have been situated northeast of Marzuk in the Fezzan in southeastern Libya.[9]

Ναγάρα, πόλις Νεγράνων, Νέγραν, or Nagran in South Arabic was a city and territory in the desert southwest of the later Mecca.[10]

Nigrae was a city and episcopal seat slightly to the north of the north bank of the Tritonian lake or marshes in what is now southern Tunisia.

---

5 See also Eph'al (1982) 65, 78, and 220. According to Ptolemy, VI. 7.32, Γειράθα was five-days travel inland from Γέρρα: three in the center of Arabia. It appears to have been the later el Ḫarǧatān, "Two Oases." Thus, the final -θα may well indicate a Proto-Arabic dual.

6 Polybios V. 46.

7 See Pliny, *Nat. Hist.* VI. 1457; Strabo XVI. 766, and others.

8 Ptolemy IV. 6, 13.16.31.

9 Pliny *Nat. Hist.* V.5.36; Ptolemy I. 8.5.

10 Ptolemy VI.7.37 and Strabo 16, 781-82.

According to Ptolemy and Pliny, Νίγειρα, or Nigira, was the capital of the Nigritai, who lived on the Niger. This leads us to the name Niger itself. Both Pliny and Ptolemy refer to a river called Niger flowing into the Sahara. They are not, however, the same. Ptolemy apparently used Νίγειρ as the name of the present Wadi Saoura, which flows intermittently from the western Atlas into the Sahara.[11] Pliny seems to have called this Ger.[12]

By contrast, Pliny called a short wadi pointing south from the Aurés Mountains in eastern Algeria "Niger," while Ptolemy used Γείρ to refer to a river—some thought connected to the former— that occasionally flooded north from the Hoggar Mountains in the Central Sahara.[13] He saw this as flowing through the Νιγρῖτις λίμνη, marshes in the plateau of Tassili n'Ajjer to the north of the Hoggar mountains.

Münzer, in his entry on "Niger," explained the confusion as follows:

> Der Widerspruch in der Namengebung bei Plinius und Ptolemaios ist nur scheinbar. Denn die berberische Wurzel *ghor, gher, ghir, ghar* ist identisch mit den Worten *Niger, Nigir, Nigris.* Diese bedeuten nichts weiter als ein Wasser, das fließt, und hydrographisch das dazu gehörende Tal...[14]

As is appropriate in an encyclopedia, Münzer was stating conventional wisdom. The French historical geographer Charles Joseph Tissot had proposed this solution in the 1880s, and it has been accepted ever since.[15] There is no doubt that all of the toponyms are connected with water. Furthermore, *'ger* with the prefix *n-* "of" does exist in Tamashek, the Berber language of the Tuaregs, as in the place-name mentioned above Tassili *n'ajjer*, "Plateau of Rivers."[16] However, apart from the fact that many Berber speakers live in deserts, the hypothesis does not explain why the toponyms

---

11 Ptolemy IV.6, 14.

12 Pliny *Nat. Hist.* V.1.14. A depression leading into the Saoura valley is called Gourara today and may well belong to the same cluster.

13 Ptolemy IV.6, 13.

14 See Münzer (1936) col. 197.

15 See Tissot (1884) 97; Gsell (1914–1928) Vol. I. 316 and Law (1978) 143 n. 3.

16 See Cortade (1968) and Lhote (1959) 40.

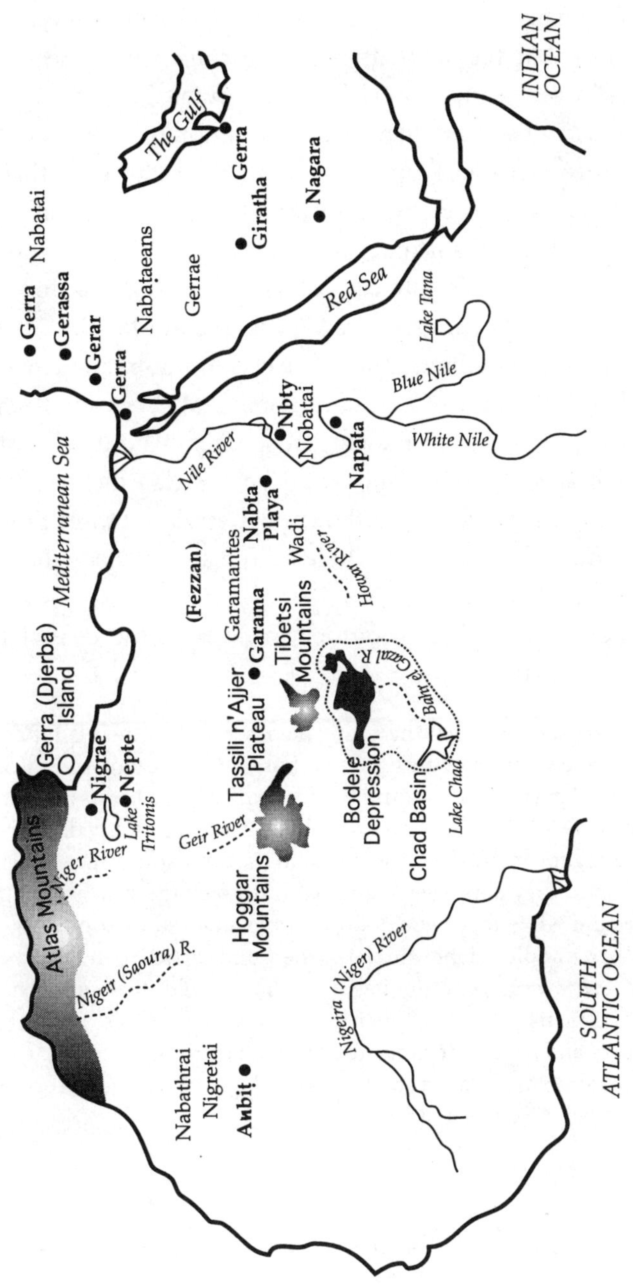
INDIAN OCEAN
The Gulf
Gerra
Nagara
Giratha
Nabatai
Gerra
Gerassa
Gerar
Gerra
Nabataeans
Gerrae
Red Sea
Lake Tana
Blue Nile
White Nile
Nbty
Nobatai
Napata
Nile River
Mediterranean Sea
Nabta Playa
Wadi
Howar River
Garamantes
(Fezzan)
Garama
Tibetsi Mountains
Bahr el Gazal R.
Gerra (Djerba) Island
Nigrae
Nepte
Lake Tritonis
Tassili n'Ajjer Plateau
Bodele Depression
Chad Basin
Lake Chad
Geir River
Niger River
Atlas Mountains
Hoggar Mountains
Nigeir (Saoura) R.
Nigeira (Niger) River
SOUTH ATLANTIC OCEAN
Nabathrai
Nigretai
Anbiṭ

should be restricted to them. Furthermore, it does not explain the Gerr and Nagar place-names in Southwest Asia where Berber has never been spoken, and the fact that the alternation *ger/niger* meaning "streams" or, more precisely, "oases" is found in Hebrew and Arabic.

There is a possibility that *(n)gr* is common to Semitic and Berber, as both are Afroasiatic languages. It is more likely, however, that the Berber *gher* is one of its many loanwords from Phoenician and that *n'gher* simply coincided with the Canaanite *niger.* Speakers of Berber and Northwest Semitic were in contact with each other in the Maghreb from at least 900 B.C.E. to 700 C.E. The most plausible explanation for the Classical place-names is that *ger* and *niger* were relatively common terms for "oases" and "rivers that disappear (into the sand)," and that Greek and Roman geographers learned them from Phoenician speakers who lived on the African coast but traded some distance into the desert. Athenæus' story of the Carthaginian Mago who crossed the waterless desert three times is impossible in some of its details, but there is no reason to deny that expeditions of this type took place.[17]

Herodotus described a journey made by some coastal Libyans or, specifically, Nasamonians:

> The story then was that the young men, sent off by their companions on their travels with a good supply of food and water, passed through the inhabited parts of the country to the region of wild beasts and then came to the desert, which they proceeded to cross in a westerly direction. After travelling for many days over the sand they saw some trees growing on a level spot; they approached and began to pick the fruit which the trees bore, and while they were doing so were attacked by some little men of less than middle height who seized them and carried them off. The speech of these dwarfs was unintelligible, nor could they understand the Nasamonians. They took their captives through a vast tract of marshy country and beyond it came to a town, all the inhabitants of which were of the same small stature, and all black. A great river with crocodiles in it flowed from west to east.[18]

---

17 Athenaeus II.44.e.

18 II.32 trans. as *Herodotus: The Histories,* by A. de Sélincourt, rev. by A. A. Burn, (1972) 141.

Herodotus accepted the view of the Ammonian king Etearchus, who told him the story that this river was a source of the Nile. This version did not disappear even though that of the source in the "Mountains of the Moon" in East Africa was probably more popular. In any event, the view that the Nile rose in the Moroccan Atlas was repeated by many later writers,[19] the melting of the known snows in the Atlas being given as the explanation for the Nile flood.

Most modern scholars, however, have associated Herodotus' river with the Gers and Nigers of Pliny and Ptolemy, and to have assumed that the river was the modern Niger, which is indeed, "A great river with crocodiles in it [that flows]...from west to east."[20]

Naturally, there has been some resistance to the idea of crossing the Sahara among the positivists and minimalists of the mid-twentieth century. Hennig suggested that the Nasamonians had merely reached the Fezzan. As Lloyd points out, however, that this is extremely implausible because the Garamantes who lived there were generally seen as living in the region of wild beasts, which was only the second zone through which the travellers had passed.[21] Instead, Lloyd has accepted a compromise view put forward by Rhys Carpenter, that the marshes were in what is now the dry Bodele depression to the northeast of Lake Chad.[22]

Carpenter and Lloyd could be correct about the marshes. Later research has shown that the climate of the greater Chad basin was significantly wetter during the first half of the first millennium B.C.E.[23] On the other hand, they have some difficulty in finding Pygmies there, though the same is true of the Upper Niger. It is probable that this part of the story was added from a widespread knowledge among North Africans and Greeks that there were

---

19 Pliny *Nat. Hist.* V.296, VI.35; Strabo XVII.3, 4; Diodorus I.37; Cass. Dio, LXXV, 15 and the Arab Edrisi I.206.

20 For a list of these, see Lloyd (1976) 138.

21 Hennig (1934) 206 and Lloyd (1976) 137.

22 Lloyd (1976) 136-39.

23 See Servant and Servant-Vildary (1980) 133-62.

Pygmies in Central Africa. More seriously, however, the Bodele hypothesis goes against the two geographical directions given in the story: that the Nasamonians travelled west, and that the river flowed from west to east. Heading southwest would have led them to the Niger bend. Lloyd dismisses this: "The ancients are careless in such matters … and the tale is third hand anyway. The direction might even be the result of inference." All these factors are indeed reasons for caution. However, Lloyd himself shows similar carelessness when he refers to the "swampy sea … having been *watered from the W.* by the Bahr el Gazal."[24] In fact, Herodotus does not refer to a river running into the swamps, but refers simply to it as flowing next to the town:

> παρὰ δὲ τὴν πόλιν ῥέειν ποταμὸν μέγαν, ῥέειν δὲ ἀπὸ ἑσπέρης αὐτὸν πρὸς ἥλιον ἀνατέλλοντα…[25]

More importantly, the Bahr el Gazal—when it flows—does not flow into the Bodele, but away from it to the south towards Lake Chad. It is not only the Ancients who could be careless! Carpenter and Lloyd's case does not seem strong enough to challenge the earlier conventional wisdom. However, this debate is not important to the argument being made here. What is significant is that ancient geographers knew about rivers in, or to the south of, the Sahara, to which they gave the names Ger or Niger, and that the banks of—at least the latter—were inhabited by black people.

Ethnography

The place-names Ger and Niger were applied also to peoples, some of whom have been mentioned above. The Garamantes, whose capital was called Garama, were based on the present Wadi al Agial in the Fezzan. They practiced agriculture, but were also prosperous traders and famous charioteers. In his studies of the Garamantes, Charles Daniels has plausibly supposed that they were Berber speakers and that their physical remains reveal a

---

24 Lloyd (1976) 138.

25 Herodotus II.32.

population that was Mediterranean, negroid, and hybrid.[26] The specialist in deserts and their irrigation, Pietro Laureano, sees them "probably" as the antecedents of the modern Touareg.[27] Herodotus refers to their using four-horse chariots to hunt τρωγλοδύται Αἰθίοπες. The specific troglodytes referred to were probably related to the Teda, a people who still use caves as refuges in the Tibesti Mountains in northern Chad. The fact that they speak a Nilo-Saharan language would explain why Herodotus' Afroasiatic-speaking informants described them "as speaking a language like no other and squeaking like bats."[28]

In any event, the Garamantes were less dark than Herodotus' "Ethiopians." This leads us to the more general and vexing question of the identity of the Αἰθίοπες, or "Ethiopians." Professor Snowden has argued forcefully that the term did not merely mean "dark" or "black-skinned," but was restricted to "Negroes" or stereotypical West Africans. As he puts it, "*all* Ethiopians were black or dark *but not all peoples* described as black or dark were designated as Ethiopians" [his italics].[29] While this is undoubtedly true, there are a number of problems with his schema. The most notable of these is that the statement does not deal with the fact that Greeks frequently saw two sets of Ethiopians. As Homer put it at the beginning of the *Odyssey*, the Ethiopians:

> are sundered in twain, the farthermost of men, some where Hyperion sets and some where he rises.[30]

Herodotus explained where the latter came from:

> The Eastern Ethiopians—for there were two sorts of Ethiopians in the army—served with the Indians. These were just like the southern Ethiopians except for their language and their hair: their hair is straight, while that of the Ethiopians of Libya is the crispest and curliest in the world.[31]

---

26 See Daniels (1975) and Keita (1990) 37.

27 Laureano (1995) 52.

28 Herodotus IV.183, trans. de Sélincourt, p. 332. See also Blench (1993) 92.

29 Snowden (1993) 320.

30 *Odyssey* I.22-25.

31 Herodotus VII.71, trans. de Sélincourt, p. 468.

The fact is that the term *aithiops* was as uncertain in Classical antiquity as "Black" is today. At times, it was restricted to stereotypical West Africans, which is the way in which Snowden generally, but not always, interprets it. At other times, however, it was used much more broadly, to include any people substantially darker than the Greeks and Romans themselves.[32] In Roman times "Aethiops" was even used synonymously with "Aegyptius."[33]

As mentioned above, classical writings on the Sahara refer to a people known variously as Nigretae, Νιγρῖται, or Νιγρῆτες. These names were associated with the river Niger, wherever that was placed. Even this is probably too specific. They seem to have been simply the people of the *niggårôt,* oases and rivers of the central and southern Sahara.[34] Herodotus describes these as follows:

> Up country further to the south lies the region where the wild beasts are found and beyond that there is a great belt of sand stretching from Thebes in Egypt to the pillars of Heracles. Along this belt separated from one another by about ten days' journey, are little hills formed of lumps of salt, and from the top of each gushes a spring of cold sweet water. Men live in the neighbourhood of these springs—beyond the wild beasts—region. They are the furthest south, towards the desert, of any human beings.[35]

The connection of Nigr- with such distant regions appears later in Pliny's description, which even he admits to be fantastic, of the "Nigroe" on the banks of the Upper Nile [which for him could have been south of the Sahara] whose king had one eye in his forehead.[36] By the first century, however, his choice of name may well have been influenced, if not determined, by the Latin word *niger* itself.

---

32 See Law (1978) 141.

33 See Thompson (1989) 80.

34 It is conceivable that there was a *nisba* form *Niggerôty meaning precisely "people of the oases." However, it is normal in Canaanite to place the gentilic *-y* on the singular forms of dual or plural place-names. See Gordon (1965) 62.

35 Herodotus IV.181, trans. de Sélincourt, p. 331. Laureano (1995) 52 sees nothing improbable in this description.

36 Pliny VI.30.

Nbty, Napata, and Nabataeans.

This, of course, was not the case with the name Nigretai, which is attested in Greek as well as Latin. The hypothesis that originally Nigret- was simply a Phoenician name for the "men of the oases" is strengthened by some Asiatic, Egyptian, and Libyan parallels. There were the G(h)errae, the name given by Classical authors to traders and raiders in the deserts of eastern Arabia, presumably based on the cities called Gerra.[37] Long before this, one of the more frequently used Egyptian terms for "barbarians" was Wḥꜣtyw "people of the Wḥꜣt, oasis region." Much later, there are references to the Napatans, inhabitants of Upper Nubia and the surrounding deserts.

At this point, we should consider a cluster of names that, although of different origins, came to be confused with each other. The earliest attested of these are the Egyptian place-names Nbt and Nby(t). These were two towns in Upper Egypt known later as Ombos and Ombi, the name being an adjectival form based on *nbw* "gold." Ombos, on the edge of the desert, was the most important cult center of Seth, who was frequently known as 'He of Ombos' or Nbty.[38]

In the sixteenth century B.C.E., during the early eighteenth Dynasty, the southernmost extension of the Egyptian empire, just below the fourth cataract, was known as Npt, which later became the famous and long-lasting Nubian kingdom of Napata.[39] According to Procopius, writing in the sixth century, more than two centuries earlier, in 294 C.E. Diocletian had invited the Nobadai or Nobatai living in the oases to the west to migrate to the Upper Nile to protect the empire.[40] The early twentieth-century historian of the Sudan, Arkell, suggested that there might be a connection between this name and Napata.[41] Equally, however, the Nobatai could be tied to Seth

---

37 See Bibby (1972) 318, 330.

38 See Gardiner (1947) II.5, 28-29, 70. Gauthier (1925–31) III.84 derives the name from *nbi* "modeling," which includes both metal-casting and pottery.

39 Gauthier (1925–31) 86-87; see also Adams (1977) 246-59.

40 Procopius, *De Bello Persico* I.19.

41 See Arkell (1961) 178.

Nbty as god of the desert and its people and animals, or to the Semitic *nbṭ*, which will be discussed below. For the moment, however, we shall stick to Seth and other parallel divinities of the desert.

According to Herodotus, not only the *quadriga* but its patron god Poseidon came to Greece from Libya: "for the Libyans are the only people who have always known Poseidon's name and always worshipped him."[42] Alan Lloyd, in his commentary on Herodotus' *Book Two* concerning Egypt, can make nothing of this statement. Working within the Aryan Model, Lloyd maintains that Poseidon's "Indo-European/Gk. provenance is beyond doubt, and dated his introduction to Greece to at least the Achaean period [Late Bronze Age]."[43] My tentative hypothesis, deriving Poseidon's name from the Egypto-Semitic hybrid P*ꜣ*(w) Ṣidôn (He of Ṣidôn), has been mentioned in the first volume of *Black Athena.* In any event, I see a connection with the West Semitic god of hunting and waters Ṣid, the divinity of Ṣidôn.[44] Thus, I do not accept that his name was either Indo-European or Libyan, though his cult was clearly practiced among the latter people. Poseidon was also the hidden counterpart of the Egyptian Seth, who by Classical times was considered to be the epitome of evil. This would explain why Herodotus' Egyptian informants seem to have been so adamant in denying Poseidon, a respectable god in Greece, a place in the Egyptian pantheon, and why they saw him as the divinity of the outside wilderness, hence a Libyan god. Possibly following Egyptian informants, Herodotus linked Poseidon to the river Tritôn and Lake Tritônis in Libya or further west.[45] Thus, the god would seem to be associated with inland water, within Libya, as well as with the hunting, horses and chariots of the oases' turbulent inhabitants. Interestingly, there was a city called Nepte on the southern and desert side of Lake Tritôn.[46]

---

42 Herodotus II.50.

43 Lloyd (1976) 237-38.

44 See Bernal (1987) 67.

45 Herodotus IV.180 and 188.

46 See Findlay (1847) pl.17. Ptolemy IV.3.21 and 6.20 refers to a people on the coast of Libya called Ναβάθραι, and Pliny V.21 to the Nabades in Morocco.

At this point, we should consider the name of Poseidon's Italic counterpart Neptune and the Semitic root *nbṭ*. The Etruscan city of Nepete near Rome had a river and springs and, as the antiquarian George Dennis described it in the 1840s:

> He [the traveller] has left the open wastes of the Campagna and entered a wooded district. It is one of the few portions of central Italy that will remind him, if an Englishman, of home. Those sweeps of bright green sward … The whole forms a lively imitation of—what is most rare on the Continent—English Park scenery, …[47]

It was, in fact, an oasis. In a later work, I shall try to make a case for the existence of many plausible Semitic etymologies of toponyms around Rome, including that of the city itself—from the common Canaanite toponym Råmå(h).[48] Thus, the derivation of Nepete from a Semitic root, which would seem to be extremely appropriate semantically, cannot be easily dismissed. With the West Semitic personal and gentilic suffixes *-ån* or *-ôn*, Nepete makes one very plausible origin for Neptune—the other chief candidate being the Egyptian Seth Nbty.[49]

Now let us turn to southwest Asia and the Semitic root *nbṭ*. The Nabataeans, who lived in the northern Arabian desert, called themselves Nbṭw. They clearly derived their name from *nbṭ* found in Sabaean *nbṭ*, "dig a well," and Arabic *nabaṭa* "well out, gush out, stream forth."[50] In Islamic times, the

---

47 Dennis (1848) I.109.

48 See Bernal (forthcoming). This etymology is now considered quite possible by the linguist John Pairman Brown (1995) 24 n. 72.

49 For the gentilic suffix *-n*, see Gordon (1965) 63. There is no reason why the Etruscan Nethun should be older than the Latin Neptune, rather than *vice versa*. For Roman knowledge of the Egyptian connection between Seth as an ass, and as Nbty as "golden" shown by Apuleius' title *Golden Ass*, see Winkler (1985) 309-21.

50 It has been widely suggested that these were the same as the Nabaitai living in the Syrian desert referred to in seventh-century Assyrian sources. However, Eph'al (1982) 221-23 is not convinced because of the distinction between the /ṭ/ and the /t/, which he now sees as reinforced by the discovery of the name Nbyt on a sixth-century inscrip-tion from the Jebel Ghunaiym in an ancient Arabic dialect. I am not so tolerant of coincidences; that two peoples in the same ecological zone should have such similar names seems highly implausible.

root was also used in the western Sahara. Early Arab geographers referred to a people there interchangeably as ᵓAnbiṭ or ᵓAswad, “Blacks.” The modern historian John Wansbrough explains that ᵓAnbiṭ was not used in reference to pigmentation but to the occupation of agriculturalist.[51] Thus, it is likely that here too the root *nbṭ* was used to describe the inhabitants of the oases. However, the parallel suggests that a significant number of them were black.

The western Sahara was the region where the Classical authors reported the presence of Nigretai. In the first century C.E., Strabo—presumably basing his statement on earlier sources—wrote that the Nigretai were neighbors of the Pharusai in an area that seems to be in the modern Mauritania. The name Pharusai can be plausibly derived from the Canaanite פָּרָשִׁים, or the construct,*פָּרְשֵׁי horsemen.”[52] If this is the case, they were well named. According to Strabo, the two peoples, riding horses—with bladders tied to their girths, so that they could cross the desert—and with chariots with scythes attached to their wheels, had raided and destroyed 300 Tyrian (Phoenician) cities on the coast, apparently that of Morocco.[53]

Strabo claimed that the Nigretai lived to the west of the Ethiopians. Pliny, on the other hand, maintained that they were the westernmost Ethiopians.[54] If they were uncertain, so are modern physical anthropologists. Some hold that as the Sahara expanded and contracted it acted as a pump causing population admixture, others that the peoples of the inland Maghreb represent a survival of undifferentiated population before the division into Africans and “Caucasians.”[55] Whatever the cause, and the two are

---

The Greek νάφθα probably derives from *nbṭ*. Pliny 2.235 described *naphthaita appelatur circa Babylonem et in Austacenis Parthiae profluens bituminis liquidi modo.* Although the second place-name reinforces the supposition that it derives from the Avestan *napta*, and the hypothetical Iranian **nafta* “wet,” the Semitic *nabata*, “issue forth,” fits better in both its phonetics and its semantics.

51 Wansbrough (1970) 91.

52 For the similarity of Hebrew and Phoenician construct forms, see Harris (1936) 61.

53 Strabo XVII.3.3-7. See also Law (1978) 143-45.

54 Pliny V.43.

55 Personal communication by telephone Shomarka Keita (January 21st, 1997).

perfectly compatible, rock paintings in the Tassili Massif and elsewhere, dating back to the fourth and fifth millennia B.C.E., as well as human remains from that period and later, indicate that the inhabitants of the Sahara were mixed in appearance, but predominantly Black, some "negroid" others not.[56] Many are strikingly similar to the Fulani, who today live around the southern rim of the Sahara.[57] Indeed, some anthropologists have even claimed to see similarities between a scene in one of the paintings and a contemporary Fulani initiation ceremony.[58]

The Fulani are classified by physical anthropologists with the Nuer, Shilluk, and Tutsi as "elongated Africans," tall with thin facial features. However, unlike the others, the Fulani have a relatively light skin. And, in this respect, they seem to differ from the people portrayed in the Saharan rock paintings, who appear considerably darker.[59] The latter seem closer to the typical Sudanic Africans and have a blue-black pigmentation, darker than that of the peoples living further south. This type is predominant among the Haratîn found in the central Saharan oases today, who are plausibly thought to be the descendents of the original Saharans of the early Holocene.[60]

The few early physical remains from the Sahara tend to indicate a rather heavier physical type with wider nasal passages, suggesting contact with, or derivation from, people from the forests to the south.[61] The consensus among physical anthropologists is that the "elongated African" type devel-

---

56 This type is described by Hiernaux (1975) 127-39. Muzzolini (1986) 60 consistently tries to play down the number of "Negroid" types drawn on the rock paintings. He concedes their presence at Tassili, but attempts to deny that they were represented in those from Tadrart Acacus some 100 miles to the east. Elsewhere, however, he has to concede their presence not only there, but in some tombs of the Garamantes, even further west (pp. 236 and 252).

57 Lhote (1959) 81; see also Laureano (1995) 273.

58 Hampate and Dieterlein (1961).

59 As I have not seen any of the originals, my judgment here is based on the reproductions in Lhote (1959) and Mori (1965).

60 Hiernaux (1975) 127-39 and Keita (1990) 36.

61 Chamla (1968) and Henneberg, Piontek, and Strzalko (1980) 389-92.

oped in the Sudanic region to adapt to the intense dry heat and exposure to the sun in the savanna and desert rim.[62] In any event, the inhabitants of the Central Sahara have tended to be very dark though with varied heights, weights, and physiognomies. This would seem to fit with the ancient writers' references to "Ethiopians" there.

The situation on the northern rim of the Sahara during Classical times was more complicated. As Desanges put it, in old-fashioned terms, in the UNESCO history of Egypt:

> Libyco-Berbers (Mauri and Numidians on the coast, Getules on the Plateaux), white or half-bred Saharans on the borders of the desert—such as Pharusians, Nigrites or Garamantes, "Ethiopians" scattered from the Sous to the Djerid—these were the peoples of Africa Minor at the time of the first Phoenician sea voyages, and as such remained throughout antiquity.[63]

Even so, there is little doubt whatever, that despite the variation in their actual color and pigmentation, the Nigretai as western Ethiopians, or their neighbors and allies, were seen by the inhabitants of the coastal Maghreb as Blacks.

The greatest west Phoenician city, Carthage, clearly contained a Black population. Carthaginian evidence tallies closely with that of the rest of the non-Saharan Maghreb. The physical anthropologist Marie-Claude Chamla estimates that between 10% and 20% of its population was "negroid."[64] The role of these Blacks was disproportionately significant as soldiers and slaves. Frontinus, an author of the first century C.E., described some Carthaginian auxiliaries of the fifth century B.C.E. as *nigerimme.* Whether or not this is an anachronism, we know, from literary references, coins and other represen-

---

62 Hiernaux (1975) 137. Hiernaux's suggestion that the light and reddish complexion of the Fulani is a climatic adaptation contradicts his conclusion earlier in the book (p. 77) that "skin colour tends to be darker in the savanna than in the forest, in which less sunlight actually reaches the ground."

63 Desanges 423-40.

64 Chamla (1975) 659-92 and (1976) 97. The range comes from her estimating 12% as "negroid" and a further 7% as "Mechta Afalou," the epipaleolithic population of northern Africa, whose position on modern "racial" spectra is ambiguous.

tations that African Blacks were a significant presence in Hannibal's invading army in Italy.[65]

As the Phoenicians appear to have been the pioneers of "Slave Society," and remained ardent slavers and employers of slaves, it is also virtually certain that Carthaginians enslaved Blacks from the Sahara and further south.[66] Thus, the following statements by Gsell appear very plausible:

> Il y avait certainment des nègres à Carthage et il est vraisemblable que la commerce punique en vendait aux grecs at aux Italiens.[67]

Niger *as a Color*

According to the lexicographers of Latin Ernout and Meillet:

> Sauf pour "rouge" les noms de couleurs ne sont d'ordinaire pas Indo-européens:

They wrote this in the entry for "albus." Under "niger" they concluded:

> Étymologie inconnue. Du reste, il n'y a pas d'adjectif indo-européen commun attesté pour "noir."[68]

Certainly neither *ater* nor *niger*, the most frequent Latin words covered by the English "black," has a known Indo-European derivation, and the latter is found only in Latin.[69] Both words are old and appear in the works of Ennius in the third century B.C.E. In the early period, however, *ater* was much more common. In his *Étude sur les termes de couleur dans la langue latine*, André made a fascinating comparison between the semantic fields

---

65 See Snowden (1970) 130-31.

66 For the first claim, see Bernal (1993) 243-50.

67 Gsell *Histoire* IV. p.140.

68 André (1985). Ernout, Meillet, and André disregarded—presumably on phonetic grounds—the tradition expressed in Tucker (1931). Tucker attempted to preserve the European identity of *niger* by linking it to the Sanskrit *nila*, "dark-colored," the Gothic *nidwa*, "dark," and the Old English *nipan*, "to be dark."

69 *Ater* is attested in other Italic languages; Ernout and Meillet concede that any relationship between *ater* and the Irish *ath*, "furnace," is dubious.

of the two words. Before about 100 B.C.E. *ater* was the opposite of *albus.* The pair were simply "black" and "white," without any reference to luminosity. *Ater* was the word for "shade" and "darkness" with somber and sinister connotations, hence the adjective *atrox*, "atrocious."

The opposite of *niger* was *candidus*, "glowing white." Where *ater* was matte, *niger* was brilliant. According to André:

> *Niger* est un noir brilliant doué de la beauté de son éclat.[70]

In this early period, *niger* was used to describe ebony, opals, and other mainly southern products. Sometimes it connoted a violet tinge and was the color of mulberries and dark wine.[71] Although it is not attested at this time to describe men and women, this luminous color would fit well with that of the people of the Central and Southern Sahara and hence the coastal stereotype of the Nigretai. Thus, a derivation of *niger* from Nigretai—and of the latter from *niggårôt* and *ngr*—fits very well, in terms of both phonetics and semantics.

Because Rome has been seen as an epitome of European civilization, anti-Semitism in European society and among some classicists has, until recently, made it ideologically impossible for scholars to imagine that there could have been a substantial number of Semitic loans into Latin. Phoenicians were present in the central Mediterranean at least from the early tenth century B.C.E.[72] There is also strong evidence of Phoenician involvement in the earliest Roman cults.[73] The three alliances between Carthaginians and

---

70 André (1948) 47.

71 André (1948) 53.

72 Niemeyer (1988) 201-4 believes that Phoenician colonization was no earlier than the Greek. The positivist and minimalist Maria Eugenia Aubet (1993) 177-84 tends to favor an early ninth-century date on archaeological grounds. On the other hand, the *doyen* of Phoenician studies, Sabatino Moscati, (*e.g.*, [1985] 179-87) argues for Canaanite activities in the western Mediterranean in the fourteenth and thirteenth centuries, and Phoenician ones in the tenth. Frank Cross (1979) 97-123, basing himself on epigraphic evidence, would go even higher, to the eleventh century. The more cautious archaeologist, John Boardman (1990) 178 sees Phoenician expansion in the Mediterranean as having taken place in the tenth or ninth centuries.

73 Van Berchen (1959-60) 61-68 and (1967) 73-109, 307-36.

Romans after 509 B.C.E., the year after the Etruscan kings had been driven out, indicate considerable official and popular contact between the two peoples and their allies.[74] It is als.o likely that there was a "colony" of Phoenicians in Rome from the seventh century B.C.E., and it is possible that this was continuous until the attested presence of a Punic, Canaanite-speaking population in Rome in the early second century.[75] Later still, there was the Roman colonization of the West Phoenician world. Given all this, it would be amazing if there had not been a substantial number of West Semitic loanwords in Latin. The failure to investigate this can be explained very easily in terms of the sociology of knowledge.[76] Even today there are scattered concessions of individual loanwords, *mapalia,* "hut," *mappa,* "napkin," and, interestingly, *ave.* Given the lack of Indo-European roots for colors, it would not be surprising to find that some of these too come from Semitic. Looked at in Indo-European terms, the relationship between the Greek μαλάχη and the Latin "malua" is puzzling. Both mean "mallow" and "mauve," but though generally similar, their phonetics have a curious discrepancy. It is generally admitted that they both come from a Mediterranean language. The Italian linguist Vincenzo Cocco indicated that the origin was the Georgian *malokhi* and the Semitic מַלוּחַ with the same meaning.[77] It is more probable that the Greek word was borrowed before the merger of ḫ>ḥ in Canaanite, and the Latin after it had taken place, from the form in Hebrew. There is an even more exact parallel, though into a different language. This is the origin of the Later Greek μαῦρος, the word for "black" that displaced all others. It derives partly from the Classical ἀμαυρός, "dim or faint," but also from Μαῦροι, the Moors or inhabitants of Mauritania. All in all, there is nothing anomalous in the hypothesis that *niger* was borrowed from a Punic proper name.[78]

---

74 See Polybius. III.22-25.

75 Rebuffat (1966) 7-48 For the later date, see Plautus' Poenulus.

76 See Bernal (1987), esp. 367-99.

77 Cocco (1955) 10-28.

78 There is also the parallel between the Latin *albus* and the Greek ἀλφός, "white, leprous," and the Semitic roots *ḥlb*, "milk," and lbn, "white." As *ḥlb* is deeply rooted

The mode of transmission is much less clear. The absence of *ngr in this sense from West Phoenician is not surprising given the extremely limited and repetitive corpus of Punic inscriptions. Nevertheless, it is plausible to suppose that it was used on the coast of the Maghreb as a general term for Black people. It is also possible —though less likely—that Romans took the ethnic name as a general term to describe the Blacks in Carthaginian armies. The attestation of *niger* in Ennius' works makes it impossible for this to have happened as late as Hannibal's invasion of Italy.

During the first century B.C.E., the popularity of the more vivid word replaced *ater* and *niger* became the standard Latin word for "black," with all its connotations.[79] As such, it passed on to the Romance langauges as the Old French *nigre, negre, neire,* and *noir*; the Spanish and Portuguese *negro*; and the Italian *nero.* It is possible, but unlikely, that any sense of the specific original meaning of "Black People" survived.

The Names Negro, Niger, and Nigger

In some ways, medieval Europeans had a remarkably vague sense of ethnography. The outstanding example is Wolfram von Eschenbach's noble infidel king Feirefiz, who was pied black and white like a magpie.[80] British pub signs for "the Turk's Head" still portray a West African. With much less inaccuracy, the patron saint of soldiers, and in particular of the Teutonic Knights, was St. Maurice, a soldier from Upper Egypt of the third century C.E., who was always portrayed as a "negro."[81] Furthermore, when precision was

---

in Afroasiatic, the connection is probably genetic, but the Latin and Greek forms could be the result of loans.

79 André (1948) 53.

80 *Parzival* 15. von Eschenbach clearly had moral reasons for this description. He began his work with the claim that all men are "motley like a magpie," "Heaven and Hell having equal part in him." This illustrates the association of the Christian moral color scheme with skin color, and, in particular, the curious identification of "white" with the pinko-gray complexions among northern Europeans in the early Middle Ages and later.

81 See Drake (1990) 213-20.

needed, a vocabulary was available. The names Moor and Saracen were frequently used interchangeably. On the other hand, they could be employed to distinguish Maghrebi Berbers from Arabs. Moreover, despite the absence of any clear difference in pigmentation, the "Moors" were definitely seen as darker. In England, "Moor" or "Blackamoor" remained an alternative name for Black Africans until the nineteenth century.

There were many different forms of *niger* in Old French: *nigre, negre, necre, neir,* and *noir.* It is interesting to note that in the *Chanson de Roland,* composed about 1100 C.E., the name Nigres was used to describe an infidel people. Whether there was continuity in the special sense of an African people, or whether it was a reflux from the general sense "Black," it is clear that in this case it was pejorative and meant "black."[82] In other contexts, however, the term was used positively. *The Catalan Atlas* of 1375 contains the portrait of a splendid Black king holding a golden nugget with the inscription:

> This negro lord is Mussa Mally (Mansa Musa king of Mali) *Senyor de los negros de Guineia.*[83]

Within a hundred years, however, a new and indelible aspect to the word was added. During the middle of the fifteenth century, Portuguese explorers needed to distinguish between the Moors or Moroccans, who had cross-bows and arquebuses, and the people south of the Senegal river, who lacked these and therefore could be kidnapped and enslaved. The latter were called "Negros." Thus, unlike the name "Ethiopian," which has generally retained some semblance of dignity, from this point on, "Negro" was associated not merely with Africans south of the Sahara, but with chattel slavery.[84] It was also seen by Europeans as the epitome of ugliness and evil.

---

82 *Chanson de Roland* laisse 237 line 3229. Brault (1978/84) vol. 2 197 translates *Nigres* as "negroes." Moignet (1989) 231 has *nègres.* The list of peoples in which this appears includes a number recognized by their dark colors, Bruns, Blos, Ermins. The vicious "racism" of the text can be seen in other passages such as those in laisses 143 and 144.

83 See Sanders (1978) frontispiece and p. 6.

84 Moore (1960).

The facts that Iberians dominated the slave trade until the late sixteenth century, that Portuguese formed the basis for the creole used in the slave trade, and that the Spaniards owned many of the early Caribbean plantations, meant that *negro* was introduced or re-introduced into French as *nègre,* and into Dutch and German as *neger.* This term was also used in English. The "gallant Elizabethan sea-dog," Sir John Hawkins, pioneered the English slave trade in the1560s. In the following decades, there are attestations of the Iberian "negro," as well as "neger," "neager," "neeger," and "niger."[85]

With the establishment of race-based slavery, in the second half of the seventeenth century, "negro" and "niger" became synonymous with "slave." Interestingly, the earliest attestation of the form "nigger" occurs in late eighteenth-century Scots (not English!), by which time the identification of blackness with slavery was complete. Paradoxically it appears in the works of Robert Burns, who composed a moving poem against the evils of slavery.[86] Elsewhere, he wrote *Disputation,* in which he wrote:

> How graceless Ham leugh at his Dad, which made Canaan a nigger.

This brings us back to the Bible and the beginning of this long and twisted story.

---

85 See the *Oxford English Dictionary* and Jordan (1968) 3-20.

86 "The Slaves Lament," Burns 1909, IV 109.

Bibliography

Adams, W. Y. (1977) *Nubia: Corridor to Africa.* London, Princeton. **André, J.**, ed. (1948) *Étude sur les termes de couleur dans la langue Latine.* Paris. (1985) *Dictionnaire êtymologie de la langue Latine: Histoire des mots.* Paris. 4th edition. **Arkell, A. J.** (1961) *History of the Sudan to 1821.* London. **Apuleius** *The Golden Ass.* **Athenaeus** *The Deipnosophists.* **Aubet, M. E.** (1993) *The Phoenicians and the West: Politics, Colonies, and Trade.* Cambridge, UK. **van Berchen, D.** (1959-60) Hercule-Melqart à L'Ara Maxima, Rendiconti della Pontifica Accademia Roman di Archaeologia, serie III, Vol. 33: 61-68. (1967) Sanctuaires d'Hercules-Melqart, Contribution à l'étude de l'expansion phénicienne en Méditerranaée. *Syria* 44: 73-109, 307-36. **Bernal, M.** (1987) *Black Athena: The Afroasiatic Roots of Classical Civilization: The Fabrication of Ancient Greece: 1785–1985.* London. (1991) *Black Athena: The Afroasiatic Roots of Classical Civilization, Vol II: The Archaeological and Documentary Evidence.* New Brunswick, London. (1993) Phoenician Politics and Egyptian Justice in Ancient Greece. In Raaflaub 1993: 243-50. (forth.) *Black Athena: The Afroasiatic Roots of Classical Civilization. Vol 3: The Linguistic Evidence.* New Brunswick, London. **Bibby, G.** (1972) *Looking for Dilmun.* Hardmondsworth. **Blench, R.** (1993) Ethnographic and Linguistic Evidence for the Prehistory of African Ruminant Livestock Horses and Ponies. In Shaw 1993: 71-103. **Boardman, J.** (1990) Al Mina and History. *The Oxford Journal of Archaeology* 9: 169-90. **Brault, G.** (1978/84) *The Song of Roland: An Analytical Edition,* 2 Vols. University Park, London. **Brown, J. P.** (1995) *Israel and Hellas.* Berlin. Cassius Dio *Roman History.* **Chamla, M.-C.** (1968) *Les populations anciennes du Sahara et des régions limitrophes: Étude des restes osseux humain néolithiques et protohistoriques.* Paris. (1975-76) Les hommes des sepultures proto-historiques et puniques, d'Afrique du Nord (Algerie et Tunisie) I. *L'Anthropologie* 79: 659-92, and II., 80: 75-116. **Cocco, V.** (1955) D'un antichissima designazione Mediterranea della "malva": Preell. "pianta magica," "malva." *Archivio Glottologica Italiano* 40: 10-28. **Cortade, J. M.** (1968) *Lexique Franáaise Touareg.* Paris. **Cross, F. M.** (1979) The Early Alphabetic Scripts. In *Symposia Celebrating the Seventy-fifth Anniversary of the American School of Oriental Research, 1900–1975,* ed. F. M. Cross. Cambridge, Mass.: 97-123. **Dalby, D.**, ed. (1970) *Language and History in Africa: A Volume of Collected Papers Presented to the London Semina on Language and History in Africa Held in the Schools of Oriental and African Studies 1967–69.* New York. **Daniels, C.** (1975) *The Garamantes of Southern Libya.* Stoughton, Wisc. **Dennis, G.** (1848) *The Cities and Cemeteries of Etruria,* 2 Vols. London. **Desanges, J.** (1981) The Proto-Berbers. In Mokhtar: 423-40. Diodorus *Library of History.* **Drake, St. C.** (1990) *Black Folk Here and There,* Vol. II. Los Angeles. **Eph'al, I.** (1982) *The Ancient Arabs: Nomads on the Borders of the Fertile Crescent, 9th–5th Centuries* B.C. Jerusalem, Leiden. **Findlay, A.** (1847) *Classical Atlas to Illustrate Ancient Geography.* London. **Gardiner, A. H.** (1947) *Ancient Egyptian Onomastica,* 3 Vols. Oxford. **Gauthier, H.** (1925-31 *Dictionnaire des noms géographiques contenus dans les textes hiéroglyphiques,* 7 vols. Cairo. **Gordon, C.** (1965) *Ugaritic Textbook.* Rome. **Graves, R., and R. Patai** (1964) *Hebrew Myths: The Book of Genesis.* London. **Gsell, S.** (1914–28) *Histoire ancienne de* *l'Afrique du Nord.* Paris. **Hampate Ba, A. and G. Dieterlein** (1961) *Koumen: Texte iniatique des pasteurs Peul.* Paris. **Harris, Z.** (1936) *A Grammar of the Phoenician Language.* American Oriental Series 8. New Haven. **Henneberg, M., J. Piontek, and J. Strzalko** (1980) Biometrical Analysis of the Early Neolithic Human Mandible for Nabta Playa (Western Desert of Egypt). In Wendporf 1980: 389-92. **Hennig, R. M.** (1934) *Die Geographie des homerischen Epos: eine Studie über erdkundlichen Elemente der Odyssee.* Leipzig, Berlin. **Herodotus** (1972) *The Histories,* tr. A. de Sélincourt, rev. by A. A. Burn. London. **Hiernaux, J.** (1975) *The People of Africa.* New York. Homer *Odyssey.* **Jordan, W.** (1968) *White over Black: American Attitudes towards the) Negro, 1550–1812.* New York, London. **Keita, S. O. Y.** (1990) Studies of Ancient Crania from Northern Africa. *Journal of Physical Anthropology* 83: 35-48. **Laureano, P.** (1995) *La Piramide Rovesciata: Il modello dell' oasi per il pianeta Terra.* Torino. **Law, R. C. C.** (1978) North Africa in the Period of Phoenician and Greek Colonization, c. 800 to 323 B.C. *Cambridge History of Africa,* Vol. II, *From 500 B.C. to A.D. 1050.* London. **Lhote, H.** (1959) *The Search for the Tassili Frescoes.* New York. **Lloyd, A. B.** (1976) *Herodotus Book II. Commentary 1-98.* Leiden. **Moignet, G.** (1989) *La Chanson de Roland, texte originale et traduction.* Paris. **Mokhtar, G.**, ed. (1981) *The UNESCO General History of Africa.* Vol. II. Paris. **Moore, R. B.** (1992) *The Name "Negro": Its Origin and Evil Use.* Baltimore. **Mori, F.** (1965) *Tadart Acacus: Arte rupestre e cultura del Sahara preistorico.* Torino. **Moscati, S.** (1985) I Fenici e il mondo Mediterranaeo al tempo di Omero. *Rivista di Studi Fenici* 13: 179-87. **Münzer** (1936) *Niger.* Pauly-Wissowa-Kroll XVII. **Muzzolini, A.** (1986) *L'art rupestre préhistoriques des massifs centraux sahariens.* Oxford. **Niemeyer, H. G.** (1988) Les Phéniciens dans l'ouest. *Revue Archéologique*: 201-4. **Pliny** *Natural History.* **Polybius** *The Histories.* **Procopius** *De Bello Persico.* Ptolemy *Geographia.* **Raaflaub, K.**, ed. (1993) *Anfänge politischen Denkens in der Antike.* Munich. **Rebuffat, R.** (1966) Les Phéniciens à Rome. *Mélanges d'archéologie et d'histoire de l'école française de Rome* 78: 7-48. **Sandars, R.** (1978) *Lost Tribes and Promised Lands: The Origins of American Racism.* Boston, Toronto. **Servant, M., and S. Servant-Vildary** (1980) L'environnement quarternaire du bassin du Tchad. In Williams and Faure 1980: 133-62. **Shaw, T., *et al.***, eds. (1993) *The Archaeology of Africa.* Routledge. **Snowden, F.** (1970) *Blacks in Antiquity: Ethiopians in the Greco-Roman Experience.* Cambridge, Mass. (1993) Response. *Arethusa* 26.3: 319-27. **Strabo** *The Geography.* **Thompson, L.** (1989) *Romans and Blacks.* Routledge. **Tissot, C. J.** (1884) *Géographie compareé de la province Romaine d'Afrique.* Vol. I. Paris. **Tomback, S.** (1978) *A Comparative Semitic Lexikon of the Phoenician and Punic Languages.* Society of Biblical Literature Dissertation Series 32. Missoula. **Tucker, T. G.** (1931) *A Concise Etymological Dictionary of Latin.* Halle. **Wansbrough, J.** (1970) Africa and Arab Geographers. In Dalby 1970: 89-101. **Wendporf, F., and R. Schild**, eds. (1980) *Prehistory of the Eastern Sahara.* New York. **Williams, M. A. J. , and H. Faure** (1980) *The Sahara and the Nile: Quarternary Environments and Prehistoric Occupation in Northern Africa.* Rotterdam. **Winkler, J. J.** (1985) *Auctor and Actor: A Narratological Reading of Apuleius's The Golden Ass.* Berkeley.

Šulgi in Simurrum*

Robert D. Biggs
The Oriental Institute
The University of Chicago

The conquest of Simurrum[1] by the Ur III king Šulgi has been known from his year names for the years 25, 26, 32, 44, and 45,[2] though the wording of the name for year 44 ("Simurrum and Lulubum were destroyed for the ninth time") indicates that there were other campaigns which did not figure in the year names. Other than the succinct statement of the year names, our only source for Šulgi's activities in Simurrum has been passages in Old Babylonian extispicy texts mentioning a man known from contemporary Ur III sources to be associated with Simurrum, Tappan-Daraḫ.[3] The omen passages are: *a-mu-ut* ^{d}*Šul-gi ša* TAB.BA-*an-da-ra-aḫ ik-mu-ú*, "omen of Šulgi who captured Tappan-Daraḫ," in YOS 10 24: 35[4] and 40, with a variant spelling ^{m}TAB.BA^{pa}-*da-ra-aḫ* in 26 i 32 and *a-mu-ut* ^{d}*Šul-*

* Abbreviations used are: MAD: Materials for the Assyrian Dictionary (2 = Gelb [1961]), 3 = Gelb [1957]); MSL: Materials for the Sumerian Lexicon (14 = Civil [1979]); YOS 10: Yale Oriental Series (10 = Goetze [1947a]).

1 The location of Simurrum has been discussed a great deal. See Edzard and Farber (1974) and more recently Astour (1987) 40-41 and D. Frayne in this volume.

2 I disregard the mu-ús-sa names which refer to the campaigns commemorated in these year names. For Ur III dates, I follow the convenient listing of the year names given in Sigrist and Gomi (1991) 319-73.

3 My transcription of the name as Tappan-Daraḫ is purely conventional. See below for comments on interpretations of the name.

4 The divine determinative before Šulgi's name is omitted in line 35.

gi ša A-pa-Da-ra-aḫ i-ni-ru, "omen of Šulgi who slew Appa-Daraḫ," YOS 10 26 iv 10.[5]

It appears to me that we may now have an independent literary account of Šulgi's campaigns against Simurrum in a text datable to the Neo-Assyrian period.[6] Three small fragments published by D. J. Wiseman and J. A. Black in *Literary Texts from the Temple of Nabû,*[7] although frustratingly broken, lead me to suggest that they are concerned with events in the reign of Šulgi. I will suggest below that they may belong to the composition known as the Šulgi Prophecy.

The first clue that these fragments might involve Šulgi is mention of Simurrum (here written *Ši-mu-ur-ri*) in No. 65: 6′, well known from the above-mentioned year names of Šulgi. Second is the apparent mention of Tappan-Daraḫ (only TAB.BA-*an*- preserved),[8] known from the Old Babylonian omen passages cited above[9] as well as from Ur III documents.[10] A. Goetze was the first to suggest Tappan-Daraḫ's specific connection with Simurrum (although I. J. Gelb in *Hurrians and Subarians* came very close[11]). Goetze further suggested that the omens concerning the defeat and capture of Tappan-Daraḫ reflected Šulgi's destruction of Simurrum recorded in his year 45.

---

5 In all cases, the protasis of the omen involves tissue (*šīrum*) located in the part of the sheep's liver called *bāb ekallim,* "palace gate." It should be noted that the statement that Šulgi slew Appadaraḫ may not be literally true since he was apparently still alive in Šu-Sin's second year (see the texts cited in n. 18 below) and even as late as Šu-Sin, year 8. We should perhaps bear in mind that the verb *nêru* often refers to defeating countries and that such a meaning may be intended in our omen passage.

6 Of course, we do not know the date of composition (as opposed to the approximate date of our copy).

7 Wiseman and Black (1996) Nos. 64, 65, and 69. The authors suggest that the three fragments are from the same tablet and add that No. 69 appears to join No. 65, although they do not indicate at what point the pieces might join.

8 In No. 65: 5′ we apparently have a name ending in r]a-aḫ, but he appears to be identified as a king of a country beginning with the sign KI, so not necessarily Tappan-Daraḫ of Simurrum.

9 See Goetze (1947b) 259-60.

10 See Gelb (1944) 114 and n. 82. For additional occurrences, see below.

11 Gelb (1944) 114.

There are a number of Ur III occurrences of a man from Simurrum (lú Si-mu-ur-ru-um, the usual way of designating a ruler) whose name appears to be written MAN-ba-an-da-ra-aḫ.[12] It seems obvious to me that the apparent MAN must be a graphic variant for the sign TAB, that is, TAB is written with either horizontal or oblique wedges.[13] This has, in fact, already been suggested by W. W. Hallo[14] and by I. J. Gelb.[15] In *Hurrians and Subarians* Gelb cites the writing Da-ba-da-ra-aḫ from the Oriental Institute text A. 5947.[16] Most[17] occurrences of Tappan-Daraḫ known to me in texts dated during the reign of Šulgi are in the special group of Drehem texts sometimes called "the archive of Šulgi-simti."[18] Sigrist refers to this group of texts as involving the "endowed institution of Šulgi-simti,"[19] explaining that she served as the head of a foundation which functioned through the contribu-

---

12 See references in Edzard and Farber (1974) 167.

13 Note, however, that Sigrist in Sigrist (1992) 233 transcribes the name as Manbadaraḫ, without comment, even though the reading *man* is not attested until Middle Babylonian.

14 Hallo (1957) 231 n. 15.

15 Gelb (1961) 67, No. 90 (TAB). Miguel Civil points out to me that the reading tab (*i.e.*, *tab*$_4$) is attested lexically for MAN. See Ea II 218 in MSL 14 256 and 261: 17′.

16 Gelb (1944) 114. See Markus Hilgert (forthcoming). A. 5947, dating to Šulgi year 34, is included as No. 21. He also includes A. 5910 as No. 24, dating to Šulgi year 36, where the wife of Tappan-Daraḫ is listed: dam TAB.BA-d[a-ra-aḫ] (TAB written with the ordinary two horizontal wedges). Both texts belong to the group designated "Archive of Šulgi-simti." Belonging to the same archive is Schneider (1932) No. 40 (republished in Molina [1993] as No. 40), where we have dam TAB.BA-da-ra-aḫ (line 4) (Šulgi, year 38). In Hallo (1963-1973) 15: 3 we also have TAB.BA-Da-ra-aḫ (Šulgi, year 34). In Sigrist (1990) No. 93: 7 we have Da-ba-da-ra-aḫ (Šulgi, year 33). A daughter of Tappan-Daraḫ is mentioned in Kang (1972) no. 188: 37 and 119 in connection with sá-dug$_4$ offerings at the ki-a-nag of Ur-Nammu. I owe the reference to the daughter of Tappan-Daraḫ to Markus Hilgert. The date of the tablet is not preserved.

17 Sigrist (1990) No. 93 cited in the previous note is an exception.

18 See Marcel Sigrist's chapter, "La 'fondation' Šulgi-simti," in Sigrist (1992) 222-46. See also the section entitled "Archiv der Königin Šulgisimtum," in Sallaberger (1993) vol. 1 18-25 and Hilgert's book mentioned in n. 14. There is an extensive bibliography dealing with Šulgi-simti, wife of Šulgi. See, for example, Steinkeller (1981) 78-79.

19 Sigrist (1995) 21-27.

tions of leading persons of the country. Šulgi-simti, a wife of Šulgi, first appears in a text in Šulgi's year 32. She died apparently shortly after Šulgi (her "libation place" [ki-a-nag] is attested early in the first year of Amar-Sin[20]), so later texts in which Tappan-Daraḫ occurs do not mention her.[21]

R. Zadok is of the opinion that Tappan-Daraḫ is not a Hurrian name and that the theophoric element is the river name Ṭab(b)an.[22] Michael Astour, on the other hand, reads Tab-ba-^{d}Da-ra-aḫ and, relying on Sumerian tab-ba and Akkadian *tappû*, "companion," understands the name as "companion of the god Daraḫ."[23] Even though a deity Daraḫ is apparently otherwise unknown, it seems easier to explain AN as the optional divine determinative. On the other hand, it is possible that -an is an element of a name of uncertain linguistic affiliation. The name of the goddess Bēlat-Deraban, apparently introduced into Sumer by Šulgi-simti from her native area,[24] comes to mind. See also names ending in -an occurring in the Ḫabiru prism of king Tunip-Teššup[25] and other names with -an as an element in Shemshara texts.[26] Whatever the correct interpretation of the name may be

20 See Sallaberger (1993) vol. 1 181.

21 See, for example, Çiğ, Kizilyay, and Salonen (1954) No. 605 rev. 4. It is dated Šu-Sin year 1. Also dated to Šu-Sin 1 is Gomi (1990) No. 271 rev. 1 (transliteration: Man-ba-an-da-ra-aḫ). Note that Ki-ri-ip-pu-ul-m[e] also occurs in this text (rev. 3) and the two men are described together as lú Si-mu-ru-um^{ki}-me, "men of Simurrum." Dated to Šu-Sin 2 are Sigrist (1990) No. 83: 13 (TAB4.BA-an-da-[ra-aḫ]) and Yildiz and Gomi (1988) No. 904: 8 (TAB4.[BA-an-da-ra]-aḫ), Schneider (1930) No. 36 (TAB4.BA-an-da-ra-aḫ, specifically identified as Lú Si-mu-ru-um^{ki}). Dated to Šu-Sin, year 8 is Schneider (1932) No. 44: 5 (republished in Molina [1993] as No. 44) (TAB4.BA-an-da-ra-aḫ).

22 See R. Zadok (1993) 224. See also Nashef (1982) 117-41. Nashef, while citing other names from the Akkadian and Ur III periods (Nashef [1982] 118-19), does not cite this name.

23 See M. Astour (1987) 41. For Old Akkadian and Ur III Akkadian names with *tappāʾum* (*tappûm*), "comrade" (written logographically as TAB.BA only), see Gelb (1957) 298.

24 See Sallaberger (1993) vol. 1 19.

25 Salvini (1996) 38-47.

26 See list of names in Eidem (1992) 90-100 and discussion of the onomastic material pp. 46-50.

and whatever its linguistic affiliation, Tappan-Daraḫ was certainly a ruler of Simurrum.

Gelb also cites the name Kirip-ulme (he is also designated lú Si-mu-ur-ru-um^{ki}) from three unpublished Ur III texts in the Oriental Institute.[27] A. 4904 and A. 5369 are Drehem texts dated to Šu-Sin year 1; A. 2852, also a Drehem text, is dated to Amar-Sin, year 9.[28] Other published texts mentioning Kirip-ulme cited by D. O. Edzard and G. Farber[29] are dated Amar-Sin 8,[30] Amar-Sin 9,[31] and Šu-Sin 2.[32] This suggests that Kirip-ulme—whose name is undeniably Hurrian—may have been a successor of Tappan-Daraḫ as ruler in Simurrum, though it should be noted that the two men appear together in a text dated to Šu-Sin year 1 (cited in n. 21) and that Tappan-Daraḫ is attested as late as year 8 of Šu-Sin.

To summarize the evidence from Ur III administrative texts (undoubtedly there are additional occurrences of which I am not aware), the name Tappan-Daraḫ is attested in the years Šulgi 33, 34, 36, and 38[33] and Šu-Sin years 1, 2, and 8. Kirip-ulme is attested in years Amar-Sin 8 and 9 and Šu-Sin years 1 and 2.

A striking feature of our three Nimrud fragments is the occurrence of Hurrian names, not unexpected in the area of Simurrum in the late third millennium and in the second millennium. It is interesting that a record or

---

27 Gelb (1944) 114.

28 Boson (1936) No. 203, cited by Gelb (1944) 114 (republished by Archi and Pomponio [1990] as No. 260) involves the same people and is dated one day later.

29 Edzard and Farber (1974) 167.

30 TCL 2 5500 iii 9 (= Genouillac [1911]), BIN 3 173: 14 (= Keiser [1971]). Also from Amar-Sin 8 is Yildiz and Gomi (1988) No. 1147: 3.

31 *SET* 66: 21 (= Jones and Snyder [1961]). Kang (1972) No. 169: 9 is also from Amar-Sin, year 9.

32 Genouillac, *Bab.* 8 pl. VII 30: 5 (= Genouillac [1924]). In one undated text, Jones and Snyder (1961) No. 297: 71, we have a reference to his wife, dam Ki(!)-ri-ip-ul-me. Exceptionally, this text deals with beer rather than deliveries of animals. It is not clear to me why the authors consider this a Lagaš text.

33 However, in years 36 and 38, it is specifically his wife (dam) who is listed in the documents.

memory of specifically identifiable Hurrian names was apparently preserved for more than a millennium in sources used by the author of this composition. Ḫa-mi-Te-šu-up occurs in No. 64: 8′ and 16′[34]; mŠu-ni-Te-šu-up in No. 65: 11′; a name beginning with Ḫa-ši-ip in No. 65: 4′[35]; and several other names having Teššup as the theophoric element (No. 64: 4′, 9′, No. 65: 3′ and probably 14′, No. 69: 3′).[36] Probably other Hurrian names occurred in this text, even if we cannot confidently restore them.

The Nimrud composition appears to be a first-person narrative (note *ēpuš*, "I did/made" in No. 65: 8′). If this text does deal with Šulgi, there is a possibility that it belongs to the Šulgi Prophecy (ancient designation: *anāku Šulgi*, "I, Šulgi" or "I am Šulgi"), likewise having first-person narrative in the first part of the text.[37] It is only after the account of Šulgi's deeds in the first two columns that the "prophecies" begin in col. iii. If our Nimrud fragments are part of the Šulgi Prophecy, they probably belong in the gap at the end of col. i or the beginning of col. ii (Borger's edition, p. 14). The lack of Šulgi's name in our text would not be surprising if it is indeed the Šulgi Prophecy. In preserved portions of the text, his name occurs only once, in the first line of the composition, "I am Šulgi."

I am not able to suggest a specific relationship among the three Nimrud fragments. If they do indeed belong to the Šulgi Prophecy, it is likely that the fragments would belong to the same column of the text since they appear to narrate related events connected with rulers or officials having predominantly Hurrian names. Apparently distinct episodes are separated by a ruling, but because we do not know the spatial relationship among the fragments, we cannot tell if there are two episodes, three episodes, or even

---

34 Depending on how much is missing on the left and right of the preserved portion of No. 65, it may be that Šuni-Teššup is identified as a son of Tappan-Daraḫ.

35 For names beginning with Ḫa-ši-ip, see Gelb *et al.* (1943) 57-58. For an interpretation of such names, see Wilhelm (1996) 182.

36 In Ur III examples (*e.g.*, Te-šup-še-la-aḫ in Schneider [1932] 44: 9, republished in Molina [1993] as No. 44) and most occurrences in Nuzi, Teššup is written Te-šup, whereas our text has the more explicit writing Te-šu-up.

37 See Borger (1971) 13-17. An English translation is given in Foster (1993), vol. 1 270-72.

four. LUGAL, "king," occurs several times, but in no case are both the name of the king and the name of his country preserved. Perhaps in No. 65: 6′ we should restore [Tappan-Daraḫ] LUGAL Ši-mu-ur-ri but, since his name apparently occurs in line 10′, there might be instead the name of his predecessor, of whom we know nothing whatever. In line 5′, as mentioned above, apparently there is a name ending in r]a-aḫ before LUGAL and the name of a country beginning Ki-i[š(?).[38] In line 3′ of the same text there may be a name ending in Te-š]u-up before LUGAL and the name of a country beginning with KA, for which I can suggest no likely restoration. In two instances apparently LUGAL occurs preceding a personal name (No. 64: 8′ and No. 65: 4′). The preserved parts appear to give filiations of several persons (DUMU.UŠ in No. 64: 9′ and 17′, No. 65: 11′).

It may be worth noting that col. ii 2′ of the Šulgi Prophecy states (in the first person) that he ruled the four quarters from east to west. I would connect this statement with Goetze's and Hallo's observation that it was after Šulgi's campaigns against Simurrum that he first claimed the title "king of the four quarters."[39]

Whether or not these fragments prove to belong to the Šulgi Prophecy, they appear to narrate events occurring in Šulgi's campaigns against Simurrum, of which no details are otherwise known. Little else can be said with any confidence. It appears that hatching for some damaged areas in No. 64 was inadvertently omitted, making this fragment especially problematic. Often it is unclear how the signs are to be combined. For example, if SAG.

---

38 Probably not the place-name Kiškati, for which see Edzard and Farber (1974) 106.

39 Goetze (1947a) 260 and Hallo (1978) 74. This conquest may also be reflected in another Old Babylonian omen concerning Šulgi, DIŠ *iz-bu-um ki-ma* ANŠE.KUR.RA *a-mu-ut* ^{d}*Šul-gi ša pa-at* 4-*bi i-bi-lu-ú*, "if the malformed newborn (sheep) is like a horse, it is an omen of the divine Šulgi who ruled the four regions," YOS 10 56 iii 10. There seems to be some special connection between Šulgi and horses; it is even possible that the king's name means "horse" or "horseman" (this suggestion for an interpretation of Šulgi's name I owe to Miguel Civil). Note also that in the hymn Šulgi A, near the end of the section with -me-en, "I am," Šulgi is described as being a horse. See Klein (1981) 188: 17. For omens concerned with Šulgi's demise, see Hallo (1991) 157-59.

GIŠ.RA, the logogram used in Sargonic inscriptions for the verb *nêru*, "slay," were to be read in No. 64: 11′ and No. 65: 13′, we would be left with an unexplained A.[40] A reading *a-šag-giš*, "like something taboo," is another possibility. Other lines are equally problematic. For example, it is not obvious in No. 65: 8′ whether to read *ni-qa-ti*, "offerings," or to understand the signs *qa-ti* here as "hand."

Borger has suggested that the Marduk Prophecy was composed in the time of Nebuchadnezzar I (ca. 1127–1105).[41] We know from the catchline of the Marduk Prophecy that it was followed by *anāku Šulgi* in the sequence established by Assurbanipal's scholars, but that is hardly evidence that the Šulgi Prophecy is from the same time. It seems more likely that at least the narrative portion of the text recounting the deeds of Šulgi derives from sources in Sumerian that were approximately contemporary with Šulgi, to which a later author added the prophetic part of the text. The phrase *anāku Šulgi* recalls [d]Šul-gi-me-en, "I am Šulgi," in the Sumerian Šulgi hymns.[42] Because the first part of the Šulgi Prophecy is so poorly preserved, it would be difficult on present evidence to claim that it is directly dependent on any of the Sumerian Šulgi hymns, despite some similar phraseology.

I hope that, after I have been able to examine the originals in Baghdad and London, I will be able to present at least a tentative edition of these most intriguing fragments.

---

40 Apparently, however, SAG.GIŠ.RA is not used as a logogram after the Akkadian period.

41 Borger (1971) 21.

42 In Šulgi A it occurs in lines 2, 26, and repeatedly in expanded formulations in this text. See Klein (1981) 188-90. See also Castellino (1972) 30: 12 (Šulgi B) and 248: 2 (Šulgi C). For other Sumerian compositions concerning Šulgi, see Klein (1981) 36-49.

Bibliography

Archi, A., and F. Pomponio (1990) *Testi cuneiformi neo-sumerici da Drehem, N. 0001-0412.* Milan. **Astour, M.** (1987) Semites and Hurrians in Northern Transtigris. In D. I. Owen and M. A. Morrison, eds., *Studies on the Civilization and Culture of Nuzi and the Hurrians* 2. General Studies and Excavations at Nuzi 9/1. 3-68. Winona Lake. **Borger, R.** (1971) Gott Marduk und Gott-König Šulgi als Propheten. *Bibliotheca Orientalis* 28: 1-24. **Boson, G.** (1936) *Tavolette cuneiformi sumere degli archivi di Drehem e di Djoha dell'ultima dinastia di Ur.* Università Catolica del Sacro Cuore, Pubblicazioni, serie 12. Scienze orientali 2. Milan. **Castellino, G. R.** (1972) *Two Šulgi Hymns (BC).* Studi semitici 42. Rome. **Çiğ, M., H. Kizilyay, and A. Salonen** (1954) *Die Puzriš-Dagan-Texte der Istanbuler Archäologischen Museen, Teil 1: Nrr. 1-725.* Annales Academiae Scientiarum Fennicae B/92. Helsinki. **Civil, M.** (1979) Ea A = *nâqu,* Aa A = *nâqu, with Their Forerunners and Related Texts.* Materials for the Sumerian Lexicon 14. Rome. **Eidem, J.** (1992) *The Shemshāra Archives 2: The Administrative Texts.* Det Kongelige Danske Videnskabernes Selskab, Historisk-filosofiske Skrifter 15. Copenhagen. **Edzard, D. O., and G. Farber** (1974) *Die Orts- und Gewässernamen der Zeit der 3. Dynastie von Ur.* Répertoire géographique des textes cunéiformes 2. Beihefte zum Tübinger Atlas des Vorderen Orients, Reihe B (Geisteswissenschaften) 7. Wiesbaden. **Foster, B. R.** (1993) *Before the Muses: An Anthology of Akkadian Literature.* Bethesda. **Gelb, I. J.** (1944) *Hurrians and Subarians.* Studies in Ancient Oriental Civilization, No. 22. Chicago. (1957) *Glossary of Old Akkadian.* Materials for the Assyrian Dictionary 3. Chicago. (1961) *Old Akkadian Writing and Grammar.* Second edition. Materials for the Assyrian Dictionary 2. Chicago. **Gelb, I. J., P. Purves, and A. MacRae** (1943) *Nuzi Personal Names.* Oriental Institute Publications 57. Chicago. **Genouillac, H. de** (1911) *Tablettes de Dréhem publiées avec inventaire et tables.* Textes cunéiformes du Louvre 2. Paris. (1924) Choix de textes économiques de la collection Pupil. *Babyloniaca* 8: 37-40. **Goetze, A.** (1947a) *Old Babylonian Omen Texts.* Yale Oriental Series, Babylonian Texts 10. New Haven and London. (1947b) Historical Allusions in Old Babylonian Omen Texts. *Journal of Cuneiform Studies* 1: 253-65. **Gomi, T.** (1990) *Selected Neo-Sumerian Administrative Texts from the British Museum.* Abiko (Japan). **Hallo, W. W.** (1957) Review of M. Çiğ, H. Kizilyay, and A. Salonen, Die Puzriš-Dagan-Texte der Instanbuler Archäologischer Museen, Teil I. *Bibliotheca Orientalis* 14: 230-32. (1963-73) *Sumerian Archival Texts.* Tabulae cuneiformes a F. M. Th. de Liagre Böhl collectae, Leidae conservatae 3. Leiden. (1978) Simurrum and the Hurrian Frontier. *Revue hittite et asianique* 36: 71-83. (1991) The Death of Kings: Traditional Historiography in Contextual Perspective. In Mordechai Cogan and Israel Eph^{c}al, eds. *Ah, Assyria . . .: Studies in Assyrian History and Ancient Near Eastern Historiography Presented to Hayim Tadmor.* Scripta Hierosolymitana 33. 148-65. Jerusalem. **Hilgert, M.** (forth.) *Drehem Administrative Documents from the Reign of Šulgi.* Economic Texts of the Ur III Period in the Oriental Institute 1. Chicago. **Jones, T. B., and J. W. Snyder** (1961) *Sumerian Economic Documents from the Third Ur Dynasty.* Minneapolis. **Kang, S.** (1972) *Sumerian Economic Texts from the Drehem Archive.* Sumerian and

Akkadian Cuneiform Texts in the Collection of the World Heritage Museum of the University of Illinois 1. Urbana, Chicago, and London. **Keiser, C. E.** (1971) *Neo-Sumerian Account Texts from Drehem.* Babylonian Inscriptions in the Collection of James B. Nies 3. New Haven and London. **Klein, J.** (1981) *Three Šulgi Hymns: Sumerian Royal Hymns Glorifying King Šulgi of Ur.* Ramat-Gan. **Molina, M.** (1993) *Tabillas administrativas neosumerias de la Abadía de Montserrat (Barcelona) copias cuneiformes.* Materiali per il vocabolario neosumerico 18. Rome. **Nashef, Kh.** (1982) Der Ṭaban-Fluss. *Baghdader Mitteilungen* 13: 117-41. **Sallaberger, W.** (1993) *Der kultische Kalender der Ur III-Zeit.* Berlin and New York. **Salvini, M.** (1996) *The Ḫabiru Prism of King Tunip-Teššup of Tikunani.* Documenta Asiana 3. Rome. **Schneider, N.** (1930) Die Geschäftsurkunden aus Drehem und Djoḫa in den Staatlichen Museen (VAT) zu Berlin. *Orientalia* 47-49. (1932) *Die Drehem- und Djoḫa-Texte im Kloster Montserrat (Barcelona).* Analecta Orientalia 7. Rome. **Sigrist, M.** (1990) *Tablettes du Princeton Theological Seminary Epoque d'Ur III.* Occasional Publications of the Samuel Noah Kramer Fund 10. Philadelphia. (1992) *Drehem.* Bethesda. (1995) *The Administration at Drehem.* Neo-Sumerian Texts from the Royal Ontario Museum 1. Bethesda. **Sigrist, M., and T. Gomi** (1991) *The Comprehensive Catalogue of Published Ur III Tablets.* Bethesda. **Steinkeller, P.** (1981) More on the Ur III Royal Wives. *Acta Sumerologica* 3: 77-92. **Wilhelm, G.** (1996) L'état actuel et les perspectives des études hourrites. In Jean-Marie Durand, ed., *Mari, Ébla et les Hourrites: dix ans de travaux.* Amurru 1: 175-87. Paris. **Wiseman, D. J., and J. A. Black** (1996) *Literary Texts from the Temple of Nabû.* Cuneiform Texts from Nimrud 4. London. **Yildiz, F., and T. Gomi** (1988) *Die Puzriš-Dagan-Texte der Istanbuler Archäologischen Museen, Teil II: Nr. 726-1379.* Freiburger Altorientalische Studien 16. Stuttgart. **Zadok, R.** (1993) Hurrians as well as Individuals Bearing Hurrian and Strange Names in Sumerian Sources. In A. F. Rainey, ed., kinattūtu ša dārâti: *Raphael Kutscher Memorial Volume.* 219-45. Tel Aviv.

Naṣbum in the Khana Contracts from Terqa*

Mark W. Chavalas
University of Wisconsin-La Crosse

Khana legal contracts, which have been known for a century,[1] contain certain clauses which have been considered unique, with no definite parallels yet known.[2] The unique features in the Khana contracts are found predominantly in those concerning transfer of real estate.[3] A recurring formula in these texts is *naṣbum*[4] *ša lā baqrim u lā*

* I dedicate this paper to Michael C. Astour, whom I have come to regard as a friend and colleague. In the many times we have shared a room at conferences, I have been impressed by the depth and breadth of his knowledge of the ancient Mediterranean and Near Eastern worlds. I want to thank the University of Wisconsin-La Crosse for a Small Research Grant which helped in the completion of this paper, as well as J. Platt, J. Hayes, G. Beckman, and K. Veenhof, all of whom made suggestions on various portions of this work. I delivered a draft of this research at the 1991 meeting of the American Oriental Society (Berkeley, 5 March).

Abbreviation list: GC: Buccellati, *et al.* (1984); M: tablets in the collections of the Bayerische Staatsbibliothek, Munich; RBC: tablets in the Rosen Babylonian Collection; TFR: Rouault (1984).

1 Since Thureau-Dangin (1897). For the Khana contracts and the Khana period in general, see Goetze (1957); Rouault (1984); Buccellati, Podany, and Rouault (1984); Buccellati (1987); Chavalas (1988) 343-78; and Podany (1988) 252-77. For Old Babylonian contracts in general and loan contracts in particular, see Skaist (1994) 172-80.

2 Podany (1988) 254. See n. 25 for the possibility that some of the Khana terms were used at Mari. For research in part concerning the Mari contracts, see Charpin (1990).

3 Podany (1988) 255.

4 The infinitive *naṣābu*, "to suck" (*cf.* CAD N/2 33), as well as the related substantive

andurārim, a phrase meant to describe properties, first recognized by Thureau-Dangin in 1897 in a Khana contract concerning a bequest of a house by King Išar-Lim to one of his servants.[5] Thureau-Dangin provided a partial translation,[6] but could not make satisfactory resolution of the phrase, and thus left *nazb(p)um*, a term used as an adjective associated with *bītum*, untranslated.[7] More Khana contracts were discovered by Thureau-Dangin,[8] Ungnad,[9] and Bauer,[10] who all left *naṣbum* without a translation.

---

naṣṣabu, "water outlet, or drain pipe" (*cf.* CAD N/2 52-53), are both attested from the Old Babylonian period. There is no evidence, however, that the Khana term *naṣbum* has a related meaning ("irrigated field") since it is associated with other types of property.

5 (1897) 85-86; AO 2673 = GC1: 1, and Kohler and Ungnad (1909) 128; #458, who give a translation with no commentary; Thureau-Dangin (1910) n. 237, who provides a cuneiform copy; and Schorr (1910) 302, n. 219, who gives a transliteration and translation, but with no commentary on the phrase. *Naṣbum* is normally spelled *na*-AZ-BU-*um*, but also has the variant readings: (a) *na*-AZ-BU-*ú*-*um*, Rouault (1984) 36; TFR 1 6: 20; (b) *na*-AZ-BA-*am*, *idem.* 10,14; TFR 1 2: 10, TFR 1 2E (envelope), and without mimation; and (c) *na*-AZ-BU: M 1 = Bauer (1928/29) 5, obv. 18. Because of comparisons with other Semitic languages which have *nṣb*, I have transcribed the root in Akkadian as *naṣbum*, although *nasbum* and *nazbum* are possible.

6 Also, *cf.* *TCL* 1 n. 237.

7 (1897) 85. This is still the case for the lexical entry *nazbum* in CAD N/2 141, where it is described as a legal term of real estate. In 1990, Charpin wrote, "Sans doubte le cle de cette clause se trouve-t-elle dans le qualificatif *naZBum* accole au champ, que l'on ne comprend malheureusment toujours pas" (p. 262, n. 34).

8 This was a Khana contract concerning the sale of a field dated to the period of Kashtiliashu (1909) 149-54; AO 4656. The cuneiform text was published by Thureau-Dangin (1910) n. 238. (Also, *cf.* Ungnad [1909a] 151-54: obv. 28-29; Schorr [1910] 266; and Kohler and Ungnad [1911] n. 1150.) Thureau-Dangin again left the term *nazb(p)um* untranslated, stating that the meaning of the term was uncertain, but that it might be equivalent to *ša lā andurāri.* He understood the term to be about real estate in general (associated with *eqlum* or *bītum*), and translated the phrase *eqlum* (or *bītum*) *naṣbum* as "la maison, le champ tributaire" (1909) 154. San Nicolò also saw this (1922) 22, 163, n. 4.

9 In the same year as Thureau-Dangin (1909), Ungnad published another Khana contract, a bequest of field of a certain Ammi-Madar ([1909a] 82, n. 204; GC1: 4 = VAT 6685). Ungnad also published the cuneiform text ([1909b] 26-32; *cf.* Kohler and Ungnad [1909] 128-29 #459 [#458, 459, 775], and [1911] #1150 all have *ša lā baqrim u lā andruārim* without the term *naṣbum*]). Ungnad, like Thureau-Dangin, was

Bauer,[11] however, was the first to propose that it was derived from a West Semitic root,[12] which was echoed by J. Lewy years later.[13]

The purpose of this paper is to determine the meaning of *naṣbum*, by reevaluating its meaning in the context of the Khana contracts, considering its etymology in other Semitic languages, and by noting its similar usage to related phrases in Akkadian.

The term *naṣbum*, of course, cannot be separated from its context in the Khana contracts. Other than the previously mentioned attestations, *naṣbum* was found once more before excavations began at Terqa in 1975,[14]

---

unable to make complete sense of the phrase (obv. 30-32), and referred back to Thureau-Dangin's article of twelve years earlier ([1897] 31, n. 30).

10 Bauer (1928-29) proposed that *nazbum* was "ostkanaanäisch" (5, z. 18, obv. 18-19). M1 = GC1: 17; the text is possibly the same as Sayce (1912) 52 in a contract for the sale of a house. Bauer (1928-29) 5 considered that *nazbum* may be a synonym for Akkadian *zakû.*

11 Two years earlier he noted a Hebrew root *nṣb*, which he translated as "einsetzen" (in the PN Ia-aṣ-ṣi-ib-Dagan; [1926] 32, 79) but made no connection between this root and the Khana term.

12 Evidence of a Northwest Semitic origin for *naṣbum* and its derivatives is found in a wide chronological and geographical sphere, ranging from the third millennium B.C. to the present. In most cases, the term has the basic meaning "stand," "set," or "establish":

I. *Canaanite:* {a} *Amorite* [Gelb (1980) 166, 335]; {b} *Ugaritic* [Gordon (1955) 77: 34, 107: 7, 125: 52, 127: 25, 27, 446: 1685]; {c} *Phoenician* [Harris (1936) 125]; {d} *El-Amarna* [EA 147: 11, 148: 42, 151: 42]; {e} *Biblical Hebrew* [Gen 18: 2, 37: 7, Ex 7: 15, 15: 18]).

II. *Aramaic:* {a} *Nabatean* [Cantineau (1930) 122]; {b} *Mandaic* [Fitzmeyer and Harrington (1978) 320, #108]; {c} *Samaritan* [Ben-Hayyim (1967) 8]; {d} *Ma'lūla* [Spitaler, (1967) 91].

III. *Southwest Semitic:* {a} *Arabic* [H. Wehr (1976) 968-69]; {b} *Sabean* [Biella (1982) 311].

IV. *Northeast Semitic:* {a} *Old Akkadian* [Gelb (1957) 205-7]; {b} *Emar* [Arnaud (1985) 215: 22]).

13 Lewy (1958) 21*-31* referred to *nazbum* (p. 24*, n. 33) and believed it could be compared to West Semitic roots, since in this period a good part of the population of Khana may have been Western Semitic.

14 Thureau-Dangin and P. Dhorme conducted archaeological investigations at Terqa for five days in 1923 (pp. 265- 93). They found no tablets, but did publish a number

in a Khana contract concerning a garden (KIRI$_6$; Akkadian: *kirû*) published by Nougayrol in 1960.[15] Since then, more than one dozen contracts have been uncovered by the recent excavations at Terqa that exhibit the phrase *naṣbum ša lā baqrim u lā andurārim.*[16] Rouault, following Thureau-Dangin, has left *naṣbum* untranslated.[17] All the excavated contracts deal with fields.[18] In one instance,[19] *naṣbum* is found without *ša lā baqrim u lā andurārim*, and instead, is juxtaposed with the Sumerian phrase šám.til.la.bi.sè ("for its full price"). More recently, G. Beckman has observed a text identified as a Khana contract,[20] where the phrase is applied to an adopted son, and is perhaps part of an adoption proceeding.[21] Also, H. Kümmel has published a Middle Assyrian text reputedly coming from Terqa or its surroundings that employs the legal terminology in question.[22] In this case, however,

of texts which had reputedly come from this site. The Joint Expedition, directed by G. Buccellati and M. Kelly-Buccellati, began operations in 1976, with O. Rouault (who has published the excavated Khana texts [1984]) becoming field director in 1987.

15 1960; GC1: 22 = location unknown. Nougayrol added no new information about the item "*nazbum*," except that it was associated with various types of property (*eqlum*, *bītum*, and *kirûm*; other items, such as *ṭuppum* and *mārum*, would be found in more recently discovered texts; see notes 21- 23).

16 Rouault (1979), (1984). Rouault's publication (1984) was concerned with texts coming from the 1976-79 seasons. There are at least two more excavated Khana texts employing *naṣbum* and the subsequent phraseology. These have yet to be published (see n. 24).

17 Rouault (1979) 6 l.16, Roualt (1984) 9, l.16.

18 *Cf.* Rouault (1979) 2, 9 l. 1′, where the phrase has survived in part without *naṣbum.* In one case *andurārum* is spelled as *uddurārim*; TFR 1: 1: 16-17, Rouault (1984) 6. Another text, which is a legal contract concerning the sale of a house for its full price, does not contain this legal terminology: TFR 1 5; Rouault (1984) 28.

19 TFR 1 2: 10-11; Rouault (1984) 10.

20 Podany, Beckman, and Kolbow (1991-93).

21 RBC 779: 11′-12′; DUMU *na-az-bu ša la ba-aq-ri / ù la an-du-ra-ri.*

22 Kümmel (1989) especially pp. 197-99. The relevant phrase (obv. 22-24) is *ṭuppu na-az-bu ša* [*la*]*-a ba-aq-ri u l*[*a*]-[*a*] AMA-AR-GI. Although the cylinder seal on the text is dated on stylistic grounds to the late Old Babylonian period, the text itself is written in the Middle Assyrian script and is dated to the eponym of a Libur-zanin-Assur, a name which is found during the reigns of Tukulti-Ninurta I and Shalmaneser I (13th-

naṣbu(m) is applied to a tablet (*ṭup-pu*). Based upon TFR 1 6: 20, where *naṣbum* is written *na*-AZ-*bu-ú-um*, Kümmel suggested either *sb'* (*saba'um* "schwanken"; *i.e.*, incontestable), or *ṣb'* (*ṣaba'um* "ziehen" *i.e.*, cultivated, in regards to a field) as possible roots for the term. Kümmel noticed that *ṣaba'um* was often concerned with military service (*i.e.*, *naṣbum* was then property granted in return for military service). However, *naṣbum* has been attested as *na-aṣ-bu-ú-um* in only a single case thus far, and so the suggestions of these alternative roots is problematic. Moreover, Kümmel postulated that *naṣbum* (if the root is derived from *ṣb'*) could have had a usage similar to *ilkum* and *dikûtum*. However, these terms were used in a narrower sense concerning corvée labor, and were not concerned with property in general. In spite of this, the Middle Assyrian text shows that the phrase had a wider chronological distribution than once thought.[23]

In sum, the *naṣbum* legal phrase (*ša lā baqrim u lā andurārim*) has been found at least twenty times in the published Khana contracts.[24] Most of these occurrences have involved fields, but there were also two houses, one garden, one tablet, and an adoption. There is also an unclear reference in a list of transactions at Mari (KÙ.UD *an-né-em iš-qú-ul* / *u na-aṣ-ba-am iṣ-ṣí-ib-*[*šu*]).[25] The *naṣbum* phrase (*ša lā baqrim u lā andurārim*) seems then to have been used for various types of acquired property.[26] Some of these

---

12th centuries, B.C.E.; *cf.* C. Saporetti [1979] 105).

23 Podany has begun a re-evaluation of the chronology of the Khana period (1991-93), and a larger treatment on the subject (forthcoming).

24 There are at least two occurrences of this phrase in un-published Khana texts excavated since the 1978 season. (I wish to thank Giorgio Buccellati for access to this material.) More Khana texts have been discovered by Rouault after 1987 (see Rouault 1991, 1992, 1994, 1996) and Rouault *et al.* (1997). Rouault has informed me that many of the contracts found since 1990 use *naṣbum* and related terms, but these occurrences do not seem to alter the findings of this paper.

25 Kupper (1983) 328: II 1-2. Also see Charpin (1987). It is tempting to postulate that *iṣṣib* stems from *naṣābum*, although there is no hard evidence for the existence of this verb. Based upon the Khana texts, Charpin (1990) 264 has reconstructed the term *naZBum* in a fragmented Mari contract concerning a field (ARM VIII 6, 7′: [*na-aZ-B*]*u-um* A-ŠÀ *la ú-da-ra-*[*ri-im*]).

26 Podany (1988) 255.

contracts are donations from the Crown, but the application of the phrase does not appear to be different from its use in other contracts.[27]

In a typical Khana contract concerning the sale of a field, the dimensions and location of the field are given, then both the buyer, seller, and terms of sale are noted. In the contracts with *naṣbum ša lā baqrim u lā andurārim*, the buyer has paid the complete price for the property (Sum. šám.til.la.bi.sè), after which the property is described as *naṣbum.*

Naṣbum ša lā baqrim u lā andurārim is often followed by *baqir ibaqqaru* ("one who formulates a claim").[28] *Andurārum* (from *darāru* "to become free"[29]) is normally concerned with the remission of debts or manumission.[30] Although the terminology in the Khana texts is the same, the inferred meaning appears somewhat different, since *andurārum* is used in connection with real estate, indicating that in some circumstances the Crown released purchased property back to its original owner, invalidating the real estate transaction.[31]

---

27 Khana contracts that have *naṣbum* and related terms and, in fact, involve donations include AO 2673 (*cf.* Thureau-Dangin [1897] 85-86), a donation by King Išar-Lim, and VAT 6685 (*cf.* Ungnad [1909a] 82), a bequest of King Ammi-madar.

28 *Cf.* Buccellati (1991) 93-94; Podany (1988) 255; and AHw 104; *paqāru.* Buccellati understands *eqel lā baqrim* as referring to a field (or property) which is declared to have a title clear of repossession limitations.

29 CAD D: 109; Meissner (1910) 539 #4275. *Darāru* is also found in Hebrew; *derôr* and Arabic, Lewy (1958) 21*.

30 Sumerian ama.ar.gi; Edzard (1957) 91, n. 445; Deimel (1930) 481 no. 52; Weidner (1936) 120; Driver and Miles (1952) 224; Westbrook (1971) 210-17; Lemche (1979) 15-21); Kraus (1984) 99; and Charpin (1987), (1990).

31 CAD A/2 115-17, AHw 51. *Baqārum* may be the result of private initiative, while *andurārum* the result of state intervention (Buccellati [1991] 94-95). It is now known that the Khana texts are not unique with regard to the usage of *andurārum* in contracts; *cf.* M.11264 and A.2654, Mari contracts published by Charpin (1990) 256; also see *idem.* (1987) 38a. A.2654 also exhibits the phrase, KÙ-BABBAR *la ud-du-ra-ri-im* (line 2), which Charpin believes may be similar in function to A-ŠÀ *ša la ba-aq-ri-im.* Kraus lists six contracts from Alalakh that also exhibit *andurārum* (for references and variants, see [1984]107). These contain the phrase, KÙ-BABBAR *šu-ú ú-ul ú-ṣa-ab ù ú-ul it-ta-ra-ar.* The usage of *andurārum* in the context of contracts was apparently widespread.

Andurārum was in use in the Old Babylonian, Old Assyrian, and Middle Assyrian periods concerning the lifting of trade restrictions.[32] Because of the *naṣbum* clause in the Khana period, landed property was probably not liable to reversion to its former owner; thus, property could not be repossessed as a result of a royal edict pertaining to a remission of debts.[33] The parties involved at Khana (*i.e.*,Terqa) agreed that the law of release would be inoperative in their case. The buyer may not have been subject to *andurārum* since the property was paid for in full; all of the properties in the aforementioned Khana texts are paid for in full (this, of course, was the norm in most cuneiform records of sales).[34] If the sale was forfeited, it would normally go back to the original owner.[35] A buyer who has paid the full price indicates that he wishes to acquire absolute property, and the seller's acceptance of the full price implies his readiness to part with his property once and for all.[36] Sales contracts concerning the payment of the full price appear to involve sellers resolved not to recover their former property. Although the Khana kings may have seen it as their duty to enact *andurārum* (enabling the impoverished to recover their landed estates) immovable properties were exempted from release. This may as well clarify the nature of the donations previously mentioned.[37]

What, then, is the meaning of *naṣbum* in the context of the Khana contracts? We have seen that it is used in reference to various types of immovable property, as well as in part of an adoption formula. Lewy's idea that the term signified "possession" or "landed estate" is thus too generic and not specific enough.[38] In context with the remainder of the legal

---

32 Lewy (1958) 23*; a more recent and detailed study of *andurārum* (*addurārum*) has been made by Larsen (1976) 65-80.

33 See Buccellati (1991) 94-95.

34 Sumerian, šám.til.la.bi.sè ("for its full price").

35 Without the clause: *ANET* 184: 44; Driver and Miles (1987) 287; David (1952) 170; and Koschaker (1928) 104.

36 Lewy (1958) 26*.

37 Lewy (1958) 29*; AO 4656, M1, *etc.*

38 Lewy (1958) 24*.

formula at Terqa, Thureau-Dangin may have been correct in assuming that *naṣbum* was synonymous with *ša lā baqrim u lā andurārim.*[39] As we have seen, property which was considered *ša lā baqrim u lā andurārim* was not liable to reversion to the former owner, *i.e.*, the law of *andurārum* was not in force.[40] The sold property remained with the new owner, who had paid the full price for the acquisition.[41] The owner need not worry about the property being recovered by the original owners, since it was now *naṣbum* property, which was guaranteed, or irrevocable.[42] The determination of *naṣbum* as meaning irrevocable in the Khana contracts can be verified by comparing it to related expressions in Akkadian.[43] In sum, the phrase *naṣbum ša lā baqrim u lā andurārim* may best be understood as irrevocable property (not only land) which could not be repossessed, either by means of a private claim (*baqārum*) or a state edict (*andurārum*).[44]

39 (1909) 153-54.

40 Buccellati (1991) 94-95.

41 Similar to its use in Psalm 119: 89, "Forever, O LORD, thy word is firmly fixed in the heavens."

42 On *naṣbum* as property guaranteed by a clear title, see Buccellati (1991) 94-95.

43 *E.g.*, compare with *ṣamit* clause in the Akkadian documents from Ugarit (*ṣamit adi/ana dārīti* "alienated forever"; *cf.* CAD Ṣ 93-95 *s.v. ṣamātu*), which was concerned with land that was permanently unredeemable (see Westbrook [1991] 113-15). The *šūduti* clause from Nuzi is also similar (*ina arki sūduti ina pāni abulli šaṭir*; *e.g.*, *HSS* 5, 56; 5, 60; 19,16 146; *JEN* 4, 345; 5, 470, 485), and is paralleled with *andurāru* (*HSS* 19, 118: 17; *HSS* 9, 103: 30; *AASOR* 10 [1928-29] 12).

44 Buccellati (1991) 94-95. It is not clear what happened to *naṣbum* property after it was inherited, or whether it was associated primarily with the *awīlum* or *muškēnum* class.

Bibliography

Arnaud, D. (1985) *Recherches au pays d'Aštata: Textes sumérians, et accadiens, Emar* VI, 1, 3. Paris. **Bauer, T.** (1926) *Die Ostkanaanäer.* Leipzig. (1928/29) Neues Material zur 'Amoriter'-Frage. *Mitteilungen der Altorientalischen Gesellschaft* 4: 1-8. **Ben-Hayyim, Z.** (1967) Samaritan Glossary. In Rosenthal 1967: 1-12. **Biella, J.** (1982) *Dictionary of Old South Arabic-Sabaean Dialect.* Harvard Semitic Series 25. Chico, Calif. **Buccellati, G.** (1987) The Kingdom and Period of Khana. *Bulletin of the American Schools of Oriental Research* 270: 43-61. (1991) A Note on the Muškēnum as a Homesteader. In Ratner, *et al.* 1991: 91-100. **Buccellati, G., A. Podany, and O. Rouault** (1984) *Terqa Data Bases I. Old Babylonian and Khana Texts through the Fourth Season of Excavation,* GC I. **Cantineau, J.** (1930) *Le Nabatean* II. Paris. **Charpin, D.** (1987) Les Décrets Royaux à l'époque paléo-babylonienne à propos d'un ouvrage récent. *Archiv für Orientforschung* 34: 36-44. (1990) L'Andurārum à Mari. *Mari, Annales de Recherches Interdisciplinaires* 6: 253-70. **Chavalas, M.** (1988) *The House of Puzurum.* Ph.D. dissertation, UCLA. **David, M.** (1952) Eine Bestimmung über das Verfallspfand in den mittelassyrischen Gesetzen. *Bibliotheca Orientalis* 9: 170-72. **Deimel, A.** (1930) *Šumerisches Lexikon* II. Rome. **Driver, G., and J. Miles** (1952) *The Babylonian Laws* I. Oxford. (1987) *The Assyrian Laws.* Oxford. **Edzard, D. O.** (1957) *Die 'Zwiete Zwischenzeit' Babyloniens.* Wiesbaden. **Fitzmeyer, J., and J. Harrington** (1978) *A Manual of Palestinian Aramaic Texts.* Rome. **Gelb, I. J.** (1957) *Glossary of Old Akkadian.* Materials for the Assyrian Dictionary 3. (1980) *Computer-Aided Analysis of Amorite.* Assyriological Studies 21. Chicago. **Goetze, A.** (1957) On the Chronology of the Second Millennium B.C. *Journal of Cuneiform Studies* 11: 53-73. **Gordon, C.** (1955) *Ugaritic Manual.* Analecta Orientalia 35. **Harris, Z. S.** (1936) *A Grammar of the Phoenician Language.* American Oriental Series 8. New Haven. **Johns, C.** (1907) A Marriage Contract from the Chabour. *Proceedings of the Society of Biblical Archaeology* 29: 177-84. **Kohler, J., and A. Ungnad** (1909) *Hammurabis Gesetz* III. Leipzig. (1911) *Hammurabis Gesetz* V. Leipzig. **Koschaker, P.** (1928) *Neue keilschriftliche Rechtsurkunden aus der El-Amarna-Zeit.* Leipzig. **Kraus, F. R.** (1984) *Königliche Verfüngen in altbabylonischer Zeit.* Studia et documenta ad iura Orientis Antiqui pertinentia XI. **Kümmel, H.** (1989) Ein Kaufvertrag aus Hana mit mittelassyrischer Līmu-Datierung. *Zeitschrift für Assyriologie* 79: 191-200. **Kupper, J. R.** (1983) *Documents adminstratifs de la salle 135 du palais de Mari.* Archives royales de Mari, texts. XXII/1, 2. **Larsen, M. T.** (1976) *The Old Assyrian City-State and its Colonies.* Mesopotamia 4. Copenhagen. **Lemche, N.** (1984) Andurārum and Mišārum: Comments on the Problem of Social Edicts and their Application in the Ancient Near East. *Journal of Near Eastern Studies* 38: 11-22. **Lewy, J.** (1958) The Biblical Institution of Derôr in the Light of Akkadian Documents. *Eretz Israel* 5: 21*-31*. **Meissner, B.** (1910) *Seltene assyrische Ideogramme.* Leipzig. **Nougayrol, J.** (1960) Documents du Ḫabur. *Syria* 37: 205-14. **Podany, A.** (1988) *The Chronology and History of the Ḫana Period.* Ph.D. dissertation, UCLA. (1991/93) A Middle Babylonian Date for the Ḫana Kingdom. *Journal of Cuneiform Studies* 43: 53-62. (forth.) *Kings of Ḫana: An Analysis of their Time and Place in Syro-Mesopotamian History.*

Bibliotheca Mesopotamica. Malibu, Calif. **Podany, A., G. Beckman, and G. Kolbow** (1991/93 An Adoption and Inheritance Contract from the Reign of Iggid-Lim of Ḫana. *Journal of Cuneiform Studies* 43: 39-51. **Ratner, R. J., *et al.***, eds. (1991) *Let Your Colleagues Praise You: Studies in Memory of Stanley Gevirtz, Maarav* 7. **Rosenthal, F.**, ed. (1967) *An Aramaic Handbook*, II/2. Wiesbaden. **Rouault, O.** (1979) *Terqa Preliminary Reports 7. Les documents épigraphiques de la troisième saison.* Syro-Mesopotamian Studies 2/7. Malibu, Calif. (1984) *Terqa Final Reports 1. L'archive de Puzurum.* Bibliotheca Mesopotamica 16. Malibu, Calif. (1991) Terqa. In Weiss 1991, "Archaeology in Syria," *American Journal of Archaeology* 95: 727-29. (1992) Cultures locales et influences extérieures: la cas de Terqa. *Studi micenei ed egeo-anatolici* XXX 247-56. (1994) Terqa. In H. Weiss, "Archaeology in Syria," *American Journal of Archaeology* 98: 142-43. (1996) Terqa et l'époque des Šakkanakku. In Tunça and Deheselle 1996. **Roualt, O., *et al.*** (1997) Terqa: Rapport Préliminaire (1987-1989), *MARI* 8: 71-103. **San Nicolò, M.** (1922) *Die Schlussklauseln der altbabylonischen Kauf-und Tausch-vertrage* Munich. **Saporetti, C.** (1979) *Gli eponomi medio-assiri.* Bibliotheca Mesopotamica 9. Malibu, Calif. **Sayce, A.** (1912) A New Date from the Kingdom of Khana. *Proceedings of the Society of Biblical Archaeology* 34: 16, 52. **Schorr, M.** (1910) Ein Kaufkontrakt aus Ḫana. *Babyloniaca* 3: 266-67. (1913) *Urkunden des altbabylonischen Zivil- und Prozessrechts.* Leipzig. **Skaist, A.** (1994) *The Old Babylonian Loan Contract: Its History and Geography.* Ramat Gan, Israel. **Spitaler, A.** (1967) The Aramaic Dialect of Ma'lūla: Glossary. In Rosenthal 1967: 82-96. **Thureau-Dangin, F.** 1897) Tablets chaldeénes inedites. *Revue d'assyriologie et d'archéologie orientale* 4: 69-86. (1909) Un contrat de Ḫana. *Journal asiatique* (10th series) 14: 149-55. (1910) *Lettres et contracts de l'époque de la première dynastie babylonienne.* Textes cunéiformes du Louvre 1. Paris. **Thureau-Dangin F., and P. Dhorme** (1923) Cinq jours de fouilles à 'Asharah'. *Syria* 5: 265-93. **Tunça, Ö and D. Deheselle**, eds. (1996) *Tablettes et images aux pays de Sumer et d'Akkad, Mélanges offerts au Professeur H. Limet. Liège* **Ungnad, A.** (1909a) *Altbabylonische Urkunden.* Vorderasiatische Bibliothek VII. Leipzig. (1909b) Zur Geschichte der Nachbarstaaten Babyloniens zur Zeit der Hammurapi-Dynastie. 4. Ḫana. *Beiträge zur Assyriologie* VI/5: 26-32. **Wehr, H.** (1976) *A Dictionary of Modern Written Arabic.* Ithaca. **Weidner, E.** (1936) Ilušumas Zug nach Babylonien. *Zeitschrift für Assyriologie* 43: 114-23. **Westbrook, R.** (1971) Jubilee Laws. *Israel Law Review* 6: 209-25. (1991) *Property and Family in Biblical Law.* Sheffield, UK.

Achilles in Anatolia: Myth, History, and the Aššuwa Rebellion

Eric H. Cline
Xavier University

I am delighted to have been asked to participate in this session honoring Michael Astour.[1] Dr. Astour's learned work on Interconnections has long been an inspiring example, such as his 1966 article in *American Journal of Archaeology* on the "Aegean List" of Amenhotep III, his 1964 article in *Journal of Near Eastern Studies* on Greek names in the Semitic world and Semitic names in the Greek world, and his various articles on connections between Ugarit and the Bronze Age Aegean. The second, revised, edition of his book *Hellenosemitica* was particularly thought-provoking and served as a catalyst first during my graduate studies and then during the writing of my own book, *Sailing the Wine-Dark Sea.*[2] Over the years, Dr. Astour's work has continued to provoke and inspire all those involved in the field of Interconnections, showing the possibilities inherent in combining mythology, linguistics, history, and archaeology.

The present paper had its origins during the summer of 1992, when I was first alerted by Dr. Judith Binder to the existence of a possible Mycenaean

---

1 I would like to thank Gordon D. Young, Mark W. Chavalas, and Richard E. Averbeck for the invitation to participate in these proceedings. Acknowledgments cited in the first footnote of Cline (1996) are herein reiterated, with thanks in particular to the following: R. H. Beal, J. Binder, T. R. Bryce, B. J. Collins, C. D. Fortenberry, O. R. Gurney, V. D. Hanson, D. Harris, J. P. Holoka, G. L. Huxley, J. Klinger, R. Maxwell-Hyslop, J. D. Muhly, A. E. Raubitschek, P. Rehak, N. K. Sandars, A. and S. Sherratt, T. F. Strasser, A. Ünal, E. T. Vermeule, J. Younger, and E. Zangger.

2 Astour (1964), (1966), (1967), (1973), (1981); Cline (1994).

sword which had been found in 1991 at Hattušaš, capital city of the Hittites. On the blade of the bronze sword is an inscription in Akkadian which states that it was dedicated at Hattušaš by Tudhaliya II following his successful quelling of the Aššuwa rebellion in northwestern Anatolia *c.* 1430 BCE:

> *i-nu-ma* ^{m}*Du-ut-ḫa-li-ya* LUGAL.GAL KUR ^{URU}*A-aš-šu-wa ú-ḫal-liq* GÍR$^{ḪI.A}$ *an-nu-tim a-na* ^{D}*Iškur be-lì-šu ú-še-li*
>
> As Duthaliya the Great King shattered the Aššuwa-Country, he dedicated these swords to the Storm-God, his Lord.[3]

Once having ascertained to my satisfaction that the sword might well be of Mycenaean manufacture, or at least reflects substantial Mycenaean influence, I began to research what possible connection there could be between the Bronze Age Aegean and the coalition of northwestern Anatolian states known as Aššuwa. The majority of my findings concerning possible Mycenaean involvement in the Aššuwa rebellion against the Hittites *c.* 1430 BCE will appear in an article to be published in *Annual of the British School at Athens*, but I would like to take this opportunity to enlarge upon some of the issues raised in that paper, to further explore a few fascinating, yet rather more speculative, issues connected with this topic, and to dedicate my discussions to Michael Astour.[4]

Aššuwa in Late Bronze Age Texts

The coalition of twenty-two northwest Anatolian city-states known as Aššuwa appears to have been located immediately south of the Troad, with its lower border at the Caicus River (see discussion below).[5] Although in existence only briefly, before its demise came at the hands of Tudhaliya II *c.* 1430 BCE,[6] Aššuwa apparently was known to several of the major powers

---

3 Translation and transliteration following Ünal *et al.* (1991) 51; Ünal (1993) 727-28; Ertekin and Ediz (1993) 721. *Cf.* Cline (1996) for full references and further discussion.

4 Cline (1996); the present reader is invited to peruse the two papers in concert.

5 See Cline (1996) for full discussion and references.

6 As noted in Cline (1996) n. 31, it is conceivable that Aššuwa may have had a longer

of the time, for references to Aššuwa are found in Hittite, Aegean, and Egyptian records.

Most of the Hittite references to Aššuwa, of which there are six, are directly concerned with the Rebellion.[7] The texts in question have been the focus of re-dating efforts in the recent past and are now all generally accepted as either dating from the time of Tudhaliya II (*c.* 1450–1420 BCE) or as later references to events occurring during his reign.[8] The Annals of Tudhaliya II (KUB XXIII 11 ii 13-39, iii 9-10) provide the most information, recording that the rebellion apparently began *c.* 1430 BCE as Tudhaliya was returning from a military campaign against the west Anatolian polities of Arzawa, Hapalla and the Seha River Land (KUB XXIII 11 ii 2-12).[9] Tudhaliya defeated the Aššuwa coalition quickly, and took the Aššuwan king(?) Piyama-^{d}KAL, his son Kukkuli, 10,000 Aššuwan soldiers, and 600 teams of horses with their Aššuwan charioteers back to Hattušaš as prisoners of war and booty. Aššuwa was then reestablished, this time as a vassal state to the Hittite Kingdom, with Kukkuli in place as a subject king. But rebellion broke out again. This second attempt at revolt also failed. Kukkuli was put to death, and the coalition of Aššuwa was destroyed.

In the Bronze Age Aegean, there are a number of possible references to Aššuwa in both Linear A and Linear B texts.[10] Within Linear A texts on Crete, *a-su-ja* is likely to be related to Aššuwa; if so, it may well be a contem-

---

life span, if the coalition were formed sometime *prior* to the reign of Tudhaliya II; but there are no data currently available to support such a suggestion, for there are no known documents which deal with this area of Anatolia from the time of Ammuna (c. 1550 BCE) until that of Tudhaliya II, a period of nearly 100 years (R. H. Beal, E-mail communication, 14 March 1994).

7 KUB XXIII 11; KUB XXVI 91; KUB XL 62 I + XIII 9; KUB XXIII 14 II:9; KUB XXXIV 43:10; and the text on the sword at Hattušaš. *Cf.* Cline (1996) for full discussions and *cf.* previously the compilation in del Monte and Tischler (1978) 52-53. A seventh text, KBo XII 53 rev. 7′, is mentioned by del Monte and Tischler, but appears to have little, if any, direct relevance.

8 On the re-dating, *cf.* summary by Easton (1984) 30-34; *idem* (1985) 189.

9 Full transliteration and translation in Carruba (1977) 158-61.

10 *Cf.* Cline (1996) for full discussion, references, and tablet numbers.

porary reference. In Linear B tablets found at Mycenae, Pylos, and Knossos, *a-si-wi-ja*, *a-si-wi-jo*, *a-si-ja-ti-ja*, *a-*64-ja*, and *a-*64-jo* may all be references to Aššuwa. Although Aššuwa had ceased to exist well before the time of most of these tablets, it seems to have already bequeathed its name to that particular area of Anatolia and beyond, for it is now fairly certain that the name 'Aššuwa' gave rise to the Greek name 'Asia' ('*Aššuwa*' = Hittite *A-aš-šu-wa* ⇒ '*Aswiā*' = Linear B *A-si-wi-ja* and other variations ⇒ Greek 'Ασια = '*Asia*'). 'Asia', as used by later Greek authors, originally referred only to the region of Lydia, but was later extended to include most of West Anatolia.[11]

An additional, tentative, textual link between the Bronze Age Aegean and Aššuwa might be found in a letter (KUB XXVI 91) sent by Arnuwanda I (or, alternatively, either Mursili II or Muwatalli) to an unknown king. The letter makes a veiled reference to a victory by a Tudhaliya, perhaps a reference to the campaign of Tudhaliya II in western Anatolia, and twice mentions the king of Aššuwa. Interestingly, the letter also mentions both Ahhiyawa, probably to be identified with Bronze Age Mainland Greece, and the king of Ahhiyawa.[12] The letter is so damaged and incomplete that it would be dangerous to read too much into the occurrence of both Aššuwa and Ahhiyawa within the same text. But it is extremely likely that we have here an indication that Aššuwa and Ahhiyawa were associated in some manner during the reign of Tudhaliya II. Ünal, in fact, believes that the letter:

> strongly suggests that the king of Ahhiyawa was involved in some way with the Aššuwan campaign of Tudhaliya. Tudhaliya seems to have subdued him.[13]

---

11 See, *e.g.*, Bossert (1946); Georgacas (1969); and additional references given in Cline (1996).

12 *Cf.* Sommer (1932) 268; Ünal (1991) 20 no. 12, 30. *Cf.* Cline (1996) for full discussion.

13 Ünal (1991) 20. See also earlier comments by Huxley (1960) 5, 38; Page (1959) 108.

Aššuwa apparently also was known in contemporary New Kingdom Egypt, during the time of Thutmose III (*c.* 1479–1425 BCE).[14] There it seems to have been recorded as *J-s-jj*, better known as *Isy*, or even as *A-si$_x$-ja*. The last rendition, argued most recently by Helck, bears a remarkable similarity to Linear A *a-su-ja*, Linear B *a-*64-ja*, and the later term 'Asia'.[15] An identification of *Isy* with Aššuwa seems more likely than an identification with Cyprus, which has been frequently suggested in the past. Indeed, the Egyptian name for Cyprus most likely was not *Isy*, but *'irs3* (Alašia).[16] The most strident of the previous objections raised to identifying *Isy* with Aššuwa, *e.g.* by Stevenson Smith,[17] have since been nullified as a result of the re-dating to the 15th century BCE of the Hittite texts mentioned above.

Thutmose III mentions *Isy* (Aššuwa) at least four times in various inscriptions. First, and perhaps most intriguing in the context of the present discussions, *Isy* is mentioned in the company of *Keftiu* (Crete) in Thutmose III's Poetic Stele/Hymn of Victory (Cairo Mus. no. 34010), which was a compilation of the entire world as known to the Egyptians at that time:

> I have come to let You smite the West, Keftiu and Isy being in awe, and I let them see Your Majesty as a young bull, firm of heart, sharp of horns, whom one cannot approach.[18]

It is unlikely that the Poetic Stele reflects actual Egyptian domination of Crete and Aššuwa,[19] but it does indicate a knowledge of those peripheral areas and political entities—even one which existed as briefly as did Aššuwa.

---

14 Kitchen (1987) 52.

15 Vercoutter (1956) 179-82; Helck (1971) 290; *idem* (1979) 28-29, 34-35; Strange (1980) 16- 20 no. 1; Haider (1988) 17; Bernal (1991) 231-34, 452.

16 *Cf.* Muhly (1972) 208-9; Cline (1994) 60, with references.

17 Stevenson Smith (1965) 10.

18 Translation following Strange (1980) 16-20 no. 1. *Cf.* also Vercoutter (1956) 11, 51-53 no. 5; Lichtheim (1976) 35-39; Helck (1979) 28, 34-35.

19 Liverani (1990) 261; on Egyptian exaggeration and hyperbole concerning "domination" of foreign areas, *cf.* now Pritchett (1993) 111-12, 248-50.

Thutmose III also reports in his Annals that *'inw*, frequently translated as 'tribute' but perhaps better understood as 'supplies' or 'gifts',[20] was received on three separate occasions from *Isy* (Aššuwa).[21] The first mention of *Isy* in these Annals is found in the records of his Ninth Campaign, in Year 34 (1445 BCE)—the "Chief of Isy" is said to have brought *inw* consisting of 108 blocks of pure copper (2,040 deben), five or more blocks of lead, 110 deben of lapis lazuli, one ivory tusk, and two staves of wood.[22] Goods from Retenu (Syro-Palestine) and Kush (Sudan) are also mentioned, indicating that the Annal entry for this year is not solely concerned with the actual "campaign," but is also a record of the various taxes, tribute, and supplies received by Thutmose III. This is also the case when *Isy* next appears. In the Annals record for Thutmose III's Thirteenth Campaign in Year 38 (1441 BCE)—the "Prince of Isy" is said to have brought *inw* consisting of crude copper and horses. Again, goods from Syria and Kush are grouped together with that from *Isy*.[23] The last entry in the Annals concerning *Isy* is found in the description of Thutmose III's Fifteenth Campaign in Year 40 (1439 BCE), where goods from *Isy*, Kush, and Syria are once again listed in order—the "Chief of Isy" is said to have brought *'inw* consisting of forty bricks of copper, one brick of lead, and two tusks of ivory.[24] It should not be surprising perhaps that Egypt and Aššuwa were in contact during the time of Thutmose III, as his reign overlapped the brief period of time that Aššuwa was in existence. There are also later New Kingdom references to *Isy* in lists of Seti I, Ramses II, and Ramses III, but these lists are considered to be copies and bear little resemblance to reality; certainly, the coalition known as Aššuwa had ceased to exist long before the time of Ramses II.[25]

---

20 Bleiberg (1981); *idem* (1984); Müller-Wollermann (1983); Boochs (1984); Schulman (1988) 57-58; Liverani (1990) 255-66.

21 For text, *cf. Urk.* IV 647-72 (Stücke I), 684-734 (Stücke V-VI); for English translations, *cf.* primarily Breasted (1962).

22 Bossert (1946) 9; Breasted (1962) 206; Hellbing (1979) 52.

23 Bossert (1946) 10; Breasted (1962) 210; Hellbing (1979) 52.

24 Bossert (1946) 10; Breasted (1962) 212; Hellbing (1979) 52.

25 See Bossert (1946) 6-8; Vercoutter (1956) 86-95 nos. 17, 19, 139-41 no. 41; Hellbing (1979) 53; Strange (1980) 27-31 nos. 4, 6; Haider (1988) 18; *idem.* (1989) 12.

What, precisely, was this *'inw* sent by *Isy* (Aššuwa) to Egypt during the reign of Thutmose III? As noted above, *'inw* (*Wb.* I, 14) is probably better translated as 'supplies' or 'gifts' than as 'tribute'.[26] Other rulers listed as supplying or presenting *'inw* to the Pharaoh in the Annals of Thutmose III include the heads of Hatti, Assur, and Babylon. All of these were independent kingdoms or political entities which would not have been sending 'tribute' to Egypt. As Bleiberg, Liverani, and others have noted, *'inw* apparently function within the medium or context of gift-exchange, rather than redistribution, and were exchanged only irregularly.[27] In particular, Liverani notes that:

> The 'translation' of the Egyptian terminology into our own is not a small problem, since translation implies an evaluation of the economic, political, [and] ideological implications of the term...for 'inw the problem is serious, the two current translations as 'tribute' or as 'gift' being the result of a misleading and misguided approach. It is a misleading approach when the political status of the supplying country is deduced from such a translation: as a subject (if one translates 'tribute') or as an independent country (if one translates 'gift'). It is a misguided approach when the translation is based on the knowledge of the political status of the supplying country (*e.g.* translating 'gift' if Hatti or Assyria are in cause, and 'tribute' in the case of Retenu). In both cases, we apply a classificatory opposition of our own to a word which is clearly indifferent in this respect. The Egyptian sorting of goods supplies, while very attentive in separating supplies from a directly administered territory from the external supplies, is not at all concerned with the status of foreign kingdoms as 'dependent' or 'independent'.[28]

Indeed, the goods described in Thutmose III's Annals as coming irregularly from *Isy* were almost certainly meant as gifts from the prince or chief of Aššuwa to Thutmose III, for there is no other evidence that Aššuwa ever sent, or needed to send, 'tribute' to Egypt. The *'inw* listed as coming from

---

26 Bleiberg (1981); *idem* (1984); Müller-Wollermann (1983); Boochs (1984); Schulman (1988) 57-58; Liverani (1990) 255-66.

27 Bleiberg (1981) 107-10; Müller-Wollermann (1983) 81-93; Liverani (1990) 257-58, 262- 63.

28 Liverani (1990) 260.

Isy are commodities known to have originated, or been available as trade goods, in northwestern Anatolia—horses, copper, lead, ivory, and lapis lazuli—and were typical of items commonly found in high-level gift-exchanges across the Bronze Age Near East.[29] The above textual data, although subject to many possible interpretations, might well be an indication that Aššuwa was actively searching for diplomatic contacts with other major powers during the decade before its great rebellion *c.* 1430 BCE, perhaps in actual anticipation of the looming troubles with the Hittites. Moreover, it may be further suggested that the Egyptians were perhaps not the only power to whom the Aššuwans appealed.

Neoanalysis and the Aššuwa Rebellion

The re-dating of the Hittite texts which document the Aššuwa rebellion now means that Aššuwa was defeated in the 15th century BCE, some 200 years before the traditional date of the Trojan War. Prior to the re-dating of these texts, when they were all still thought to date to the reigns of Tudhaliya IV and Arnuwanda III in the 13th century BCE, scholars used them as specific indications for Mycenaean involvement in the Trojan War and of Hittite knowledge of that involvement.[30] Now that many of these texts are dated to the reigns of Tudhaliya II and Arnuwanda I, they should probably be seen to indicate Hittite knowledge of Mycenaean involvement in Anatolia not during the Trojan War, but some 200 years prior to that war—unless the Trojan War itself is to be re-dated to the 15th century BCE.[31]

Since at least the time of Homer, and more likely back into the Bronze Age itself, the Greeks have told stories about Achaean warriors fighting on

---

29 *Cf.* Liverani (1990) 258 and n. 20.

30 *E.g.*, Page (1959); Huxley (1960); *cf.* also discussion in Muhly (1974) 137-38.

31 As Easton (1984) 34 has stated,

> despite the shortcomings of the various dating criteria, we are probably justified in regarding the Madduwattas text, the Annals of Tudhaliyas and the Annals of Arnuwandas as historical sources for the Early Empire period, and not for the period of the Trojan War.

Cf. Vermeule (1986) 87-88 and Mellink (1986) 95-96, 99, for discussions on the possibility of re-dating the Trojan War to the LH II-IIIA1 period (Troy VIF-H).

Anatolian soil.[32] The saga of the Trojan War is the most famous example, as recorded in Homer's *Iliad.* But even within this epic there are hints of warriors and events from an era considered by the Greek authors to be even more ancient. It is well known that a few elements found in Homer actually predate the traditional setting of the Trojan War in 1250 BCE, perhaps by as much as several centuries. These include the warrior Ajax and his Tower Shield (*cf. Il.* VII.219-20; XI.485; XVII.128), a shield type which had been replaced long before the 13th century BCE, as well as various heroes using 'silver-studded' swords (*phasganon arguroelon* or *xiphos arguroelon*; *cf. Il.* II.45; III.361; VII.303-4), an expensive type of weapon which had also gone out of use long before; Idomeneus, Meriones, and Odysseus may also be earlier figures incorporated into this epic.[33] A prime example is the mythical story of Bellerophon (*Il.* VI.178-240), a Greek hero almost certainly of pre-Trojan War date, who was sent from Tiryns to Lycia by Proteus, King of Tiryns. After completing three tasks and overcoming numerous additional obstacles, Bellerophon was eventually awarded a kingdom in Anatolia by Iobates, father-in-law of Proteus.[34] T. B. L. Webster saw in the story of Bellerophon, whom he regarded as a Mycenaean warrior originally dating back to at least the 14th century BCE, "some connection with the troubles in Lycia about which the king of the Hittites wrote to the king of Ahhiyawa."[35]

A predominantly European school of thought known as "Neoanalysis" may be of particular relevance and assistance in interpreting these 'early',

32 See Cline (1995) 270-73 for a full discussion of the supporting archaeological evidence for Mycenaeans fighting overseas as mercenaries in Anatolia, and in Egypt as well, during the Late Bronze Age. To those discussions should now be added Schofield and Parkinson (1994).

33 Vermeule (1983) 142; Vermeule (1986) 83, 85-86, 88-90; West (1988) 156, 158-59; *cf.* also Cauer (1921-23) 263; Nilsson (1932) 158; Lorimer (1950) 134, 152-53, 273-75; Webster (1958) 92, 101, 113-17; Page (1959) 232-38; Bowra (1960) 16-23; Luce (1975) 101-7, 119, plate XI.

34 *Cf.* Grote (1846) 166-68; Graves (1960) 252-54; Kirk (1974) 35, 97, 111, 150-52; also comments by Webster (1958) 25, 67, 117, 179-80, 185-86.

35 Webster (1958) 67. See now Smit (1988) 56 n. 49 and Liebig (1993) 492-93, on this same topic.

pre-Homeric, elements. Perhaps best represented to date by the work of Wolfgang Kullmann, Neoanalysis is

> a critical approach to the Iliad which takes into account the stories and themes of the epic cycle as sources of or as background for the Homeric poem.[36]

In other words, some portions of the *Iliad* may originally have been part of (or are imitations of) other epic cycles which dealt with events from a pre-Trojan War era. As Kullmann has concisely stated,

> according to this [the neoanalytical] approach, certain motifs found in Homer were taken from earlier poetry;

and thus

> ...the contexts of the Cyclic epics seems to be more ancient and nearer the legends of the oral singers than the contents of the Iliad.[37]

Indeed, stories of earlier 'Trojan Wars' conducted by Heracles and by Achilles are described by Homer and other Greek epic poets.[38] For example, Greek tradition, as recorded by Homer in the *Iliad*, held that in the time of Priam's father Laomedon, Heracles sacked Troy, using only six ships (*Il.* V.638-642):

> Of other sort, men say, was mighty Heracles, my father, staunch in fight, the lion-hearted, who on a time came hither [to Troy] by reason of the mares of Laomedon with but six ships and a scantier host, yet sacked the city of Ilios and made waste her streets.[39]

A similar description is found in Apollodorus (II.6.4):

---

36 Clark (1986) 379, 383. See Kullmann (1960), (1981), (1984), (1991); Latacz (1986) 99-100; Holoka (1991) 467; also references given by Clark (above) in an extensive review of relevant bibliography through 1986.

37 Kullmann (1984) 309 and 321-22.

38 *Cf.* Grote (1846) 388-89, 396-97; Finley (1956) 46; Andrews (1965) 28-37; *cf.* also Webster (1958) 116-17, 120, 125-26; Vermeule (1987) 122, 131.

39 Translation following Fagles (1990) 185.

> And having come to port at Ilium, he [Heracles] left the guard of the ships to Oicles and himself with the rest of the champions set out to attack the city....[40]

An alternate tradition mentioned by Apollodorus (II.6.4) and Diodorus (IV.32) held that Heracles had eighteen, rather than six, ships with fifty rowers in each—for a total of 900 men, hardly a "scanty" contingent![41]

Heracles' sack of Troy was thought to have taken place at least sixty, and perhaps as many as ninety, years prior to Homer's Trojan War, for Priam's rule spanned three generations. Bloedow has suggested that this "so-called First Trojan War" may be seen in the destruction of Troy VIh, now dated to the LH IIIA2/B transition, *c.* 1340 BCE. This era is, perhaps coincidentally, indeed some ninety years prior to the traditional 1250 BCE date for the Trojan War.[42] Alternatively, Vermeule has suggested several times that evidence for an Achaean attack such as that attributed to Heracles might be seen in the "vigorous housecleaning" visible in House VIF at Troy, which dates to the late LH II or early LH IIIA1 period, *c.* 1400 BCE—a time which is, again perhaps coincidentally, close to that of Tudhaliya II and the Aššuwa rebellion.[43]

In addition, the first, ill-fated, Achaean expedition sent to rescue Helen at Troy resulted in Mycenaean warriors fighting in northwestern Anatolia some time immediately prior to the Trojan War itself (ancient and modern

---

40 Translation following Frazer (1921) 245-47.

41 Nilsson (1932) 196-98 does not believe in the authenticity of any of these accounts, but he seems to be in the minority; *cf.* other discussions in Webster (1958) 125-26; Andrews (1965); Luce (1975) 135-36; Schachermeyer (1982) 93-12; Bloedow (1988) 48-51; Morris (1989) 517-18; Bernal (1991) 270; Hiller (1991) 145-48, 150-53; Zangger (1994) 192-94.

42 Bloedow (1988) 48-49, 51; also Andrews (1965) 28-32; Hiller (1991) 152. On the date of Troy VIh and the Mycenaean pottery found within, *cf.* Blegen *et al.* (1953) 20 and *passim*; Mee (1978) 146-47; *idem* (1984) 45. The date of the LH IIIA2/B transition is a matter of some debate; for a date of *c.* 1340 BCE, *cf.* Warren and Hankey (1989) 169; Cline (1994) 7.

43 Vermeule (1972) 275-76; Vermeule (1983) 142-43; *idem* (1986) 87-88; Hiller (1991) 153. On the date of Troy VIf and the Mycenaean pottery found within, *cf.* Blegen *et al.* (1953) 19 and *passim*; Mee (1978) 146-47; *idem* (1984) 45; Hiller (1991) 152.

estimates for the elapsed time between the expeditions range from a few weeks to eight years). The story is recounted in the *Cypria*, as recorded in Proclus, *Chrestomathy* i:

> All the leaders then meet together at Aulis and sacrifice....After this, they put out to sea, and reach Teuthrania and sack it, taking it for Ilium. Telephus comes to the rescue and kills Thersander the son of Polyneices, and is himself wounded by Achilles.[44]

Achilles, and Ajax too, later went raiding in this area again, during the Trojan War. According to Strabo (*Geography* XIII.1.7):

> ...along with other places, Achilles also sacked the country opposite Lesbos in the neighborhood of Thebe and Lyrnessus and Pedasus, which last belonged to the Leleges, and also the country of Eurypylos the son of Telephus. 'But what a man was that son of Telephus who was slain by him with the bronze', that is, the hero Eurypylus, slain by Neoptolemus.[45]

Strabo (*Geography* XIII.1.7) further locates the 'country of Eurypylos' as follows:

> ...one might include in the Lyrnessian Cilicia the territory subject to Eurypylus, which lay next to the Lyrnessian Cilicia. But that Priam was ruler of these countries, one and all, is clearly indicated by Achilles' words to Priam....[46]

The above passages might be readily linked to a pre-Trojan War era, particularly if the "Neoanalysis School" is correct in its interpretation of

---

44 Translation following Evelyn-White (1954) 492-93. *Cf.* discussion in Garstang and Gurney (1959) 97; Kullmann (1960) 189-203.

45 Translation following H. L. Jones (1927) 14-15. Homer, in speaking of Neoptolemus, Achilles' son (*Od.* XI.518-21), says:

> ...and many men he slew in dread combat. All of them I could not tell or name, all the host that he slew in defence of the Argives; but what a warrior was that son of Telephus whom he slew with the sword, the prince Eurypylus! Aye, and many of his comrades, the Ceteians, were slain about him, because of gifts a woman craved (translation following Rieu [1991] 174).

Cf. also Pindar's *Olympian Odes* IX.60. Huxley (1960) 40 has a brief discussion of the translation of "Ceteian" as "Hittite" and mentions the hypothesis that Telephus might be a Hittite name (Telepinus).

46 Translation following H. L. Jones (1927) 20-21.

these as 'early', pre-Homeric, passages. The above story of the expedition to Teuthrania in particular is seen by Neoanalysts as a pre-Homeric episode.[47] Is it mere chance that the area of northwestern Anatolia called Teuthrania (and/or the 'country of Eurypylos') sounds suspiciously similar to the area which the Hittites knew as Aššuwa? The battle in Teuthrania, during which Achilles wounded Telephus, King of Mysia, is thought to have taken place on a plain at the mouth of the Caicus River.[48] The Caicus River is frequently identified as the southern boundary of Aššuwa by those scholars who locate Aššuwa on the coast between the Troad and the Arzawa Lands; a location which is here considered to be correct. If this is so, then the Teuthrania of the *Cypria* might well have been located in the same approximate geographical region as the Aššuwa of the Hittite texts.[49]

Indeed, the description of the coalition of northwest Anatolian states known as Aššuwa, as listed in the Annals of Tudhaliya II, does bear a resemblance to the 'Trojan Catalogue' found in Homer's *Iliad* (II.926-89), which is itself thought to be an authentic survival of the Late Bronze Age.[50] Albright put it most concisely, stating:

> If the Aššuwan Confederacy was really centered in the northwestern part of the peninsula...it corresponded strikingly in makeup and geographical extension to the Trojan confederation in the Iliad.[51]

---

47 Kullmann (1960) 189-203; Clark (1986) 382.

48 Garstang and Gurney (1959) 97 and n. 1; *cf.* Wood (1985) 22, 206.

49 On the location of Classical Teuthrania, see Pauly-Wissowa, *sv.* "Teuthrania"; Grundy (1904) Maps XI-XII; Garstang and Gurney (1959) 96-97; Hammond (1981) Map 13. Note that Garstang and Gurney (1959) 97, Map 1, who locate Aššuwa inland, place the Seha River Land, rather than Aššuwa, in the Caicus Valley. However, Gurney (1990) 107, Map 1 locates Aššuwa closer to, or possibly on, the northwestern coast of Anatolia, with its southern border apparently at the Caicus River. In addition, Macqueen (1986) 38-39, figure 21 places Aššuwa with its southern border at the Caicus River on his "alternative map of Anatolia in Hittite times." Both Macqueen (above) and Bryce (1989) 21, Map 1 locate the Seha River Land further to the south, just above Miletus, at the next major river flowing westward to the Mediterranean. *Cf.* also maps in Wood (1985) 179, 182.

50 *Cf.* Huxley (1960) 31-36; Luce (1975) 92-93; Bryce (1977) 30-32; Zangger (1994) 59-60.

51 Albright (1950) 169.

Could it be that Homer's account of the 'first', ill-fated, Achaean expedition to the Troad region is a dimly remembered reflection of a Mycenaean attempt to aid Aššuwa in their rebellion against the Hittites? As we have seen, the geographical area involved is approximately the same, the participants are relatively similar, the timing of both is prior to the "real" Trojan War, and both "expeditions" end in apparent failure. Are all of these to be taken as merely coincidences? Although the first expedition led by Achilles is recorded as having occurred only shortly before the Trojan War, it is certainly tempting to imagine that this story, like that of Heracles' sack of Troy, might reflect events which belong to an earlier period in time—perhaps as early as the Aššuwa rebellion against the Hittites in the 15th century BCE. Indeed, Morris has recently intimated that the LM IA Thera Frescoes might provide evidence that small, ship-borne Achaean expeditions were taking place even earlier, perhaps as far back as the 17th/16th century BCE:

> The Iliad itself commemorates earlier expeditions undertaken by Herakles and the generation which fathered Homeric heroes like Diomedes (5.640-643), famous in the "first" Trojan War. The Thera frescoes hint at such historical expeditions translated into poetry, then into art, and not because the South Fresco fleet has the number of ships Herakles did, or because topography and landscape indicate Anatolia. These paintings contribute to a coincidence of evidence—from Hittite records, Luwian poems, Anatolian and Mycenaean pottery, and pre-Homeric patterns in epic poetry—which points to an earlier date for the first expeditions to Asia and the Troad and to a poetic, even heroic account of these expeditions, on both sides of the Aegean.[52]

Many of the observations cited above have long been known, for scholars have been discussing the pre-Homeric elements found in the *Iliad* and elsewhere in Greek literature for much of this century. However, it is only with the recent re-dating of the Aššuwa rebellion that one may begin to search for a "kernel of truth" underlying such pre-Homeric elements and tales. Thus, it might now be suggested that if one were to search for an

---

52 Morris (1989) 534, *cf.* also 515-22, 531-33, figure 4.

historical event with which to link pre-Homeric traditions of Achaean warriors fighting on the Anatolian mainland, the Aššuwa rebellion *c.* 1430 BCE would stand out as one of the largest military events within northwestern Anatolia prior to the Trojan War, and as one of the few events to which the Mycenaeans (Ahhiyawans) might be tentatively linked via textual evidence (*e.g.*, the Hittite letter KUB XXVI 91 mentioned above). We might well wonder, therefore, if it were not this incident which was the historical basis for the contemporary Hittite tales of Mycenaean (Ahhiyawan) warriors or mercenaries fighting in Anatolia and which generated the stories of earlier, pre-Trojan War, military endeavors of the Achaeans on the Anatolian mainland.

Anatolian/Aššuwan Ancestors for the Atreidai?

But why would such Mycenaean warriors have been helping Aššuwa in their rebellion against the Hittites? Most likely, Mycenaean motives would have been political and economic in nature; concerned with access to the Black Sea and to areas rich in agricultural products and raw materials such as metals. Similar scenarios have been suggested concerning Mycenaean motives for the Trojan War *c.* 1250 BCE.[53]

However, there exists another, more tenuous, possibility as well. The most questionable, and yet undeniably fascinating, potential evidence for contacts between Aššuwa and the Aegean are the mythological traditions regarding the western Anatolian origins or connections of several of the Bronze Age dynasties in the Argolid.[54] Could it be that Mycenaean warriors were helping Aššuwa in their rebellion against the Hittites because of the western Anatolian connections, later recalled in legend, of Mycenae, Tiryns, and Argos?

First, concerning Tiryns, Strabo (VIII.6.11) says:

---

53 Bloedow (1988).

54 *Cf.* Grote 1846) 120-25, 210-20; also discussions by Bryce (1989) 13; Bernal (1991) 452- 56.

> Now it seems that Tiryns was used as a base of operations by Proteus, and was walled by him through the aid of the Cyclopes, who were seven in number...and they came by invitation from Lycia.[55]

Apollodorus (II.2.1) gives further details:

> ...and Proteus went to Lycia to the court of Iobates or, as some say, of Amphianax, and married his daughter, whom Homer calls Antia, but the tragic poets call her Stheneboea. His father-in-law restored him to his own land with an army of Lycians, and he occupied Tiryns, which the Cyclopes had fortified for him. They [Proteus and his brother Acrisius] divided the whole of the Argive territory between them and settled in it, Acrisius reigning over Argos and Proteus over Tiryns.[56]

Proteus and Acrisius themselves were understood to be the great-grandsons of the Egyptian brothers Danaus and Aegyptus, who had emigrated to Mainland Greece several generations earlier (see figure 1). Apollodorus (II.2.2) goes on to note that Proteus had a son by Antia/Stheneboea, named Megapenthes—who was thus part Lycian, part Egyptian, and part Greek. Meanwhile, Acrisius had a daughter Danae, who in turn gave birth to a son named Perseus—who was thus part Egyptian and part Greek (Apol. II.2.2, II.4.1).[57] These cousins, Megapenthes and Perseus, exchanged the territories over which they ruled, so that, according to Apollodorus (II.4.4),

> Megapenthes ruled over the Argives, and Perseus reigned over Tiryns after fortifying also Midea and Mycenae.[58]

and, according to Pausanias (II.16.3),

> Perseus, ashamed because of the gossip about the homicide [of his father], on his return to Argos induced Megapenthes, the son of Proteus, to make

55 Translation following H. L. Jones (1927) 169.

56 Translation following Frazer (1921) 145-47. *Cf.* also Paus. II.16.2 and II.25.7-8 Loeb edition by W. H. S. Jones (1918) 329, 383.

57 Frazer (1921) 147-49, 153-55. The father of Perseus was unknown, but was speculated to be either Proteus (Danae's own uncle) or Zeus. Thus, Perseus is ⅜ Egyptian and ⅝ Greek if Proteus is his father, but ⅛ Egyptian and ⅞ Greek if Zeus is his father (assuming Zeus is Greek). Megapenthes is ½ Lycian, ¼ Egyptian, and ¼ Greek.

58 Translation following Frazer (1921) 163.

> an exchange of kingdoms; taking over that of Megapenthes, he founded Mycenae.[59]

Tiryns therefore had links to Anatolia through Proteus' Lycian wife Antia/Stheneboea and their hybrid son Megapenthes, but was then ruled by Perseus, who was of mixed Egyptian and Greek descent. Argos, which had been originally taken over by the Egyptian Danaus (Apol. II.1.4), was later ruled by this same Megapenthes who was of mixed Lycian, Egyptian, and Greek descent.[60] Therefore, according to the Greeks, by the time of the Late Bronze Age, both Tiryns and Argos had legendary links of some kind to Anatolia.

Perhaps most important is the legendary connection of the Atreid dynasty at Mycenae with Anatolia. According to Thucydides (I.9.2), Pelops, father of Atreus, came to Greece from Asia.[61] As noted above, the name 'Asia', which refers to Lydia in its earliest attestations by Greek authors and was later extended to include most of West Anatolia, is thought to derive from the Hittite name 'Aššuwa'. Thucydides says, specifically,

> ...it was by means of the great wealth which he [Pelops] brought with him from Asia into the midst of a poor people that Pelops first acquired power, and, consequently, stranger though he was, gave his name to the country [Peloponnesos], and that yet greater things fell to the lot of his descendants.[62]

We may note that Pindar (*Olympian Ode* I.24) also has a reference to "the Lydian Pelops,"[63] while Pausanias (V.1.7) refers to "Pelops the Lydian, who crossed over from Asia."[64]

Concerning Pelops' descendants, Thucydides continues (I.9.2):

---

59 Translation following W. H. S. Jones (1918) 329.

60 *Cf.* Frazer (1921) 135-37.

61 *Cf.* also discussion in Huxley (1960) 49; Bernal (1991) 452-53, 455, 459; Zangger (1994) 160.

62 Translation following Smith (1919) 15-17.

63 *Cf.* Sandys (1946) 7.

64 *Cf.* W. H. S. Jones (1918).

> Atreus was entrusted by Eurystheus with Mycenae and the sovereignty because he was a kinsman; and when Eurystheus did not return, Atreus ...received the sovereignty over the Mycenaeans and all who were under the sway of Eurystheus. And so the house of Pelops became greater than the house of Perseus.[65]

Thus, according to the legends of the ancient Greeks, Mycenae, Tiryns, and Argos all traced at least part of their ancestry back to the same area of Anatolia wherein lay the coalition of states known as Aššuwa.

I have suggested elsewhere that Mycenaean warriors or mercenaries may have been helping Aššuwa in their rebellion against the Hittites, perhaps because of these western Anatolian connections, later recalled in legend, of Mycenae, Tiryns, and Argos. Mycenaean aid to Aššuwa might thus be seen as a reaction to Tudhaliya II's campaigns in the Achaean dynasts' ancestral homelands. At the very least, such legendary connections could have served as a convenient excuse while more blatant economic and political motives remained concealed.

---

65 Translation following Smith (1919) 17.

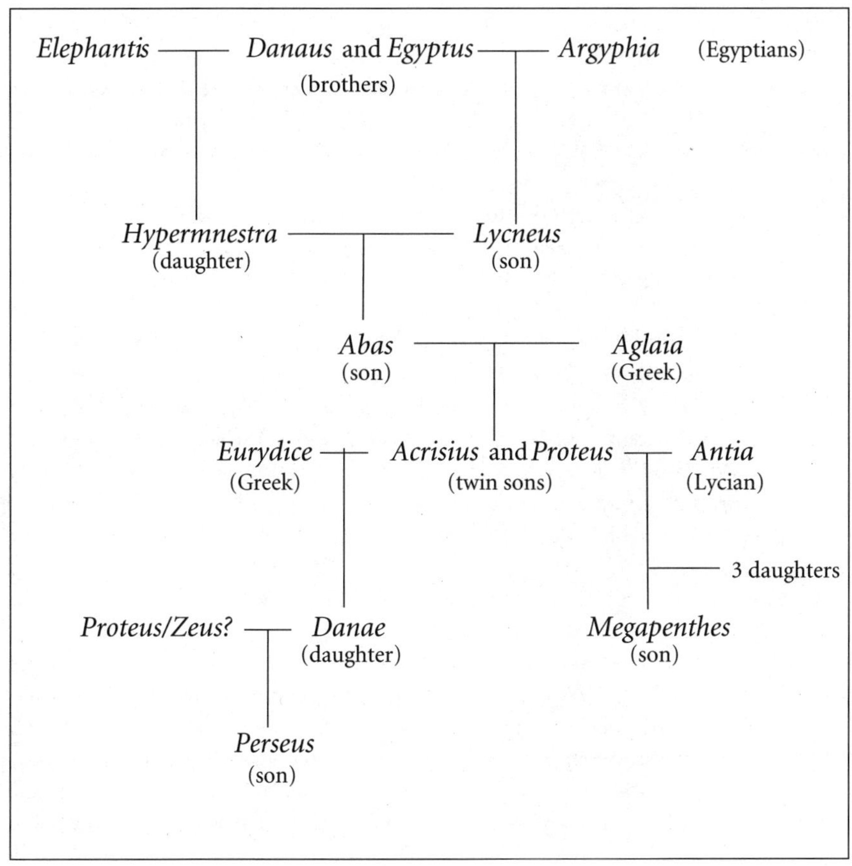

Figure 1.

PROPOSED FAMILY TREE FOR PERSEUS AND MEGAPENTHES
(following Apollodorus II.1.5 - II.4.1)

Bibliography

Albright, W. F. (1950) Some Oriental Glosses on the Homeric Problem. *American Journal of Archaeology* 54: 162-76. **Andrews, P. B. S.** (1965) The Falls of Troy in Greek Tradition. *Greece and Rome* 12: 28-37. **Astour, M. C.** (1964) Greek Names in the Semitic World and Semitic Names in the Greek World. *Journal of Near Eastern Studies* 23: 193-201. (1966) Aegean Place-Names in an Egyptian Inscription. *American Journal of Archaeology* 70: 313-17. (1967) *Hellenosemitica.* 2nd ed. Leiden. (1973) Ugarit and the Aegean. In Hoffner 1973: 17-27. (1981) Ugarit and the Great Powers. In Young 1981: 3-29. **Åström, P.**, ed. (1987) *High, Middle or Low? (Acts of an International Colloquium on Absolute Chronology Held at the University of Gothenburg 20th-22nd August 1987), Pt. 1.* Göteborg. **Bernal, M.** (1991) *Black Athena: The Afroasiatic Roots of Classical Civilisation. Vol. II: The Archaeological and Documentary Evidence.* New Brunswick, N.J. **Blegen, C. W., J. L. Caskey, and M. Rawson** (1953) *Troy III.* Princeton. **Bleiberg, E.** (1981) Commodity Exchange in the Annals of Thutmose III. *Journal of the Society for the Study of Egyptian Antiquities* 11: 107-10. (1984) The King's Privy Purse: An Examination of INW. *Journal of the American Research Center in Egypt* 21: 155-67. **Bloedow, E.** (1988) The Trojan War and Late Helladic IIIC. *Prähistorische Zeitschrift* 63: 1-41. **Boochs, W.** (1984) Weitere Bemerkungen zu den sogenannten Tributen. *Göttinger Mizszellen* 71: 61-66. **Bossert, H. T.** (1946) *Asia.* Literarische Fakultät der Universität Istanbul no. 323, Forschungsinstitut für altvorderasiatische Kulturen no. 2. Istanbul. **Bowra, C. M.** (1960) Homeric Epithets for Troy. *Journal of Hellenic Studies* 80: 16-23. **Breasted, J. H.** (1962) *Ancient Records of Egypt, v. II.* New York. **Bryce, T. R.** (1977) Ahhiyawa and Troy—A Case of Mistaken Identity? *Historia* 26: 24-32. (1989) The Nature of Mycenaean Involvement in Western Anatolia. *Historia* 38: 1-21. **Carruba, O.** (1977) Beiträge zur mittelhethitischen Geschichte I: Die Tuthalijas und die Arnuwandas. *Studi micenei ed egeo-anatolici* 18: 137-74. **Cauer, P.** (1921-23) *Grundfragen der Homerkritik.* 3rd ed. *Prähistorische Zeitschrift.* **Clark, M. E.** (1986) Neoanalysis: A Bibliographical Review. *Classical World* 79/6: 379-94. **Cline, E. H.** (1994) *Sailing the Wine-Dark Sea: International Trade and the Late Bronze Age Aegean.* B.A.R. International Series 591. Oxford. (1995) Tinker, Tailor, Soldier, Sailor: Minoans and Mycenaeans Abroad. In Niemeier (1995) 265-87. (1996) Aššuwa and the Achaeans: The 'Mycenaean' Sword at Hattušaš and Its Possible Implications. *Annual of the British School at Athens* 91 (1996) 137-51. **del Monte, G. F., and J. Tischler** (1978) *Die Orts- und Gewassernamen der hethitischen Texte.* Wiesbaden. **Easton, D. F.** (1984) Hittite History and the Trojan War. In Foxhall 1984: 23-44. (1985) Has the Trojan War Been Found? *Antiquity* 59: 188-96. **Ertekin, A., and I. Ediz** (1993) The Unique Sword from Bogazköy/Hattuša. In Mellink, Porada, and Özgüç 1993: 719-25. **Evelyn-White, H. G.** (1954) *Hesiod. The Homeric Hymns and Homerica.* Loeb edition. London. **Fagles, R.** (1990) *Homer: The Iliad.* New York. **Finley, M. I.** (1956) *The World of Odysseus.* New York. **Foxhall, L., and J. K. Davies**, eds. (1984) *The Trojan War: Its Historicity and Context.* Bristol. **Frazer, J. G.** (1921) [*Pseudo.*]*-Apollodorus.* Loeb edition, vol. 1. London. **Garstang, J., and O. R. Gurney** (1959) *The Geography of the Hittite Empire.*

London. **Georgacas, D. J.** (1969) The Name Asia for the Continent: Its History and Origin. *Names* 17: 1-90. **Graves, R.** (1960) *The Greek Myths: 1.* New York. **Grote, G.** (1846) *History of Greece, vol. 1.* London. **Grundy, G. B.** (1904) *Murray's Small Classical Atlas.* New York. **Gurney, O. R.** (1990) *The Hittites.* 2nd ed. New York. **Haider, P. W.** (1988) *Griechenland-Nordafrika.* Darmstadt. (1989) Zu den ägyptisch-ägäischen Handelsbeziehungen zwischen ca. 1370 und 1200 v. Chr.: II. Handelsgüter und Handelswege. *Münstersche Beiträge zur Antiken Handelsgeschichte* 8: 1-29. **Hammond, N. G. L.** (1981) *Atlas of the Greek and Roman World in Antiquity.* Park Ridge, N.J. **Helck, W.** (1971) *Die Beziehungen Ägyptens zu Vorderasien im 3. und 2. Jahrtausend v. Chr.* Darmstadt. (1979) *Die Beziehungen Ägyptens und Vorderasiens zur Ägäis bis ins 7. Jahrhundert v. Chr.* Darmstadt. **Hellbing, L.** (1979) *Alasia Problems. Studies in Mediterranean Archaeology* 47. Göteborg. **Hiller, S.** (1991) Two Trojan Wars? On the Destructions of Troy VIh and VIIa. *Studia Troica I*: 145-54. Mainz am Rhein. **Hoffner, H. A., Jr.**, ed. (1973) *Orient and Occident: Essays Presented to Cyrus H. Gordon on the Occasion of His Sixty-fifth Birthday.* Alter Orient und altes Testament 22. Neukirchener. **Holoka, J. P.** (1991) Homer, Oral Poetry Theory, and Comparative Literature: Major Trends and Controversies in Twentieth-Century Criticism. In Latacz 1991: 456-81. **Huxley, G. L.** (1960) *Achaeans and Hittites.* Oxford. **Jones, H. L.** (1927) *The Geography of Strabo.* Loeb edition. London. **Jones, W. H. S.** (1918) *Pausanias I.* Loeb edition. London. **Karageorghis, V.**, ed. (1972) *Acts of the 1st International Congress of Cypriot Studies, v. 1.* Nicosia. **Kirk, G. S.** (1974) *The Nature of Greek Myths.* New York. **Kitchen, K. A.** (1987) The Basics of Egyptian Chronology in Relation to the Bronze Age. In Åström 1987: 37-55. **Kullmann, W.** (1960) *Die Quellen der Ilias.* Hermes Einzelschriften, Heft 14. Wiesbaden. (1981) Zur Methods der Neoanalyse in der Homerforschung. *Wiener Studien* 15: 5-42. (1984) Oral Poetry Theory and Neoanalysis in Homeric Research. *Greek, Roman and Byzantine Studies* 25: 309-23. (1991) Ergebnisse der motivgeschichtlichen Forschung zu Homer (Neoanalyse). In Latacz 1991: 425-55. **Latacz, J.** (1986) News from Troy. *Berytus* 34: 97-112. **Latacz, J.**, ed. (1991) *Zweihundert Jahre Homer-Forschung: Rückblick und Ausblick: Colloquium Raurica Band 2.* Stuttgart. **Lichtheim, M.** (1976) *Ancient Egyptian Literature. Volume III: The New Kingdom.* Berkeley. **Liebig, M.** (1993) Lyker und Achäer—Ein Beitrag zur Ahhijawa-Frage. *Historia* 42/4: 492-93. **Liverani, M.** (1990) *Prestige and Interest: International Relations in the Near East ca. 1600-1100 B.C.* Padua. **Lorimer, H.** (1950) *Homer and the Monuments.* London. **Luce, J. V.** (1975) *Homer and the Heroic Age.* New York. **Macqueen, J. G.** (1986) *The Hittites and Their Contemporaries in Asia Minor.* 2nd ed. London. **Mee, C.** (1978) Aegean Trade and Settlement in Anatolia in the Second Millennium BCE. *Anatolian Studies* 28: 121-56. (1984) The Mycenaeans and Troy. In Foxhall and Davies 1984: 45-56. **Mellink, M. J.** (1986a) Postscript. In Mellink 1986b: 93-101. **Mellink, M. J.**, ed. (1986b) *Troy and the Trojan War.* Bryn Mawr. **Mellink, M. J., E. Porada, and T. Özgüç**, eds. (1993) *Aspects of Art and Iconography: Anatolia and Its Neighbors. Studies in Honor of Nimet Özgüç.* Ankara. **H.I.H. Prince Takahito Mikasa**, ed. (1991) *Essays on Ancient Anatolian and Syrian Studies in the 2nd and 1st Millennium B.C.* Bulletin of the Middle Eastern Culture Center in Japan, v. IV.

Wiesbaden. **Morris, S. P.** (1989) A Tale of Two Cities: The Miniature Frescoes from Thera and the Origins of Greek Poetry. *American Journal of Archaeology* 93: 511-35. **Muhly, J. D.** (1972) The Land of Alashiya: References to Alashiya in the Texts of the Second Millennium B.C. and the History of Cyprus in the Late Bronze Age. In Karageorghis 1972: 201-19. (1974) Hittites and Achaeans: Ahhiyawa *Redomitus. Historia* 23: 129-45. **Müller-Wollermann, R.** (1983) Bemerkungen zu den sogenannten Tributen. *Göttinger Mizszellen* 66: 81-93. **Niemeier. W.-D., and R. Laffineur**, eds. (1995) *Politeia: Society and State in the Aegean Bronze Age.* Aegaeum 12. Liège. **Nilsson, M. P.** (1932) *The Mycenaean Origin of Greek Mythology.* Berkeley. **Page, D.** (1959) *History and the Homeric Iliad.* Berkeley. **Pritchett, W. K.** (1993) *The Liar School of Herodotus.* Amsterdam. **Redford, D. B.**, ed. (1988) *The Akhenaten Temple Project v. 2: Rwd-Mnw, Foreigners and Inscriptions.* Toronto. **Rieu, E. V.** (1991) *Homer: The Odyssey.* Revised by D. C. H. Rieu and P. V. Jones. New York. **Sandys, J.** (1946) *The Odes of Pindar.* Loeb edition. London. **Schachermeyer, F.** (1982) *Die Ägäische Frühzeit, vol. V. Die Levante im Zeitalter der Wanderungen vom 13. bis zum 11. Jahrhundert v. Chr.* Österreichische Akademie der Wissenschaften, phil.- hist. Klasse, Sitzungsberichte 387. Wien. **Schofield, L., and R. Parkinson** (1994) Of Helmets and Heretics: A Possible Egyptian Representation of Mycenaean Warriors on a Papyrus from El-Amarna. *Annual of the British School at Athens* 89: 157-70. **Schulman, A. R.** (1988) Hittites, Helmets and Amarna: Akhenaten's First Hittite War. In Redford 1988: 54-79. **Smit, D. W.** (1988) Backgrounds to Hittite History—Some Historical Remarks on the Proposed Luwian Translations of the Phaistos Disc. *Talanta* 18/19: 49-62. **Smith, C. F.** (1919) *Thucydides I.* Loeb edition. London. **Sommer, F.** (1932) *Die Ahhijawa-Urkunden.* Munich. **Stevenson Smith, W.** (1965) *Interconnections in the Ancient Near East.* New Haven. **Strange, J.** (1980) *Caphtor/Keftiu.* Leiden. **Ünal, A.** (1991) Two Peoples on Both Sides of the Aegean Sea: Did the Achaeans and the Hittites Know Each Other? In H.I.H. Prince Takahito Mikasa 1991: 16-44. (1993) Bogazköy Kilicinin Üzerindeki Akadca Adak Yazisi Hakkinda Yeni Gözlemler. In Mellink, Porada, and Özgüç 1993: 727-30. **Ünal, A., A. Ertekin, and I. Ediz** (1991) The Hittite Sword from Bogazköy-Hattusa, Found 1991, and Its Akkadian Inscription. *MÜZE* 4: 46-52. **Vercoutter, J.** (1956) *L'Égypte et le monde égéen préhellènique.* Cairo. **Vermeule, E. T.** (1972) *Greece in the Bronze Age.* Chicago. (1983) The Hittites and the Aegean World: 3. Response to Hans Güterbock. *American Journal of Archaeology* 87: 141-43. (1986) Priam's Castle Blazing: A Thousand Years of Trojan Memories. In Mellink 1986b: 77-92. (1987) Baby Aigisthos and the Bronze Age. *Proceedings of the Cambridge Philosophical Society* 213: 122-52. **Warren, P. M., and V. Hankey** (1989) *Aegean Bronze Age Chronology.* Bristol. **Webster, T. B. L.** (1958) *From Mycenae to Homer.* London. **West, M. L.** (1988) The Rise of the Greek Epic. *Journal of Hellenic Studies* 108: 151-72. **Wood, M.** (1985) *In Search of the Trojan War.* New York. **Young, G. D.**, ed. (1981) *Ugarit in Retrospect: Fifty Years of Ugarit and Ugaritic.* Winona Lake, Ind. **Zangger, E.** (1994) *Ein Neuer Kampf um Troia: Archäologie in der Krise.* München.

Der Vertrag zwischen Ir-Addu von Tunip und Niqmepa von Mukiš*

M. Dietrich – O. Loretz
Münster

1. Vorbemerkungen

1938 hat Sir L. Woolley einen weitläufigen Palast der Schicht IV von Tell Atchana/Alalaḫ freigelegt, den er aufgrund seiner Fundobjekte dem Herrscher Niqmepa, dem Sohn des Idrimi, zuweisen konnte[1]. Dort fand er an den Stufen zum Palasttor innerhalb des Hofes[2] den in zwei Teile zerbrochenen Vertragstext, den D. H. Wiseman (1956) als Nr. 2 in seiner Ausgabe der Alalaḫ-Tafeln[3] vorgestellt hat: im CATALOGUE (S. 26-30) mit Umschrift und Übersetzung und im Tafelteil mit einer Autographie (PLATE II-III).

---

* Abkürzungen: AASOR: The Annual of the American Schools of Oriental Research; AHw: W. von Soden, *Akkadisches Handwörterbuch*; Al.T.: Wiseman (1953); AOAT: Alter Orient und Altes Testament; ATT: Tafelsignatur Tell Atchana/Alalaḫ; BWL: Lambert (1967); CAD: *The Assyrian Dictionary of the Oriental Institute of the University of Chicago*; DNWSI Hoftijzer and Jongeling (1995); GAG: W. von Soden (1952); GLH: Laroche (1980); HSS: Harvard Semitic Series; JCS: *Journal of Cuneiform Studies*; LE : Goetze (1956); RGTC: Répertoire Géographique des Textes Cunéiformes; TUAT: Texte aus der Umwelt des Alten Testaments.

1 Woolley (1955) 106-31.

2 Woolley (1939) 114, wenn die dort angegebenen Tafelsignaturen ATT/38/34-42,72 in irgendeiner Weise mit den von Wiseman (1953) 26 ("courtyard") AT.211 + AT.212 zusammenzubringen sind.

3 Wiseman (1953) 26-31.

Wegen seines schlechten Erhaltungszustands konnte dieser Vertragstext zwischen Niqmepa von Alalaḫ/Mukiš und Ir-Addu von Tunip, obwohl er einer der wenigen 'internationalen' ist, die bis *dato* in Syrien ans Tageslicht gekommen sind, sich nicht in wünschenswerter Weise einen festen Platz in der modernen Geschichts- und Sprachforschung der Altorientalistik sichern. So liegt nach der Erstveröffentlichung durch Wiseman als umfassende Übersetzung nur die von E. Reiner im Sammelband *Ancient Near Eastern Texts Relating to the Old Testament* (3. Aufl.) vor.[4] Von gelegentlichen Zitaten eines oder mehrerer Paragraphen sei hier zunächst nur auf die Studie M. Liveranis hingewiesen, die von der Auslieferung von Flüchtlingen handelt.[5]

Würdigungen zahlreicher Details aus dem Vertragstext lassen sich in historischen und philologischen Studien zu den Alalaḫ-Texten nachweisen: So widmete sich auf seiten der Historiker etwa H. Klengel den erschließbaren Implikationen zwischen Niqmepa und seinem Nachbarn Ir-Addu[6], W. Helck den eher indirekten Berührungen zwischen Ägyptern und Tunip[7], und auf seiten der Philologen G. Giacumakis Phänomenen der mittelbabylonischen Koine[8] sowie A. Draffkorn dem Reflex des Hurritischen in der Vertragsformulierung[9].

Unsere folgende Studie über Al.T. 2 fußt auf zwei Kollationen des Originals in den Jahren 1964 und 1965, einer zweifachen fotographischen Erfassung in denselben Jahren sowie einer 1965 angefertigten Autographie (O. Loretz) im Hatay-Museum zu Antakya, wo die Tafel heute aufbewahrt wird und unter den Inventarnummern 8997a und 8999b registriert ist.

Die beiden getrennt aufbewahrten Tafel'hälften' lassen sich am linken Rand über einen schmalen Steg zusammenschließen, so daß die Größe der

---

4 Reiner (1969) 531-32.

5 Liverani (1964).

6 Klengel (1965) 220-21, 232-33; vgl. Klengel (1992) 89.

7 Helck (1971) 118, 295-97, etc.

8 Giacumakis (1970) *passim.*

9 Draffkorn (Kilmer) (1959).

Tafel sowie die Anzahl der auf ihr zwischen Querstrichen erfaßten Paragraphen bekannt ist.

Da auf der rechten Tafelhälfte der Mittelteil verkrustet und großteils herausgebrochen ist, erweist sich eine ganze Reihe der Paragraphen als nicht mehr voll lesbar. Das beeinträchtigt die Arbeit an dem Vertragstext und behindert eine Bestimmung seiner literarischen Besonderheit erheblich.

Es erscheint geboten, unsere Ergebnisse trotz der erwähnten Schwierigkeiten mitzuteilen und damit der Forschung an den philologischen und historischen Aussagen der Tafel neuen Auftrieb zu geben.[10] Als Beleg für die vorgetragenen Lesungen liefern wir am Ende des Beitrags Fotos mit. Die Autographie wird in einem Kopienband veröffentlicht.

Wenn wir diese Studie als Beitrag zur Festschrift des hochverehrten Jubilars M. C. ASTOUR ausgewählt haben, dann tun wir das im Bewußtsein, daß er die Alalaḫ-Forschung stets mit besonderem Interesse verfolgt und sie vielfach entscheidend gefördert hat.[11]

---

10 Wir danken unserem Kollegen Walter Mayer für wertvolle Hinweise.

11 Gleichzeitig kommen wir unserer Ankündigung nach, eine Neubearbeitung von Al.T. 2 vorzulegen: Klengel (1969) 94.

2. Umschrift und Übersetzung (mit Gliederung)

Umschrift

^{na_4}KIŠIB *ša* ^{m}*Ir*-^{d}IM LUGAL-RU ^{uru}*Tu-ni-ip*^{ki}

(Abrollung eines breitbandigen Siegels mit Spiralmuster)

PRÄAMBEL

1 *ṭu*[*p-p*]*u ša ni-iš* DINGIR^{meš} *ša* ^{m}*Níq-me-pa* LUGAL KUR *Mu-ki-iš-ḫé*
2 [*ù ša*] ^{m}⸢*Ir*⸣-^{d}IM LUGAL ^{uru}⸢*Tu*⸣-*ni-ip*^{ki} *ki-ia-am* ^{m}*Níq-me-pa ù* ^{m}*Ir*-^{d}IM
3 [x x x xx x *t*]*a an-na-t*[*i*] ⸢*i*⸣-[*n*]*a bi-ri-šu-nu i-pu-šu*

§ 1

4 [*šum-ma* . . .]*x mi-in-d*[*ì* ^{lú}DAM.]GÀR^{meš} *mi-in-dì* ERÍN^{meš} ^{kur}*Zu-ti*^{ki}
5 [. . .]⸢*ka*⸣-*ak-k*[*u* x x x x *m*]*a-la na-ak-ru-ka*
6 [. . .]-*ia la na*[-*ak-r*]*a-ta šum-ma* ŠE-*IM* ZÍZ$^{ḫi.a}$ GIŠ.Ì^{meš}
7 [. . . *ú-k*]*à-al* ⸢*ù*⸣[x x x]⸢*kan*⸣-*ka-am*
8 [. . .] x x [*ta-na-*]*an-din*

---

§ 2

9 [. . . *i*]*b-bá-aš-ši*
10 [. . . *ta-*]*dáb-bu-bá-a*
11 [. . . *ša*] URUDU
12 [. . .]*lu-ú tu-bá-á'-a-šu-nu*
13 [. . .] x x [. . .]⸢*i*⸣-*qá-ab-bu-ú*
14 [. . .]⸢*i-na*⸣ KUR *Mu-ki-iš-ḫé*^{ki} *ni-*⸢*i*⸣[-*nu* . . .]
15 *šu*[*m-m*]*a* ERÍN^{meš} *a-na-mu-ú la ta-ad-du-uk-šu*[-*nu*]

---

§ 3

16 *šum-ma ma-am-ma-an iš-tu lìb-bi* KUR-*ia i-*[*na* KUR-*ka i-ir-ra-ab*]
17 *šum-ma at-ta te-še-em-me-šu šum-ma la ta*[-*ṣa-bat-šu ù la*] *tu-ba-sar-an-n*[*i*]
18 *ù šum-ma i-na lìb-bi* KUR^{ki}-*ka aš-bu šum-ma* [*la ta*]-⸢*ṣa-bat*⸣ *ù la ta-n*[*a-an-di-na-šu*]

Übersetzung

Siegel des Ir-Addu, des Königs von Tunip.

(Abrollung eines breitbandigen Siegels mit Spiralmuster)

Präambel

1 Tafel über den Gotteseid zwischen Niqmepa, König des Landes Mukiš,
2 [und zwischen] Ir-Addu, dem König von Tunip. Folgendermaßen haben Niqmepa und Ir-Addu
3 [. . .] diese [. . .] unter sich durchgeführt:

§ 1

4 [Wenn . . .]x seien es die Händler, seien es die Sūtû-Leute,
5 [. . .] Waffen$^{?}$ [. . ., sov]iele dir feind sind,
6 [. . .] meiner [. . .] darfst du nicht feindlich sein! Ob er nun Gerste, Emmer, Olivenöl
7 [. . .] zurückhält oder [. . .] eine gesiegelte [. . .]
8 [. . .]. . .[. . .] mußt du (her)geben.

---

§ 2

9 [. . .] aufkommt,
10 [. . .] werdet ihr anklagen
11 [. . .] aus Kupfer
12 [. . .] sollt ihr sie suchen.
13 [. . .] . . . [. . .] werden sie sagen:
14 ["'. . .] aus Mukiš sind wi[r." . . .]
15 Diese Leute mußt du töten.

---

§ 3

16 Wenn irgendeiner aus meinem Land in [dein Land eintritt,]
17 mußt du ihn, wenn du von ihm hörst, ergreifen und mir melden.
18 Und wenn er in deinem Land ansässig ist, mußt du (ihn) ergreifen und mir übergeben.

---

§ 4

19 *šum-ma šal-la-tum ša* KUR-*ia i-na* KUR^{ki}-*ka ša i-pa-aš-ša-ru ib-bá-aš-š*[*i*]

20 *šum-ma qa-du ša i-pa-aš-ša-ru-šu-ma la ta-ṣa-bat ù a-na ia-ši la ta*[*-na-an-di-na-šu*]

---

§ 5

21 *šum-ma* ^{lú}*mu-un-na-ab-tù* ÌR^{meš} GEMÉ^{meš} *ša* KUR-*ia a-na* KUR-*ka in-na*[*-ab-bi-it*]

22 *šum-ma la ta-ṣa-bat ù la tu-te-er-šu šum-ma ma-am-ma-an iṣ-ṣa-bat-ma*

23 *ù a-na ka-ša ú-ba-al-šu i-na* É *ki-lì-ka šu-k*[*u-un*]-⸢*šu*⸣-*mi*

24 *im-ma-ti-me-e* EN-*šu i-il-la-kám ù ta-na-din a-na š*[*a-š*]*u*

25 *šum-ma la aš-bu* ^{lú}*a-lik pa-ni-šu ta-na-din i-na a-i-im-me-e* ⸢URU⸣ *ki aš-bu*

26 *ù li-iṣ-bat-šu la aš-bu-ma-a* ^{lú}*ḫa-za-an-nu qa-du* 5 $^{\text{lú.meš}}$ŠI.BU^{meš}-*šu*

27 *a-na ni-iš* DINGIR^{meš} *i-za-ka*$_4$*-ru šum-ma* ÌR-*ia i-na lìb-bi-ku-nu aš-bu ù tu-ba-sà-ra-ni-mi*

28 *šum-ma i-na ma-mi-ti-ia la i-ma-ga*$_5$*-ru ù* ÌR-*šu ut-te-er-šu*

29 *šum-ma i-tam-mu-šu-nu ar-ka*$_4$*-nu* ÌR-*šu ú-še-el-la-šu (*x x *ru x)*

30 *ù šar-ra-qú \ up-su-qà ri-it-ta-an*

31 6 *li-im* URUDU *a-na* É.GAL *in-na-an-din-šu (*⸢x x⸣*)*

---

§ 6

32 *šum-ma* LÚ *lu* LÚ.SAL-*tum* GU$_4$ ANŠE *ù šum-ma* ANŠE.KUR.RA *iš-tu* É *ma-an-nim* [0]

33 *jú-dá-šu ù i-qáb-bi a-na ši-mi-im-mi el-qí-šu-mi* [0]

34 *šum-ma* ^{lú}DAM.GÀR-*ma ú-še-el-la-šu* ⸢*ù*⸣ *za-ku ù šum-ma* ^{lú}[DAM.GÀR-*ma*]

§ 4

19 Wenn es jemanden gibt, der Raubgut aus meinem Land in deinem Land verkaufen will,

20 dann mußt du (ihn) mitsamt dem, der ‘es’ verkaufen wollte, fassen und mir übergeben.

---

§ 5

21 Wenn ein Flüchtling—ein Sklave, eine Sklavin—aus meinem Land in dein Land flieht,

22 dann mußt du (ihn) ergreifen und zurückgeben. Wenn ihn irgendein anderer ergreift,

23 dann soll er ihn zu dir bringen. Du setze ihn (dann) im Gefängnis fest!

24 Wann immer sein Herr kommt, dann wirst du ihn ihm geben.

25 Wenn er nicht ansässig ist, dann wirst du seinen Anführer geben. Ist er in einer bestimmten Stadt ansässig,

26 dann soll man ihn fassen; ist er nicht (in einer bestimmten Stadt) ansässig, dann wird der Bürgermeister mitsamt seinen fünf Zeugen

27 einen Gotteseid leisten: Wenn mein Sklave unter euch lebt, dann werdet ihr mir Nachricht geben.

28 Wenn sie in meinen Schwur nicht einwilligen, dann wird ihm (: dem früheren Besitzer) sein Sklave zurückgegeben.

29 Wenn sie ihnen (falsch) schwören, später ihm seinen Sklaven produziert,

30 dann sind sie Diebe, beide Hände (von ihnen) werden abgetrennt.

31 6.000 (Sekel) Kupfer wird (zudem) dem Palast für ihn gegeben.

---

§ 6

32 Wenn ein Mann oder eine Frau ein Rind, einen Esel oder gar ein Pferd aus dem Haus(stand) irgendjemandes

33 erkennt und sagt: “Zu einem Kaufpreis habe ich es entgegengenommen!”,

34 (dann) ist er unschuldig, wenn er einen Händler aufbietet. Wenn er aber einen [Händl]er

35 *la ú-še-el-la ša jú-dá-šu i-li-q*[*í-*]⸢*e*⸣*-šu*[*ù* 0$^{?!}$]
36 *a-na ni-iš* DINGIR^{meš} *i-za*[*-k*]*àr-šu šum-m*[*a . . .-mi*]

u.Rd.

37 *ù šum-ma a-na ma-mi-ti la i-ma-gàr* ⸢*ù*⸣ [*šar-ra-qú*]

---

§ 7

38 *šum-ma* LÚ *ta-na-aṣ-ṣa-ru it-ti* LÚ *ta-*[. . . *i-na qa-ti-ka*]
39 *i-il-la-ak šum-ma* ^{giš}GÌR*-šu i*[*-pe-et-ti-ma kán-na-šu . . .*]

Rs.

40 *ab-bu-ut-ta-šu ú-gal-li*[*-bu . . .*]
41 *ù iṣ-bat-šu ù šar-ra-qú šum-ma i-qáb*[*-bi . . .*]
42 *ù ki-ia-am a-na ni-iš* DINGIR^{meš} *i-za-*ka_4*-ru šum-ma i*[-x x]*-ta-*[x x x x x x (x)]
43 *šum-ma a-na ma-mi-ti la i-ma-*ga_5*-ru ù ša*[*r-ra-*]*qú ki-ma šar-ra-q*[*í . . .*]
44 *šum-ma* ^{lú}*ši-nu šum-ma* LÚ.SAL*-tum ù šum-ma ṣú-ḫa-ru i-n*[*a qa-*]*ti-šu i-il-la-ak* [*ù* EN*-šu*]
45 *iṣ-bat-šu ù šar-ra-qú ki-ia-am* EN*-šu i-tam-mu-šu*
46 *šum-ma iš-tu* ŠU*-šu i-na* KASKAL*-ni la aṣ-bat-šu* (x x x)

---

§ 8

47 *šum-ma* ^{lú}*šar-ra-qú ša* KUR^{ki}*-ka i-na* KUR^{ki}*-ia i-šar-ra-qú-m*[*a*]
48 É *ù* URU^{ki} *i-pá-al-la-š*[*u*] *ù i-ṣa-ba-tù a-na* É *ki-lim* [*išakkanū-šunu*]
49 *ma-*ti_4*-me-e* EN*-šu*[*il-la-k*]*ám* EN*-el* É *ki-ia-am a-na ni-iš* DINGIR^{meš} *i*[*-za-*ka_4*-ar*]
50 *šum-ma-mi iš-tu pá-al-ši* \ *ḫa-at-ḫa-ar-re la ta-aṣ-bat-šu-mi*
51 $^{\text{lú.meš}}$*ši-bu-te-šu ú-še-el-la-šu-nu ḫi-iṭ-a-šu a-na* SAG.DU*-šu*
52 *i-ša-ak-*ka_4*-nu ù i-ḫap-pí-tu-šu ù* ÌR*-du*
53 *la i-tam-mu-nim-ma-a ù za-ku*

---

35 nicht aufbieten kann, das, was er gefunden hat, aber mitnimmt, [dann]

36 wird er einen Gotteseid vor ihm leisten: “Bestimmt [. . . !”]

u.Rd.

37 Wenn er aber in den Eid nicht einwilligt, dann [ist er ein Dieb[?].]

---

§ 7

38 Wenn ein Mann, den du in Gewahrsam hast, mit einem Mann, den du [. . ., deine Verfügung]

39 verläßt—wenn einer seine Fußfessel [öffnet und sein Band . . .,]

Rs.

40 nachdem(?) er seine Locke rasiert hat[, . . .]

41 und ihn aufgenommen hat, dann ist er ein Dieb. Wenn er sagt[: “. . .”,]

42 dann werden sie folgendermaßen einen Gotteseid leisten: “Bestimmt [. . .]. [. . . !”]

43 Wenn sie (jedoch) in den Eid nicht einwilligen, dann sind sie Diebe. Wie Diebe [. . .]

44 Wenn ein Fremder, wenn eine Frau oder wenn ein junger Mann seine Verfügung verläßt [und sein (ehemaliger) Herr]

45 seiner habhaft wird, dann ist er ein Dieb. So soll sein Herr ihm schwören:

46 “Ich habe ihn gewiß nicht aus seiner Hand während eines (Handels-)Zuges gefaßt!”

---

§ 8

47 Wenn Diebe aus deinem Land in meinem Land stehlen und

48 in ein Haus oder in die Stadt einbrechen und dabei (etwas) wegnehmen, dann [wird man sie] ins Gefängnis [werfen.]

49 Sobald sein Herr [auftr]itt, wird der Herr des Hauses folgendermaßen einen Gotteseid [leisten:]

50 “Aus der Einbruchstelle hast du es genommen!”

51 Zeugen wird er aufbieten, sie werden sein Vergehen auf sein Haupt

52 laden und ihn überführen. Dann wird er ein Sklave.

53 (Wenn) sie aber nicht gegen ihn schwören, dann ist er frei.

---

§ 9

54 [*šum-ma* L]Ú-*ia i-na lìb-bi* KUR^{ki}-*ka a-na bu-tal-lu-ṭì i-ru-ba-am*
55 ⸢*šum-ma*⸣ *ki-ma* KUR^{ki}-*ka la ta-na-aṣ-ṣa-ar-šu-nu šum-ma ki-ma* KUR^{ki}-*ka*
56 *la ta-ta-kal-šu-nu ma-ti*$_{4}$-*me-e i-na* KUR^{ki}-*ia id-*⸢*dá*⸣[-*ar-r*]*a-ru*
57 *ta-ba-aḫ-ḫar-šu-nu ù tu-te-er-ra-šu-nu i-n*[*a* KUR^{ki}-*ia*]
58 *ù* 1^{en} É *i-na lìb-bi* KUR^{ki}-*ka la ta-kal-l*[*a-šu*]

---

§ 10

59 *šum-ma* LÚ *ša* KUR^{ki}-*ka i-na* KUR^{ki}-*ia a-na bu-ta*[*l-lu-ṭì i-ru-ba-am*]
60 *i-dáb-bu-ub šum-ma* URU^{ki}-*ia a-na* x[. . .]
61 ^{lú}EN-*el ḫi-iṭ-i*[. . .]
62 *ú-še-ri-b*[*u* . . .]
63 *ta-a-*x[. . .]
64 x[. . .]
65 [. . .]
66 *ša*[. . .]
67 *ù* ^{lú}[. . .]. . .[. . .] (x x)

---

§ 11

68 *šum-ma* URU[x x x x]*x it*$^{?}$ *šum-ma mu-*[x x (x) *i*]*b-ba-aš-ši*
69 *it-ti* ERÍN[^{meš}-*ia i-na lìb-b*]*i* URU-*ia aš-bu* x[x x *t*]*a-aš-šu-ša-an-ni*
70 URU *a-na* x[x x x x -]*at*$^{?}$-*mu ù i-na ar-*x[x x x]-*ku la ta-ṣa-bat-šu-nu*
71 *i*[*š*]-*tu* [*x*] *šu un nu* KI *aš-li-im*[x x x *l*]*a ta-ṣa-bat-šu-nu*

---

§ 9

54 [Wenn Leu]te von mir, um zu überleben, in dein Land eingetreten sind,
55 dann mußt du sie, als wären sie Angehörige deines Landes, in Schutz nehmen, mußt ihnen, als wären sie Angehörige deines Landes,
56 Vertrauen entgegenbringen. Sobald sie freien Lauf in mein Land wollen,
57 wirst du sie überprüfen und sie in [mein Land] zurückkehren lassen.
58 Nicht eine einzige Familie darfst du in deinem Land zurückhalten!

---

§ 10

59 Wenn ein Mann aus deinem Land mein Land, um zu über[leben, betritt und]
60 sagt: "Meine Stadt ist gewiß gegenüber x [. . .!",]
61 dann ist er ein Frevler. [. . .]
62 sie haben hineingebracht[. . .]
63 . . . [. . .]
64 [. . .]
65 [. . .]
66 von [. . .]
67 und der [. . .]. . .[. . .] (Rasur: x x)

---

§ 11

68 Wenn die Stadt [. . .]. . . wenn . . .[. . .] entsteht,
69 sich bei [meinen?] Leuten [inmitte]n meiner Stadt aufhält,[. . .] du versetzt mich in Trübsal,
70 eine Stadt [. . .]. . . und in . . .[. . .]. . . mußt du sie ergreifen,
71 Aus . . . mit einem Seil . . . mußt du sie ergreifen!

Treuegelöbnis

72 [*šum-m*]*a* ERÍN.MEŠ *Ḫur-ri* EN-*lí šum-ma it-ti* LUGAL ERÍN.MEŠ *Ḫu*[*r-r*]*i na-kir ù a-na-ku*

73 [*m*]*a-mi-it-šu ša* LUGAL ERÍN.MEŠ *Ḫur-ri* EN-*ia la a-ḫa-ap-pí*

74 ⸢*a*⸣*-na-mu-ú a-wa-te*^{meš} *iš-tu ma-*⸢*mi*⸣*-ti lu-ú i-pá-aš-šar*

$^{\text{na}_4}$KIŠIB *ša* ^{m}*Níq-me-pa* LUGAL ^{uru}*A-la-la-aḫ*^{ki}

(Abrollung des Dynastiesiegels—Legende siehe unten)

lk.Rd.

Fluch

75 *ma-an-nu-um-me-e a-*[*wa-t*]*e*^{meš} *an-nu-ut-ti uš-bal-kàt-šu-nu* ^{d}IM E[N *bi-r*]*i* ^{d}UTU EN-*el di-ni*

76 ^{d}30 *ù* DINGIR^{meš} GAL.GA[L.E.NE] *ú-ḫal-liq-šu* MU-*šu ù* NUMUN-*š*[*u li-ḫa*]*l-liq i-na* KUR$^{\text{ki.meš}}$

77 ^{giš}GU.ZA-*šu ù* ^{giš}P[A-]*šu li-iš-bal-kat-šu a*[*k-x-*^{d}I]M DUB.SAR

(Legende des Dynastiesiegels:)

1 *Ab-ba-an* LUGAL KALA.GA

2 DUMU *Šar-ra-an*

3 ÌR ^{d}IM

4 *na-ra-am* ^{d}IM

5 *sí-ki-il-tum*

6 *ša Ḫé-pat*

Treuegelöbnis

72 Wenn sich (mit) den Ḫurru-Leuten mein Herr, wenn mit dem König sich die Ḫurru-Leute verfeinden, so werde ich selbst
73 den Eid gegenüber dem König der Ḫurru-Leute, meinem Herrn, niemals brechen,
74 (es sei denn, daß) dieser die Worte aus dem Eid auflöst!

Siegel des Niqmepa, des Königs von Alalaḫ.

(Abrollung des Dynastiesiegels—Legende siehe unten)

lk.Rd.

Fluch

75 Wer diese Worte überschreitet, den werden Addu, der He[rr der Opfer]schau, Šamaš, der Herr über die Rechtsprechung,
76 Sîn und die gro[ßen] Götter, (gewiß) vernichten! Seinen Namen und seinen Nachkommen [möge er] aus den Ländern entfernen!
77 Seinen Thron und sein Szepter möge er umstürzen! Ak[-x]-Addu ist der Schreiber.

(Legende des Dynastiesiegels:)

1 Abban, der mächtige König,
2 der Sohn des Šarran,
3 der Diener des Addu,
4 der Liebling des Addu,
5 Kleinod[12]
6 der Ḫepat.

[12] Wörtl.: “Erwerb”.

3. *Bemerkungen zum Text*

ÜBERSCHRIFT DES SIEGELS VON IR-ADDU VON TUNIP

Die Lesung von dIM im Namen des Herrschers von Tunip, Ir-dIM, ist in der bisherigen Diskussion kontrovers: Während D.J. Wiseman[13] und E. Reiner[14] dIM nicht umschreiben, lesen M. Liverani[15] und H. Klengel[16] Ir-Teššub, W. Helck dagegen Ir-Addu[17]. Zur Verdeutlichung der Problematik seien im folgenden die in Alalaḫ syllabisch belegten PNN aufgelistet, die die Elemente Ir-/Ar- und -Addu/-Teššub aufweisen: *I-ri-(i)a-du* (2x; vgl. *I-ri-ia* oft) : : *Ir-te-šu-ba* / *Ir-te-eš-šu-ub* (je 1x; vgl. *Ir-te* oft); *A-ri-(i)a-du* (1x; vgl. *A-ri-ia* oft) : : *Ar-te-šu-bá* (1x; nie **Ar-te*)[18].

Dieser Aufstellung ist hinsichtlich der beiden Namenselemente zu entnehmen:

1. Das theophore Element kann sowohl "Addu" als auch "Teššub" heißen, wobei "Addu" möglicherweise der Vorzug gegeben werden könnte, weil es eine größere Belegbreite hat.
2. Das Verbalelement lautet gleichermaßen ar= und ir= und steht für das hurr. ar= "geben"[19]. Also ist ar=/ir= ein weiterer Beleg für die auch sonst gut belegte Austauschbarkeit der Vokale *a* und *i* im Anlaut.

Über die Person des Ir-Addu von Tunip, dessen Siegel Spiralmuster in einem breiten Band zeigt, ist uns über die hier gemachten Aussagen hinaus

---

13 Wiseman (1953) 26-31; in der Vorbemerkung (S. 26) verweist D.J. Wiseman auf *Iri-adu in seinem Namensindex.

14 Reiner (1969).

15 Liverani (1964).

16 Klengel (1965) 297: Index; Klengel (1969) 80, 88; Klengel (1992) 89-90, bietet die Alternative Ir-Adad/Teshup.

17 Helck (1971) 118, 603: Index.

18 Vgl. *arttb* in alphabetischen Texten aus Ugarit (13. Jh.).

19 GLH 52f.

nichts bekannt[20]: Er wurde von Niqmepa mit *bēlī* "mein Herr" (Z. 72) angesprochen, was zumindest eine Gleichrangigkeit, möglicherweise sogar eine höhere Stellung signalisiert, und unterstand seinerseits dem König der Hurriter (LUGAL ERÍN.MEŠ *Ḫur-ri*, Z. 72. 73) als Oberherrn.

In dem Titel LUGAL-*RU* ^{uru}*Tu-ni-ip*^{ki} ist die Schreibweise LUGAL-*RU* für ein Regens im Genitiv auffallend: Es scheint ein gemischtes Sumero-Akkadogramm zu sein, dessen Aussprache durch das Silbenzeichen *RU* (: |šarru|?) nicht festgelegt ist; vielleicht steht LUGAL-*RU* für ein westliches |malik| oder ein hurritisches |ewre|.

Aus der Tatsache, daß sowohl Niqmepa von Mukiš als auch Ir-Addu von Tunip dem "König der Hurri-Leute" unterstellt waren, ergeben sich Rückschlüsse auf eine grobe Datierung für den Vertragsabschluß Al.T. 2, wie W. Helck vor Augen führt: vielleicht schon während der späten Jahre des Pharao Thutmosis III. (1490–1436), zumindest aber ab den frühen von Amenophis II. (1438–1412), als Tunip bestimmt nicht mehr unter ägyptischer Oberhoheit stand[21] und in die der Hurri-Könige gewechselt war[22].

Die Lage des Ortes Tunip im Grenzbereich ägyptischer und mitannischer Interessen ist unsicher: H. Klengel[23] und W. Helck[24] vermuten es im Süden von Mukiš, und zwar jenseits des direkten Nachbarn Niya. Diese Lokalisierung von Tunip erscheint im Hinblick auf die in vorliegenden Vertrag angesprochenen Regelungen problematisch, weil diese doch eher eine direkte als eine indirekte Nachbarschaft voraussetzen.

---

20 Klengel (1969) 88-89.

21 Helck (1971) 293.

22 Klengel (1965) 234-35; Klengel (1969) 90-91.

23 Klengel (1969) 75-77: nordwestlich von Ḥoms; vgl. auch del Monte-Tischler (1978) 440 (mit Nennung von weiterer Literatur).

24 Helck (1971) 150-56, 308 (Karte).

Präambel (Z. 1-3)

1 Niqmepa war nach Al.T. 15 Sohn und Nachfolger des Idrimi[25] und hat um die Mitte des 15. Jh.s geherrscht. Ihm lag daran, ein ungetrübtes Vasallenverhältnis zum hurritischen Oberherrn Sauštatar zu wahren (unten, Z. 72-73).

Die Schreibung KUR *Mu-ki-iš-ḫé* besagt, daß KUR nicht als Determinativ, sondern als Regens in einer Genitivverbindung verstanden wurde, dem der um die hurritische Nisbe =ḫe erweiterte Landesnamen Mukiš zugeordnet ist: *māt Mukiš=ḫe* "das Land von Mukiš, das Mukiš'sche Land".

2 Für eine erwogene Ergänzung ^{uru}*A-la-la-aḫ* am Anfang der Zeile[26] fehlt der Platz.

3 Da hier auf Vertragsworte angespielt wird, könnte am Zeilenanfang [*a-ma-*]*ta* zu ergänzen sein, dem das Demonstrativpronomen *anna-t*[*i*] folgt.

Paragraph 1 (Z. 4-8)

Der 1. Paragraph schließt direkt an die Präambel an und scheint sich mit der Beschaffung von Lebensmitteln zu befassen. Welche Rolle dabei die Händler und Nomaden spielen, läßt sich nicht mehr sagen—möglicherweise stehen sie in Opposition zu einander.

4 Die Gegenüberstellung von ^{lú}DAM.GÀR^{meš} und ERÍN^{meš} *zu-ti*^{ki} zeigt an, daß wir es bei *zu-ti* trotz des Determinativs KI nicht mit einem geographisch begrenzbaren Begriff zu tun haben, sondern mit der für diese Zeit neben *Aḫlamû/Aramû* gut belegten Bezeichnung von Nomaden allgemein[27].

---

25 Klengel (1965) 232-33.

26 Reiner (1969) 531.

27 Kupper (1957) 83ff.; Klengel (1972) 69-73; nach Klengel (1977) wäre es auch vorstellbar, daß die hier vorgenommene Parallelsetzung von ^{lú}DAM.GÀR^{meš} und ERÍN^{meš} *zu-ti*^{ki}, Händlern und Nomaden, auf einen durch Nomaden getragenen Handel hinweist.

Paragraph 2 (Z. 9-15)

Der 2. Paragraph handelt offenbar von Überläufern, die sich fälschlicherweise zu Mukiš bekennen und mit dem Tod bestraft werden sollen.

12 Die Austauschbarkeit der Objekts- und Possessivsuffixe gehört zu den typischen Merkmalen der mittelbabylonischen Koine Syriens.[28]

15 Zur häufig wiederkehrenden Ausdrucksweise *šumma lā* im Eid mit positiver Aussage s. GAG § 185g.

Für das—hier offensichtlich nicht deklinierte—*a-na-mu-ú* s. CAD A/2 125b.[29]

Die Form *ta-ad-du-uk-šu*[*-nu*] ist ein Pf. im promissorischen Eid s. GAG Nachträge § 185g.

Paragraph 3 (Z. 16-18)

Der 3. Paragraph regelt die Auslieferung von Umsiedlern nach Tunip.

16 Die Ergänzungen wurden in Anlehnung an Al.T. 3, dem Vertrag zwischen Idrimi von Alalaḫ und Pilliya wohl von Kizzuwatna, vorgenommen, wo in den Abschnitten Z. 23-25 und Z. 29-32 von Überläufern gehandelt wird.

17 Die Ergänzung la *ta*[*-ṣa-bat-šu*] geschieht in Anlehnung an die sonst übliche Diktion in diesem Text, vgl. z.B. Z. 18, 20, 22, etc.; mit dem Suff. 3.Pl. Z. 70—die Anhängung des Suff. der 3.Pers. erfolgt, wie üblich, ohne die graphische Veränderung des *š* in Kontaktstellung mit *t*.

Zum positiv promissorischen Eid im Bedingungssatz ohne Nachsatz mit dem Prs. (*šumma . . . lā taṣabbat-šu* "du wirst ihn ganz gewiß ergreifen!", "du mußt ihn ergreifen!") s. GAG § 185g.

---

[28] Vgl. Giacumakis (1970) 33-34: § 4.25; Huehnergard (1989) 132; Adler (1976) 27-28 (#15 b) für die Tušratta-Briefe.

[29] Vgl. Giacumakis (1970) 35: § 4.35; für Ugarit: Huehnergard (1989) 136.

18 Die Form *ašbu* weist, da hier kein St. im Subj. gemeint sein kann, auf ein (Vb.-)Adj.

Paragraph 4 (Z. 19-20)

Der 4. Paragraph stellt klar, daß Leute, die Beutegut aus Mukiš in Tunip zu veräußern gedenken, ausgeliefert werden müssen.

19 Wörtliche Übersetzung des epigraphisch klaren Bedingungssatzes[30]: "Wenn—Beute aus meinem Land ist in deinem Land—(wenn) es jemanden gibt, der (sie) verkaufen will".

Das Wort *šallatum* "Beute" läßt zunächst offen, ob mit ihm außer Sachgut auch Menschen gemeint sind, wie das folgende *pašāru* "lockern, (auf)lösen"[31] und das diesem in Z. 20 angehängte Suffix *-šu* suggeriert. Ein Argument dafür könnte das Thema Sklavenflucht im nächsten Paragraphen sein.

Paragraph 5 (21-31)

Der 5. Paragraph trifft Regelungen für flüchtige Sklavinnen oder Sklaven.

22-23 In *iṣṣabat-ma u . . . ubbal-šu* liegt die übliche Konstruktion der Gesetzestexte vor: Das Pf. des *šumma*-Bedingungssatzes wird im Nachsatz durch ein Prs. fortgeführt. Die Einleitung des Nachsatzes geschieht hier nach dem Muster der mB Koine Syriens durch die 'doppelte Konjunktion' *-ma u* "dann"; *-ma u* kann, wie dieser Paragraph noch vor Augen führt, entweder durch ein einfaches *u* ersetzt werden (z.B. Z. 24, 26) oder ganz entfallen (z.B. Z. 25).

Die Anrede an den Vertragspartner wird durch das affigierte *-mi* der direkten Rede am Imp. *šukun-šu* "setze ihn!" unterstrichen.

25 Die Tatsache, das ein Flüchtling *lā ašbu* "nicht ansässig" sein muß, weist gewiß darauf hin, daß er sich, um nicht erkannt zu werden, in der Gruppe der *ḫapīru*-Leute aufhält. Von daher erklärt es sich

---

30 Vgl. Reiner (1969) 531 Anm. 4 zu einer Lesung *la* [*i-pa-aš*]*-ša-ru ib-bá-aš-*[*ši*].

31 AHw. 842b: *pašāru(m)* G 3c.

auch, daß der Vertragspartner anstelle des Flüchtlings dessen *ālik pānī* "Anführer" auszuliefern hat.

Die einleitende Konditionalpartikel *šumma* "wenn" fehlt in den nächsten beiden Bedingungssätzen; offensichtlich übernimmt deren Funktion das *šumma* am Anfang von Z. 25.

26 Die Sg.-Form *liṣbat-šu* "möge ihn fassen" antizipiert entweder das Subjekt *ḫazannu* "Bürgermeister" des nächsten Satzes, oder es wird das unpersönliche Subjekt hier durch den Sg. ausgedrückt. Das akkadische Pseudoideogramm $^{\text{lú.meš}}$ŠI.BU^{meš} wird in Z. 51 syllabisiert: $^{\text{lú.meš}}$*ši-bu-te.*

Das Poss.-Suff. -*šu* nach $^{\text{lú.meš}}$ŠI.BU^{meš} weist zurück auf den Bürgermeister, der Zeugen für seine Angaben braucht.

27 Subjekt von *izakkarū* "sie werden sprechen" sind der Bürgermeister und seine fünf Zeugen.

Die Formulierung des Schwursatzes, der durch das affigierte -*mi* als direkte Rede gekennzeichnet ist, geschieht wider Erwarten aus dem Blickwinkel des Vertragspartners aus Mukiš.

28 Die Form *ut-te-er-šu* dürfte trotz der Schreibweise mit *e* eher ein Prs. als ein Prt. von Dt sein; darauf läßt u.a. *uše͏lla-šu* "er wird ihm vorbringen" des nächsten Konditionalsatzes schließen.

29 Hier beinhaltet *tamû* "schwören" den Meineid.

Die kaum leserlichen vier Zeichen nach *ú-še-el-la-šu* sind offensichtlich eine Rasur.

30 Der nominale Nachsatz *u šarrāqū* "dann sind sie Diebe" führt den *šumma*-Satz von Z. 29 fort.

Äußerst problematisch ist der auf *šar-ra-qú* folgende Abschnitt: D.J. Wiseman liest ihn *u up-ta-ka ri-it-ta-an* "and his hands shall be bound?"[32]; E. Reiner übersetzt ihn "and their hands are cut off"[33] und setzt dabei offenbar die in CAD B 165a vorgeschlagene Lesung

---

32 Wiseman (1953) 27, 29.

33 Reiner (1969) 531.

u ub-ta-<ta->ka ri-it-ta-an voraus; in CAD Š/2 (s.v. *šarrāqu*) findet sich eine geringfügige Abwandlung: *u butaqqa rittān* "and his hands will be cut off"[34]. Bei dieser Lesung können sich die Interpreten auf das hinlänglich bekannte Phänomen des Abschneidens der Hände von Delinquenten stützen.

Bei genauem Studium der Tafel ergeben sich allerdings starke Zweifel an den bisherigen Lesungen: 1. Bei dem Keil zwischen *šar-ra-qú* und **ub-ta-qà* handelt es sich nicht um einen Winkelhaken, der hier, vollends ungebräuchlich, als Konjunktion *u* "und" gedeutet worden ist, sondern um einen diagonalen Glossenkeil; 2. das zweite Zeichen der Verbform ist ein deutliches ZU und nicht ein in dieser Form sonst nicht bekanntes TA. Also haben wir es hier mit einem Glossenkeilwort *uB-Zu-Ka* zu tun, an das sich das epigraphisch sichere *ri-it-ta-an* anschließt.

Die Tatsache, daß wir es bei *uB-Zu-Ka* mit einem Glossenkeilwort zu tun haben, lenkt unsere Blicke aus dem engeren Rahmen der mB Koine hinaus: Wir müssen bei einem solchen Wort entweder mit einem fremden, westsemitischen oder einem hurritischen Wort rechnen. Obwohl letzteres aufgrund zahlreicher Belege nicht nur in Alalaḫ (siehe unten Z. 50) sondern auch in Ugarit und in Emar am nächsten liegt[35], unterbreiten wir nachfolgend eine Erklärung auf der Basis eines westsemitischen Substrats in Nordsyrien:

In Hinblick auf die Verbindung mit dem nachfolgenden *ri-it-ta-an* liegt es nahe, in *uB-Zu-Ka* eine Verbform mit einem *ā*-Auslaut zu erkennen, versuchsweise *up-zu-qà* zu lesen und |upsuqā| zu deuten; dabei bezöge sich der *ā*-Auslaut auf den—archaisierenden —Du. von *rittān*. Dieser Verbform könnte ein 'inneres Passiv'

---

34 CAD Š/2 70b, *s.v. šarrāqu* a); W. von Soden betrachtet die Stelle als 'unklar': AHw. 990a, *s.v. rittu* 2b.

35 Als mögliche Analyse wäre hierbei zu erwägen ups=ukka: Partizip des Zustands mit der Negationsformans =kk= von einer Basis ups=, von der weder Lautung noch Bedeutung bekannt ist: "sind nicht *ups=*".

(|jupsaq|) zugrundeliegen, wie sie auch für das Ugaritische angenommen wird[36], bei dem das unbetonte *a* der mittleren Silbe zu *u* enttont worden wäre. Damit bekämen wir die Voraussetzung für eine westsemitische finite Verbform, die von einer Wurzel PSQ abzuleiten wäre, die im Aram. stets etwas mit Abschneiden, Abtrennen, u.ä., zu tun hat[37]. Als Übersetzung böte sich "die beiden werden abgetrennt werden" an.

31 Die Reste von zwei Zeichen am Zeilenende gehören zu einer Rasur.

Paragraph 6 (Z. 32-37)

Der 6. Paragraph regelt die Behandlung zugelaufener Tiere.

33 Epigraphisch ist weder hier noch in Z. 35 ein Zweifel an der Lesung *jú-dá-šu* möglich, weil in beiden Fällen das Zeichen WA deutlich ist. Also haben wir es auch hier mit einer Verbform zu tun, deren Präfix westsemitisch anlautet.

34 Das enklitische *-ma* nach lúDAM.GÀR, das auch am Zeilenende zu ergänzen sein dürfte, hat eine hervorhebende Funktion.

37 Die Ergänzung [*šar-ra-qú* "ist ein Dieb"] legt sich sachlich nahe.

Paragraph 7 (Z. 38-46)

Der 7. Paragraph hat die Menschenhehlerei zum Thema, die grenzübergreifend praktiziert wurde.

38 Die Verbindung LÚ *ta-na-aṣ-ṣa-ru*, in der das finite Verbum den selten auftretenden Subjunktiv aufweist, stellt einen asyndetischen Relativsatz dar. Möglicherweise liegt eine ebensolche Konstruktion in der zweiten, am Ende weggebrochenen, Zeilenhälfte vor, die mit *it-ti* LÚ *ta-*[...] beginnt.

---

36 Vgl. Segert (1984) § 54.31.

37 Vgl. etwa aAram. *psq*$_1$, DNWSI 923.

Für die Deutung von *naṣāru* "bewachen, schützen, bewahren", das an dieser Stelle Sklaven zum Objekt hat, ist der Hinweis auf einen einschlägigen Paragraphen des Ešnunna-'Kodex' aufschlußreich—§ 52: SAG.ÌR *ù* GEMÉ *ša it-ti* DUMU *ši-ip-ri-im na-aṣ-ru-ma* KÁ.GAL *Èš-nun-na*.KI *i-te-er-ba-am ka-an-nam maš/ma-aš-ka-nam ù ab-bu-tam iš-ša-(ak-)ka-an-ma a-na be-lí-šu na-ṣir/ṣi-ir* "Ein Sklave oder eine Sklavin, die unter Bewachung eines Boten das Stadttor von Ešnunna betritt, wird mit Band, Fessel und 'Haarlocke' versehen und für seinen Herrn in Gewahrsam gehalten"[38].

Die Ergänzung [*i-na qa-ti-ka*] "[aus deiner Hand]" am Zeilenende erfolgt nach Z. 44. "Hand" steht hier in übertragenem Sinne für "Verfügung(sgewalt)".

39 Bei dem Bemühen, die bisher nicht erschlossene Lesung des Sumerogramms ^{giš}GÌR "Fußfessel" zu ermitteln, ist der eben zitierte Ešnunna-Paragraph 52 hilfreich: Dort treten als Sklavenmerkmale die Begriffe *kannum* "Binde, Band"[39], *maškanu(m)* "Tenne; Ort, Stätte; Fessel; Pfand"[40] und *abbuttu* "Haarlocke"[41] auf, von denen im vorliegenden Text zwei erhalten sind: ^{giš}GÌR (Z. 39) und *abbuttu* (Z. 40). Daraus läßt sich folgern, daß ^{giš}GÌR entweder *kannu* "Band" oder *maškanu* "Fessel" sein dürfte. Zieht man die Gebrauchsweisen dieser beiden Begriffe in Betracht, dann fällt die Entscheidung recht eindeutig zugunsten von *maškanu* "Fessel". Als mögliche Stütze dafür könnte auch gelten, daß die normalerweise aus Metall gefertigte *maškanu* "Fessel" einerseits auch aus Holz bestehen konnte[42]

---

38 LE § 52: A IV 10-13 || B IV 14-16; aus der Version B stammen die orthographischen Varianten.

39 AHw. 438: *kannu(m)* II; CAD K 156-57: *kannu* B "fetter, band, rope, belt, wisp of straw to bind a sheaf".

40 AHw. 626-27: *maškanu(m)* 3 "eine Fessel"; CAD M/1 372: *maškanu* 6 "fetter (for a slave)".

41 AHw. 5-6: *abbuttu(m)* I; CAD A/1 48-50.

42 AHw. 627a: $^{\text{(giš)}}$KAB = *iṣ maš-ka-ni*; CAD M/1 369a lex.

und daß *maškanu* "Fessel" nach *Ludlul bēl nēmeqi* II 98 zudem auf die Füße des Klagenden bezogen wird: *maš-kan ram-ni-ia muq-qu-ta še-pa-a-a* "in der Fessel meiner selbst sind gestrauchelt meine Füße"[43].

Für die weggebrochene zweite Hälfte von Z. 39 kann somit festgestellt werden, daß dort eine Bemerkung über *kannu* "Band" gestanden haben muß.

Die Restaurierung des Verbums, das wegen des sicher lesbaren *i-* doch wohl nur im Prs. gestanden haben kann und auf die Öffnung der Fußfessel angespielt haben könnte, ist unklar: Denkbar wären beispielsweise **ipette* "öffnet" oder **ipaṭṭar* "löst".

40 Die Prt.-Form *ú-gal-li-*[*bu*] scheint gegenüber dem Prs. in Z. 39 eine Vorzeitigkeit auszudrücken.

42 Wegen des zerstörten Kontextes ist das pluralische Subjekt von *izakkarū* "sie sprechen", dem *imaggarū* "sie willigen ein" (Z. 43) entspricht, nicht mehr bestimmbar.

44 Problematisch ist die Deutung von *ši-nu*, das neben LÚ.SAL-*tum* "Frau" und *ṣú-ḫa-ru* "junger Mann, Bursche" steht. Möglicherweise handelt es sich um eine ungewöhnliche Nebenform von *šanû* "anderer, Fremder"[44], bei der das unbetonte *a* in Kontaktstellung mit *š* zu *e* umgelautet worden ist.

46 Die letzten drei Zeichenreste sind eine Rasur.

PARAGRAPH 8 (Z. 47-53)

Der 8. Paragraph handelt vom grenzübergreifenden Diebstahl, den ein Mann aus Tunip in Mukiš begeht.

---

43 In Parallele zu *il-lu-ur-tú ši-ri-ia na-da-a i-da-a-a* "in die Fessel meines Leibes sind gelegt meine Arme" BWL 44: 97-98; von Soden (1990) 125, übersetzt Z. 98: "durch Selbstfesselung befallen sind meine Füße".

44 Wiseman (1953) 27.29, liest *amêlu lim-nu* und übersetzt "a wicked person"; Reiner (1969) 531: "criminal"—also liest offensichtlich auch sie **lem-nu* "böse, schlecht". Kaum wahrscheinlich ist die Lesung IGI.NU(.TUKU) "Blinder".

47 Da die Verbformen *išarraqū* "sie stehlen" (Z. 47)[45] sowie *ipallašū* "sie brechen ein" und *iṣabbatū* "sie nehmen weg" (Z. 48) eindeutig im Plural stehen, handelt es sich bei [lú]*šar-ra-qú* offensichtlich um einen kollektiven Singular.[46]

48 Die Textrestitution erfolgt nach Z. 23. Der dabei postulierte Wechsel zwischen den Präp. *i-na* und *a-na* läßt sich auch sonst nachweisen[47].

49 Zum asyndetischen Anschluß des Nachsatzes s. zu Z. 22-23.

50 Der auf *iš-tu pá-al-ši* "aus der Bresche, Einbruchstelle" folgende Keil ist kein Winkelhaken mit der sonst nicht belegbaren Deutung *u* "und", sondern ein Diagonaler. Also haben wir es hier wie in Z. 31 mit einem Glossenkeil zu tun, der vor ein Wort gesetzt ist, das dem Koine-Babylonischen fremd ist und das vorangehende *palšu* "Bresche" glossiert: *ḫa-at-ḫa-ar-ri.*

Beim Versuch, das Glossenwort zu analysieren, stößt man auf den in Nuzi belegten zusammengesetzten hurro-akkadischen Infinitivausdruck *ḫatḫumma epēšu*, dessen Deutung den akkadischen Wörterbüchern Schwierigkeiten bereitet: Das AHw. (336a) notiert dafür "töten(?)", das CAD (Ḫ 149b) "mng. uncert."; bei der Behandlung der Belegstellen aus HSS 13, 422, wird hier die Übersetzung LÚ.MEŠ *sarrūtu ša bīt qarīti* . . . *ḫatḫumma īpušū* "the criminals from the storehouse who committed the crime" vorgeschlagen, woraus für den besagten Ausdruck eine Übersetzung "commit a crime" ableitbar wäre. E. Laroche (GLH 88) führt im Hinblick auf diesen Ausdruck eine für ihn fragliche hurr. Wortbasis *ḫad-*, die er, wohl in Anlehnung an das AHw., "tuer?" übersetzt.

---

45 ŠRQ ist hier in der Ablautklasse konjugiert.

46 Denkbar ist es auch, daß der Schreiber es versäumt hat, das Determinativ [lú] mit dem Pl.-Zeichen [meš] zu versehen.

47 Für Alalaḫ vgl. Giacumakis (1970) 39, *s.v. ana* (5.3i, mit Anm. 3) sowie *s.v. ina* (5.8d).

Die Nuzi-Belege lassen zweierlei erkennen: Die Wortbasis ist ein um =ḫ= erweitertes ḫat/d= und wird im Zusammenhang mit Diebstahl gebraucht, den Verbrecher (*sarrūtu*) begingen, indem sie Vorratslager (*bīt qarīti*) aufbrachen und plünderten. Nichts liegt bei diesem Sachverhalt näher, als eine Brücke zum *ḫatḫarre* ≈ *palšu* in Alalaḫ zu schlagen und in ḫat=ḫ= den Weg zum Diebstahl zu sehen: die "Bresche, Einbruchstelle", durch die die Einbrecher zum Vorrat gelangen konnten. Der Ausdruck *ḫatḫumma epēšu* könnte dann wörtlich "das Einbrechen, einen Einbruch machen, eine Bresche schlagen" heißen und für alle Nuzi-Belegen einen glatten Sinn ergeben: LÚ.MEŠ *sarrūtu ša bīt qarīti* . . . *ḫatḫum-ma īpušū* "die Einbrecher, die ins Lagerhaus einbrachen".

Nun wieder zu *ḫatḫarre* ≈ *palšu*: In *ḫatḫarre* liegt die erweiterte Basis ḫat=ḫ= vor, an die ihrerseits das Element =ar= angetreten ist, das als Wurzelaugment faktitiv wirkt; dieses Konglomerat wurde schließlich durch =ne determiniert: ḫat=ḫ=ar=re "das Einbrechen, der Einbruch". Trifft diese aus der Analyse gewonnene Deutung für das hurritische Glossenwort zu, dann erscheint die Übersetzung "Einbruchstelle"[48] für das babylonische *palšu* zu konkret. Angesichts der Konstruktion *ištu* . . . *ṣabātu* "aus . . . herausholen" ist nach dem Prinzip *concretum pro abstracto* jedoch trotzdem die Übersetzung "Einbruchstelle" vorzuziehen.

Hinsichtlich der Verwendung von Glossenkeilen im vorliegenden Text zu festzuhalten: In Z. 31 soll der Glossenkeil nur darauf aufmerksam machen, daß nach ihm ein Wort folgt, das der mB Koine fremd ist, in Z. 50 liegt hingegen ein Übersetzungswort vor, das dem hurritischen Umfeld entstammt und offensichtlich eher geeignet war, einen Sachverhalt zu präzisieren, als das 'klassische' *palšu*.

51 Das Suffix -*šunu* nimmt offenbar das unmittelbar vorangehende Objekt *šībūtē-šu* auf.

---

[48] AHw. 816b; für "Einbruch(stelle), Loch, Bresche" kennt das Akkadische normalerweise *pilšu* (s. AHw. 863-64).

52 Zur bildlichen Rede *ḫiṭ'a ana qaqqadi šakānu* "die Verfehlung (d.h. die Folgen aus der Verfehlung) aufbürden" siehe Malul (1988) 266-67 mit Anm. 167.

In dieselbe Richtung weist das folgende *i-ḫap-pí-tu-šu* "sie werden übermächtig für ihn", d.h. "sie überführen ihn": Dieser Verbform liegt die Wurzel *ḫapātu* "übermächtig sein, werden"[49] zugrunde, die eine Wurzelvariante von *kabātu* "schwer sein, werden"[50] sein dürfte.

Paragraph 9 (Z. 54-58)

Der 9. Paragraph bestimmt das Verhalten des Ir-Addu gegenüber Wirtschaftsflüchtlingen aus Mukiš.

54 Die Lesung [L]Ú ist trotz der dazu passenden Spuren unsicher; gestützt wird die Annahme eines LÚ allerdings durch den nächsten Paragraphen (§ 10), in dem ebenfalls von der Wirtschaftsflucht, diesmal allerdings in umgekehrter Richtung, die Rede ist.

LÚ ist hier kollektiv gebraucht, wie die zugehörige Verbform *īrubam* "eingetreten ist" im Vergleich mit den nachfolgenden Formen—z.B. *idd*[*arr*]*arū* (Z. 56), *tanaṣṣar-šunu* (Z. 55), *tatakkal-šunu*—und vor allem der Ausdruck 1-*en* É "eine einzige Familie (von ihnen)" (Z. 58) zeigt.

Die Form des kontextlich erforderlichen Pron.-Suff. 1.Sg. am Subjekt [L]Ú, -*ia*, ist orthographisch, wie in der mB Koine üblich, nicht von der des Genitivs zu unterscheiden.

55 *ki-ma* KUR^{ki}-*ka* bedeutet wörtl.: "wie dein (eigenes) Land".

56 Da die Regenten von Zufluchtsgebieten gegenüber Überläufern stets mißtrauisch waren, ist die Bestimmung, Ir-Addu solle Wirtschaftsflüchtlinge aus Mukiš wie eigene Landeskinder behandeln und ihnen Vertrauen entgegenbringen (*lā tatakkal-šunu* im *šumma*-

---

49 AHw. 321b (i/i); CAD Ḫ 11f. *s.v. ḫabātu* C "to triumph(?), prevail(?)".

50 AHw. 416f.; CAD K 14-18.

Eid mit positiver Aussage: "du mußt ihnen vertrauen!"[51]), von größter Wichtigkeit und bedingt gleichzeitig, sie zu versorgen.[52]

Die Zeichenreste am Zeilenende legen die Lesung *id-*⸢*dá*⸣[*-ar-r*]*a-ru* "sie wünschen freien Lauf"[53] nahe.

57 AHw. 108a bringt den vorliegenden Beleg unter *bâru* I "fangen" (G 4 Ende); CAD B 2-4 verweist dafür von *ba'āru* "to catch fish, to fish, etc." (Ende, S. 4b oben) auf *bêru* "to select, choose; to examine" (S. 212f.), kommt dort aber nicht mehr auf diese Stelle zu sprechen. Der vom CAD suggerierte Bedeutungsansatz "prüfen"[54] ist kontextlich auf jeden Fall dem des Einfangens (AHw.) vorzuziehen, weil die Leute aus Mukiš schon die Rückkehr wünschten und nicht für eine Rücksendung eingefangen werden mußten. Eine Stütze dafür ist zudem die Aufforderung an den Vertragspartner, nicht eine einzige Familie zurückzuhalten (Z. 58).

Die Orthographie mit einem festen *ḫ* (*ta-ba-aḫ-ḫar*) erschwert den Anschluß an die Wurzel *bêru* (ass. *be'āru*). Möglicherweise liegt hier ein Substrateinfluß des Nordwestsemitischen vor, weil die Wurzel dort BḤR lautet.

Paragraph 10 (Z. 59-67)

Der 10. Paragraph, dessen Text fast ganz verlorengegangen its, bestimmt das Verhalten des Niqmepa gegenüber Wirtschaftsflüchtlingen aus Tunip.

---

51 Vgl. AHw. 1305a: *takālu* G II 1c.

52 Reiner (1969) 532, übersetzt: "feed them"; es erscheint unmöglich, die Bedeutung "zu Essen geben" an den G von *akālu* "essen" (AHw. 26-27; CAD A/1 245-57) anzuschließen.

53 AHw. 163a; CAD D 109; vgl. auch Dietrich (1993) 51.

54 Nach AHw. 122b unsicher nur fürs aA. — Vgl. auch die 'Nebenwurzel' *pâru* I "suchen", für deren Gt auch die Bedeutung "prüfen" ermittelt ist (AHw. 836b).

Paragraph 11 (Z. 68-71)

Der 11. Paragraph befaßt sich mit Bewohnern von Tunip, die sich gegenüber Mukiš feindlich verhalten; da große Teile des Textes zerstört sind, sind die Aussagen nicht mehr sicher zu erfassen.

69 Wenn die Lesung am Zeilenende zutrifft, dann haben wir es hier mit der transitiven Bedeutung von *ašāšu* "sich betrüben" (AHw. 79b) zu tun, wie sie in G^2 des CAD (A/2 423b) vorgeschlagen wird: "in Betrübnis versetzen". Inhaltlich ist hier offenbar davon die Rede, daß Ir-Addu bei Nichthandeln seinen Vertragspartner Niqmepa erzürnen kann.

70/71 Die beiden Feststellungen *la ta-ṣa-bat-šu-nu* dürften zu einem Eid mit positiver Aussage gehören, deren einleitendes *šumma* nicht erhalten ist.

71 Die Lesung und Deutung von *aš-li-im* ist unsicher: Wenn wir es mit dem Substantiv *ašlu* "Seil" zu tun haben, dann liegt hier wegen der Mimation offensichtlich ein Akkadogramm vor (: *AŠ-LI-IM*).

Treuegelöbnis (Z. 72-74)

Niqmepa gelobt dem hurritischen Oberherrn absolute Treue auch dann, wenn sich seine Kollegen gegen den Hurriter entscheiden sollten.

73 In *lā aḫappe* wird der Prohibitiv offensichtlich im Sinne des assertorischen Eides gebraucht.

Fluch (Z. 75-77)

Die drei Zeilen des Fluchs[55] stehen auf dem linken Tafelrand und werden durch den Namen des Schreibers abgeschlossen.

75 / 76 Da die Namen der Schwurgötter ideographisch geschrieben sind, ist es nicht mehr mit Sicherheit zu sagen, welche Lesung ihnen zugrundeliegt: Da die Epitheta und der Globalbegriff für das Pan-

---

55 Vgl. zu Flüchen allgemein: Sommerfeld (1993).

theon der Hochgötter in der traditionell mesopotamischen Weise auftreten, liegt es nahe, ^{d}IM als "Addu", ^{d}UTU als "Šamaš", ^{d}30 als "Sîn" und DINGIR^{meš} GAL.GA[L.E.NE] als "*ilū rabûtu*" zu lesen; es ist aber ebenso gut denkbar, daß wir bei den Götternamen die hurritische Form aufgreifen müssen: Teššub, Šimige und Kušuḫ.

^{d}IM und ^{d}UTU werden mit Epitheta angesprochen, ^{d}30 nicht. Die Epitheta von ^{d}UTU, EN-*el di-ni* "Herr über die Rechtsprechung", und ^{d}IM, E[N *bi-r*]*i* "Herr über die Opferschau", sind für diese Gottheiten im mesopotamischen Kulturkreis gut bezeugt.[56]

76 Die Verbform *ú-ḫal-liq-šu* dürfte fehlerhaft sein: Wir brauchen entweder ein Prs. *uḫallaqū-šu* "sie (: die Götter) werden ihn (bestimmt) vernichten!" oder einen Prk., *liḫalliqū-šu* "sie (: die Götter) mögen ihn vernichten!". Am leichtesten ist die Brücke zu *uḫallaqū-šu* zu schlagen, wenn wir unter der Voraussetzung eines *a*-*i*-Wechsels bei der unbetonten dritten Silbe (*liq* = *laq*$_{x}$) eine Lesung *ú-ḫal-laq*$_{x}$*-šu* postulieren und den Sing. mit einer *Constructio ad deum* erklären—vgl. die beiden folgenden Verbformen. Mit denselben Phänomenen haben wir es in Z. 77 zu tun, wo die Schreibweise *li-iš-bal-kat-šu* für ein erwartetes *lišbalkitū-šu* steht. Unter diesem Aspekt ist die in Anlehnung an das folgende *li-iš-bal-kat-šu* vorgenommene Ergänzung der Prk.-Form [*li-ḫa*]*l-liq* nicht unproblematisch: Es könnte hier durchaus [*ú-ḫa*]*l-liq* gestanden haben.

77 Der Name des Schreibers, dessen theophores Element ^{d}IM ist, kann nicht mehr sicher rekonstruiert werden.

Dynastiesiegel von Alalaḫ und Mukiš (mit Legende)

Es ist als ein besonderes Merkmal für Niqmepa zu werden, daß er das Siegel von Abban, dem Sohn des Šarran und Dynastiegründer von Mukiš-Alalaḫ, benützte.[57]

---

[56] Für *Šamaš bēl dīni* vgl. AHw. 172a (*dīnu* 2), CAD D 152 (*dīnu* 1b); für Addu/Adad *bēl bīri* vgl. AHw. 130a (*bīru* b), CAD B 265 (*bīru* A c).

[57] Siehe Landsberger (1954) 55.

Al.T. 2

Al.T. 2

Bibliography

Adler, H.-P. (1976) *Das Akkadische des Königs Tušratta von Mitanni.* AOAT 201. **del Monte, G., and J. Tischler** (1978) *Die Orts- und Gewässernamen der hethitischen Texte.* RGTC 6 Wiesbaden. **Dietrich, M.** (1993) *Die Frage nach der persönlichen Freiheit im Alten Orient, in: Mesopotamica – Ugaritica – Biblica. Festschrift für Kurt Bergerhof.* AOAT 232, 45-58. **Dietrich, M., and O. Loretz** (1981) Die Inschrift der Statue des Königs Idrimi von Alalaḫ. *UF* 13: 201-69. **Draffkorn (Kilmer), A.** (1959) *Hurrians and Hurrian at Alalaḫ. An Ethnolinguistic Analysis* (Ph.D. dissertation). Philadelphia. **Giacumakis, G.** (1970) *The Akkadian of Alalaḫ.* Janua Linguarum 59. Den Hague. **Goetze, A.** (1956) *The Laws of Eshnunna.* AASOR 31. New Haven. **Helck, W.** (1971) *Die Beziehungen Ägyptens zu Vorderasien im 3. und 2. Jahrtausend v.Chr.* Ägyptologische Abhandlungen 5. Wiesbaden. **Hoftijzer, J., and K. Jongeling** (1995) *Dictionary of the North-West Semitic Inscriptions* (HdO I 21 1/2). Leiden. **Huehnergard, J.** (1989) *The Akkadian of Ugarit.* Harvard Semitic Monographs. Atlanta, Ga. **Klengel, H.** (1965) *Geschichte Syriens im 2. Jahrtausend v.u.Z.* Teil 1 - Nordsyrien. Berlin. (1969) *Geschichte Syriens im 2. Jahrtausend v.u.Z.* Teil 2 - Mittel- und Südsyrien. Berlin. (1972) *Zwischen Zelt und Palast. Die Begegnung von Nomaden und Seßhaften im alten Vorderasien.* Wien. (1977) Nomaden und Handel. *Iraq* 39, 163-69. (1992) *Syria 3000 to 300 B.C. A Handbook of Political History.* Berlin. **Kupper, J.** (1957) *Les nomades en Mésopotamie au temps des rois de Mari.* Paris. Lambert, W. G. (1967) *Babylonian Wisdom Literature.* Oxford. **Landsberger, B.** (1954) Assyrische Königsliste und "dunkles Zeitalter". *JCS* 8: 31-73. **Laroche, E.** (1980) *Glossaire de la langue Hourrite.* Paris. **Liverani, M.** (1964) L'estradizioni dei rifugiati in AT 2. *Rivista degli Studi Orientali* 39: 111-15. **Malul, M.** (1988) *Studies in Mesopotamian Legal Symbolism.* AOAT 221. **Reiner, E.** (1969) Akkadian Treaties from Syria and Assyria. In J. B. Pritchard, ed., *Ancient Near Eastern Texts Relating to the Old Testament. 3.* Princeton: 531-41. **Segert, S.** (1984) *Basic Grammar of the Ugaritic Language.* Berkeley. **von Soden, W.** (1952) *Grundriß der akkadischen Grammatik,* AnOr 33. (1990) "Weisheitstexte" in akkadischer Sprache. TUAT III/1, 110-88. **van Soldt, W. H.** (1991) *Studies in the Akkadian of Ugarit. Dating and Grammar.* AOAT 40. **Sommerfeld, W.** (1993) *Flüche und Fluchformeln als Quelle für die altorientalische Kulturgeschichte, in: Mesopotamica - Ugaritica - Biblica, Festschrift für Kurt Bergerhof.* AOAT 232, 447-63. **Speiser, E. A.** (1954) The Alalakh Tablets. *Journal of the American Oriental Society* 74: 18-25. **Wiseman, D. J.** (1953) *The Alalakh Tablets.* Occasional Publications of the British Institute of Archaeology at Ankara. London. **Woolley, Sir L.** (1955) *Alalakh. An Account of the Excavations at Tell Atchana in the Hatay, 1937–1949. Reports of the Research Committee of the Society of Antiquities of London XVIII.* Oxford.

On the Location of Simurrum

Douglas R. Frayne
University of Toronto

1. *Introductory Remarks*

Michael Astour has provided scholars with many insightful studies on the geography of the ancient Near East, and it may be fitting, therefore, to honour the celebrant on the occasion of his eightieth birthday with a paper dealing with geographical matters—in specific terms—the question of the location of the ancient city of Simurrum.[1]

---

1 The city name was written in early periods Simurrum; by Old Babylonian times the writing had changed to Šimurrum. The designation Simurrum used throughout this article is conventional. Throughout this paper we have cited the toponyms without the postfixed KI determinative.

2. *Simurrum in Pre-Kassite Times*

2.1 *Early Dynastic Period*

If we can believe the evidence of a proverb known from two Old Babylonian period tablet copies, Simurrum was already the target of a military campaign during the Early Dynastic period.[2] The text in question deals the taking of Simurrum by a certain king Nanna, who, following Hallo,[3] is likely to be identified with the Early Dynastic period king of Ur named A-ane-pada. The relevant line in the Oxford[4] and Philadelphia[5] exemplars of the proverb reads as follows:

si-mu-ru.KI i-dib gú-bi nu-mu-un-da-gíd-x	(Nanna) took Simurrum, but was not able to carry off its tribute.

Unfortunately, very little historical information can be gleaned from this laconic statement.

2.2 *Sargonic Period*

2.2.1 *Sargon*

A Sumerian year name of Sargon of Akkad attested on two tablets from Nippur deals with a military campaign against Simurrum.

mu *śar-um*-GI śi-mur-um.KI-šè ⸢ì⸣-gin-⸢na-a⸣	The year Sargon went (on a campaign) to Simurrum.[6]

Because we have so little historical data for the reign of Sargon, even the relative placement of this year name within the evidently long reign of Sargon is unclear.

---

2 Gurney and Kramer (1976) 38-39 and 105 Proverb no. 5.

3 Hallo (1978) 73.

4 Gurney and Kramer (1976) 105 obv. line 13.

5 Legrain (1922) no. 50 col. ii line 4′.

6 Pohl (1935) no. 151 rev. lines 10-12. Westenholz (1975a) no. 151 lines 10-12. Westenholz (1975b) no. 145 obv. lines 3′-4′.

2.2.2 *Narām-Sîn*

Two Akkadian year names of Narām-Sîn of Akkad (here designated as [i][7] and [ii][8]) deal with campaigns against Simurrum; a third Sargonic year name (iii) does not mention Simurrum by name, but may possibly be connected with an attack on the city.

(i) [*i*]*n* 1 MU [^{d}]*na-ra-am-*^{d}⸢EN.ZU⸣ *a-na* KASKAL.⸢KI⸣ *śi-mu-ur*$_{4}$*-rí-im*.KI *i-li-ku*	The year Narām-Sîn went on the Simurrian campaign.
(ii) *in* 1 MU ^{d}*na-ra-am-*^{d}E[N.ZU] REC448bis *śi-mu-ur*$_{4}$*-ri-*[*im*.KI] *in ki-ra-šè-ni-we iš*$_{11}$*-a-ru ù ba-ba* ÉNSI *śi-mu-ur*$_{4}$*-ri-im*.KI *dub-ul* ÉNSI *a-ra-me*.KI *ik-mi-ù*	The year Narām-Sîn was victorious over Simurrum at Kirašeniwe and captured Baba, governor of Simurrum, (and) Dubul, governor of Arame.

The Baba who appears as governor of Simurrum in year name (ii) is likely to be connected with the Baba who is named as governor of Simurrum in a temporal clause in a mace-head inscription in Akkadian from Sippar. The text, which is likely to be attributed to Narām-Sîn, reads:

Lacuna	... when he (Narām-Sîn[?]) [...]
1′) [*ì*]*-nu*	[Ba]ba, [gove]rnor of [Sim]ur[rum].[9]
2′) [ba]-ba	
3′) [PA.T]E.SI	
4′) [*śi-m*]*u-ur*$_{4}$-[*ri-i*]*m*.KI	
Lacuna	

(iii) The Baba of the year name and mace-head inscription, in turn, may possibly be connected with the partially preserved PN b[í]-bí which appears in a Sargonic period year name:

7 Cohen (1976) 227-28.

8 Gelb (1952) no. 217 lines 2-8 and no. 220 lines 1-10.

9 Winkler (1897) 545 no. 3. Walker and Collon (1980) 100 and pl. 26 no. 40.

[*in* 1 MU ...] ti-[...] [b]í-bí-[...] *en-a-*[*ru*] *ù* REC448bis *śa-dú-a-tim* [*in*] *ḫa-śi-ma-ar*.KUR [*iš*$_{11}$]-*a-ru*	[The year ... defe[ated] [B]ibi[...] and was [vic]torious over the mountain lands [in] Ḫaśimar.[10]

The expression "mountain lands in Ḫaśimar" in this year name is almost certainly to be connected with the Mount Ḫašimur named in Neo-Assyrian sources.[11] Mount Ḫašimur was the mountain crossed by the Assyrian king Šalamaneser III just before his triumphal entry into the city of Namri.[12] N. Hannoon, in his unpublished dissertation entitled "Studies in the Historical Geography of Northern Iraq During the Middle and Neo-Assyrian Periods," has analyzed the data concerning Mount Ḫašimur. He writes:

> In any event, the texts of Shalmaneser III and Šamši-Adad V, mentioned above, indicate that (a) the Ḫašimur mountain was east of the Diyala, (b) it was to the west or south-west of the land Namri, which might be located east of modern Khanaqin .... This leads us to suggest the area east south-east of Khanaqin as far as the Iraq-Iran border as the location of Mt. Ḫašimur. In that area Mt. Darewishkeh and its western extension just south of Khanaqin seem likely to be Ḫašimur.[13]

The point where the Diyālā River cuts through the Darāwīsh-Kuh[14] is a mere nine kilometers west of modern Khāniqīn. Now, in our discussion

---

10 de Genouillac (1921) pl. 54 no. 9625 rev. lines 3′-9′.

11 Parpola (1970) 155 sub ḪAŠIMUR.

12 Michel (1954–59) 154. Levine (1973b) 134 notes: "The proposed identification of Ḫ[ašimur] with Ḫašmar is untenable."

13 Hannoon (1986) 362.

14 The mountain name appears as Darewishkeh in Hannoon's dissertation (p. 362), and as Jabal Darawishkah in the 1: 253,440 topographical map published by the Directorate of Military Survey of the British Army (date sometime in the 1940's). According to notes of Professor R. M. Savory of the University of Toronto, who kindly helped me with the transcription of the modern geographical names in this study: "Dārwīsh is a spurious Arabic broken plural of the Persian word Darwīsh, and it is just possible that the Kah stands for the Persian Kūh = 'mountain'. Jabal would then be redundant."

below, we suggest that Khāniqīn marks the location of ancient Niqum. Of interest, then, is the find of a few mace-heads (some made of stone, and one of bronze) incised with an inscription of a governor of Niqum who acknowledges Narām-Sîn as his overlord.[15] If the suggested connection between Darāwīsh-Kuh and Mount Ḫaśimar be true, then Niqum was likely conquered during the same campaign that was commemorated in year name (iii). Further, the point where the Diyālā River cuts through the Darāwīsh-Kuh lies only 39 km south of Simurrum (according to our geographical reconstruction; see §4.4 below). If these site identifications prove to be correct, they could account for the appearance of both Bibi (=[?] Baba, governor of Simurrum) and Mount Ḫaśimar in year name (iii).

2.2.3 *Sargonic Period*

A reference to the people of Simurrum is found in a Sargonic period letter from Gasur:

ù śum-ma si-mur-ur₄-rí-ù.KI *a-dì da-ni-iś* ŠE *la i-ma-ḫa-ru in qer-bí-śu a-na* ŠE.BA *li-dì-in*	And if the people of Simurrum cannot hunt up any grain at all, then he should provide it as a grain ration from it (the seed grain).[16]

2.3 *Lagaš II or Early Ur III Period*

Two tablets from Girsu of probable late Lagaš II or early Ur III[17] date record rations accorded to a important group of foreign visitors at Girsu. They included men from Simurrum and guests from the eastern cities of Ḫuḫnuri and Lullubu. Steinkeller has suggested that the foreigners might be members or dependents of the Elamite royal family[18]; they are qualified

15 Dossin (1962)158-59 and pl. XXV. Lambert (1968) 85-86 and pls. VIII-IX.

16 Meek (1935) pl. 11 no. 5 lines 1-14. See also Kienast and Volk (1995) 182-84 Ga 3 lines 1-14.

17 Thureau-Dangin (1903) 97 no. 249 and Grégoire (1981) pl. 31 no. 92.

18 Steinkeller (1988) 53 n. 21.

in the texts as being: dumu šim-bí-iš-ḫu-<me>[19] (variant: šim-bí-iš-me[20]) "sons Šimbi-išḫu<k>." Šimbi-išḫuk, in turn, as Steinkeller notes, is the Elamite king who was the father of Kutik-Inšušinak.[21] The aliens' presence at Girsu at this time may possibly be connected with Ur-Nammu's victory over Kutik-Inšušinak; the triumph is recorded in a royal inscription known from a tablet copy from Isin.[22]

2.4 *Ur III Period*

2.4.1 *Year Names*

(i) Šulgi 25: mu śi-mu-ru-um.KI ba-ḫul
"The year Simurrum was destroyed."[23]

(ii) Šulgi 26: mu śi-mu-ru-um.KI a-rá-2-kam-ma-aš ba-ḫul
"The year Simurrum was destroyed for a second time."[24]

(iii) Šulgi 32: mu śi-mu-ru-um.KI a-rá-3-kam-ma-aš ba-ḫul
"The year Simurrum was destroyed for a third time."[25]

According to W.W. Hallo:

> The third defeat of Simurrum may have involved Šulgi's crowning military achievement, to judge from the Old Babylonian omen tradition.[26]

The ruler of Simurrum conquered by Šulgi is known to have been a certain Tappa(n)-Daraḫ; Hallo has examined various Ur III and later sources that refer to this ruler.[27] Three omens published by Goetze deal with

---

19 Grégoire (1981) pl. 31 no. 92 obv. ii line 4′.

20 Thureau-Dangin (1903) 97 no. 249 obv. ii line 5′.

21 For example in Scheil (1900) pl. 12 line 7.

22 Wilcke (1987) 109-10 rev. col. v′.

23 Schneider (1936) 15 no. 23.

24 *Ibid.* 15 no. 24.

25 *Ibid.* 15 no. 30.

26 Hallo (1978) 74.

27 *Ibid.* 74-75. See also Biggs in this volume.

the capture of Tappa(n)-Daraḫ.[28] As noted by Hallo,[29] a PN *tap-pá-da-ra-aḫ* is found in a Drehem tablet dated to Š 34[30] and a daughter of Tappa(n)-Daraḫ is mentioned in a text dated to Š 33.[31] Tappa(n)-Darah's wife appears in a tablet dated to Š 33[32]; later references noted by Hallo date to the time of Šū-Sîn. [33] Further, an omen known from a Middle Assyrian copy dated by Nougayrol to the time and library of Tiglath-pileser I refers to the defeat of Tappa(n)-Daraḫ: [... *tab*]-*ba-gar ù*(!) *rab-si-si* MAN.MEŠ *šá* x [...] / [...] x *su-nu-ti-ma* ŠEŠ ŠEŠ-*šú* GAZ "[...Tab]ba-gar and Rabsisi, kings of ... [...], he [...] and brother killed brother."[34] In addition, a chronicle text from Seleucid Uruk retains a memory of Šulgi's attack against Tappa(n)-Daraḫ: [x ^{d}š]ul-gi LUGAL ŠEŠ.UNU.KI A ^{m}ur-^{d}nammu / [*šar*]-*ru-tu* KUR.KUR *ka-la-ši-na i-pu-uš* / [*tab*]-*ban-ga-ár u* ^{m}*rab-si-si* LUGAL.MEŠ *šá* KUR SU.BIR$_4$.KI *i-be-el* "Šulgi, king of Ur, son of Ur-Nammu, exercised [ki]ngship over all the lands, [Tab]bangar and Rabsisi, kings of the land of Subartu, he overpowered."[35]

(iv) Šulgi 44: mu śi-mu-ru-um.KI ù lu-lu-bi.KI a-rá-10-LAL-1-kam-aš ba-ḫul

"The year Simurrum and Lullubu were destroyed for a ninth time."[36]

(v) Šulgi 45: mu ^{d}šul-gi nita-kala-ga lugal-uri$_5$.KI-ma lugal-an-ub-da-límmu-ba-ke$_4$ ur-bí-lum.KI śi-mu-ru-um.KI lu-lu-bu.KI ù kára-ḫar.KI-ra AŠ-eš šu du$_{11}$-ga šu-tibir-ra im-mi-ra

---

28 Goetze (1948) 259-60 nos. 25-27.

29 Hallo (1978) 74-75.

30 Hallo (1973) pl. V no. 14 line 3.

31 Schneider (1932) 16 no. 53 line 21. See also Molina (1993) pl. XX no. 53 line 22.

32 Schneider (1932) 12 no. 40 line 4. See also Molina (1993) pl. XIV no. 40 line 4.

33 Hallo (1978) 75 nn. 40-41.

34 Walker (1972) pl. 53 BM 122643 rev. lines 14-15.

35 Hunger (1976) 19 and 123 no. 2 pl. lines 3-5.

36 Schneider (1936) 20 no. 42.

"The year Šulgi, mighty man, king of Ur, king of the four quarters, having overtaken Urbillum, Simurrum, Lullubu, and Karaḫar as a single group, struck them down."[37]

(vi) Ibbi-Sîn 3: mu ^{d}*i-bí*-^{d}EN.ZU lugal-uri$_5$.KI-ma-ke$_4$ śi-mu-ru-um.KI mu-ḫul

"The year Ibbi-Sîn, king of Ur, destroyed Simurrum."[38]

2.4.2 *City Governors*

2.4.2.1 *Mentioned in Seal Inscriptions*

An important official named Ṣilluš-Dagān is named (generally without title) in a few archival texts dating to the period of Š 43 to IS 1.[39] A seal impression on a tablet envelope dated to AS 6 ii indicates that he was governor of Simurrum. The inscription reads:

1) *ṣi-lu-uš*-^{d}*da-gan*	1) Ṣilluš-Dagān,
2) énsi-	2–3) governor of Simurrum:
3) śi-mu-ru-um.KI-ma	
4) *i-bí*-^{d}IŠKUR	4) Ibbi-Adad,
5) dub-sar	5) scribe,
6) ir$_{11}$-zu	6) (is) your servant.[40]

A second seal inscription mentioning Ṣilluš-Dagān as governor of Simurrum is found on an undated tablet envelope from Drehem.[41]

2.4.2.2 *Mentioned in Archival Texts*

In addition to Ṣilluš-Dagān, two other Ur III rulers of Simurrum are attested in archival sources, namely: Kirib-ulme and Tappan-daraḫ.[42]

---

37 *Ibid.*, 22 no. 43 B e (restored from duplicates).

38 *Ibid.*, 37 no. 3 B a.

39 Goetze (1962) 13-14 no. 7.

40 Keiser (1971) pl. LXXIX no. 627.

41 Scheil (1926) 36-37 no. 4.

42 For references, see Edzard and Farber (1974) 166-67 sub Simurum.

2.5 *Early Old Babylonian Period*

2.5.1 *Iddi(n)-Sîn of Simurrum*

With the collapse of the Ur III empire, the state of Simurrum apparently regained its independence. Evidence supporting this supposition is found in an archival text from Isin dated to late in the reign of Išbi-Erra. It records the disbursement of a royal gift (of Išbi-Erra) to an unnamed king of Simurrum; the tablet also mentions a messenger from Simurrum.[43] Of further note in this connection is a roughly contemporaneous Akkadian letter from Ešnunna published by Whiting.[44] It contains a report of a military campaign in the eastern mountains. The letter indicates that a certain Iddi(n)-Sîn had been defeated in the east by the enemy troops of DUMU-*ḫu-dam*.[45] The letter unfortunately gives no indication of who Iddi(n)-Sîn or DUMU-*ḫu-dam* were. While DUMU-*ḫu-dam* is otherwise unknown, the Iddi(n)-Sîn of this letter is almost certainly to be identified with the Iddi(n)-Sîn who has left us four inscriptions carved into a rock-face near the town of Bardi Sanjian in the Bītwāta region of the Rāniyyah plain. Three of the rock-cut inscriptions, now housed in the Iraq Museum, were published by Al-Fouadi,[46] and one, in the Israel Museum, remains unpublished.[47] The Bītwāta region is clearly quite distant from the city of Simurrum, and the rock reliefs attest to the wide sphere of influence of Simurrum during the reign of Iddi(n)-Sîn. Another rock-cut inscription, probably belonging to Iddi(n)-Sîn (or to his son Zabazuna), has been found, much closer to the city of Simurrum, on a cliff just north of the modern village of Sar-i Pul-i Zuhāb on the Alwand (Ḥulwān) River.[48] While no royal name appears in the extant text of the Sar-i Pul-i Zuhāb inscription, the fact that its concluding formula is virtually

---

43 Crawford (1954) pl. LXXI no. 421 lines 10 and 16.

44 Whiting (1987) 3738 no. 2.

45 *Ibid.*, lines 4′-7′.

46 Al-Fouadi (1978) 122-29.

47 We eagerly await A. Shaffer's publication of this inscription.

48 Hrouda (1976) 6 and pl. 1 and 6a.

identical with that found in the Iddi(n)-Sîn inscriptions from the Bītwāta region argues for its attribution to Iddi(n)-Sîn (or Zabazuna). According to our geographical reconstruction, the city of Niqum lay about 32 kilometres south of Simurrum. Of interest, then, is the mention of the cities of Niqum (and Ḫalman) in the above cited Ešnunna letter.[49] Unfortunately, the city names appear in a broken context; a possible interpretation takes them to be cities once held (and subsequently lost?) by Iddi(n)-Sîn.

3. *Cities on the Section of the Great Khurāsān Road beside the Alwand (Ḥulwān) River.*

3.1 *Introduction*

Chart 1 lists various ancient cities (cited as 1-8 in the header of the chart) which, to judge from a variety of evidence, lay northeast of the Jebel Ḥamrīn on a land route that ran beside the Diyālā and Alwand (Ḥulwān) Rivers. The region is shown in the map.

A productive analysis of this material results from: (a) considering those sites that can be identified on the basis of inscriptional finds, and (b) by taking into account the evidence of the relevant, apparently geographically arranged, sections of: (i) the LGN, and (ii) the geographical list from Tall Ḥarmal.

3.2 *Sites Identified on the Basis of Inscriptional Finds*

In this section we consider three sites.

3.2.1 *Site* 1: *Mê-Turran = Tall Ḥaddād and Tulūl al-Sīb*

Tablets found in Iraqi salvage excavations at the mounds of Tall Ḥaddād and Tulūl al-Sīb have positively identified the combined mounds as the site of ancient Mê-Turran.[61] The published inscriptional material excavated at neighboring Tall Baradān,[62] on the other hand, is insufficient to determine if Tall Baradān comprised part of greater Mê-Turran or was a differently named neighboring city.[63]

---

49 Whiting (1987) 3738 no. 2 lines 2 and 5.

50 Pettinato (1978) 54-73; *ibid.*, (1981) 217-41. Entry numbers are given on the chart.

CHART 1: Cities along the Combined Courses of the Diyālā and Alwand Rivers

Source	1) Mê-Turran	2) Batir	3) Niqum	4) Namar	5) Madar	6) Karaḫar	7) Padan	8) Ḫalman
LGN[50]		258: ba-tá-ar	—	237: na-mar	241: ma-dar	242: kak-kà-ra		244: ʾà-ir-rìm
Old Akkadian Texts: Tall al-Sulaymah[51]		ba-tá-rí no. 29 line 10 no. 42 line 12		na-ma-rí no. 5 col. ii line 9		kà-kà-ra-an no. 5 col. I line 6	pá-da-ni no. 34 line 8	
Early Old Babylonian letter from Ešnunna[52]		—	ni-qi_4-[im] Letter 2 line 2	—	—	—	—	ḫa-al-⸢ma-ni⸣ Letter 2 line 5
Tall Ḫarmal Geographical List[53]	me-tu-ra-an line 78	—	ni-qum line 77	—	—	kára-ur line 76	—	—
Tamītu text mentioning Ḫammu-rāpi[54]	—	—	—	—	—	—	URU.pad-ni lines 5 and 10	KUR.ḫal-man line 24
Mustafa, O.B. Texts Mê-Turan no. 916[55]	—	—	—	na-mar	—	kára-ḫar	—	—
Mustafa, *op. cit.* no. 114	me-tu-ra-an	ba-ti-ir	—	—	—	—	—	—
Samsu-ilūna Genealogy[56]	—	—	—	—	ma-da-ra	ḫa-ar-ḫa-ar	—	—
MB kudurru[57]	—	—	—	na-mar	—	—	—	ḫal-man
MB kudurru[58]				na-mar				ḫal-man
Agum-Kakrime Inscription[59]							pa-da-an	al-ma-an
ḪAR-gud[60]	—	—	—	—	—	—	pa-din	ár-man

3.2.2 *Site* 2: *Batir* = *Tall al-Sulaymah*

An inscribed brick found in the course of salvage excavations at Tall al-Sulaymah gives the titulary of an apparently local ruler; he styles himself: *ra-bí-an* x x / *ša ba-*⸢*ti*⸣*-ir.*[K]I "... chief of Batir."[64] Further, a lapis-lazuli seal found in the same excavations bears the seal inscription of a certain Apil-kīn, who is named as "anointed priest of the goddess Batirītum (Lady of Batir)" (GUDU$_4$ ^{d}*ba-ti-ri-tum*).[65] The combined evidence of the brick and seal provides a compelling, if not conclusive, argument for an identification of Tall al-Sulaymah with ancient Batir. Previously, F. Rashid had suggested that the mound might mark ancient Awal,[66] but the evidence of the LGN, as interpreted by the author, points to a location of ancient Awal in the vicinity of Qarā Tappah.[67]

Although it cannot be used for identification purposes, we may note that the GN *ba-ti-rí* does, in fact, appear in two archival texts from Tall al-

---

51 Rashid (1981) *passim.*

52 Whiting (1987) 37 no. 2. Line numbers are given in the chart.

53 Landsberger, Reiner, and Civil (1974) 87 col. iii lines 74-86. Line numbers are given in the chart.

54 K3703+5966+9957+16238: transliteration courtesy W. G. Lambert.

55 Mustafa (1983).

56 Schroeder (1917) no. 156 line 3′.

57 Borger (1970) 2 col. i line 14.

58 Pinches (1880) 33 col. 1 lines 37-38.

59 King (1912) 35 col. ii lines 22-23.

60 Landsberger, Reiner, and Civil (1974) 36 Recension B Tablet V line 6.

61 Anonymous (1985) 220.

62 Kessler (1995) 281-88.

63 Kessler (1995) 282-83 conjectures that LGN 33: ^{d}ra-sa-ap.KI—a city whose name clearly links it with the god Nergal—may be connected with Mê-Turan, in light of the unequivocal textual evidence attesting to the cult of Nergal at Mê-Turan.

64 Frayne (1990) 702.

Sulaymah.[68] In this case, a reading Batiri rather than a conceivable Patiri is indicated by the writing Batir found in Old Babylonian sources.[69]

3.2.3 *Site* 8: *Ḫalman = Sar-i Pul-i Zuhāb*

A *kudurru* (boundary stone) found, probably *in situ*, near the famous rock relief of Annu-banini near Sar-i Pul-i Zuhāb bears an inscription which names a certain Šitti-Marduk as governor of Namar and Ḫalman.[70] According to its editor, R. Borger: "Das heißt natürlich, daß der neue Grenzstein die Gleichsetzung Ḫalman (Arman) = Ḥulwān = Sarpol-e Zohāb endgültig sichert."

The positive identification of sites 1, 2 and 8 enables us to bracket a specific section of the Great Ḫurāsān Road that ran beside the Alwand (Ḥulwān) River.

3.3 *The Evidence of Geographically Organized Texts*

3.3.1 *The List of Geographical Names* (LGN)

Entries 241-44 in the LGN, according to the interpretation of the author, are to be identified with cities lying along the stretch of the Great Khurāsān Road that ran beside the Alwand (Ḥulwān) River. Because we have shown in our previous study of the LGN that many (if not all) sections of the LGN list cities in a geographical order, we have assumed that the same holds true for entries 241-44. In the following discussion we consider three sites: nos. 4, 6 and 8.

---

65 Al-Gailani Werr (1992) 47 no. 87.

66 Rashid (no date) 55-56.

67 Frayne (1990) 56.

68 Rashid (1981) 199 no. 29 line 10; 106 no. 42 line 12.

69 While a value pá (BA) is attested in Old Babylonian, it is rare.

70 Borger (1970) 2 col. i line 14.

3.3.1.1 *Site* 4: *Namar/Namri*

LGN 237: *na-ma-ar* is to be identified with the important city of Namar; the GN is well attested in Middle Babylonian and Neo-Assyrian sources. It occurs already in Sargonic times in a tablet from Tall al-Sulaymah[71] along with a mention of *kà-kà-ra-an*[72] (Karaḫar); this corresponds to a mention of *na-mar* and *kára-ḫar* in an Old Babylonian period tablet from Mê-Turran.[73] In a detailed study of the location of Namri (= Namar) Levine concludes: "… the evidence points at the present time to a location for Namri along the Diyala somewhere between the Hamrin and the Qara Dagh."[74] Postgate adds: "… a location close to the Hamrin basin, but on the Khorasan road, seems to fit the facts best to us, pointing to the Khanaqin area or a little further east."[75] If our proposed identifications of LGN 242: *kak-kà-ra* and LGN 244 *ʾà-ir-rìm* with Karaḫar and Arman/Ḫalman respectively, hold true, then a location of Namar/Namri somewhat to the west of Sar-i Pul-i Zuhāb and a little to the east of Khāniqīn would be indicated.

3.3.1.2 *Site* 6: *Karaḫar* = (?) *Qaṣr-i-Shīrīn*

While an Ur III variant spelling ḫar-ḫar for káraḫar is known,[76] this ḫar-ḫar (= Karaḫar) is to be kept distinct from Assyrian Ḫarḫar, which Levine has indicated[77] is to be located much further east, namely, on the Great Khurāsān Road in the area of the central or eastern Mahidasht. Again, based on the correlation of LGN *kak-kà-ra* with Karaḫar, Karaḫar should be located on the Great Khurāsān Road somewhere between Namar (Khāniqīn region) and Ḫalman (Sar-i Pul-i Zuhāb). Modern Qaṣr-i-Shīrīn ("Palace of Shīrīn," Shīrīn being the name of the mistress of the Sasanian king Khosrau

71 Rashid (1981) no. 5 col. ii line 9.

72 *Ibid.* no. 5 col. i line 6.

73 Mustafa (1983) no. 916.

74 Levine (1973a) 22-24.

75 Postgate (1979) 592.

76 Gelb (1944) 57 n. 72. The identification is confirmed by Whiting JCS 28 (1976) 181 n. 21.

II) lies at the point where the road from Khāniqīn meets the Alwand (Ḥulwān) River. It likely marks the location of ancient Karaḫar.

3.3.1.3 *Site* 8: *Ḫalman = Sar-i Pul-i Zuhāb*

Assuming that LGN 244: *ʾà-ir-rìm* connects with Arman/Ḫalman, then this city should lie on the Great Khurāsān Road east of Namar and Karaḫar. As noted, the proposed location for ancient Ḫalman at Sar-i Pul-i Zuhāb is virtually certain.[78]

3.3.2 *The Evidence of the Geographical List from Tall Ḥarmal*

As argued in our study of the LGN,[79] col. iii lines 74–86 of the geographical list from Tall Ḥarmal[80] apparently lists cities in geographical order along a road that proceeded up the Diyālā valley to Simurrum and thence northwest along the "Kirkūk corridor" to Arrapḫa.

In this section we will consider three sites, nos. 1, 3, 6. Line iii 78 of the Tall Ḥarmal list: *me-tu-ra-an* gives the name of site 1: Mê-Turran. Line iii 77 *ni-qum* corresponds to site 3: Niqum. Its position in the Tall Ḥarmal list indicates that Niqum should lie somewhere between Mê-Turran and Karaḫar. A location of this city just west of Namar accords well with the mention of the city of Namarum together with the king of Niqum in an Old Babylonian letter from S̱ hamsẖāra.[81] Line iii 76: *kára-ur* is to be connected with site 6: Karaḫar.

3.4 *The Evidence of the Samsu-ilūna Genealogy*

An unexpected source for this discussion is a royal inscription of Samsu-ilūna; it apparently opens with a genealogy of the king. Although only two names: *ḫu-ar-ḫa-ar* and *ma-da-ra* are preserved in the genealogical section,[82]

77 Levine (1974) 116-17.

78 Borger (1970) 1.

79 Frayne (1990) 67-70.

80 Levy (1947) 50-63 and 74-83. See also Landsberger, Reiner, and Civil (1974) 56-59.

81 Laessøe (1966) 103-4 no. 69.

82 Schroeder (1917) 64 no. 156 line 3′.

they can plausibly be connected with two proper names occurring in the Assyrian king list, namely: (a) *ḫar-ḫa-ru* and *man-da-ru* in the Khorsabad exemplar,[83] and (b) *ḫar-ḫa-u* and *man-da-ru* in the "Seventh Day Adventist" exemplar.[84] Since Finkelstein has shown that some names in the Amorite genealogies can be connected with tribal or geographical names,[85] we may further connect the proper names *ḫa-ar-ḫa-ar* and *ma-da-ra* of the Samsu-ilūna genealogy with LGN 242: *kak-kà-ra* and LGN 241: *ma-dar*. If this be true, then the ancient city of Madar probably lay not far west of Karaḫar.

3.5 *The Neighboring Cities of Padan and Ḫalman*

Three sources indicate that neighboring cities of Padan and Ḫalman were situated at the point where the section of the Great Khurāsān Road that runs beside the Alwand (Ḥulwān River) terminates. The first source, a *tamītu* text recording an oracular query to the gods Šamaš and Adad in connection with a campaign of king Ḫammu-rāpi, mentions the cities Padni (= Padan) and Ḫalman.[86] In a second source, the so-called "Agum-Kakrime" inscription, the author of the text styles himself "king of Padanu and Alman" (LUGAL *pa-da-nu u al-ma-an*).[87] Finally, the proper names *ár-man* and *pa-din* occur as an entry in a Kuyunjik copy of the lexical list ḪAR-gud corresponding to "Tirgan in front of the mountain" ([t]i-ir-ga-an igi ḫur-sag.KI).[88]

---

83 Gelb (1954) 210 Khors. list i 3-4.

84 Gelb (1954) 211 SDAS List i 3.

85 Finkelstein (1966) 99.

86 K. 3703+. See Leichty (1964) 83. The line numbers are cited from a transliteration of the *tamītu* kindly provided by W. G. Lambert.

87 Pinches (1880) 33 col. i lines 37-38.

88 Landsberger, Reiner and Civil (1974) 36 Recension B Tablet V col. iii line 6.

4. *The Location of Simurrum*

4.1 *General Considerations*

While scholars have not been able to determine a precise location for the city of Simurrum, all have agreed that the city was located near ancient Mount Ebih, that is, the modern Jabal Ḥamrīn.

4.2 *Previous Scholarship*

4.2.1 *Overview*

For a list of the extensive literature on the question of the location of Zabban/Simurrum, see Nashef (1982) 279-80; there the important studies of Meissner (1919) cols. 69-70, Weidner (1945–51) 75-89, and Goetze (1953) 120, among others, are noted. To these we should add the article of W. W. Hallo entitled "Simurrum and the Hurrian Frontier" (Hallo [1978] 71-83).

4.2.2 *Meissner, OLZ 22 (1919) cols. 69-70*

Meissner made the important observation that late lexical lists equate the GN Simurrum with the GN Zabban; *cf.* Reiner and Civil (1974) 35 line 18: si.úr.ru ki = ŠU = URU *za-ban* and *ibid.* 36 line 3: si.mur.ra ki = *zab-ban.* Simurrum is evidently the earlier term; it appears in texts dating to Sargonic, Ur III, and early Old Babylonian times. We cannot say with precision when the change of name from Simurrum to Zabban occurred, but we may note, that in the archive of economic texts from ancient Mê-Turran dating to the time of the Ešnunna rulers Ṣillī-Sîn and Ilūni,[89] only the GN Zabban appears—Simurrum is never mentioned. It may be, then, that by the time of Ṣillī-Sîn of Ešnunna the GN Simurrum had been replaced by Zabban.

---

89 Mustafa (1983).

4.2.3 *Weidner, AfO 15 (1945–51) 75-80*

In his survey of then available sources referring to Simurrum and Zabban, Weidner singled out for attention an archival text from Sippar dating to year four of Apil-Sîn of Babylon [90]; it mentions both Simurrum (line 2) and Zabban (line 19) in comparable contexts. From this fact Weidner concluded[91] that Simurrum was the name of a land, and that Zabban was its chief city.

Weidner also addressed the question of the locations of Simurrum and Zabban. He noted[92] an inscription of king Šalmaneser III that records a campaign in which the Assyrian king marched from Aššur in a southeasterly direction along the flank of Mount Ebiḫ (the modern Jabal Ḥamrīn) to the city of Mê-Turnat. Weidner tentatively placed Mê-Turnat near the confluence of the Nārīn Su River with the Diyālā River.[93] As it turns out, Mê-Turran lies exactly where Weidner and others had suggested it should be; the mounds of Tall Ḥaddād and Tulūl al-Sīb lie just east of the confluence of Nārīn Su River with the Diyālā River. The fact that Simurrum appeared in the Šalamaneser III inscription as a stopping point on the road from Aššur to Mê-Turnat led Weidner to conclude that Simurrum should be located near the Jabal Ḥamrīn, somewhere on the road between Aššur and the Diyālā River. He posited a location for the city at a point where the Nahr-al-ᶜUẓaym river breaks through the Jabal Ḥamrīn.[94]

4.2.4 *Nashef, RGTC 5: 279-80*

In an excellent survey of the literature concerning the GN Zabban (var. Zamban) that is found in Middle Babylonian and Middle Assyrian sources,

---

90 Pinches (1898) pl. 47a (Bu 88-5-12, 711).

91 Weidner (1945–51) 78: “Da Zaban ohne Zweifel ein Stadtname war, bleibt eigentlich nur noch de Möglichkeit, Simurrum als den dazu gehörigen Landschaftsnamen aufzufassen, der später nach der Einverleibung des Gebietes in das babylonische Staatsgebilde ausser Gebrauch kam.”

92 Weidner (1945–51) 76.

93 *Ibid.*, 76 n. 11.

94 Weidner (1945–51) 79: “Meines Erachtens ist sie am ehesten in der Gegend anzusetzen, wo der Schaṭṭ el-Adhêm das Gebirge durchbricht.”

Nashef noted that the account of the fourth campaign of Šamšī-Adad V against Babylon is a primary source for determining the location of Zabban. Nashef writes:

> In 1 R 31 IV 2f. wird nämlich berichtet, daß der Herrscher, nachdem er den Kleinen Zab überquert hatte, ein Gebiet zwischen Zaddu und Z[abban] passierte, den Ebeḫ überquerte und schließlich die Stadt Mê-Turnat belagerte. Zum Verlauf des Feldzuges s. J.A. Brinkman, AnOr 43, 208f. Šamšī-Adad V. überquerte, bevor er das am Diyālā gelegenen Mê-Turnat (Mê-Turran) erreichte, das Ḥamrīn-Gebirge. Für diese Überquerung können nur die von J.N. Postgate, Sumer 35, 593 (auch dort zur gesamten Route) erwähnten Engpässe Sākāl Tutān und ᶜĒn Lēlān in Frage kommen, die nicht weit voneinander entfernt sind. Wenn man dazu nun die Aussage in VS 19, 9, 37 heranzieht (vgl. H. Freydank, AoF 1, 82, der den Weidnerschen Vorschlag modifizierte, indem er Z[abban] eine Ausdehnung nach bis zum Diyala zuwies), dann käme als Lage für Z[abban] das unmittelbar vor den erwähnten Pässen liegende Gebiet in Frage. Es ist etwa die Hügellandschaft zwischen Kifrī und Qarā Tepe. Daß Z[abban] nicht am Kleinen Zab lag, zeigt auch die Reihe von Städten, die sich gegen Slm. III. empörten (1 R 29 I 48f.; etwa von Süden nach Norden); wo Zabban vor Lubdu vorkommt, das schon nördlich des Nahr al-ᶜUẓēm bzw. dessen Verlängerung dem Ṭawūq Čāy lag.[95]

In summary, Nashef postulated a location for Zabban/Zamban (= Simurrum) in the hilly country between the modern towns of Kifrī and Qarā Tappah.

4.3 *Criteria for Determining the Location of Simurrum*

4.3.1 *Location on the Diyālā River*

While our survey of references to Simurrum is restricted in this brief study to sources dating from the Early Dynastic to Old Babylonian periods,[96] a text that sheds important light on the question of the location of Simurrum is a Middle Assyrian period archival text from KārTukultī-Ninurta (VAT

95 Nashef (1982) 280.

96 Later references have been collected by Weidner (1945–51) 75-77 and Nashef (1982) 279-80.

18000).[97] The tablet mentions (line 36): KUR.*za-am-ba-an a-aḫ tu-ra-an* "the land (or mountain[?]) of Zamban on the bank of the Diyālā River." If *za-am-ba-an*.KI here, as seems most likely, refers to the Zamban equated with Simurrum in the lexical texts cited in §3.2.2 above, then the city of Simurrum must have lain, not on the banks of the Nahr-al-ᶜUẓaym, as Weidner suggested, but rather on the Diyālā River.

Indeed, Diyālā connections for Simurrum are suggested by a number of sources. A year name of Narām-Sîn of Akkad, cited in §2.2.2 (ii) above, commemorates the defeat of the two cities of Arame and Simurrum. Now, according to the evidence of the Tall Ḥarmal geographical list as interpreted by the author,[98] the city of Arame likely lay on the Diyālā River south of the point where the river broke through the Jabal Ḥamrīn. This proposed location for Arame accords well with the evidence of an archival text dated to Š 48 that mentions troops (érin) of Arame together with those of Ešnunna.[99] In the campaign commemorated in the aforementioned Narām-Sîn year name, the Akkadian army likely proceeded up the Diyālā River from the city of Arame to Simurrum. Further, the fact that Ṣilluš-Dagān, the Ur III governor of Simurrum, is attested as commanding not only the army of Simurrum but also troops of Išīm-Šulgi[100] again argues for Simurrum-Diyālā connections, since Išīm-Šulgi is well known as a locality in the Diyālā region.[101]

4.3.2 *Location on the Road Leading from the Kirkūk Corridor*

The fact that the Ur III period governor of Simurrum, Ṣilluš-Dagān, was responsible for conveying booty taken during Šulgi's last campaigns (as for example in a Drehem tablet dated to 17 vii Š 45)[102] suggests that Simurrum

---

97 Freydank (1974) 78-83 (edition); Freydank (1976) pl. IX no. 12 (copy).

98 Frayne (1992) 70.

99 Deimel (1920) 62 Wengler Collection no. 22: A. Deimel, *Orientalia* 2 (1920) p. 62.

100 Maeda (1992) 153.

101 Edzard and Farber (1974) 87: "Ort in Diyālagebiet."

102 Limet (1976) obv. line 5 gìr *ṣe-lu-uš-*ᵈ*da-gan* "conveyed by Ṣilluš-Dagān"; rev. 5-6: *ṣe-lu-uš-*ᵈ*da-gan* / nam-ra-ak ur-bìl-lum.KI-ma: "Ṣelluš-Dagān, booty of Urbillum."

had important connections, presumably by a land route, with the mountain lands of Kimaš, Ḫurtum, and Urbillum that lay to the northwest of Simurrum.[103] Our expectation is that the city was located at a strategic point, possibly a mountain pass, on the road from Madga (almost certainly modern Kifrī[104]) to the Diyālā. This led Nashef, as noted, to posit a location of Simurrum in the hilly country between the modern towns of Kifrī and Qarā Tappah. It is important to note (as is shown in the Map) that there were, in fact, five potential routes leading southward from the area of Kifrī to the Diyālā River. One road proceeded from Kifrī to Qarā Tappah and then split into two branches; one branch headed west to cross the Jabal Ḥamrīn through either the Sākāl Tūtān Pass (route 1), the ᶜAyn Laylān Pass (route 2), or the Abū Ḥajar Pass (route 3). Another road proceeded from Kifrī to Qarā Tappah and then on to meet the Diyālā near modern Qizil Rubaṭ (route 4—the dotted line shown running west of the Jubbah Dāgh in the Map). Yet another road from Kifrī continued, not by way of Qarā Tappah, but rather in an easterly direction, following the pass formed by the valley of the Pūngla River to meet the upper course of the Diyālā at the modern village of Qalᶜah Shīrwānah (route 5—the dotted line shown running east of the Kushki-Zang in the Map). In modern times the upper course of the Diyālā at this point is given the name Sirwān. Our expectation, then, is that Simurrum lay at a point along one of these five routes that linked Madga/Kifrī to the Diyālā River.

4.3.3 *Close Connections with the City of Karaḫar*

The fact that the campaigns against Karaḫar (Š 24) and Simurrum (Š 25) were the first to be noted with consistency in the Šulgi year names[105] suggests that Karaḫar and Simurrum lay relatively close together.

---

103 On the important road linking the area of Kirkūk with the Diyālā regions, see Postgate (no date) 151.

104 Frayne (1992) 57.

105 The year name of Š 21b dealing with the destruction of Dēr is attested so far only in an Ur III period date list (Wilcke [1985] 299-303) and in a Nippur tablet (Owen [1982] pl. 87 no. 351).

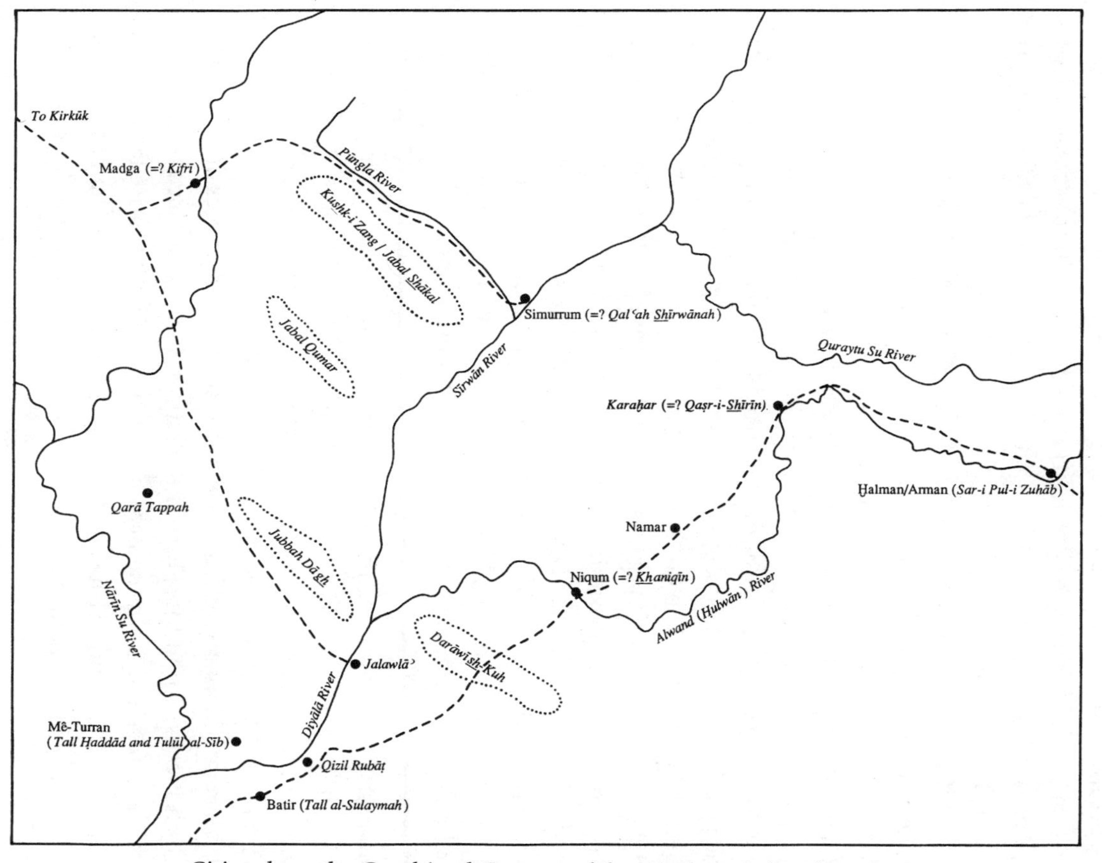

Cities along the Combined Courses of the Diyālā and the Alwand Rivers

4.4 *The Location of the City of Simurrum*

If we consider the three criteria noted in §4.2 above, then Simurrum should be situated: (i) on the Diyālā River, (ii) at a point where the river was crossed by one of the land routes leading south from Kifrī to the Diyālā, and (iii) not too far from ancient Karaḫar.

As it turns out, only routes 4 and 5 satisfy these criteria. Routes 1–3, while indeed crossing the Jabal Ḥamrīn, do not lead directly to the Diyālā; rather they afford general access to the greater Diyālā basin west of the Jabal Ḥamrīn. If we add the restriction of Simurrum's being located near a mountain pass (there is actually no concrete evidence for this assumption), then only route 5 would fit. If so, Simurrum would be situated at the point where the pass formed by the Pūngla River meets the upper Diyālā (or Sirwān) River. A key argument favoring this choice is the fact that the modern name of the mountain range lying immediately to the west of the Pūngla River is modern Kushki Zang (Mount Zang; variant Jabal Šākal); it gives its name to the Zangana district. Now, an alteration between (ancient) b and (modern) q is found in Eidem's equation[106] of the ancient GN Burullum (of the Mari texts) and Burulli(we) (mentioned five times in the Šemšāra archives) with the modern mound named Quralla; it lies about 10 km south of Tell Šemšāra.[107] By assuming a similar development, we could see the modern GN Zang(ana) as a reflex of the ancient GN Zamban. Further, bearing in mind the alternation between w and m, the GN (Qalᶜah) Shīrwānah and the river name Sirwān are likely modern reflexes of the ancient GN Simurrum: *siwurr+ān> sirwān.

It now becomes reasonably clear that the two tributaries of the Diyālā which meet at a point just east of the Jubbah Dāgh (see Map) bear names which are derived from the names of ancient cities that once lay on their banks. The Alwand (Ḥulwān) River is almost certainly named for the ancient city of Ḫalman. If our connection of Simurrum with Sirwān holds

---

106 Eidem (1992) 56. For the g / b alternation in Sumerian, see Civil (1973) 57-61.

107 Eidem (1992) 55 Map 2.

true, then the Sirwān River would have been named for the ancient city of Simurrum.

Simurrum on the Sirwān commanded access to the road that led to the "Kirkūk Corridor" and points west and, by way of the Quraytu Su River and a small portage, to the Alwand (Ḥulwān) River and the Great Khurāsān Road that led to points east. It is little wonder that the Ur III kings battled so long (and so frequently) to try to keep their hold on the strategically located city of Simurrum.

Bibliography

Anonymous (1985) Excavations in Iraq. *Iraq* 47: 215-39. **Borger, R.** (1970) Vier Grenzsteinurkunden Merodachbaladans I. von Babylonien. *Archiv für Orientforschung* 23: 1-62. **Civil, M.** (1973) From Enki's Headaches to Phonology. *Journal of Near Eastern Studies* 32: 57-61. **Cohen, M. E.** (1976) A New Sumerian Date Formula. *Journal of Cuneiform Studies* 28: 227-32. **Crawford, V.** (1954) *Sumerian Economic Texts from the First Dynasty of Isin.* Babylonian Inscriptions in the Collection of James B. Nies 9. New Haven. **Deimel, A.** (1920) Miszellen. *Orientalia* 2: 53-64. **Dossin, G.** (1962) Bronzes inscrits du Luristan de la collection Foroughi. *Iranica Antiqua* 2: 149-64. **Edzard, D. O., and G. Farber** (1974) *Die Orts- und Gewässernamen der Zeit der* 3. *Dynastie von Ur.* Répertoire Géographique des Textes Cunéiformes 2. Tübinger Atlas des Vorderen Orients, Reihe B (Geisteswissenschaften) 7/2. Wiesbaden. **Eidem, J.** (1992) *The Shemshāra Archives 2: The Administrative Texts.* Copenhagen. **Finkbeiner, Dittmann, and Hauptmann**, eds. (1995) *Beitrage zur Kulturgeschichte Vorderasiens: Festschrift für Rainer Michael Boehmer.* Mainz. **Finkelstein, J.** (1966) The Geneaology of the Hammurapi Dynasty. *Journal of Cuneiform Studies* 20: 95-118. **Al-Fouadi, A. H.** (1978) Inscriptions and Reliefs from Bītwāta. *Sumer* 34: 122-29. **Frayne. D.** (1990) *Old Babylonian Period (2003–1595 BC).* The Royal Inscriptions of Mesopotamia, Early Periods Volume 4. Toronto. (1992) *The Early Dynastic List of Geographical Names.* American Oriental Series 74. New Haven. **Freydank, H.** (1974) Zwei Verpflegungstexte aus Kār-Tukultī-Ninurta. *Altorientalische Forschungen.* Inschriften zur Geschichte und Kultur des alten Orients 11. Berlin. (1976) *Mittelassyrische Rechtsurkunden und Verwaltungstexte.* Vorderasiatische Schriftdenkmäler der Staatlichen Museen zu Berlin Neue Folge 3 (19). Berlin. **Al-Gailani Werr, L.**, ed. (1992) Old Babylonian Cylinder Seals from Hamrin. *Edubba* 2. London. **Gelb, I. J.** (1944) *Hurrian and Subarians.* Studies in Ancient Civilizations 22. Chicago. (1952) *Sargonic Texts from the Diyala Region.* Materials for the Assyrian Dictionary 1. Chicago. (1954) Two Assyrian King Lists. *Journal of Near Eastern Studies* 13: 209-30. **Genouillac, H. de** (1921) *Epoque présagonique, époque d'Agade, époque d'Ur.* Inventaire des tablettes de Tello 5. Paris. **Goetze, A.** (1948) *Old Babylonian*

Omen Texts. Yale Oriental Series. Babylonian Texts 10. New Haven. (1953) Hulibar of Duddul. *Journal of Near Eastern Studies* 12: 114-23. (1962) Two Ur-Dynasty Tablets Dealing with Labor. *Journal of Cuneiform Studies* 16: 13-16. **Grégoire, J.-P.** (1981) *Inscriptions et archives administratives cunéiformes* 1. Materiali per il Vocabulario Neosumerico 10. Rome. **Gurney, O., and S. N. Kramer** (1976) *Sumerian Literary Texts in the Ashmolean Museum.* Oxford Edition of Cuneiform Texts 5. Oxford. **Hallo. W. W.** (1973) *Tabulae Cuneiformes a F.M.Th. de Liagre Böhl Collectae, Leidae Conservatae* 3. Leiden. (1978) Simurrum and the Hurrian Frontier. *Revue Hittite et Asianique* 36: 71-83. **Hannoon, N.** (1986) *Studies in the Historical Geography of Northern Iraq During the Middle and Neo-Assyrian Periods.* Ph.D. dissertation, University of Toronto. **Hrouda, B.** (1976) *Sarpol-i Zohāb. Die Felsreliefs I-IV.* Iranische Denkmäler 7/2. Iranisches Felsreliefs C. Berlin. **Hunger, H.** (1976) *Spätbabylonische Texte aus Uruk* 1. Ausgrabungen der Deutschen Forschungsgemeinschaft in Uruk-Warka 9. Berlin. **Kessler, K.** (1995) Drei Keilschrifttexte aus Tell Baradān. In Finkbeiner *et al.* 1995: 281-88. **Keiser, C.** (1971) *Neo-Sumerian Account Texts from Drehem.* Babylonian Inscriptions in the Collection of James B. Nies 3. New Haven. **Kienast, B., and K. Volk** (1995) *Die sumerischen und akkadischen Briefe der* III. *Jahrtausends aus der Zeit vor der* III. *Dynastie von Ur.* Freiburger altorientalische Studien 19. **King, L.** (1912) *Babylonian Boundary Stones and Memorial-Tablets in the British Museum.* London. **Laessøe, J.** (1966) *Det Første Assyriske Imperium: Et Aspekt.* Copenhagen. **Lambert, M.** (1968) Masses d'armes de pierre au nom de Naramsîn. *Orientalia* n.s. 37: 85-86 and pls. VIII-IX. **Landsberger, B, E. Reiner, and M. Civil** (1974) *The Series ḪAR-ra = ḫubullu Tablets XXX-XXIV.* Materials for the Sumerian Lexikon 11. Rome. **Legrain, L.** (1922) *Historical Fragments.* University of Pennsylvania, the Museum, Publications of the Babylonian Section 13. Philadelphia. **Leichty, E.** (1964) *A Bibliography of the Cuneiform Tablets of the Kuyunjik Collection in the British Museum.* London. **Levine, L.** (1973a) Geographical Studies in the Neo-Assyrian Zagros I. *Iran* 11: 1-28. (1973b) Ḫašimur. *Reallexikon der Assyriologie und Vorderasiatischen Archäologie* 4: 134. (1974) Geographical Studies in the Neo-Assyrian Zagros II. *Iran* 12: 99-124. **Levy, S.** (1947) Harmal Geographical List. *Sumer* 3 50-63, and 74-83. **Limet, A.** (1976) *Texts sumeriens de la* IIIe *dynastie d'Ur.* Documents du Proche Orient ancien. Epigraphie 1. **Maeda, T.** (1992) The Defence Zone during the Rule of the Ur III Dynasty. *Acta Sumerologica* 14: 135-72. **Meek, Th.** (1935) *Old Akkadian, Sumerian and Cappodocian Texts from Nuzi.* Excavations at Nuzi 3. Harvard Semitic Studies 10. Cambridge, Mass. **Meissner, B.** (1919) Simurru. *Orientalische Literaturzeitung* 22: cols. 69-70. **Michel, E.** (1954) Die Assur-Texte Salmanassars III. (858–824). 7. Forsetzung. *Die Welt des Orients* 2: 137-47. **Molina, M.** (1993) *Tablillas administrativas neosumerias de la Abadía de Montserrat* (*Barcelona*). *Copias cuneiformes.* Materiali per il Vocabolario Neosumerico 18. Rome. **Mustafa, A.** (1983) The Old Babylonian Tablets from Me-Turan (Tell al-Sib and Tell Haddad), Ph.D. dissertation, University of Glasgow. **Nashef, Kh.** (1982) *Die Orts- und Gewässernamen der mittelbabylonischen und mittelassyrischen Zeit.* Répértoire Géographique des Textes Cunéiformes 5. Tübinger Atlas des Vorderen Orients, Reihe B (Geisteswissenschaften) 7/5. Wiesbaden. **Owen, D. I.** (1982) *Neo-Sumerian Archival Texts Primarily from Nippur in the*

University Museum, the Oriental Institute, and the Iraq Museum. Winona Lake, Ind. **Parpola, S.** (1970) *Neo-Assyrian Toponyms.* Alter Orient und Altes Testament 6. Neukirchen-Vluyn. **Pettinato, G.** (1978) *L'Atlante Geografico del Vicino Orient Antico attestato ad Ebla e ad Abū Ṣalābīkh* (I). Orientalia, n.s. 47: 50-73. (1981) *Testi lessicali monolingui della biblioteca L.* 2769. Istituto Universitario orientale di Napoli, Seminario di studi Asiatici, Series maior 3. Materiali epigrafici di Ebla 3. Naples. **Pinches, Th.** (1880) *The Cuneiform Inscriptions of Western Asia, Vol. V: A Selection from the Miscellaneous Inscriptions of Assyria and Babylonia.* Prepared for Publication ... by Major-General Sir H. C. Rawlinson ... Assisted by Theophilus G. Pinches. London. (1898) *Cuneiform Texts from Babylonian Tablets ... in the British Museum* 4. London. **Pohl, A.** (1935) *Vorsargonische und sargonische Wirtschafttexte.* Texte und Materialen der Frau Professor Hilprecht Collection of Babylonian Antiquities in Eigentum der Universität Jena 5. Leipzig. **Postgate, N.** (1979) The Historical Geography of the Hamrin Basin. *Sumer* 35: 591-94. (1983) The Historical Geography of the Hamrin Basin. *Sumer* 40: 149-59. **Rashid, F.** (1983) Akkadian Texts from Tell Sleima. *Sumer* 40: 55-56. **Scheil, V.** (1900) *Textes éslamites-sémitiques* 1. Mémoires de la Délegation en Perse 2. Paris. (1926) Raptim. *Revue d'Assyriologie et d'Archéologie Orientale* 23: 35-48. **Schroeder, O.** (1917) *Altbabylonische Briefe.* Vorderasiatische Schriftdenkmäler der königlichen Museen zu Berlin. Leipzig. **Schneider, N.** (1932) *Die Drehem- und Djoḫatexte im Kloster Montserrat (Barcelona).* Analecta Orientalia 7. Rome. (1936) *Die Zeitbestimmungen der Wirtschaftsurkunden von Ur* III. Analecta Orientalia 13. Rome. **Steinkeller, P.** (1988) The Date of Gudea and His Dynasty. *Journal of Cuneiform Studies* 40: 47-53. **Thureau-Dangin, F.** (1903) *Receuil de tablettes chaldéennes.* Paris. **Walker, C. B. F.** (1972) *Miscellaneous Texts.* Cuneiform Texts from Babylonian Tablets in the British Museum 51. London. **Walker, C. B. F, and D. Collon** (1980) Hormuzd Rassam's Excavation for the British Museum at Sippar in 1881–82 in de Meyer, L., *Tell ed-Dēr* 3. *Sounding at Abū Ḥabbah (Sippar).* Leuven. **Weidner, E.** (1945–51) Simurrum und Zaban. *Archiv für Orientforschung* 15: 75-80. **Westenholz, A.** (1975a) *Early Cuneiform Texts in Jena. Pre-Sargonic and Sargonic Documents from Nippur and Fara in the Hilprecht-Sammlung vorderasiatischer Altertümer.* Det Kongelige Danske Videnskabernes Selskab Historik-Filosofiske Skrifter 7, 3. Copenhagen. (1975b) *Old Sumerian and Old Akkadian Texts in Philadephia Chiefly from Nippur. Part One: Literary and Lexical Texts and the Earliest Administrative Documents from Nippur.* Bibliotheca Mesopotamica 1. Malibu, Calif. **Whiting, R.** (1976) Tiš-atal of Nineveh and Babati Uncle of Shu-Sin. *Journal of Cuneiform Studies* 28: 173-82. (1987) *Old Babylonian Letters from Tell Asmar.* Assyriological Studies 22. Chicago. **Wilcke, Cl.** (1985) Neue Quellen aus Isin zur Geschichte der Ur-III Zeit und der I. Dynastie von Isin. *Orientalia* n.s. 54: 299-318. (1987) *Isin-Išān Baḫrīyāt* 3. *Die Ergebnisse der Ausgrabungen 1983–1984.* Bayerische Akademie der Wissenschaften, Philosophisch-Historische Klasse, Abhandlungen N. F. 94. **Winckler, H.** (1897) Einige altbabylonische inschriften(sic!). *Altorientalische Forschungen* 1/6: 544-47. Leipzig.

Father's Sons and Mother's Daughters:
The Problem of Indo-European–Semitic Relationships*

Cyrus H. Gordon

On 13 March, 1989, at a session of the annual meetings of the American Oriental Society in New Orleans, Calvert Watkins concurred with Harry Hoffner in interpreting the following pair of Hittite expressions: *atta-neknes*, "brothers (sired by one) father," and *anna-neknes*, "sisters (borne by one) mother."[1] It remains to be pointed out that this pair of expressions reflects an institution whereby a husband and wife blessed with children of both sexes could form a duplex family divided into a male sub-family and a female sub-family. In Hebrew there is terminology reflecting such an institution; to wit, the *bêt-ᵓab*,[2] "house of a father," and *bêt-ᵓem*,[3] "house of a mother." In each of these divisions of a family, there could be a hierarchy of children, paralleling each other.[4]

* Abbreviations used are: IE: Indo-European; PRU III: *Le palais royales d'Ugarit* III = Nougayrol (1955); RS: Ras Shamra, ancient Ugarit; UT: *Ugaritic Textbook* = Gordon (1965).

1 The transliteration does not distinguish *k* from *g*, nor *s* from *š*.

2 This term can refer not only to the house of any individual's father, but can designate the extended family in a patriarchal system. Cf. למשפחתיו אל־בית אבתיו (Numbers 2:34), "according to his clans by his patriarchal households"; note that the plural of the technical term בית־אב is בית־אבות with the second element pluralized. Normal usage calls for pluralizing the first element as in בני־ישׂראל, "the Children of Israel."

3 Examples with the possessive suffix "her" are in Genesis 24:28 and Ruth 1:8 mentioned below.

4 Please note that I write "could be" and not "were." There were alternative life-styles

A complete family consisted of a father with a number of sons, of which one (usually, but not necessarily, the firstborn[5]) was the fratriarch with the largest inheritance, plus leadership over his siblings. After him came the vice-fratriarch,[6] then the third in line, and so forth with the fourth, fifth, etc. The father had one or more wives, each of whom could head a sub-family of daughters, who constituted a parallel hierarchy normally, but not necessarily, with the eldest as sororarch followed by others in sequence down to the youngest.

However, the father, as patriarch, could elevate a younger child (male or female) over his or her seniors. In the case of polygyny, one wife outranked the others so that the patriarch's successor had to be chosen from her brood. In that case, the patriarch could select, or approve of, the one to succeed him. This veto power was limited; he was not free to make a son of any of his other wives his successor. This system was of special importance at the royal level, where only one woman in the royal harem was contractually entitled to bear the crown prince.[7]

A clear case of the institution of the parallel households of (1) the father with his sons, and of (2) the mother with her daughters, is provided by the Epic of Kret, unearthed at Ugarit, a satellite of the Hittite Empire from the 15th century down to the destruction of Hattusas and Ugarit around 1185 B.C.E. The hero, King Kret, won a divine covenantal promise that his dynasty would endure through the progeny to be borne to him by his destined bride, Ḥry.[8] The promise, which was fulfilled, included *bn krt*, "the sons of Kret,"

---

and I have tried throughout this article not to give the false impression of monolithic institutions.

5 The distinction between the בכור, "firstborn," and ראש "fratriarch," is clearly brought out terminologically in Chronicles (cf. especially 1 Ch 26:10). See Gordon (1935), esp. 228, and Spanier (1989).

6 The classical designation is משנהו "his second-in-command" (with reference to the fratriarch).

7 At Ugarit, the wife contractually entitled to bear the crown prince was called the *rabîtu*; *cf.* Gordon (1988).

8 For the annotated translation of the Kret Epic, see Gordon (1977) 34-59 with constant references to the Ugaritic source in UT.

and *bnt ḥry*, "the daughters of Ḥry."[9] It would not have been "worthy of saga" if the eldest son, Yṣb, proved to be deserving, and succeeded his father on the throne. Instead, the eldest proved to be undeserving, while a younger son, Ilḥu, emerged as worthy.[10] As for the girls, it was not the eldest, but Ṯtmnt, "Octavia," the eighth and youngest daughter, who was elevated to the rank of sororarch.[11]

When Rebecca met Eliezer, her father (Bethuel) and fratriarchal brother (Laban) were alive and present, but she ran to bring the news to "the house of her mother"[12] and not to the men's abode. When Naomi advised her widowed daughters-in-law, Ruth and Orphah, not to accompany her to Judea, but to remain with their own people in Moab, she urged them to return, each to the house of her mother.[13] Daughters could thus belong to their mothers' houses, not only before marriage, but even after being bereft of their husbands.

The dichotomy of "father's sons" and "mother's daughters" is not limited to the ancient Near East. I have come across examples of this among Shiites in Iraq and Iran. (1) My student, the late Dr. Izzu-d-Din al-Yasin (an Iraqi) divorced his first wife (an Iranian) who had borne him four sons but no daughters. There was no question of child-custody. He kept all four sons in his Baghdad home, while she was sent back to her family in Iran with none of her children. (2) The first marriage of General Jahanbani (of Iran) was a *siǧeh* (or *mutᶜa*), or "temporary marriage," contracted for him by his mother and sister for the duration of his summer vacation while he was a cadet at the Russian Military Academy. The brief union produced a daugh-

9 For the *bn krt and bnt ḥry*, see UT 128: III: 23-24.

10 Yṣb tried to usurp his sick father's kingship, while the devoted Ilḥu was distressed by Kret's suffering.

11 For the series of Kret's daughters to be born by Ḥry, see UT 128: III: 7-12, and Gordon (1977) 48. For the statement that the youngest of the girls was to be elevated to the position of sororarch, *cf.* UT 128: III: 16, *ṣǵrthn abkrn*, "I shall make the youngest (f.) of them (f.) the firstborn (= sororarch)."

12 Genesis 24:28.

13 Ruth 1:8.

ter, who automatically remained in the custody of her mother. All of the parties involved in both of these marriages were Shiites.

The closest form of siblingship is that of children sharing the same father and mother.[14] Half-brothers and sisters were sometimes permitted to marry each other if they were agnatic, but not uterine (*i.e.*, sharing the same father, but of different mothers).[15] The assignment of boys to the father's house and the daughters to the mother's house is, as noted above, attested in "Hattu," *i.e.*, in Hittite Anatolia and among Northwest Semites.[16]

Whether the divisions between "father's sons," and "mother's daughters" moved from the Northwest Semites to the Hittites is still an open question. Unless and until it is found in Indo-European (IE) society outside of the Hittite sphere, we should not insist that it is of IE origin. However, there are other elements in Northwest Semitic society that are definitely of IE derivation.

Levirate marriage is widespread among the Indo-Europeans (Indics, Greeks, Romans, Hittites). So far it has not been detected in the ancient Near East prior to the era of IE impact. Thus it does not occur in the Sumerian and Old Babylonian law codes.[17] After the advent of the Indo-Hittites,[18]

---

14 Thus Kret's full brothers are called "brothers—sons of a (= one) mother." *Cf. dšbᶜ* [*a*]*ḫm lh ṯmnt bn um*, "he who had seven brothers; (altogether) eight sons of one mother" (UT Krt: 8-9).

15 For the Patriarchal Age, note Genesis 20:12; for the Age of the United Monarchy, see 2 Samuel 13:13.

16 I have not come across it among the Arabs. An Islamic household is traditionally divided into (1) the men's quarters for the adult male members of the household, and (2) the *ḥarîm*, for the women and the children of both sexes. A socially and economically solid Muslim who has more that one wife should provide each of them with separate quarters (tent, room, apartment or house as *modus vivendi* and material means prescribe). But the boys remain in the *ḥarîm* only through their pre-adolescent years, whereupon they are classified as "men."

In Iran, the Persian terminology is: *andirûn*, "women's quarters," and *berûn*, "men's quarters."

17 Hammurapi's Code was promulgated after the early IE presence in the Near East. However, the Code is conservative. Thus while the horse and camel were already known, they do not appear in the Code's repertoire of animals (kine, sheep, goats, pigs and asses).

18 I use this term to highlight the Hittite factor. I do not imply the existence of a hypo-

it appears in the Assyrian as well as Hittite Laws,[19] in cuneiform tablets such as those from Nuzi[20] and Ugarit[21] and in the Hebrew Bible. In the Bible, it occurs in three divergent forms:

In Deuteronomy 25:5-10 it is formulated as a law to the effect that if a married man (provided that he is living in a fratriarchal enclave) dies childless, his brother should marry the widow, and their first child was to be reckoned as the son of the deceased so that no name shall be obliterated from Israel.

The second case occurs in the Scroll of Ruth, which is set in the period of the Judges. Ruth married her deceased husband's closest available kinsman who was willing and able to redeem the estate of the deceased. The firstborn son of the union perpetuated the name and line of the deceased on the latter's estate (4:5).

---

thetical Proto-Indo-Hittite plus a hypothetical Proto-Indo-European, as was the fashion in certain circles back in the nineteen-twenties and thirties.

19 Hittite Laws: tablet II #193 (trans. Hoffner [1995] 236); Middle Assyrian Laws: tablet A #33 (trans. Roth [1995] 165).

20 See Gordon (1936) 163 and *passim* in numerous recent studies.

21 By means of a curse invoking Baal, Arḫalbu, King of Ugarit, to ensure a legitimate succession, would prevent anyone except his brother from marrying his widow, Kubaba. The tablet (RS 16.144; PRU III, p. 76) was written while Arḫalbu was alive, but before a crown prince was borne by his wife who was contractually entitled to bear the next king.

Obverse

: 1)	*iš-tu ûmi*$^{\text{I-kam}}$ *a-ni-im*	On this day
: 2)	^{m}*ar(i)-ḫal-bu šar* ^{âl}*u-ga-ri-it*	Arḫalbu, King of Ugarit
: 3)	*a-kán-na iq-ta-bi*	declares thus:
: 4)	*šum-ma ú-ra še-ra*	"If in the future
: 5)	*a-na-ku* (BA.BAT^{meš}) mi-ta-ku	I die,
: 6)	*ù ša* ^{f}*ku-ba-ba mârat ták-a-an*	and anyone, Kubaba
		daughter of Takan,
: 7)	*aššati-ia iš-tu aḫi-ia*	my wife, from my brother,
: 8)	*ša i-ḫu-uz-ši*	takes,
: 9)	^{d}IM *li-ra-ḫi-iṣ-šu*	May Baal drown him!
: 10)	^{iṣ}*kussâ la ú-ra-bi*	May he not enhance the throne!
: 11)	É^{ḫá} *la i-ši-ib*	May he not inhabit the palace!
: 12)	^{d}IM *bêl ḫuršân ḫa-zi*	May Baal, the Lord of Mount Cassius,
: 13)	*li-ra-ḫi-iṣ-šu*	drown him!"

The third case (in Genesis 38) is set still earlier, in the Patriarchal Age. Judah was living among members of the local population. His wife bore him three sons. Judah married off the eldest, named Er, to a local girl named Tamar. But Er died childless, so that Tamar, in accordance with the custom of levirate marriage, automatically[22] became the wife of Er's brother, Onan. The latter, unwilling to provide a surrogate son and heir for his dead brother, practiced *coitus interruptus.*[23] For this selfishness, God is said to have terminated Onan's life (verse 10). Judah's third son, Shelah, was still a minor, and so Judah sent Tamar back to her father's house, ostensibly to wait until the boy became mature enough to marry, but actually because he feared she would bring him bad luck, causing the death of the third son too (verse 11).

Time went by and Shelah grew up, but Judah continued to withhold him from performing his levirate duty with Tamar. Tamar was not deceived by Judah's tactics and decided to assure her right to become the mother of the next head of Judah's family, by guile. Judah's wife had recently died, and after the customary period of mourning, he attended a sheep-shearing celebration where wine and other pleasures were the rule. Tamar disguised herself as a prostitute and attracted Judah's attention by waiting alongside the road she knew he would take. Her ruse worked and they agreed on the price: a kid. As a security for the payment, Judah left with Tamar three personal articles: his seal, cord,[24] and staff.

Judah had unwittingly impregnated Tamar during their one encounter. Soon after, he wanted to pay her the stipulated fee for her services and dispatched a friend of his to convey the kid to the harlot. But no harlot could

---

22 Levirate marriage is not considered a new marriage. It is simply an automatic continuation of the original marriage, with the יבם "levir," taking his dead brother's place to produce the latter's heir.

23 The reason for being unwilling to produce a son for the dead brother is that Onan, who would otherwise become the fratriarch and chief heir, would lose that position, with all of its prerogatives, to the son of the dead Er.

24 This "cord" might possibly be the chain for suspending the seal. However, I am more inclined to compare it with the Akkadian *sissiktu,* "fringe," impressed like a seal or fingernail on clay tablets, as we affix our signature to validate a document.

be found in the vicinity and Judah became apprehensive because his seal, cord and staff would reveal his identity. It was not long before news of Tamar's pregnancy reached Judah's ears, and he was outraged that his daughter-in-law had conceived through whoring. He demanded that she be expelled from her father's house to be burned to death.[25] She then revealed that the father of the fetus was the owner of the three personal articles left as security. Judah thereupon realized and confessed his guilt, saying, צדקה ממני "She is in the right; not I" (verse 26). That he was her father-in-law would not exclude him from serving in place of the levir according to the Hittite Code.[26] Accordingly, Genesis 38 provides a link with the Indo-European Hittites. The other IE ties are provided by India, where *sati*, "suttee," as well as *niyoga*, "levirate marriage," is honorable for widows.

In the other biblical examples of levirate marriage, as well as in all of the post-biblical Jewish sources, the widow and the levir go on living together as man and wife. It is only in Genesis 38:26 that the "levir" (Judah), having impregnated the widow, never touches her again, exactly as in India, where the union lasts only until the impregnation[27] which fulfills the purpose of *niyoga*: to provide an heir for the dead.

The interpenetration of the Indo-Hittite and Semitic spheres is complex and extended over many periods, and via several channels of transmission by land and sea.[28] Though the subject is still in its infancy, it is a foregone conclusion that its investigation will inevitably contribute significantly to our understanding of the Indo-Europeans and ancient Near Easterners as we come across them since the earliest written sources.

---

25 This can only mean that her father's household accepted the demand as justified.

26 Tablet II, #193 (trans. Hoffner [1995] 165).

27 It was my student, Claire Gottlieb, who called my attention to this peculiarity of *niyoga*.

28 The connections began in prehistoric times. In the Achaemenian Age (6th to 4th centuries B.C.E.), the Persian Empire extended at it height "from India to Ethiopia" (Esther 1:1), with excellent roads and fast courier service (a sort of "pony express").

The Elamite language is demonstrably connected with Tamil. So we must regard the Elamites as a channel of transmission.

Note also Gordon (1958).

Bibliography

Eslinger, L. and G. Taylor, eds. (1988) *Ascribe to the Lord: Biblical and Other Studies in Memory of Peter C. Craigie.* Journal for the Study of the Old Testament, Supplement Series 67. Sheffield. **Gordon, C. H.** (1935) Fratriarchy in the Old Testament. *Journal of Biblical Literature* 54: 223-31. (1936) The Status of Women Reflected in the Nuzi Tablets. *Zeitschrift für Assyriologie* N. F. 9 (43): 146-69. (1958) Indo-European and Hebrew Epic. *Eretz-Israel* 5: 10-15. (Benjamin Mazar Festschrift) (1965) *Ugaritic Textbook.* Analecta Orientalia 38. Rome. (1977) Poetic Legends and Myths from Ugarit. *Berytus* 25: 5-133. (1988) Ugaritic *rbt/rabîtu.* In Eslinger and Taylor 1988: 127-32. **Hoffner, Harry A.** (1995) Hittite Laws. In Roth 1995: 213-47. **Nougayrol, J.** (1955) *Le palais royale d'Ugarit III. Textes accadiens et hourrites des archives est, ouest et centrales, avec des Ètudes de G. Boyer et K. Laroche.* Mission de Ras Shamra 6. Paris. **Roth, M. T.** (1995) *Law Collections from Mesopotamia and Asia Minor.* SBL Writings from the Ancient World Series 6. Atlanta. **Spanier, K.** (1989) *Aspects of Fratriarchy in the Old Testament.* Ph.D. dissertation, New York University, (University Microfilms, Ann Arbor, Mich.)

The Form and Structure of the Solomonic District List in 1 KINGS 4: 7-19*

Richard S. Hess
Denver Seminary

In 1913 Alt argued for historical value to the Solomonic District list in 1 Kings 4: 7-19 on the basis of its form as an administrative document.[1] This opinion has been followed by most scholars who have attempted to use the text for the study of historical geography. However, it has recently been challenged by Ash who has argued that it "should be seen as the product of an oral/scribal transmission which selected, abbreviated and garbled its source(s)."[2]

When Alt wrote, there were available no extrabiblical West Semitic sources that could provide administrative documents for comparison. Specifically, no such administrative evidence existed containing lists of both personal and place-names. This has now changed. The West Semitic archives of both Ugarit and Alalakh provide examples of just such administrative texts.[3] It is therefore surprising that no systematic study and comparison of

---

* It is a delight to dedicate this study to Michael Astour, whose own contributions to the scholarly understanding of historical geography also emphasized the importance of administrative texts from Ugarit and Alalakh.

1 Alt (1913).

2 Ash (1995), esp. p. 84.

3 Texts from Ugarit will be cited according to excavation number (RS). The abbreviations KTU and KTU[2] denote publication in Dietrich, Loretz, and Sanmartín (1976) (1995) respectively. Texts from Alalakh will be cited according to AT number as found in Wiseman (1953). A bibliography for additional publications of these texts may be found in Hess (1988) (1992). For AT 457, see Wiseman and Hess (1994). Some unpublished texts from Alalakh will also be referred to. These include two texts

these texts with the district list of 1 Kings 4 have been made. Despite this absence of comparative studies, conclusions have been drawn about the form of the text and its date and function. It is essential that such a study be done in order to establish the relationship.

This study will consider the form and structure of 1 Kings 4: 7-19. The results will be compared with West Semitic administrative texts, especially those from the Late Bronze Age archives of Ugarit and Alalakh. This will lead to some conclusions that will argue the importance of an awareness of the comparative literature before drawing conclusions about editorial work and the "garbling" of texts in their transmission from the original documents.

I. The Masoretic Text (with RSV Translation)

The decision to choose the Masoretic Hebrew text for the study of 1 Kings 4 is based on its general acceptance as an early witness to the original text. Other early versions such as the LXX and the Peshitta preserve a similar form to the district list, although they contain important variations in content.

1 Kgs 4:7 וְלִשְׁלֹמֹה שְׁנֵים־עָשָׂר נִצָּבִים עַל־כָּל־יִשְׂרָאֵל וְכִלְכְּלוּ אֶת־הַמֶּלֶךְ וְאֶת־בֵּיתוֹ חֹדֶשׁ בַּשָּׁנָה יִהְיֶה עַל־אֶחָד [הָ][אֶחָד] לְכַלְכֵּל ס	Solomon had twelve officers over all Israel, who provided food for the king and his household; each man had to make provision for one month in the year.
1 Kgs 4:8 וְאֵלֶּה שְׁמוֹתָם בֶּן־חוּר בְּהַר אֶפְרָיִם	These were their names: Ben-hur, in the hill country of Ephraim;

without AT numbers: 76 and 81/20. 78/2 and 83/13 are published by Dietrich and Loretz (1970) 104-5, 108.

1 Kgs 4:9 בֶּן־דֶּקֶר בְּמָקַץ וּבְשַׁעַלְבִים וּבֵית שָׁמֶשׁ וְאֵילוֹן בֵּית חָנָן ס	Ben-deker, in Makaz, Sha-albim, Beth-shemesh, and Elonbeth-hanan;
1 Kgs 4:10 בֶּן־חֶסֶד בָּאֲרֻבּוֹת לוֹ שֹׂכֹה וְכָל־אֶרֶץ חֵפֶר ס	Ben-hesed, in Arubboth (to him belonged Socoh and all the land of Hepher);
1 Kgs 4:11 בֶּן־אֲבִינָדָב כָּל־נָפַת דֹּאר טָפַת בַּת־שְׁלֹמֹה הָיְתָה לּוֹ לְאִשָּׁה ס	Ben-abinadab, in all Naphath-dor (he had Taphath the daughter of Solomon as his wife);
1 Kgs 4:12 בַּעֲנָא בֶּן־אֲחִילוּד תַּעְנַךְ וּמְגִדּוֹ וְכָל־בֵּית שְׁאָן אֲשֶׁר אֵצֶל צָרְתַנָה מִתַּחַת לְיִזְרְעֶאל מִבֵּית שְׁאָן עַד אָבֵל מְחוֹלָה עַד מֵעֵבֶר לְיָקְמֳעָם ס	Baana the son of Ahilud, in Taanach, Megiddo, and all Beth-shean which is beside Zarethan below Jezreel, and from Beth- shean to Abel-meholah, as far as the other side of Jok- meam;
1 Kgs 4:13 בֶּן־גֶּבֶר בְּרָמֹת גִּלְעָד לוֹ חַוֹּת יָאִיר בֶּן־מְנַשֶּׁה אֲשֶׁר בַּגִּלְעָד לוֹ חֶבֶל אַרְגֹּב אֲשֶׁר בַּבָּשָׁן שִׁשִּׁים עָרִים גְּדֹלוֹת חוֹמָה וּבְרִיחַ נְחֹשֶׁת ס	Ben-geber, in Ramoth-gilead (he had the villages of Jair the son of Manasseh, which are in Gilead, and he had the region of Argob, which is in Bashan, sixty great cities with walls and bronze bars);

1 Kgs 4:14 אֲחִינָדָב בֶּן־עִדֹּא מַחֲנָיְמָה	Ahinadab the son of Iddo, in Mahanaim;
1 Kgs 4:15 אֲחִימַעַץ בְּנַפְתָּלִי גַּם־הוּא לָקַח אֶת־בָּשְׂמַת בַּת־שְׁלֹמֹה לְאִשָּׁה	Ahima-az, in Naphtali (he had taken Basemath the daughter of Solomon as his wife);
1 Kgs 4:16 בַּעֲנָא בֶּן־חוּשָׁי בְּאָשֵׁר וּבְעָלוֹת ס	Baana the son of Hushai, in Asher and Bealoth;
1 Kgs 4:17 יְהוֹשָׁפָט בֶּן־פָּרוּחַ בְּיִשָּׂשכָר ס	Jehoshaphat the son of Paruah, in Issachar;
1 Kgs 4:18 שִׁמְעִי בֶן־אֵלָא בְּבִנְיָמִן ס	Shime-i the son of Ela, in Benjamin;
1 Kgs 4:19 גֶּבֶר בֶּן־אֻרִי בְּאֶרֶץ גִּלְעָד אֶרֶץ סִיחוֹן מֶלֶךְ הָאֱמֹרִי וְעֹג מֶלֶךְ הַבָּשָׁן וּנְצִיב אֶחָד אֲשֶׁר בָּאָרֶץ 1 Kgs 4:20 יְהוּדָה	Geber the son of Uri, in the land of Gilead, the country of Sihon king of the Amorites and of Og king of Bashan. And there was one officer in the land of Judah.

II. The Structure of the List

The general form of this text is that of a list of personal names, each of which is attached to one or more place-names. A more detailed examination of the list reveals the following features of its structure.

1. SUMMARY INTRODUCTION

An introduction (v. 7) specifies that the document is concerned with the royal household and the administration of taxes that are paid to the palace. The text specifies the number of individuals referred to in the list (12), their occupation (officers), and the general territory covered by the place-names (all Israel).

2. SECOND INTRODUCTION

The first two Hebrew words of v. 8 form a second introduction that introduces the list as an onomastic one, "These were their names."

3. "SON OF X"

Each entry in the list begins with a personal name. Five of the names are of the form "*ben* X" ("son of X"). Six of the remaining names are followed by a patronym. Two of these are named Baana and so their different patronyms distinguish them. Geber son of Uri could also be confused with an earlier Ben-geber. Although Ahinadab son of Iddo and Ben-abinadab might sound alike, Ahinadab's name, as well as the names Jehoshaphat and Shime-i, are not duplicated in the list. In summary, eleven of the twelve personal names include the element, *ben* "son of," either as the first part of the name or after the personal name as the means of introducing the patronymic element.

4. PREPOSITION BEFORE THE PLACE-NAME

Each personal name is followed by the preposition *beth*, which introduces the place-name in nine cases. The three examples where this is omitted (vv. 9, 11-12) introduce names of towns rather than regions or tribal territories. Where more than one place-name is associated with an officer, the additional names may be introduced by *beth* prepositions (vv. 9 and 16) but not if the first place-name omits the preposition (v. 12).

5. ADDITIONAL NOTES

Additional notes, other than additional place-names, are found associated with six of the officers. Two of these, vv. 12 and 19, describe the regions associated with the officer's assignment. In v. 12 this is done by means of place-names contained within the territory and prepositions which connect the place-names. This may appear to resemble the border descriptions of tribal territories found in Joshua 13-19. However, the prepositions "below" (*mittaḥat*) and "beside" (*ʾēṣel*) do not occur in Joshua. The same is true for the note in v. 19. The expression "Sihon king of the Amorites" occurs only in Joshua 12:2; 13:10, 21. In these cases it is followed by the place-name Heshbon, where Sihon ruled. Its usage in 1 Kings 4: 19 is different, connected with Og and with the Gilead. Thus these notes are distinctive and use a vocabulary unrelated to other place-name lists in the Bible.

6. NOTES ABOUT ADDITIONAL REGIONS

The notes in vv. 10 and 13 are introduced by *lôʾ* "to him." They refer to additional towns and regions that formed part of the administrative district of the officer named.

7. NOTES ABOUT SPOUSES

Notes appended to the administrators named in vv. 11 and 15 designate the wives of the officers and note that they are daughters of Solomon.

8. DISTINCTIVE LAST ITEM

There is no concluding summary at the end of this list. However, an additional unnamed officer is mentioned at the end of v. 19 and the first word of v. 20.[4] This figure is simply identified as "one other

---

4 This interpretation follows the RSV. The LXX and Peshitta both understand the final clause in v. 19 as referring to an additional ruler, although the LXX moves Jehoshaphat (v. 17) to the end of the list. Naʾaman (1986) 174-76 also interprets this last phrase as referring to an additional ruler, although he regards most of v. 19 as an interpolation. The NJPS translates the last phrase of v. 19, "and one prefect who was in the land." This is different from the NIV, which connects the final phrase with the preceding governor (Geber), "He was the only governor over the district." Naʾaman's suggestion is based on his historical reconstruction of the list which was determined

officer who was in the land of Judah." The absence of a personal name, the use of a connective *waw*, and the designation of the person as "one other officer" are all distinctive elements of this entry. However, the form of noting a single person and of a place-name introduced by "beth" are common to all of the other entries in this list. The unique form and the fact that this is a thirteenth entry in a list whose heading identifies twelve officers suggest that this last item is distinctive.

III. An Administrative Context for the Form of the List

When the administrative texts from Ugarit and Alalakh are examined, it is noted that some published documents have a structure like 1 Kings 4, where a list of personal names occurs, with each name followed by one or more place-names. In Ugaritic text KTU 4.288 [RS 17.293] the personal name is replaced by the expression *skn*, "governor of," plus place-name.[5] Among the administrative texts of the Late Bronze Age archive at Alalakh (level IV), the majority that list place-names occur where the place-name follows a personal name or some other expression. Thus many of the texts contain a personal name followed by a place-name as part of each item on the list. The place-name can directly follow the personal name on each line,[6] or there can occur an intervening expression.[7] Some texts specify the people named as warriors or some other social class.[8] Others begin each line with a number, sometimes referring to persons, houses, grain, horses, sheep, asses, or quantities of silver.[9]

---

in the absence of any formal comparison with other administrative documents. The NIV also seems unaware that such an interpretation of the Hebrew text is unattested in comparable administrative documents.

5 This and the texts that follow are the second type of administrative list, discussed in Hess (1996).

6 AT 141, AT 161, AT 166, and 76 (an unpublished fragment).

7 These include *i-na* "from" (AT 457), *i-na* É "from the house of PN at GN" (AT 162), DUMU "son of" (AT 152 and AT 184), and LÚ "man (*i.e.*, citizen) of" (AT 220).

8 Mariannu are mentioned in AT 152 and AT 220. Hapiru appear in AT 180, AT 181, AT 182.

9 A number followed by a place name occurs in lines of 81/20. Numbers of persons

A survey of these texts reveals a variety of points of similarity in the overall structure and in the anomalies as noted in the structural elements of the district list in 1 Kings 4.

1. SUMMARY INTRODUCTION

A summary introduction is preserved in the first two lines of AT 180, a text containing a list of personal names with place-names attached to many of them. The introduction is, ERÍN.MEŠ LÚ.SA.GAZ EN.GIŠ.TUKUL.MEŠ *ša* URU *mar-ma-ru-ku-um*^{ki} "armed SA.GAZ troops who [captured?] Marmarukum." Like the summary introduction of 1 Kings 4 this title introduces the people named by identifying their common function and therefore the reason for their inclusion in this list. Note also AT 457 which begins, DUMU.MEŠ URU *ta-i*[*a*?...] "Citizens of Taia?" Similar introductions occur at the beginning of AT 181, AT 182, AT 188, and AT 220.

2. SECOND INTRODUCTION

The 1 Kings 4 "These are their names" (Hebrew וְאֵלֶּה שְׁמוֹתָם) resembles the content of introductions such as *annû ša* URU *Ḫazirpa* "These are from Hazirpa" (AT 141). See also AT 184 and AT 224. Instead of a second introduction immediately following the first one, some administrative texts have a second identification of the list occurring at the end of each subsection of the document. For example, AT 180, which introduces its list with two lines, summarizes each subsection of its list with a solid line drawn across the tablet and the identification of the particular class of each group named above the line. This is found at lines 24, 27, 31, and 34-35. See also AT 182.

(LÚ.MEŠ) are listed in AT 163 (reverse), AT 223, and AT 224. Numbers of houses are found in AT 185, AT 187, and fragment 78/2. *Cf.* also fragment 83/13, where "house" is followed by a place name on each line. Amounts of grain are found in AT 287 and in the Old Babylonian text AT 271. Texts mentioning numbers of horses include AT 329, AT 330, AT 338, and AT 339. Numbers of sheep and asses occur in AT 341, AT 342, AT 343, and AT 352. Quantities of silver are listed in AT 395.

3. "SON OF X"

Naveh has reviewed the collected evidence and discussions of this name form in biblical, epigraphic, and rabbinic Hebrew.[10] He concludes that the data agree with the material that Heltzer collected from Ugarit personal names and administrative documents.[11] In the West Semitic world of the second and first millennia, the names of adult males could be written as "X son of Y," as "X," as "son of Y," or as any of these where Y could be a nickname or a gentilic. For example, at Ugarit two documents contain an identical list of eight priests. In one list they are identified only by patronyms (son of Y; KTU 4.69 VI 25-32) whereas in the other document the first name occurs with the patronym (X son of Y; RS 16.257 + 16.258 + 16.126 III 37-44 [Nougayrol [1955]). In a list of eleven names in AT 141 every name has a patronym, whereas in KTU 4.76 a list of names includes "X," "X son of Y," and "son of Y" forms, just like the list in 1 Kings 4. In another example, AT 220 provides a list of charioteers whose twelve names are followed (in some cases) by their place of origin. Two of these are of the form, "son of Y," ^IDUMU *ku-uk-ki* and ^IDU[MU *b*]*i-im-me-né-e*.[12] The form of these names does not provide any certainty about the social status of the name bearers, nor are the linguistic possibilities of the "Y" name in the form "son of Y" any more restricted than the possibility of personal names formed without the "son of" element.[13]

---

10 Naveh (1990).

11 Heltzer (1982) 113, 133-34.

12 AT 220 lines 8 and 11. The reading of the second name was first suggested by Dietrich and Loretz. My collation at the British Museum in July 1991 agreed with this reading.

13 Ash (1995) 82-83 argues that Ben-Abinadab of 1 Kings 4:11 has been "abbreviated and garbled" because it has the unique form *ben* + theophoric + perfect tense verb; and because names constructed with *bn* as the first element should consist of a divine name, plant, animal, or place name as their second element. The first argument is specious because there are no limitations on the types of names that can be formed with *ben* as the first element. The second argument refers to paragraph 8.69 in the grammar of Gordon (1965). However, there are examples of names that do not fit these categories as Gordon's glossary (paragraph 19.481, *bn.ǵlmt*) illustrates. See also Gröndahl (1976) 34, 381-84. Of course, the question is much broader than Ugaritic personal names, since the names of 1 Kings 4 are not related to Ugarit.

4. PREPOSITION BEFORE THE PLACE-NAME

Although some administrative lists with personal names and associated place-names occur without any intervening prepositions, this is not always the case. AT 162 provides a list of mostly feminine names, in which each is normally followed by *i-na* + place-name + *i-na* + É + personal name, which can be translated, "PN1 from GN from the house of PN2." However the function of this text is to be interpreted, it is clear that West Semitic administrative texts do use prepositions before place-names.

5. ADDITIONAL NOTES

The presence of notes that disturb the regularity of the text has led to conclusions about editorial insertions. However, when compared with administrative lists from West Semitic archival sources, these assumptions need to be reconsidered. AT 161 preserves a list of personal names, many of which are associated with place-names that immediately follow. However, this is not always the case. Some personal names are followed by notes telling the reader more about the name bearer. For example, a certain *iz-zi* (obv. 3) is designated as a LÚ.SIMUG (*nappāḫu*) "smith." Another name, now broken, is designated as a LÚ.GIŠ.GIGIR "charioteer." Some names are followed by the names of their fathers in the manner already discussed. Thus a variety of notes providing further means of identifying the person named appear throughout the document. The same variety of recording also occurs in AT 166, AT 180, AT 182, and AT 188. These were not editorial insertions added later but appear to have formed part of the scribe's original record.

6. NOTES ABOUT ADDITIONAL REGIONS

These are not found in West Semitic administrative texts.

7. NOTES ABOUT SPOUSES

Insofar as these notes serve to further identify the name bearers by specifying a family relationship, they may be compared to the patronyms that occur in several of the administrative texts, where the addition of the expression, "son of Y," can replace either a place-name or occupation of the name bearer. See AT 161, AT 166, AT 180, and AT 182.

8. DISTINCTIVE LAST ITEM

The specific form of the final line in 1 Kings 4: 19 is found in administrative texts. For example, AT 224 is a list that has an introduction followed by a series of lines, each of which includes a number of unnamed people (LÚ.MEŠ) associated with (*a-na*) a place-name or person. In at least two cases the number of people is one (lines 17 and 20), similar to 1 Kings 4: 19.

One additional text is relevant for this feature of a distinctive final entry to the list. Ugaritic text KTU 4.288, which contains the list of *skn* "town mayors" on its obverse, is significant as one of the few texts that provides a list of leaders and the place-names associated with their area of rule. According to the transcription of Dietrich, Loretz, and Sanmartín (1995) 322, the text is as follows:

1. *spr blblm*
2. *skn uškn*
3. *skn šbn*
4. *skn ubrᶜ*
5. *skn ḫrṣbᶜ*
6. *rb.ntbtš*

rev.

7. *w.ᶜbd{.}r[ ]*
8. *arbᶜ.kk[r]*
9. *ṯlṯ.ktt*

Several features parallel the list of governors in 1 Kings 4. First, there is an introduction that refers to the contents of the following list and that designates the individual referred to in a special way, as *blblm*. Second, there is a formal list of five individuals who, although not named, are indicated by their title and the place-name where their jurisdiction reaches. Third, there is a distinctive final line to this list, line 6. Like the final figure referred to in the 1 Kings 4 list, it also is different containing a different title for the figure so designated. In fact, this title, *rb*, may be synonymous with *skn.*[14]

---

[14] Rainey (1962) 92-93; (1966) 426-28.

Nevertheless, it is distinctive and appears at the end of the list. Of course, this does not suggest that there was some sort of standard literary form that required the last line of such a list to be different. In KTU 4.288 the scribe was given the task of recording a group of individuals in leadership positions. One individual was distinct in terms of the title of office. Rather than placing this individual at the beginning or in the middle of the list, the scribe chose to reserve the entry until the end and to add it there. It would appear that the same method was used in the list of 1 Kings 4. The Judean official lacked a single personal name for some reason. Perhaps at the time of the writing of the list, no individual had been designated. Perhaps the name had been lost or forgotten. Just as the reason for the different title in the Ugaritic list is not clear, so the reason for the absence of a personal name in the 1 Kings 4 list is no longer apparent. However, in both cases the distinctive nature of the entry led the scribe to follow an identical procedure. It was reserved for the end of the list.

IV. Conclusion

In general, the Solomonic district list of 1 Kings 4: 7-19 resembles administrative texts from Ugarit and Alalakh. The overall form of a list with introductory comments, a series of entries of a personal name followed by a preposition and place-name(s), and a concluding entry distinctive from its predecessors are all elements found in other administrative lists. Thus there is no basis for arguing that the list as a whole cannot be archival.[15]

Distinctive to 1 Kings 4 are the notes about spouses and descriptions of additional territories. However, the ancient Near Eastern administrative texts have been shown to contain notes regarding the family relationships of the name bearer and additional information about the name bearer.

---

15 Ash (1995) 83-85. The assumptions about an absence of literacy in early Israel which Ash makes on the basis of some recent publications lead him to argue that the list is a product of a garbled oral transmission. These assumptions need to be qualified in the light of the actual epigraphic evidence from Israel and its contemporary neighbors (*cf.* Millard [1995] 207-17).

Also of interest are those administrative lists, or lists that resemble administrative texts, that form part of a larger document. AT 228 provides a list of towns with numbers of individuals associated with each town. On the opposite side of the tablet there is a description of how these individuals, Suteans, were held on charges of theft. Ugaritic text KTU 1.91 [RS 19.15] includes a list of towns with quantities of wine and other items from each town. The other side of the tablet describes sacrifices to various deities. KTU 4.288, discussed above, describes quantities of copper on its reverse side. These texts demonstrate that the presence of additional material associated with the administrative lists, but not part of the form of the list, could occur on the same tablet as the administrative document.

There may be other evidence for the presence of editorial insertions, such as the relationship of historical geography to places named on the list. However, many items that at first might appear to be intrusive to the form of an archival administrative document are found, upon closer inspection, to have antecedent parallels in the same type of document occurring in West Semitic cultures of the Late Bronze Age. Therefore, their presence in the list of 1 Kings 4: 7-19 cannot be taken as *prima facie* evidence for editorial insertions or for distortions in the transmission of the document.

Bibliography

Alt, A. (1913) Israels Gaue unter Salomo. In *Alttestamentliche Studien Rudolf Kittel zum 60. Geburtstag dargebracht*, 1-19. Leipzig. Reprinted in *Kleine Schriften zur Geschichte des Volkes Israel*, 2: 76-89. Munich (1953). **Ash, P. S.** (1995) Solomon's? District? List. *Journal for the Study of the Old Testament* 67: 67-86. **Dietrich, M., and O. Loretz** (1970) Die soziale Struktur von Alalakh und Ugarit (IV). Die E_2 = *bītu*-Listen aus Alalakh im 15. Jh. v. Chr. *Zeitschrift fur Assyriologie* 60: 88-123. **Dietrich, M., O. Loretz, and J. Sanmartín** (1976) *Die keilalphabetischen Texte aus Ugarit. Einschließlich der keilalphabetischen Texte außerhalb Ugarits. Teil 1. Transkription.* Neukirchener. (1995) *The Cuneiform Alphabetic Texts from Ugarit, Ras Ibn Hani and Other Places.* Second edition. Münster. **Gordon, C. H.** (1965) *Ugaritic Textbook. Grammar.* Rome. **Gröndahl, F.** (1976) *Die Personennamen der Texte aus Ugarit.* Rome. **Heltzer, M.** (1982) *The Internal Organization of the Kingdom of Ugarit.* Wiesbaden. **Hess, R. S.** (1988) A Preliminary List of the Published Alalakh Texts. *Ugarit Forschungen* 20: 69-87. (1992) Observations on Some Unpublished Alalakh Texts, Probably from Level IV. *Ugarit Forschungen* 24: 113-15. (1996) A Typology of West Semitic Place Name Lists with Special Reference to Joshua. *Biblical Archaeologist* 59:3 160-70. **Millard, A. R.** (1995) The Knowledge of Writing in Iron Age Palestine. *Tyndale Bulletin* 46: 207-17. **Na'aman, N.** (1986) *Borders and Districts in Biblical Historiography.* Biblical Studies 4. Jerusalem. **Naveh, J.** (1990) Nameless People. *Israel Exploration Journal* 40: 108-23. **Nougayrol, J.** (1955) *Textes Accadiens et Hourrites des archives est, ouest et centrales.* Le palais royal d'Ugarit, 3. Paris. **Rainey, A. F.** (1962) *The Social Stratification of Ugarit.* Ph.D. dissertation, Brandeis University. Ann Arbor, Mich. (1966) ^{LU2}MAŠKIM at Ugarit. *Orientalia* NS 35: 426-28. **Wiseman, D. J.** (1953) *The Alalakh Tablets.* London. **Wiseman, D. J., and R. S. Hess** (1994) Alalakh Text 357. *Ugarit Forschungen* 26: 501-8.

On Homicide in Hittite Law*

Harry A. Hoffner, Jr.
The Oriental Institute
The University of Chicago

Not all homicide is criminal. To quote *Black's Law Dictionary*: "homicide may be committed without criminal intent and without criminal consequences, as, where it is done in the lawful execution of a judicial sentence, in self-defense, or as the only possible means of arresting an escaping felon. The term 'homicide' is neutral; while it describes the act, it pronounces no judgment on its moral or legal quality."[1]

When modern readers first look into an ancient law collection, one of the subjects which most attracts them is homicide. Several questions arise in their minds: "How did this society deal with homicides? And did they punish criminal homicide with cruel or unusual means?" Modern readers tend to impose their own contemporary views and moral judgments on societies remote in time and place. To a degree, there is even a certain morbid interest in this subject, which I do not propose to titillate.

It is well known in fact that the best-known ancient Near Eastern law collections devoted little space to the subject of homicide. Various explanations have been given for this fact, including the assumption that

* Abbreviation of Hittite text publications in this article are: CHD = *Chicago Hittite Dictionary*; KBo = Keischrifttexte aus Boghazköi (6 = Hrozny 1922, 34 = Otten 1991); KUB = Keilschrifturkunden aus Boghazköy (1 = Figulla 1921, 8 = Weidner 1924, 32 = Ehelolf 1942, 58 = Popko 1988); StBoT = Studien zu den Bogazköy-Texten (32 = Neu [1996]).

1 Black (1991) 506.

premeditated homicide was normally handled by private "justice," that is, by revenge. As we shall see, there is good reason to assume this for Hittite society.

Still, the law collections of early Mesopotamia and Anatolia are not silent on the subject of homicide. In particular, over ten of the 200 paragraphs of the Hittite laws are devoted to the subject. The organization of the collection is such that not all of these situations (or "cases") are found in one place.

Laws 1-4

The first group of laws touching upon the subject are the opening ones in the collection: §§1-6. They deal with unlawful or criminal homicide.

One of the characteristics of the organization of the Hittite laws is the conspicuous attention to conditions under which an offense takes place, and to the relative social status, age, and gender of both the perpetrator and the victim. In some instances a given offense—for example, abduction—is described in four consecutive laws, in each of which the combination of factors differs slightly: the perpetrator is a free man, a free woman, a male slave, a female slave; the victim is one of these four types; the crime occurs in Ḫatti, or in a nearby allied country, or in a remote land with no diplomatic ties to Ḫatti.

So it is also with the first six laws. Two factors—the free or unfree social status of the victim and the intentionality of the act—combine in various ways to determine the sequence of the first four laws. The victim is either free or unfree. The compensation for the free victim is twice that for the unfree. The act is committed either in the heat of anger—the term is "because of a quarrel"—or completely by accident—the expression is "only his hand sins." The compensation for death caused in anger is twice that of death inflicted accidentally. When both factors are applied, the cases show a compensation ratio of 4: 2: 2: 1.

But while this tells us something about the textual composition of the law collection, what, if anything, does it tell us about legal thinking? The choice of factors is significant: in any action for damages one must recognize the principle of economic worth. Regardless of the inevitable variations in individual "net worth"—the size of one's estate and the success of one's business—every individual Hittite had a standard and uniform "worth." And as in the section of the law collection stating prices for common commodities and livestock, so also here a uniform value is placed on a human life. In setting the value of livestock, the laws considered group characteristics: species, gender, and age, while disregarding individual variables, such as whether or not a particular bull, stallion, or buck was noticeably successful in impregnating females in its herd. So the law does not attempt to gauge the particular value of individual adults other than on the basis of free or unfree social status—the gender or financial status of the victim is not taken into consideration. In the later parallel text of this law (§II)—formulated several centuries after the main recension—allowance is made for the gender of the victim. Unfortunately, due to breaks at key points in the text, we cannot ascertain whether the Late Parallel version of this law considered cases which differentiated among free man, free woman, male slave, and female slave, or only between the two cases of a free or unfree female victim. The translation of [*tá*] *k-ku* MUNUS-*za-ma* GÉME as "but if the woman is a slave" is problematic, since elsewhere a GÉME is never referred to as a MUNUS-*za* "woman." But regardless of this uncertainty, it cannot be unimportant that the victim's gender is specified. This suggests that the earlier concept—that only social status mattered in determining victim loss—had evolved to take into consideration the relative value of male versus female. As we shall see, a similar development is found in the New Hittite period, as reflected in law 6 and its late parallel. The essential philosophy which informs Hittite law is that the consideration of victim status should aid in determining how much compensation was needed to offset the *economic* loss. The intentionality of the perpetuation was also taken into consideration, but the emotional suffering or social loss encumbered by the victim's family was not a legal concern.

Much has been claimed about the enlightened approach of Hittite law, which is more concerned with compensating victims than punishing offenders. But if only the first concern had existed, there should have been no gradation of payments based upon the perpetrator's motives. Yet such was not the case. Hittite law did attempt to punish culpability and protect innocence—intent was a consideration. Although the victim's family assuredly suffered just as much from the loss of a provider from an accidental act as from a malicious act, equal consideration had to be given to the perpetrator's intention.

Having considered the framework of laws 1-4, let us examine a few of the details. What is the medium of compensation? In all four cases it is "persons." The Hittite text uses the Sumerogram SAG.DU, "heads." As everyone agrees, this denotes slaves of either sex. Nothing is specified about the age or sex of these slaves, only their number. The lack of detail suggests that the principal concern of the laws is not precisely how each offender will discharge his debt, but rather the relative gravity of the offense and of the loss entailed. It is possible that, in practice, slaves were required whose sex and age matched those of the victim. But laws 1-4 are primarily concerned with establishing the theoretical basis of Hittite homicide law.

Laws 1-2 differ from laws 3-4 in the choice of the verb to describe the homicide. In laws 1-2 the expression is *šullannaz kuenzi*, "kills in a quarrel." We have already taken into account the force of the words "in a quarrel" as indicating an impulsive act committed in the heat of anger. Other examples of the verb *kuen-*, "to kill," qualified by an ablative of cause, are known, but none describes premeditated murder.[2] Simple *kuen-* without ablative complement does describe murder.[3] But usually murder is described with the phrase *ešḫar iya-*, "to shed blood." This would seem to have as its implied but unexpressed counterpart an act committed coolly and deliberately.[4]

---

2 *UL≈war≈an≈kan tuetaza memiyanaz kuennir.* "Did (Gilgamesh and Enkidu) not kill it (*i.e.*, the bull of heaven) at your word?" KUB 8.48 i 12 (Gilgamesh), transliterated in Laroche (1969) 131, and *apūn≈kan* LUGAL-*un gimri zaḫḫiyaz kunanzi* "they will kill that king in the field as a result of battle" KBo 34.130 ii 8.

3 See, for example, the examples of *kuen-* in the Edict of Telepinu edited in Hoffman (1984) 17-19, 21-22 (Telepinus).

4 But did the Hittites ever verbalize such a motivation for homicide or are we merely spinning out an imaginary scenario? Archi (1979) has assembled textual evidence which comprised the Hittites' ideal conception of a ruler: a man who could feel compassion for others. This royal ideology is well expressed in a negative mirror image in

But if the word *šullannaz* supplies an ameliorating motive to the act in laws 1-2, the verb *kuenzi*, "kills," attributes to it a degree of intention greater than the phraseology in laws 3-4. The deed is anger-driven, but it is intended. Laws 3-4 employ the expression "strikes (a person) so that he/she dies, with only his/her hand sinning," *i.e*, the blow was not intended to kill, but only to inflict pain or injury.[5]

Among other lexical considerations, we have to note that the verb translated "sins"—*waštai*—does not have the flavor of moral depravity associated with the English word. Like the Greek *hamartanō*, Hittite *wašta-* has the root meaning "to miss the mark," "to fail to achieve what is intended." Thus it is used quite literally in an archery scene in which one archer misses the target (*waštai*), while another hits it (*ḫazzizzi*).[6] What the text says then is not that the hand was morally depraved and committed a sinful act, but that it failed to achieve what it attempted—to inflict pain—and instead caused death.

Laws 5-6

Although law §5 appears to introduce another victim status, namely the merchant, I do not believe that this is strictly the case. Although the

---

the Old Kingdom monarch Ḫattušili I's description of his heir apparent, who is described as unworthy of becoming king. Speaking of his son, the king wrote: *apāš ≈ma* DUMU-*aš* UL *uwawaš uwattat* / UL *išḫaḫruwattat* UL≈*aš genzuwait* / *ekunaš≈aš n≈aš* UL *genzuwalaš*, "But he showed himself a child unworthy to be seen. He shed no tears; he felt no compassion; he was cold; he had no feelings" (KUB 1.16 ii 5-7). Other parts of this king's narrative make it clear that this coldness manifested itself in causing or allowing the deaths of innocent people. For this reason Ḫattušili would disinherit his son and adopt in his stead the man who would become King Muršili I.

5 It is not true, as once was proposed, that a Hittite expression which literally means "a sin of the head" is the intentional counterpart to "only his hand sins." This interpretation was based upon a misunderstanding of the context in which the expression "sin of the head" is found. But whether or not one can conceive of a literal pendant to "his hand sins," the fact that this describes an accidental homicide cannot be doubted.

6 MUNUS ^{GIŠ}BAN / ^{LÚ}*ḫartaggan* GI-*it* 1-*ŠU šiezzi* / *t≈an waštai tān≈a šiezzi* / *t≈an ḫazziazzi ta ḫalzai* / [*aw*]*aya awaya* KUB 58.14 rev. left col. 24-28.

compensation is very high, the factors which cause this are of another order from those which govern the first four laws. I therefore believe that laws 1-4 are intended to cover the entire spectrum of human victims, and laws 5 and 6 are supplemental, introducing special cases.

One can safely assume that a merchant is a free person. But he is much more than this. At times he functioned as the representative of his king. And so, there may be considerations other than his free status or his wealth which might make compensation for his death very high.

That this case is not simply a part of a pattern begun in laws 1-4 is indicated by the different medium of compensation. Nothing is said of "persons." Rather, compensation is in silver: 100 minas (=4,000 shekels),[7] a truly princely sum. However, it is not the large amount of compensation which is significant; it is the form: silver rather than persons.

Laws 1-4 make no mention of the locus of the death, presumably because it was assumed to be close to the victim's home. In the case of a merchant, who, by virtue of his occupation, is frequently away from home, the locus needs to be mentioned. It becomes an issue chiefly because of the peripheral issue of the loss of his goods, which must be returned by the perpetrator whether the killing took place in Ḫatti or in an allied land. Instead of stating simply "in a foreign land," the text mentions two specific countries—Luwiya and Pala. Why is this? Luwiya is again singled out for mention as both the locus of a crime and as the homeland of a potential perpetrator in laws §§19-23, where the subject is the abduction, capture, and return of fugitive slaves. There, various combinations of factors—the nationality of the perpetrator, victim, and finder; the location from and to which the abduction, flight, and return took place—are used to grade offenses from most to least serious, and rewards from largest to smallest. In these laws Luwiya assumes a position between Ḫatti and KUR *kurur*ī, "an

---

[7] The Hittite mina was 40, rather than 60, shekels. Friedrich (1959) 16 n. 2 once proposed to emend the text from 1 *ME* MA.NA to 1½ MA.NA (that is, 60 shekels). But the same error would have had to be made twice in the Old Hittite copy A and at least once in copy B, which according to other evidence was not made using copy A as its model. The reading 1 *ME* then seems unimpeachable.

enemy country." This makes sense only if we assume that extradition was possible from a land such as Luwiya because of a treaty, while no extradition was possible from an "enemy country" with which no treaty was in force. We assume that in law §5 the lands of Luwiya and Pala are mentioned as examples of countries with whom the Hittites had a treaty relationship. Such countries could be counted on to see to it that the dead merchant's goods were returned. Obviously, the same requirement held for a homicide committed in Ḫatti itself. But, in this latter instance, there exists a clause concerning the return of the merchant's body—it would be unthinkable to return an unembalmed corpse from a foreign country, but possible within Ḫatti itself.

Late Parallel to Law 5

In the corresponding law from the Late Parallel version (§III) the three variant scenarios do not consider location, but, rather, intention—a criterion borrowed from laws 1-4. In the first case a person is killed intentionally in order to rob him, in the second he is killed in a quarrel, and in the third he dies because the perpetrator's "hand sins," *i.e.*, in an accident. The amount of silver imposed in case one is, unfortunately, unknown, due to a textual break. In case two 6 minas are imposed, in case three 2. Unless the missing figure in the first case is much higher than the remaining two, it appears that the 100 mina compensation of the Old Hittite formulation was drastically reduced in the New Hittite version. But despite the obvious influence of the intentionality clauses from laws 1-4 in the New Hittite version of law 5, compensation remains silver rather than "persons."

Although the amount of silver paid to compensate for the homicide may have been reduced from the Old Hittite 100 minas, the stolen goods are replaced not simply onefold, but threefold. This is because the loss of the goods is now considered theft, a second offense, and is subject to its own separate penalty. Whereas the earlier onefold restoration of the goods was not considered a penalty, the threefold replacement obviously is.[8]

---

8 See the threefold compensation for theft in §XXXV (=late version of §§45 and 71).

Law 6

Law 6 shares with law 5 the status of a supplement to the basic legal statement on homicide contained in laws 1-4. Whereas law 5 deals explicitly with a merchant, law 6 deals with any person—man or woman—who is killed in "another city" (*takīya* URU-*ri*). Even though the law does not state that the homocide occurs in another country, it belongs together with law 5 thematically. Both are extensions of the basic framework of laws 1-4. Both involve deaths away from the victim's home.

The word *takiya* (translated "another") is not the term usually found: *tamedani* for this context. And although it might be just an archaic synonym to the latter, there is always the possibility of a different connotation or more precise meaning than "another." To date, *taki-* is found only in the laws (in published or announced unpublished texts). In laws 191 and 196 *takiya* occurs in the correlate construction *takiya utne ... takiya utne* and *takiya* URU-*ri ... takiya* URU-*ri*. Both laws concern the separation of two partners to an abominable sexual act called *ḫurkil*. It is easy to see how Goetze could have suggested to Sturtevant and Bechtel (1935) 224f. a translation "distant," although the usual term is *tuwala-*. The late parallel text (KBo 6.4) has generalized the situation to include persons found dead on another's property, even within the same city. The fine imposed in §6 (equivalent to 8¼ shekels—for the price of land see §183) is greatly increased in §IV (all his land plus 60 shekels). Although both A and B agree in reading 1 *ME* GIŠ*gipeššar* (12,000 m² = 3 acres),[9] Sturtevant and Bechtel (1935) objected that this was too high and "would amount to a whole field." But that is just the point. The land is not to be used, as Sturtevant thought, as a "burial plot," but is compensation to the heirs. In the Old Babylonian laws of Hammurabi §§23-24, the town in which a robbery or a homicide was committed was responsible for compensation to the victim or his heirs, and in the case of a homicide, the payment was one mina (60 shekels) of silver. Still, this amounts to much less than the sums for killing a merchant. Everything points to a very high status of the merchant in early Hittite society.[10]

9 The reading 1 *ME* (100) is also accepted by Hout (1990) 521f.

10 Hoffner (1968), Klengel (1979), Haase (1978).

This was the Old Hittite law. The Late Parallel law makes several changes. First of all, for the first time a distinction of value based upon gender is made on the life of the victim. The Late Parallel law voices the condition "if it is a free man," specifies the required compensation, but then follows up not with the alternative "if, however, it is a slave," but rather with "if, however, it is a woman." Since no mention of social status was made in the Old Hittite law, we must assume that the law covered only free persons, since elsewhere in the main Old Hittite recension distinctions are drawn between cases in which the victim or perpetrator is slave or free. And since in the older law the victim is "a person, man or woman," it is clear that no distinction was made in the compensation on the basis of gender. The judgment that a free woman's life was worth less than a man's was taken by the author of the New Hittite version.

As in the Old Hittite law, in the late version the compensation for the homicide is required from the owner of the land on which the dead man or woman was found. In the Old Hittite law it was about 3 acres. In the New Hittite law it is: "his property, house, and 60 shekels of silver. But if (the dead person) is a woman, (the property owner) shall give (no property, but) 120 shekels of silver." No acreage is specified, but the complete forfeiture of property and buildings thereon plus a substantial payment in silver. Since the real estate might well constitute virtually all of a person's assets, he might have to sell slaves or even members of his family in order to raise the 60 shekels of silver.

It is obvious from a comparison of this law with Old Hittite laws 1-4 that in the New Hittite period the burden of responsibility for someone found dead on your property could be much higher than in the Old Hittite laws on homicide in the heat of anger or accidental homicide detailed in laws 1-4. Unfortunately the Late Parallel version of laws 1-2 (§I) is too badly broken to interpret. There is, therefore, no way we can determine if the New Hittite compensation for heat of anger and accidental homicide of free persons was as high or higher than what the late parallel to law 6 required. Compensation for the accidental homicide of a slave woman was two minas (= 80 shekels), which is ⅔ of the three minas (=120 shekels) which the late parallel to law 6 required for a free woman found dead on someone's property.

The question naturally arises: "But what if the body is not found on someone's land?" For this the late parallel offers a solution which resembles the procedures described in Deuteronomy 21: 1-9. I would translate the rest of the law as follows:

> If (the place where the dead body was found) is not (private) property, but uncultivated open country, they shall measure 3 DANNA's in all directions, and whatever town/village is determined (to lie within that radius), he shall take those very (inhabitants of the town/village).[11] If there is no town/village, (the heir of the deceased) shall forfeit (his claim).

Earlier translations have missed the significance of this passage, because they have failed to divide the clauses properly and have mistaken a key term. Goetze (1969) translated the words *ták-ku* *Ú-UL-ma* $^{\text{A.ŠÀ}}$A.GÀR *dam-me-el pé-e-da-an* as: "But if there is no other man's field (and) fallow." In so doing, he mistakenly combines two adjacent, asyndetic clauses and fails to translate *pedan.* Friedrich (1959) 51 rendered the passage this way: "Wenn aber der Ort nicht Feldflur eines anderen (ist)." At least he attempted to translate both *pedan* "place" and $^{\text{A.ŠÀ}}$A.GÀR "field and fallow." But he also mistakenly combined the two clauses. His interpretation—which is followed also by Imparati (1964) ("Ma se il luogo non <è> il campo di un altro") and Haase[12] ("Wenn aber Feld (und) Flur eines anderen nicht der (Tat)ort (sind)")—would require the Hittite to read: *ták-ku pé-e-da-an-ma Ú-UL dam-me-el* A.ŠÀ A.GÀR. Von Schuler (1982) 98 also combines the two clauses, but takes A.ŠÀ A.GÀR as the subject and *dam-me-el pé-e-da-an* as the negated predicate: "Wenn aber die Gemarkung keines anderen (Eigentümers) Ort (ist)." This interpretation would require the Hittite to read: *ták-ku* A.ŠÀ A.GÀR-*ma Ú-UL dam-me-el pé-e-da-an.* Both of these false interpretations founder on the position of *Ú-UL* and fail to understand what is most crucial here, that we are dealing with two clauses, not one. I understand *dam-me-el* in line 11 not as "of another" (genitive of *tamai-*), but as an *l*-stem adjective synon-

---

11 Or less likely: "he shall take those same (payments from the inhabitants of the village)."

12 Haase (1963), (1984).

ymous with the enlarged *i*-stem *dammeli-*, which always describes open country not yet brought under cultivation. The common locative expression *dammeli pedi*, "in an uncultivated place," "on uncultivated land," is usually attributed to the i-stem *dammeli-*, but could, on the basis of form, just as well belong to the l-stem *dammel-*. The two clauses describe the location first negatively and then positively: it is *Ú-UL-ma* $^{\text{A.ŠÀ}}$A.GÀR, "not a field and fallow," of anyone, but *dammel pedan*, "an uncultivated place."

Although this analysis is a great improvement grammatically and lexically over the previous ones, it amounts practically to the same situation. If the place where the body is found is uncultivated or virgin land, it is not the property of any particular individual who can be held accountable. But my second interpretation of this passage has a direct relevance to the disposition. I understand the compensation similar to previous interpreters. If a settlement (expressed in Hittite by the Sumerogram URU) lies within a circle of three DANNA's radius, the center of which is the find spot of the body, that settlement becomes liable for compensating the victim's heirs. But what is the amount of that settlement?

The Hittite text of the law reads: *nu apūš≈pat dāi.* All interpreters agree that the subject of the verb is the victim's heir. "He shall take those same ones." The point at issue is: what are "those same ones?" *a-pu-u-uš-pát* is understood by Friedrich (1959) as referring back to "welche Ortschaft … festgestellt wird." Von Schuler (1982) writes "eben die Stadt, die … festgestellt wird." Imparati (1964) writes "e qualunque città entro <tale raggio> sia situata, allora quelle appunto prenda." Haase (1994) translates, "so nimmt der Erbe des Toten diese [Siedlung] in Anspruch."[13] That *apūš≈pat* is plural common gender was noted by Imparati's "quelle," Haase's "gerade sie," and Goetze's (1969) "he shall take those." But Friedrich's "gerade die" and von Schuler's "eben die Stadt, die …" could be construed as feminine singular.

What is the referent of *apūš≈pat*? Friedrich and Haase thought "gerade," Imparati "appunto," and von Schuler "eben." Goetze fails to

---

13 Haase (1994) 75-76.

translate it at all. If the claimant takes the entire city or town, or all its inhabitants, this would amount to a penalty much higher than prescribed if the body is found on privately owned land. I would assume that the heir's "taking" of the entire citizenry of the settlement would include all which they possess, animate and inanimate, and would therefore represent the same phenomenon of referring to inanimate objects such as land and buildings with the common gender pronoun *apūš*. A clear parallel is ⸢*nu-uz*⸣*-za a-pu-ú-un-pát da-an-*[*zi*][14] in law 43, to be discussed below. There the heirs or legal representatives of the decedent "take" the perpetrator in the sense that he becomes their property.

Deuteronomy 21: 1-9 contains a similar Israelite law. The same procedure of measuring to the nearest town is employed, but there is no limit to the distance to be measured, and there is no mention of blood money, only the right of the town's elders to take an exculpatory oath.

This Hittite law and similar ones—such as Ḫammurapi §23—from other ancient Near Eastern societies underscore the importance of venue for liability.[15] Texts from Ugarit contemporary with the Hittite New Kingdom reveal that in cases in which the murderer was apprehended he had to make compensation for the murdered man and restore the stolen goods. When the murderer was not apprehended, the community took an oath to the effect that both the identity of the murderer and the location of any stolen goods were unknown. After this the community had to make compensation for the murdered man, but was not required to restore stolen goods. The Late Parallel Hittite law §IV likewise states that the community is to make compensation for the murdered man without any mention of a requirement to restore stolen goods.

No exculpatory oath is mentioned in Hittite law §IV, but textual evidence shows that, like other ancient peoples, the Hittites employed excul-

---

14 B iii 53 has ⸢*nu a-pu-un*⸣*-pát da-an-zi* without *-za* and C iv 15 *nu-za a-pu-un-pát da-a-i* with *-za* but a singular verb, "he shall take."

15 On the liability of the community for such a crime committed in their territory see also Klengel (1980) 193 and 196 n. 23 (with lit.).

patory oaths.[16] And in KBo 1.10, a text from the reign of Ḫattušili III describing Hittite legal procedure in the case of merchants killed abroad, we read the following: [... *aš-*]*ra ša na-pu-ul-tu*$_4$ *i-na libbī*(ŠÀ)*-šu di-ku ul-la-lu* "They shall 'purify' the place in which someone was killed" (rev. 20). This might mean that they shall determine the guilt or innocence of the inhabitants of the place, giving them an opportunity to exonerate themselves with an exculpatory oath. In Akkadian exonerating oneself is normally conveyed by a form of the verb *ubbubu* rather than its near synonym *ullulu.* But in a text composed in Akkadian by a Hittite, it is unlikely that such fine distinctions would always have been observed. In Hittite *parkunu-*, "to purify," is used in both the normal sense of cleaning something, in a magical-ritual sense, and in the judicial sense of "to exonerate, prove innocence" (*Chicago Hittite Dictionary* P: 172f., sub *parkunu-* 2a).

Other Laws concerning Homicide

After law 6 the subject changes from homicide to personal injuries. The formal treatment of homicide is now concluded. But there are other laws in the corpus which concern the subject, or at least the related issue, of compensatable deaths.

Laws 42-44

Law 42 concerns the responsibility of someone who gives no advance payment when he hires another to go on a military campaign in which the hired person dies. The Old Hittite manuscript A requires the giving of one "person" in compensation, just as law 4 required the giving of one "person" for the accidental causing of the death of a slave. The compensation is minimal, because the hirer did not himself kill the victim, but is economically responsible to compensate his heirs, since he did not give a hire in advance.

The New Hittite manuscripts B and C add: "And as hire he shall pay twelve shekels of silver. As the hire of a woman he shall pay six shekels [of

16 See the evidence assembled in the articles *link-* "to swear," *lingai-* "oath," and *linganu-* "to administer an oath to another person" in *Chicago Hittite Dictionary* L-N: 62-71.

silver]," thus showing that they do not consider the giving of "one person" to be the equivalent of the hire not paid in advance. But since copy A does not mention the paying of the hire, it is likely that the "one person" was considered to include, or be in lieu of, the agreed-upon hire.[17] It is therefore possible that—at least in the Old Hittite formulation—this was not a case of criminal homicide but of economic responsibility for an appreciable loss suffered by a party (or his representatives) with whom one has an unfulfilled contractual obligation.

Law 43

Law 43 reads: "If a man is crossing a river with his ox, and another man pushes him off (the ox's tail), grasps the tail of the ox, and crosses the river, but the river carries off the owner of the ox, (the dead man's heirs or legal representatives) shall take that very man (who pushes him off)." This is clearly a case of wrongful death. The circumstances are not generalized, as in laws 1-4, with stereotyped victim-status or motivational expressions such as *šullannaz kuenzi* or *keššaršiš waštai*. Instead, an elaborate scenario is presented in detail. This betrays the origin of the law as a precedent case. It is full of vivid details including the use of the iterative verb *zīnuškizzi* to portray a protracted action in its incomplete course: the victim was in the

---

17 The amount of the fire/wage in B and C is 12 shekels for a man and 6 for a woman. In both the Old Hittite and New Hittite versions of law 20, if a Hittite man abducts a male slave belonging to another Hittite man from the land of Luwiya, and brings him to the land of Ḫatti, and subsequently the abducted person's Hittite owner recognizes him, the abductor shall return the abducted slave and in addition pay his owner 12 shekels of silver, which must represent a kind of hire. The appropriate wage rates are also found in the Old Hittite copy A of law 24, where we read: "If a male or female slave runs away, he/she at whose hearth his/her owner finds him/her shall pay one month's wages: 12 shekels of silver for a man, 6 shekels of silver for a woman." Here the New Hittite copy substitutes: "shall pay one year's wages: 2½ minas (=100 shekels) of silver for a man, 50(?) shekels of silver for a woman)." While it is possible that there was a real difference in settling cases of harboring fugitive slaves, in which in later times a full year's wage was required even if the period of harboring was much briefer, it is equally likely that prorating was practiced, and the New Hittite versions were simply quoting wage rates for the longer period.

process of fording the river with his ox, when the incident occurred. Obviously, it is not intended that this law should only apply in identical circumstances. It represents a principle of liability which can be extended to similar cases. But although it contains vivid details, it leaves many important questions unanswered. Is the perpetrator already in the river when he knocks the victim off his ox, or does he jump onto the victim from a nearby bank? In the former case it could be argued that the perpetrator was himself trying to cross without an ox and, losing his battle with the current, knocked the victim off his ox in an attempt to save his own life. In the latter case, there would be no extenuating circumstance, since the perpetrator could have safely remained on the bank. The disposition of the case should give a clue as to the gravity, if not the precise nature, of the deed. This disposition is expressed succinctly. The Old Hittite copy A reads ⌜*nu-uz*⌝*-za a-pu-ú-un-pát da-an-*[*zi*] "they (*i.e.*, the victim's heirs or representatives) shall take that very (man)," presumably meaning the perpetrator. The New Hittite copy B has substantially the same reading, while the even later New Hittite copy C changes the plural verb to a singular: "he shall take that (man)."[18] All copies employ the particle *-pat*, which I have rendered with the word "very." This has the force of making the demonstrative "that" exclusive: "that man and no other." This means that no member of his family or slave could be substituted for the perpetrator. We are reminded of the phrase: *nu a-pu-u-uš-pát da-a-i* "he (= the victim's heir) shall take those very (persons)" which we saw above in the later parallel to law 6 (§IV, Parallel Text i 13). Presumably, since the two phrases are such a close match and occur in the same contexts, the force of the *-pat* is the same: no substitutes can be accepted in the place of the responsible parties.

The precedent case of law 43 supplements laws 1-6 in presenting another aspect of responsibility for wrongful death. It is not homicide in self-defense since the victim himself does not directly threaten the life of the perpetrator. It cannot fall into Black's category "Homicide by necessity," because the necessity to kill was not unavoidable, arising as it did through

---

18 I retract my earlier view (Hoffner [1963] 229) that the subject of the verb "they shall take" was the authorities, while the singular "he" was the victim's heir.

the misjudgment of the perpetrator that he could safely ford the river without an ox of his own. Yet neither was it due to anger (*šullannaz*) or accident (*keššaršiš waštai*). Although it may have been an unavoidable consequence of the perpetrator's attempt to save his own life, he is responsible for the death of another through his culpable misjudgment of the danger of the stream to himself. He must make compensation in a form more severe than in laws 1-6 (which require only the giving of "persons"), but in a form similar to the later parallel to law 6 (which allows the decedent's heir to take as slaves the persons held to be legally accountable for the death).

Law 44a

Law 44a reads: "If anyone makes a man fall into a fire, so that he dies, (the guilty party) shall give a son in return." Since the crucial noun "son" is preserved only in the late New Hittite copy C (KBo 6.5 iv 17), it is possible that a different word was used in Old Hittite copy A, but there is no argument to make this supposition plausible. The signs of "son" (DUMU.NITA-*an*) are damaged on the tablet, but it was the preferred reading of Hrozny (1922), Walther (1931), Neufeld (1951), Goetze (1969), Friedrich (1959), and Imparati (1964).[19] SAG.DU-*an*, given in Friedrich (1959) as an alternative reading to DUMU.NITA-*an*, and initially preferred by Güterbock,[20] was subsequently withdrawn by him.[21] It would be the only example of SAG.DU, "person," with a Hittite complement (*-an*) and without a preceding numeral.

The compensation, then, is higher for the perpetrator than the giving of one person. But the reason for this is not clear. The verb which describes the action is *peššiya-*, often translated "to push or shove."[22] A precise translation would require a better understanding of what the fire in question was

---

19 See also the remarks of Hoffner (1975) 56f.

20 Güterbock (1961) 68.

21 Güterbock (1962) 23. See also Imparati (1964) 60-62.

22 Friedrich (1952) 168 offers the following translations: "werfen, stoßen;—verwerfen; mißachten;—abschaffen."

and where it was located. My translation "causes someone to fall" is based upon several lines of evidence. Firstly, in the law collection itself we have a use of *peššiya-* which requires this meaning. In laws 17-18 (only New Hittite versions are preserved) *peššiyazi* takes a pregnant woman's unborn child (*šarḫuwanduš≈šuš*) as its object in a case of negligent action causing a miscarriage. And while the verb might be translated "shoves" if the grammatical object were the woman, it can only be translated "causes to fall" in the case of the embryo, much as one might cause unripened fruit to fall from a tree branch. Support for this interpretation can be found in the use elsewhere of the verb *mauškizzi,* "it falls," to describe a woman's habitual miscarriages[23] and *katta maušzi* to describe a normal birth.[24] In laws 17 and 18 *peššiyazi* is obviously the causative of *maušzi.* Further support is found in the use of *peššiya-* as a hunting term for felling a deer.[25] Since deer hunters do not "shove" them, this can only be derived from the same idea of causing the deer to fall.

Causing another to fall into a fire can be intentional or accidental. The only clues available to us are the size of the compensation and the position of the law in the corpus. If the reading DUMU.NITA is correct, the compensation is higher than the giving of "persons" in laws 1-4, but lower that the forfeiture/enslavement(?) of the perpetrator himself in law 43. The position of the law immediately following law 43 in which there might have been the extenuating circumstance of the perpetrator's seeking to save his own life, might incline one to understand this deed also as not deliberate.

Law 44b, which, as its number indicates, was combined in some manuscripts with 44a, makes no explicit mention of homicide. The only possibility of an association with homicide would be that the offence—disposing of the remnants of a purification ritual on another's property—was potentially life-threatening to the property owner and is labelled "sorcery"

23 See *Chicago Hittite Dictionary* L-N: 212 sub *maušš-* a 1′ d′.

24 See *Chicago Hittite Dictionary* L-N: 213 sub *maušš-* b 5′ b′ 2′′.

25 *peššiandu≈ya≈an aliyanan* ^LÚ.MEŠ^*ṢĀʾIDŪTIM* "May hunters fell it, (namely this) deer!" KBo 32.14 ii 13-14, from the Hurro-Hittite bilingual Song of Release to be edited by E. Neu in StBoT 32 (1996).

(*alwanzatar*) and "a case for the king's court," which could entail a very severe penalty. Law 44b is the first of two laws in the collection that label offences as *alwanzatar*. Law 111 concerns making an image for purposes of harmful magic to be directed against another person. In addition, law 170 bears all the earmarks of sorcery, although the word *alwanzatar* does not occur as its characterization. The offence is killing a snake while pronouncing someone else's name. The fine—here the term "compensation" seems inappropriate—is high: if the offender is a free person, he pays one mina of silver; if a slave, he must die. What this suggests for law 44b is that its penalty would also have been high, whether because the offence was sorcery or because such sorcery was life-threatening to the property-owner. In any event, it is not a typical case of homicide.

The above cases seem to exhaust the instances of criminal homicide, that is, a person's being required by Hittite law to render compensation for another person's death.

Justifiable Homicide

According to Black, "justifiable homicide" includes instances where a duly constituted judicial or police authority takes a human life in discharge of his duties. Such cases—involving the "death penalty"—are to be found in the Hittite law collection (§§92, 121, 126, 166-67, 172, 173, 187-91, 195, 197, 199), as in other ancient collections.[26]

Homicide in Self-Defense

An example of homicide in self-defense may be found in laws 37 and 38, where persons described by the word *šardiyaš*, "helper, accomplice," lose their lives in the pursuit of activities in which the law offers no guarantee of compensation in case of injury or death.[27] In both cases the verdict of the law collection is that "there will be no compensation."

---

26 For a discussion of these see Hoffner (1963) 334-36.

27 This was my opinion already in Hoffner (1963) 228. I realize that the interpretation of

Summary

How can we summarize what we have learned in this brief survey of the paragraphs of the Hittite laws which touch upon the subject of homicide? Firstly, no law in the collection directly addresses murder. As is well known and has often been stated in earlier treatments of the subject, the clearest statement about the society's procedure in the case of murder comes from a passage in the Old Hittite edict of King Telipinu: "Whoever commits murder, whatever the heir himself of the murdered man says (will be done). If he says: 'Let him die,' he shall die; but if he says: 'Let him make compensation,' he shall make compensation. The king shall have no role in the decision."[28] The distinction may seem a fine one, but it is worth observing here that it is not the law—neither the law of the official collection nor the law of this king's edict—that requires the death penalty for murder; rather it is the heir or legal representative of the victim, the person called the "lord of the blood" (*ēšḫanaš išḫāš*). This is especially remarkable, since there were other offenses described in the law collection which draw the death penalty. Murder was not the most serious offense and did not draw the most severe penalty.

---

these two cases is controversial and that according to some views the actions of the *šardiyaš*—at least in law 37—are legally more defensible than those of the man whom the *šardiyaš* pursues and threatens. There is also uncertainty as to whom the expression "you have become a wolf" applies: to the pursuing *šardiyaš* or the pursued eloper. But regardless of the party so described, the allusion is appropriate: there can be neither prosecution of a wolf for killing its human attackers, nor humans for killing the predator. Therefore, despite these uncertainties I am persuaded by the lack of compensation for the deaths of the *šardiyaš* in both laws that they were acting outside the law's sphere of protection, much as if they had been combatants in a battle. Admittedly, this is easier to visualize in law 37 than in law 38, where resort to force in a trial would seem to fall under the jurisdiction of the law.

28 Quoted in Hoffner (1995) 237. In her edition Hoffmann (1984) 52f. understands the last sentence to mean that there will be no compensation payable to the king. But while the laws attest to a compensation given to the palace (*ŠA* É.GAL-*LIM*, never **ŠA* LUGAL) in cases of bodily injury, none is ever mentioned in cases of homicide. On the other hand, since serious crimes, which certainly would include murder, often fell under royal jurisdiction, one might expect the Telipinu edict to clarify the matter by renouncing royal jurisdiction outside of special instances.

Secondly, although important supplementary laws occur later in the collection, the primary guidelines for the response to an unpremeditated homicide are laid down in the opening laws of the collection, numbers 1-4. And in these laws the emphasis is not upon punishment of the offender but on compensating the decedent's family. The compensation is not measured in silver but in "persons."

Thirdly, aside from the standard issues of victim social status and intentionality expressed in laws 1-4, other factors needed to be invoked in resolving difficult cases involving wrongful death. Among these were criminal negligence, such as presumed in the cases of the property owners or villagers in whose area a murder was allowed to transpire, and of the man who recklessly attempted to ford a river without an ox and put himself in a position where he was obliged to save his own life at the expense of another's.

Homicide is only one of the matters of concern in Hittite law. The compensations required in its rulings indicate that it was not the most serious crime. The position of the command "You shall not murder" as the sixth in the Hebrew Decalogue also is an indication that other prohibitions were of greater gravity. But the conspicuous position of the primary laws governing homicide—at the very beginning of the Hittite law collection—indicates its centrality in the legal thought of the Hittites. No other ancient Near Eastern law corpus puts homicide laws at the very beginning of the collection.[29] According to the Old Hittite Telipinu edict, "bloodshed"—by which is meant criminal homicide—which has become widespread and unpunished is the most ominous harbinger of national catastrophe. We still do not know the precise date within the Old Hittite period of the composition of the law collection. But the prominence of position given in it to the homicide laws coincides with the prominent warnings against homicide in the Telipinu edict.

---

29 The first of the laws of Hammurabi concerns not homicide *per se* but false accusation of homicide and is followed immediately by a false accusation of witchcraft, thus making it clear that the common subject of the opening laws is not homicide but false accusations.

Bibliography

Archi, A. (1979) L'humanite des hittites. In E. Masson 1979: 37-48. **Black, H. C.** (1991) *Black's Law Dictionary.* St. Paul, Minn. **Ehelolf, H.** (1942) *Kultische Texten vorwiegend in hethitischer, churrischer und luvischer Sprache aus den Grabungen 1931 und 1932.* Keilschrifturkunden aus Boghazköy 32. Berlin. **Figulla, H. H.** (1921) *Keilschrifturkunden aus Boghazköi* Vol. 1. Berlin. **Friedrich, J.** (1952) *Hethitisches Wörterbuch. Kurzgefaßte kritische Sammlung der Deutungen hethitischer Wörter.* Heidelberg. (1959) *Die hethitischen Gesetze.* Documenta et Monumenta Orientis Antiqui 7. Leiden. **Goedicke, H. and Roberts, J. J. M.**, eds. (1975) *Unity and Diversity: Essays in the History, Literature, and Religion of the Ancient Near East.* Baltimore. **Goetze, A.** (1969) The Hittite Laws. In Pritchard 1969: 188-97. **Güterbock, H. G.** (1961) Review of J. Friedrich, *Die hethitischen Gesetze. Journal of Cuneiform Studies* 15: 62-78. (1962) Further Notes on the Hittite Laws. *Journal of Cuneiform Studies* 16: 17-23. **Haase, R.** (1963) *Die keilschriftlichen Rechtssammlungen in deutscher Faßung.* Wiesbaden. (1978) Zur Tötung eines Kaufmanns nach den hethitischen Gesetzen (§§5 und III). *Die Welt des Orients* 9: 213-19. (1984) *Texte zum hethitischen Recht. Eine Auswahl.* Wiesbaden. (1994) Deuteronomium und hethitisches Recht. Über einige Ähnlichkeiten in rechtshistorischer Hinsicht. *Die Welt des Orients* 25: 71-77. **Hoffmann, I.** (1984) *Der Erlaß Telipinus.* Texte der Hethiter 11. Heidelberg. **Hoffner, H. A., Jr.** (1963) *The Laws of the Hittites.* Ph. D. Dissertation, Brandeis University. (1968) A Hittite Text in Epic Style about Merchants. *Journal of Cuneiform Studies* 22: 34-45. (1975) Propaganda and Political Justification in Hittite Historiography. In Goedicke and Roberts 1975: 49-62. (1995) The Hittite Laws. In Roth 1995: 211-47. **Hout, T. P. J. van den** (1990) Maße und Gewichte. Bei den Hethitern. *Reallexikon der Assyriologie und Vorderasiatischen Archäologie* 7: 517-30. **Hrozný, B.** (19 21) *Keilschrifttexte aus Boghazköi. Autographien.* Keilschrifttexte aus Boghazköi 6. Osnabrück. (1922) Code Hittite provenant de l'Asie Mineure (vers 1350 av. J.-C.) 1er partie. Transcription, traduction Française. Tome 1er, Premièr partie. Paris. **Imparati, F.** (1964) *Le leggi ittite.* Rome. **Keiser, O.**, ed. (1982) *Rechtsbücher.* Texte aus der Umwelt des Alten Testaments I/1. Gütersloh. **Klengel, H.** (1979) Handel und Kaufleute in hethitischen Reich. *Altorientalische Forschungen* 6: 69-80. (1980) Mord und Bußleistung im spätbronzezeitlichen Syrien. *Mesopotamia* 8: 189-97. **Laroche, E.** (1969) *Textes mythologiques hittites en transcription.* Paris. **Masson, E.**, ed. (1979) *Florilegium Anatolicum. Mélanges offerts à Emmanuel Laroche.* Paris. **Neu, E.** (1996) *Das hurritische Epos der Freilassung* I. Studien zu den Boğazköy-Texten 32. Wiesbaden. **Neufeld, E.** (1951) Notes on Hittite Laws. *Archiv Orientalni* 18/4 116-30. **Otten, H.** (1991) *Hethitische Texte vorwiegend von Büyükkale, Gebaude A/.* Keilschrifttexte aus Boğazkoy 34. Berlin. **Popko, M.** (1988) *Hethitische Rituale und Festbeschreibungen.* Keilschrifturkunden aus Boghazköy 58. Berlin. **Pritchard, J. B.**, ed. (1969) *Ancient Near Eastern Texts Relating to the Old Testament.* Princeton. **Roth, M. T.** (1995) *Law Collections from Mesopotamia and Asia Minor.* SBL Writings from the Ancient World Series 6. Atlanta. **von Schuler, E.** (1982) Die hethitischen Gesetze. In Keiser 1982: 96-123. **Smith, J. M. P.**, ed. (1931) *The Origin and History of Hebrew Law.* Chicago.

Sturtevant, E. H., and Bechtel, G. (1935) *A Hittite Chrestomathy.* Philadelphia. **Walther, A.** (1931) The Hittite Code. In Smith 1931: 246-79. Apendix 4. Chicago. **Weidner, E. F.** (1924) *Hethitische Texte verschiedenen Inhalts.* Keilschrifturkunden aus Boghazköy 8. Berlin.

Le fonctionnement de la poste et le métier de facteur d'après les textes de Mari*

Bertrand Lafont
CNRS, Paris

Comment s'y serait donc pris un sujet du roi de Mari pour envoyer un message de sympathie au savant que nous souhaitons honorer aujourd'hui et qui, notamment par ses nombreux articles de géographie historique, nous a tant fait voyager parmi les différents royaumes du Proche-Orient ancien et nous a aidés à les mieux connaître?

Une fois la tablette rédigée, comment la faire parvenir à son destinataire?

Regardons ce qu'un haut fonctionnaire, représentant à Karanâ le roi de Mari Yasmah-Addu, écrivait à son maître (*ARM* V 38)[1]:

> Dis à mon Seigneur Yasmah-Addu: ainsi parle Haṣidânum, ton serviteur.
> Le porteur de tablettes en place[?] a été muté à Mari. Maintenant son fils

* Editors' note: the abbreviation ARM used throughout refers to the series *Archives royales de Mari.* The authors/editors may be found in the bibliography. Readers unfamiliar with the Akkadian of Mari may wish to consult the parallel series of transliterations and translations, ARMT, *Archives royales de Mari Transcrites et Traduites.* Volumes cited and other abbreviations are: ARM I: Dossin (1946); ARM II: Jean (1941); ARM III: Kupper (1948); ARM IV: Dossin (1951a); ARM V: Dossin (1951b); ARM VI: Kupper (1953); ARM VII: Bottéro (1956); ARM X: Dossin (1967); ARM XIII: Dossin, *et al.* (1964); ARM XIV: Birot (1974); ARM XVIII: Rouault (1976); ARM XXIII: Bardet, *et al.* (1984); ARM 26/1 and 2: Durand, *et al.* (1988); ARM 27: Birot (1993); FM II: Durand et Charpin (1994); IM: siglum for texts in the Iraq Museum.

1 *a-na be-lí-ia ia-ás-ma-aḫ-*[d]IM (2) *qí-bí-ma* (3) *um-ma ḫa-ṣí-da-nu-um* (4) ÌR-*ka-a-*

vient de mourir et son petit-fils n'est qu'un bébé. Il faut donc que mon Seigneur envisage le cas du petit: l'enfant est en bas âge et n'a personne qui l'entretienne. Il faut que mon Seigneur le (= *le porteur de tablettes*) laisse aller.

Haṣidânum cherche donc ici à récupérer un porteur de tablettes dont il utilisait les services mais dont le roi a décidé la mutation d'office à la capitale; ce sont des raisons familiales qui sont invoquées à l'appui de cette demande, même s'il est vraisemblable que Haṣidânum espérait surtout qu'on lui rende du personnel dont on l'avait privé. Ce texte nous apprend ainsi qu'il existait bel et bien un métier spécifique de "porteur de tablettes", soit *(mâr) b/wâbil ṭuppim*, et correspondant à ce qu'est aujourd'hui notre "facteur"; comme tout fonctionnaire, ces gens étaient susceptibles d'être mutés à différents postes, en différents lieux. Et de fait, ce titre se rencontre à plusieurs reprises dans les textes de Mari[2], même si ses attestations ne sont pas aussi fréquentes que celles des *mâr šiprim* que l'on voit sillonner à cette époque, en grand nombre, les routes du Proche-Orient.

Mais à lire tous les textes si nombreux où il est question de la transmission des messages écrits d'un endroit à un autre, on constate que cette tâche est en réalité accomplie par des personnes portant des titres assez divers. Qui voit-on en effet acheminer des tablettes dans les textes de Mari? La liste suivante peut être dressée:

---

ma (5) dumu *ba-bi-il ṭup-pí-im* (6) *š*[*a qa-t*]*i-im* (7) [*a-na ma-r*]*i*^{ki} *na-si-iḫ* (8) [*i-na*]*-an-na* (9) dumu-*šu im-tú-*[*u*]*t* (10) *ù* dumu dumu-*šu* (11) *ṣe-ḫe-er i-*[*n*]*a-*[*an-n*]*a* (12) *be-lí ṣú-ḫa-ra-am* (13) *li-mu-ur-ma* (14) lú-⸢tur⸣ *ṣé-ḫe-er* (15) *ù pa-qí-da-am* (16) *ú-ul i-šu-ú* (17) *be-lí li-wa-še-er-šu.*

Pour ce texte, *cf.* J.-M. Durand (1987b) 192. La lecture de la ligne 6 (*ša qâtim* = "qui est à disposition") suit une nouvelle proposition faite dans Durand (1997) 508:326.

On remarquera que *mâr wâbil ṭuppim*, par rapport à *wâbil ṭuppim* est construit sur un mode parallèle à *mâr lâsimim* (*ARM* XXVI/2 373 et 490) par rapport à l'habituel *lâsimum*, ou à *mâr šiprim* par rapport au simple *šiprum* (qui peut signifier "messager" et non pas seulement "message", comme en *FM* II 49: 13).

2 *wâbil ṭuppim* par exemple en *ARM* I 14, II 141, IV 3, X 85, 176, XVIII 33, XXVI/2 318, 340, XXVII 82, *FM* II 55 et 56, *etc.* On remarquera par ailleurs que, à côté de l'expression *ṭuppam wabâlum*, "apporter une tablette", on rencontre également *ṭuppam našûm* (*ARM* XIV 117, XXVI/2 505, *FM* II 49).

(1) les diplomates chargés de la correspondance internationale et des échanges diplomatiques (*mâr šiprim*); particulièrement présents dans nos archives, on les voit transporter les messages de capitale en capitale; ils ont un statut d'ambassadeur et sont parfois habilités à mener des négociations; ils sont souvent accompagnés de différentes sortes d'adjoints et assistants et sont militairement escortés[3].

(2) les "coureurs" et les "chevaucheurs" (*lâsimum* et *rakbum*); les premiers (*lâsimum* ou *mâr lâsimim*, équivalents aux lú-kas$_4$ sumériens, *ARM* VI 24, 62, XIII 131, XXVI/2 373, 490, *etc.*) sont des coureurs ou des "estafettes", organisés en services spécialisés et qui dépendent directement des chancelleries des différentes capitales existant à cette époque. Ainsi voit-on par exemple le roi de Mari entretenir à Alep un bureau de poste permanent composé de ces courriers, comme le montre l'intéressant passage de la lettre A.2937[4] qui mentionne les "courriers-*lâsimum* qui sont au service de mon Seigneur (Zimri-Lim) et qui résident à Alep". On remarquera par ailleurs les *mârû lâsimi qallûtim*, "coureurs légèrement équipés?" mentionnés en *ARM* XXVI/2 373: 19. Par opposition aux "coureurs-*lâsimum*" qui accomplissent leur mission à pied, les *rakbum* (équivalents aux rá-gab sumériens, par exemple en *ARM* XXVI/2 484) sont des messagers pourvus de montures. Ils doivent, pour leur part, être distingués des *râkib imêri*, "chevaucheurs d'ânes", qui ne sont pas, en eux-mêmes, chargés d'une quelconque mission, mais représentent vraisemblablement une catégorie de dignitaires (*ARM* XXVI/1 131, XXVI/2 312, XXVII 16 et notes à ces textes).

(3) les individus spécialement attachés au service de tel gouverneur de province ou de tel haut fonctionnaire pour transporter leurs messages. C'est par exemple le cas des *našparum* (*ARM* XIV 66): ce terme, qui n'est pas très fréquent à Mari, désigne le "porteur de tablettes" affecté auprès d'un gouverneur. Ainsi cette lettre *ARM* XIV 66 nous apprend-elle que, à Saggarâtum, le gouverneur Yaqqim-Addu disposait de trois de ces agents chargés

---

3 Voir B. Lafont (1992) 167-83.

4 Voir J.-M. Durand (1990) 71, n. 177.

d'acheminer son courrier jusque chez son maître Zimri-Lim[5]. Un haut fonctionnaire comme Yamṣûm, en poste à Ilânṣurâ, bénéficiait lui aussi du service de plusieurs messagers, puisqu'on le voit demander à son correspondant: "Renvoie-moi *les* porteurs de *mes* tablettes; qu'ils ne soient pas retenus." (*ARM* XXVI/2 340). Mais ces individus au service de tel ou tel personnage important et que l'on voit "porter des tablettes" n'ont parfois pas d'autre qualification que celle de lú-tur NP, lú NP ou ìr NP, "serviteur de NP" (*ARM* II 21, 104, XXVI/2 470: 3, *etc.*); ce sont en quelque sorte des "porteurs particuliers" attachés au service d'un dignitaire.

(4) les simples facteurs (*wâbil ṭuppim*) dont on pouvait sans doute trouver au moins un spécimen dans chaque localité de quelque importance (*cf. ARM* V 38 ci-dessus et autres références rassemblées note 2).

(5) certaines catégories de soldats présents dans les garnisons locales et dont les services, en temps de paix, pouvaient être utilisés par les autorités du lieu pour l'acheminement du courrier; c'est notamment le cas des lú-diri-ga, ces "supplétifs" qui effectuent une sorte de service militaire et qui peuvent avoir, parmi leurs obligations, la charge de porter des messages comme le rappelle très explicitement Zakira-Hammû, auteur de la lettre *ARM* XXVII 44: "Depuis toujours, les supplétifs (lú-diri-ga-meš) qui demeurent à Qaṭṭunân et qui sont nourris aux frais du Palais doivent: (1) protéger les terroirs du Palais contre les buffles et les ânes sauvages, (2) assurer l'acheminement des tablettes chez mon Seigneur, (3) occuper les postes de garde". Il s'agit là d'un intéressant descriptif de la triple mission de ces "supplétifs" lorsqu'ils ne sont pas en guerre (voir également à ce sujet le parallèle *ARM* XXVII 6).

(6) On mentionnera pour finir les quelques exemples où l'on voit que, à titre exceptionnel, des gens ayant les qualifications les plus diverses peuvent être utilisés pour porter des tablettes: un palefrenier? (*kizûm* en *ARM* II 9)[6],

---

5 On pourra rapprocher avec intérêt les tablettes *ARM* XIV 66 et XXVII 44 pour voir comment étaient organisés les services dépendant du gouverneur.

6 Voir J.-M. Durand (1991) 59.

un marchand (dam-gàr en *ARM* I 93)[7], un pâtre (*nâqidum* en A.1025: 33)[8], un devin (*ARM* XXVI/1 140), ou un cuisinier (muḫaldim en *ARM* I 45)[9]. Dans ces différents cas, c'est tout simplement l'occasion offerte par le déplacement de tel ou tel agent dans le cadre de ses propres activités, qui est utilisée pour que puissent être acheminées en même temps quelques tablettes allant dans la même direction que lui. La tablette *ARM* I 45 offre une belle illustration de ce phénomène:

> Dis à Yasmah-Addu: ainsi parle Samsî-Addu, ton père.
>
> La tablette urgente qui avait été écrite pour Išhi-Addu (roi de Qaṭnâ), était à remettre à Altiš-qallu, le cuisinier; mais il est parti, sans qu'on n'ait pu lui mettre la main dessus. Maintenant donc, je t'envoie cette tablette. Il faut que deux de tes serviteurs, courriers rapides, allant à sa poursuite, la lui fassent tenir. S'il se trouve qu'ils n'ont pu rejoindre Altiš-qallu, qu'ils fassent eux-mêmes parvenir à destination cette tablette.

Altiš-qallu est donc un cuisinier qui, devant se rendre à Qaṭnâ via Mari, s'est mis en route avant qu'on ait pu lui confier du courrier à destination de cette ville. Deux facteurs s'apprêtent donc à partir à sa poursuite en espérant le rattrapper rapidement, faute de quoi ils devront faire eux-même le déplacement jusqu'à Qaṭnâ.

Il existe encore d'autres termes que l'on rencontre quand on part à la recherche des porteurs de messages. Ainsi, par exemple, le terme *naṣrum* (*ARM* XXVI/2 217, 357, 358): il s'agit de messagers d'un genre très particulier puisqu'ils sont utilisés pour la transmission de messages "secrets". Ou encore le *kallûm* (*ARM* V 40, XXVI/2 334: 5, *etc.*)[10]: il s'agit de messagers

---

7 Pour ce texte, *cf.* J.-M. Durand (1987b) 182-83, ainsi que les notes de A. Finet (1988) et F. Joannès (1988). Il existe d'autres exemples de l'utilisation des marchands en déplacement pour faire acheminer des tablettes. Ainsi profite-t-on souvent de "l'immunité" dont ils bénéficient en principe, pour faire passer "en cachette" des lettres que l'on souhaite voir circuler discrètement. Pour toutes ces questions, voir J.-M. Durand et D. Charpin (1997) 379.

8 *Cf.* J.-R. Kupper (1990) 337-47.

9 Ligne 7: *a-na qa-at al-ti-iš$_7$-qa-al-lu* muḫaldim* (collation J.-M. Durand).

10 À ne pas confondre avec l'adverbe *kallâm*, "rapidement", tel qu'il a été reconnu par Charpin (1994).

"rapides", à distinguer des individus qualifiés de *qallûtum*, signifiant sans doute "légèrement équipés" et que l'on rencontre également dans les textes (*ARM* I 39, 45, 84, 93, 97, *etc.*); mais en réalité, ce ne sont vraisemblablement pas là de nouvelles catégories à différencier des autres, ces termes pouvant fonctionner comme des épithètes qualifiant les diverses espèces de messagers dont on vient de faire la liste (*cf.* d'ailleurs les *mârû lâsimi qallûtim* d'*ARM* XXVI/2 373 rencontrés ci-dessus).

Peuvent donc être distingués, parmi les différentes sortes de "porteurs de tablettes", ceux dont c'est réellement la profession (n⁰ 1 à 4) et les "occasionnels" (n⁰ 5 et 6). Cependant, si l'on voit effectivement toutes ces personnes effectuer d'incessants déplacements, et si de nombreux échanges en tous sens nous sont attestés, on ne sait pas grand chose sur l'infrastructure elle-même des services de la poste, dont toute cette circulation laisse pourtant deviner l'existence. Par ailleurs, la particularité de notre documentation est qu'elle est palatiale. Ainsi ne peut-on savoir comment s'y prenaient les simples particuliers pour expédier du courrier, bien qu'il ne soit pas sûr que ces derniers aient eu un fréquent recours à l'écrit et à l'usage épistolaire. Si donc le courrier est essentiellement de nature "officielle", il est normal que ceux qui sont chargés de transporter les messages appartiennent à "l'administration", qu'elle soit centrale (le palais royal avec ses services de *lâsimum*), provinciale (services particuliers des gouverneurs et des dignitaires présents çà et là), ou locale (présence d'un facteur dans chaque bourgade).

Une fois cette description et ce classement établis, la différence peut sembler évidente entre la tâche dévolue à un *mâr šiprim* et celle confiée à un simple *wâbil ṭuppim*: le premier a clairement un statut de diplomate habilité à mener des négociations à un niveau international, alors que le second semble n'avoir comme simple responsabilité que de porter les plis qui lui sont confiés à un niveau local. Mais dans la réalité, la situation n'est peut-être pas aussi tranchée. Les tâches supplémentaires que l'on confie aux *wâbil ṭuppim* sont en effet nombreuses:

- Ils servent d'informateurs et peuvent rapporter des nouvelles ou des propos dont ils ont eu connaissance; il arrive même qu'on leur demande leur avis sur telle ou telle question (*ARM* II 21, 141, VI 58[11], *etc.*).
- Ils sont parfois chargés de transmettre au destinataire un message oral en plus de la tablette qu'ils ont mission de transporter et de remettre (*ARM* I 76 ou III 68 cité ci-dessous). En *FM* II 49, un courrier-*lâsimum* arrive de chez le roi sans être porteur d'une tablette, et c'est oralement qu'il délivre les instructions royales, ce qui ne manque pas d'étonner son interlocuteur, destinataire du message.
- Ils sont utilisés comme escorteurs pour accompagner telle ou telle personne. Ainsi l'expéditeur de la lettre *ARM* X 176 déclare-t-il: "Si (Dame Mennâ) se réjouit à l'idée de venir (à Alahtum), confie-la au porteur de ma présente tablette" (*wâbil ṭuppiya*). En *FM* II 120, l'auteur de la missive écrit: "NP_1 est avec toi. Puisqu'il a reçu une (nouvelle) affectation, pourquoi tarderait-il une seule nuit? Avec NP_2 le courrier (*lâsimum*) qui t'apporte ma tablette, mets-le en route et envoie-le chez moi."
- Ils sont porteurs de paquets et/ou d'objets tout autant que de tablettes. On le voit bien par exemple avec les textes *ARM* II 104, X 32 (Kirûm fait livrer à son père Zimri-Lim, par le porteur de sa tablette, les "cheveux de sa tête et la guenille arrachée à son corps"), A.3889 (ci-dessous publié), X 85, XVIII 33 (des outils en métal sont confiés au porteur de tablettes). Et cela est encore visible dans cette autre lettre de Haṣidânum au roi de Mari Yasmah-Addu où, comme dans la tablette citée au début de cet article, le fonctionnaire demande à son maître de lui rendre un autre "facteur" indûment déplacé à Mari (*ARM* V 40): "Selon les instructions du Roi (= Samsî-Addu), c'est à Qaṭṭarâ même que doit résider NP pour servir de messager rapide (*kallûm*) préposé à tous les transports."

Mais un autre indice montre la différence très ténue qui peut parfois exister entre les termes *mâr šiprim* et *wâbil ṭuppim*, et la confusion qui pouvait être faite entre les différentes fonctions ici répertoriées. Ainsi pourrait-on s'étonner de voir Yamṣûm, haut fonctionnaire de Mari détaché auprès du roi d'Ilânṣurâ, qualifier de *mâr šiprim* ceux de ses serviteurs qui sont simplement chargés de porter ses tablettes à son maître; il demande en effet au ministre mariote Sunuhra-halû (*ARM* XXVI/2 335): "Renvoie-moi rapidement mon messager (*mâr šipriya*) par qui je fais porter les tablettes

---

11 Dernière ligne du texte: [*be-lí li-ša-a*]*l-šu*, "que mon seigneur l'interroge."

à mon Seigneur." Cela montre en définitive qu'il ne faut sans doute pas établir de catégories trop rigides entre ces différentes sortes de "porteurs de tablettes".

L'accent doit être mis par ailleurs sur une notion qui paraît fondamentale dans l'acheminement du courrier, en cette époque qui se caractérise, rappelons-le, par un fort morcellement politique mais aussi par une relative homogénéité de peuplement: il s'agit de la notion de "relais". En considérant qu'un porteur de tablettes à pied ne peut guère parcourir plus d'une trentaine de kilomètres par jour, si son objectif final est lointain, il lui faut donc choisir avec soin les différentes étapes qu'il devra nécessairement effectuer. Quand il s'agit d'un ambassadeur, son ambassade est dite *êtiqtum* ("de passage") tant qu'elle est en transit dans l'un de ces relais[12]. À l'étape, le messager, qu'il soit diplomate ou simple facteur, est "pris en charge" par le responsable du lieu auquel il délivre les informations en sa possession. Celui-ci décide des conditions de la poursuite du voyage du messager. Les simples porteurs de tablettes n'ont qu'un rayon d'action limité et doivent se contenter de livrer leur message au centre le plus proche, avant de revenir au plus vite dans leur localité de rattachement, ledit message étant alors, si nécessaire, pris en charge par un autre facteur (voir par exemple *ARM* III 68 cité ci-dessous).

Plusieurs documents laissent très bien entrevoir l'organisation de ce système de relais, tant à l'époque du royaume de Haute Mésopotamie que sous le règne de Zimri-Lim. Ainsi Samsî-Addu, qui expédie son courrier depuis Šubat-Enlil, se sert-il du relais de Mari où réside son fils Yasmah-Addu pour faire parvenir son courrier à Qaṭnâ (*ARM* I 11, 48, 84 105 et I 45 ci-dessus), à Ešnunna (*ARM* I 27) ou à Babylone (*ARM* I 93, en passant par Yabliya et Râpiqum). Et l'on peut encore voir le même Yasmah-Addu être sollicité par son frère Išme-Dagan qui bataille dans les régions au-delà du Tigre et qui souhaite transmettre un message à son épouse (*ARM* IV 68).

---

12 Arrivée à destination, l'ambassade est dite *ṭêḫîtum*, "accréditée". *Cf.* Lafont (1992) 173.

D'une façon similaire, à l'époque de Zimri-Lim, les gouverneurs présents à Terqa (Kibri-Dagan), à Saggarâtum (Yaqqim-Addu) ou à Qaṭṭunân (successivement Ilušu-naṣir, Zakira-Hammû et Zimri-Addu) servent-ils de relais pour le courrier circulant entre Mari et les régions plus septentrionales (*ARM* III 59, 68, *etc.*). *ARM* III 68 est à cet égard assez révélateur: Yaqqim-Addu, qui réside donc à Saggarâtum, doit faire porter en urgence la tablette d'un certain Yapah-Lim jusqu'à Mari. Or on peut constater que le courrier fait une étape à Terqa puisque Kibri-Dagan, gouverneur de Terqa, écrit à Zimri-Lim:

> La tablette que Yapah-Lim a fait porter chez Yaqqim-Addu, Yaqqim-Addu l'a fait porter rapidement chez moi en disant: "Fais porter cette tablette chez mon Seigneur afin qu'il en prenne connaissance." Que mon Seigneur prenne donc connaissance de cette tablette.

La tablette, pour parvenir à Mari, sera donc passé entre les mains de trois facteurs successifs: de chez Yapah-Lim jusque chez le gouverneur de Saggarâtum, de Saggarâtum jusque chez le gouverneur de Terqa, et de Terqa jusqu'à Mari[13].

Un autre exemple peut être pris avec *FM* II 55 et 56 qui évoquent le rôle de relais de la ville de Qaṭṭunân, à l'occasion d'un problème de transmission du courrier entre Mari et les différents royaumes du Jebel Sinjar.

À Mari même, on voit le gouverneur local Bahdi-Lim faire suivre vers le roi de Babylone le courrier que le roi de Mari, sans doute absent plus au Nord, lui expédie (*ARM* VI 18). Et cette circulation fonctionne aussi bien dans l'autre sens, comme l'atteste la tablette *ARM* VI 53 où c'est Hammurabi de Babylone qui écrit à Zimri-Lim, toujours absent dans le Nord, en passant par le gouverneur de Mari.

Ainsi ces responsables locaux sont-ils au cœur de tout le processus de circulation des informations et des messages: il s'agit là, on le sait, d'un de leurs rôles et de l'une de leurs obligations les plus essentiels comme le souligne par exemple ce "serment d'un gouverneur" qui appelle sur lui la malé-

---

[13] Dans cette affaire de la tablette de Yapah-Lim, il y eut en réalité tout un imbroglio dont les tenants et aboutissants ont été explicités dans Charpin (1995).

diction divine "si jamais une tablette, bonne ou mauvaise, lui arrive de l'étranger sans qu'il la fasse tenir à son Seigneur Zimri-Lim"[14]. Dès lors, quand l'un d'entre eux reçoit personnellement une tablette contenant des informations susceptibles d'intéresser le roi, soit il la recopie (*ARM* XXVII 75, A.427+[15]), soit il la met sous enveloppe scellée et la fait "suivre" jusque chez le roi (*ARM* V 78, VI 58, XXVII 67, 69). C'est ainsi que nombre de missives ont été retrouvées dans les archives du palais de Mari, qui n'étaient pas directement adressées au roi mais qui lui furent transmises *pour information.* Une saine évaluation de la composition globale de ces archives passe par la prise en compte de ce phénomène important[16].

On observe donc, en définitive, à quel point la confidentialité des messages est habituellement faible. Ainsi les autorités locales qui hébergent un messager faisant étape, apprennent le plus souvent l'objet de sa mission et le contenu de son message. Cela est patent par exemple dans le cas de Yasîm-El, représentant le roi de Mari à Andarig, que l'on voit recopier *verbatim* le contenu d'un message que s'échangent deux rois et qui transite par Andarig; après son travail de recopie, il envoie ce double à son maître (*ARM* XXVI/2 435). On voit le même phénomène fonctionner encore en *ARM* VI 33 ou dans la tablette A.6[17]. C'est cette absence de discrétion qui explique par ailleurs l'existence, bien attestée, de nombreux messages et messagers secrets (*naṣrum*, *ṭuppât niṣirtim*)[18].

Toujours en ce qui concerne la diffusion des informations, il faut citer également le cas exemplaire d'Ašmad[19], le jour où le roi Zimri-Lim l'informa d'une attaque ešnunnéenne et qui recopia soigneusement en dix-sept exemplaires le contenu de la tablette qu'il avait reçue de son maître, pour

---

14 M.6182 publié dans Durand (1991) 26.

15 Cette tablette a été publiée dans Charpin (1995).

16 Voir également à ce sujet ce qu'écrit par exemple D. Charpin (1993) 166.

17 *Cf.* J.-M. Durand (1994) 15-22.

18 Pour ces deux termes, voir par exemple l'index de *ARM* XXVI/2.

19 Pour ce fonctionnaire et les diverses responsabilités qui ont été les siennes, voir *ARM* XXVI/1, p.147.

transmettre l'information à dix-sept rois alliés de Mari (A.3591)[20]; ce qui suppose par ailleurs qu'il ait pu disposer d'un grand nombre de "porteurs de tablettes", mais peut-être est-ce précisément dans ce genre de circonstances qu'un recours au contingent pouvait être effectué (voir plus haut à propos des lú-diri-ga).

Bien qu'ils ne soient pas très nombreux, certains détails existent dans nos textes qui permettent d'en savoir un peu plus sur les réalités du métier de facteur. Le texte *ARM* V 38, cité au début de cet article, montre qu'il s'agit d'une profession qui pouvait se transmettre de père en fils. Pour l'accomplir, il fallait avoir de solides qualités physiques: "Veille au choix du porteur de la tablette: qu'il soit résistant!" demande le roi en *ARM* XXVI/2 318. Et le fait qu'il s'agit d'un métier épuisant apparaît clairement quand on découvre la situation décrite en *ARM* XXVI/1 29 où les porteurs de tablettes sont tellement fatigués en arrivant à l'étape, que les autorités locales préfèrent les garder pour qu'ils se reposent, d'autres porteurs étant mis en route pour transmettre les tablettes à leur place (on remarquera que les dites tablettes sont alors mises sous scellés pour authentifier et justifier le changement imprévu de facteur dans l'acheminement du courrier). Les porteurs de tablettes doivent aussi être des individus rapides (*qallum*) et dignes de confiance (*taklum*).

Une tablette administrative (*ARM* VII 21) évoque leur entretien: "Un litre d'huile de qualité supérieure pour la toilette des hommes qui ont apporté des tablettes de chez Išme-Dagan." Mais peut-être ne s'agit-il là que d'un *extra* accordé par faveur à de valeureux courriers que l'on souhaitait récompenser, sinon pareil document devrait avoir beaucoup de parallèles.

Le plus souvent, on craint les bavardages de ces porteurs de tablettes comme le montre *ARM* IV 80, lettre d'Išme-Dagan à son frère Yasmah-Addu[21]:

---

20 *Cf.* M. Guichard (1994) 256-57.

21 La traduction donnée ici est celle de J.-M. Durand (1997) 511. Elle repose sur des collations et des interprétations dont l'auteur s'explique dans cet ouvrage. La remarque est également valable pour la lettre *ARM* III 59 présentée ci-après.

> Fais-moi porter tes tablettes de façon à cacher tes informations. Moi, je ferai porter (les miennes) chez toi de la même façon, afin que ne *soient pas connues* les nouvelles de ce pays-ci pour ce pays-là. Afin que ceux qui sont chargés de mes tablettes ne racontent pas les nouvelles de ce pays-ci à ce pays-là, je t'ai donc fait porter une petite tablette à côté de cette tablette-ci. Écoute-la.

On peut même voir un souverain n'avoir pas confiance en ses propres services de portage des tablettes et faire appel aux messagers d'un roi allié pour transmettre ses missives (*ARM* XXVII 71). Mais il s'agit sans doute là d'une situation exceptionnelle, car on a vu comment les porteurs de tablettes directement attachés à tel ou tel haut fonctionnaire étaient en réalité généralement choisis pour la confiance qui pouvait leur être accordée en toute circonstance (*ARM* II 141, *etc.*).

Le facteur qui ne fait pas bien son travail est passible de sanctions. Ainsi Kibri-Dagan, gouverneur de Terqa, fait-il part au roi de son indignation quand il constate que des porteurs de tablettes chargés d'un message pour Karanâ ont trop traîné en route, rendant ainsi inutile l'acheminement d'une lettre royale ayant perdu toute son actualité; il renvoie donc les coupables au roi afin qu'ils soient sanctionnés (*ARM* III 59):

> Dis à mon Seigneur: ainsi parle Kibri-Dagan, ton serviteur.
> La tablette de mon Seigneur que l'on devait porter à Karanâ, à Iddiyatum (ce n'est que) hier (que) les gens d'Ilum-Muluk me l'ont apportée pour que je la voie, et moi de crier: "Quel scandale! quel scandale!" Voici ce que j'ai dit: "Comment se fait-il que vous ayez gardé jusqu'à présent la tablette de mon Seigneur?" Maintenant, donc, j'ai fait conduire chez mon Seigneur cette tablette et les responsables qui, jusqu'à maintenant, l'ont retenue.

Le responsable local qui doit entretenir une correspondance suivie avec l'administration centrale et dispose pour cela d'un ou plusieurs serviteurs, sait à quel moment part le porteur de ses tablettes, mais ne sait jamais quand il va revenir. Et il a toujours crainte de devoir attendre bien longtemps son retour, ce qui représente pour lui une menace d'isolement. L'objectif est donc partout affirmé de voir le porteur de tablettes regagner son point de départ au plus vite (*ARM* IV 68, XXVI/2 340, XXVII 53, 82, *etc.*).

Quand il s'agit de faire porter des tablettes dont le contenu est jugé particulièrement important, deux possibilités s'offrent aux responsables qui décident des conditions de leur acheminement: soit assurer la sécurité des porteurs en leur adjoignant des gardes (*ARM* XIV 117), soit leur faire prendre des chemins détournés ("de nuit et en se cachant" précise le texte 72-2[22]; voir aussi *ARM* I 97). Un autre exemple de détour volontaire est donné par la "mission secrète à Ešnunna" d'un groupe de messagers benjaminites[23]. Tout cela montre que le service de la poste n'était pas épargné par certaines formes d'insécurité qui existaient alors à l'état endémique.

Les porteurs du courrier sont donc, comme on l'a vu, souvent absents et il est primordial pour le responsable de leur service de pouvoir les localiser en attendant leur retour. Dans cette perspective, il est intéressant de publier ici un inédit de Mari qui est pour l'heure unique en son genre. Il s'agit du document suivant (A.3889)[24]:

	[^{I} *a*]*r*$^{?}$*-šum*	[...a]ršum
2	*ša ṭup-pa-t*[*im*] *a-na an-da-ri-ig*$^{\circ}$	qui a porté des tablettes
	ub-lu-ú	à Andarig
4	*i-na qa-aṭ-ṭu-na-an*^{ki} *wa-ši-ib*	réside (pour l'heure) à Qaṭṭunân.
	[^{Id}]UTU*-za-ni-in*	Šamaš-zanin
6	[*ša ṭu*]*p-*[*p*]*a-tim ù ni-*[*di-tam*]	qui a porté des tablettes et la dot
R.	*a-na an-*[*d*]*a-ri-i*[*g*]	à Andarig
8	*ub-lú-ú i-na ma-*[*ri*^{ki}]	réside (pour l'heure)
	wa-ši-[*ib*]	à Mari.
10	^{I}*i-din-an-nu*	Iddin-Anu
	š[*a i*]*t-ti* ^{d}UTU*-za-ni-in*	qui est allé avec Šamaš-zanin
12	[*a-n*]*a an-da-ri-ig*^{ki}	à Andarig
	[*il-li*]*-ku i-na qa-ṭ*[*ú-na-an*^{ki}]	réside (pour l'heure)
14	[*wa-š*]*i-ib*	à Qaṭṭunân.

22 *Cf.* M. Birot (1973) 4.

23 F. Joannès (1992) 185-93.

24 Connaissant mon intérêt pour tout ce qui touche aux messagers et à la transmission des messages, c'est J.-M. Durand qui a repéré, parmi les documents inédits de Mari, cette tablette (A.3889) ainsi que celle présentée un peu plus bas (M.8887), et les a mises toutes deux à ma disposition. Qu'il en soit ici remercié.

Ce texte n'est qu'une sorte de petit *memorandum*, que l'on peut rapprocher de ceux déjà connus à Mari[25]. Il fait le point sur l'endroit où se trouvent trois porteurs de tablettes qui avaient été envoyés en mission à Andarig. Sans doute leur chef de service a-t-il jugé opportun, à un moment donné, de pouvoir les localiser précisément en fonction des informations à sa disposition, ce qui a occasionné la rédaction de cette tablette. Il faut dire que leur mission était sans doute particulièrement importante car, bien que le document ne soit pas daté, l'allusion qui y est faite au transport d'une dot (*nidittum*) jusqu'à Andarig laisse à penser que ces individus furent envoyés à l'occasion du mariage d'Ibbatum, fille du roi de Mari, avec Atamrum roi d'Andarig, mariage dont on sait qu'il eut sans doute lieu en l'an 9′ du règne de Zimri-Lim[26].

Par ailleurs, parallèlement au problème posé par la localisation des différents porteurs de tablettes dont on se désesèpre toujours qu'ils ne soient pas encore de retour, la détermination de l'adresse même du destinataire d'un message que l'on a préparé peut également être cause de soucis: ainsi Uṣur-awassu, resté à Mari alors que son maître Yasmah-Addu est en déplacement dans la région de Qabarâ, s'excuse de ne pas lui transmettre régulièrement de nouvelles faute de pouvoir établir avec précision l'endroit où il réside (*ARM* XXVI/2 291), tant il est vrai que, pour écrire à quelqu'un, il est préalablement nécessaire de connaître son adresse!

En dehors des tablettes de Mari, il existe par ailleurs un document qui intéresse de très près notre propos et apporte une éclairage particulier sur les conditions mêmes de la vie des facteurs. Il s'agit d'une lettre retrouvée à Tell Harmal (l'ancienne Šaduppum) et envoyée par le roi d'Ešnunna Ibâl-pî-El à l'un de ses fonctionnaires en poste à Šaduppum[27]:

> Dis à Tutub-mâgir: ainsi parle ton Seigneur.
>
> Parmi les courriers-*rakbû*, il y a de plus en plus de fuyards[28]. J'ai donc délibéré de la sorte: "Puisqu'il est vrai que les fuyards sont nombreux,

---

25 Voir F. Joannès (1984), et (1985).

26 *Cf.* B. Lafont (1987) 115.

27 A. Goetze (1958) 21-22, texte n⁰ 5 (IM 51251).

28 En suivant *CAD* M/1 24, sous *mâdum*, contra l'*editio princeps*.

désormais un courrier-*rakbum* qui voudra aller à son village ne devra pas partir sans être porteur d'un (sauf-conduit) à mon sceau." C'est ce que j'ai décidé et je t'ai écrit en conséquence.

À partir de maintenant, (seul) un courrier-*rakbum* qui pourra te produire un document à mon sceau pourra rester dans son village et profiter de sa maison et de son champ. Tant qu'il résidera là, un domaine (lui) sera dévolu. (Par ailleurs), avant qu'il ne revienne, NP devra le conduire au palais où il devra (r)apporter le document scellé à mon sceau pour son identification. En revanche, celui qui viendra à toi sans être porteur d'un document à mon sceau, celui-là tu ne devras pas l'autoriser à rester: tu devras l'envoyer (directement) chez moi.

Cette lettre possède une enveloppe qui porte le sceau d'Ibâl-pî-El, roi d'Ešnunna. Elle montre donc que ce souverain, inquiet de voir croître le nombre des déserteurs parmi ses propres services de messagers-*rakbû*, impose à chacun d'entre eux l'obligation d'obtenir un sauf-conduit avant qu'il puisse éventuellement être autorisé à quitter le service et à retourner dans son village. On voit par ailleurs que sont attribués à ces messagers dûment identifiés, un champ alimentaire et une maison. Il s'agit là d'un document tout à fait explicite, qui complète admirablement notre information sur la façon dont étaient organisés les services de messagers royaux à l'époque paléo-babylonienne, sur leur mode de rémunération et sur l'espoir que caressaient sans doute beaucoup d'entre eux de pouvoir échapper à leurs obligations pour retourner chez eux et travailler leur terre.

En ce qui concerne le courrier et les objets mêmes qui sont transportés, quand il s'agit d'une lettre qui doit parvenir à son destinataire, on rappellera simplement qu'elle est mise sous enveloppe scellée (*ARM* XXVI/2 490 et A.427+[29], avec l'emploi du verbe *ḫarâmum*), même si fort peu de ces missives ont été retrouvées avec leur enveloppe (voir cependant *ARM* XXVII 140 qui porte encore, adhérant à la tablette, un petit fragment de son enveloppe sur lequel on peut du reste lire une partie du sceau de son expédi-

---

29 Pour ce texte, *cf.* D. Charpin (1985).

teur; voir également la lettre de Tell Harmal ci-dessus)[30]. On remarquera que c'est d'ailleurs le sceau qui permet d'authentifier le document, notamment quand l'identité du facteur est incertaine ou inhabituelle (*ARM* XIII 144, XXVI/1 29). Un autre indice que l'on a de l'existence de ces enveloppes est que, pour pouvoir prendre connaissance de la tablette, il faut commencer par "l'ouvrir" (*petûm*, par exemple en *ARM* II 121, V 64, XXVI/2 315, A.2701[31], *etc.*). Préalablement à la mise sous enveloppe, la tablette que venait d'écrire le scribe était relue à son auteur. C'est ce que nous apprend la lettre A.427+ (*cf.* ci-dessus note 15) où une erreur dans le contenu du message est attribuée au fait que "le scribe a mis la tablette sous enveloppe sans la faire entendre", donc sans la relire à celui qui l'avait dictée.

Un autre point mérite d'être mentionné qui touche à l'existence de toute une série de documents "annexes" qui peuvent circuler avec le courrier principal. On possède ainsi de nombreuses tablettes (*ARM* III 68 et IV 80 ci-dessus, ou XXVI/2 315, *etc.*), qui ne furent rédigées que pour accompagner une missive importante et préciser les conditions dans lesquelles celle-ci devait circuler, être délivrée ou être entendue. Certaines affaires ne nous sont d'ailleurs connues, de façon détournée, que par ces annexes.

On a vu que le danger est toujours présent de voir toutes ces lettres être interceptées (*ARM* II 121, *etc.*)[32], volées, ou égarées: il est dans ce cas nécessaire d'en refaire un "double" (*ARM* X 166 et 167). Une autre occasion de faire un "double" (*meḫrum*) existe quand on veut transmettre à un tiers, "pour information", copie de l'original d'un courrier que l'on a expédié (*ARM* XXVI/1 25).

À l'administration centrale, il y a une personne tout spécialement chargée de prendre en charge et d'ouvrir le courrier reçu, ce qui permet de faire le tri, de préparer et de classer le courrier destiné à être lu en priorité au roi. Au palais de Mari, au temps de Zimri-Lim, c'est Šunuhra-halû qui s'acquitte de cette tâche[33] (voir notamment le très explicite *ARM* XXVI/2

---

30 Sur cette question en général, voir F. R. Kraus (1985).

31 Ce texte a été publié dans Charpin (1995).

32 Voir aussi Lafont (1992) 172.

33 Voir Sasson (1988) 329-35. Voir également les remarques de M. Birot (1993) 17.

396). Il semble que, auprès de Samsî-Addu, un dénommé Hulâlum ait assumé, au moins pour un temps, cette responsabilité, comme nous l'apprend un document où l'on voit cet individu se charger de réexpédier à Mari une lettre provenant de Qaṭnâ, adressée à Yasmah-Addu, mais arrivée par erreur chez Samsî-Addu (A.2701)[34]. Et auprès de ce même Yasmah-Addu, roi de Mari, trois fonctionnaires sont connus pour avoir successivement accompli ce travail de "secrétariat": Šamaš-tillassu, Ikûn-pî-Sîn et Sîn-muballiṭ[35]. Par ailleurs, en cas d'absence du fonctionnaire destinataire d'une lettre, on voit qu'un collègue peut agir "par procuration" en ouvrant le courrier et en traitant l'affaire à sa place (*ARM* V 64).

Quand se succèdent sur un rythme très rapide les informations et les contre-informations, les ordres et les contre-ordres envoyés par courrier (voir par exemple *ARM* IV 35), il est compréhensible que soit donnée par l'expéditeur l'indication de la date et de l'heure auxquelles il fait partir son message. Plusieurs suscriptions de lettres ont ainsi gardé la trace de ces détails importants indiquant le moment précis du départ du courrier. Ces mentions apposées sur les missives jouent, *mutatis mutandis*, le même rôle que nos actuels "cachets de la poste faisant foi", et informent le destinataire, qui ne reçoit souvent le message que plusieurs jours après, de la date exacte de la rédaction de la tablette. Ainsi peut-on relever sous le calame des expéditeurs de lettres les expressions suivantes: "J'ai envoyé ma présente tablette

- le *n* courant" (u_4 *n*-kam ba-zal-*ma*, ou u_4 *n*-kam *issuḫ-ma*): *ARM* I 8, 53, 60, 65, X 142, *etc.*; c'est l'expression la plus fréquente, mais plusieurs indices montrent l'impossibilité de la traduire par "au soir" comme on le fait habituellement.
- dans la matinée" (*ina muštêrtim*, ou *muštêrtam*): *ARM* VI 33, XIV 28 et 119.
- au milieu de la journée" (*ûmum mâšil*): *ARM* IV 76.

---

34 *Cf.* D. Charpin (1995).

35 Voir la contribution de P. Villard à paraître dans les Actes du Colloque tenu à Paris en 1993, "Mari, Ebla et les Hourrites: dix ans de travaux," *Amurru* 2.

- ❍ au moment chaud de la journée" (*ûmum šâḫun*)[36]: *ARM* IV 35.
- ❍ en soirée" (*ina kinsikim*): *ARM* I 67.
- ❍ au coucher du soleil" (^{d}*Šamaš erbet*): *ARM* I 10, IV 45, XXVI/2 397.
- ❍ à l'heure du repas" (*ina simân naptanim*; il s'agit sans doute du repas du soir): *ARM* XXVII 2, 14, 16 et M.8887 ci-dessous. *Cf.* aussi l'adverbe *naptanam* pour lequel voir *ARM* XXVII, p. 44 en haut.

La journée est ainsi découpée en quatre ou cinq tranches correspondant à des moments de départ du courrier. Et parallèlement, plusieurs auteurs de lettres, répondant à une missive qu'ils ont reçue, précisent à leur correspondant la date et l'heure auxquelles est arrivé le facteur. Ils utilisent pour cela les mêmes expressions et soulignent ainsi par exemple: "J'ai reçu cette tablette de toi (ou la tablette de mon Seigneur):

- ❍ le *n* à l'heure de la sieste" (*muṣlalam*): *ARM* XIV 37.
- ❍ le *n* à la nuit tombante" (*ina pân mûšim*): *ARM* XIV 70.
- ❍ le *n* au coucher du soleil" (^{d}*Šamaš erbet*): *ARM* XIV 9.
- ❍ le *n* à l'heure du repas (du soir)" (*ina siṃân naptanim*): *ARM* XIV 16.

Tout cela peut être mis en parallèle avec cette observation d'un fonctionnaire désolé d'avoir trop tardé pour accomplir les instructions du roi et qui se justifie de la sorte (*ARM* XIII 9): "Lorsque la tablette de mon seigneur est arrivée, c'était la nuit; les verrous du palais étaient mis". On voit donc que le courrier pouvait parfois passer fort tard.

Dès lors, on ne s'étonnera pas de trouver parmi les textes inédits de Mari un autre petit *memorandum* qui, tout comme A.3889 publié ci-dessus, a dû être rédigé par les services de la poste de la chancellerie mariote et qui est ainsi libellé (M.8887):

	iti *li-li-ia-tim*	Au mois de *lîliyâtum* (= IX),
2	u_4 12-kam	le 12,
	i-na sí-ma-an nì-gub	à l'heure du repas,
4	^{I}*Ib-ba-*^{d}IM	Ibba-Addu
	[*ṭup*]*-pa-am*	a fait porter
6	[*a-na ṣ*]*e-er*	une tablette

36 Selon une proposition de restitution du texte dans J.-R. Kupper (1996) 80.

R.	[*ì*]-*lí-še-me*	à destination de
8	*ú-ša-bi-lam*	Ilî-šemê

Ce qui fait pourtant la particularité de ce petit *memorandum*, c'est qu'il s'agit d'un *unicum*. Il est rare, en outre, de trouver un texte de Mari commençant par la date, mais en l'espèce, c'est précisément pour enregistrer celle-ci que la tablette a été rédigée. On peut cependant se poser la question de savoir ce qui a nécessité la rédaction de ce document inhabituel. Celui-ci a sans doute joué le rôle "d'accusé de réception" pour certifier et authentifier le départ du courrier en une occasion spécifique. Malheureusement, Ibba-Addu et Ilî-šemê sont par ailleurs parfaitement inconnus à Mari, ce qui n'aide pas à saisir le contexte de ce petit document à l'écriture peu soignée mais au contenu étonnant.

Ainsi, derrière toutes ces archives épistolaires que nous a livrées le palais de Mari, il est possible de retrouver bien des détails sur l'activité inlassable de ceux dont on ne parle presque jamais dans ces lettres mais dont le rôle fut essentiel pour qu'elles puissent exister: non seulement les scribes qui les écrivirent et qui les lurent mais aussi les messagers qui les portèrent. Précisons simplement pour finir que la rédaction de la présente contribution a été achevée en ce mois de juin 1996, u_4 27-kam ^{d}*Šamaš erbet.*

Bibliographie

Bardet, G., *et al.* (1984) *Archives administratives de Mari* 1. Archives royales de Mari 23. Paris. **Birot, M.** (1973) Nouvelles découvertes épigraphiques au palais de Mari (Salle 115). *Syria* 50: 1-12. (1974) *Lettres de Yaqqim-Addu gouverneur de Sagarâtum.* Archives royales de Mari 14. Paris. (1993) *Correspondance des gouverneurs de Qattunan.* Archives royales de Mari 27. Paris. **Bottéro, J.** (1956) *Textes administratifs de la salle 110.* Archives royales de Mari 7. Paris. **Charpin, D.** (1993) Un souverain éphémère en Idamaraṣ: Išme-Addu d'Ašnakkum. *Mari, Annales de Recherches Interdisciplinaires* 7: 165-91. (1994) kallâm "rapidement". *Nouvelles Assyriologiques Brèves et Utilitaires* 1994/62. (1995) 'Lies natürlich . . . : ' à propos des erreurs de scribes dans les lettres de Mari. Pp. 43-56 dans Dietrich et Loretz 1995. **Charpin, D. et Joannès, F.** (1991) Eds. *Marchands, Diplomates et Empereurs : études sur la civilisation mésopotamienne offertes à Paul Garelli.* Paris. (1992) Eds. *La circulation des biens, des personnes et des idées dans le Proche-Orient ancien.* Actes de la XXXVIIIe Rencontre Assyriologique Internationale, Paris, 8-10 juillet 1991. Paris. **Dietrich, M. et Loretz, O.** (1995) Eds. *Vom alten Orient zum alten Testament : Festschrift für Wolfram*

Freiherrn von Soden zum 85. geburtstag am 19. Juni 1993. Alter Orient und altes Testament 240. Neukirchen-Vluyn. **Dossin, G.** (1946) *Lettres.* Archives royales de Mari 1. Paris. (1951a) *Lettres.* Archives royales de Mari 4. Paris. (1951b) *Lettres.* Archives royales de Mari 5. Paris. (1967) *La correspondance féminine.* Archives royales de Mari 10. Paris. **Dossin, G., et al.** (1964) *Textes divers.* Archives royales de Mari 13. Paris. **Durand, J.-M.** (1987a) Ed. *La femme dans le Proche-Orient antique. Compte rendu de la 33e Rencontre Assyriologique Internationale (Paris, 7-10 Juillet 1980).* Rencontre Assyriologique Internationale 33. Paris. (1987b) Villes fantômes de Syrie et autres lieux. *Mari, Annales de Recherches Interdisciplinaires* 5: 199-234. (1988) *Archives épistolaires de Mari* I. Archives royales de Mari 26. Paris. (1990) La Cité-État d'Imâr à l'époque des rois de Mari. *Mari, Annales de Recherches Interdisciplinaires* 6: 39-92. (1991) Précurseurs syriens aux protocoles néo-assyriens. Considérations sur la vie politique aux Bords-de-l'Euphrate. Pp. 13-72 dans Charpin et Joannès 1991. (1994) L'empereur d'Elam et ses vassaux. Pp. 15-22 dans Gasche, Tanret, Janssen and Degraeve 1994. (1997) Documents épistolaires du palais de Mari, tome 1. *Littératures anciennes du Proche-Orient,* volume 16. **Durand, J.-M. et Charpin, D.** (1994) Eds. *Florilegium marianum II: recueil d'études à la mémoire de Maurice Birot.* Mémoires de Nouvelles Assyriologiques Brèves et Utilitaires 3. Paris. (1997) Aššur avant l'Assyrie. *Mari, Annales de Recherches Interdisciplinaires* 8: 367-391. **Durand, J.-M. et Kupper, J.-R.** (1985) Eds. *Miscellanea Babylonica: Mélanges offerts à Maurice Birot.* Paris. **Finet, A.** (1988) à propos d'ARM I, 93. *Nouvelles Assyriologiques Brèves et Utilitaires* 1988/18. **Gasche, H., et al.** (1994) Eds. *Cinquante-deux réflexions sur le Proche-Orient ancien: offertes en hommage à Léon De Meyer.* Mesopotamian History and Environment Occasional Publications 2. Leuven. **Goetze, A.** (1958) Fifty Old Babylonian Tablets from Harmal. *Sumer* 14: 3-78. **Guichard, M.** (1994) Au pays de la Dame de Nagar. Pp. 235-75 dans Durand et Charpin 1994. **Jean, C. F.** (1941) *Lettres.* Archives royales de Mari 2. Paris. **Joannès, F.** (1984) Textes no. 91 à 245. Pp. 87-226 dans Bardet, *et al.* 1984. (1985) Nouveaux mémorandums. Pp. 97-113 dans Durand et Kupper 1985. (1988) La ville de Hab(b)anum. *Nouvelles Assyriologiques Brèves et Utilitaires* 1988/19. (1992) Une mission secrète à Ešnunna. Pp. 185-93 dans Charpin et Joannès 1992. **Kraus, F. R.** (1985) Altbabylonische Briefe mit Siegelabrollungen. Pp. 137-47 dans Durand et Kupper 1985. **Kupper, J.-R.** (1948) *Lettres.* Archives royales de Mari 3. Paris. (1953) *Lettres.* Archives royales de Mari 6. Paris. (1990) Une lettre du général Yassi-Dagan. *Mari, Annales de Recherches Interdisciplinaires* 6: 337-47. (1996) Les différents moments de la journé d'après les textes de Mari. Pp. 79-85 dans Tunca, Ö. et D. Deheselle 1996. **Lafont, B.** (1987) Les filles du roi de Mari. Pp. 113-21 dans Durand 1987a. (1992) Messagers et ambassadeurs dans les archives de Mari. Pp. 167-83 dans Charpin et Joannès 1992. **Leichty, E., Ellis M. deJ., et Girardi, P.** (1988) Eds. *A Scientific Humanist. Studies in Memory of Abraham Sachs.* Philadelphia. **Rouault, O.** (1976) *Mukannišum: lettres et documents administratifs.* Archives royales de Mari 18. Paris. **Sasson, J. M.** (1988) Shunukhra-Khalu. Pp. 329-51 dans Leichty, Ellis et Girardi 1988. **Tunca, Ö. et D. Deheselle,** eds. (1996) *Tablettes et images aux pays de Sumer et d'Akkad, Mélanges offerts au Professeur H. Limet.* Liège.

A New Teḫip-tilla Text Fragment*

M. P. Maidman
York University

The text fragment published here comes from a private collection. It measures 21 mm in height, 59.5 mm in width (probably about 70 mm before it was damaged), and 28.5 mm in thickness. It is light brown and appears to have been baked in antiquity.

The text contains the beginning of the obverse, the end of the reverse, and the upper edge of a tablet. Internal evidence—the text genre, onomasticon, one of the seal impressions—demonstrates that this piece is most likely a Teḫip-tilla text from Nuzi.

TRANSLITERATION

Obv.

1. [*ṭup*] -*pí ma-ru-ti ša*
2. [ᵐ*x-n*] *a*? -*a-a* DUMU *Šu-ur*-ᵈ⌜IM⌝
3. [ᵐ*Te-ḫi*] -⌜*ip*⌝ -*til-la* DUMU *Pu-ḫ*[*i-še-en-ni*]

.
.
.

---

* It is a pleasure to dedicate this article to Michael Astour. Both through his publications relating to the region of Nuzi (see, *e.g.*, Astour [1968]) and our many conversations, he has stimulated my own research as well as my appreciation of the geopolitics of ancient Western Asia.

Obv.

1
2
3

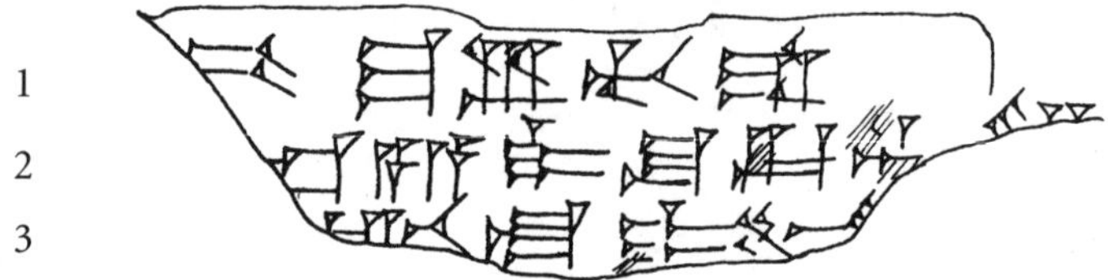

Rev.

4′

U.E.

5′

Rev.

.
.
.

(*seal impression*)

4′. [^{NA4} KIŠ]IB $^{⸢m⸣}$*Še-eš-⸢te?-pí?-a⸣?-šu*

U.e.

(*seal impression*)

5′. [^{NA4} KIŠI]B ^{m}*⸢A⸣?-[ ]-⸢a⸣-na-at-t*[*i*]?

Translation

(1-3) Tablet of adoption of X-n?aya son of Šûr-adad. [He adopted] Teḫip-tilla son of Puḫi-šenni.
(4′-5′) (*seal impression*) Seal impression of Šeštepi-ašu; (*seal impression*) seal impression of X.

Comments to the Text

The fragment contains the start and end of a tablet of real estate adoption (*i.e.*, *ṭuppi mārūti*). In all likelihood, the vendor of the unnamed real estate was x-n?aya son of Šûr-adad and the purchaser, Teḫip-tilla son of Puḫi-šenni; it therefore appears likely that it was once part of the Teḫip-tilla Family archive of rooms 15 and 16 (less likely, 13). Efforts to join this piece to any of the texts and fragments housed in the Oriental Institute of the University of Chicago have proved fruitless.[1]

---

1 This piece does *not* join JENu 22a, a real estate adoption tablet, probably of Teḫip-tilla, which lacks the start of the obverse, the end of the reverse, and the upper edge; where the vendor is one Ḫanaya (ll. 4, 5; *cf.* below, note to line 2); and where one Šeštepi-ašu is a witness (l. 21; *cf.*, in the present text, l. 4′).

It is possible, though unlikely, that the present fragment is not from a Teḫip-tilla text at all. The name of the presumed vendor/adopter seems nowhere else attested among the Chicago and Harvard Nuzi texts; neither seal impression appears in the Chicago corpus as published by Porada (1947); and Teḫip-tilla's name and patronymic, although plausibly reconstructed in line 3, is not certain (the signs might represent, for example, *"Ḫašip-tilla son of Puḫiya").

Thus the failure to find a join to this fragment in the Chicago collection (the repository of most of the Teḫip-tilla Family texts) may not be accidental.

The following is to be noted regarding the seal impressions.[2] Only the first impression is at all well preserved. It seems not to be represented in Porada (1947). However, the impression is not atypical of designs found among the Chicago texts, resembling, in different ways, Porada nos. 545, 604, 626, 627, 628, and 686. It is especially close—in fact almost identical—to no. 629.[3]

The second impression is barely preserved at all.

NOTES TO THE LINES

Line 2. If the first sign fragment is interpreted correctly, the initial PN might be Ennaya, Ḫanaya, Šennaya, or Unaya. As mentioned (n. 1), this individual is, to my knowledge, otherwise unattested in the Nuzi texts.

Line 3. This restoration of the line is most plausible, but, as already indicated (n. 1) not absolutely certain.

Line 4′. The identity of the sealer of a text of this type is usually qualified by a patronymic, indicator of profession, or the like. No such qualifier appears here or, apparently, in the next line.

Line 5′. See note to line 4.

Bibliography

Astour, M.C. (1968) Mesopotamian and Transtigridian Place Names in the Medinet Habu Lists of Ramses III. *Journal of the American Oriental Society* 88: 733-52. **Porada, E.** (1947) *Seal Impressions of Nuzi.* The Annual of the American Schools of Oriental Research 24. New Haven, Conn.

[2] The drawings of the seal impressions were made by Ellen Maidman. I wish to thank her for the drawings and for discussing with me the composition of these impressions.

[3] Note that, in no. 629, the seal is impressed so that the seal inscription appears to the left of the three figures. In the present instance, very faint traces of an inscription of at least two lines are to be seen on the far right.

Amnon and Tamar: A Matter of Honor (2 Samuel 13:1-38)

Victor H. Matthews
Southwest Missouri State University

Don C. Benjamin
Rice University

A social scientific reading of the stories of Amnon and Tamar in the books of Samuel-Kings (2 Sam 13:1-22) involves honor, virginity, and rape. Each is a technical term for a specific social institution characteristic of eastern Mediterranean cultures such as that of ancient Israel. Honor is the political power or social status of a household in a village. Virginity is the economic power of a household to provide for and to protect its own land and children, and to assist other households in its village in providing for and protecting their land and children. Rape is not only an act of violence of a man against a woman, but also is a social institution used by one household to test the honor of another. Against this background, the stories of Amnon and Tamar do not tell of unrequited love, but of a struggle for power between the households of Absalom and Amnon for the right to succeed David as monarch in Israel. The issue is more politics and economics than sex.

Honor

Honor in eastern Mediterranean cultures is distinct from honor in western European cultures in at least four ways. First, in western European cultures, the connotations of honor are personal. In these cultures, moral virtue or reputation has little to do with political power and social status. Widows, clergy, and teachers are generally regarded as honorable people in western European cultures, yet they have only modest political power and social status. Politicians and attorneys are often not regarded as honorable people, yet they have considerable political power and social status. In the village cultures of the Mediterranean the connotations of honor are political power or social status.[1]

> There are three main forms of stratification...in the Mediterranean: bureaucracy, class and honour. Each...is related to the distribution of wealth.... Of the three ways in which material differences are socially construed the first and most important is honour.[2]

Unfortunately, the definitions of honor as moral virtue or reputation and as political power or social status continue to be confused in social scientific literature today.[3] Boissevain, for example, argues that discriminating between honor as virtue and honor as status is a popular weapon among rivals in Mediterranean cultures.[4] Campbell wants to distinguish the material wealth of a household or its "prestige" from the integrity or nobility of spirit of a household, which he calls its "honor."[5] Likewise, Davis distinguishes the honor or wealth allocated to a household for its performance of explicitly sexual roles from the prestige or respect allocated to a household for its performance of asexual roles. He then argues that while prestige is characteristic of all cultures, honor is specific to Mediterranean cultures.[6]

Second, honor in Mediterranean cultures is a characteristic of villages or households, and not just of individuals. In the world of the Bible, the individual was more conscious of being one of the group than is the individual in western European cultures today.[7] The villages or households of

---

1 Cutileiro (1971); Davis (1977) 89-101; Bourdieu (1965) 228; *pace* Campbell (1964) 306.

2 Davis (1977) 76, 89.

3 Pitt-Rivers (1966) 21-77.

4 Boissevain (1965) 50.

5 Campbell (1964) 268-74.

6 Davis (1977) 89-90.

7 Robinson (1971) 45-47.

Amnon and Absalom were incorporated into individuals like Amnon and Tamar, and these individuals thought of themselves as authorized to speak in the name of the households or villages which they represented.

Third, the economies of these villages where honor plays an important social and economic role are subsistent and decentralized, rather than being based on centralized and surplus economies, as in western European cultures.[8]

Fourth, honor in western European cultures refers to a variety of moral virtues. In Mediterranean cultures honor deals primarily with the fertility of women and the fertility of the land. This focus of honor on fertility or female sexuality is reflected in the codes of honor which govern the use of political power and social status by households.[9] Even though codes vary from culture to culture, the goal of every code of honor is to maintain a household's ability to bear children and bring in a harvest. "Honor" is the preferred technical label in the social sciences for this fundamental strategy for distributing land and children which appears throughout the world of the Mediterranean and in the world of the Bible.[10]

Codes of honor govern political power both by restricting and by promoting competition between the households for land and children. Codes of honor restrict competition among men in the same household,[11] forging bonds among them so they can defend the household's land and children against attacks by men of other households.[12] Otherwise, these same men would compete with one another to seize the land and children

---

[8] For Davis (1977) 101, "...honour is not, was not, a specialty of shepherds nor of farmers with bilateral inheritance.... [Nevertheless,] ...[t]he kinds of society in which honour stratification is important seem to share the characteristic of having relatively undiversified economies: it is difficult to speak, with the sort of conviction a sociologist of England or Germany has, of occupational hierarchies when describing Vila Velha or Pisticci or the Sarakatsani: there are too many people left undifferentiated."

[9] Pitt-Rivers (1977) 1-17.

[10] Davis (1977) 98.

[11] Schneider (1971) 1-24; Davis (1977) 100.

[12] Stirling (1965) 230-33.

of their household for themselves. Codes of honor promote competition between households in the same village. Each household tries to create a unique position for itself by challenging the way other households fulfill their responsibilities. Households struggle for honor because they can, when successful, improve their access to the resources of the village. Disputes about honor occur most often where access to land and children is crucial, because either these resources are few or standards of living are changing. This kind of competition prevents the creation of a permanent hierarchy by denying any one household unchallenged dominance.[13]

Virginity

Honor is not gender specific, but more than any other members of a household, women are the living symbols of its honor. They are the incarnation of the status of their households.[14] These women are not things or possessions. They are a human portfolio, and mothers and virgins are the most significant women in the portfolio.[15]

In western European cultures today the connotations of virginity are primarily physical, whereas in the world of the Bible the connotations of virginity are primarily economic. Although honor in Mediterranean cultures expects men and women to perform or to abstain from sexual actions, the connotations of abstinence, like virginity, include much more than sexual behavior.[16]

---

13 Davis (1977) 99.

14 Zeid (1966) 247; Schlegel (1991) 727.

15 Schneider (1971) 2.

16 Peristiany (1966) 9; Gilmore (1987) 3-4; Delaney (1987) 40. For Davis (1977) 2, "...honour is not primarily a matter of sexual behaviour. True, honour can be lost more easily through sexual failings than by any other means; but more women lose honour than fornicate, and the subtle discrimination between families requires more diacritics than copulation alone can provide. Most people discriminate between men by their performance of everyday roles as strugglers to survive, between women by their performance of their roles as makers of the best of a bad job...."

Mediterranean cultures use the term "virgin" with economic connotations. A virgin is a marriageable woman.[17] She holds a label of honor and serves as a measure of the economic integrity of her household. In Mediterranean cultures, legal eligibility of men for marriage is determined by criteria other than the legal eligibility of women. Virginity is the legal guarantee of land and children.[18] It is not just a woman's physical condition, but her economic power. "Virginity (Arabic: *ird*)" is the technical term for the legal eligibility of a woman to enter a marriage, and "chastity" is the technical term for the legal compliance of a woman with the terms of her marriage covenant.[19] Chastity describes a woman's ability to bear children to her husband and contribute to the work of her household.[20]

Twelve times in the Bible female virgin or young woman (Hebrew: *bĕtûlâ*) is parallel with male virgin or young man (Hebrew: *bāḥûr*). Only when the word "virgin" is modified by the phrase "who has never known a man" is the Bible talking primarily about a woman who has never had sexual intercourse.[21] In the stories of Ba'al Peor in the book of Numbers, for example, Moses rules that the "...young girls who have not known a man by sleeping with him" (Num 31:18) have not violated Israel's covenant with Yahweh by serving Ba'al Peor. Likewise, the stories of Isaac and Rebekah in the book of Genesis use this idiom to introduce her to Abraham's slave (Gen 24:15-16).

Virgins who were marriageable represented the potential of a household for growth. The virginity of a bride was indicative that the household of her father was stable, so that the covenant between her household and the household of her husband would be productive. Her fertility represented the fertility of their covenant. It was a marriage which would produce land and children for both households.

---

17 Schmitt (1992) 853.

18 Giovannini (1987).

19 Zeid (1965) 247; Schneider (1971) 20-21.

20 Gilmore (1987) 4.

21 Gordon (1964) 378.

A teaching on a breach of covenant in the book of Deuteronomy (Deut 22:13-21) outlines a protocol for virgins in ordinary households. The teaching directs that if one household falsifies its standing when it negotiates a covenant with another by presenting the bride as a virgin when she is not, then the woman whose marriage ratified the covenant is to be executed. If a household brings ungrounded charges of fraud against another, then the husband whose marriage ratifies the covenant is to be flogged.

The Book of Job refers to a virgin of a divine household. When Job testifies: "I have made a covenant with my eyes; how then could I look upon a virgin?" (Job 31:1), he is referring not just to lust or voyeurism, but to a desire to worship Anat, the virgin of Ugarit, rather than Yahweh, the divine patron of Israel.[22] As the stories of Ba'al and Anat make clear, Anat's title does not certify that she has never had sexual intercourse, but that she is the most powerful woman in the divine assembly of Ugarit.[23]

Promiscuity threatens the economic status of a household.[24] It is not simply sexual indiscretion, but an economic crisis which puts the land and children of a household at risk. Households guard their women to keep their own economic status intact.[25] Protecting its women is a matter of honor for each household.[26] The father was responsible for the virginity or legal eligibility of the women in his household for marriage, and for the chastity or

---

22 Pope (1965) 229.

23 "Anat's body trembled with gladness, her heart filled with joy, her soul gloated with triumph, as ...she waded knee deep in warriors' blood, up to her thighs in their guts. Until, finally, these deadly games were enough for her, with the slaughter in her arena, she was content. The warriors' blood was washed from her house. The oil of peace was poured from a bowl. *The Virgin Anat* washed her hands, *Anat, Queen of All Nations,* cleaned her nails. She washed the warriors' blood from her hands, ...their guts from her nails.... She washed herself with dew from the sky, she anointed herself with oil from the earth, she bathed with rain from the Cloud Rider, with dew from the sky, with moisture from the stars" (Matthews and Benjamin [1991a] 159, *emphasis added*).

24 Schlegel (1991) 724.

25 Goody (1976) 14.

26 Baab (1962) 788; Tapper (1981) 391; Bird (1989) 77.

legal compliance of the women with the terms of their marriage covenants.[27] Few responsibilities of a household were more important.[28]

One measure of a household's honor is the evidence of virginity on the part of the bride at the time when the marriage is consummated.[29] Villages rate a father's fulfillment of his responsibility to feed and protect his household on the basis of how well he cares for and protects its virgins. Fathers of households are honorable when they are untainted by successful attacks on their women.[30]

If fathers protect the women of their household, then they are protecting its land as well. In Vila Velhans, Portugal, honor required that a man should provide for his household. Failure in one sphere leads to suspicion of failure in another.[31] Similarly, in Pisticci, if a man did not provide for his household, it was assumed that his wife was having intercourse with other men in order to support her husband's household.[32] The Mediterranean world assumes that honor and shame are transmitted physically from parents to children during conception. Sexual misconduct in women therefore jeopardizes the honor accumulated by their own household from its ancestors, whereas sexual misconduct in men destroys the honor accumulated by the household of another.[33]

Fathers enclosed their women like human fields with a variety of fences.[34] These fences restricted the activities and movement of women into the wild, natural space outside the household where fathers could not adequately control their powers of reproduction.[35] When Dinah leaves the

---

27 Pitt-Rivers (1977) 78; Davis (1973) 160; Gilmore (1987) 8.

28 Pitt-Rivers (1977) 165; Giovannini (1987) 69.

29 Delaney (1987) 41-42.

30 Pitt-Rivers (1966) 77.

31 Cutileiro (1971).

32 Davis (1977) 93.

33 Pitt-Rivers (1966) 77.

34 Delaney (1987) 40; (1991) 39.

35 Ardener (1972) 143-44.

protection of the encampment of Jacob, there is no hint that she, as a woman, fears the world outside, but her action is interpreted by Shechem, as a man, as his opportunity to rape her.[36]

Rape

The Mediterranean world assumes that women who are promiscuous have husbands who are impotent.[37] If the father of a household cannot prevent its women from having intercourse with others, then it confirms the charge that he is impotent.[38] Households use rape to challenge each other and to determine who should control the land and children of the village.[39] Like war, rape is a violent social process for redistributing the limited goods which a village or state possessed, so that it cannot be destroyed by the weakness of a single household. Disputes about honor occur when one household claims more honor than it had before, and a duel results.[40] Rape declares a household to be insolvent or shamed, and, therefore, unable to fulfill its responsibilities to the village. It confirms that the father of a household has left its mothers and virgins in harm's way, and, therefore, must be impeached.

There is a protocol for rape as an economic challenge.[41] Of course, not every wanton act of sexual violence by any man against any woman in ancient Israel qualified as a challenge to the honor of a household.[42] For the protocol of rape to be set in motion, the woman must be an official representative of the household targeted for takeover. She must either be married and a mother in the household like Rizpah (2 Sam 3:6-11), Michal (2 Sam

---

36 Delaney (1987) 41; Douglass (1984) 248.

37 Filipovic (1958) 156-67.

38 Giovannini (1987) 68.

39 Barth (1961) 34, 39.

40 Pitt-Rivers (1966) 29-31, 58.

41 Bourdieu (1979) 106; Abu-Lughod (1986) 90.

42 Zeid (1966) 246.

3:12-16), Bathsheba (2 Sam 11:3), and David's concubines (2 Sam 16:21-22), or marriageable and a virgin in the household like Dinah and Tamar. The woman could not, for example, be a widow or a child. The man must also be a representative of the household. The action could not be taken by just any male. He must be a son or prince, a man who would be capable of leadership. When rape met these qualifications it was not only an act of sexual violence, but also a hostile takeover bid. The assailant asserted the right of his household to the resources of another.

The rape must take place in the context of some activity connected with fertility such as harvesting (Gen 34:1-2; Judg 21:17-23), sheep shearing (2 Sam 13:23-28), eating (2 Sam 13:5-6), or menstruating (2 Sam 11:4). Otherwise, it was treated like any other crime (Deut 22:23-27). The basis for this criterion was the concern over a household's ability to supply food and children to its members. Tying the aggressive act to an event associated with fertility clearly identified the intention of the aggressor.

The steps which a shamed household followed to reestablish its honor were parallel to the protocol followed to challenge it. A prince or son of the shamed household assassinated a prince or son of the household which had shamed his household. The son must carry out the assassination while the prince who attacked his household is exercising the power which he seized.[43] In this way justice and the restoration of honor were matched with attention to place and the symbols of authority.

An example of this protocol is found in the story of how Levi and Simeon deliver Jacob from Shechem. By raping Dinah, the household of Hamor lays claim to her inheritance in the household of Jacob.[44] Shechem is not just infatuated with Dinah when he says: "...whatever you say of me I will give" (Gen 34:12). His household wants to take over the household of Jacob outright.[45] But the household of Jacob counters Shechem with a strategy of its own.[46] Jacob's sons, Levi and Simeon, begin negotiations with

---

43 Hoftijzer (1970) 58-60.

44 Schlegel (1991) 724.

45 Caspi (1985) 35; Wyatt (1990) 437-38.

46 Caspi (1985) 31-32; Wyatt (1990) 433.

Shechem, and then assassinate the warriors of Shechem before they recover from circumcision. Both the rape and the reprisal take place during celebrations of fertility.

Although the Bible itself says only that Dinah goes into the field with other women, the occasion is no doubt a celebration of fertility. Similar celebrations occur in the books of Joshua-Judges. In the story of Benjamin's obtaining brides from Shiloh (Judg 21:15-25), the women of Shiloh dance in their vineyards. In the story of Jephthah's deliverance of Israel from the Ammonites (Judg 11:1-40), the daughter of Jephthah and her companions "...bewail her virginity on the mountains with other women into the hills" (Judg 11:38).

The monarchs of Israel and Judah played little direct role in the competition among their sons.[47] Several reasons have been proposed for their lack of involvement. First, the father is not simply weak.[48] His inaction may be a strategy for retaining his position and increasing his own power. As part of this strategy of dissociating himself from kin allegiance and thereby present a model of national leadership, the father had to remain neutral in power struggles.[49] Second, removing the father from active participation in political challenges among the sons also guaranteed that a strong heir would emerge (even if that proved to be a danger later to the king or chief). Third, honor and shame promote competition between households in the same class, but not between one class and the other. Sons compete with one another, but not with their father, at least not until they are prepared to claim the throne outright for themselves.

The honor of households at the top and bottom of the hierarchy is more stable than the honor of households in the middle, where rivalry is greatest, and where households conspire to prevent one another from moving upward.[50] In the middle range, wealth and the ability to flout rules which

---

47 Van Seters (1987) 122.

48 Ridout (1974) 77; Flanagan (1988) 261-72.

49 Frick (1985) 79-80.

50 Schneider (1971) 9-11.

others must observe go together.[51] Challenges of honor occur chiefly in the indeterminate middle section of communities, where rank is not certain or more fluid.[52] Nonetheless, the monarch David, who is at the top of the social scale, does challenge Uriah by raping Bathsheba, just as those who would be king, such as Amnon, Absalom, and Adonijah, struggle for an edge against one another.

Stories of Amnon and Tamar (2 Sam 13:1 – 14:33)

The stories of David's successor in the books of Samuel-Kings (2 Sam 9:1 – 20:26; 1 Kgs 1:1 – 11:43) are developed by the household of Solomon to authorize its right to rule Israel. The stories begin with a trial of David (2 Sam 9:1 – 12:31) which indicts David for failing to protect and provide for the land of Israel and for its people. The stories of Meriba'al indict David for his abuse of power in taking over the land which belonged to the household of Saul. The stories of Bathsheba indict David for his abuse of power in taking over the children which belonged to the household of Uriah. In both cases, David failed to negotiate an effective covenant for his succession, and had to use force to implement his claim. He was no longer a chief who ruled Israel with the consent of its elders. He was now a monarch who wielded the absolute power of a pharaoh. He had lost the approval of Yahweh in much the same way as had Saul.

Crisis (2 Sam 13:1-14)

The stories of David's successor continue with traditions describing the unsuccessful campaigns of Amnon, Absalom, and Adonijah to succeed David.[53] The first episode (2 Sam 13:1-2) in the crisis (2 Sam 13:1-14) of the stories of Amnon and Tamar (2 Sam 13:1-22) portrays Tamar as beautiful or fertile. There were certainly sexual relationships in the world of the Bible which reflected the deep personal and emotional love of one person

---

51 Giovannini (1987) 65.

52 Davis (1977) 95-96, 99.

53 Conroy (1978); Fokkelman (1981).

for another. There was romance (Cant 8:1-4; Gen 24:67; Exod 21:7-11). But in the world of the Bible, sexual relationships were more than romance, they were politics and economics as well. Therefore, the Hebrew word describing Tamar (*yāpâ*) does not refer simply to a pleasing physical appearance.[54] In Song of Songs, *yāpâ* describes lips which can stimulate every taste of one's lover (Cant 4:10) and the graceful feet of the dancer (Cant 7:1[2]). It also expresses the maturing of Israel in the parable of Yahweh as a good parent (Ezek 16:13-14).

This label thus describes Tamar as a woman coming of age, fully capable of fulfilling her role as mother of a household. She is physically capable of sexual intercourse and the conception of a child. She has learned well from the mother of her own household the skills which she will need to manage a household of her own. She is wise, and she will demonstrate in the following episodes of the story just how wise a mother she will be.[55]

The text says that Amnon loves Tamar (2 Sam 13:1). However, he loves her as David loved Michal, the daughter of Saul, and Bathsheba the wife of Uriah. Their actions are not simply reflections of personal passion or pain, but, rather, distinct strategies in a political campaign. Tamar, a virgin and sister of Absalom, is beautiful—thus an enticement for conquest and ultimate destruction.[56]

The basic assumption of this strategy is that marriage with Tamar could endow her husband with a proportion of the resources of the household of Absalom, and could virtually guarantee him the throne of David. Thus Tamar not only arouses the passions of Amnon, but his ambition. His actions are political, not simply personal or moral. When he falls in love with Tamar, and is so tormented by her that he makes himself ill, Amnon

---

54 English translations obscure the social scientific connotations of many words referring to women. See Matthews and Benjamin (1993) 177-78: "Virgin." For Flanagan (1990) 157, translations are "...laced with sexual inferences and feeling for the castaway Tamar, which obscure the larger issues of social norms and rules addressed by the story."

55 Matthews and Benjamin (1993) 22-36.

56 Keefe (1993) 87.

is dealing not just with unrequited love, but with political ambition. He is a man who would be a monarch in Israel.[57]

Similarly, the titles by which Amnon, David, Tamar, and Absalom address each other reflect more than kinship.[58] In modern English legal usage, "brother" and "sister" refer to kinship relationships, although they do appear as membership titles and terms of affection in some communities of faith. In the world of the Bible, they identify people related by covenant, who call each other "father," "son," or "brother." Thus the issue in the story of Amnon and Tamar is power, not incest.[59] Endogamous marriages between households were common.[60] The marriage of Abraham and Sarah is endogamous (Gen 20:12). This endogamous pattern was also mandated in the post-exilic administrations of Nehemiah (Neh 13:23-27) and Ezra (Ezra 10:2-5). In contrast, Leviticus and Deuteronomy explicitly forbid endogamous marriages (Lev 18:9, 11; Deut 27:9, 22). It is still not clear when exogamous marriages replaced endogamous marriages in ancient Israel. Therefore, the laws in Leviticus and Deuteronomy may not have been in effect when the stories of Amnon and Tamar became popular.[61] But even if endogamous marriages were prohibited in general, state marriages were often exempt from such statutes.[62]

In contrast to Tamar who is beautiful, Amnon is tormented and impotent. He finds Tamar marvelous to admire, but difficult to possess. Amnon is portrayed like the pharaoh satirized in a story of Abraham and Sarah (Gen

---

57 Pitt-Rivers (1977) 78; Davis (1973) 160; Gilmore (1987) 8.

58 For Gunn (1988) 296: "…from the beginning the familial relationships are sharply focused by constant definition and redefinition of characters (as the point of view changes) in terms of 'son', 'sister', 'brother', and 'father'. This is a story of sickness within a family, where the very ties that betoken solidarity and protection are perverted into the means to commit crime."

51 *Pace* Smith (1990) 24-25, 35.

60 Murphy and Kasdan (1968) 186; Musil (1928) 137-40; Cohen (1965) 71-75, 121; Daube (1947) 77-79; de Vaux (1961) 19-20.

61 McCarter (1984) 323.

62 Flanagan (1990) 157; Hackett (1992) 94.

12:9 – 13:1), and the ruler of Gerar in a story of Isaac and Rebekah (Gen 26:6-11). He is stimulated by looking at Tamar, but he is physically unable to have intercourse with her. He burns with passion, and yet is unable to act. Tamar reduces Amnon to a voyeur. Later the storytellers say much the same of David, who burns with anger, but is unable to act (2 Sam 13:21).

The second episode (2 Sam 13:3-9a) in the crisis portrays Amnon as a fool who chooses a fool for a friend and follows the fool's advice. Jonadab is introduced as a wise man (Hebrew: *ḥākām*), who becomes a friend of Amnon. "Friend" is the title for a royal advisor (1 Kgs 4:5; Ps 45:14). Here the term "wise" is used satirically.[63] Jonadab is anything but wise. His advice destroys the household of Amnon. [64] The appointment reveals that Amnon cannot tell wisdom from foolishness.

Jonadab is also not a trickster. Tricksters first appear in stories as outcasts without land and children. But in the course of the story, they manipulate the powerful into changing their status and endowing them with land and children.[65] When Abraham and Sarah negotiate with pharaoh, they are tricksters. At the beginning of the story they are powerless.[66] By the end of the story, Abraham has used crafty negotiating skills, and Sarah has used her good looks to trick the pharaoh into giving them land and children. Jonadab is not an outcast, but a member of the royal court. His actions in

---

63 Gunn (1988) 296.

64 Amen-em-ope, who taught in Egypt between 1200–1000 BCE, considered the choice of friends to be a defining test for the wise. In his teachings, he cautioned against just the kind of flawed judgment which Amnon demonstrates in choosing Jonadab to be his friend. Campbell and Flanagan (1990) 157; *pace* McCarter (1984) 321; Smith (1990) 28. Amen-em-ope's advice is: "Do not take counsel with fools, nor seek their advice. Do not speak back to superiors, nor insult them. Do not let superiors discuss their troubles with you, nor give them free advice. Seek advice from your peers, do not ignore your equals. More dangerous are the words of fools, than storm winds on open waters.... Do not rush to embrace fools, lest their advice drown you like a storm" (Matthews and Benjamin [1991a] 194).

65 Niditch (1987) 44-50.

66 For Wilson (1951) 257, Abraham and Sarah follow a pattern of temporary employment recounted several times in Egyptian tradition.

the story are not shrewd, they are incompetent. He acquires nothing by the end of the story which he did not possess at the beginning of the story.

Absalom may have even dispatched Jonadab to the household of Amnon to seed it with bad advice. Later, David will use this strategy against Absalom and force him to chose between a friend who is wise and a friend who is a fool, in order to demonstrate that he is incompetent to rule Israel (2 Sam 15:32-37). In his bid to succeed David, Absalom carefully builds a constituency within the household of David to support his candidacy. Among Absalom's supporters is Ahithophel, an advisor of David (2 Sam 15:17; 16:23; 1 Chr 27:33-34). When David becomes aware of Ahitophel's desertion, he dispatches another advisor, Hushai the Archite, to Absalom to test his wisdom. Just as Amnon before him, Absalom fails this defining test of a ruler to choose wise friends. He takes the advice of Hushai and ignores the advice of Ahitophel, who then commits suicide.

Jonadab advises Amnon to launch his campaign to succeed David by asking him to assign Tamar to feed him. In doing this, Amnon is not simply asking for some tender loving care while he is not feeling well. His request implies that he is fearful of being slowly poisoned, and needs Tamar to supervise his kitchen to prevent it from happening again.[67]

Food plays a significant role in the stories of Amnon and Tamar. The story begins when Amnon asks for food, and ends when he is murdered eating at the table of Absalom (2 Sam 13:23-29). Storytellers want their audiences to understand that Amnon, who could neither feed nor protect himself, should not become a monarch who is responsible for feeding and protecting Israel. The bread (Hebrew: *lĕbibâ* 13: 6, 8, 10) which Tamar prepares says more about the relationship between those who eat it than about its nutritional or medicinal value. The language is both sexual and political.[68] The name "Tamar" means "date palm," a tree associated with both fertility and covenant making.[69]

---

67 Ford (1985) 381-83; Heaps (1969) 17; Gilmore (1987) 3; Gunn (1978) 98-100.

68 Hackett (1992) 93.

69 Eilberg-Schwartz (1990) 157.

Semitic vocabulary for having sexual intercourse, learning, eating, farming, fighting, and sacrificing overlap. In the stories of Adam and Eve, when the serpent asks the woman: "Did Yahweh say, 'You shall not eat from any tree in the garden?'" it means: "Are you fertile?" When it says: "When you eat of it your eyes will be opened, knowing good and evil," it means: "You will become fertile."[70] Tamar and the bread she bakes are symbols of the children and the land which the household of Absalom provides in Israel.[71]

In this episode, David is not simply a concerned parent coming to the bedside of a sick child. He is a royal magistrate hearing Amnon's petition in a court of law.[72] Unlike elders in a village assembly who listened to many witnesses and discussed a case until they reached a consensus, royal magistrates simply heard a plaintiff, and then rendered a decision. Tamar belongs to the household of Absalom, which may have made this attempt on Amnon's life, so Amnon asks David to make it directly responsible for his safety. Tamar serves the probation on which David places the household of Absalom.

When David sends her to Amnon, her safety is totally dependent on Amnon. Amnon exploits Tamar's vulnerability by telling her to bake bread for him in his presence and to have sexual intercourse with him. The request

---

70 Benjamin (1997). See also the "civilizing" of Enkidu in the Gilgamesh Epic I.iv: 1-20 (Pritchard [1969] 75).

71 In the Hittite ritual against impotence (KUB, vii, 5; KUB, vii, 8; KUB ix, 27), an *arzawa* woman takes her impotent client into the temple of Uliliyassis. There she prepares one day's rations, enriched with "...three sweet sacrificial loaves of flour, water weighing one *tarnas*, figs, grapes, ...a little of everything; the fleece of an unblemished sheep, a pitcher of wine...." (Pritchard [1969] 349). They remain in the temple for three days. Three times a day she prepares an exquisite meal for Uliliyassis, her divine patron, and for her impotent client and then has intercourse with him.

72 For Matthews and Benjamin (1993) 227-36, there was more than one judicial system in Israel as a state. There was the divine assembly over which Yahweh presided, there were assemblies in the villages and cities over which the elders presided, and there were state courts over which magistrates appointed by the monarch presided. They functioned contemporaneously, one did not review or appeal to the other (*pace* Kohler [1957] 139-40).

invites Tamar to commit Absalom's resources to Amnon's campaign to become monarch in David's place.[73] Bread is the harvest of Absalom's land, and Tamar is the child of Absalom's household.

The third episode in the crisis portrays Amnon as a fool who cannot negotiate a covenant for land and children. Amnon tries to impose a covenant on the household of Absalom by ordering Tamar to have intercourse with him and thereby ratify a covenant between their households.[74] She tells Amnon that if he wants a covenant between his household and the household of Absalom, he needs to negotiate for it.[75] Tamar's response demonstrates that she is wise,[76] while Amnon acts on impulse.

In the final episode of the crisis, Tamar, as the representative of Absalom's household, shames Amnon as being a fool for allowing his emotions to dictate his actions, and for being unable to protect a virgin in his household. Three times Tamar appeals to Amnon, assuring him that if he can be patient and negotiate with David, their marriage could ratify a covenant between the households of Amnon and Absalom.[77]

TAMAR'S USE OF "SHAMING SPEECH" (2 Sam 13:12-13, 16)

The biblical narrative is a product of a "tradition-oriented" society, which places a great deal of value on honorable behavior. Codes of correct behavior are the measure of honor or dishonor. Thus shame, guilt and embarrassment, which are the personal reflections of improper behavior, are

---

73 Johnson and Earle (1987) 208-9; *pace* Eilberg-Schwartz (1990) 161.

74 To lay claim to the throne they desire to usurp, Abner asks for Rizpah and Adonijah asks for Abishag. Although neither man consummates his sexual advance, simply asking is equivalent to the act (1 Kgs 2: 22). For Gunn (1978) 99, there is no mention of a marriage contract having been negotiated. For Phillips (1975) 241, by forcing her to have sexual relations with him, Amnon breaches a fundamental canon on which ancient Near Eastern cultures operate. For McCarter (1984) 322, Amnon acts contrary to the manners and customs by which his people are identified (Gen 20: 9; 29: 26).

75 Pitt-Rivers (1977) 165.

76 Hagan (1979) 310; Abu-Lughod (1990) 45.

77 Frymer-Kensky (1992) 135.

based on social experience, are reinforced by rituals and shared attitudes, and are a product of group processes endowed with the power of coercion.[78] Shame and shaming are less likely to be concealed in traditional societies than in modern ones.[79]

This is particularly true of a household, the primary social unit in ancient Israelite society. Each member of a household has an obligatory social role of upholding the honor of the household through speech and action. If a member of the household has performed or is about to perform some action that would reflect badly on the household, it is the responsibility of every other member to attempt to prevent a repetition of the dishonorable action or to convince deviants to reconsider their action(s) and come back into compliance with honorable behavior. In addition, each member must also protect the household's honor against insults by outsiders—both physical and verbal.

Aside from physical retorts in defense of the household, the principal method used is "shaming speech." Unlike insults and taunts, which are components of aggressive behavior and may or may not be rationally based,[80] shaming speech is a social control mechanism designed through reasoning or the "vocabulary of embarrassment"[81] to make the prodigal or the enemy rethink his plans. It calls on him to behave honorably, with prudent actions, not in the manner of a fool who acts in the height of passion, without considering the consequences of his act . Generally, shaming speech will take the form of a wisdom argument, calling on traditional practice, social codes, and covenantal allegiance.

Embarrassment or shaming can thus be conceived as a positive process, designed to maintain social order and personal civility.[82] It can elicit a

---

78 Cahill (1992) 3-5; Goffman (1971).

79 Scheff and Retzinger (1991).

80 Felson (1993) 307.

81 Goffman (1972) 98.

82 Cahill (1992) 1.

reevaluation of actions, feelings, or behavior, and a self-acknowledgment of having done wrong.[83]

At times it is necessary to embarrass a person using shaming speech publicly, in order to draw upon the energies and backing of a desired audience.[84] The aim is the same as in the private setting, to sustain public order, and may be employed by either male or female characters. It should be noted that embarrassment, guilt, and shame all elicit similar behavior reactions and thus will not be greatly distinguished here.[85] Shame can elicit the strongest reactions and is based on the most serious charges, but it, like the others, is intended as a form of behavior modification.

In the "wisdom contest" between Amnon and Tamar, Amnon demonstrates his foolishness because he is impatient to consummate his control over Tamar and become the uncontested heir to the throne of David. Amnon directly orders Tamar to have intercourse with him. He is proposing to seed a female field which is not his, taking possession of this resource just as he has taken a portion of the produce of Absalom's actual fields. Normally, by having intercourse together, Amnon and Tamar would ratify a marriage covenant between their households and strengthen Amnon's claim to the throne of David. However, forced intercourse has only one value—it weakens Absalom's household.

Tamar's response to Amnon's ultimatum is quite proper and demonstrates that she is the wise one in this narrative.[86] Tamar does not reject their union, only their union without proper arrangements.[87] Amnon is proposing an action which is contrary to the manners and customs by which his people are identified.[88] Consequently, Tamar accuses him of acting like the

---

83 Sharkey (1992). Of course, shaming speech can be used to harass and dominate someone, but in such cases the intent is not to uphold honorable behavior, and is better termed malicious speech.

84 Kuzmics (1991) 3.

85 Bedford (1986) 21.

86 Hagan (1979) 310.

87 Pitt-Rivers (1977) 165.

88 McCarter (1984) 322; Gen 20: 9; 29: 26.

fool, a person who knowingly violates the law (Deut 21:18-21).[89] What distinguishes Tamar and Absalom from Amnon is their patience.[90] Tamar urges Amnon to be patient and to negotiate a covenant with her father for their marriage, rather than to act impulsively and rape her. Absalom advises Tamar to wait patiently for the occasion to restore the honor of their household, rather than impulsively seek revenge.

The long dialogue between Tamar and Amnon highlights Tamar as a wise woman. Resistance to and denunciation of Amnon's dishonorable proposal portray her as politically astute.[91] Like the wise woman in the Book of Proverbs (Prov 3:13-18), Tamar is capable of providing riches, long life, peace, and happiness. Like the wise woman of Abel (2 Sam 20:16-22), Tamar offers a fair settlement to a dispute between brothers.[92] Tamar's speech is by no means unique for women in the Bible. Eve's dialogue with the serpent (Gen 3:1-6), Rebekah's coaching of Jacob on deceiving Isaac (Gen 27:5-17), Rahab's statement of acquiescence to Joshua's spies (Josh 2:8-14), and the mother of Samson reporting to her husband, Manoah, on the angel's prediction that they would have a son (Judg 13:3-23) all portray women speaking with authority. However, there is a difference between these speeches which examine a question or make plans for future action and the speech of Tamar.

Tamar's speech is designed to shame a male, who is culturally-defined as the more powerful of the two. In the same way, the woman from Shunam shames Elisha (2 Kgs 4:8-37), Michal shames David (2 Sam 6:20-23), and Jezebel shames Jehu (2 Kgs 9:30-37) in the books of Samuel-Kings.[93] Tamar

---

89 Matthews and Benjamin (1991b) 222-24.

90 In both the teachings of Amen-em-ope and the Book of Proverbs, the wise act with deliberation. Fools, on the other hand, are impulsive. "A fool despises a parent's instruction, but the one who heeds admonition is prudent" (Prov 15: 5). The wise know when to talk and when to listen (Arabic: *'agl*). Fools are hot-tempered because they let passion run or ruin their lives (Matthews and Benjamin [1991a] 194; Abu-Lughod [1986] 90).

91 Abu-Lughod (1990) 45.

92 Frymer-Kensky (1992) 135.

93 Matthews (1994) 12-13.

refers to Amnon as "my brother" to remind him that they are social equals and that he owes her the proper conduct due her rank. She pleads with him not to "force" her because it is not the custom in Israel.

Obviously, taking brides by force is not unknown, but apparently it was considered a non-Israelite custom by the time of the monarchy.[94] Her description of rape as shameful tells Amnon that he will be counted among the fools (Hebrew: *nĕbālîm*, a term employed in the story of Abigail and Nabal [1 Sam 25:2-22] which applies to men without honor).[95] Three times Tamar appeals to Amnon, assuring him that by following the proper protocol and maintaining social customs David would sanction the marriage.

Although Tamar is technically a member of Absalom's household and represents his honor, David, her father and king, will determine her actual political placement through marriage. Marriage was a delicately negotiated covenant, sealing a significant political or economic contract.[96] It was designed to bring together two households willing to exchange substantial goods and services with each other over a significant period of time. The father of the household was responsible for safeguarding the status of the men and women in his household, and decided which were eligible to marry one another.[97] David's choice of Tamar's husband would thus be a significant political decision.

CLIMAX (2 Sam 13:14-19)

The climax to the story is reached when Amnon ignores Tamar's refusal and rapes her (2 Sam 13:14-19).[98] By this act of sexual violence, Amnon lays claim to the power, wealth, goods, and service which she represents, and issues a political challenge to Absalom.[99]

---

94 Kressel (1992) 35.

95 Levenson (1978) 14.

96 Pitt-Rivers (1977) 160; Levenson and Halpern (1980) 508.

97 Peristiany (1966) 9; Gilmore (1987) 3-4; Giovannini (1987) 67.

98 Ridout (1974) 80-84; Fokkelmann (1981) 99-114.

99 McCarter (1984) 324; Smith (1990) 37.

Having shamed Tamar, Amnon dismisses her, using the legal term for divorce (Hebrew: *šlḥ*). Tamar is sent back to her household in shame to demonstrate that it no longer possesses status equal to the household of Amnon.[100] In so doing, she becomes the process server of this new political situation.

Amnon's shift from want to hate is dramatic and predictable. Just as the aggression of the rape evidences his foolish nature, so too the embarrassment of Tamar's shaming speech simply adds to his determination to take what he wants and then discard the woman as no longer of any consequence.[101] Still Tamar must voice a final protest. Once a household is challenged, it is entitled to redeem its honor. Tamar demands this right. She has been shamed, but her household should not be politically destroyed.[102]

Amnon is unrelenting and Tamar, in her frustration and shame, tears her clothes to mourn the lost honor of Absalom's household (2 Sam 13:19). This young woman, who had been a symbol of the fertility and honor of the household, now has become a symbol of its impotence and shame (Gen 37:29-35; 39:11-15).

David's rights to control her marriage covenant have also been circumvented, but there is no proof of rape since there are no witnesses. The law

---

100 McCarter (1984) 324; Smith (1990) 37.

101 Tangney (1992).

102 Tiglath-Pileser I (1115–1077 BCE) promulgated the Middle Assyrian Law Code which outlines the same due process for which Tamar appeals. Article 55, authors' translation:

> If a virgin, who is the daughter of a citizen, who is living in her father's house, who is not engaged to be married, and who is not collateral for any of her father's debts, is kidnapped and raped by another citizen, either in the city, in the country, in the street at night, in a granary or at a city festival, then her father must kidnap and rape the wife of her assailant.
>
> If the assailant has no wife, then the father may give his daughter to her assailant in marriage, and the assailant must pay the bride price and marry her without the opportunity for divorce.
>
> If the father does not wish to marry his daughter to her assailant, then he can keep the bride price and marry his daughter to whomever he wishes.

See also Driver and Miles (1935).

which requires that the rapist marry his unbetrothed victim (Deut 22:28-29) can thus not be enforced.

Denouement (2 Sam 13:20-22)

In the denouement of the stories of Amnon and Tamar (2 Sam 13:20-38), Tamar cries out, and Absalom hears her cry.[103] He silences her only for the time being. He is not refusing to answer Amnon's challenge, only refusing to answer it in a rage or without deliberation. While Absalom waits, Tamar and his household remain shamed in Israel.[104]

Only after two years is Absalom ready to restore the honor of his household by challenging Amnon to a duel at the sheepshearing.[105] David delays sending Amnon to the sheepshearing, hoping to avoid admitting that Absalom has challenged the honor of Amnon by inviting him.[106] Eventually Absalom convinces David to offer Amnon a chance to defend his honor.[107]

---

103 Absalom is not refusing to answer Amnon's challenge, only refusing to answer it in a rage or without deliberation (*pace* Hackett [1992] 94).

104 For Van Seters (1987) 53 and Trible (1984) 422, David also hears Tamar's cry, but does nothing. Some ancient versions add "...but he did nothing to vex his son Amnon because he loved him, for he was his firstborn," (McCarter [1984] 319) which assumes that David had already designated Amnon as his heir, and so simply confirms or loves Amnon as his heir or firstborn after his assault on the household of Absalom.

105 Abu-Lughod (1986) 65-66.

106 For Pitt-Rivers (1966) 57, "In all situations of challenge a man's honour is what obliges him to respond by resenting the affront, yet a challenge is something which can only be given by a conceptual equal...."

107 For Gunn (1988) 297, "....[d]id he really suspect nothing, as Absalom pressed him to let Amnon go to the sheepshearing (13: 24-27, especially v. 26)...?" David's "... attitude toward both Amnon and Absalom may thus be complex. A hidden factor becomes evident only when we remember the larger setting of the story. David's hands are tied by his own evil (chap. 11), for the sons have merely mimicked the king, their father. To function as judge [and sentence Amnon to death for raping Tamar, or Absalom for killing Amnon] would thus be to expose himself fatally to a charge of hypocrisy. He would then be like his ancestor Judah, condemning the other Tamar to death (Genesis 38) [for a crime which he himself committed]."

Absalom assassinates Amnon at Ba'al Hazor, which is six miles northeast of Bethel.[108] David's other sons flee back to Jerusalem, along the road from the twin villages of upper Beth-Horon and lower Beth-Horon, which are northwest of Gibeon. By assassinating Amnon, Absalom makes his own bid to be David's heir and invites David's other sons to endorse him. However, not one of the sons of David stands by either Amnon or Absalom. Each mounts a royal ass to return to Jerusalem.

For many, Tamar remains shamed. They see her silenced by Absalom. Without witnesses to her assault and without the opportunity to indict Amnon publicly for failing to protect her, they consider her abused by David who sends her, Amnon who rapes her, and Absalom who ignores her. They understand Tamar like Michal, who upholds the honor of Saul's household (2 Sam 6:20-23), but forfeits her own. For them, Tamar never regains her status as a virgin, never becomes the mother of a household.[109] Instead, she spends her days in domestic captivity, a pawn and a victim of a much larger political game.[110]

The stories of Amnon and Tamar say nothing of Tamar after the assassination of Amnon. Ancient, as well as modern, interpreters have pondered her fate. A genealogy of Absalom lists one daughter: "...there were born to Absalom three sons, and one daughter whose name was Tamar; she was a beautiful women (2 Sam 14:27)." The sister of Absalom may have been the

---

108 The final episode of the denouement (2 Sam 13: 34-38) is poorly preserved (Wevers [1971] 176). The clause "Absalom departed" is repeated three times (2 Sam 13: 34, 37, 38), and 2 Sam 13: 37-38 are repetitious and do not fit with 2 Sam 13: 39, which belongs with the next story.

109 For Bird (1989) 77; Gottlieb (1989) 63; Keefe (1993) 91-92. For Gunn (1988) 296, "...Shechem, who raped Dinah, ...ends by loving her, ...(Gen 34: 1-4). But ...her brothers will not consider a marriage, since her honor (by which they really mean their own) has been slighted. Shechem is slaughtered and Dinah disappears from view, locked up in perpetual dependency upon her do-nothing father and dominating brothers. A similar fate awaits the now unmarriageable Tamar, shut up, desolate, in the house of her brother Absalom (2 Sam 13: 20) while her angry father, like Jacob (Gen 34: 30-31), does nothing."

110 Matthews (1994) 14.

birth mother of this woman, or simply her ancestor. By naming his daughter, Tamar, Absalom may have celebrated the restoration of his sister's honor in the household. A genealogy of Abijam identifies his mother and father as Rehoboam and Maacah, "...the daughter of Abishalom," or Absalom (1 Kgs 15:2; 2 Chr 11:20-22). Consequently, some Septuagint Greek and Old Latin manuscripts read "Maacah" instead of "Tamar" in the genealogy of Absalom (2 Sam 14:27).[111] Abishalom is probably not Absalom, and therefore, Maacah is not Tamar. Nonetheless, the identification of the two women and their fathers reflects an ancient conviction that eventually the daughter or the namesake of Tamar, the sister of Absalom, became the mother of a household, thus fully restoring the honor of her ancestor and the honor of the household of Absalom in Israel.

Bibliography

Abu-Lughod, L. (1986) *Veiled Sentiments: Honor and Poetry in a Bedouin Society.* Berkeley. (1990) The Romance of Resistance: Tracing Transformations of Power through Bedouin Women. *American Ethnologist* 17: 41-55. **Achtemeier, P.**, ed. (1988) *The Harper's Bible Commentary.* San Francisco. **Ardener, E.** (1972) Belief and the Problem of Women. In J. LaFontaine 1972: 135-54. **Attema, D.**, ed. (1970) *Schrift en Uitleg.* Kampen. **Baab, O. J.** (1962) Virgin. In G. A. Buttrick, ed., *The Interpreter's Dictionary of the Bible* 4. Nashville. **Baines, J., and J. Malek.** (1980) *Atlas of Ancient Egypt.* New York. **Barth, F.** (1961) *Nomads of South Persia. The Basseri Tribe of the Khamseh Confederacy.* Oslo and Boston. **Bedford, E.** (1986) Emotions and Statements about Them. In Harre 1986: 15-31. **Benjamin, D. C.** (1983) *Deuteronomy and City Life.* Lanham, Md. (1997) The Stories of Adam and Eve (Gen 2: 4b-4: 2). In H. T. C. Sun and K. L. Eades 1997: 38-58. **Bird, P.** (1989) "To Play the Harlot": An Inquiry into an Old Testament Metaphor. In Day 1989: 75-94. Philadelphia. **Bohanan, P., and J. Middleton**, eds. (1968) *Marriage, Family and Residence.* Garden City, N.Y. **Boissevain, J.** (1965) *Saints and Fireworks. Religion and Politics in Rural Malta.* London. **Bourdieu, P.** (1966) The Sentiment of Honour in Kabylie Society. In Peristiany 1966: 191-242. (1979) The Sense of Honour. In *Algeria 1960*, 95-132. Cambridge. **Braudel, F.** (1949) *La Mediterranee et le Monde Mediterraneen a l'epoque de Philippe II.* Paris. **Brown,**

[111] McCarter (1984) 342

R. E., *et al.*, eds. (1990) *New Jerome Biblical Commentary.* Englewood Cliffs, N.J. **Cahill, S. E.** (1992) Embarrasability and Public Civility: Another View of a Much Maligned Emotion. Unpublished paper presented to the 1992 Annual Meeting of the Midwest Sociological Society. **Campbell, A. F., and J. W. Flanagan.** (1990) 1-2 Samuel. In Brown 1990: 145-59. **Campbell, J. K.** (1964) *Honour, Family and Patronage. A Study of Institutions and Moral Values in a Greek Mountain Community.* Oxford. **Caspi, M. M.** (1985) The Story of the Rape of Dinah: the Narrator and the Reader. *Hebrew Studies* 26: 25-45. **Cohen, A.** (1965) *Arab Border-Villages in Israel: a Study of Continuity and Change in Social Organization.* Manchester. **Conroy, C.** (1978) *Absalom, Absalom*! Analecta Biblica 81. Rome. **Cutileiro, J.** (1971) *A Portuguese Rural Society.* Oxford. **Daube, D.** (1947) *Studies in Biblical Law.* Cambridge. **Davis, J.** (1973) *Land and Family in Pisticci.* London. (1977) *People of the Mediterranean: an Essay in Comparative Social Anthropology.* Boston. **Day, P.**, ed. (1996) *Gender and Difference in Ancient Israel.* Philadelphia. **Delaney, C.** (1987) Seeds of Honor, Fields of Shame. In Gilmore 1987: 35-48. (1991) *Seed and the Soil: Gender and Cosmology in Turkish Village Society.* Berkeley. **Douglass, C. B.** (1984) Toro Muerto, Vaca Es: An Interpretation of the Spanish Bullfight. *American Ethnologist* 11: 242-58. **Driver, G. R., and J.C. Miles** (1935) *The Assyrian Laws, Edited with Translation and Commentary.* Oxford. **Eades, K.**, ed. (1996) *Problems of Old Testament Theology: A Festschrift for Rolf P. Knierim on His 65th Birthday.* Grand Rapids, Mich. **Eilberg-Schwartz, H.** (1990) *The Savage in Judaism: an Anthropology of Israelite Religion and Ancient Judaism.* Bloomington, Ind. **Felson, R. J.** (1993) Shame, Anger, and Aggression. *Social Psychology Quarterly* 56: 305-9. **Filipovic, M. S.** (1958) Vicarious paternity among Serbs and Croats. *Southwest Journal of Anthropology* 14: 156-67. **Flanagan, J. W.** (1988) *David's Social Drama.* The Social World of Biblical Antiquity Series, 7. Sheffield. (1990) 2 Samuel. In Brown 1990: 154-59. **Fokkelmann, J. P.** (1981) *King David (II Sam 9-20 & I Kings 1-2).* Vol. 1 of J. P. Fokkelmann, *Narrative Art and Poetry in the Books of Samuel.* Netherlands. **Ford, F. L.** (1985) *Political Murder: From Tyrannicide to Terrorism.* Cambridge, Mass. **Freedman, D. N.**, ed. (1992) *Anchor Bible Dictionary* 6. New York. **Frick, F. S.** (1985) *The Formation of the State in Ancient Israel.* The Social World of Biblical Antiquity Series 4. Sheffield. **Frymer-Kensky, T.** (1989) Law and Philosophy: The Case of Sex in the Bible. *Semeia* 45: 89-102. (1992) *In the Wake of the Goddesses: Women, Culture and the Biblical Transformation of Pagan Myth.* New York. **Gardiner, A.** (1966) *Egypt of the Pharaohs.* New York. **Gilmore, D. D.** (1987) Introduction: The Shame of Dishonor. In Gilmore, D. D., ed., *Honor and Shame and the Unity of the Mediterranean,* 2-21. Washington, D.C. **Giovannini, M. J.** (1987) Female Chastity Codes in the Circum-Mediterranean: Comparative Perspectives. In Gilmore 1987: 61-74. **Goffman, E.** (1971) *Relations in Public.* New York. (1972) Embarrassment and Social Organization. In *Interaction Ritual: Essays in Face to Face Behavior,* 97-112 London. **Goody, J.** (1975) *Character of Kinship.* Cambridge. (1976) *Production and Reproduction.* Cambridge. **Gordon, M. M.** (1964) *Assimilation in American Life: the Role of Race, Religion, and National Origins.* New York. **Gottlieb, C.** (1989) *Varieties of Marriage in the Bible and Their Analogues in the Ancient World.* Ph.D. dissertation, New York University. **Gunn, D. M.** (1978) *The*

Story of King David: Genre and Interpretation. Journal for the Study of the Old Testament Supplement Series 6. Sheffield. (1988) 2 Samuel. In Achtemeier 1988: 287-304. **Hackett, J. A.** (1992) 1 and 2 Samuel. In Newsom and Ringe 1992: 85-95. **Hagan, H.** (1979) Deception as Motif and Theme in 2 Sm 9-20; 1 Kgs 12. *Biblica* 60: 301-26. **Harre, R.**, ed. (1986) *The Social Construction of Emotions.* New York. **Heaps, W. A.** (1969) *Assassination: a Special Kind of Murder.* New York. **Hoftijzer, J.** (1970) Absalom and Tamar: A Case of Fratriarchy? In Attema 1970: 54-61. **Jackson, J., and M. Kessler**, eds. (1974) *Rhetorical Criticism.* Pittsburgh. **Johnson, A., and T. Earle** (1987) *The Evolution of Human Society: From Forager Group to Agrarian State.* Stanford. **Keefe, A. A.** (1993) Rapes of Women/Wars of Men. *Semeia* 61: 79-97. **Kohler, L.H.** (1957) *Hebrew Man.* Nashville. **Kressel, G.** (1992) Shame and Gender. *Anthropological Quarterly* 65: 34-46. **Kuzmics, H.** (1991) Embarrassment and Civilization: On Some Similarities and Differences in the Work of Goffman and Elias. *Theory, Culture and Society* 8: 1-30. **LaFontaine, J.**, ed. (1972) *The Interpretation of Ritual.* London. **Laymon, C. M.**, ed. (1971) *Interpreter's One-Volume Commentary on the Bible.* Nashville, Tenn. **Levenson, J. D.** (1978) I Samuel 25 as Literature and as History. *Catholic Biblical Quarterly* 40: 11-28. **Levenson, J. D. and B. Halpern** (1980) The Political Import of David's Marriages. *Journal of Biblical Literature* 99: 507-18. **Long, B. O.** (1981) Wounded Beginnings: David and Two Sons. In B. O. Long, ed., *Images of Man and God.* Bible and Literature Series 1, 26-34. Sheffield. **McCarter, K.** (1984) *II Samuel.* Anchor Bible 9. New York. **Marks, J. H., and R. M. Good**, eds., (1987) *Love and Death in the Ancient Near East.* Guilford, Conn. **Matthews, V. H.** (1987) Entrance Ways and Threshing Floors: Legally Significant Sites in the Ancient Near East. *Fides et Historia* 19: 25-40. (1994) Female Voices: Upholding the Honor of the Household. *Biblical Theology Bulletin* 24: 8-15. **Matthews, V. H., and D. C. Benjamin** (1991a) *Old Testament Parallels: Laws and Stories from the Ancient Near East.* Mahwah, N.J. (1991b) The Stubborn and the Fool. *The Bible Today* 29.4: 222-26. (1993) *The Social World of Ancient Israel 1250-587 BCE.* Peabody, Mass. **Murphy, R. F., and L. Kasdan** (1968) The Structure of Parallel Cousin Marriage. In Bohanan and Middleton 1968: 185-201. **Musil, A.** (1928) *Manners and Customs of the Rwala Bedouins.* New York. **Newsom, C. A., and S. H. Ringe**, eds. (1992) *The Women's Bible Commentary.* Louisville, Ky. **Niditch, S.** (1987) *Underdogs and Tricksters: a Prelude to Biblical Folklore.* San Francisco. **Oller, G. H.** (1992) Tamar. In Freedman 1992: 315. **Patai, R.** (1959) *Sex and Family in the Bible and the Middle East.* Garden City, N.Y. **Peristiany, J. G.** (1966) Introduction. In J. G. Peristiany, ed., *Honour and Shame: The Values of Mediterranean Society*, 9-18. Chicago. Phillips, A. (1975) NEBALAH—A Term for Serious Disorderly and Unruly Conduct. *Vetus Testamentum* 19: 237-41. **Pitt-Rivers, J.** (1966) Honour and Social Status. In Peristiany 1966: 21-77. (1975) The Kith and the Kin. In Goody 1975: 89-105. (1977) *The Fate of Shechem or The Politics of Sex: Essays in the Anthropology of the Mediterranean.* Cambridge. **Pope, M. H.** (1965) *Job.* Anchor Bible 15. Garden City, N.Y. **Pritchard, J. B.**, ed. (1969) *Ancient Near Eastern Texts Relating to the Old Testament.* Princeton. **Ridout, G.** (1974) Rape of Tamar: A Rhetorical Analysis of 2 Sam 13: 1-22. In Jackson and Kessler 1974: 75-84. **Robinson, H. W.** (1971) *Corporate Personality in Ancient Israel.* Philadelphia. **Scheff, T. J.**,

and S. M. Retzinger (1991) *Emotions and Violence: Shame and Rage in Destructive Conflicts.* Lexington, Mass. **Schlegel, A.** (1991) Status, Property, and the Value of Virginity. *American Ethnologist* 18: 719-34. **Schmitt, J. J.** (1992) Virgin. In Freedman 1992: 853-54. **Schneider, J.** (1971) Of Vigilance and Virgins: Honor, Shame and Access to Resources in Mediterranean Societies. *Ethnology* 10: 1-24. **Sharkey, W. F.** (1992) Use and Responses to Intentional Embarrassment. *Communication Studies* 43: 257-76. **Smith, J.** (1990) The Discourse Structure of the Rape of Tamar (2 Samuel 13: 1-22). *Vox Evangelica* 20: 21-42. **Stirling, A. P.** (1965) *Turkish Village.* London. **Sun, H. T. C. and K. L. Eades**, eds. (1997) *Problems of Old Testament Theology: Essays in Honor of Rolf Knierem.* Grand Rapids, Mich. **Tangney, J. P., *et al.*** *(1992)* Shamed into Anger? The Relation of Shame and Guilt to Anger. *Journal of Personality and Social Psychology* 62: 669-76. **Tapper, N.** (1981) Direct Exchange and Brideprice: Alternative Forms in a Complex Marriage System. *Man* 16: 387-407. **Trible, P.** (1984) *Texts of Terror.* Philadelphia. **Van Seters, J.** (1987) Love and Death in the Court of David. In Marks and Good 1987: 121-24. **de Vaux, R.** (1961) *Ancient Israel.* New York. **Wevers, J. W.** (1971) The Second Book of Samuel. In Laymon 1971: 170-80. **Wikan, U.** (1984) Shame and Honour: a Contestable Pair. *Man* 19: 635-52. **Wilson, J.** (1951) *The Culture of Ancient Egypt.* Chicago. **Wyatt, N.** (1990) Story of Dinah and Shechem. *Ugarit-Forschungen* 22: 433-58. **Zeid, A. M. Abou** (1966) Honour and Shame among the Bedouin of Egypt. In Peristiany 1966: 245-59.

Ur III Geographical and Prosopographical Notes*

David I. Owen
Cornell University

It is difficult to find a subject in which Michael Astour has, at one time or another, not worked. Among those, one area stands out among the many—historical geography—and it is to that subject that I wish to turn and offer these new texts and comments as a small token to my teacher and friend for all I have learned from him and for all the support and encouragement he has provided to me over three decades.

* Abbreviations list: AUCT: Andrews University Cuneiform Texts (1 = Sigrist [1984], 2 = Sigrist[1988a], 3 = AUCT 3); BCT: *Catalogue of Cuneiform Tablets in Birmingham City Museum* (1 = Watson [1986]); BIN: Babylonian Inscriptions in the Collection of James B. Nies (3 = Keiser/Kang [1971]); CT: Cuneiform Texts from Babylonian Tablets in the British Museum (32 = King [1912]); CTMMA: Cuneiform Texts in the Metropolitan Museum of Art (1 = *Tablets, Cones, and Bricks of the Third and Second Millennia*); CTU: Cuneiform Texts from the Ur III Period in the Oriental Institute: (1 = *Drehem Administrative Documents from the Reign of Shulgi*, 2 = *Drehem Administrative Documents from the Reign of Amar-Suena*); DV: *Drevnosti Vostočnyja* (Moscow); MVN: Materiali per il vocabolario neosumerico (1 = Pettinato and Waetzoldt [1974], 3 = Owen [1975], 8 = Calvot and Pettinato [1979], 11 = Owen [1982], 15 = Owen [1991]); NPN: *Nuzi Personal Names.* Oriental Institute Publications 57; NRVN: *Neusumerische Rechts- und Verwaltungsurkunden aus Nippur* 1 (1 = Çığ and Kızılyay [1965]); PDT: *Die Puzriš-Dagan Texte der Istanbuler Archäo-ligischen Museen* (1 = Çığ, Kızılyay, and Salonen [1954], 2 = Yildiz and Gomi [1988]); RGTC: Repertoire géographique de textes cunéiformes (2 = Edzard and Farber [1974]); SACT: *Sumerian and Akkadian Cuneiform Texts in the Collection of the World Heritage Museum of the University of Illinois*; SCCNH: *Studies on the Civilization and Culture of Nuzi and the Hurrians* 1981–; SCT: *Smith College Tablets*, Gordon (1952); SEL: *Studi*

The toponomy of the Ur III empire may be divided into two major areas—the heartland, *i.e.*, Sumer proper, and the periphery, particularly the frontier areas of the north, northeast, and northwest. The tens of thousands of archival texts surviving from this period provide numerous references to toponyms in all these areas.[1] But the Puzriš-Dagan texts in particular provide frequent references to places otherwise poorly known from either contemporary or other sources. Messengers, workers, taxes, and booty from frontier regions and towns are mentioned often with little or no indication of the localization of the individual places from which they came. Thus the discovery of new references to geographical names (GNs), especially when recorded in clusters, offers additional possibilities to establish general or actual locations. Michael Astour has devoted much of his productive career to the identification and elucidation of both obscure and well-known toponyms. He never shirks from this difficult task and brings to bear a lifetime of study of sources from all periods of antiquity. I trust that this modest offering will not only be of interest but will also stand up to his scrutiny.

In 1914, in what was then a pioneering study, William N. Nesbit published his Columbia University dissertation on 30 Ur III tablets of various content.[2] Nesbit did not continue in the field of Assyriology, choosing instead to devote his life to the Methodist ministry.[3] In June 1996, I received a call from Ms. Susan Nelson who informed me that her husband's grandfather was William Nesbit and that the tablets he published and owned had

---

Epigrafici e Linguistici; SET: *Sumerian Economic Texts from the Third Ur Dynasty*, Jones and Snyder (1961); TCL: Textes Cuneiformes. Musée de Louvre–Department des Antiquities Orientales (2 = Genouillac [1911b]); TPTS: *Tablettes du Princeton Theological Seminary Époque d'Ur III*; UET: Ur Excavations, Texts (3 = Legrain [1937/47]).

1 Admirably collected by D. O. Edzard and G. Farber in RGTC 2, with supplements by Owen (1981) 244-69.

2 *Sumerian Records from Drehem*, Columbia University Oriental Series 8 (New York, 1914).

3 For his career, see the introduction to my forthcoming publication of the Nesbit tablets.

been found in a box in his attic. Upon examination of the contents, it was determined that in addition to the 30 published tablets, another group of texts also existed. Thanks to the generosity of the family, the tablets have been turned over to me for publication. This preliminary publication consists of four texts and is a preview of this important group of mostly Puzriš-Dagan and Nippur texts. I am very grateful to Susan Nelson for making these texts available for publication.[4]

Some of the texts from the Nesbit Collection contain a number of rare or unique place and personal names. They continue to add to an ever growing list of toponymic and onomastic sources from the Ur III period.

Nesbit A

Deliveries (mu-DU) of animals, mostly by soldier-workers (érin) from towns in the trans-Tigris area. Archival account from Puzriš-Dagan listing taxes in the form of cattle and sheep. It is dated to Amar-Suen 8/iv/13 and is from the archive of Lugal-amarku.

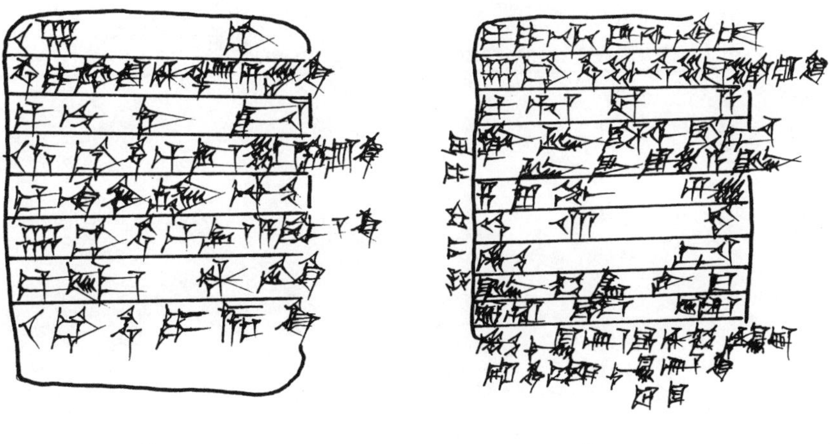

Obverse Reverse

[4] Copies and commentaries to all of the Nesbit tablets will be published in a separate study in the near future.

obv.

1. 17 gu_4
2. érin-i-šim-^{d}šul-gi^{ki}
3. ugula nu-ni-da
4. 10-lá-1 gu_4 érin-maš-kán-šar-ru-um^{ki}
5. ugula na-aḫ-šum-bala
6. 8 gu_4 érin-maš-gán-a-bí^{ki}
7. ugula inim-^{d}nanna
8. 10 gu_4 érin-i-NANGA(LÁL×NIGIN)^{ki}

rev.

9. ugula i-ṭi-ib-ši-na-at
10. 8 gu_4 érin-pu-ut-tu-li-um^{ki}
11. ugula ḫu-pá-a
12. gìri lú-ša-lim gàr-du / lú-kin-gi_4-a-lugal
13. 4 udu bu-zi
14. u_4-13-kam
15. mu-DU
16. lugal-amar-kù ì-dab_5
17. iti u_5-bí-kú
18. mu en-nun-e ^{d}amar-^{d}suen-/ra ki-ág-en-eridu^{ki} / ba-ḫun

side

19. 52 gu_4 4 udu

Nesbit B

Account of a large number of sheep and goats in Tasil and Maškan-Šarrum[5] brought with his brand(?). No date. Presumably from Puzriš-Dagan.

obv.

1. 844 udu-máš-/ḫi-a
2. 31 udu-niga
3. šà tá-si-il/^{ki}

rev.

4. [n má]š-ú
5. 240 udu-niga
6. šà maš-kán-šar-ru-/um^{ki}
7. šu sum-ma / si-im-da-ni

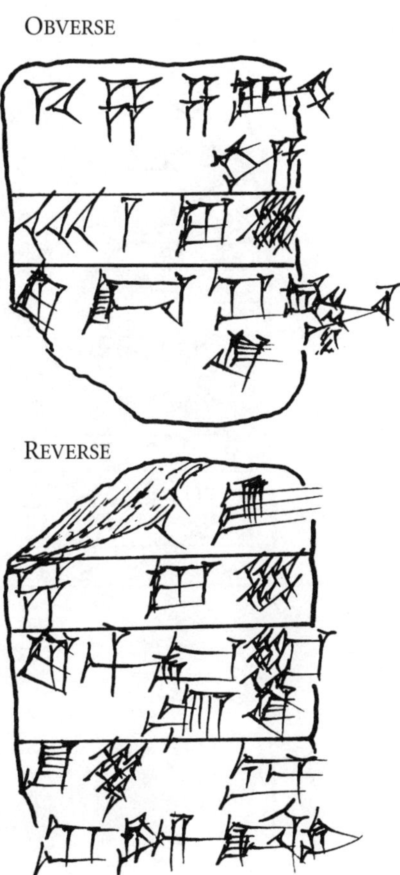

5 This line appears to be unique among the account texts from Puzriš-Dagan. If si-im-da-NI is a personal name, it is a hapax.

NESBIT C

Upper half of a well-preserved four-column summary account of animal disbursements (ba-zi) from Puzriš-Dagan listing standard taxes in the form of cattle, sheep and goats. It is dated to AS 7/x/-. From the extensive archive of Abbasaga.

OBVERSE

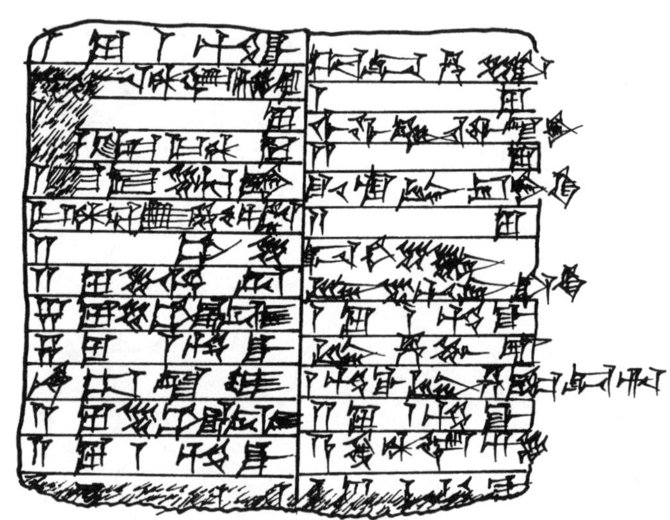

REVERSE

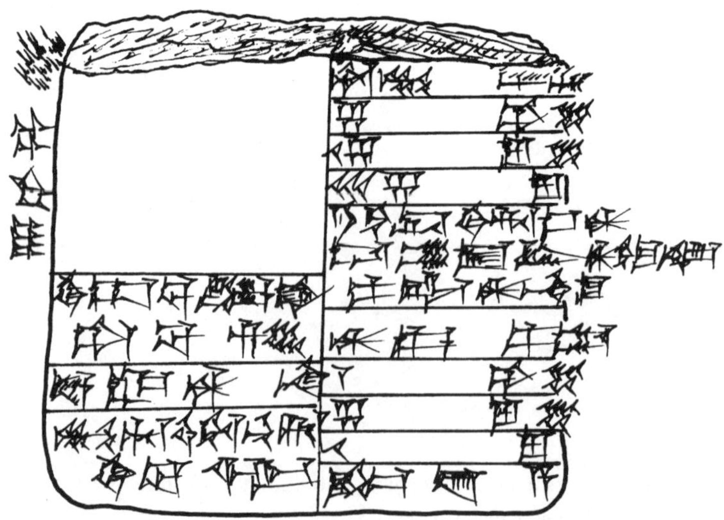

I.

1. 1 udu 1 máš-gal
2. m[u-D]U-^{d}šul-gi-ra
3. 1 udu
4. [ki] a-nag-ur-^{d}namma
5. 1 sila$_{4}$ é-uz-ga
6. [u]r-^{d}ba-ba$_{6}$ muḫaldim maškim
7. 2 gu$_{4}$-niga
8. 2 udu-niga-sig$_{5}$-ús
9. 4 udu-niga-gu$_{4}$-e-ús-sa
10. 4 udu 1 máš-gal
11. na-ab-la-núm
12. 2 udu-niga-gu$_{4}$-e-ús-sa
13. 2 udu 1 máš-gal
14. [....]

remainder of col. I destroyed

II.

1. ad-da-ḫa-li
2. 1 udu
3. ši-wi-il-wa-la-aḫ
4. 2 udu
5. šu-eš$_{4}$-tár lú-kára-ḫar^{ki}
6. 2 udu
7. tá-ḫi-še-in / lú-še-ti-ir-ša^{ki}
8. 1 udu 1 máš-gal
9. lú-ḫa-bu-ra
10. 1 máš-gal lú-ḫa-pi$_{5}$-tá-tal
11. 2 udu 1 máš-gal
12. a-mur-^{d}šul-gi
13. 1 udu 1 máš-gal
14. [....]

remainder of col. II destroyed

III.

x+1. árad-mu maškim

x+2. 4 gu_4-niga
x+3. 15 udu-niga
x+4. 35 udu
x+5. níg-mussa(MUNUS.ÚS.SA) ri-iṣ-ilum / rá-gaba é-lú-^{d}nin-šubur / šabra-an-na-šè
x+6. ilum-dan maškim
x+7. 1 gu_4-niga
x+8. 5 udu-niga
x+9. 10 udu
x+10. bí-zu-a

IV.
upper half of column IV destroyed
blank space
1. ki ab-ba-sa_6-ga-/ta ba-zi
2. iti ezem-an-na
3. mu ḫu-ùḫ-nu-ri/^{ki} ba-ḫul
4. 6 gu_4 240[+? udu]

Nesbit D

An account disbursement (ba-zi) of five sheep from four foreigners. It is dated to ŠS 2/xi/14 and stems from the extensive Puzriš-Dagan archive of the chancellor Aradmu, who deals mostly with foreigners arriving at Puzriš-Dagan.[6]

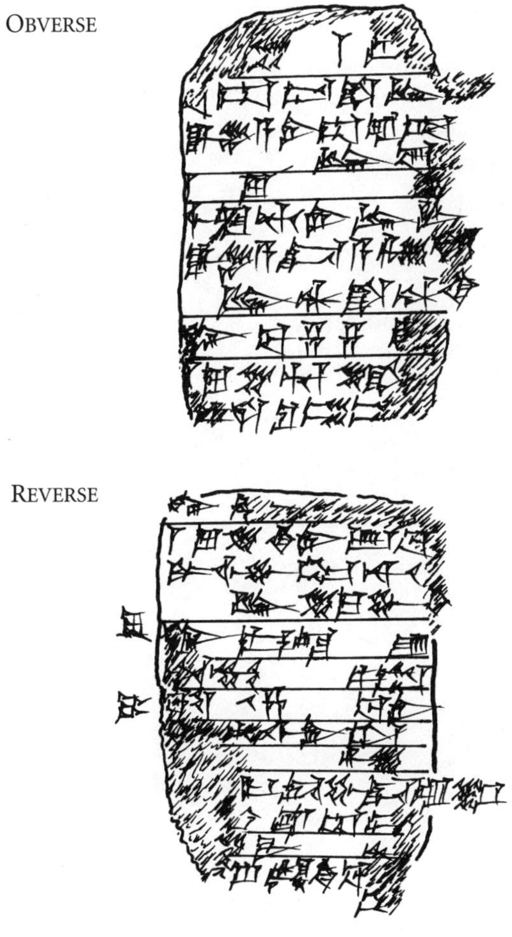

[6] Restorations are based on Genouillac (1924) plate VII, no. 30 (see appendix II), which is clearly related to our text although dated 10 days earlier. The Genouillac text is not cited in RGTC 2, sub Anšan.

1. [1 udu-n]iga 1 u[du]
2. [b]a-ab-du-ša lú-k[in]-/gi$_4$-a ìa-ab-ra-at / lú-šimaški(SU)$^{[ki]}$
3. 1 udu-n[iga]
4. ši-la-ti-ir lú-kin-/gi$_4$-a da-a-zi-t[e] / lú-an-ša-an^{ki}
5. gìri ba-za-za su[kkal]
6. 1 udu-niga ḫu-li-[bar] / énsi-du$_8$-d[u$_8$-li^{ki}]

rev.

7. gìri ḫa-[x-x sukkal]
8. 1 udu-niga ki-ir-ib-b[a] / dumu ši-bu-úr-ti lú-še-ku-bu^{ki}
9. gìri kal-la sukkal
10. á[rad-m]u maškim
11. iti-u$_4$-14 ba-zal
12. k[i a-ḫ]u-we-er-ta
13. [ba]-zi
14. [gìri] ur-uš-gíd-da dub-sar
15. [ù] ma-n[ú]m-ki-^{d}šu[l-g]i / šár-ra-ab-d[u]
16. [iti] še-kin-[ku$_5$]

u.e.

17. [m]u má-^{d}en-ki ba-[ab]-/d[u$_8$]

side

18. 5 udu

Cumulative Commentary

The unusual personal and geographical names from the above texts are commented upon collectively in alphabetical order.

Ad-da-ḫa-li: Adda-ḫali appears to be a new addition to the Ur III onomastica.

A-mur-^{d}šul-gi: probably the same individual known elsewhere to come from Mari or associated with individuals from Mari (possibly the same individual written as A-mi-ir-^{d}šul-gi, although Amir-Šulgi appears in texts only late in the reign of Šulgi). For references, see my collection of data in Chavalas and Hayes (1992) 125 *s.v.*

An-ša-an^{ki}: Anšan is in Elam and known now to be located at Tall-i-Malyān. However, very few Ur III personal names from this kingdom are known. Both the messenger Šilatir and his superior Dazite have been overlooked among the personal names from Elam. They should be added to the nearly exhaustive lists compiled in Zadok (1991) 225-37 and (1994) 31-51.

[B]a-ab-du-ša: Babduša, the messenger of Iabrat, the Šimaškian, is known from SET 66: 28$^{!}$ (see appendix II); de Genouillac (1924) plate VII, 30: 2 (see appendix II); Gelb (1956) 384, note 1 (Schrijver 42 rev. 1); and Zadok (1991) 229 sub no. 40.

Bí-zu-a: the sister of the queen (nin$_9$-nin) and a balag-singer is known from a handful of references. See my comments with previous bibliography in Owen (1979) 64 and MVN 11, p. 14, comments to no. 215. Add now Hallo (1981) 70-71 and Owen (1988) 114b.

Da-a-zi-t[e]: see above sub Anšan and de Genouillac (1924) plate VII, 30: 3 (see appendix II), where the copy has da-a-GI-te. The zi in our text is perfectly clear.

Du$_8$-du$_8$-[li^{ki}]: for ḫu-li-bar / énsi-du$_8$-du$_8$-li^{ki}, see Goetze (1953) 114-23.

Ḫa-pi$_5$-tá-tal: appears to be a new addition to the Hurrian(?) Ur III onomastica. For a comprehensive collection of Hurrian onomastica updating Gelb (1944), see Zadok (1993) 219-45. The name may be composed of the Anatolian(?) element ḫapi (NPN 214 *s.v.*) and the Hurrian(?) element tatal (NPN 263 *s.v.*), although the independent existence of this element is uncertain.

Ḫu-li-[bar]: see above sub Duduli.

I-NANGA(LÁL×NIGIN)^{ki}: this GN is otherwise unknown. I am unable to associate it with any other place name unless it is to be read i-šur$_6$^{ki} and interpreted as a variant writing for a-šur$_5$^{ki}.

I-šim-^{d}šul-gi^{ki}: probably to be located in the Diyālā region.[7] There are six known ensis of this city: Lugal-pae,[8] Nanna-isa, Ur-Utu, Ur-sasaga, Aḫu-waqar, and Ku-Šara.[9] This is only the second time érin-workers are documented from Išim-Šulgi. In CT 32 103398 they are mentioned along with Abibana,[10] Kakkulatum,[11] Tutub,[12] Maškan-abi,[13] Qišqati,[14] Simudar,[15] Šame,[16] Tumbal,[17] Puḫziqar,[18] Maškan-

---

7 See RGTC 2 86 *s.v.* and note that the reference to unpubl. HTS 139, that has now appeared as SACT 1 188: 132 (Š 48).

8 For Lugal-pae, see Sollberger (1976) 446, note 33.

9 See my chart in Owen (1988) 121.

10 In the unpublished Drehem text, YBC 3635 (courtesy W. W. Hallo and M. Sigrist) column iv, we have: 4 gu$_4$ 30 udu / 10 máš / érin-a-bí-ba-na^{ki} / 4 gu$_4$ 20 udu / 20 máš / érin-kak-ku-la-tum^{ki}. This twelve-column, one-month summary account is from the archive of Abbasaga and dates to AS 2/xi/2-30. Also found in BIN 3 101: 3 and MVN 11 182: i 8. See also RGTC 2 1 *s.v.*

11 See preceding note and RGTC 2 89 *s.v.* and the comments of Röllig (1976-80) 288 *s.v.*

12 See the discussion by Harris (1955) 45-46.

14 So read by Harris (1955) 45-46. See RGTC 2 106 *s.v.* Known only from two references in CT 32 103398.

15 Located east of the Tigris in the Diyālā region. Possibly, it is the endpoint of the wall (*mūriq-tidnim*) built by Šu-Suen to keep the Martu out of Sumer. See RGTC 2 167 *s.v.*

16 Known from CT 103398 and Delaporte (1911) 185, no. 4: 8 (see appendix II) where two individuals, šu-gu$_5$-bu-um ugula 60 and his brother Á-ni-da/id, are designated lú-ša-mi^{ki}-me. See RGTC 2 177 *s.v.* where their names are not listed, and Owen (1981) 264 *s.v.* where one should read gu$_5$(KU) and not gu$_8$.

17 See RGTC 2 198 *s.v.* Probably also to be located in the Diyālā region.

18 See RGTC 2 153 *s.v.* Known only from CT 103398 and PDT 1 448: 4 (see appendix

šuri[19] and Pūt-šadar.[20] To the references add now AUCT 2 281: 3 (Š 48/viii/-, see appendix II) and AUCT 3 253: 2, env. (AS 9/vii/30, see appendix II) and 254: 2, tab. (AS 9/vii/30, see appendix II).

I-ṭi-ib-ši-na-at: for this name, see AUCT 1 93: 5 (AS 5/iv/10, see appendix II) who also occurs together with Naḫšumbala in this text dated three years earlier than ours. Compare PDT 2 913, i: 24, I-ṭib-mi-šar.

Kára-ḫar[ki]: possibly to be identified with Ḫarḫar on the Diyālā south of Kirkuk. For a different location in the vicinity of present day Kermanšāh, *cf.* Levine (1972-75) 120-21. Šu-Eštar is the first official known from Karaḫar other than the ensis Ea-rabi and Arad-Nanna (*cf.* Owen [1988] 121).

Ki-ir-ri-ba: son of Šiburti. The PN is otherwise unknown and should be added to the lists compiled by Zadok (1993). Possibly to be compared with the foreign name, Kiribulme. See below sub Šekubu[ki].

Lú-ḫa-bu-ra: presumably a personal name or simple designation, "man from the (city of) Ḫabur." Such a city existed in the upper Ḫabur area and is associated with Mardaman. See my comments in Owen (1988) 112b and the documentation in Astour (1987) 42-44. Note érin-ḫa-bu-ra[ki] in BCT 1 4: 3 (ŠS 3/iii/18). Given the pattern of this text, the interpretation, the "man from the (city of) Habur" is likely. *Cf.* Zadok (1993) 226.

Maš-kán-a-bí[ki]: otherwise known only from four references in CT 32 103398 (i: 16; vi: 13, 14, 22) a large summary account dated to Ibbi-Suen 2. It is to be located probably in the Diyālā area (*cf.* RGTC 2 [1974] 131 *s.v.*). The text was discussed briefly by Harris (1955) 45-46 because of the cluster of GNs associated with Tutub (Ḫāfāği) and

II). Probably to be located in the Diyālā region.

19 Known only from CT 32 103398 and probably located in the Diyālā region. See RGTC 2 132 *s.v.*

20 Known only from CT 32 103398 and probably located in the Diyālā region. See RGTC 2 154 *s.v.*

all of which she located in the Diyālā region.[21] Many of the GNs are found in the later Harmal geographical list and nearly all were known previously only from this Ur III text. Thus the new reference to Maškan-abi, clustered with additional GNs and from an earlier Ur III date, assumes special significance. See above under Išim-Šulgi.

Maš-kán-šar-ru-um^{ki}: Whiting (1976) 178 locates Maškan-šarrum "north of Eshnunna, where the Tigris enters the plain," and again later (*ibid.*, p. 180), "somewhere east of the Tigris and north of Eshnunna." Babati was the military governor (šagana/šakkanakkum) of Maškan-šarrum as well as governor (énsi) of Abal.[22] *Cf.* also RGTC 2 131 *s.v.* Maškan-šarrum.

Na-ab-la-núm: Nablānum is the well-attested Amorite (mar-tu) known from numerous texts, particularly, from the Puzriš-Dagan archives. His active role in the Ur III period has not been subjected to any comprehensive study.

Pu-ut-tu-li-um^{ki}: Pūt-tuli'um is known otherwise only from Dhorme (1912) 9 63 14: 5 (ŠS 7/iii/22, see appendix II) and AUCT 1 743: 2 (Š 47/ix/9, see appendix II and add reference to RGTC 2 154, *s.v.*) where érin are mentioned. It is interesting to note that Pūt-tuli'um was under the control of the Ur III empire from at least Šulgi's 47th year with Šu-Suen 7 the latest reference recorded. It is difficult to

---

21 See below sub Tašil.

22 I have pointed out elsewhere (Owen [1981] 66) that Whiting's conclusions on the interchange of the spellings Abal/Awal in the Ur III period are based on a misreading by Goetze (1963) 5 where he cited a-wa-al^{ki} in NMW 30376. My subsequent collation and transliteration published in Owen (1981) 65-66 showed clearly that the spelling in that text is a-ba-al^{ki} (correct accordingly RGTC 2 20). Thus the grounds for Whiting's conclusions based on a comparison with ASM 12059, where it is also written a-ba-al^{ki}, are incorrect as also noted by Walker (1983) 94. But Whiting's conclusion, based on other considerations, that Abal is to be located in the vicinity of Maškan-šarrum remains correct. Walker, *ibid.*, notes that the "Recent Iraqi excavations at Tell Suleimeh in the Hamrin area suggest the identification of Awal [N.B. Abal in the Ur III period] with that site."

narrow its location since it is associated in the cited texts with towns both in the Diyālā area (Tutub, etc.) as well as at least one town in Elam (Sabum). Compare the form of the GN with Pūt-šadar (RGTC 2 154, *s.v.*), which has been located in the Diyālā region by Harris but might be much further north according to D. Frayne (personal communication).

Ri-iṣ-ilum: Riṣ-ilum, the courier, is a well-known official in the Puzriš-Dagan archives, with close connections to the royal family (see appendix I).[23] In Šulgi 47/viii/22, he is characterized as an "easterner" (sa$_{12}$-ti-um)[24] when he provides bridewealth for his marriage into the household of Dayyani, the cook, and again three days earlier (Š 47/viii/19) in MVN 8 108, probably for the same marriage. He is described as the "queen's courier" (rá-gaba-nin) in MVN 11 183(HSM 911.10.121): 8 (AS 8/-/-)[25] and often functions as a maškim-official in exchanges involving female members of the royal family.[26] His marriage into the family of Lu-Ninšubura, the major-domo of (the temple-houselhold of) An,[27] is an important additional bit of information on his life and activities. In MVN 3 232 (see appendix II), Ur-Baba, the son of the king (dumu-lugal), marries into the same family and Riṣ-ilum is the maškim-official in that transaction. Nesbit C is dated one year later and suggests that Riṣ-ilum had by then married into the extended royal family. But Riṣ-ilum also had a son by the name of Ur-Baba who was already an adult in AS 8/iv/- (BIN 3 482). Is prince Ur-Baba and Ur-Baba

23 See Michalowski (1978) 7.

24 See Steinkeller (1980) 1 and below, appendix. Note also Greengus (1990) 39, sub no. 9.

25 Michalowski (1978) 13, no. 8 but left out in his transliteration on p. 14.

26 For references, see Michalowski (1978).

27 Note also AUCT 1 327: 14, where Lu-Ninšubur receives bridewealth as he does from Ur-Baba in MVN 3 232: 4 (see appendix II). No doubt his position, coupled with a number of daughters, made marriage into his houselhold an attractive proposition.

son of Riṣ-ilum one and the same? Could this be additional proof that dumu-lugal can be both prince as well as an honorific title?[28]

Si-im-da-NI: If this is a PN it is new to the onomastica of the period and may originate in the region of the two toponyms in the text. On the other hand, it may be the noun si-im-da+(a)ni, "his mark/brand" and may refer to the mark/branding iron without the determinative URUDU and may have something to do with the marking of these animals. For ^{urudu}si-im-da, see Foxvog (1995) 5-6 with previous bibliography. In either case, no parallel texts are known to me.

Še-ku-bu^{ki}: The determinative ki is worn and faint. This GN is otherwise unknown, as is the case with the PNs Kiribba and his father Šiburti. For Šame, see above sub Išim-Šulgi.

Še-ti-ir-ša^{ki}: Taḫišen is known from TCL 2 5515 rev. 1 and A 3297 (Gelb [1944] 113, note 67 = Hilgert [forthcoming] 92.[29] See appendix II). It may be compared to Taḫašen (UET 3 936) for which see Zadok (1993) 230 sub 2.2.5. The GN Šetirša is known from only one other text, Contenau (1915) 6, iii, 12. See RGTC 2 180, *s.v.*

Ši-bu-úr-ti: father of Kirriba. The PN is otherwise unknown and should be added to the lists compiled by Zadok (1993). See above sub Še-ku-bu^{ki}.

Ši-la-ti-ir: see above sub Anšan. See de Genouillac (1924) plate VII, 30: 3 (ŠS 2/xi/24, see appendix II).

Ši-wi-il-wa-la-aḫ: probably an Elamite name and new to the corpus. Add to the lists compiled by Zadok (1993).

Šu-Eštar: see above sub Karaḫar.

Taḫišen: see above sub Šetirša.

---

28 The Nesbit C reference to "bridewealth" (níg-mussa) should be added to the comprehensive study by Greengus (1990) 25-88.

29 I am grateful to Markus Hilgert for making his transliterations of the relevant CTU texts available to me in advance of his publications.

Tá-si-il^{ki}: Previously known only with the spelling tá-ši-il^{ki} as cited in RGTC 2 30 *s.v.* To those references add: Nat.Mus.Washington 303276 = Owen (1981) 63-68 as NMW 303276, de Genouillac (1911a) 54.ii.2 (see appendix II) and YBC 16651 (Owen [1981] 68) where the "elders" (abba) of Tašil, Tutub,[30] and the otherwise unattested Maškan-kallātum are mentioned. R. Whiting has shown that Tašil is to be located in the upper Tigris region, where it is associated with Aššur,[31] Terqa (al-^{c}Ašāra),[32] Urguḫalam,[33] and other sites. Since it also occurs in YBC 16651 together with Tutub and Maškan-kallātum, I have suggested that its position be further localized in the upper eastern region of the Tigris, perhaps in the Diyālā area (see Owen [1981] 66).

---

30 See RGTC 2 201 *s.v.* and Harris (1955) 45-46.

31 See RGTC 2 18 *s.v.*

32 Known only from Genouillac (1911a) 54, i, 3 (see appendix II).

33 Otherwise known only from Genouillac (1911a) 54: iii, 4′ (see appendix II).

APPENDIX I

Career of Riṣ-ilum, the (Queen's) Courier[34]

Date unknown

He arrives in Sumer from somewhere in the east since later he is designated as a foreigner, satium.

Šulgi 43/iv/6

In the first attestation for Riṣ-ilum (Hilgert [1997] 150 [A3251], see appendix II), he appears as an àga-ús and provides two sheep and a goat.

Šulgi 47/viii/22

Four years after his initial appearance in the Puzriš-Dagan sources he marries into the household of Dayyani, the cook (Steinkeller [1980] 1-2, A 4723 = Hilgert [1997] 316, see appendix II). Bridewealth for the marriage of Riṣ-ilum is recorded in another text of the same day (MVN 8 108, see appendix II).

Amar-Suena 4/iii/24

Riṣ-ilum is the maškim-official in a transaction concerning expenditures of goats for various gods and goddesses (AUCT 1 132, see appendix II).

Amar-Suena 4/vii/1x

In Amar-Suena's fourth year he appears as a maškim-official in the extraordinary account summary dealing with many of the royal daughters, wives, and wetnurses (Sigrist, *apud* Spar [1988] 17: 56).

Amara-Suena 4/vii/27

Later in the same month Riṣ-ilum appears once again as a maškim-official in a delivery of a sheep of Šu-kab-tá (BIN 3 81).

---

34 I am grateful to Markus Hilgert for sharing his list of references to Riṣ-ilum and providing the references to his forthcoming volumes of Ur III texts in the Oriental Institute, Chicago.

Amar-Suena 5/viii/18

After a year without any references, Riṣ-ilum appears as a maškim-official in a transaction involving a number of sheep and goats for Abi-simti (Gomi [1980] 46, no. 28, see appendix II).

Amar-Suena 6/iii/-

Early in Amar-Suena's sixth year, Riṣ-ilum serves as a maškim-official in Sollberger (1956) 22, no. 11: 3 (see appendix II), which is an account concerning gifts of silver rings to the dowager queen, Abi-simti, and silver rings and bronze objects to others.

Amar-Suena 6/x/14

Later in Amar-Suena's sixth year, Riṣ-ilum is the maškim-official for the transfer of the bridewealth of Ur-Baba, the son of the king (dumu-lugal), to the household of Lu-Ninšubur, major-domo (of the temple-household) of An (MVN 3 232, see appendix II).

Amar-Suena 7/ix/27

After an absence of references for nearly a year, Riṣ-ilum appears as šarrabdu and functions as a giri-official involving a goat for Sagdana taken in charge by Šu-Mama (DV 5 461: 15, see appendix II).

Amar-Suena 7/x/[?]

In Amar-Suena 7 Riṣ-ilum marries for the second(?) time, this time into the household of Lu-Ninšubur, the major-domo (of the temple-houselhold) of An (Nesbit C, see above).

Amar-Suena 8/i/22

At the beginning of this year Riṣ-ilum is the maškim-official when DINGIR.BI, a royal lukur (lukur-lugal), enters (the palace?) (SCT 24, see appendix II).

Amar-Suena 8/ii/9

The following month Riṣ-ilum is the maškim-official in a transaction involving a royal cook (muḫaldim-lugal) possibly Dayyani, his father-in-law (AUCT 2 238, see appendix II).

Amar-Suena 8/iv/-

By Amar-Suena 8 Riṣ-ilum has become the queen's courier (rá-gaba-nin) (MVN 11 183[HSM 911.10.121] = Michalowski [1978] 13, see appendix II).

Amar-Suena 8/iv/-

Riṣ-ilum has a grown son, Ur-Baba, who is the recipient(?) of a bronze-covered table (BIN 3 482, see appendix II).

Amar-Suena 8/vii/2

Later in the same year, according to PDT 1 548: 3 (see appendix II), Riṣ-ilum is a maškim-official in a text dealing with Bizua, the queen's sister (nin_9-nin), along with numerous other foreign delegates and officials from northern and northeastern towns, including Amorites (mar-tu).

Amar-Suena 9?/xi/16

Nearly a year later Riṣ-ilum appears in Gomi (1990) 297: 3 (see appendix II) as the maškim-official in a transaction concerning the offering of one fattened gu_4-e-ús-sa-sheep for the wife of Beli-arik.

Šu-Suen 2/ix/3

In the first reference during the reign of Šu-Suen, Riṣ-ilum appears without any official title in an agricultural account from Umma (MVN 15 129[Brooklyn Mus. 74.71.9]): 23. But since he is classed here as an érin, it is unlikely that he is the same person.

Šu-Suen 2/[x]/-

The restoration of the name Riṣ-ilum šár-ra-ab-du in MVN 15 303(MKL 2): 26 is conjecture and cannot be substantiated. But compare CTMMA I 17: 56.

Šu-Suen 6/vii/10

Riṣ-ilum occurs without title in a list of boatmen in an Umma text (MVN 1 95). Like MVN 15 129 quoted above, this Umma reference is probably not to our Riṣ-ilum.

Šu-Suen 9/viii/-

In UET 3 1647: 5 (see appendix II), Riṣ-ilum is a supervisor (ugula) in an account concerning textiles and involving, among others, the princess Šat-Suen.

Ibbi-Suen 1/xii/-

In UET 3 1654: 8, a Riṣ-ilum nar provides two cloths for the corenation of Ibbi-Suen. It is unlikely that this is the same person as our Riṣ-ilum.

[date broken]

In MVN 11 180(HSM 911.10.112): i, 15, Riṣ-ilum, without title, delivers(?) three(?) sheep.

APPENDIX II

Selected Quoted Sources[35]

Çığ, Kızılyay, and Salonen, PDT 1 448

(1) 1 amar-mašda (2) lú-sún-zi-da (3) 1 gu_4 10 udu (4) érin-pu-úḫ-zi-qàr^{ki} (5) ugula a-mur-é-a (6) 4 udu-niga šar-ru-um-ba-ni (7) 2 $sila_4$ (rev. 8) $puzur_4$-^{d}suen nu-bànda (9) 1 $sila_4$ énsi-umma^{ki} (10) 1 amar-mašda (11) é-a-ì-lí (12) 2 $sila_4$ zabar-dab_5 (13) mu-DU (14) na-sa_6 ì-dab_5 (15) itu še-gur_{10}-ku_5 (16) mu ús-sa ki-maš^{ki} ba-ḫul (l.e.) u_4-9-kam (Š 45/xii/-)

Çığ, Kızılyay, and Salonen, PDT 1 548

(1) 1 udu-niga-sig_5 išib-^{d}ištaran (2) gìri á-pil-lí rá-gaba (3) ri-iṣ-ilum maškim (4) 2 gu_4-niga 2 udu-niga-sig_5 (5) 5 udu-niga-gu_4-e-ús-sa (6) 3 udu 2 máš-gal (7) na-ab-la-núm mar-tu (8) 1 udu-niga-gu_4-e-ús-sa 1 udu

---

35 For convenience sake, relevant related texts are provided here in revised transliterations. Comments to these texts have been kept at a minimum. Most of the remaining texts quoted but not included in the appendix may be found in the collection of electronic transliteration files of Ur III texts compiled by Bram Jargisma and Remco de Maaijer at the Near East Institute at Leiden University. Access to these files is available through the World Wide Web at http: //oasis.leidenuniv.nl/ub/sta/ur3/ur3.htm.

(9) ad-ga-nu-um mar-tu (10) 1 udu-niga-gu$_4$-e-ús-sa 1 udu (11) zu-zu lú-še-er-šum^{ki} (12) 1 gu$_4$-niga 2 udu-niga-gu$_4$-e-ús-sa 3 udu (13) it-ḫi-pá-tal lú-ḫi-bí-la-at^{ki} (14) 1 udu lú-kin-gi$_4$-a ad-da-gi-na lú-ḫa-ar-ši^{ki} (15) 1 udu lú-kin-gi$_4$-a it-kùš-ilum mar-tu (16) 1 udu lú-kin-gi$_4$-a ḫu-li-bar lú-du$_8$-du$_8$-lí^{ki} (17) 1 udu lú-kin-gi$_4$-a gu-u$_4$ lú-ù-ul^{ki} (rev. 18) 1 udu-niga-gu$_4$-e-ús-sa 1 udu (19) šu-ištar lú-NI.ḪI^{ki} (20) 3 udu a-mur-^{d}šul-gi (21) 2 udu ak-ba-ìa (22) 2 udu ^{d}šul-gi-a-bí (23) 1 udu ^{d}šul-gi-ì-lí (24) gìri na-ra-am-^{d}iškur sukkal (25) 1 gu$_4$-niga 2 udu-niga 3-kam-ús (26) 3 udu-niga 5 udu (27) en-^{d}inanna (28) árad-mu maškim (29) 1 gu$_4$-niga 2 udu-niga 3 udu (30) bí-zu-a (31) li-ni-si-in maškim (32) 1 udu ki a-nag-ur-^{d}namma 33) gìri an-na-ḫi-li-mu (34) ur-^{d}ba-ba$_6$ muḫaldim maškim (35) u$_4$-2-kam (36) ki ab-ba-sa$_6$-ga-ta ba-zi (37) iti ezem-^{d}šul-gi (38) mu en-nun-e-^{d}amar-^{d}suen-ra ki-ág-en-eridu^{ki} ba-ḫun (side 39) 5 gu$_4$ 52 udu (AS 8/vii/2)

Delaporte (1911) 185, no. 4, tab.

(1) 1 sag-níta šar-ru-a mu-ni-im (2) nì-šám-bi 6 5/6 gín kù-babbar (3) ar-ši-aḫ GUR lugal-a-ni-ir (4) lú-^{d}suen-ke$_4$ (5) in-ši-s[a$_{10}$] (6) DIŠ šu-gu$_5$-bu-um GUR (7) DIŠ Á-ni-da{env. has id} (8) lú-ša-me^{ki}-me (9) DIŠ á-gu (10) DIŠ al-du$_{10}$-ga (11) DIŠ ur-^{d}maḫ-di-an-ka (rev. 12) DIŠ kù-sa$_6$-ga (13) DIŠ ur-sukkal (14) DIŠ ḫa-an-du kurušda-lugal (15) lú-inim-ma-bi-me (16) iti NE-izi-gar-ra (17) mu ^{d}amar-^{d}suen lugal-àm (AS 1/v/10 [Nippur])

Delaporte (1911) 185, no. 4, env.

(1) 1 sag-n[íta šar-ru-a mu-ni-im] (2) nì-šám-[bi 6 5/6 g]ín kù-babbar(3) ar-ši-aḫ GUR lú-ša-me^{ki}-ka lugal-a-ni-ir (4) lú-^{d}suen-ke$_4$ (5) in-ši-sa$_{10}$ (6) DIŠ šu-ku-bu-um GUR (7) DIŠ á-ni-id šeš šu-ku-bu-um-ma (8) lú-ša-me^{ki}-me (9) DIŠ á-gu (10) DIŠ al-du$_{10}$-ga (rev. 11) DIŠ ḫa-an-du kurušda-lugal (12) DIŠ ur-^{d}maḫ-di-an-ka (13) [lú]-inim-ma-bi-me (14) iti NE-izi-gar-ra u$_4$-10-zal-la (15) mu ^{d}amar-^{d}suen (16) lugal-àm (seal) ar-ši-aḫ / dumu en?-at-AK / ugula [....] (AS 1/v/10 [Nippur])

Dhorme (1912) 63, no. 14

(1) 10 udu-ú (2) šar-ru-um-ba-ni nu-bàn[da] (3) 72 udu-ú (4) 8 máš-gal-ú (5) érin-pu-ut-tu-li-um^{ki} (6) ugula ib-ni-^{d}šul-gi (7) gìri ad-da-mu lú-kin-gi$_4$-a-lugal (8) dur?-TÙN-da (rev. 9) mu-DU (10) in-ta-è-a (11) ì-dab$_5$ (12) gìri ^{d}nanna-ma-ba dub-sar (13) u$_4$-22-kam (14) iti šeš-da-kú (15) mu

^{d}šu-^{d}suen lugal uri$_5$^{ki}-ma-ke$_4$ (16) [m]a-da za-ab-ša-li^{ki} mu-ḫul (side: 90 udu) (ŠS 7/iii/22)

de Genouillac (1924) plate VII, 30

(1) 1 udu-[ni]ga 1 udu (2) [b]a-ab-du-ša lú-ki-gi$_4$-a [ìa]-ab-ra-at lú-šimaški(SU)^{ki} (3) [1] udu-niga ši-la-ti-ir lú-kin-gi$_4$-[a] da-a-GI-te lú-an-ša-an^{ki} (4) gìri ba-za-za sukkal (5) [1] udu-niga ki-rí-ib-ul-me lú-si-mu-ru-um^{ki} (6) gìri šu-ku-bu-um sukkal (7) 1 udu-niga a-ri-du-bu-uk lú-ša-aš-ru^{ki} (8) gìri la-qí-pu-um sukkal (9) 1 udu-niga (rev. 10) še-et-pá-tal lú-gi-gi-ib-ni^{ki} (11) gìri la-la-mu sukkal (12) árad-mu maškim (13) 1 sila$_4$-ga a-bí-sí-im-ti (14) ku-ub-za-gi-mu maškim (15) [i]ti u$_4$-24-kam ba-zal (16) ki a-ḫu-we-er-ta ba-zi (17) gìri ur-^{d}lugal-bàn-da (18) ù a-ḫa-ni-šu šár-ra-ab-du (19) iti ezem-me-ki-gál (20) mu má-^{d}en-ki ba-ab-du$_8$

de Genouillac (1911a) 54

I. (1) [n] udu-ú (2) 9 máš-gal-ú (3) érin-te-er-qá^{ki} (4) [ugula] šeš-kal-la (5) [n] udu-ú (6) [ugula ^{d}addad]-da-ni (7) [....]-ú (8) [ugula ....] (9) [....]-ú (remainder of column I lost) II. (1) šà 1 (2) érin-tá-ši-il^{ki} (3) ugula ^{d}addad-da-ni (4) 10 udu-ú u$_4$-20 (5) [ugul]a? si-zum (6) 10 udu-ú (7) URU×PA-da-bi-u?-ù? (8) 2 gu$_4$-ú šà-a (9) 14 udu-ú (10) 5 máš-gal (remainder of column II lost) III. (beginning of column III lost) (1′) [n ....] (2′) 17 udu-ú (3′) 3 máš-gal-ú (4′) érin-ur-gu-ḫa-lam^{ki} (5′) 1 gu$_4$-ú (6′) 9 udu-ú (7′) 1 máš-gal-ú (8′) érin-maš-kán-ga-raš$_x$(KASKAL×gunû)-šar^{ki} (9′) udu a-ḪAR-àm (10′) 10 udu-ú IV. (beginning of column IV lost) (1′) [....]-mu-um / [...]-x-ù (2′) [n g]u$_4$-ú (3′) [n ... n] máš-ú (4′) [érin?-a?]-šur$_5$^{ki} / [....] (5′) [... nu]-úr-^{d}suen / [lú-kin]-gi$_4$-/a (remainder lost)

Gomi (1980) 46, no. 28

(1) 8 udu-niga (2) 4 máš-gal-niga (3) 2 ^{munus}áš-g[àr]-niga (4) 16 [sila$_4$?-niga?] (5) 1 máš (6) a-bí-sí-i[m]-/ti (7) blank line (8) ri-iṣ-ilum rá-gaba / maškim (rev. 9) 1 ^{munus}áš-gàr-niga é-u[z-ga] (10) a-a-kal-la maškim (11) š[à m]u-DU-ra-ta (12) u$_4$-18-kam (13) ki ab-ba-sa$_6$-ga-ta (14) ba-zi (15) iti šu-eš$_5$-ša (16) mu en-u[nu$_6$]-gal-/^{d}inanna-unug$^{k[i]}$ [ba]-ḫun (side 17) 32 (sic!)

Gomi (1990) 297

(1) 1 udu-niga-gu$_4$-e-ús-sa (2) é-muḫaldim (3) IGI+KÁR mu dam-be-lí-/a-rí-ik-šè (4) ri-iṣ-ilum rá-gaba maškim (5) 1 udu-niga (6) mi-gir-^{d}nin-líl-tum (rev. 7) é-gi$_4$-a-na-ni-pá-tal (8) gìri ba-za-za sukkal (9) árad-mu maškim (10) iti-u$_4$-16 ba-zal (11) ki zu-ba-ga-ta ba-zi (12) gìri ad-da-kal-la / dub-sar-zì (13) iti ezem-me-ki-gál (14) [mu en-^{d}kar-zi-d]a! ba-ḫun[36] (side 15) 2 udu (AS 9?/xi/16)

Gordon, SCT 24[37]

(1) 1 udu 4 gu$_4$! DINGIR.BI lukur-lugal (2) u$_4$ ku$_4$-ra-ni-a (3) gìri ri-iṣ-ilum rá-gaba (4) ilum-dan! sukkal! maškim (5) 2 udu 7 u$_8$ (6) mu kaš$_4$-é-ne-šè (7) ur-^{d}ba-ba$_6$! muḫaldim maškim! (8) 3 udu 10-lá-1 u$_8$ (9) mu gàr-du-e-ne-šè (10) šu-gíd é-muḫaldim-šè! (11) u$_4$-22-kam (12) ki du$_{11}$-ga-ta (13) ba-zi (14) iti maš-dù-kú (15) mu en-eridu^{ki} ba-ḫun (side 16) 22 udu 4 gu$_4$ (AS 8/i/22)

Hilgert, CTU 1 150

(1) 2 udu 1 máš (2) ri-iṣ-ilum àga-ús (3) 2 udu 1 máš-gal (4) 2 sila$_4$ (5) ú-ú-kal-la sipa (6) 1 sila$_4$ énsi-šuruppag^{ki} (7) 1 šeg$_9$-bar-munus (rev. 8) ur-ni$_9$-gar (9) 1 sila$_4$ ur-tilla$_5$(AN.AŠ-tenû.AN) (10) blank space (11) mu-DU (12) iti ki-síg-^{d}nin-a-zu (13) mu en-^{d}nanna / maš-e ì-pàd (side 14) u$_4$-6-kam (Š 43/iv/6)

Hilgert, CTU 1 316

(1) 1 sila$_4$ ^{d}utu (2) mu-DU ad-da-tur (3) 1 sila$_4$ mu-DU šu-^{d}nin-šubur (4) 1 sila$_4$ mu-DU ur-ni$_9$-gar (5) ^{d}inanna (6) zabar-dab$_5$ maškim (7) 1 amar-mašda é-uz-ga (8) mu-DU énsi-marad^{ki} (9) a-a-kal-la maškim (10) 1 gu$_4$ 6 udu 4 máš (11) níg-mussa(MUNUS.ÚS.SA) ri-iṣ-ilum sa$_{12}$-ti-um (rev. 12) é-da-a-a-ni muḫaldim-šè (13) árad-mu maškim (14) 2 gu$_4$ 4 áb (15) 8 udu 20 u$_8$ 2 úz (16) šu-gíd é-muḫaldim mu àga-ús-e-ne-šè (17) ur-ni$_9$-gar šu ba-ti (18) u$_4$-22-kam (19) ki na-sa$_6$-ta ba-zi (20) iti šu-eš-ša (21) mu ús-sa ki-maš^{ki} ba-ḫul (Š 47/viii/22)

---

36 The date follows the restoration by Gomi. Zubaga (line 11) is attested, according to Sigrist (1992) 336-38, from AS 8/v to ŠS 1, which accords well with the restoration.

37 This text requires collation.

Hilgert, CTU 2 92

(1) 1 gu$_4$ tá-ḫi-še-en (2) 5 gu$_4$ érin-ši-ti-ir-/ša^{ki} (3) ugula tá-ḫi-še-en (4) 1 sila$_4$ énsi-/nibru^{ki} (rev. 5) 1 sila$_4$ igi-an-na-ke$_4$-z[u] (6) 1 maš-dà (7) ama eš$_4$-tár-il-šu (8) u$_4$-11-kam (9) mu-DU (10) ab-ba-sa$_6$-ga ì-dab$_5$ (11) iti ezem ^{d}šul-gi (12) mu en-unu$_6$-g[al]-/^{d}inanna unug^{ki} <ba-ḫug> (side 13) 10-lá-1 (AS 5/vii/11)

Jones and Snyder, SET 66[38]

(1) 3 [udu....] (2) 2 [udu....] (3) 1 udu-niga zà-gú-lá šà é-[...] (4) a-tu sagi maškim (5) 2 udu ^{giš}gu-za-^{d}amar-^{d}suen (6) 1 gu$_4$-niga (7) 2 udu (8) 3 máš-gal a-rá-1-kam (9) 4 udu-niga (10) 1 ^{munus}áš-gàr a-rá-2-kam (11) mu gìri-ke$_4$-ne-šè (12) 1 udu-niga mu na-ab-la-núm mar-tu-šè (13) é-muḫaldim-šè (14) gìri ur-^{d}ba-ba$_6$ muḫaldim (15) 1 ^{munus}áš-gàr u$_4$-ná-a-ka é-gal-la ba-an-ku$_4$! (16) a-bí-sí-im-ti (17) uri$_5$^{ki}-ma-šè (18) gìri zu-ba-ga (19) 1 udu-niga šu-a-gi-na (20) 1 udu-niga nì-dirig-a (21) ki$^{!}$-ri-ib-ul-me$^{!}$ lú-si-mu-ru-um^{ki} (rev. 22) gìri ba-za-za sukkal (23) 1 udu-niga na-ab-la-núm mar-tu (24) gìri ^{d}šul-gi-uru-mu sukkal (25) 1 udu-niga (26) wa-la-la lú-ma-ḫi-li^{ki} (27) gìri ^{d}suen-kà-ši-id sukkal (28) 1 udu-niga ba-ab-du-ša lú-šimaški (SU)$^{!}$ (29) lú? ìa-ab-ra-at lú-šimaški(SU) (30) gìri šu-^{d}šul-gi sukkal (31) 1 udu-niga bàn-da-du dumu bí-lí-ib-ba énsi-é-gu-la^{ki} (32) gìri la-qí-ip sukkal (33) árad-mu maškim (34) 2 udu-niga-gu$_4$-e-ús-sa (35) ur-ni$_9$-gar lú-nam-dumu (36) gìri ba-ba-ti maškim (37) iti u$_4$-26-ba-zal (38) ki zu-ba-ga-ta ba-zi (39) gìri ad-da-kal-la dub-sar (40) iti šeš-da-kú (41) mu en-^{d}nanna-kar-zi-da ba-ḫun (side 42) 1 gu$_4$ 28 udu (AS 9/ii/26)

Keiser and Kang, BIN 3 81

(1) [1 udu] é-uz-ga (2) mu-DU lugal-má-gur$_8$-re (3) ur-^{d}ba-ba$_6$ maškim (4) 1 udu-lullum$_x$(LÚ.ÙLU-um)-niga mu-DU / ṣe-lu-uš-^{d}da-gan (5) 1 u$_8$-niga 1 ^{munus}áš-gàr-niga mu-DU / a-bu-NI (6) [1 x mu-D]U á-da-a (7) [1 x mu-D]U énsi-/[ur]ua^{ki} (8) [1 x mu-DU] ab-ba-^{d}en-líl / [kù?]-dím (rev. 9) [1 x m]u-DU ur-^{d}suen (10) [^{d}šu]l-gi-sí-im-ti (11) [1 x] išib-^{d}ištaran (12) mu-

[38] This text requires extensive collation. Some corrections are suggested in the transliteration.

DU šu-kab-tá (13) ri-iṣ-ilum rá-gaba / maškim (14) u_4-27-kam (15) ki ab-ba-sa_6-ga-/ta ba-zi (16) [iti eze]m-^{d}šul-gi (17) [mu e]n-maḫ-al-an-na-/ [e]n-^{d}nanna ba-ḫun (side 18) 10-lá-1 (AS 4/vii/27)

Keiser and Kang, BIN 3 482

(1) [1?] banšur-LAM / zabar-gar-ra (2) ur-^{d}ba-ba_6 dumu / ri-iṣ-ilum (3) ilum-dan maškim (4) ki a-ḫu-ni-ta (5) ba-zi (blank line) (6) iti ki-síg-^{d}nin-a-zu (7) mu [e]n-eridu^{ki} / ba-ḫun (AS 8/iv/-)

Legrain, UET 3 1647

(1) 1 túg-uš-bar (2) a-ḫu-ni (3) mu i-ti-èr-ra-šè (4) 1 túg ša-at-^{d}suen (5) ugula ri-iṣ-ilum (6) 1 túg ^{d}nanna-kam (7) [....]-bu-un-ke_4 (8) [mu]-DU (rev. 9) [?] ^{d}nanna-ḫi-li (10) šu+nígin 3 túg mu-TAG (11) lú-^{d}nin-šubur (12) šu ba-an-ti (13) iti ezem-^{d}šul-gi (14) mu GS 9 (ŠS 9/viii/-)[39]

Nikol'skij, DV 5 461

(1) 3 $sila_4$ kíg-gi_4-a (2) 6 $sila_4$ 6 máš (3) má-lugal gub-ba (4) 3 u_8 $sila_4$-nu-a 1 ud_5 máš nu-a (5) 10-lá-1 máš giš-dù (6) má-muḫaldim gub-ba (7) sag-da-na-ta (8) 28 (9) šà-bi-ta (10) [1] u_8 $sila_4$ nu-a é-muḫaldim (rev. 11) [x] $sila_4$ ^{d}nanna-igi-du_8-[a?] (12) zi-ga u_4-27-kam (13) 1 u_8 $sila_4$-nu-a sag-da-na-šè (14) šu-ma-ma ì-dab_5 (15) gìri ri-iṣ-ilum šár-ra-ab-du (16) 10-lá-1 $sila_4$-máš(sic!) uri^{ki}-šè / má-a ba-a-DU gìri ur-gar (17) 1 $sila_4$ 1 máš má-lugal-ta / LÚ-ša-lim ba-an-zuḫ(KA) (18) NI-tam-ma íb-gi-né (19) 1 u_8 $sila_4$ nu-a gìri a-ḫu-um-ba-<ni?> (20) du_{11}-ga ì-dab_5 (21) 25 (22) zi-ga (23) lá-ì 3 máš-$sila_4$ (24) èn-bi tar-re-dam (side 25) ki-bi gi_4-a udu / má-lugal gub-ba (26) iti ezem-maḫ (27) mu ḫu-úḫ-nu-ri^{ki} / ba-ḫul (AS 7/ix/27)

Owen, MVN 3 232

(1) 6 udu (2) 10-lá-1 máš-gal (3) níg-mussa(MUNUS.ÚS.SA) ur-^{d}ba-ba_6 dumu-lugal (4) é-lú-^{d}nin-šubur šabra-an-na-šè (5) ri-iṣ-ilum rá-gaba

---

39 There is a problem with the date of this text. On the copy it is indicated as being GS 9. But in UET 3 Index, p. 277 the text number does not appear under Year, Gimil-Sin 9. However, on p. 270, sub 1647-1648, the two texts are dated together as GS 9/viii but the months are different, 1648 being the third Ur month of šeš-da-kú. Collation is required.

maškim (rev. 6) u$_4$-14-kam (7) ki in-ta-è-a-ta (8) ba-zi (9) iti ezem-an-na (10) mu ša-aš-ru^{ki} ba-ḫul (side 11) 15 udu (AS 6/x/14)

Owen, MVN 11 183(HSM 911.10.121) =
Michalowski (1978), p. 13, no. 8[40]

(1) 2 ḫar kù-babbar 10-lá-1 gín-ta (2) a-na-a lukur-na-wi-ir-ilum a-zu[41] (3) E.ER-be-lí[42] maškim (4) 1 ḫar kù-babbar 8 gín-ta (5) a-tu-ma-ma (6) 1 ḫar ur-^{d}nanše šeš-a-ni (7) má-laḫ$_4$-me (8) ri-iṣ-ilum rá-gaba-nin maškim (9) u$_4$ ki ^{d}sumuqan-[an]-d[ùl] / ba-n[a-DU?-a][43] (10) ù na-wi-ir-[ilum][44] (11) ba-a-ak-a (12) in-be$_6$-e-éš (13) ki lú-dingir-ra-ta (14) ba-zi (15) šà puzur$_4$-iš-^{d}da-gan (16) mu en-^{d}nanna ^{d}amar-^{d}suen-ki-ág-an-na ba-ḫun (AS 8/iv/-)

Calvot and Pettinato, MVN 8 108

(1) 6 udu 4 máš (2) nì-mussa / ri-iṣ-ilum (3) 8 udu 20 u$_8$ (4) 2 uz (5) é-muḫaldim u$_4$-22-kam (6) żi-ga ki ur-nun-na (7) iti šu-eš-ša (8) mu-ús-sa ki-maš^{ki} / ba-ḫul (Š 47/viii/22)

Sigrist, AUCT 1 93

(1) 2 máš-gal-niga lú-šimaški(SU) (2) ḫa-ši-pá-tal (3) 2 sila$_4$ énsi-nibru^{ki} (4) 2 sila$_4$ wa-da-ru-um sanga (5) 2 sila$_4$ i-ṭi-ib-ši-na-at (6) 1 sila$_4$ na-aḫ-šum-bala (7) 1 sila$_4$ lú-^{d}nanna (8) 1 sila$_4$ šar-ru-um-ba-ni (9) 1 sila$_4$ i-ri-bu-um

40 This transliteration differs somewhat from that of Michalowski's, which contains a number of typographical errors.

41 Michalowski prefers an Elamite interpretation for this name: na-pi-ir-^{d}a-zu, for which see now also MVN 15 244(SI 303277): 20, but MVN 15 274(Auburn 16): 3 and again MVN 15 287(Auburn 28): 5 where he occurs without a-zu, suggests an Akkadian interpretation with occupational designation, a-zu, "physician."

42 On names with E.ER, see MVN 11, pp. 12-13 sub comments to no. 141 and Hallo, (1981) 69-70. Names with this spelling so far attested are: E.ER-^{d}addad (MVN 11 141: 12); E.ER-be-lí (YBC 16650: 7 = Hallo [1981] 75); E.ER-^{d}en-líl-lá (NRVN 1 135: 4 and seal). See also my related remarks in Zevit (1995) 578 comments to line 12.

43 The ba-n[a- signs are clearly indicated in both my and Michalowski's copies, but they are not indicated in Michalowski's transliteration.

44 The space indicated in the copy is insufficient for the reconstructed three signs. Collation of the text is required. See my copy in MVN 11 183 for a different perspective.

(10) 1 sila$_4$ gù-dé-a énsi (11) 1 sila$_4$ ib-ni-^{d}addad (12) 1 sila$_4$ šà-bi (13) [1] sila$_4$ ^{d}šára-kam énsi (14) [1]3 udu-lullum$_x$(LÚ.ÙLU-um) (rev. 15) 30 máš-[ga]l1[ú-šimaški(SU)] (16) udu ṣe-lu-uš-^{d}[da]-gan-ta (17) 20 udu (18) udu ur-^{d}nin-šubur-ta (19) 20 udu (20) udu ḫa-ši-pá-tal-ta (21) 30 udu (22) udu ur-^{d}iškur [é]nsi-ḫa-ma-zé^{ki}-ta (23) gìri a-da-làl lú-kaš$_4$ (24) u$_4$-10-kam (25) mu-DU (26) ab-ba-sa$_6$-ga ì-dab$_5$ (27) iti ki-síg-^{d}nin-a-zu (28) mu en-unu$_6$-gal-^{d}inanna ba-ḫun (side 29) 128 (AS 5/iv/10)

Sigrist, AUCT 1 132

(1) 1 sila$_4$ ^{d}en-líl (2) 1 sila$_4$ ^{d}nin-líl (3) mu-DU ur-^{d}tìlla sanga (4) 1 sila$_4$ ^{d}nin-urta (5) mu-DU énsi-nibru^{ki} (6) ri-iṣ-ilum rá-gaba / maškim (7) u$_4$-24-kam (8) ki an-na-sa$_6$-ga-/ta ba-zi (9) iti u$_5$-bí-kú (10) mu-ús-sa gu-za-/^{d}en-líl-lá ba-dím (11) 3 (AS 4/iii/24)

Sigrist, AUCT 1 743

(1) 12 gu$_4$ (2) érin-pu-ut-tu-li-um^{ki} (3) u$_4$-4-kam (4) 29 gu$_4$ (5) érin-sa-bu-um^{ki} (6) u$_4$-9-kam (rev. 7) mu-DU (8) ki na-sa$_6$-ta (9) ^{d}en-líl-lá ì-dab$_5$ (10) iti ezem-maḫ (11) mu ḫa-ar-ši^{ki} ù ki-maš^{ki} ba-ḫul (Š 47/ix/9)

Sigrist, AUCT 2 238

(1) 4 udu da-da gala (2) u-tá-mi-šar-ra-am maškim (3) 2 amar-mašda-nita (4) ^{d}da-gan muḫaldim-nin-šè (5) ri-iṣ-ilum rá-gaba maškim (rev. 6) šà mu-DU-ra-ta (7) u$_4$-10-lá-1-kam (8) ki lugal-amar-kù-ta (9) ba-zi (10) iti šeš-da-kú (11) mu en-nun-e ^{d}amar-^{d}suen-ra-ki-ága-en-eridu^{ki} ba-ḫun (side 12) 6 (AS 8/ii/9)

Sigrist, AUCT 2 281

(1) 10 anše-BAR+AN-níta (2) 4 anše-BAR+AN-munus (3) ki lugal-pa-è énsi-i-šim-^{d}šul-gi-ra-ta (4) mu-DU (rev. 5) na-ra-am-ì-lí ì-dab$_5$ (6) úga(A.KA) na-sa$_6$-ka ba-a-gá-ar (7) iti šu-eš-ša (8) mu ḫa-ar-ši^{ki} (9) ḫu-mur-ti^{ki} ù ma-da-bi u$_4$-1-a ba-ḫul (Š 48/viii/-)

Sigrist, AUCT 3 253, env.

(1) 2 gu$_4$-niga 20 udu kù-^{d}šára énsi- (2) i-šim-^{d}šul-gi^{ki} (3) 1 gu$_4$-niga 10 udu ^{d}nisaba-an-dùl šabra (4) šu lá-a (5) kìšib nu-tuku (6) [inim-^{d}šára-kam-t]a (7) [ki ab-ba-sa$_6$-ga]-ta (8) ba-zi (rev. 9) kìšib lú-bi-ne (10) ^{d}šára-

kam-e (11) túmu-dam (12) iti ezem-^{d}šul-gi (13) mu en-^{d}nanna ba-ḫun (AS 9/vii/30)

Sigrist, AUCT 3 254, tab.

(1) 2 gu$_{4}$-niga 20 udu (2) kù-^{d}šára énsi-i-šim-^{d}šul-gi^{ki} (3) 1 gu$_{4}$-niga 10 udu ^{d}nisaba-an-dùl šabra (4) šu lá-a (l.e. 5) kìšib nu-tuku (rev. 6) inim-^{d}šára-kam-ta (7) ki ab-ba-sa$_{6}$-ga-ta ba-zi (8) kìšib lú-bi-ne (9) ^{d}šára-kam-e (10) túmu-dam (11) iti ezem-^{d}šul-gi (12) mu en-^{d}nanna ba-ḫun (AS 9/vii/30)

Sigrist, TPTS 1 81

(1) 1 sila$_{4}$ mu-DU ur-^{d}en/-gal-du-du (2) 1 sila$_{4}$ mu-DU a-da-tum (3) 1 sila$_{4}$ mu-DU ḫu-un-/^{d}šul-gi (4) 1 sila$_{4}$ mu-DU ur-sa$_{6}$-/sa$_{6}$-ga (5) 1 sila$_{4}$ mu-DU ^{d}šul-gi-/^{d}lama-mu kuš$_{7}$ (6) 1 sila$_{4}$ mu-DU lú-maḫ-^{d}šára (7) 1 sila$_{4}$ mu-DU á-da-a (8) 1 u$_{8}$-niga 1 ^{mí}áš-gar-niga 1 sila$_{4}$ (9) mu-DU i-ti-ib-/si-na-at (10) a-bí-sí-im-ti (11) ri-iṣ-ilum rá-gaba maškim (12) 1 sila$_{4}$ mu-DU za-zi (13) 1 sila$_{4}$ mu-DU lú-kù-zu (14) é-uz-ga (15) ur-^{d}ba-ba$_{6}$ maškim (16) u$_{4}$-26-kam (17) ki an-na-sa$_{6}$-ga-ta ba-/zi (18) iti ezem-maḫ (19) mu en-maḫ-gal-an-na / en-^{d}nanna na-ḫun (AS 4/ix/26)

Sollberger (1956) 22, no. 11

(1) 2 ḫar kù-babbar 8 gín-ta (2) nu-ḫi-ilum sukkal a-bí-sí-im-ti (3) ri-iṣ-ilum maškim[45] (4) 2 ḫar kù-babbar 8 gín-ta (5) 1 dalla kù-babbar (6) dumu-munus lugal-an-na-ab-tum dam šar-ru-um-ì-lí nu-bànda lú-šušina^{ki}-ka (7) ši$_{x}$(SIG$_{4}$)-te-lá-ni maškim (rev. 8) u$_{4}$ ba-ná-ša-a (9) 1 GAL zabar (10) a-ḫa-an-si-bu ^{giš}pan? (11) in-ba (12) [?] maškim (13) ki lú-dingir-ra-ta (14) ba-zi (15) šà puzur$_{4}$-iš^{iš}-^{d}da-gan (16) iti u$_{5}$-bí^{mušen}-kú (17) mu ša-aš-ru^{ki} ba-ḫul (side 18) 6 (AS 6/iii/-)

45 Contra Michalowski (1978) 7, where he notes that "he occurs, without title in connection with a messenger (sukkal) of Abi-simti." Perhaps he meant without the title "courier" (rá-gaba) as opposed to "maškim-official."

Steinkeller (1980) 1-2, A 4723, see above CTU 1 316.

Watson, BCT 1 4[46]

(1) 8 áb 15 gu_4 (2) érin-ḫa-bu-ra^{ki} (3) 4 áb 2 [g]u_4 (4) ḫi-l[i-i]š lú-RI-$mu\check{s}^{ki}$ (5) 1 gu_4 1 udu (6) [da]m ri-ma-nu-um mar-tu (rev. 7) 1 áb 1 gu_4 (8) érin-ni-nú-a^{ki} (9) 1 gu_4 érin-ú-r[a?]-e^{ki} {or ú-UR[U×A]-e^{ki}; Waetzoldt, ú-[sar]-e^{ki}]} (10) mu-DU (11) u_4-18-kam (12) iti u_5-bí-kú (13) mu ús-sa má-dàra-abzu ba-ab-du_8 (side 14) 33 gu_4 áb-ḫi-a 1 udu (ŠS 3/iii/18)

APPENDIX III
Riṣ-ilum Dossier

AUCT 1 132.
AUCT 2 238.
BIN 3 81.
BIN 3 482.
CTMMA 1 17.
CTU 1 150.
CTU 1 316 = Steinkeller (1980) 1-2, A 4723.
DV 5 461.
Gomi (1980) 46, no. 28.
Gomi (1990) 297.
Michalowski (1978) 13, no. 8 = MVN 11 183.
MVN 1 95.
MVN 3 232.
MVN 8 108.
MVN 11 180.
MVN 11 183 = Michalowski (1978) 13, no. 8.
MVN 15 129.
MVN 15 131.
Owen (1981) 63-68, NMW 303276.
PDT 1 548.
SCT 24.
Steinkeller (1980) 1-2, A 4723 = CTU 1 316.
TPTS 1 81.
UET 3 1654.

46 For comments to this text, see Owen (1988) 113a.

Bibliography

Astour, M. (1987) Semites and Hurrians in Northern Transtigris. *SCCNH* 2: 3-68. **Calvot, D., and G. Pettinato, *et al.*** *(1979) Textes économiques du Sellus-Dagan du Musée du Louvre et du College de France / Testi economici dell'Iraq Musseum Baghdad.* MVN 8. Rome. **Chavalas, M., and J. Hayes**, eds. (1992) *New Horizons in the Study of Ancient Syria.* Bibliotheca Mesopotamica 25. Malibu, Calif. **Contenau, G.** (1915) *Contribution à l'histoire économique d'Umma.* Bibliothèque de l'École des Hautes Études 219. Paris. **Delaporte, L.** (1911) Tablettes de Drehem. *Revue d'Assyriologie et d'Archeologie Orientale* 8: 183-98. **Dhorme, E.** (1912) Tablettes de Drehem à Je'rusalem. *Revue d'Assyriologie et d'Archéologie Orientale* 9: 39-63. **Edzard, D. O., and G. Farber** (1974) *Die Orts- und Gewässernamen der Zeit der 3. Dynastie von Ur.* RGTC 2. Wiesbaden. **Eichler, B., *et al.***, eds. (1976*) Kramer Anniversary Volume.* AOAT 25, 435-50. Neukirchen-Vluyn. **Foxvog, D.** (1985) Sumerian Brands and Branding-Irons, *Zeitschrift für Assyriologie* 85. **Gelb, I. J.** (1944) *Hurrians and Subarians.* Studies in Ancient Oriental Civilization 22. Chicago. (1956) New Light on Hurrians and Subarians. *Studi orientalistici in onore di Giorgio Levi della Vida* 1: 378-92. **Genouillac, H. de** (1911a) *La trouvaille de Drehem.* Paris. (1911b) *Tablettes de Dréhem publiées avec inventaire et tables.* TCL 2. Paris. (1924) Choix de textes économiques de la collection Pupil. *Babyloniaca* 8: 37-40. **Goetze, A.** (1953) Hulibar of Duddul. *Journal of Near Eastern Studies* 12: 114-23. (1963) Šakkanakkus of the Ur III Empire. *Journal of Cuneiform Studies* 17: 1-31. **Gomi, T.**, *et al.* (1980) Administrative Texts of the Third Dynasty of Ur in the Merseyside County Museums, *Orient* 16: 1-110. (1990) *Neo-Sumerian Administrative Texts of the Hirose Collection.* Potomac, Md. **Gordon, C. H.** (1952) *Smith College Tablets: 110 Cuneiform Texts Selected from the College Collection.* Smith College Studies in History 38. Northampton. **Greengus, S.** (1990) *Bridewealth in Sumerian Sources.* Hebrew Union College Annual 61: 25-88. **Hallo, W. W.** (1981) Appendix to David Owen: Tax Payments from Some City Elders in the Northeast. *Acta Sumerologica* 3: 69-76. **Harris, R.** (1955) The Archive of the Sin Temple in Khafajah (Tutub). *Journal of Cuneiform Studies* 9: 31-88. **Hilgert, M.** (1997) *Cuneiform Texts from the Ur III Period in the Oriental Institute, Volume 1: Drehem Administrative Documents from the Reign of Shulgi* (Oriental Institute Publications 115). Chicago: Oriental Institute. (forth.) *Cuneiform Texts from the Ur III Period in the Oriental Institute, Volume 2: Drehem Administrative Documents from the Reign of Amar-Suena* (Oriental Institute Publications). Chicago: Oriental Institute. **Jones, T., and J. W. Snyder** (1961) *Sumerian Economic Texts from the Third Ur Dynasty.* Minneapolis. **Kang, S. T.** (1972) *Sumerian Economic Texts from the Drehem Archive, Sumerian and Akkadian Cuneiform Texts in the Collection of the World Heritage Museum of the University of Illinois*, Vol. 1. Urbana. **King, L. W.** (1932) Cuneiform Texts from Babylonian Tablets in the British Museum, Part 32. London. **Legrain, L.** (1937/47) *Business Documents of the Third Dynasty of Ur.* Ur Excavation. Texts 3. London. **Levine, L.** (1972-75) Harhar. *Reallexikon der Assyriologie.* 4: 120-21 **Limet, H.** (1968) *L'Anthroponymie Sumerienne dans les documents de la 3*[e] *dynastie d'Ur.* Paris. **Michalowski, P.** (1978) The Neo-Sumerian Ring

Texts. *Syro-Mesopotamian Studies* 2: 43-58. **Nesbit, W. N.** (1914) *Sumerian Records from Drehem.* Columbia University Oriental Series 8. New York. **Nikol'skij, M. V.** (1915) *Dokumenty chozjajstvennoj otčetnosti drevnej Chaldei iz sobranija N.P. Lichačeva Čast' II: Ėpocha dinastii Agade i ėpocha dinastii Ura. Drevnosti Vostočnyja* 5. Moscow. **Owen, D. I.** (1975) *The John Frederick Lewis Collection Texts from the Third Millennium in the Free Library of Philadelphia.* Materiali per il Vocabolario Neosumerico, Vol. 3. Rome. (1979) A Thirteen Month Summary Account from Ur. In Sack *et al.* 1979: 57-70. (1981a) Review of RGTC 2. *Journal of Cuneiform Studies* 33: 244-69. (1981b) Tax Payments from Some City Elders in the Northeast. *Acta Sumerologica* 3: 63-68. (1982) *Selected Ur III Texts from the Harvard Semitic Museum.* Materiali per il Vocabolario Neosumerico, Vol. 11. Rome. (1988) Random Notes on a Recent Ur III Volume. *Journal of the American Oriental Society* 108: 111-22. SEE P. 5. (1991) *Neo-Sumerian Texts from American Collections.* Materiali per il Vocabolario Neosumerico, Vol. 15. Rome. (1992) Syrians in Sumerian Sources from the Ur III Period, 107-76. In Chavalas and Hayes, eds. (1995) Pasūri-Dagan and Ini-Teššup's Mother. In Zevit 1995: 573-83. **Purves, P. M.** (1943) Elements Other than Akkadian and Sumerian. *Nuzi Personal Names*: 183-280. **Rainey, A. F.**, ed. (1993) *kinattutu ša darāti: Raphael Kutscher Memorial Volume.* Tel Aviv University Institute of Archaeology Occasional Publications 1, 219-45. Tel Aviv. **Röllig, W.** (1976–80) Kakkulātum, Kar-Kakkulāti(m). *Reallexikon der Assyriologie.* 5: 288-89. **Sack, R., *et al.***, eds. (1979) *Studies in Honor of Tom B. Jones.* AOAT 203. Neukirchen-Vluyn. **Sigrist, M.** (1984) *Neo-Sumerian Account Texts in the Horn Archaeological Museum.* AUCT 1. (1988a) *Neo-Sumerian Account Texts in the Horn Archaeological Museum.* AUCT 2. (1988b) *Neo-Sumerian Account Texts in the Horn Archaeological Museum.* AUCT 3. (1990) *Tablettes du Princeton Theological Seminary Époque d'Ur III.* Philadelphia. (1992) *Drehem.* Bethesda. **Sollberger, E.** (1956) Selected Texts from American Collections. *Journal of Cuneiform Studies* 10: 203-76. (1976) Legal Documents of the Third Dynasty of Ur. In Eichler, *et al.*, 1976: 435-50. **Spar, I.** (1988) *Tablets, Cones, and Bricks of the Third and Second Millennia. Texts in the Metropolitan Museum of Art,* Vol. 1. New York. **Steinkeller, P.** (1980) The Old Akkadian Term of 'Eastener'. *Revue d'Assyriologie et d'Archeologie Orientale* 74: 1-9. **Walker, C.** (1983) Another Babati Inscription. *Journal of Cuneiform Studies* 35: 91-96. **Watson, P. J.** (1986) *Neo-Sumerian Texts from Drehem. Catalogue of Cuneiform Tablets in Birmingham City Museum,* Vol. 1. Warminster. **Whiting, R. M.** (1976) Tiš-atal of Nineveh and Babati, Uncle of Šū-Sîn. *Journal of Cuneiform Studies* 28: 173-82. **Zadok, R.** (1991) Elamite Onomastics. *Studi epigrafici e linguistici sul Vicino Oriente antiqua* 8: 225-37. (1993) Hurrians as well as Individuals Bearing Hurrian and Strange Names in Sumerian Sources. In Rainey 1993: 219-45. Tel Aviv (Originally to have appeared in *Tel Aviv* 18 [1991] according to Zadok 1991: 229 sub F.). (1994) Elamites and Other Peoples from Iran and the Persian Gulf Region in Early Mesopotamian Sources. *Iran* 32: 31-51. **Zevit, Z., *et al.***, eds. (1995) *Solving Riddles and Untying Knots: Biblical, Epigraphic, and Semitic Studies in Honor of Jonas C. Greenfield.* Winona Lake, Ind.

The Meaning of EN at Ebla*

Wayne T. Pitard
University of Illinois at Urbana-Champaign

It is a great pleasure for me to dedicate this paper to Professor Astour, whom I greatly admire and whose career has been a model for scholarly emulation. His contributions have been and continue to be made in an extraordinary range of fields, only a few of which would I dare to enter. I want to wish him well in this eightieth year of his life.

Over the past several years I have been studying issues related to the concepts of death and afterlife in ancient Syria-Palestine. I first envisioned this project as a limited and short-term one, but it has proved complex enough to lead me into numerous unexpected areas of research that have captured my interest and opened new aspects of the issue to me. Among those unexpected areas, I have found myself delving into the difficult and perilous subject of Eblaic studies, where, among other things, I discovered that my research required an examination of the issue of the meaning of the Sumerogram EN in the Ebla tablets.

At first glance, it might seem that the meaning of EN should have little to do with the issue of the afterlife at Ebla, but in fact, the identity of persons

---

* I wish to thank Drs. Michael Astour and Lorenzo Vigano for making a number of valuable comments and suggestions on a penultimate draft of this paper. The interpretations and any errors still remaining are, of course, my own responsibility.

Abbreviation list: ARET : *Archivi reali di Ebla, Testi* (I = Archi [1985]; III = Archi and Biga [1982]; VII = Archi [1988]; IX = Milano [1990]; XI = Fronzaroli [1993]); MEE: *Materiali Epigrafici di Ebla* (I = Pettinato [1979]; X = Mander [1990]); TM: siglum for Ebla texts.

designated by this term has been a crucial element in the current discussion of the cult of the dead at this site. Tell Mardikh/Ebla has produced a considerable amount of material, both epigraphic and archaeological, that several scholars have interpreted as documenting royal Eblaic funerary practices. The extraordinary archives found in the great Early Bronze IV palace produced a number of tablets that have been interpreted as providing evidence for a complex cult of the deified royal dead at Ebla. Among them are god lists which are said to include references to deified "fathers" and "kings," offering and rations lists which appear to include deceased kings among the beneficiaries, and a ritual tablet listing offerings to what have been identified as ten deified kings of Ebla. Many of these proposed deceased royal ancestors are identified in the tablets by the Sumerogram EN, plural EN-EN.

It would not be surprising to find evidence for a cult of deified royal ancestors at Ebla. After all, similar cults are well attested in Mesopotamia during the second half of the third millennium B.C.E., contemporary with the archive at Ebla.[1] However, the existence of such a cult in Sumer does not ensure the existence of a similar religious phenomenon in northern Syria. Over the past three years I have come to the conclusion that the evidence adduced for a royal funerary cult at Ebla is far more ambiguous than many scholars have supposed, and that the texts do not so clearly imply the existence of such a cult. Surprisingly, the assumption that the word EN in these texts refers exclusively to kings at Ebla is one of the primary foundations of the current reconstruction of the funerary cult at Ebla. Thus a study of the semantic range of this word is quite important. In this paper I would like to look at the texts that bear on this issue.

The most prominent piece of evidence for the worship of deified kings at Ebla is the tablet, *ARET* VII: 150 (TM.75.G.2628), found in the main archive of the palace, Room 2769. It is composed of a list of offerings that were to be made in a ceremony at the city of Daritum.[2] The first set of offer-

1 *Cf.* Hallo (1992b) 387-91.

2 Archi reads the name of the city as *Da-ri-íb* (1986) 214. However, Astour ([1992] 20,

ings described in the tablet (the beginning is broken, but presumably it is a series of sheep offerings) is made to a group of ten deities referred to as DINGIR, followed by a proper name (I: 3-III: 5). The ten names in this series have been identified by A. Archi, the editor of the text, as kings of Ebla, since the group of names is summarized in obv. III: 6 by the term EN-EN, which he renders, "kings." In addition, the first two names on the list are known from other documents to have been those of Eblaite kings.[3] Since each name is preceded by a DINGIR ("god")-sign, Archi concluded that these kings were deceased and deified, and that the tablet thus shows that they received offerings as gods. This section of the tablet is followed by an enumeration of offerings to other deities and concludes after a broken passage, with a reference to "the gods of the cities which reside in Daritum." The text reads as follows:

Obv. I [ ]
[ ]
[k]ab-[d]a-mu
[dingi]r
[I]g-rí-[i]š-LAM
dingir
A-dub-da-mu

II dingir
Kum-Da-mu
dingir
I-sar-Ma-lik
dingir
En-ár-Da-mu
dingir

Rev. I *wa*
^{d}Gu-la-du
1 udu
[r]a-ru$_{12}$
[ ]rí-[í]b^{ki}
[ud]u
$^{[d]}$GA×SIG$_{7}$-ra

II lú da-da(-)EN
[á]š-da
1[ ]
[ ]
[ ]

---

n. 108) has argued forcefully for reading the city name *Da-ri-tum*, rather than *Da-ri-íb*, since the sign read *íb* by Archi normally has the value *tum* in the final position of place-names. This, of course, affects Archi's identification of the town in *ARET* VII: 150 with modern Atareb (Archi [1987] 41). Although it is not significant to the present study, Astour's caveat seems well founded.

3 Archi, Biga and Milano (1988) 215-17.

Ba-Da-mu
dingir

III I-bí-Da-mu
dingir
A-gur-Li-im
dingir
A-bur-Li-im
en-en
2 udu
^{d}NI-da-KUL

IV *wa*
^{d}BE-MÍ
2 udu
^{d}Ra-sa-ap
wa
^{d}A-dam-ma
2 udu
^{d}A-gú

III (broken)
x +1 dingir-dingir-dingir
uru-uru
al$_{6}$-tuš

IV *in*
Da-rí-tum^{ki}

There are problems, however, with Archi's interpretation. The first is the way in which the DINGIR-sign relates to the names of the ENs. The scribes of the Eblaic tablets used the Sumerian technique of surrounding each individual word, or sometimes phrase, with a rectangular case or register. These cases could be as small or as large as necessary to hold the entire word or phrase. When the DINGIR-sign (or any other sign) was used as a determinative for a word, it was written in the same case with the word it determined. This can be seen in the section of *ARET* VII: 150 that lists offerings to known deities (obv. III: 8-rev. I: 7), where the DINGIR-sign, as a determinative, is written in the case with each god name. However, in the list of ENs, the DINGIR is always written in a separate register, never in the one that holds the proper name. This shows that the DINGIR-sign is to be understood as a separate word, not as a determinative for the succeeding name. Thus, dingir *A-dub-Da-mu* must mean "the god of Adub-Damu," rather than "(the god) Adub-Damu."

But exactly who or what is the "god of" a person? Archi recognized that dingir PN must be rendered "the god of PN," but argued that the phrase should be understood as "the deified spirit of the departed.[4] The term "god" in this case would work semantically like the word "ghost" does in English, "the ghost of Jacob Marley." But there is no supporting evidence for such an interpretation of this phrase. Such a meaning cannot be substantiated in any Near Eastern language or culture of which I am aware.[5] I know of no examples in any Near Eastern text where a being called "the god of PN" is clearly shown by context to be the spirit of that person, *i.e.*, PN him/herself, and I am unaware of any other evidence that the term "god" is ever used to mean the "divine essence" of a being. It is never used in that way with known divinities, *i.e.*, "the god (divine essence) of Baal," or "the god (divine essence) of Enlil," *etc.* This interpretation is plausible only if there is other strong evidence that the ENs listed in *ARET* VII: 150 were viewed in Ebla as deities. But without it, there is no obvious reason to interpret this phrase in such an unexpected way.

The most plausible understanding of the phrase is that it designates the personal or patron deity of the one named. The concept of the personal deity was widespread throughout the Near East, and such a god was regularly referred to as "the god of PN" or "my/your/his god." Attestations of these phrases applied to personal gods are found in Sumerian and Akkadian texts, as well as in the Hebrew Bible.[6] In spite of the fact that a few scholars

---

4 Archi (1988) 106-7.

5 This issue is too large to discuss here, but will be addressed in detail in my forthcoming monograph on the concepts of death and afterlife in Syria-Palestine.

6 See conveniently, Vorländer 1975. Note, however, that Vorländer's example from Ugarit (1975) 151, "the gods of Daniel," is a mistake. See also the discussion in Schmidt (1994) 15-27.

The issue of "the god of PN" is a complex one at Ebla. Besides this text, there are a few others that make reference to DINGIR/PN, most notably the recently published ritual texts for the enthronement of the king of Ebla, *ARET* XI, Texts 1 and 2, where a number of offerings are given to such gods as the new royal couple travels through various towns on their way to Binasu, where the enthronement ceremony reaches its climax. These texts deserve extensive treatment that cannot be done here. Suffice it to say that *ARET* XI: 1 and 2 also regularly place the DINGIR in a separate case and that there is no clear indication exactly who the PNs referred to in the texts are. The editor, P. Fronzaroli, has identified all the offerings to the DINGIR PN in these texts as

have argued that the "god of Abraham, the god of Isaac and the god of Jacob," should be understood as referring to the deified spirits of the three patriarchs,[7] it is clear that the Bible always identifies the god of the patriarchs with their patron deity. The absence of evidence supporting the former interpretation, along with the common attestation of the phrase to designate personal gods makes it most reasonable to understand the first part of *ARET* VII: 150 as a list of the patron deities of the ten persons named, each of which was to receive an offering at the Daritum ceremony. This is also compatible with the fact that the summary identification of the ten individuals, EN-EN, is not given a DINGIR-determinative, as we might expect if the ENs themselves had been understood as deities.

We may thus doubt the deified nature of these ENs. But we should also ask if the list is thus describing offerings to the patron deities of the dynasty of Eblaite kings. Is it appropriate to interpret these names as a list of Ebla's rulers? To determine this, we must examine the use of the term EN within the Eblaic corpus. Although there was some initial controversy as to whether EN was ever to be translated as "king,"[8] there can now be no doubt that the ruler of Ebla was regularly designated by the EN-sign in the Ebla tablets.[9] Thus the rendering, "king" is an appropriate translation value for EN. With this in mind, it is plausible to identify the EN-EN in *ARET* VII: 150 as Eblaite kings. However, there is considerable evidence in the tablets that EN also could designate high royal officials other than the king.

---

funerary offerings to deified deceased kings (*ARET* XI: pp. 39-41). An important element of his interpretation centers on the identity of the building at the city of Binasu, where most of these offerings are made. It is called the É *ma-tim*, which Fronzaroli interprets as "mausoleum," literally, "house of death." Such a location would, of course, be quite appropriate for funerary rituals. Vigano (1995) 218 n. 20, however, has pointed out that *ma-tim*, also written *ma-da* and *ma-da-am*$_6$, is better interpreted as the adjective "great, large," and that the enthronement ceremony is better and more appropriately understood to take place in the "Great House/Temple," rather than in the "mausoleum."

7 On this interpretation, see the discussion in Bloch-Smith (1992) 123.

8 See the early and insightful discussion of this issue by Michalowski (1985), esp. 294-97.

9 See Archi (1987) 37-43.

The EN-sign was commonly used in Mesopotamia for the Akkadian *bēlum*, "lord," a word that could be applied to a ruler, but also to any person of high rank. At Ebla, it seems most likely that EN stood for *māliku*,[10] which in West Semitic became the standard word for "king," while in East Semitic it was used to designate a high official, and is usually rendered, "counsellor, advisor." There are indications, however, that *māliku* at Ebla was used with both meanings, somewhat like *bēlum* in Mesopotamia.[11]

The strongest evidence for the use of the term as a designation of high officials of the court comes from several ration lists recording the distribution of food to a number of ENs within the palace administration. Several of these were published in *ARET* IX (see Texts 9, 10, 13, 14, 16, 18, 26, 27 and 32). In all cases, the plural group of ENs (written EN-EN, as in our offering text) are distinguished from the king, who is listed separately as the EN. They also appear in context with the other high officials of the court. For example, in Text 10 (TM.75.G.266) the following recipients of rations are named in order: the EN and the EN-EN; Irak-Damu (a high official, or prince[12]); the queen (*ma-lik-tum*); the elders (ABxAŠ); messengers; the city of Armi (Armi's regular appearance in the food lists suggests that its ruler may have been at Ebla for an extended period of time); Ilzi (an official); the KA.DI official; a person named Raizu and two others, BE-dulum and his guard (obv. I: 1-III: 4).

In Text 19 (TM.75.G.411) rations are provided to the EN (*i.e.*, the king), the queen, the EN-EN, the sons of the EN-EN, Dubuḫu-Hadda (a son of Ibi-zikir), Iptura and Ilzi (two high officials), the EN's son, the EN's daughter, the elders, the "friend" (attendant/assistant?) of the EN-EN of the city Armi, the KA.DI official, the *ašadara* (meaning unknown), the "friend" of Armi, the city of Arḫadu (presumably to the king or a representative of the town),

10 Archi (1987) 37.

11 As far as I know, Michalowski (1985) 279; (1988) 270 was the first to suggest that EN at Ebla probably had a more general meaning of "person in charge," and that the title could be held by various heads of organizations in the city, not just the king.

12 *Cf.* Archi, Biga and Milano (1988) 225.

Ritimu, the "friend" of the EN, BE-dulum and his guard, the nurse and two groups of elders (obv. I: 1-rev. I: 2) In Text 16 (TM.75.G.527) the first set of entries (I: 1-II: 6) lists rations to the EN, the elders, the god Kura and the gods in general (DINGIR-DINGIR-DINGIR). In the second section (obv. II: 7-rev. I: 7), the tablet registers rations for the EN, the EN-EN, the sons of the EN-EN, the elders, the queen, Ilai and Iptura, and Dubuḫu-Ḫadda, *etc.* The EN-EN also appear alongside the king, his family and other high officials as providers of offerings in a text (TM.75.G.1764) listing offerings to the gods made by various persons.[13] Obv. XI: 20-rev. I: 4 records offerings by the EN-EN of 20 sheep to Rasap of the city Atani and 18 sheep to Ada (Haddu). That the latter ENs belong to the palace personnel seems clear, since the entry follows the form used to record the offerings of the rest of the palace officials, while a distinct form is used in the following lines to register offerings from foreign rulers (rev. I: 5-17). In the latter entry, the offering is referred to as a "tax" (šu-du_8-máš).

So who were these EN-EN? There can be little doubt that they were living people, since their rations and their offerings to the gods are recorded in the midst of other clearly live persons and groups who function within the palace. If they were deified ancestors, we would expect to find their rations listed alongside those of the god Kura and "the gods" (DINGIR-DINGIR-DINGIR), who regularly occur in these lists, but usually in a completely separate entry (see, for example, Text 10: obv. IV: 9-V: 3; Text 14: rev. I: 6-II: 4; Text 16: obv. I: 7-II: 2).

Pettinato suggested that the EN-EN of the rations and offering lists were living, former kings of Ebla. He argued that at Ebla, rulers were elected to seven-year terms and that after they retired they continued to receive rations from the palace.[14] However, his evidence for limited terms of kingship at Ebla is extremely dubious.[15]

---

13 Pettinato (1979) 129-45, *esp.* 136-37.

14 Pettinato (1981) 78-80.

15 *Cf.* Michalowski (1985) 295.

Archi, while insisting on the identification of the EN-EN in *ARET* VII: 150 as deceased kings, proposed that the EN-EN in the provisions lists were kings visiting from other towns.[16] The primary evidence for this interpretation consists of six texts that show that kings indeed visited other cities (five in [1987] 43, n. 21; one in Archi, Biga and Milano [1988] 218). But none of these really illuminate the situation here. One text lists a "gift for the EN (probably the king of Ebla) when he came to Abarsil" (TM.75.G.2361 obv. X: 3-9). TM.75.G.10183 rev. II: 2-13 notes the number of garments given to the ENs of Emar and Burman "who came to the feast of Ibi-Zikir at the palace." TM.75.G.1381 mentions the arrival of ZugaLUM, queen of Harran, at the palace,[17] which indicates that queens too travelled on state visits. The fourth will be discussed below, and the last two of the six examples (TM.75.G.1704 and 2443) have proved to be irrelevant, since they record journeys by Ibi-zikir, once thought to be a king of Ebla, but now known to have been a high Eblaite official.[18]

While there can be no doubt that various rulers came to visit the king of Ebla and that the Eblaite king himself travelled to other cities on state visits, it seems unlikely that the common appearance of the unnamed EN-EN and sons of the EN-EN should refer to such visits. The occurrence of the EN-EN in the rations lists suggests that they are long term, regular recipients rather than unusual visitors. In fact, the occasional, important visitors appear to have been specifically named in the rations lists. For example, ambassadors and other high officials are listed by their titles ("the KA.DI-official of Ku-se-ku, the EN of Ḫutimu" [Text 13: obv. IV: 9-V: 1]; "the *ku-li*-official of the ENs of Armi" [Text 19: obv. III: 9-10], "the *ku-li* -official of Armi" [Text 19: obv. IV: 6-7]). And a few city names by themselves appear as recipients in several texts, *e.g.*, Armi (*ARET* IX: Text 9, 10, 13, 14, *etc.*); Ḫutimu (Text 14); Arḫadu (Text 16, 19); Kish and Ibal (Text 26). Since the size of the rations indicates that they were intended for individuals, and

---

16 Archi (1987) 43, n. 21; Archi, Biga and Milano (1988) 218.

17 Archi (1987) 43, n. 21.

18 Archi, Biga, and Milano (1988) 207-21.

since lower officials seem to be designated by their titles, it is reasonable to propose that the rations listed simply under the name of a city were intended for the visiting king. In any event, the listing of so many specific visitors makes it difficult to propose that the term EN-EN also refers to visiting rulers. And it would seem odd to specifically list the lower officials by their title and their home town, while lumping royal visitors into a communal category without even mentioning the cities they ruled.

Archi's final example for his interpretation of the EN-EN as visiting foreign kings[19] comes from a list of disbursements of olive oil (TM.75.G.541, now published as *ARET* IX: 82), from which he quotes obv. I: 1-II: 6:

> [x] sila of fine oil for (the cities) Raak, Burman, Tub, Imar, Lumnanu, Inebuni, Ursa'um, Garmu and Gudadanum. Total: 21 sila of oil: issue for the EN-EN. [x] jars [of oil] for the messengers.

Archi seems to assume that the issuance of oil here must have taken place within the palace at Ebla and that these ENs must therefore have been in residence. I see no evidence for this assumption. In fact, the texts dealing with consignments of oil published in *ARET* IX (Texts 74-84) argue strongly against such a view. Most of these texts register gifts of oil to foreign destinations (Texts 74-78 and 81-84), in several cases (Texts 75-77 and 83-84) referring to the foreign rulers by the collective term EN-EN,[20] as in Text 82. There can be little doubt that these gifts were sent to the cities listed rather than distributed to the rulers in the palace at Ebla. Several of the texts list shipments made to the EN-EN over periods of several months. For example, Text 75 records provisions to the EN-EN for three consecutive months, while 76 does the same for three other months, and 77 for two others. In addition, the disbursement of oil to the nine cities in Text 82 is dated to the month of *ḫur-mu* (January-February–*ARET* IX: 353), while the gifts to the same cities in Text 81 are dated to the month of *Kur*$_6$ (March-April). It is highly unlikely that the kings were required to be in residence at Ebla month after

---

19 Archi, Biga, and Milano (1988) 218.

20 Milano (1990) 241-42 is certainly correct that in texts 75, 76, and 77 the references to the EN-EN refer to the kings of the nine cities listed in full in Texts 74, 81 and 82.

month to receive these gifts. It is much more probable that they were sent to the rulers of these nine cities via messengers, who, at least in Text 82: obv. II: 4′-6′, were given gifts of oil as well.[21]

Although the foreign kings in the oil texts are designated as EN-EN, one cannot equate them with the EN-EN in the bread and drink rations lists. In the oil texts where EN-EN are mentioned, there is no registration of rations for the royal family of Ebla, for the elders, or for any of the other officials who are regularly provided for in the bread and drink rations lists. The oil lists deal almost entirely with external personages, not with people in the palace. The context is thus sufficiently different to distinguish the EN-EN of Ebla from the foreign EN-EN of the oil texts.[22]

Ebla is not the only city that has multiple contemporary ENs attested in the tablets. The city of Azu is said to have two ENs, as is the city of Manuwat; tablets list at least four contemporary officials of Ibal called ENs, and the cities of Armi and Dugurasu are listed as having EN-EN, all clearly alive.[23] At the same time, an individual ruler of any of these cities could be referred to alone as EN of that city. See, for example, *ARET* I: 12: obv. II: 4-6, "Atian,

---

21 Pettinato (1981) 161 identifies the shipment of fine oil in IX: 74 (TM.75.G.217) as evidence of exportation of olive oil. But Astour (1992) 57 is certainly correct that the amounts shipped in these consignments show that they were gifts, not commerce. *Cf.* also Astour's discussions of the political and religious significance of gifts of oil in the Ebla tablets (1988) 149, n. 69; (1992) 31.

22 In addition, virtually all these cities are listed in *ARET* I: 1-9, texts detailing shipments of textiles to the kings of numerous cities and their elders and other high officials. It is not likely that these people were all required to be present at Ebla to receive these goods. Oil, along with garments and other items, was easily transportable and there is no reason to assume, as Archi does, that the kings in *ARET* IX: 82 were visitors at Ebla when the oil was granted to them (*cf.* Astour [1992] 57-58).

23 Archi (1987) 42· From Archi (1987) 42, see TM.75.G.411, obv. III: 8-10, "1 ration of bread for the ambassadors (*ku-li*) of the EN-EN of the city Armi"; TM.75.G.10188, obv. VII: 9-13, which refers to gifts given to the EN-EN of Armi; TM.75.G.10182, obv. XXI: 19-23: "2 ingots to the two ENs of Azu, at Riḫati"; TM.75.G.1701, obv. I: 2-10, which lists clothing for Iga-Lim, Enbuš-Damu, Irpeš-Lim and KA-gadu, "four ENs of the city Ibal," while TM.75.G.10077, rev. XIII: 3-8 lists the following ENs from Ibal: Dubuš-Damu, Iga-Lim, KA-gadu, and Ilum-ariḫu. In addition, numerous tablets refer to the two ENs of the city of Manuwat (see the list in Archi [1987] 42).

EN of Ebal"; *ARET* I: 11: obv. VIII: 8-10: Enna-Damu, EN of Manuwat"; *ARET* I: 10: obv. VIII: 4-6: "a gift for the EN of Dugurasu." Thus, references to both an EN and to EN-EN at Ebla are not at all unique.

ARET IX: 17 (TM.75.G.570), in fact, may refer to a high official other than the king as an EN. This text is a rations list that also includes the records of some offerings to various gods, among them an offering to the dingir EN é-siki. This phrase is ambiguous and may be translated either as "the (patron) god of the EN of the House of Wool" or "the (patron) god of the EN, at the House of Wool." The House of Wool was a major royal storehouse,[24] and if the former translation of the passage is correct, this EN presumably would have been the official in charge of it.

Actually, EN was not the only Sumerian ideogram for a high office at Ebla that was used with some elasticity. Archi has pointed out that Iga-Lim, a person listed as an EN of the city Ibal, is also referred to as an ugula, "overseer" in other tablets.[25] Astour notes a similar fluidity with the designations lugal, "governor," and ugula, "overseer,"[26] in texts mentioning a certain Ennail, sometimes with the title lugal igi-nita-igi-nita, "governor of the bulls(?)," and sometimes with ugula igi-nita, "overseer of the bulls(?)." The scribal practice of using the Sumerogram EN both for "king" (either domestic or foreign) and for "person(s) in charge," like *bēlum* in Akkadian, is quite reasonable and would not likely have caused any confusion among the scribes charged with keeping the records.

The most natural interpretation, then, is to see the term EN-EN in the ration lists as a general designation of certain high officials within the palace administration, provided with food and drink from the palace stores along with all the other important personages in the palace, and responsible, like the rest, for making offerings to the gods. This means that the EN-EN of *ARET* VII: 150 need not necessarily be identified as deceased kings at all, but may have been prominent officials of Ebla or the surrounding towns,

---

24 See *ARET* I: 281-82; Astour (1992) 53.

25 Archi (1987) 42-43.

26 Astour (1988) 150-51.

who took part in a ceremony at the city of Daritum, which involved making sacrifices to their own patron deities, as well as to the gods of Daritum.

There is further evidence that needs to be considered. One major argument used to support the identification of the ten as kings of Ebla is the appearance of these names, in the same order, on what appears to be a school exercise tablet (TM.74.G.120), which lists over sixty other names as well.[27] The ten are preceded by one name and are followed by eleven others that some scholars have identified as a continuation of the king list. If this identification were correct, the tablet, then, would provide the names of 22 Eblaic kings. In addition, it has been suggested that the next five to thirteen names, which seem to be those of cities and towns, could actually belong to the list as eponymous ancestors of the Eblaic dynasty. [28]

However, there are some caveats that must be considered when interpreting TM.74.G.120. As mentioned above, the tablet is generally believed to be a school exercise text. Following the thirty-five names mentioned above, the text shifts gears and begins to list personal names arranged according to their first element, *i.e.*, ten names beginning with *du-bí*, followed by five names beginning with *du-bù-ḫu*, *etc.* (obv. V: 3ff.). This type of school exercise is well attested in Sumer,[29] and it indicates that the latter part of the tablet came from a different source than the earlier section. Once this is recognized, it becomes clear that we cannot tell whether the first columns were compiled from one or several sources. There is no way to determine whether the names that follow the attested ENs are a continuation of that list, or whether they came from an entirely different source. The same may be said of the set of apparent city names. The student scribe may simply have copied names from various available tablets in the archive, moving from one to the next as he exhausted each, before finally making use of the more traditional list of names that begins in obv. V. It thus seems inappropriate to identify all these persons as former rulers of Ebla without additional evidence.

---

27 Archi, Biga, and Milano (1988) 212-15.

28 See Biga and Pomponio (1987); Astour (1992) 20-24; Hallo (1992a) 142-43.

29 *Cf.* Pettinato (1981) 43-44.

Nonetheless, we still have ten persons identified as ENs who appear on two tablets found in different rooms of the palace. This seems to suggest that the names and their order were a relatively fixed set.[30] Might this not argue in favor of interpreting them as the dynasty of Ebla? Unfortunately, not very strongly. The Ebla tablets contain lists of numerous groups of people, both members of the royal family and others, that are repeated with little or no variation from tablet to tablet. For example, several lists of the sons of the EN are virtual duplicates,[31] and the names of chief singers of the royal court found in three different tablets (*ARET* I: 6 and 8 and *ARET* III: 457) have sections that are identical in order.[32] So the appearance of the ten names in two documents does not illuminate the meaning of the term EN and neither proves nor disproves the thesis that they belong to a king list.

On the other hand, there are some indications that the people listed on the tablet were contemporary with one another, rather than successors to an office. Several tablets mention Igriš-Ḫalam and Irqab-Damu together in contexts that indicate that they were high officials and colleagues in the royal court before either became king.[33] They received garments from the

---

30 It is possible, of course, that *ARET* VII: 150 was actually the source tablet used by the student who wrote TM 74.G.120.

31 See Archi, Biga, and Milano (1988) 231-32. Note that the lists 26, 27 and 28 show a high degree of duplication, as do lists 33 and 34, and 36, 37, and 39.

32 Archi, Biga, and Milano (1988) 279, lists 3, 4, and 5.

33 Archi, Biga, and Milano (1988) 216. Biga and Pomponio (1990) 179-86 have argued that the references to Igriš-Ḫalam and Irkab-Damu together occur only in texts datable to a period after they had both died, and that the provisions given to them in the texts are actually funerary offerings. Their arguments are not compelling. First, the entries referring to these two officials are in no way distinct from the entries describing clothing provisions to anyone else in the texts, and it is quite clear that the others were alive. Secondly, their conclusions are based on their ability to date two of the tablets which refer to Igriš-Ḫalam and Irkab-Damu to the period of the last king of Ebla, some years after the deaths of the two kings. To do this, they attempt to show that *ARET* IV: 19 and the as-yet unpublished TM.75.G.1335, both of which list provisions for the two, were written in the same year as TM.75.G.1860 (now published as *MEE* X: 20), which they date to the early part of the reign of Išar-Damu, whom they identify as the archive's final king. The evidence they put forward for relating *ARET* IV: 19 to TM.75.G.1860 is the fact that each contains an entry in which a similar (but

palace along with others, often in contexts that link them with the high official Ebrium, once thought to have been a king of Ebla. In addition, *MEE* I: 1724, a registration of receipts of gold and silver from various governors,[34] lists the following contributions: "4869 minas of silver in ingots, 39 minas of gold in 20 ingots from Kum-Damu and Igriš-Ḫalam." These names are numbers 2 and 4 on the list, and the context clearly indicates that neither is king of Ebla, but that they are high officials working together.[35] This tablet

far from identical) provision of items is given to Giminizatu, the sister of the queen of Ebla (Biga and Pomponio [1990] 183-85). Biga and Pomponio believe that the two entries refer to the same provision because they both mention that the offerings are *si-in* É×PAP, which they interpret as meaning, "for the funeral" of Giminizatu. However, Baldacci, in his study of the term É×PAP (1991), has shown that it has nothing to do with funerary contexts, but is an administrative term for some kind of allotment. Therefore, there is no reason to assume that the two provisions date to the same year. Similarly, the parallel they find between TM.75.G.1860 and TM.75.G.1335 is another pair of allotments, not identical, this time to Ayagidu, a daughter of the EN, and also *si-in* É×PAP. But again there is no reason to insist that the two entries are describing the same allotment.

Examination of the names of recipients found in TM.G.75.1860 and *ARET* IV: 19, also fails to support the contemporaneousness of the tablets. Of the 66 names in *ARET* IV: 19 (the smaller text), only seven of them are found in TM.75.G.1860, including Ibrium and Ibi-zikir. One of them is the high official, Aya-Damu, whose representative at Ebla in *ARET* IV: 19 section 29 is a certain Dubi-zikir, while in TM.75.G.1860 obv. 19: 3-4, it is one Ingar. One may also note that while Ibi-zikir plays a very small role in *ARET* IV: 19 (in fact, he doesn't receive rations in this list), he is clearly at the height of his power in TM.75.G.1860, in which he receives numerous provisions (obv. 6: 20, 8: 3; 9: 19; 10: 16; 15: 4; 20: 23; rev. 9: 15; 11: 24; 18: 18).

Thus there is no valid reason to argue that Igriš-Ḫalam and Irkab-Damu are deceased kings receiving funerary offerings of clothing in either *ARET* IV: 19 or TM.75.G.1335, or in the several other texts in which they are mentioned together (see Archi, Biga, Milano [1988] 216).

34 Pettinato (1991) 66-67, 244.

35 Biga and Pomponio (1990) 196 propose that the accounting of gold and silver from these two might be "a considerable left-over from the accounting of two previous reigns." But there is no evidence for such an interpretation. The listing of the contribution of Kum-Damu and Igriš-Ḫalam is no different from that of Ibrium or Gigi, the other two officials named on the list, both of whom are assumed to be alive. Kum-Damu also appears in a fragmentary list of garment rations as a recipient in

is also contemporary with Ebrium, who is recorded here as contributing some silver. In *ARET* I: 11, a provision list of garments and other items distributed to various officials, many located in nearby towns, an Adub-Damu of Irar, a town very closely linked with Ebla, is listed (obv. IX: 6),[36] the name paralleling #3 on the "king" list. This text is also contemporary with Ebrium. Another text from the time of Ebrium, *ARET* III: 465, lists an Ibi-Damu (number 8 on the list) among the officials receiving clothing. An Enar-Damu (#6) is mentioned as recipient of a mina of gold in *MEE* X: 4 obv. IX: 5-10, a text which, in the previous column (obv. VIII: 6-11), also records an allotment of gold for Irkab-Damu (#1), thus indicating that these two were contemporaries.[37] An Išar-Malik (#5) is mentioned in several distribution lists (*ARET* III: 70: II: 1-2; 320: II: 4; 386: II: 3; 458: rev. VI: 1; 468: obv. III: 18; 470: obv. III: 4; and 826: I: 4). In *ARET* III: 70, he is identified as a nar-maḫ, a "chief singer," an important religious position. In 386, he appears in a context in which the queen is mentioned in the previous, fragmentary column. This also indicates his high status.

It is, of course, possible that these high officials simply had names identical to those of the earlier kings. But it is striking that people with the names of seven of the ten ENs on the "king" list can be shown to have been contemporary high officials receiving rations from the Eblaite palace. Unfortunately, *ARET* VII: 150 is not specifically dated, but it is certainly not unreasonable to suggest that it is likely to belong to the period of Ebrium as well.

To summarize, then. There is substantial evidence that the term EN was not used exclusively to designate the king. It also referred to other high offi-

---

ARET III: 334: obv. III: 6. Here, too, there is no hint of his being the king.

36 Irar, whose location is not yet ascertained, appears often in the Ebla texts. The king of Irar sent special gifts to the king of Ebla at his anointing (Pettinato [1991] 107), and appears to have had close relations (*cf.* Pettinato [1991] 151).

37 Mander, in *MEE* X: 31, renders the section concerning Irkab-Damu as follows: "Total: 7 gold minas and 30 shekels, expense on occasion of the end of Irkab-Damu's destiny." If his rendering of the latter part is correct (*ši-mi* TIL-*su* is obscure), then it suggests that Irkab-Damu has died and that Enar-Damu therefore outlived the former!

cials in the Eblaic court (as well as in the courts of other cities), who, along with their families, received regular rations from the king. The lists of dignitaries in *ARET* VII: 150 and TM.74.G.120 need not be identified as kings, but are more likely to have been contemporary officials who, in the case of *ARET* VII: 150, took part in the ceremonies described in the tablet. Other published documents, in fact, show that seven of the ten persons in the *ARET* VII list were likely contemporaries. Even the two persons generally identified as kings of Ebla, Igriš-Ḫalam and Irqab-Damu, are known to have been linked together when both were high officials in the administration. All other references to these two together date to the time before either was king. This text too perhaps belongs to the period before their reigns, rather than after. So *ARET* VII: 150 may be reasonably interpreted as beginning with a list of offerings to the personal deities of ten high officials (primarily Eblaite) who took part in the ceremony for which this tablet was designed to prepare. It does not provide any evidence for the deification or cult of deceased kings at Ebla, nor can it easily be used to establish the succession of Eblaic kings.

Bibliography

Arbeitman, Y. L., ed. (1988) *Fucus: A Semitic/Afrasian Gathering in Remembrance of Albert Ehrman.* Amsterdam/Philadelphia. **Archi, A.** (1985) *Testi Amministrativi: Assegnazioni di Tessuti (Archivio L. 2769).* Archivi Reali di Ebla, Testi I. Rome. (1986) Die Ersten zehn Könige von Ebla. *Zeitschrift für Assyriologie* 76: 213-17. (1987) Les titre de *EN* et *LUGAL* à Ebla et des cadeaux pour le roi de Kish. *Mari, Annales de Recherches Interdisciplinaires* 5: 37-52. (1988a) *Testi Amministrativi: Registrazioni di metalli e tessuti (L. 2769).* Archivi Reali di Ebla, Testi VII. Rome. (1988b) Cult of the Ancestors and Tutelary God at Ebla. In Arbeitman 1988: 103-12. **Archi, A., and M. G. Biga** (1982) *Testi Amministrativi di vario contenuto (Archivio L. 2769: TM.75.G.3000-4101).* Archivi Reali di Ebla, Testi III. Rome. **Archi, A., M. G. Biga, and L. Milano** (1988) Studies in Eblaite Prosopography. In *Eblaite Personal Names and Semitic Name-Giving.* Archivi Reali di Ebla, Studi I, 205-306. Rome. **Astour, M.** (1988) The Geographical and Political Structure of the Ebla Empire. In Waetzoldt and Hauptmann 1988: 138-58. (1992) An Outline of the History of Ebla (Part 1). In Gordon and Rendsburg 1992: 3-82. **Baldacci, M.** (1991) ExPAP and the Eblaite Administrative Terminology. *Welt des Orients* 22: 10-20. **Biga, M. G. and F. Pomponio**

(1987) Iš'ar-Damu, roi d'Ebla. *Nouvelles Assyriologiques Brèves et Utilitaires* No. 4: 60-61. (1990) Elements for a Chronological Division of the Administrative Documentation of Ebla. *Journal of Cuneiform Studies* 42: 179-201. **Bloch-Smith, E.** (1992) *Judahite Burial Practices and Beliefs About the Dead.* Journal for the Study of the Old Testament Supplement Series 123. Sheffield, UK. **Fishbane, M., and E. Tov**, eds. (1992) *Sha'arei Talmon: Studies in the Bible, Qumran, and the Ancient Near East Presented to Shemaryahu Talmon.* Winona Lake, Ind. **Gordon, C. H., and G. A. Rendsburg**, eds. (1992) *Eblaitica: Essays on the Ebla Archives and Eblaite Language,* Vol. 3. Winona Lake, Ind. **Hallo, W. W.** (1992a) Ebrium at Ebla. In Gordon and Rendsburg 1992: 139-50. (1992b) Royal Ancestor Worship in the Biblical World. In Fishbane and Tov 1992: 381-401. **Franzaroli, P.** (1993) *Testi rituali della regalita (Archivio L. 2769).* Archivi Reali di Ebla, Testi XI. Rome. **Mander, P.** (1990) *Administrative Texts of the Archive L. 2769.* Materiali epigrafici di Ebla 10. Rome. **Michalowski, P.** (1985) Third Millennium Contacts: Observations on the Relationships Between Mari and Ebla. *Journal of the American Oriental Society* 105: 293-302. **Milano, L.** (1990) *Testi amministrativi: Assegnazioni de prodotti alimantari (Archivio l.2712–Parte I).* Archivi Reali di Ebla, Testi IX. Rome. **Pettinato, G.** (1979) *Catalogo dei testi cuneiformi di Tell Mardikh-Ebla.* Materiali epigrafici di Ebla 1. Naples. (1981) *The Archives of Ebla: An Empire Inscribed in Clay.* Garden City, N.J. (1991) *Ebla: A New Look at History.* Trans. from the Italian by C. Faith Richardson. Baltimore. **Schmidt, B.** (1994) *Israel's Beneficent Dead: Ancestor Cult and Necromancy in Ancient Israelite Religion and Tradition.* Tübingen. **Vigano, L.** (1995) Rituals at Ebla. *Journal of Near Eastern Studies* 54: 215-22. **Vorländer, H.** (1975) *Mein Gott: Die Vorstellungen vom persönlichen Gott im Altern Orient und im Alten Testament.* Alter Orient und Altes Testament 23. Kevelaer. **Waetzoldt, H., and H. Hauptmann**, eds. (1988) *Wirtschaft und Gesellschaft von Ebla.* Heidelberger Studien zum Alten Orient 2. Heidelberg.

Some Shared Traditions between Ḫana and the Kassites*

Amanda H. Podany
California State Polytechnic University, Pomona

Was the region known as Ḫana around Terqa in Syria home to a small Kassite kingdom during the late years of the First Dynasty of Babylon? A king named Kaštiliašu ruled there before his namesakes occupied the throne in Babylon. It seems that there must be a connection between them, but exactly what it was still eludes us. Some scholars have been convinced by Kaštiliašu's name that he was a member of the later Kassite dynasty,[1] others have stated that the Kassites founded a short-lived kingdom at Terqa,[2] and still others have seen no real connection between Terqa's Kaštiliašu and the Kassites at all.[3] Professor Astour gave a thought-provoking talk on this topic in 1988 at the annual meeting of the American Oriental Society, in which he argued against the idea that Ḫana was a stronghold of Kassite power in the Old Babylonian period.[4] His

---

* Abbreviation list: AO: tablets in the collections of the Musée du Louvre; ARM: *Archives royales de Mari* (8 = Boyer [1957] = TCL 29, 22 = Kupper [1983]); BBS: King, *Babylonian Boundary Stones* (1912); CAD: *Chicago Assyrian Dictionary*; MDP: *Mémoires de la Délégation en Perse* (2 = Scheil [1900]); MLC: tablets in the collections of the J. Pierpont Morgan Library; TFR: *Terqa Final Reports* (1 = Rouault [1984]); TQ: Terqa texts (see n. 52); VAT: Vorderasiatischen Abteilung der Staatlichen Museen, Berlin; YBC: tablets in the Babylonian Collection, Yale University Library.

1 Smith (1940) 23; Parrot (1953) 369-74.

2 Sommerfeld (1995) 918.

3 *E.g.*, Buccellati (1983) 14, who suggested that a local king might have adopted a Kassite name.

4 Astour (1988).

analysis provided the impetus for this paper, as we continue to try to understand the role of the Kassites, if there was one, in the Middle Euphrates, and it is an honor to offer this study for the volume in his honor.

It was F. Thureau-Dangin who, in 1908, first noted the existence of king Kaštiliašu; he was named in the oath and date formula of a contract for the sale of a piece of property.[5] Although the kingdom ruled by this monarch was not named in the text, Thureau-Dangin concluded that it must have been Ḫana since the text included many parallels to one that he had published in 1897, which dated to the reign of Išar-Lim, king of Ḫana.[6] Kaštiliašu's name, unlike that of Išar-Lim, or of any other king of Ḫana known at the time, was Kassite. In the decades that have passed since Thureau-Dangin's publication, many other Ḫana texts have been uncovered and published, so that we now have the names of at least fifteen kings who ruled Ḫana.[7] Still, however, Kaštiliašu is the only ruler known to have borne a Kassite name, and Kassite names are also unknown among the rest of the population in published texts.

The majority of documents which have been recognized as belonging to the Ḫana tradition pertain to real estate, and record the purchases and gifts of fields, orchards, and houses. The distinctive clauses found in these documents were used over a long period of time,[8] from the reign of Yāpaḫ-Sūm[u-X], who was probably a contemporary of Samsu-iluna,[9] to the time of Tukulti-Ninurta I,[10] a span of perhaps five centuries. The kings mentioned in these texts were sometimes local, independent rulers, but at other times, the area was subject to foreign domination (see Fig. 2 for a listing of known kings). Most of the extant texts in the Ḫana tradition have been retrieved from excavations over the past two decades at Terqa, on the Euphrates

---

5 Thureau-Dangin (1908).

6 Thureau-Dangin (1897).

7 Rouault (1992).

8 Podany (1991–93) 54.

9 TFR1 8/8E in Rouault (1984).

10 Kümmel (1989).

north of Mari.[11] The few documents that were published prior to modern excavations also seem to have come from the same region.

In spite of the dearth of Kassite names in Ḫana documents, a few other intriguing clues seem to link Ḫana, however remotely, to the Kassites. For example, the seal impressions of the Ḫana kings Išar-Lim, Iggid-Lim, Isiḫ-Dagan, and Ḫammurapiḫ show similarities to Kassite glyptic traditions,[12] although they also resemble Old Babylonian seals. Also, a votive object is shown by its inscription to have been dedicated by King Ammurapi of Ḫana (possibly the same king as Ḫammurapiḫ) to a god whose name is read variously Duzagaš or Duzabi.[13] Thureau-Dangin and Dhorme proposed that Duzagaš might be a Kassite god,[14] but K. Balkan argued against this.[15] A similar disagreement surrounds the name of the "*Ḫabur-ibal-bugaš*" canal mentioned, again, in the reign of Ḫammurapiḫ.[16] *Bugaš* might be the Kassite word for "prince,"[17] or, as Astour has suggested, it could have a Semitic etymology.[18]

Another intriguing parallel exists between Ḫana real estate transaction documents and *kudurrus* from the kingdom of the Kassites in Babylon. This is the awarding of land grants by the king, which seems to have been a prominent feature of the economy in both societies. Even the terms used in describing the borders of the land are closely related in Ḫana and Kassite documents. This has not been explored in depth in previous studies and warrants closer examination.

---

11 See Buccellati (1979) and Buccellati and Kelly-Buccellati (1983) for the first eight seasons. The more recent seasons are described in Rouault, *et al.* (1996).

12 Beran (1958) 257; Goetze (1957) 63ff.; Porada (1976) 38ff.; Podany, Beckman and Colbow (1991–93) 44.

13 AO 9047 in Thureau-Dangin and Dhorme (1924) 275-76.

14 Thureau-Dangin and Dhorme (1924) 276.

15 Balkan (1954) 105.

16 MLC 613: 31 in Johns (1907).

17 Balkan (1954) 102-4; Landsberger (1954) 62.

18 Astour (1988).

In Kassite Babylonia, the system of royal land grants has sometimes been seen as so prominent a feature of the economy that the whole society has been termed "feudal."[19] W. Sommerfeld recently argued persuasively against this characterization.[20] He writes that "granting lands is but an interesting manifestation in the conferral of royal favor, one that played a striking, but not decisive, role within the total context of social relations."[21]

A similar situation seems to have existed during the kingdom of Ḫana, with its roots in the earlier Terqa kingdom that flourished during late Old Babylonian period. During the earlier period, in the reigns of the kings from Yāpaḫ-Sūm[u-X] to Ammi-madar, the majority of real estate transaction contracts known are for the sale of land. Nevertheless, a few royal land grants are attested. One was a donation of many acres of fields by king Ammi-madar to "his servant" Pagirum.[22] Another was the donation of several fields by king Zimri-Lim to Sin-imguranni,[23] a bequest which was confirmed by king Kasap-ili in a subsequent contract.[24] Later, during the kingdom of Ḫana, in the reigns of the kings from Išar-Lim to Ḫammurapiḫ, royal land grants seem to have become more common and, in contrast to the earlier texts, an impression of the king's seal appears on most or, perhaps, all of them.[25]

Only one contract for the sale of land has been published from the period of the kingdom of Ḫana,[26] but there are three published bequests. One records a gift of a house by king Išar-Lim to his servant Abi-ḫunni.[27]

---

19 Balkan (1943).

20 Sommerfeld (1995) 920-25.

21 *Ibid.*, 925.

22 VAT: 6685 published by Ungnad (1909).

23 TQ12 17, mentioned by Rouault (1992) 251.

24 TQ12 11, *ibid.*

25 This is true of those published to date, but may not be true of the new texts to be published by Rouault. He does not mention whether they were sealed by the king or not.

26 Schaeffer 2 in Nougayrol (1960).

27 AO 2673 in Thureau-Dangin (1897).

The other two, although broken, can also be classed as bequests because of the features they share with that of Išar-Lim: borders to the property belong largely or entirely to "the palace"; the king's seal appears in the margin; and (although this is preserved only in one instance) the owners of the land are listed as a number of gods and the king.[28] Rouault notes that many of the recently discovered texts from the excavations at Terqa record royal land grants, and that in each case the land is bounded by palace property, and the property is listed as belonging to gods and the king (the same gods who appear in the oath formula).[29]

None of the published land grants stipulates any service that was expected of the recipient. The "servants" to whom the lands were given, including Sin-imguranni[30] and Pagirum,[31] were heads of prominent Terqa households, but no reason is given for their being chosen to receive lands from the king. Besides the fact that, as mentioned above, the owners of the land were given as gods and the properties tended to flank palace land, the contracts were almost identical to land sale contracts. Only the fourth clause of the agreement differs between the two groups of texts; this is the section which, in a sale document, gives details of the price. Generally, the documents have a standard format (see Fig. 1).[32]

Even though the evidence is limited to only a few contracts, the fact that such a high proportion of the known documents from the kingdom of Ḫana record bequests suggests that, as in Kassite Babylonia, they played an impor-

---

28 YBC 6518 in Stephens (1937), dating to the reign of Ḫammirapiḫ, and AO 20162 in Nougayrol (1947), dating to the reign of Isiḫ-Dagan. The owners of the field are missing in YBC 6518, and the text is broken before the king's name at the end of the list of gods owning the field in AO 20162.

29 Rouault (1992) 254-55.

30 *Ibid.* 251.

31 VAT 6685: 27.

32 Not all published texts follow this pattern exactly, but it is common to most. Rouault (1992) 251 notes that some of the more recently excavated texts from Terqa vary from the Ḫana tradition and include Babylonian formulas. He proposes that these were written during a time of Babylonian control of Terqa.

	BEQUEST		LAND SALES
1.	Size and location of the property or properties	1.	Size and location of the property or properties
2.	Identification of the four borders of each property (often E_2.GAL)	2.	Identification of the four borders of each property
3.	Name of owner of the property (list of gods and RN, the king)	3.	Name of PN_1, owner of the property
4.	RN, the king gave the property to PN_1 (recipient's name), his servant (RN LUGAL *a-na* PN_1 IR_3-*šu* E_2/A.$ŠA_3$ IN.NA.AN.BA)	4.	From PN_1 (owner's name), PN_2 (buyer's name) bought the property for its full price (KI PN_1 LUGAL E_2/A.$ŠA_3$ PN_2 E_2/A.$ŠA_3$ IN.ŠI.IN.$ŠAM_2$ $ŠAM_2$.TIL.LA.BI.$ŠE_3$)
5.	(no payment)	5.	amount paid
6.	The property is incontestable and free from claims or release (*naṣbum ša la baqrim u la andurārim*)	6.	The property is incontestable and free from claims or release (*naṣbum ša la baqrim u la andurārim*)
7.	He who makes a claim (*baqir ibaqqaru*) ...	7.	He who makes a claim (*baqir ibaqqaru*) ...
8.	because they have sworn an oath by (list of gods) and RN ...	8.	because they have sworn an oath by (list of gods) and RN ...
9.	he will pay 10 minas of silver to the palace	9.	he will pay 10 minas of silver to the palace
10.	hot asphalt will be smeared on his head.	10.	hot asphalt will be smeared on his head.
11.	List of witnesses	11.	List of witnesses
12.	Date	12.	Date

Fig. 1

tant role in the economy and society. Land sales were, however, still known, at least in the reign of Ḫammurapiḫ.[33]

Donation of land by a king to his civil servants was probably a local tradition,[34] which was not shared by Babylonian monarchs of the First Dynasty. Only after the Kassites came to power did this practice become common in Mesopotamia, reflecting, as in Ḫana, a greater centralization of power over land in the hands of the king.[35]

The king was prominent in many aspects of Kassite society and economy,[36] and the same may prove to be true of the kings of Ḫana. Impressions of kings' seals have been found on documents that seem to have no direct connection to the king or the palace, including a will[37] and a contract for adoption and inheritance.[38] (A similar phenomenon is seen at Ugarit, where many documents are described as having been drawn up "in the presence of" the king.[39])

Given these parallels between the kingdoms of Ḫana and the Kassites, what might be the relationship between the two kingdoms? There is no direct evidence that the Kassite kings developed their system of royal land grants as a result of influence from the earlier kings who ruled Terqa during the Old Babylonian period or from the Ḫana kings who probably ruled during the early Middle Babylonian period. Aside from the enigmatic Kaštiliašu, the Terqa and Ḫana kings seem not to have been Kassites, so we cannot posit that the commonalties derived from a shared background on the part of the kings (also, the earliest known Terqa bequest comes from before the reign of Kaštiliašu).

---

33 Schaeffer 2, published by Nougayrol (1960).

34 Rouault (1992) 252.

35 Sommerfeld (1995) 923-25.

36 *Ibid.* 925.

37 MLC 613 in Johns (1907), from the reign of Ḫammurapiḫ.

38 RBC 779 in Podany, Beckman, and Colbow (1991–93), from the reign of Iggid-Lim.

39 Heltzer (1982) 178.

There is, however, intriguing indirect evidence for a connection between the two kingdoms in the way that land was described in the transaction documents (tablets in Ḫana and *kudurrus* in Babylonia). Although *kudurrus* are very different in formulation from Ḫana bequest contracts, the terms used to identify the borders are almost identical. Almost all Ḫana texts refer to the first two sides of a field, house, or orchard as US$_2$.SA.DU AN.TA ("upper border") and US$_2$.SA.DU KI.TA ("lower border"). The only exceptions are in two contracts, one from the time of Ḫammurapiḫ[40] and one from the Middle Assyrian period,[41] both of which use the form US$_2$ AN.TA and US$_2$ KI.TA. The third and fourth sides were usually SAG.KI AN.TA ("upper side") and SAG.KI KI.TA ("lower side"). The exceptions to this are found in the earliest two documents, which use SAG.KI 1 KAM and SAG.KI 2 KAM ("first side" and "second side")[42]; and in the latest, Middle Assyrian text, which has SAG AN.TA and SAG KI.TA.[43] In each case, the term is followed by the name of the adjoining property (either the name of its owner or the name of the river, canal, road, square, or other geographical feature).

Kassite and later Neo-Babylonian *kudurru* inscriptions recording royal land grants provide the closest known parallels to the terminology found in the Ḫana contracts. In *kudurrus*, the borders to the property are usually labeled US$_2$ AN.TA, US$_2$ KI.TA, SAG.KI AN.TA, and SAG.KI KI.TA.[44] Each of these terms is usually followed by the designation north, south, east or west, which in turn is often followed by US$_2$.SA.DU, then the name of the building, field, canal or other feature marking that border. A standard description of a border therefore might read SAG.KI AN.TA TU$_{15}$.MAR.TU US$_2$.SA.DU E$_2$-PN: "the upper side to the west adjacent to GN."[45] The "upper" sides tend to be

---

40 Nougayrol (1960).

41 Kümmel (1989).

42 TFR1 8E: 6, 7; TFR1 9: 5, 6 in Rouault (1984).

43 Kümmel (1989).

44 See, for example MDP 2, 99ff, Pl. 21-24: Col. I 42-53; BBS n VIII: Col. I 14-21; MDP 6, 31 ff.: Col. I 12- Col. II 2; BBS n VII: Col. I 3-9.

45 CAD I, 314, quoting MDP 6 pl. 9 i 20.

the north and west sides, the "lower" sides tend to be south and east, although this is not invariably the case. In both Kassite and Ḫana documents all four sides of the property are always accounted for.

Texts from Late Bronze Age Emar show some similarities with those from Terqa and with Kassite *kudurrus*, especially in field and orchard contracts.[46] The first two sides of a field or orchard were labeled as the "upper border" and "lower border" (US$_2$.SA.DU AN.TA....US$_2$.SA.DU KI.TA). The third and fourth sides were the "first side" (SAG 1 KAM or SAG.KI 1 KAM) and the "second side" (SAG 2 KAM or SAG.KI 2 KAM). The borders of houses were perceived differently, however.[47] Their sides were described (in order) as ZAG-*šu* ("its right"), GUB$_3$-*šu* ("its left"), EGIR-*šu* ("its back") and *pa-nu-šu* ("its front"). As might be expected, the fourth side or "front" was where the street, square, or other access was usually listed, in contrast to earlier practice in Mesopotamia and Syria where this generally appeared on the third side.

The amount of detail is greater in the Kassite descriptions of property than in Ḫana and Emar examples, since in the latter the cardinal points are not mentioned. Kassite, Emar, and Ḫana texts are all, in turn, more precise in identifying borders to the property in question than Old Babylonian contracts recording real estate transactions. Many of the latter (especially from southern cities) list just one or two sides to a piece of property, often designated only DA ("side"), for houses, and DA, *i-ta* or US$_2$.SA.DU ("border") for fields and orchards. Even when all four sides to the property are listed, the identification of "upper" and "lower" sides is not found. The third and fourth sides to both houses and fields are usually designated SAG.BI ("its front"), sometimes with the qualification "first" and "second." One might have expected contracts from Mari to be more similar to those from Ḫana, but few are available. Of those published, most list no borders to the prop-

46 Arnaud (1986) texts 1, 2, 3, 11, 12, 89, 90, 137.

47 Arnaud (1986) texts 9, 10, 20, 76, 80, 85, 94, 96, 97, 109, 111, 122, 125, 126, 130. In text 110, exceptionally, the sides are listed as US$_2$.SA.DU AN.TA / US$_2$.SA.DU KI.TA/ EGIR-*ša*/*pa-nu-ša*

erty.[48] One Mari text does, however, list sides of a piece of property as being "upper" and "lower."[49]

Figure 3 lists the usual terms used for the boundaries to fields and orchards in Old Babylonian contracts from some major cities in Mesopotamia.[50] The differences between Old Babylonian and Kassite scribal traditions for identifying the borders of property are dramatic. They suggest that the Kassite scribal tradition for defining real estate boundaries came from outside Babylonia. Either the Kassite scribal tradition shared a common source with the scribal practice in Ḫana texts, or perhaps Kassite terminology derived from Ḫana tradition.

In conclusion, long before the Kassite kings of Babylon began granting land to powerful subjects and extending their control over land acquisition, the same phenomenon was found in the region around Terqa. Much of the land adjoining the fields and houses being granted was described as belonging to "the palace" and, during the height of the Ḫana kingdom, the king's own seal impression appeared on almost all known documents.[51] The kings of the Middle and Neo-Babylonian periods required greater precision in accurately identifying the borders of the land grants than did earlier Old Babylonian buyers and sellers of property. For this purpose they adopted (perhaps indirectly) the terminology used earlier at Terqa, including the designation of "upper" and "lower" sides, and they increased the specificity of the description by adding reference to compass directions. Although some similarities exist between the terms used in Kassite *kudurrus* and those found in land-sale contracts from Emar, the parallels are much closer with texts from Ḫana.

---

48 *E.g.*, ARM VIII 4 (house), ARM VIII 5, ARM VIII 11 (both for fields) and five of the sixteen fields listed in ARM XXII 328.

49 ARM VIII 6.

50 These charts are based on a survey of over 400 published Old Babylonian real estate contracts. The terms listed reflect those found most often in the texts from each region; terms that are found infrequently are not listed.

51 The one exception is Schaeffer 2, the text published by Nougayrol (1960) from the time of Ḫammurapiḫ.

This still does not imply that Ḫana was a Kassite kingdom, but it does indicate that there may have been close ties between the two regions. The parallels between the two cultures described here might have resulted from Kassite influence on Ḫana, but might also have resulted from Ḫana influence on the Kassites.

The Main Phases of Ḫana History *

I. *A period of probable local autonomy contemporary with the reigns of Samsu-iluna, Abi-ešuḫ, and Ammi-ditanna of Babylon*

Yāpaḫ-Sūm[u-X]
Iṣi-Sūmu-Abu
Yadiḫ-Abu
Zimri-Lim, son of Yadiḫ-Abu **
Kasap-ili
Kuwari
Kaštiliašu
Ḫanaya (vassal of Ya'usa?)
Šunuḫru-Ammu
Ammi-madar, son of Šunuḫru-Ammu

II. *Babylonian interregnum*

Ammi-Ṣaduqa
Samsu-ditana

III. *The kingdom of Ḫana, probably during the 16th century* ***

Idin-Kakka
Išar-Lim, son of Idin-Kakka
Iggid-Lim, son of Išar-Lim
Isiḫ-Dagan, son of Iggid-Lim

IV. *A period of apparent vassalage to the kingdom of Mitanni*

Qiš-Addu, vassal of Paratarna and Saustatar

V. *Re-emergent kingdom of Ḫana, perhaps in the 15th or 14th century*

Ḫammurapiḫ, son of Azilia(?)

VI. *Region subject to Middle Assyrian empire*

Tukulti-Ninurta I of Assyria

Fig. 2

* This sequence of kings is based on arguments made by Podany (1991–93), Rouault (1992), and Charpin (1995). A listing of all Ḫana texts found prior to the ninth season excavation at Terqa is found in Podany (1991–93) 53 n. 4, 54 n. 8; Rouault (1992) describes texts found since then. The sequence given here agrees with that of Charpin (1995), with the exception of the placement in the chronology of kings Ḫanaya and Qiš-Addu. The text listed as having an oath by Ḫanaya and Ya'usa (TQ12 14) is from the family archive of Sin-imguranni, since that man's son appears in the document (Rouault [1992] 252-53). Sin-imguranni lived during the reign of Zimri-Lim (*Ibid.* 251). Since Kasap-ili and Kuwari must have ruled right after Zimri-Lim, Ḫanaya probably ruled after them, either soon before or after Kaštiliašu. Most of these kings must have had relatively short reigns; a single generation of brothers (sons of Yašub-Dagan) lived through the reigns of all the kings from Yāpaḫ-Sūm[u-X] to Kaštiliašu (Podany [1988] 348-52). I have placed Qiš-Addu before Ḫammurapiḫ (unlike Charpin) on the basis of the physical appearance of one text from his reign (TQ12 6: Rouault and Masetti-Rouault [1993] 338, 460) which has more in common with texts from the time of Išar-Lim's dynasty than with those from Ḫammurapiḫ's time.

** According to Rouault (1992) 251-52, Terqa may have been subject to Babylon during part of the reign of Zimri-Lim.

*** For the royal inscriptions of Išar-Lim, Iggid-Lim, Isiḫ-Dagan, and Ḫammurapiḫ, see Frayne (1990) 730-34. Idin-Kakka's royal title is mentioned by Rouault (1992) 253.

Examples of some regional traditions for terms used to define boundaries of fields and orchards

OLD BABYLONIAN PERIOD

	Side 1	*Side 2*	*Side 3*	*Side 4*
Larsa	US_2.SA.DU or DA	ù US_2.SA.DU (or omitted)	usually omitted	usually omitted
Ur	US_2.SA.DU or DA	DA or ù DA or US_2.SA.DU	usually omitted	usually omitted
Nippur	US_2.SA.DU (fields) ZAG (orchards)	usually omitted	usually omitted	usually omitted
Sippar	*i-ta*	*ù i-ta*	SAG.BI1.KAM or SAG.BI (or often omitted)	SAG.BI 2.KAM (or often omitted)
Dilbat	US_2.SA.DU or DA	ù DA or ù US_2.SA.DU	SAG.BI	SA.KU.BI
Terqa	US_2.SA.DU AN.TA	US_2.SA.DU KI.TA	SAG.KI AN.TA	SAG.KI KI.TA

Fig. 3A

Examples of some regional traditions for terms used to define boundaries of fields and orchards

MIDDLE BABYLONIAN PERIOD

	Side 1	*Side 2*	*Side 3*	*Side 4*
Ḫana	US_2.SA.DU AN.TA	US_2.SA.DU KI.TA	SAG.KI AN.TA	SAG.KI KI.TA
kudurrus	US_2 AN.TA	US_2 KI.TA	SAG.KI AN.TA	SAG.KI KI.TA
Emar	US_2.SA.DU AN.TA	US_2.SA.DU KI.TA	SAG.KI 1 KAM or SAG 1 KAM	SAG.KI 2 KAM or SAG 2 KAM

Fig. 3B

Bibliography

Arnaud, D. (1986) *Recherches au pays d'Aštata Emar* VI.3 *Textes Sumériens et Accadiens.* Éditions Recherche sur les Civilisations. Paris. **Astour, M.** (1988) The Kingdom of Ḫana and the Kassites. Paper presented at the 198th meeting of the American Oriental Society, 1988. **Balkan, K.** (1943) *Studies in Babylonian Feudalism of the Kassite Period* (translated by B. Foster and D. Gutas, Monographs on the Ancient Near East 2.3, 1986). (1954) *Kassitenstudien* I. *Die Sprache der Kassiten* . American Oriental Society 37. New Haven. **Beran, Th.** (1958) Die babylonische Glyptik der Kassitenzeit. *Archiv für Orientforschung* 18: 255-78. **Boyer, G.** (1958) *Textes juridiques.* Archives royales de Mari VIII. Paris. **Buccellati, G.** (1979) *Terqa Preliminary Reports* 10: *The Fourth Season: Introduction and the Stratigraphic Record.* Bibliotheca Mesopotamica 10. Malibu. (1983) *Terqa: An Introduction to the Site* (Preprint on the occasion of the symposium of Der ez-Zor). Der ez-Zor. **Buccellati G., and M. Kelly-Buccellati** (1983) Terqa: The First Eight Seasons. *Annales Archéologiques Arabes Syriennes* 33/2: 47-67. **Charpin, D.** (1995) À propos des rois de Ḫana. *Nouvelles Assyrio-*

logiques Brèves et Utilitaires 1 (Mars): 19-20. **Frayne, D. R.** (1990) *Old Babylonian Period (2003-1595 BC)*. The Royal Inscriptions of Mesopotamia : Early Periods, vol. 4. **Goetze, A.** (1957) On the Chronology of the Second Millennium B.C. *Journal of Cuneiform Studies* 11: 53-61, 63-73. **Heltzer, M.** (1982) *The Internal Organization of the Kingdom of Ugarit.* Wiesbaden. **Johns, Rev. C. H. W.** (1907) A Marriage Contract from the Chabour. *Proceedings of the Society of Biblical Archaeology* 29: 177-84. **King, L. W.** (1912) *Babylonian Boundary-Stones and Memorial Tablets in the British Museum.* London **Kümmel, H. M.** (1989) Ein Kaufvertrag aus Ḫana mit mittelassyrischer *limu*-Datierung. *Zeitschrift für Assyriologie* 79: 191-200. **Kupper, J.-R.** (1983) *Documents administratifs de la salle 135 du palais de Mari.* Archives royales de Mari XX11, vols. 1 and 2. Editions Recherche sur les Civilisations. Paris. **Landsberger, B.** (1954) Assyrische Königsliste und "dunkles Zeitalter." *Journal of Cuneiform Studies* 8: 31-45, 47-73. **Nougayrol, J.** (1947) Textes et documents figurés IV. Un nouveau roi de Ḫana. *Revue d'Assyriologie et d'Archéologie Orientale* 41: 42-46. (1960) Documents du Habur, I. Une nouvelle tablette du Ḫana. *Syria* 37: 205-9. **Parrot, A.** (1953) *Archéologie mesopotamienne: technique et problèmes.* Paris. **Podany, A. H.** (1988) *The Chronology and History of the Ḫana Period.* (Unpublished UCLA Ph.D. dissertation.) Los Angeles. (1991–93) A Middle Babylonian Date for the Ḫana Kingdom. *Journal of Cuneiform Studies* 43-45: 53-62. **Podany, A. H., G. Beckman, and G. Colbow** (1991–93) An Adoption and Inhertance Contract from the Reign of Iggid-Lim of Ḫana. *Journal of Cuneiform Studies* 43-45: 39-51. **Porada, E.** (1976) Seal Impressions on the Cuneiform Tablets. In *Ancient Mesopotamian Art and Selected Texts*, 35-42. The Pierpont Morgan Library. New York. **Rouault, O.** (1984) *Terqa Final Reports* 1: *L'archive de Puzurum.* Bibliotheca Mesopotamica 16. Malibu. (1992) Cultures locales et influences extérieures: le cas de Terqa. *Studi Micenei ed Egeo-Anatolici* 30: 247-56. **Rouault, O., and M. G. Masetti-Rouault** (1993) *L'Eufrate e il tempo.* Milano. **Rouault, O., *et al.*** (1996) Terqa: Rapport Préliminaire (1987–1989) *MARI, Annales de Recherches Interdisciplinaires* 8: 73-103. **Sasson, J. M.**, ed. (1995) *Civilizations of the Ancient Near East.* 4 Vols. New York. **Scheil, V.** (1900) *Textes Élamites-Sémitiques.* Mémoires de la Délégation en Perse, tome 2. Paris. **Smith, S.** (1940) *Alalakh and Chronology.* London. **Sommerfeld, W.** (1995) The Kassites of Ancient Mesopotamia: Origins, Politics, and Culture. In Sasson 1995: 2 917-30. **Stephens, F. J.** (1937) A Cuneiform Tablet from Dura-Europos. *Revue d'Assyriologie et d'Archéologie Orientale* 34: 184-90. **Thureau-Dangin, F.** (1897) Tablettes chaldéennes inédites. *Revue d'Assyriologie et d'Archéologie Orientale* 4: 69-78, P. XXXII. (1908) Un nouveau roi de Ḫana. *Orientalische Literaturzeitung* 11: 93. **Thureau-Dangin, F. and R. P. Dhorme** (1924) Cinq jours de fouilles à Asharah. *Syria* 5: 265-93. **Ungnad, A.** (1909) Zur Geschichte der Nachbarstaaten Babyloniens zur Zeit der Hammurapi-Dynastie. 4. Ḫana. *Beiträge zur Assyriologie und semitischen Sprachwissenschaft* VI/5: 26-32.

The Early History of Israel

Gary A. Rendsburg
Cornell University

In an article such as this, the topic of "The Early History of Israel" cannot be treated with all the necessary detail. Instead, this article represents an outline, incorporating ideas previously published by others and myself. It is, in short, a synthesis. Michael Astour has distinguished himself as a historian of the ancient Near East throughout his illustrious career. Researchers in the field have learned much from his many and varied studies. And although my own expertise is in language and literature, I offer this foray into history as a tribute to our honoree, with sincere wishes that he may enjoy many more years of good life and productive scholarship.

Anyone who approaches the early history of Israel must do so with all due caution. There are, of course, no Israelite records contemporary with the events and processes to be discussed herein. Instead, the historian must approach the topic with the realization that the main document, the Torah, (a) was composed at a later time, and (b) did not have as its main goal the presentation of history in the modern sense of the word. In my estimation, the date of this composition is the tenth century B.C.E., that is, the period of David and Solomon,[1] and the main goal was a combination of elements,

---

1 Rendsburg (1986) 107-20, and Rendsburg (1996). These two works deal with Genesis only. There is less evidence in the remaining books of the Torah that points to a tenth-century B.C.E. composition, but still an occasional datum in Exodus through Deuteronomy confirms this view. See, for example, the reference to Agag in Num 24: 7,

including aesthetic literature, history text, theological treatise, and political propaganda.[2]

But the presence of additional factors in biblical narrative does not necessitate rejecting the historical evidence contained therein altogether. All it means is that the historian must be cautious in his or her evaluation of the material. The Old English poem *Beowulf* works well as an analogy. It is based on historical events that can be dated to the sixth century C.E., the poem itself was written in the eighth century C.E., and the earliest manuscript (in fact the only ancient manuscript) dates to the late tenth or early eleventh century C.E.[3] My colleague Robert Farrell has written as follows:

> *Beowulf* is a work of heroic history, i.e. a poem in which facts and chronology are subservient to the poet's interest in heroic deeds and their value in representing the ethics of an heroic civilization. A poet writing in this mode does not disregard absolute historical fact, history, that is, as we know it. He rather sees it as less important than other considerations… . His account will sometimes mesh reasonably well with history, as in the episode of Hygelac's raid on the Frisian shore. But more often, his work will be a freely-woven structure in which the characters and actions of the past will be part of an ethically satisfying narrative.[4]

The same words could apply to the Torah. The narrative is based on historical facts known to the author, but the author is more interested in presenting an "ethically satisfying narrative," which in the case of biblical narrative is one based on the theological thread that runs throughout (along with the other elements noted above). So while the author "does not disregard absolute historical fact, history, that is," these facts take a back seat to the main thrust of the story, the demonstration of Yahweh's role in that history. Furthermore, as with *Beowulf*, the composition of the Torah is to

---

and the law of the king in Deut 17: 14-17, which can only be a reaction to the excesses of Solomon. For the linguistic evidence on the date of the Torah, see Rendsburg (1980).

2 See Rendsburg (1996).

3 For details, see Jack (1994) 1-12.

4 Farrell (1970–73) 229.

be dated to several centuries after the events themselves, and our earliest manuscripts come from a still later epoch.[5]

In short, the Torah and books such as Joshua and Judges cannot be taken at face value for the recovery of ancient Israelite history. But at the same time, especially when a variety of sources from the ancient Near East confirms elements of the biblical narrative, we are absolutely justified in using the Bible as a source for recovering the early history of Israel.

A good example of where the Torah cannot be taken at face value is the basic structure of the nation of Israel. Nations simply do not descend from the offspring of one man.[6] Instead, as with most nations, Israel was comprised of peoples of diverse origins. We are able to identify some of these origins (on which see further below), though no doubt others are beyond our present ability to isolate. But one point seems clear: the people that gave Israel its ultimate identity must have been a group that wandered the desert regions south (and east) of the arable land of Canaan.

An assemblage of evidence supports this conclusion. First, the Bible states very plainly that the people of Israel entered the land from the outside, specifically from the desert. In fact, the desert ideal remained a part of Israel throughout its history.[7] Furthermore, various peoples associated with the desert fringe in some biblical texts (Kaleb, Qenaz, Yeraḥme'el, etc.) appear in other biblical texts to be part and parcel of the tribes of Israel, in particular, the dominant southern tribe of Judah.[8]

---

5 Of course, in the case of the Torah, the distance from date of composition to earliest manuscripts, viz. the Dead Sea Scrolls, is considerably greater than the distance between composition of *Beowulf* and the earliest manuscript. But this is a factor of preservation. The discovery of the seventh-century B.C.E. Ketef Hinnom silver amulets containing the priestly benediction (Davies [1991] 72-73), though not verbatim what appears in Num 6: 24-26, is a tiny step towards the recovery of earlier Torah texts.

6 See Sarna (1966) 196.

7 Though he has a different opinion on the matter, a good survey may be found in Talmon (1966), reprinted in Talmon (1993) 216-54.

8 For discussion, see de Vaux (1978) 534-37.

Second, the national god of Israel, Yahweh, is a deity associated in a variety of biblical texts with the desert region: Seir, Edom, Sinai, Paran, Teman (Deut 33: 2, Judg 5: 4-5, Hab 3: 3, Ps 68: 8, etc.).

Third, Egyptian topographical lists from Soleb and ʿAmarah (both in Nubia), dated to the New Kingdom period, refer to *t3 š3sw ya-h-wa* "the land of the Shasu of Yahweh," in conjunction with other Shasu locales, among them *t3 š3sw sa-ʿ-r-ir* "Shasu of the land of Seʿir."[9] However one is to explain Yahweh here, for it appears to be a place name in the Soleb and ʿAmarah lists, the collocation of Yahweh and Seir in these lists conforms well with the biblical evidence associating the deity with Seir, Edom, etc.[10] Furthermore, as we shall see below during our discussion of P. Anastasi VI, there is additional reason to associate the Israelites, or at least the desert people portion thereof, with the Shasu, the general Egyptian term for the nomads and semi-nomads of the desert.

Fourth, notwithstanding some difficult experiences with desert people such as Amaleq (Exod 17: 8-15, Deut 25: 17-19) and even Midian on occasion (e.g., Num 25: 16-18), generally the Israelites enjoyed close ties with desert folks such as Midian (Exod 2: 16-22, 18: 1-12, Num 10: 29-32), the Qenites (Judg 1: 16, 5: 24, 1 Sam 15: 6), and the Rekhabites (2 Kgs 10: 15-16, Jer 35, 1 Chr 2: 55).

Fifth, the excavations at Timna, in the southern Negev (30 kilometers north of Eilat), revealed a cultic center with features reminiscent of Israelite religious practices as described in the Bible. Most important are (a) the evidence of a tent sanctuary, akin to the biblical *mishkan*, or Tabernacle (described in Exodus 25-31, 35-40); and (b) the presence of a copper snake

---

9 For the primary data, see Giveon (1971) 26-28, 74-77. I must respectfully disagree with Astour (1979), who argued that these toponyms are to be located in Syria, not in the desert regions south of Canaan. See the comments in Redford (1992) 272 n 67. I will cite Redford (1992) often in the notes below, for it is an excellent treatment incorporating a wealth of information. However, it must be used cautiously due to the bias that the author brings to the biblical material; see Rendsburg (1995). My transcription of the Egyptian syllabic orthography is based on the catalogue of signs in Hoch (1994) 505-12.

10 See Herrmann (1967).

mounted on a standard, so close to the description in Num 21: 4-9 that it may be considered a virtual depiction thereof.[11]

Sixth, Herodotus (3: 8) describes the Arabs of his day as practicing a blood covenant ritual in which blood from the thumbs of the participants was smeared on the holy stones which stood before them. While not agreeing in every detail, this calls to mind the covenant ceremony conducted by Moses in Exod 24: 1-8 in which both twelve stone pillars and blood play a prominent role.[12]

The picture which emerges from these diverse points is that a significant portion of the nation of Israel that later would emerge in the land of Canaan had desert origins. These desert people, "semi-nomads" is the best term for them, wandered the desert fringe with their flocks of sheep and goats, engaged in some seasonal agriculture, and at times settled in the arable regions of the land of Canaan. This pattern can be seen still today among the Bedouin, and it is reflected in the Bible for certain non-Israelites. Note, for example, how the Qenites are associated with the desert in 1 Sam 15: 6, but how individual families from this group settle in the sown in Judg 1: 16, 4: 11.

At some point in time, semi-nomadic Israelites[13] arrived in Egypt. The story of Joseph in Genesis 37-50 focuses on the individual family members and thus is an example of "heroic history," but the overall picture is confirmed by Egyptian records. In the New Kingdom in particular, peoples from Asia arrived in the Delta in unprecedented numbers. Some came as captives, the prize of Egyptian military success in Western Asia under the

---

11 See Rothenberg (1993) 1483.

12 On this specific parallel and on the picture in general, see Weinfeld (1987) 483-86. For the mention of a blood ritual among Semites dwelling in Egypt, see Černy (1955).

13 An objection might be raised that "Israel" is specifically a name reserved for the nation after it emerged as a national entity in the land of Canaan, and that these semi-nomads of the desert should be called something else, such as "proto-Israelites." But I prefer to eschew such terms and to keep matters simple by using the term "Israel-(ites)" to refer to the semi-nomads as well. Moreover, the name "Israel" is attested already in the Merneptah Stele, on which see further below, so that the entity already existed in the late thirteenth century B.C.E.

conquering Pharaohs of the 18th and 19th Dynasties; some were sent to Egypt as slaves, either by Canaanite city-state kings loyal to the Pharaoh or even by their own kinfolk (as with Joseph!); while still others came freely, either as merchants seeking to ply their trade or as Bedouin seeking grazing land for their animals.[14] It is this last group of individuals that interests us most, for the biblical account emphasizes the animal husbandry of the newly-arrived Israelites in Egypt (Gen 46: 31-47: 6).

There is, moreover, a striking parallel to the arrival of the Israelites in Egypt in an Egyptian document from the reign of Merneptah (1214–1205). The text, alluded to above, P. Anastasi VI 4: 11-5: 5, reads as follows: [15]

> The scribe Enana greets his master, the treasury scribe Qa-ga[b] … Life, prosperity, health! This is a dispatch of information for my master, to wit: I have carried out every commission placed upon me, in good shape and strong as metal. I have not been lax. Another communication to my master, to wit: We have finished admitting the Shasu tribes of Edom at the fortress of Merneptah Hotephirmaat, life, prosperity, health, which is in Tjeku, to the pools of Per-Atum of Merneptah Hotephirmaat, which are in Tjeku, to keep them alive and to keep their flocks alive, by the great Ka of Pharaoh, life, prosperity, health, the good sun of every land, in the year 8, day 5, of [the birth of] Seth. I have had sent a report to my master, with the other days specified when the fortress of Merneptah Hotephirmaat, life, prosperity, health, which is in Tjeku, may be passed.

The parallel between this text and the general picture portrayed in the Bible is obvious.[16] In the former, a group of Shasu from Edom are allowed to pass the fortress that marked the Egyptian border with the Sinai desert and settle (at least temporarily), along with their flocks, in Per-Atum. In the biblical account, we read that the Israelites are given the same permission and that eventually they are resident in the city of Pithom (Exod 1: 11), no doubt

---

14 See Redford (1992) 214-29 for an overview.

15 For the text, see Gardiner (1937) 76-77. For translations and comments, see Caminos (1954) 293-96, Redford (1992) 228, and *ANET* 259.

16 The recent attempt by Goedicke (1987) to deny the similarity, to place these "Edomites" near Suez, and to assume that they were allowed to enter Egypt for only one day, is quite unsatisfactory.

the Hebrew equivalent of Per-Atum.[17] When one keeps in mind that the aforecited Egyptian topographical lists refer to Shasu of Yahweh and Shasu of Seir, and that Seir equals Edom in the Bible (Gen 32: 4, 36: 8-9, etc.), and that Yahweh is portrayed as shining or marching forth from both Seir and Edom (Deut 33: 2, Judg 5: 4), the parallel is even more striking (though one should resist the temptation to invoke the law of transitivity and to associate the Shasu of this frontier official's report with the Israelites of the Bible). Clearly, the two references, the one about the Edomites in P. Anastasi VI and the one about the Israelites in the Torah, are part of the same general movement of Shasu arriving in the eastern Delta to sustain both themselves and their animals. Here it is important to keep in mind the strong biblical tradition that Israel and Edom were closely related kindred nations, descended from twin brothers according to the epic tradition (Gen 25: 23-24, Num 20: 14). The Torah naturally focuses on Israel's experiences, but Edom's must have been very similar, as we learn from P. Anastasi VI.

Accordingly, we conclude that a group of Israelites, whom the Egyptians would have classified as Shasu along with other semi-nomads settled in Egypt sometime in the New Kingdom period. Exactly when in the New Kingdom period cannot be determined with certainty, but a suggestion can be made here. The Israelites must have arrived in Egypt sometime earlier than the reign of Rameses II, for this king is the leading candidate for the Pharaoh represented in Exodus 1 as the Pharaoh of the slavery (see next paragraph). If the statement in Exod 1: 8 is interpreted to mean immediate succession, then the Pharaoh during whose reign the Israelites arrived in Egypt must have been Seti I (1291–1279), father and immediate predecessor of Rameses II. The book of Genesis suggests this in several ways. First, the text implies that the Israelites' settlement in Goshen, that is, the eastern Delta in general or the Wadi Tumilat in particular, was near the pharaoh's residence (see Genesis 45 especially); and the 19th Dynasty monarchs ruled from this region.[18] Second, the expression "land of Rameses" occurs in Gen

17 In Late Egyptian, final *r* was weakened, as reflected in the Hebrew *pîtôm*. For the phonological process, see Loprieno (1995) 38.

18 The preceding 18th Dynasty monarchs ruled from Thebes in Upper Egypt. The

47: 11, and while this term could be an anachronism, it may be noted that the name Rameses already was in use by the founder of the 19th Dynasty, Rameses I (1292–1291), father of Seti I.

Within a relatively short period, the Israelites who had settled in the Delta, became slaves to the Egyptians.[19] The Torah, of course, ascribes this change in status to a change in royal administration in Egypt (Exod 1: 8-11). We cannot place this next stage of Israelite history within known Egyptian history, but again we are able to cite Egyptian texts that corroborate the general picture. Exod 1: 11 informs us that the Israelites were put to work building the store cities of Pithom and Rameses. Based on the latter name, I (along with many other scholars) assume that the Pharaoh of Egypt at this time was Rameses II (1279–1214), the great builder whose major achievement in the Delta region was the construction of the city Per-Rameses.[20] From this king's reign comes a text, P. Leiden 348, a collection of letters (probably model letters) discussing building activities. Recto 6: 6 reads as follows: "Issue grain to the men of the army and to the ʿApiru who are drawing stone(?) for the great pylon of the [house?] of Rameses."[21] Much has been written about a possible connection between the term "ʿApiru" in Egyptian texts (equals "Ḫabiru" in cuneiform texts) and the term "Hebrew" of the Bible. Simply stated: there are too many hurdles (philological, ethnic-social, and historical) to equate the two.[22] Yet in an

---

earlier Hyksos also ruled from the eastern Delta, and thus many scholars consider this period as the most likely one for the Israelite arrival in Egypt (especially if there is any historicity to the figure of Joseph, a Semite elevated to high station in the Egyptian royal administration). But the Hyksos period is far too early for the origins of Israel, especially as it would place the Patriarchs (again, assuming any historicity for them) even earlier. Everything points to the Late Bronze Age, not the Middle Bronze Age, for the era of the Patriarchs (literary parallels from Ugarit, socio-legal parallels from Nuzi, etc.); see Gordon (1954).

19 I do not treat here the exact nature of that enslavement. Most likely it was a corvée system.

20 See Bietak (1984).

21 See Wilson (1933) 276, and Greenberg (1955) 56. For the original text, see Leemans (1843) Plate 148.

22 See the summary discussion in Greenberg (1955) 91-96.

example such as the Egyptian text before us, with the specific reference to ʻApiru building the city of (Per-)Rameses, I am inclined to see a more direct correlation in this instance. Also of interest is the fact that the biblical account utilizes the term "Hebrew" at times (Exod 1: 15, 16, 19; 2: 11, 13; 5: 3), though of course this is not unique to this narrative.[23]

A second Egyptian text which is germane here is the Merneptah Stele. This victory stele of Merneptah is concerned mainly with his defeat of Libya to the west. But at the end of the inscription comes a short passage boasting of Merneptah's victories over peoples in Canaan. The names of all of the defeated peoples in this portion of the text are accompanied by the determinative indicating "foreign land" (thus for large entities such as Hatti and Canaan, and for smaller entities such as Ashqelon, Gezer, and Yanoʻam). The exception, as is well known, is Israel, which is determined by a group of signs indicating "people." This peculiarity demonstrates that at the time of the inscription Israel was a people without a land.

Most scholars conclude that this refers to Israel during the wandering period, that is, after the Exodus from Egypt. But as I have argued elsewhere,[24] an alternative approach is possible. I prefer to interpret the mention of Israel in the Merneptah Stele as a reference to the slavery.[25] It is important to note that the "people" determinative following the phonetic writing of Israel includes the "woman" determinative. This unique usage points to the fact that the Israelites are not just another people defeated in battle (at the Reed Sea or in the desert, as most scholars would suggest), but are a people in the true sense of the word, that is, with women (and children), though without a land. While this would be true of Israel even during the wandering, that is, with women (and children) accompanying the men, other considerations, mostly chronological ones to be treated below, argue

---

23 The term "Hebrew" is typical in contexts between Israelites and non-Israelites in the biblical corpus.

24 Rendsburg (1992) especially 517-18.

25 This interpretation was offered by some scholars already in the years immediately following W. M. F. Petrie's discovery of the stele. For discussion, see Engel (1979) 396-97.

in favor of the Merneptah Stele as a reference to Israel enslaved in Egypt. The scribe of this inscription knew that the Israelites had associations with Canaan, and thus he mentioned them in the course of describing Merneptah's victories in Canaan. But he was careful to distinguish Israel as an enslaved people in Egypt from the locales mentioned in the rest of the passage.

Another piece of Egyptian evidence is relevant here. I refer to the battle scenes on the outer western wall of the Cour de la Cachette at Karnak depicting Merneptah's military victories. There is a debate between Frank Yurco and Anson Rainey as to which individual scene or scenes depicts the Israelites. Yurco argued that the fourth scene portrays Israelites, in which case they are an urban people, not distinguishable from other Canaanites.[26] Rainey, on the other hand, argued that the Israelites are to be found in the fifth through eighth scenes, which portray Shasu folk.[27] From what I have written above, it is clear that I agree with Rainey on this point. But even if Yurco's position is accepted, there is no major problem, because, as intimated above and as we shall discuss below in greater detail, Israel was of diverse origins and there is evidence that a portion thereof was settled in Canaan and never participated in Shasu culture or, as the Torah story tells it, in the sojourn in and exodus from Egypt.

After several generations as slaves in Egypt, the Israelites left Egypt upon gaining their freedom. The Torah describes these events as "heroic history" in the extreme, with Moses as Yahweh's prophet before Pharaoh. What actually occurred we cannot say with any certainty. But chronology is helpful in allowing us to speculate.[28] Recent archaeological work in Israel demonstrates clearly that the emergence of Israel in the land of Canaan occurred only in the mid-twelfth century B.C.E.,[29] and this would suggest that the Israelites did not leave Egypt until early in the twelfth century.

---

26 Yurco (1990), and Stager (1985).

27 Rainey (1991).

28 For much of what follows in greater detail, see Rendsburg (1992).

29 See most importantly Finkelstein (1988).

Genealogical material in the Bible supports that date. The lineage of David (Ruth 4: 18-22, 1 Chr 2: 5-15) informs us that he had a great-great-great-grandfather named Nahshon, and this individual in turn is mentioned in the Torah in two contexts: as the brother-in-law of Aaron (Exod 6: 23) and as the prince of Judah during the wandering period (Num 1: 7). Using 30 years as the average generation,[30] and dating David to c. 1000 B.C.E., we arrive at a date of c. 1150 B.C.E. for Nahshon.

A crucial passage in this discussion is Exod 13: 17: "God did not lead them the way of the land of the Philistines though it was near, for God said, 'Lest the people change their minds when they see the fighting and then return to Egypt'." The mention of the Philistines here is often thought to be an anachronism, but such need not be the case. Rather, the reference to Philistines, war, and the coastal route suggests that the Israelites left Egypt when the Philistines were attacking the Egyptians along the coast as part of the major Sea Peoples assault during the reign of Rameses III (1182–1250), specifically c. 1175 B.C.E. The records of this Pharaoh, both textual and pictorial, demonstrate clearly to what extent Egypt was involved in defending itself against this invasion.[31] This would have been a propitious time for the Israelites to leave Egypt.

Another biblical passage that supports this reconstruction of history is Josh 13: 2, where the districts of the Philistines are reckoned among "the great amount of land remaining to be taken" (v. 1). This passage too is often seen as anachronistic, but I prefer to take the evidence at face value. The Philistines and their Sea Peoples allies were repelled by the Egyptians and made their way to the coast of Canaan c. 1175 B.C.E. Thus they were settled there before the Israelites arrived in the land, which, again based on the archaeological work, points to a time several decades or perhaps a half-century later.

The evidence thus points to an Israelite exodus from Egypt during the reign of Rameses III. It is this chronological argument that suggests the

---

30 For this figure, see Rendsburg (1992) 522-24. On the reliability of the biblical genealogies, see Rendsburg (1990a).

31 See Edgerton and Wilson (1936) 35-58.

above interpretation of the Merneptah Stele: during the reign of Merneptah the Israelites were still slaves in Egypt.

Of some interest is another Egyptian document, P. Anastasi V 19: 2-20: 6 from the reign of Seti II (1205–1200). This text includes the report of another frontier official, also stationed at Tjeku. After the typical formalities at the beginning of the letter, we read as follows: [32]

> Another matter, to wit: I was sent forth from the broad halls of the palace, life, prosperity, health, in the 3rd month of the 3rd season, day 9, at evening time, following after two slaves. Now when I reached the wall of Tjeku on the 3rd month of the 3rd season, day 10, they told me that to the south they were saying that they [i.e. the slaves] had passed by on the 3rd month of the 3rd season, day 10. When I reached the fortress, they told me that the scout (?) had come from the desert stating that they had passed the walled place north of Migdol of Seti Merneptah, life, prosperity, health, beloved like Seth. When my letter reaches you, write to me about all that has happened to them. Who found their tracks? Which watch found their tracks? What people are after them? Write to me about all that has happened to them and how many people you sent out after them.

Once more there are parallels between an Egyptian document and the biblical account. Regardless of the manner in which the Torah presents Israel's history, it is noteworthy that the account includes an Egyptian force sent to pursue escaped slaves (Exod14: 5-9). The above document informs us that this was perfectly natural, in fact, when even only two slaves escaped. Moreover, the route of the two escaped slaves is significant. The two sites mentioned are Tjeku and Migdol. Though some scholars are still skeptical, there is no objection to equating Tjeku with biblical Sukkot,[33] the very site mentioned as the Israelites' point of departure (Exod 12: 37; 13: 20). Migdol, meanwhile, is also mentioned in the biblical account (Exod 14: 2). One gains the impression that the Israelites were utilizing a route well traveled by escaping slaves, a type of "underground railway."[34]

---

[32] For the text, see Gardiner (1937) 66-67. For translations and comments, see Caminos (1954) 254-58, and *ANET* 259.

[33] See Redford (1992) 203 for the equation.

[34] I owe this point to Manuel Gold of the Bureau of Jewish Education in New York City.

About the trek through the desert we can say little. The Torah remains our sole source for this period of Israel's history. But the general picture is reliable. The Israelites wander from place to place with their flocks, they engage in some seasonal agriculture, they have dealings with other peoples of the desert or desert fringe, they construct a portable tent shrine typical of desert folk, they eat manna (a substance still utilized by the Bedouin today), and so on. Eventually, this group of semi-nomads reaches the sown, first the less arable land east of the Jordan River, and then eventually the more arable land west of the Jordan. The biblical account, found mainly in the Book of Joshua, describes the emergence of Israel in Canaan as a military conquest. Archaeological work belies this view, however, and instead points to a different approach, what scholars call the peaceful settlement or peaceful infiltration model.[35] According to this view, as the archaeological surveys in Israel have shown, most of the central hill country which the Israelites occupied was open terrain, very sparsely settled before the arrival of the Israelites. The Israelites simply moved in from the desert and established themselves in the region. Again, as remarked earlier, this is a pattern known throughout history, even in the recent past, as Bedouin groups exchange their nomadic ways for a sedentary life-style (never, however, losing sight of their Bedouin origins, as is the case with many Bedouin groups in regions such as the Galilee today).

The earliest settlements in the central hill country were elliptical sites reminiscent of the Bedouin desert encampments. The Israelites shifted from tents to stone walls, but the "city planning" was the same, an outer circle of dwellings with a large open area inside for the protection of the flocks at nighttime. Only with the passage of time did Israel shift from these elliptical sites to more urban-type settlements, as the process of acculturation to a sedentary lifestyle took hold.

At the same time, however, it must be admitted that the conquest tradition in the Bible is a very strong one. It is hard to imagine that Israel did not have to fight at all upon its arrival in Canaan. Though the terrain was

---

35 See Finkelstein (1988).

sparsely populated, we can assume that on occasion the Israelites needed to obtain territory by military conquest. Moreover, the lack of archaeological evidence to substantiate the biblical record is not a hindrance to accepting the basic outline preserved in the Bible. Comparative analysis reveals that in other instances well-documented historical conquests also cannot be substantiated by archaeological fieldwork.[36]

Given the two methods of achieving territorial advantage, peaceful settlement and military conquest, it is only natural that Israelite authors would choose the latter to glorify in their poetic and prose compositions. This will explain why the national epic preserved in the Bible emphasizes the military approach, even if these battles represent less than the whole truth about the emergence of Israel in Canaan.[37]

To return to the chronological discussion: it is noteworthy that never does the Bible refer to an encounter between the Israelites and the Egyptians in the land of Canaan. Egypt had ruled Canaan, with garrisons stationed there, for most of the 18th and 19th Dynasties. Had Israel arrived in Canaan at anytime prior to 1200 B.C.E., it is difficult to imagine that they would not have encountered the Egyptian military. The Bible's silence in this regard bolsters the view expressed above that the Israelites left Egypt under the reign of Rameses III, that is, during the 20th Dynasty, and arrived in Canaan c. 1150 B.C.E., after the glory years of the Egyptian Empire.[38] Again, there is reference to the presence of Philistines already, and this would assume a twelfth-century setting.

Actually, the Bible may refer to Egypt in Canaan, but in a most interesting and subtle way. Three biblical passages (Exod 23: 28, Deut 7: 20, Josh 24: 12) refer quite enigmatically to God's having sent forth the *ṣir'āh* "hornet" before the Israelites to drive out the population of Canaan. John Garstang was the first to suggest that *ṣir'āh* is a reference to Egypt,[39] and this

36 See most importantly Isserlin (1983).

37 Compare the American epic treatment of "How the West was won," even if, in some cases, open territory was peacefully settled.

38 On the Egyptian rule over Canaan, see Weinstein (1981).

39 Garstang (1931) 258-60.

interpretation has been revived by more recent scholars.[40] This view is based on the fact that the hieroglpyh for the king of Lower Egypt was either a bee or a hornet (depending on one's view of the depicted insect), which the biblical authors then utilized as a symbol for the Pharaoh and for Egypt. The aforementioned presence of Egyptian troops in Canaan, with some mighty military campaigns during the New Kingdom period, would have weakened both the moral resolve and the fighting capabilities of the Canaanites. Under such circumstances, the entrance of the Israelites into Canaan was accomplished with greater ease.

An additional item of interest in this regard is the toponym *maʿyan mê neptôaḥ*, literally "the spring of the waters of Nephtoah," but more accurately "the spring of Merneptah," mentioned in Josh 15: 9, 18: 15, as marking the border between Benjamin and, Judah (modern-day Lifta, three miles west of Jerusalem).[41] Here we have sure evidence that Merneptah campaigned not only in Canaan in general, but in the very area settled by the Israelites at an early stage.

The picture presented to this point represents only a part of the whole. We have followed the main biblical tradition and have commented on its various components with collateral evidence from Egyptian documents and archaeological fieldwork. But the picture is much more complicated. At the outset, I stated that Israel was comprised of peoples of diverse origins, though until now the nation has been treated as rather homogeneous. The evidence for diversity comes from different sources.

At the very time when we assume that the Israelites, that is, the desert or Shasu component thereof, were in Egypt, enslaved under Rameses II, there is evidence that the tribe of Asher was resident in Canaan. P. Anastasi I, dated by most authorities to the reign of Rameses II, is a satirical letter written by the master scribe Hori addressed to a second scribe named Amenemopet, in which the former chastises the latter for his ignorance regarding the topography of Canaan. In the course of his "tour" of the land,

40 Yadin (1979) 67-68, and Borowski (1983).

41 See Rendsburg (1981).

Hori mentions Reḥob and Megiddo and soon thereafter states: "Your name becomes like Qadjardy chief of Asher, when the hyena(?) found him in the *baka*-tree" (lines 23: 6-7).[42] Not everyone agrees that the Egyptian writing *ʾa$_2$-sa-ru$_2$* refers to Asher, but this is by far the most probable interpretation. First, the tribal allotment of Asher,[43] as described in Josh 19: 24-31 is in this very area and includes (apparently) two cities named Reḥob (vv. 28, 30). Second, the tree written as *bi-ka-ʾi* recalls the biblical phrase in Ps 84: 7 *ʿēmeq habbākāʾ* "valley of the *baka*-tree" (thus the traditional interpretation), a northern locale, perhaps to be associated with the city of Baka, located in the Galilee, mentioned by Josephus (*Jewish Wars* 3: 39).[44]

Accordingly, if Asher was resident in northern Canaan during the time of Rameses II, it could not have participated in the events experienced by the desert component of the nation that would emerge as Israel. This is a crucial piece of information for us, and allows us to presume that other elements of the people of Israel were similarly resident in Canaan throughout this period. We can only speculate what must have transpired. The desert folk entered the land of Canaan, and in time elements within Canaan itself came to align themselves with the newly arrived people. What factors would have led to such an alignment we cannot determine. Most likely they were socio-economic, but one cannot rule out the religious factor. Possibly Israel's unique worship of a single god who manifests himself in human history and who protects the underprivileged rung a resonant chord with others in the area.

At a later time we see the same process more clearly. The best example is Jerusalem, which was incorporated into Israel by King David c. 1000 B.C.E. The city was not destroyed, the population was not killed; rather, the residents simply became part of the nation of Israel. This fact would be remembered centuries later when the prophet Ezekiel would address the city with

---

42 For translation and original text, see Gardiner (1911) 25*, 70.

43 For a survey of opinions, see Fischer-Elfert (1986) 199-200.

44 On the Egyptian word, see Hoch (1994) 112-13. On Ps 84: 7 and the Josephus passage, see Goulder (1982) 40 and Rendsburg (1990b) 52-53.

the words, "Your origin and your birthplace is from the land of the Canaanites, your father was an Amorite and your mother was a Hittite" (Ezek 16: 3).

A second tribe of Israel whose origins can be traced is Dan. Here we return to the Sea Peoples invasion of Egypt. Among the allies of the Philistines who attacked Egypt during the reign of Rameses III was a group called the Danuna. Most scholars agree that this group is to be equated with the people known as Danaoi in Greek, Adanawana in Luwian, and *dnnym* in Phoenician (the latter two from the Karatepe bilingual inscription). As noted above, when the Sea Peoples were repulsed by the Egyptians, they were forced to find a new home on the coast of Canaan. Thus, the Philistines settled on the southern coast, and the Egyptian tale of Wenamon (c. 1100 B.C.E.) informs us that the Tjeker (another member of the coalition) settled in Dor. The experience of the Danuna must have been similar, and there is good reason to identify them with the tribe of Dan known from the Bible.[45]

Several lines of evidence converge to argue in favor of this position. First, the original territory ascribed to Dan in Josh 19: 40-46 is on the coast, adjacent to Philistine territory. Second, Judg 5: 17 "and Dan, why do you dwell in ships" connects the tribe to a maritime life. Third, the greatest of Danite heroes, Samson, has intimate relations with the Philistines (Judges 14-16). Fourth, Gen 49: 16 "Dan shall judge his people like one of the tribes of Israel" implies that until this point Dan is not a tribe of Israel and is in the process of joining the tribal league. Fifth, notwithstanding the allotment granted Dan in the Book of Joshua, Judg 18: 1 states that "the tribe of Dan was seeking for itself a land grant in which to dwell, because a land grant had not fallen to it until this day among the tribes of Israel." Sixth, and finally, of all the tribes of Israel, Dan has the least developed genealogy. In fact, Gen 46: 23, Num 26: 42, and 1 Chr 7: 12 each record only one name (either Ḥushim or Shuḥam).

The conclusion to be drawn is that Dan originates with the Sea Peoples Danuna group that reached the land of Canaan by sea at approximately the same time (or slightly earlier [see the above discussion about the Philis-

---

45 Suggested originally by Gordon (1963) 21, and developed by Yadin (1965).

tines]) that the main Israelite group reached Canaan by land. The experience of the Sea Peoples groups will be similar to some extent, but will be different once they settled on the Canaanite coast. For whereas the Philistines in time became the archenemy of the Israelites,[46] the Danites elected to join the Israelite coalition. Again, as with Asher above, we cannot determine for what reasons Dan chose this course. Though in this case it might have been the common enemy, the Philistines, that led Dan to join Israel. For while the Philistines and the Danuna may have been allies during the Sea Peoples attack against Egypt, such cordial relations may have ended once this common enterprise ceased.[47] From passages such as Gen 49: 16, Judg 18: 1, and the evidence of genealogies (or lack thereof), it would appear that Dan was the last of the tribes to join what eventually became the twelve tribes of Israel.

This ends the presentation of the evidence. If we had more information at our disposal, most likely we would be able to speak of the origins of still other Israelite tribes. But the picture that we have presented allows us to reconstruct the early history of Israel along the following lines. The main group of what would emerge as the nation of Israel was a desert group, classified by the Egyptians among the Shasu, who after experiences in the desert and a period of dwelling in Egypt itself, surrendered its desert life-style and settled in the relatively open central hill country of the land of Canaan. There they were joined by other groups to create the nation that the Bible portrays. Among these groups were some, like Asher, which always had lived in Canaan, and some, like Dan, which reached Canaan through other means (even by sea).

To unify these tribes of diverse origins, Israelite literati created a national epic that portrayed the entire nation as experiencing the same

---

46 As long as the Philistines remained in the coastal plain and as long as the main body of Israelites dwelled in the hill country, the two groups could live without hostility. But when both groups began to expand and to contend over the foothills that separate the two concentrations, enmity was the result.

47 How often this is true in the history of the modern Middle East! The most recent example: Jordan, one of the few Arab countries to side with Iraq during the 1991 Gulf War, now allies itself with the United States and Israel.

history. The ancestry of all of Israel can be traced back to one man, Jacob/Israel. All of Israel was enslaved in Egypt. All of Israel experienced the exodus from Egypt, the revelation at Sinai, the wandering through the desert, and the entrance into Canaan from the east. The exodus in particular became the great unifying event for these disparate groups, and Passover became the national holiday *par excellence*, the equivalent of American Thanksgiving (commemorating both a harvest and a new start) and Independence Day rolled into one. All Israelites, no matter of what origin, were to see themselves as having experienced these great events. As such, we can compare the Israelites and Passover with Americans and Thanksgiving. The American people was formed by an on-going series of migrations to this country,[48] yet the single migration central to the American epic tradition is the voyage of the Pilgrims in 1620. Accordingly, all Americans[49] celebrate Thanksgiving and reenact the first Thanksgiving as if their ancestors were on the Mayflower. Similarly, all Israelites were to celebrate Passover as if their ancestors exited Egypt.

I have not referred at all to the biblical tradition which places the homeland of the patriarchs to the far northeast, in Aram Naharaim, essentially modern-day northern Syria and southern Turkey, centered around the cities of Haran and Ur(fa). How this link is to be fit into our picture is beyond our treatment. Should we assume that other Israelite elements migrated to Canaan from Aram? Or that the desert group extended not only to the south and east of Canaan but also to the northeast, essentially following the line at which the Fertile Crescent adjoins the desert?[50] Can we thus explain the many typological parallels between Mari civilization and ancient Israel?[51] Should we incorporate into this picture the fact that Yahweh is attested as a divine name among the Amorites of Syria in the Old

---

48 This includes an element of native Americans as well, but since their history is unique and not related to the present context, I omit them from the discussion.

49 I apologize for the slight exaggeration, but it remains true that Thanksgiving is the single most-widely celebrated holiday in the United States.

50 See Astour (1979) for evidence of Shasu in Syria.

51 See Malamat (1989).

Babylonian period and at Hamath in the 1st millennium B.C.E.?[52] All of these are questions for another time.

Bibliography

Astour, M. C. (1979) Yahweh in Egyptian Topographic Lists. In M. Görg and E. Pusch, eds., *Festschrift Elmar Edel*, 17-34. Bamberg. **Bietak, M.** (1984) Ramsesstadt. In W. Helck, ed., *Lexikon der Ägyptologie* 5: 128-46. Wiesbaden. **Borowski, O.** (1983) The Identity of the Biblical *ṣir'â*. In C. L. Meyers and M. O'Connor, eds., *The Word of the Lord Shall Go Forth: Essays in Honor of David Noel Freedman in Celebration of His Sixtieth Birthday*, 315-19. Winona Lake, Ind. **Caminos, R. A.** (1954) *Late-Egyptian Miscellanies.* Brown Egyptological Studies 1. Oxford. **Černy, J.** (1955) Reference to Blood Brotherhood among Semites in an Egyptian Text of the Ramesside Period. *Journal of Near Eastern Studies* 14: 161-63. **Dalley, S.** (1990) Yahweh in Hamath in the 8th Century B.C.: Cuneiform Materials and Historical Deductions. *Vetus Testamentum* 40: 21-32. **Davies, G. I.** (1991) *Ancient Hebrew Inscriptions: Corpus and Concordance.* Cambridge. **Edgerton, W. F., and J. A. Wilson** (1936) *Historical Records of Ramses III.* Chicago. **Engel, H.** (1979) Die Siegestele des Merneptah. *Biblica* 60: 373-99. **Farrell, R.** (1970–73) Beowulf, Swedes and Geats. *Saga-Book of the Viking Society for Northern Research* 18: 220-96. **Finkelstein, I.** (1988) *The Archaeology of the Israelite Settlement.* Jerusalem. **Fischer-Elfert, H.-W.** (1986) *Die satirische Streitschrift des Papyrus Anastasi I.* Wiesbaden. **Gardiner, A. H.** (1911) *Egyptian Hieratic Texts.* Leipzig. (1937) *Late-Egyptian Miscellanies.* Bibliotheca Aegyptiaca 7. Brussels. **Garstang, J.** (1931) *Joshua and Judges.* London. **Giveon, R.** (1971) *Les Bédouins Shosou des Documents Égyptiens.* Leiden. **Goedicke, H.** (1987) Papyrus Anastasi VI 51-61. *Studien zur altägyptische Kultur* 14: 83-98. **Gordon, C. H.** (1954) The Patriarchal Narratives. *Journal of Near Eastern Studies* 13: 56-59. (1963) The Mediterranean Factor in the Old Testament. In *Congress Volume Bonn 1962*, 19-31. Supplements to Vetus Testamentum 9. Leiden. **Goulder, M. D.** (1982) *The Psalms of the Sons of Korah.* Journal for the Study of the Old Testament Supplement Series 20. Sheffield. **Greenberg, M.** (1955) *The Ḫab/piru.* American Oriental Series 39. New Haven. **Herrmann, S.** (1967) Der Name JHW3 in den Inschriften von Soleb. In *Fourth World Congress of Jewish Studies* 1: 213-16. Jerusalem. **Hoch, J. E.** (1994) *Semitic Words in Egyptian Texts of the New Kingdom and Third Intermediate Period.* Princeton. **Isserlin, B. S. J.** (1983) The Israelite Conquest of Canaan: A Comparative Review of the Arguments Applicable. *Palestine Exploration Quarterly* 115: 85-94. **Jack, G.** (1994) *Beowulf: A Student Edition.* Oxford. **Leemans, C.** (1843) *Monumens égyptiens du Musée d'Antiquités des Pays-Bas à Leide* 2. Leiden. **Loprieno, A.** (1995) *Ancient Egyptian: A Linguistic Introduction.* Cambridge. **Malamat, A.** (1989) *Mari and the Early Israelite Experience.* The Schweich Lectures 1984.

52 The former is widely discussed. On the latter see Dalley (1990).

Oxford. **Rainey, A. F.** (1991) Rainey's Challenge. *Biblical Archaeology Review* 17/6: 56-60, 93. **Redford, D. B.** (1992) *Egypt, Canaan, and Israel in Ancient Times.* Princeton. **Rendsburg, G. A.** (1980) Late Biblical Hebrew and the Date of 'P'. *Journal of the Ancient Near Eastern Society* 12: 65-80. (1981) Merneptah in Canaan. *Journal of the Society for the Study of Egyptian Antiquities* 11: 171-72 (with corrigenda published as Supplement to *JSSEA* 12). (1986) *The Redaction of Genesis.* Winona Lake, Ind. (1990a) The Internal Consistency and Historical Reliability of the Biblical Genealogies. *Vetus Testamentum* 40: 185-206. (1990b) *Linguistic Evidence for the Northern Origin of Selected Psalms.* Society of Biblical Literature Monograph Series 43. Atlanta. (1992) The Date of the Exodus and the Conquest/Settlement: The Case for the 1100s. *Vetus Testamentum* 42: 510-27. (1995) Review Essay of Donald B. Redford, *Egypt, Canaan, and Israel in Ancient Times.* In J. Neusner, ed., *Approaches to Ancient Judaism,* New Series 7: 203-14. South Florida Studies in the History of Judaism 110. Atlanta. (1996) Biblical Literature as Politics: The Case of Genesis. In A. Berlin, ed., *Religion and Politics in the Ancient Near East,* 47-70. Bethesda, Md. **Rothenberg, B.** (1993) Timnaʿ. In E. Stern, ed., *The New Encyclopedia of Archaeological Excavations in the Holy Land* 4: 1475-86. Jerusalem. **Sarna, N. M.** (1966) *Understanding Genesis.* New York. **Stager, L. E.** (1985) Merneptah, Israel and Sea Peoples: New Light on an Old Relief. *Eretz Israel* 18 (Nahman Avigad Volume): 56*-64*. **Talmon, S.** (1966) The "Desert Motif" in the Bible and in Qumran Literature. In A. Altmann, ed., *Biblical Motifs.* Cambridge, Mass. (1993) *Literary Studies in the Hebrew Bible.* Jerusalem. **de Vaux, R.** (1978) *The Early History of Israel.* Philadelphia. **Weinfeld, M.** (1987) Israelite Religion. In M. Eliade, ed., *The Encyclopaedia of Religion* 7: 481-97. New York. **Weinstein, J. M.** (1981) The Egyptian Empire in Palestine: A Reassessment. *Bulletin of the American Schools of Oriental Research* 241: 1-28. **Wilson, J. A.** (1933) The ʿEperu of the Egyptian Inscriptions. *American Journal of Semitic Languages and Literatures* 49: 275-80. **Yadin, Y.** (1965) "And Dan, Why Do You Dwell in Ships." In *Western Galilee and the Coast of Galilee,* 42-55. Jerusalem (in Hebrew). (1979) The Transition from a Semi-Nomadic to a Sedentary Society in the Twelfth Century B.C.E. In F. M. Cross, ed., *Symposia Celebrating the Seventy-fifth Anniversary of the Founding of the American Schools of Oriental Research,* 57-68. Cambridge, Mass. **Yurco, F. J.** (1990) 3,200-Year-Old Picture of Israelites Found in Egypt. *Biblical Archaeology Review* 16/5: 20-38.

Nabonidus of Babylon

Ronald H. Sack
North Carolina State University

Anyone who has ever read Second Kings or the books of Daniel and Jeremiah of the Old Testament is familiar with the name of Nebuchadnezzar, the king of Babylon who conquered the kingdom of Judah and destroyed Solomon's temple. As the second member of the Chaldean dynasty of Mesopotamia (626–539 BCE), he ruled for forty-three years (605–562 BCE), during which time he also organized a number of building projects that were to transform Babylon into one of the seven wonders of the ancient worlds. Tales of these legendary achievements, as well as those of his father, Nabopolassar (626–605 BCE), also found their way into the narratives of a number of Greek, Roman, and medieval historians and chronographers many centuries later. Yet despite the predominance of Nebuchadnezzar in these sources, perhaps the most intriguing figure of sixth-century BCE Babylonia is Nabonidus (556–539 BCE), the last monarch of the Chaldean period, whose reign was brought to an abrupt end through the conquest of Babylon by Cyrus the Great of Persia in 539 BCE. Like his famous predecessor, Nabonidus campaigned in foreign lands and supervised building activities in Babylon and elsewhere. Yet his name is almost totally absent from a number of the sources that comment extensively on the achievements of Nebuchadnezzar. On the other hand, so many strange events occurred during his reign that he became the subject of more varied characterizations in his own contemporary written sources than any other monarch of the Chaldean period. In view of the unevenness of the written record, one might wonder why he is so prominent in one body of source material, yet so conspicuously absent from the other. For this and other reasons, we will examine the surviving accounts of Nabonidus of Babylon, while placing emphasis on the highly unusual aspects of the reign of this fascinating individual.

When undertaking an examination of Nabonidus' reign, we are immediately confronted with a major problem. While the origins of Nebuchadnezzar and Nabopolassar can easily be determined,[1] those of Nabonidus cannot. We do know that he succeeded Labaši-Marduk and that he ruled as king of Babylon for seventeen years.[2] Yet while Berossus, in his *Babyloniaca*, notes that he was not related to any of his predecessors, Nabonidus himself tells us he was a legitimate successor of Nebuchadnezzar and Neriglissar (560–556 BCE).[3] An even bigger problem is that of determining how he seized power in the first place. Neriglissar died shortly after his campaign in Cilicia in early April of 556 BCE. His son and successor, Labaši-Marduk, ruled for another two months before Nabonidus took control.[4] The dated cuneiform contract tablets support this conclusion, since cities from Nippur to Babylon and Sippar dated their documents to the accession year of Nabonidus. While there is no direct evidence to support the contention that Nabonidus' son, Belshazzar, had something to do with the murder of Labaši-Marduk, it is certainly possible that he had a hand in the accession to the throne of his father, with the ultimate goal in mind of becoming king himself. We know, after all, that Belshazzar had business dealings with prominent banking families that were famous for their activities during the

1 Wiseman (1985) 5ff. The discussion here deals in great detail with the ancestry of the Chaldean Dynasty. Although many of the conclusions drawn are controversial, it is the best discussion of the sources available. For an even more controversial treatment of the rise of Nabopolassar to prominence, see Zawadski (1987) 3ff.

2 The most complete treatment of all sources available is Beaulieu (1989). A discussion of the datable contract tablets is also available in Parker and Dubberstein (1956) 5ff.

3 See Langdon (1912) Cylinder 8, Column 5. See also Berger (1973) 384-86. For a discussion of the contributions of Berossus and other classical sources to Nabonidus scholarship, see Beaulieu (1989).

4 Parker and Dubberstein (1956) 5.

reigns of Nebuchadnezzar and Neriglissar.[5] He may even have profited from the confiscation of property belonging to Neriglissar following Labaši-Marduk's death.

Although the suggestion has been made that Nabonidus may have been related to the Chaldean dynasty through marriage to one of Nebuchadnezzar's daughters,[6] the fact remains that Nabonidus' own inscriptions do support Berossus' contention that he "was not related to the royal line." He probably came from the western fringes of the Chaldean kingdom and was certainly well advanced in age when he ascended the throne. He claims to have been an only child, who had no followers and no desire to become king.[7] To some degree, this view finds support in the famous "biography" of Adad-guppi, Nabonidus' mother, which was unearthed many years ago at Haran in Syria.[8] It, like other significant inscriptions, was erected there by Nabonidus himself following his return to Babylonia from Arabia. While centering on the restoration of the Ehulhul temple of Sin, it contains the assertion that Adad-guppi was responsible both for acquainting Nabopolassar and Nebuchadnezzar with her son, and for his subsequent advancement to a position of higher authority. This may, indeed, be true, since there is no evidence that Nabonidus himself had any ties to prominent Babylonian business interests (unlike his predecessor, Neriglissar),[9] or that he had held a position in a temple bureaucracy.

Normally, one need only consult surviving royal inscriptions to recover details of a Chaldean monarch's early years. However, such is not the case with Nabonidus. In fact, such sources as the *Verse Account of Nabonidus*[10]

---

5 In addition to the discussion in Beaulieu (1989), see Dougherty (1929), which is still a useful treatment of the activities of both men during the years prior to Cyrus' seizure of power in Babylon.

6 Wiseman (1985) 11ff.

7 Langdon (1912) Cylinder 8. See also the important analysis of the Nabonidus inscriptions in Tadmor (1965).

8 See Gadd (1958) 35ff., as well as Pritchard (1979) 106-9.

9 See Sack (1994) 222ff.

10 See Pritchard (1950) 313.

and the *Nabonidus Chronicle*[11] are incomplete or are not preserved in good condition. It is clear, nevertheless, that Nabonidus not only can be credited with a number of significant achievements but he also acted in a way that fit the role of a traditional Babylonian monarch. For example, he campaigned in Cilicia, attended to the building of fortifications around his capital city, and excavated the foundations of a number of temples in his kingdom, including the Egipar in Ur and the Ebabbar in Sippar.[12] He also restored or reinstated religious practices associated with Marduk in Sippar and Uruk. In doing this, Nabonidus repeatedly linked himself with the accomplishments of a number of his predecessors, and his royal inscriptions stressed his "antiquarian" interests as well as his reign's continuity with the past.[13] It also appears that he allowed the bureaucracies of such major temples as Eanna in Uruk to function largely as they had prior to his accession to the throne. Although the subject of his possible extensive "reorganization" or "intervention" in the affairs of Eanna has precipitated much debate,[14] there is very little evidence that anything "new" really took place. Temple administrative documents clearly do contain mention of such officials as the *šar rēš šarri bēl piqitti Eanna*; this should not be surprising, since opposition to the succession of a number of monarchs apparently emerged at various times. It is also true that the majority of previously-published texts from the Chaldean period suggest an absence of this "official" prior to 555 BCE. However, evidence from the Eanna temple clearly shows that this title not only did not first appear with the reign of Nabonidus, but also

---

11 See Grayson and Redford (1973) 117-28.

12 See a discussion of this text in Beaulieu (1989) and also Tadmor (1965) no. 22.

13 See Langdon (1912) Cylinder no. 5 and the interesting discussion in Grayson and Redford (1973) 117ff.

14 See most recently Frame (1991) 65ff. This article includes a convenient bibliography of virtually all significant literature published on the subject, as well as a discussion of the meanings associated with official titles. This subject was also treated in Joannès (1982, as well as by others. Unfortunately, Frame's conclusions regarding the extent of the reorganization of the Eanna temple during the first year of Nabonidus are not entirely supported by all available evidence. See Sack (1995) 431.

that it was well established as early as the reign of Nebuchadnezzar[15] and that control exercised by the palace over temple activities was common throughout the Chaldean period. Evidence such as this raises serious doubts concerning not only the nature of the "reorganization" of the Eanna temple hierarchy in the time of Nabonidus, but also the extent of that reorganization. If anything, royal intervention or control of temple affairs was an established fact long before Nabonidus became king. Our picture of the relationship of temple and palace has simply been heretofore distorted by the relatively small number of Chaldean administrative documents published to date. Indeed, Nabonidus may have acted according to a tradition going back to at least the Neo-Assyrian period.

In 553 BCE, after a second Cilician campaign, Nabonidus left Babylon for Syria, Anti-Lebanon and Arabia. Belshazzar, his son and co-regent, ruled in his father's stead for at least ten years.[16] Although the subject of the king's sojourn to the oasis of Tema and Arabia has generated much literature over the past several decades,[17] the purpose of the visit remains unclear. While we do know that Nabonidus made Tema his principal residence and stationed troops there, the evidence from Tema itself published to date still leaves many questions unanswered. Nevertheless, Assyrian kings had long been aware of the immense economic resources of northern Arabia.[18] Also, while the name of Nabonidus is not preserved in any Arabic source, Nebuchadnezzar's name occurs in several places. The most interesting of these is to be found in the *Annales (Tarikh al-Rusul wal-Muluk)* of Muham-

---

15 As to problems that may have arisen related to succession of monarchs of the Chaldean period in Uruk, see Hunger and Kaufman (1975) 371ff. Since then, a number of scholars have taken issue with their interpretation of this interesting text. See Wiseman (1985) 101ff.

16 See most recently the thought-provoking study of Beaulieu (1995).

17 The literature on this topic is immense. See, for example, Dougherty (1922), and the bibliography associated with this topic in Beaulieu (1995).

18 Assyrian monarchs from Tiglath-Pileser III (745–727 BCE) to Sennacherib (705–681 BCE) recognized the immense potential of the area and tried to exploit its resources in various ways.

mad b. Jarir Aṭ-Ṭabari (written in the tenth century A.D.). It is here that one finds a fascinating account of a raid said to have been conducted by Nebuchadnezzar against the Arabs. It reads as follows:

> So Bukht Naṣr (=Nebuchadnezzar) fell on those in his country of the merchants of the Arab, and they used to come with traders and merchants and trade grain and dates and cloth and other things, and he gathered those he seized of them guards and keepers. Then he announced to the people the raid, and they prepared for that. The account spread out among those near them of the Arab. So groups of them came to him surrendering and asking protection.[19]

Whether the above account actually refers to a raid in Arabia conducted by Nebuchadnezzar II is, of course, open to question. It does, nevertheless, suggest that control of the trade routes from Arabia to Mesopotamia may have been a motivating factor in Nabonidus' decision to reside in Tema for at least a decade.

Additional information regarding Nabonidus' sojourn to Tema can be found in the chronicles and contract tablets datable to the king's reign. These sources differ markedly from the rather one-sided characterizations of the Persian sources (to be discussed shortly), since they are rather dry, event-by-event records of happenings associated with each year. Both the *Nabonidus Chronicle* and the economic texts contain numerous references to the king's journey to Tema; both note the monarch's absence from Babylon during at least a three-year period of time. We know that the Persians associated his lengthy journey with a neglect of his kingly responsibilities;[20] anyone devoted to Marduk would hardly have avoided being present during the celebration of the New Year's festival, thus necessitating the cancellation of such an essential event. This fact was certainly worthy of note in both the contract tablets and the *Nabonidus Chronicle*, where we read:

---

19 See Goeje (1881–82) 671. I am indebted to Dr. Gordon Newby of Emory University for this translation.

20 See A. L. Oppenheim's translation of the *Verse Account of Nabonidus* in Pritchard (1950) 313.

> The seventh year: The king (was) in Tema (while) the prince, his officers and his army (were) in Akkad. [The king] did not come to Babylon [in the month of Nīsan]. Nabû did not come to Babylon. Bēl did not come out. The [Akitu festiv]al [did not take place].
>
> The ninth year: Nabonidus, the king, (was) [in] Tema (while) the prince, the officers, (and) the army (were) in Akkad. The king did not come to Babylon in the month of Nisan. Nabû did not come to Babylon. Bēl did not come out. The Akitu festival did not take place. The offerings were presented (to) the gods of Babylon and Borsippa as in normal times in Esagil and Ezida.[21]

What, then was the king's justification for his own absence? The answer is to be found in his account displayed in Haran—namely, he was commanded to do so by his god until a ten-year period of time elapsed, after which he could re-enter his capital city. As he explains:

> He (Sin) decimated the inhabitants of the country, but he made me leave my city Babylon on the road to Tema, Dadanu, Padakku, Hibra, Jadihu even as far as Jatribu. For ten years I was moving around among these (cities) and did not enter my own city Babylon .... As to the land of the Arabs which [is the eternal enemy] of Babylonia [and which] was (always) *ready* to rob and carry off its possessions, Nergal broke their weapons upon the order of Sin, and they all bowed down at my feet.[22]

In the words of Nabonidus, he was merely carrying out the orders of Sin; he did only what he was instructed to do by divine command. Thus, while the Persians could exploit the absence of the king from Babylon to their own propagandistic advantage, the inhabitants of Haran were witnessing the acts of a perfectly normal monarch doing only what a devout servant of Sin would be expected to do. The accounts of these deeds, then, naturally carry forth the positive tradition that emphasizes the king's piety.

Further mention of the king's journey to Tema can be found in the so-called *Prayer of Nabonidus*—an Aramaic document found four decades ago at Qumrân. While the date of this manuscript is, relatively speaking, late

---

21 Grayson (1975a) 106-7.

22 See Pritchard (1979) 109-12.

(first century, BCE), it contains descriptions that are at least similar to those of the Persian sources discussed below. These characterizations suggest a continuity that spanned several centuries and kept alive a folkloristic image that was to be characteristic of several of the Hebrew sources, especially the Book of Daniel.

> The words of the prayer that Nabonidus, king of A[ssyria and Ba]bylon, the [great] king, prayed [when he was smitten] with a bad inflammation by the decree of the [Most High God] in [the city of] Tema. [With a bad inflammation] I was smitten for seven years and from [men] I was put away. But when I confessed my sins and my faults, He (God) allowed me [to have] a soothsayer. This was a Jewish [man of the exiles in Babylon. He] explained [it] and wrote [me] to render honor and g[reat glor]y to the name of the [Most High God. Thus he wrote: 'When] you were smitten with a b[ad] inflammation in [the city of] Tema [by the decree of the Most High God] for seven years, [you we]re praying to gods of silver and gold, [of bronze], iron, wood, stone, (and) clay...that th[ese] gods...'[23]

This incredible piece (which is, of course, midrashic in genre) identifies Nabonidus and Daniel (he must be the Jewish man of the text) and mentions Babylon and Tema—all the aspects of a historical reconstruction. The purpose of the text is clear—namely, to magnify the God of Heaven while emphasizing the skill and sagacity of the Jewish sage. This seems to indicate that the Old Testament in general, and the Book of Daniel in particular, assume far greater importance (both from a folkloristic and an historical point of view) than the somewhat imaginary reconstructions found in the later *Midrash Rabbah*. Hence, while the name of Nabonidus does not occur anywhere in the Old Testament, the *Prayer of Nabonidus* illustrates that the Jews of the Post-Exilic period were familiar with the Tema tradition and made ample use of it in describing the madness of Nebuchadnezzar in the Book of Daniel. It also found its way into the *Lives of the Prophets*, where there can be no mistaking the origin of the characterization of Nebuchadnezzar with the historical Nabonidus and his son Belshazzar:

---

23 See Hartman (1978) 174ff. See also Milik (1978).

> He made great supplication in behalf of Nebuchadnezzar whose son Belshazzar besought him for aid at the time when the king became a beast of the field, lest he should perish. For his head and foreparts were those of an ox, his legs and hinder parts those of a lion. The meaning of this marvel was revealed to the prophet: the king became a beast because of his self indulgence and his stubbornness. This is the manner of tyrants, that in their youth they come under the yoke of Satan; in their latter years they become wild beasts, snatching, destroying, smiting and slaying.[24]

The City of Babylon and Nabonidus

We noted earlier that Nebuchadnezzar initiated a number of important building projects for which his reign was justly famous. Not only were the massive fortification walls surrounding Babylon built, but Marduk's temple, Esagila, and the king's own palaces did not escape his attention. "I plated the furnishings of Esagil with red gold," he writes, "and the processional boat with yellow gold and (precious) stones (so that it was studded) like the heavens with stars." In like manner, Nebuchadnezzar "completed the work on Ezida and decorated (it) with platings of silver (and) gold and studdings of precious stones."[25] As to the image of Marduk in Esagila he "placed (various) stones on the top of his crown, (with other stones) I studded his crown." In all these instances, the emphasis rests on the king's serving as the provider of the gods, and the statement "Nebuchadnezzar indeed provides for our sanctuaries"[26] turns up in many of his inscriptions. Therefore it would seem, on the surface at least, that these building projects of Nebuchadnezzar, once brought to a successful conclusion, would have necessitated little in the way of further construction by his successors. By 562 BCE, Babylon was heavily fortified; elaborate palaces housing the royal family were now in evidence, and Marduk's temple once more stood as a symbol of the god's power and the Chaldean king's greatness. However, only seven years after Nebuchadnezzar's death, a series of strange events occurred. Nabonidus, the last king of the dynasty, bore no relation to the

---

24 Torrey (1946) 39.

25 Langdon (1912) no. 126 iii 11.

26 Langdon (1912) 118.

royal line. Although he tells us in his own inscriptions that he considered himself to be a legitimate successor of Nebuchadnezzar and Neriglissar, the fact remains that his origins are still unknown and they clearly served as a source of friction that would eventually result in Persian conquest. Nevertheless, like his predecessors, Nabonidus channeled great energy into the rebuilding of temples in cities throughout his realm. In fact, his inscriptions abound with details of excavation and temple building that find few parallels in the records of other earlier Mesopotamian monarchs. The Esagila in Babylon required and received appropriate attention. So did the temple of Shamash in Sippar, and one of our cuneiform texts details his rebuilding of the Ebabbar, which had fallen into ruins:

> The inscription of Naram-Sin, son of Sargon (of Akkad), I discovered but did not alter. Anointing it with oil and making sacrifices, I deposited it with my inscriptions and thus returned it to its proper place.
>
> Ebabbar, the temple of the god Shamash, which had long ago become dilapidated and become like a hill of ruins....In the reign of Nebuchadnezzar II, a former king son of Nabopolassar, the sand and mounds of dust which had accumulated on the city and that temple were removed and Nebuchadnezzar discovered the foundation of Ebabbar from the time of Burnaburiash, a former ancient king, but he did not discover the foundation of an older king who preceded Burnaburiash although he looked for it. So he rebuilt Ebabbar on the foundation of Burnaburiash. Then Shamash...commanded me, ...Nabonidus, ...to restore Ebabbar...the sand which had covered the city and that temple was taken away...its foundation appeared and its layout was exposed. I found therein the inscription of Hammurapi, an old king who seven hundred years before Burnaburiash had built Ebabbar and the temple-tower upon an old foundation for Shamash. I was overcome with awe.
>
> He (the god) showed Nabonidus, his reverent servant who looks after his shrines, the foundation of Naram-Sin, son of Sargon (of Akkad). In that year, in a favourable month, on a propitious day, without altering it one finger-length, Nabonidus laid its base on the foundation of Naram-Sin, son of Sargon—the foundation of Ebabbar, temple of Shamash. He discovered the inscription of Naram-Sin and, without altering it, restored it to its proper place. He deposited it with his own inscriptions.[27]

---

27 Grayson and Redford (1973) 126-27.

Yet the overriding concern was the sanctuaries of Sin, the god of the moon worshipped under the name Nanna in Sumerian times, and later a primary deity of the *Aramu*, or northern Aramaeans. In the third millennium BCE, the city of Ur was not only a cult center of Nanna, but also the capital of the Third Ur Dynasty. Thus we should not be surprised to see Nabonidus attempting to rebuild his temple, even to the extent of tracing its original foundations. His own account of the work reads as follows:

> Nabonidus, king of Babylon, patron of the temples Esagil and Ezida, worshipper of the great gods, I: Elugalgalgasisa, the temple-tower of the Egishnugal in the city of Ur, which the ancient king Ur-Nammu had built but not completed so that his son Shulgi had to complete the work; I examined the inscriptions of Ur-Nammu and his son Shulgi and realized that Ur-Nammu had built but not completed that temple-tower so that his son Shulgi had to complete the work; now that temple-tower had become old. Using as a base the old foundation which Ur-Nammu and his son Shulgi had built, I repaired the damage to that temple-tower, as in olden days, with bitumen and baked brick. For the god Sin, lord of the gods of heaven and underworld, king of the gods, god of the gods who dwell in the highest heaven, lord of Egishnugal in the city of Ur, my lord, I rebuilt it.
>
> O Sin, lord of the gods, king of the gods of heaven and underworld, god of the gods who dwell in the highest heaven, when you joyfully enter that temple may there be on your lips blessings for Esagil, Ezida, and Egishnugal, the temples of your great divinity. Reverence for your great divinity instill in my people that they might not sin against your great divinity. May their foundations be as firm as those of heaven. Deliver me, Nabonidus, king of Babylon, from sinning against your great divinity and grant me long life. In Belshazzar, my own offspring, my eldest son, instill reverence for your great divinity that he might have no sin and enjoy an abundant life.[28]

This preoccupation with the god Sin was explained both by Nabonidus himself and by his mother, Adad-guppi—a votaress of Sin in the Syrian city of Haran. In her "autobiography," she not only tells the story of the restoration of Sin's temple, the Eḫulḫul, but also associates this act with the rise of Nabonidus to power in Babylon:

---

28 Grayson and Redford (1973) 118.

> (Eventually) his wrathful heart quieted down and he became reconciled with the temple Ehulhul, the temple of Sin in Haran, the divine residence in which his heart rejoices, and he had a change of heart. Sin, king of all the gods, looked with favor upon me and called Nabonidus, my only son, whom I bore, to kingship and entrusted him with the kingship of Sumer and Akkad, (also of) all the countries from the border of Egypt, on the Upper Sea, to the Lower Sea. Then I lifted my hands to Sin, the king of all the gods [I asked] reverently and in a pious mood: (ii) "Since you have called to kingship [Nabonidus, my son, whom I bore, the beloved of his mother,] and have elevated his status, let all the other gods—upon your great divine command—help him (and) make him defeat his enemies, do (also) bring to completion the (re)building of the temple Ehulhul and the performance of its ritual!" In a dream Sin, the king of all the gods, put his hands on me saying: "The gods will return on account of you! I will entrust your son, Nabonidus, with the divine residence of Haran; he will (re)build the temple Ehulhul and complete this task. He will restore and make Haran more (beautiful) than it was before! He will lead Sin, Ningal, Nusku and Sadarnunna in solemn procession into the temple Ehulhul!
>
> I heeded the words which Sin, the king of all the gods, had spoken to me and saw (them come true). Nabonidus, the only son whom I bore, performed indeed all the forgotten rites of Sin, Ningal, Nusku and Sadarnunna, he completed the rebuilding of the temple Ehulhul, led Sin, Ningal, Nusku and Sadarnunna in procession from Babylon (*Shuaana*), his royal city, installed (them again) in gladness and happiness into Haran, the seat which pleases them.[29]

This highly unusual act, like the king's journey to Tema, provided the Persians with an opportunity to capitalize on the discontent generated among Nabonidus' own subjects. After Cyrus II entered Babylon in 539 BCE, he went to great lengths to woo dissatisfied elements unhappy with what had happened during the preceding years. He immediately allied himself with the Marduk party by not destroying the capital city of the former Chaldean kingdom and respecting local custom, administrative organization, and religious rites.[30] As a consequence, the priest-scribes in Esagila

---

29 Pritchard (1975) 106. For the most recent treatment of the Adad-guppi material, see d'Agostino (1994), which treats the king's relationship to the cult of Sin.

30 See the interesting article of Amélie Kuhrt (=Kuhrt [1990]) in Beard and North (1990).

produced propagandistic accounts of the events of the last years of Nabonidus' reign that were to cast the king in a negative light. Here, naturally, Nabonidus is blamed not for being inattentive to the responsibility of caring for and restoring temples in various urban centers, but for neglecting Marduk and attempting to institute the worship of a new god (*i.e.*, Sin of Haran) whom no one had ever seen in the land. Such an unusually critical attitude appears in the *Verse Account of Nabonidus*, an editorialized inscription composed to justify the end of the Chaldean dynasty and the rise of Persia to prominence. The relevant section reads as follows:

> [He had made the image of a deity] which nobody had (ever) seen in (this country)
> [He introduced it into the temple] he placed (it) upon a pedestal;
> [...] he called it by the name of Nanna,
> [...it is adorned with a...of lapis] lazuli, crowned with a tiara,
>
> [...] its appearance is (that of) the eclipsed moon,
> [...the gest]ure of its hand is like that of the god Lugal.ŠU.DU,
> [...] its head of hair [reac]hes to the pedestal,
> [...in fr]ont of it are (placed) the Storm (*abûbu*) Dragon and the Wild Bull.[31]

Subsequently, the king's famous journey to Tema is portrayed, with emphasis on the consequences rather than the causes of it, especially the termination of the celebration of the New Year's festival. It reads:

> He let (everything) go, entrusted the kingship to him
> And, himself, he started out for a long journey,
> The (military) forces of Akkad marching with him;
> He turned towards Tema (deep) in the west.
>
> He started out the expedition on a path (leading) to a distant (region). When he arrived there,
> He killed in battle the prince of Tema,

Here one finds a discussion of the Babylonian "culture" in general. Some of Kuhrt's conclusions (especially those dealing with Nabonidus' relationship to the worship of Sin) are, in this author's opinion, not supported by available evidence.

31 Pritchard (1950) 313.

> Slaughtered the flocks of those who dwell in the city (as well as) in the countryside,
> And he, himself, took his residence in [Te]ma, the forces of Akkad [were also stationed] there.[32]

Similar to the *Verse Account* is the *Cyrus Cylinder*, a type of royal inscription extolling Cyrus and detailing the transfer of power from Nabonidus. Like the preceding account, the evil deeds of the last Neo-Babylonian monarch are detailed, with emphasis being placed on the positive elements in the Achaemenid conquest of Babylonia. Passages related to our subject read as follows:

> The chief of the gods (Marduk) was enraged by their complaints (and he left) the region. The gods who dwelt amongst them left their sanctuaries, angered that Nabonidus had brought them into Babylon.
>
> But the god Marduk...took pity on the people of Sumer and Akkad who had become like corpses, he was appeased and had mercy. Carefully looking through all lands he sought an upright prince after his own heart. Taking him by the hand he pronounced his name: "Cyrus, king of Anshan." He designated him for rule over everything. At his feet he subdued the Qutu and all the Ummanmanda. The black-headed people which Marduk had allowed him to conquer he always administered in truth and justice. The god Marduk, the great lord, guardian of his people, looked with joy upon his good works and upright heart. He commanded him to march to his city Babylon.[33]

In examining these accounts, and considering the contents of Nabonidus' own inscriptions (both in Babylon and Haran), it is not hard to understand why the later classical writers considered Nabonidus to be only a name in a list, while the Persians viewed him as an example of something never to be repeated again. The Achaemenids did not consider either the construction or restoration of sanctuaries that were characteristic of Nabonidus to be significant, since they were considered the traditional responsibilities of Babylonian monarchs. Instead, the activities of the king

32 Pritchard (1950) 313-14.

33 Pritchard (1950) 313.

amounting to behavior that went *contrary* to the traditional will of a god had to be emphasized. Cyrus II, of course, had to cast his own image in a favorable light; having taken Babylon through force and betrayal, it was necessary to be propagandistic in justifying his success. Such, therefore, were the circumstances surrounding the creation (by the priest-scribe of Marduk in Babylon) of an account which focused on the outright heretical acts of the last king of the Chaldean period.

Nebuchadnezzar's forty-three-year reign was one in which devotion to Marduk was accepted fact; Nabonidus, on the other hand, not only halted the New Year's festival but also forsook his kingdom for a sojourn to Tema. But the most hated act of all was his preoccupation with the god Sin of Haran, a preoccupation that, as we have just seen, formed an integral part of the king's own elaborate accounts. Thus, while Nabonidus (in one quarter of his kingdom, at least) may have been viewed as a monarch devoted to the worship of Sin and to the care and upkeep of his sanctuaries, to the *Babylonians* (under Persian rule) and the Jews of the Post-Exilic period, Nabonidus was, literally, mad and, consequently, did not deserve the devotion of his subjects. As a result, many of these hostile characterizations in the Achaemenid portrayals were to be incorporated into other sources where they were employed for different reasons.

The Fall of Babylon

By the time Nabonidus returned to Babylon in 543 BCE, Cyrus of Persia had already conquered the kingdoms of Media and Lydia, which left Babylonia open to invasion from virtually all sides. Unfortunately, the surviving cuneiform sources are either fragmentary or say nothing of substance about the events that may have taken place between 543 and 540 BCE. In fact, strangely, Nabonidus' name is missing from what does survive.[34] Nevertheless, there is no evidence of engagements between Chaldean and Persian forces prior to 543 BCE. Belshazzar, Nabonidus' son and co-regent, had been left in charge of affairs in Babylonia during his father's absence. Belshazzar's

---

34 Dougherty (1929) 114ff.

name occurs in a number of contract tablets and letters datable to the first fourteen years of Nabonidus' reign.[35] These comment on his business dealings with certain prominent banking houses or "families," most notably Egibi and Nur-Sin. In addition, they document Belshazzar's rise to power prior to Nabonidus' eleventh year, and outline some of his official duties as co-regent after 545 BCE. He appears to have had ample authority to give orders to temple officials in Uruk and Sippar, and could even lease temple land. His name disappears from the contract tablets in Nabonidus' thirteenth year; it has been suggested that this coincides with Nabonidus' return to Babylonia from Tema.[36] Whatever the case, we do know that Belshazzar commanded Babylonian troops in the vicinity of Sippar when Cyrus II conquered Anatolia (545 BCE), yet nothing is known of his activities after 543 BCE. There is some evidence that Belshazzar had already sided with the Marduk priests in Babylon prior to his father's return to the capital; hence he may have stood in opposition to Nabonidus' "heretical" acts in order to strengthen his own position.

Despite a raid into southern Babylonia from Elam in 546 BCE, the Chaldean kingdom was still relatively strong when Nabonidus returned from Tema. Uruk and its vicinity were still in the king's camp, and it was only after Anatolia was secured by Cyrus II that things began to crumble.[37] Cyrus' own pro-Persian propaganda contributed to his success, since he repeatedly insisted that Nabonidus tried to alter traditional religious beliefs by replacing Marduk with Sin, who now became the supreme god of Babylonia. The pro-Persian party in the capital city may have fomented resistance to Nabonidus, thus making the capture of Babylon that much easier. Whatever the case, Cyrus' armies eventually took Babylon in 539 BCE and

---

35 Dougherty (1929) 114ff. For a brief discussion of the relationship of Nabonidus to Belshazzar while the king was absent from the capital, see Beaulieu (1995) 976.

36 Unfortunately we know next to nothing about what political or military events took place during Nabonidus' absence from Babylon.

37 Of course, Herodotus' *Histories* I, 17 makes clear that Lydia and the kingdom of the Medes were firmly in Cyrus' hands before Babylon was taken in 539 BCE.

the Chaldean kingdom came to an end. The later classical Greek sources assert that Nabonidus died in another part of the Persian empire some time after Babylon fell.[38] Within a year of Cyrus' takeover, the Hebrews, who had been led into captivity by Nebuchadnezzar II in 586 BCE, returned to Judah and their period of exile ended.[39]

Nabonidus' name does not occur anywhere in the Hebrew Bible, in the *Apocrypha*, or in the *midrashim* forming what is known as the *Midrash Rabbah*. His reign was not forgotten by the Hebrew writers, however. The Maccabean author(s) of the Book of Daniel, four centuries removed from the Chaldean period, chose to substitute the name of Nebuchadnezzar for that of Nabonidus (especially in Daniel 2-6), not because of an ignorance of history or because the events of the Exilic period were forgotten,[40] but due to the fact that Nebuchadnezzar was the architect of the Captivity and a didactic commentary could best realize its objectives through a portrayal of a king that combined history and fiction. To the Hebrew writer, it did not matter whether a characterization harmonized with historical accuracy; the events of the reign of Nabonidus could be combined with an account of the destruction of the city of Jerusalem by Nebuchadnezzar in order to construct an image of a king that could easily be related to the rule of any monarch at any point in time. Nabonidus appeared in his own and later sources in such a way as to *fit* the situation involving Nebuchadnezzar that was being described. Certainly, the Achaemenids needed to (and did) emphasize Nabonidus' lack of attention to Marduk; when the Hebrews returned to Palestine, they carried with them their own hatred for Nebuchadnezzar, plus the Persian hostility toward Nabonidus, and, as a consequence, transformed them both into a story of a conqueror-king who would forsake his god and require the worship of another by his subjects (Daniel 3: 1-3). The subsequent account of the madness of Nebuchadnezzar (Daniel

38 For a convenient summary of these sources, see Beaulieu (1989).

39 The Book of Ezra, chapter 6, records the decree allowing the Hebrews to return to Judea after the Babylonian Captivity (initiated by Nebuchadnezzar II in 586 BCE).

40 See von Soden (1935) 88-89.

4: 33) reflects the contents of the *Lives of the Prophets* and the *Wisdom of Ahiqar*, and also echoes the *Prayer of Nabonidus* quoted earlier, where the king is said to have lived apart from men for seven years. Not limited by either time or space, the events of the reign of Nabonidus became applicable to all periods of history.

Bibliography

Beard, M., and J. North, eds., (1990) *Pagan Priests: Religion and Power in the Ancient World.* London. **Beaulieu, P.-A.** (1989) *The Reign of Nabonidus, King of Babylon (556-539 B.C.).* New Haven. (1995) King Nabonidus and the Neo-Babylonian Empire. In Sasson 1995: 969-79. **Berger, P. R.** (1973) *Die neubabylonischen Königsinschriften, Königsinschriften des ausgehenden babylonischen Reiches (626–539 a. Chr.).* Alter Orient und Altes Testament, 4/1. Neukirchen-Vluyn. **d'Agostino, F.** (1994) *Nabonedo, Adda Guppi, il deserto e il dio luna: storia, ideologia e propaganda nella Babilonia del 6. sec. a. C.* Pisa. **Dietrich, M., and O. Loretz**, eds. (1995) *Vom alter Orient zum alten Testament: Festschrift für Wolfram Freiherrn von Soden zum 85. geburtstag am 19. Juni 1993.* Alter Orient und altes Testament 240. Neukirchen-Vluyn. **Dougherty, R. P.** (1922) Nabonidus in Arabia. *Journal of the American Oriental Society* 42: 305-14. (1929) *Nabonidus and Belshazzar.* Yale Near Eastern Researches 15. New Haven. (1933) Tema's Place in the Egypto-Babylonian World of the Sixth Century, B.C. *Mizraim* 1: 140-43. **Foster, B. F.** (1983) Nabonidus at Kesh. *Revue d'assyriologie et d'archéologie* 77: 92-93. **Frame, G.** (1991) Nabonidus, Nabû-šarra-uṣur and the Eanna Temple. *Zeitschrift für Assyriologie und vorderasiatische Archäologie* 81/1: 37-86. **Gadd, C. J.** (1958) The Haran Inscriptions of Nabonidus. *Anatolian Studies* 8: 35-92. **Goeje, M. J., *et. al.***, eds. (1881-82) *Annales*, Prima Series. Vol. 2. Leiden. **Grayson, A. K.** (1975a) *Assyrian and Babylonian Chronicles.* Texts from Cuneiform Sources, 5. Locust Valley, N.Y. (1975b) *Babylonian Historical-Literary Texts.* Toronto. **Grayson, A. K. and D. B. Redford** (1973) *Papyrus and Tablet.* Englewood Cliffs, N.J. **Güterbock, H. and T. Jacobsen**, eds. (1965) *Studies in Honor of Benno Landsberger on His Seventy-fifth Birthday, April 21, 1965.* Assyriological Studies 16. Chicago. **Hartman, L. F.** (1978) *The Book of Daniel.* The Anchor Bible. Vol. 23. Garden City, N.Y. **Hunger, H. and S. Kaufman** (1975) A New Akkadian Prophesy Text. *Journal of the American Oriental Society* 95/3: 371-75. **Kuhrt, A.** (1990) Nabonidus and the Priesthood of Babylon. In Beard and North 1990: 117-55. **Kuhrt, A. and H. Sancisi-Weerdenburg**, eds. (1990) *Center and Periphery: Proceedings of the Groningen 1986 Achaemenid History Workshop.* Achaemenid History 4. Leiden. **Joannès, F.** (1982) *Textes économiques de la Babylonie récente.* Paris. **Lambert, W. G.** (1969) A New Source for the Reign of Nabonidus. *Archiv für Orientforschung* 22: 1-8. (1972) Nabonidus in Arabia. In *Proceedings of the Fifth Seminar for Arabian Studies: Held at the Oriental Institute, Oxford,*

22nd and 23rd September, 1971, 53-64. London. **Langdon, S.** (1912) *Die neubabylonischen Königsinschriften.* Vorderasiatische Bibliothek, Heft IV. Leipzig. **Milik, J. T.** (1978) Prière de Nabonide (4Q or Nab). *Revue de Qumrân* 9/4: 483-95. **Olmstead, A. T.** (1925) The Chaldean Dynasty. *Hebrew Union College Annual* 2: 29-55. **Parker, R. and W. H. Dubberstein** (1956) *Babylonian Chronology 626 B.C.-A.D. 75.* Brown University Studies 19. Providence, R.I. **Pritchard, J. B.** (1950) *Ancient Near Eastern Texts Relating to the Old Testament.* Princeton. (1975) *The Ancient Near East.* Volume II. *A New Anthology of Texts and Pictures.* Princeton. **Röllig, W.** (1964) Nabonid und Tema. In *Compte-rendu de l'onzieme Rencontre Assyriologique Internationale*, 21-32. Leiden. **Sack, R. H.** (1982) Nebuchadnezzar and Nabonidus in Folklore and History. *Mesopotamia* 17: 67-131. (1994) *Neriglissar—King of Babylon.* Alter Orient und Altes Testament 236. Neukirchen-Vluyn. (1995) Royal and Temple Officials in Eanna and Uruk in the Chaldean Period. In **Dietrich and Loretz** 1995: *Vom Alten Orient zum Alten Testament*, 425-32. **Sasson, J. M.** (1995) *Civilizations of the Ancient Near East.* 4 Volumes. New York. **Tadmor, H.** (1965) The Inscriptions of Nabunaid: Historical Arrangement. In Güterbock and Jacobsen 1965: 351-64. **Torrey, C. C.** (1946) *The Lives of the Prophets: Greek Text and Translation.* Society of Biblical Literature Monograph Series 1. Journal of Biblical Literature Monograph Series 1. Philadelphia. **von Soden, W.** (1935) Ein babylonische Volksüberlieferung von Nabonid in den Daniel zählungen. *Zeitschrift für die alttestamentliche Wissenschaft* 53: 81-89. (1983) Kyros und Nabonid. Propaganda und Gegenpropaganda. In *Archäologische Mitteilungen aus Iran.* Ergänzungsband 10, 61-68. Berlin. **Wiseman, D. J.** (1985) *Nebuchadrezzar and Babylon.* Oxford. **Zawadski, S.** (1987) *The Fall of Assyria and Median-Babylonian Relations in Light of the Nabopolassar Chronicle*, Poznan.

The Vow of Mutiya, King of Shekhna* [1]

Jack M. Sasson
University of North Carolina at Chapel Hill

Vows to the gods and the grief they create when they are neglected (or tardily fulfilled) have generated a literary theme that was well-cultivated in antiquity and is nicely studied in our time. In honoring my beloved teacher Michael Astour, I want to launch into this topic by focusing on an Old Babylonian letter found at Tell-Leilan by a Yale expedition.

The letter (L87-1317) is edited in an article by Jesper Eidem who kindly placed page-proofs at my disposal.[2] It was sent to Til-Abnu (also known as Tillaya) who ruled Apum, a region in the eastern portion of the Khabur triangle, from his capital Shekhna, now Tell-Leilan. A number of eponymal dates plus a synchronism with Babylon allow us to slot our letter around 1745 B.C.E., so within a few years after the death of Hammurabi of Babylon.

---

* Abbreviations list: A: Siglum for tablets from Mari; AbB: Altbabylonische Briefe. See Frankena (1966); ARM: Archives royales de Mari; FM2: Charpin and Durand (1994); KTU: *Die Keilalphabetischen Texte aus Ugarit*; L: Siglum for tablets from Tell-Leilan, (see Eidem [1991], Ismail [1991], and Vincente [1991]; MARI: *Mari. Annales de Recherches Interdisciplinaires*; NABU: *Nouvelles Assyriologiques Brèves et Utilitaires*; OB: Old Babylonian; SI: Samsu-iluna; ZL: Zimri-Lim.

1 This is a lightly revised version of a presentation given at one of the sessions of the Middle West Branch of the American Oriental Society honoring Professor Michael C. Astour (February 11, 1996).

2 Edition and brief discussion in Eidem Forthcoming. Eidem has translated the text in his (1991) 125, and in Matthews and Eidem (1993) 204.

The writer of the letter is Ea-Malik, about whom more will be said below. The burden of his message does not come until line 14 of the letter. So I skip the opening paragraph to read what Ea-malik is counseling Til-Abnu:

> Now it is you [Til-Abnu] whom the goddess has touched with her finger, and you have ascended the throne of your father's house. Within 14 days, the goddess plans to leave her temple so that boundary markers could be set in place. (*They should be set as the goddess heads to Alā.*) You must grant, and not withhold, whatever is the need of the goddess. You may wish to offer an excuse such as, "Troops are badgering us!" or "We are destitute!"; but you must not think it! Satisfy the goddess with what is at your disposal, and this goddess will keep you healthy.

Ea-Malik is writing just before a festival in which the great goddess Bēlet-Nagar leaves her temple, presumably in Nagar (a town at or near Tell Brak), and heads toward a shrine at a nearby town. Her trip may have had to do with setting up boundary markers for estates or villages. Although by the Old Babylonian period Nagar's prestige was no longer what it was half a millennium earlier, its goddess Bēlet-Nagar continued to be widely venerated and her frequent peregrinations drew many regional rulers who paid her homage at her many stops.[3] Thus, about twenty years earlier, a local ruler wrote to Zimri-Lim of Mari,

> I have heard the tablet my lord sent me. My lord wrote to me about a festival, saying, "Come here!" However, from this region Bēlet-Nagar...will be taken on a tour. I must welcome her in the town of Iluna-akhi itself while Khaya-sumu (king of Ilanṣura) must welcome her in Mishkilum. As for me, I must also welcome her on behalf of Khaya-abum [of Shekhna], and make sacrifices to her in Khazakkanum itself. For this reason I have not come to meet my lord, but I have just dispatched to him Ewri, who knows what is going on.[4]

We do not know what else beyond sacrifices a full homage to Bēlet-Nagar entailed; but in our particular case, Ea-Malik who had obviously

---

3 See Matthews and Eidem (1993), but especially Guichard (1994) 269-72.

4 See Guichard (1994) 238, #122.

heard enough excuses in his lifetime, did not leave the choice up to Til-Abnu: he must give whatever the goddess says she needs, he tells Til-Abnu, nor must he reduce or delay his gifts.[5] The specifics about this gift are not spelled out; but to prepare Til-Abnu for the proper decision, Ea-Malik tells him,

> Now then, I am (also) sending to you the priest of Bēlet-Nagar, your lady. Send him back to me after you have advised him of your full intent, whatever it is.

I wish I could be precise about the identity of this Ea-Malik. Jesper Eidem has told me of an unpublished treaty in which the king of Kakhat (Yamṣi-Khatnu) is joined by Ea-Malik when exchanging oaths with Til-Abnu of Shekhna. Ea-Malik, then, would have been in line to become king of Kakhat and may have written his letter while honing his skills at Nagar, a town downstream of Kakhat, as was the common practice of the time.[6]

Whatever his true affiliation, Ea-Malik could demand fealty to the goddess not because in the past Til-Abnu had also made a vow, but because, as Ea-Malik claims, the latter owes his throne to Bēlet-Nagar. He writes that the goddess touched Til-Abnu—metaphorically, but likely also physically—and thus made it possible for him to ascend his father's throne.[7] The

---

5 In his edition of the text, Eidem speculates that Bēlet-Nagar expects to receive a town.

6 The only published text known to me that could link Ea-Malik to Kakhat is L87-710 (=Ismail [1991], #115), a record of disbursement of gifts to many dignitaries, "when the king (=Til-Abnu) met with the 'man' of Kakhat." Recorded first is "a silver vessel, weighing 10 shekels, a Babylonian-style uṭ.ba (*tuttubatum*) garment to Ea-Malik." An Ea-Malik, messenger from Karkamish, is mentioned in Vincente (1991) 222 #85. Mari records know of a number of Ea-Maliks, none of whom seems a candidate for equation with our letter-writer.

7 *Lapātum*, "to touch," could be made into a metaphor for selection. For example, in FM2: 50: 5-9, Akshak-magir writes the king, "Ever since my lord selected me in Samanum, I have remained observant of my lord's utterances and have indulged neither in the commission nor omission of a crime. In fact, my lord has rewarded me freely."

To connote an intimate involvement in the selection, *lapātum* could be construed with *suqtum*, "chin," as in A.450: 5ff. (cited Durand, [1988] 378; see comments in Veenhof [1989]/40: 27), "My lord has given me a very large responsibility, but I am not up to it. Just as it is God who 'calls' human beings, now me—a mere worm at the

idiom Ea-Malik uses in line 16, *ana kussi bīt abīka tērub*, literally meaning "you have come into your ancestor's throne," evokes a rather precise climb to power. However, despite our rather limited knowledge of the period, the idiom cannot be taken literally, for on his cylinder seal Til-Abnu gives Dari-Epukh as his father's name. Had this Dari-Epukh ruled in the Khabur area or elsewhere, he would have had to be a contemporary of Zimri-Lim. Yet despite their loquacity about political matters in the Khabur Triangle, the Mari records have so far nothing to say about him. In fact, we have a pretty extensive list of people who ruled Shekhna since the days of Shamshi-Addu, and none of them is called Dari-Epukh.[8] Moreover, we know that Til-Abnu succeeded not his father, but a Muti-Abikh, also called Mutiya.[9] As this Mutiya was the subject of the object lesson Ea-Malik wished to draw, we should get back to Ea-Malik's opening paragraph and read what it says,

---

base of a wall—my lord majestically (lit. "in accordance with his divinity") 'touched my chin,' to send me out toward (important) men."

The intimacy conveyed by the idiom as used in Mari is not easily paralleled in another OB text, AbB2: 154: 14-17 (= Frankena [1966]), where it occurs third in the sequence "going to someone's aid," "giving him encouragement," and "touching his chin"; the whole is contrasted to destraining his slave.

8 Here is a tentative list:

From texts found in Mari

Samiya	Sumu-Yamam—Zimri-Lim (at transition)
Turum-nadki	barely a couple of years
Susu	after viii.ZL3′
Khaya-abum	ZL4′-9′
Kunnam	an Elamite, is "lord of Shubat-Enlil" ZL9′
Qarni-Lim	of Andariq, via Shamash-Dayyan his aide, had a household there [information from Leilan documents]
Atamrum	ZL9′-11′
Khimdiya	ZL11′-12′+ ; includes Azamkhul (=? Mohammed Diyab?, see FM2, 242)

From texts found at Leilan

Mutu-Abikh	(Mutiya) son of Halumpimu
Til-Abnu	(Tillaya), son of Dari-Epukh (once ruled Shurnat)
Yakun-Ashar	his brother, briefly also ruling at Ilanṣura; defeated by Samsu-Iluna (SI23).

9 Eidem speculates that Til-Abnu was a nephew of Mutiya. See lastly, Eidem forthcoming: ms 5.

> In the past, before he could ascend his throne, Mutiya kept on making the following vow, "If I were to ascend my throne, I shall donate silver, gold, cups of silver, cups of gold, and skillful maids to Bēlet-Nagar, my Lady!" This is what he kept on vowing. (Yet) when this man did ascend his throne, he totally ignored the goddess and did not even visit her once!

While we cannot evaluate Ea-Malik's full intent when he crafted this passage, we nevertheless can observe that he used language that was far from pedestrian. We notice first that since he was addressing Mutiya's immediate successor, it was hardly necessary for him to open on *pānānum*, "in the past." Yet, it is this adverb that draws Til-Abnu from immediate events and thus invites him to reflect on lessons taught by history. We further notice that because the entire clause in lines 3-4, "before he could ascend his throne" (*lāma ana kussîšu irrubu*), depends on a durative construction, it sharpens the futurity of a past declaration and thus effectively invites Til-Abnu to observe Mutiya as he ponders his avenues for kingship.[10]

Three times in this passage, Mutiya is said to be after a "throne," *kussûm*, (*kussîšu*, lines 3 and 10; *kussîya*, line 5), but not after a "dynastic throne," *kussi bīt abim*, as when said about Til-Abnu in line 16. Although the distinction between phraseologies remains to be fully grasped, it may not have been an inconsistency on Ea-Malik's part when, in speaking of Til-Abnu's own rise to power in the middle paragraph of his letter, he chose the more complete idiom.[11] He may well have sought to flatter Til-Abnu by giving him a ruling ancestry. But, again, from what we now know about the succession at Shekhna, it looks like we should have doubts about the legitimacy of Mutiya no less than that of Til-Abnu. In fact, Mutiya's own father was called Halumpimu, and this Halumpimu hardly makes an appearance

---

[10] Another reference to the formula is in M.11072, Durand [CEO8} 1995: 441. Interestingly, it is not attached to a royal figure!, "I have written to my lord, 'Ever since Yakbar-Lim has taken his throne (*ana* ^{giš}GU.ZA-*šu īrub*), this man does not harbor goodwill toward me'."

[11] The formula *ana bīt abīšu īrub* occurs at Leilan in an *inūma* clause (Vincente [1991] #63 [L 87-761]; see p. 184), "A half mina of silver, delivery of [x], from Yatti[m$^?$], when Lawila-Addu, from Shuppa, came to power."

in the Mari records even when he must have been an exact contemporary of Zimri-Lim and Shamshi-Addu.[12]

Although the Akkadian word for a vow-containing appeal, *ikribum*, does not occur in Ea-Malik's letter, we find in lines 4 and 9 two iterative forms of a cognate verb *karābum* encasing Mutiya's pledge. In choosing iteratives, Ea-Malik intimates that Mutiya has had to repeat his pledge many times before the goddess was convinced of his sincerity. But by using these forms, Ea-Malik may also be justifying how knowledge of the vow reached him: Mutiya repeated his pledge, probably as the goddess was making her rounds. If so, it must have occurred within hearing of a priesthood which, as observed above, was beholden to Ea-malik.[13]

The vow itself turns out to be direct and fairly standard. As expected, the condition (protasis) of lines 6-7, "If I were to ascend my throne" (*šumma ana kussīya ēterub*), includes a verb in the perfect. However, the promise (apodosis) in lines 7 to 8, "I shall donate silver and gold, silver and gold cups, and skillful maids to Bēlet-Nagar, my Lady!," which is unexceptionally controlled by a precative, has a rather curious content: it is specific in pledging silver, gold, precious vessels, and pretty maidens; yet it fails to set limits on the amount to deliver. This comment requires a brief excursus.

A painstaking, though probably not complete, review of pre-Roman near eastern vows (but not oaths) allows me to distinguish between those

---

12 The information comes from the inscription of a cylinder seal cited in Vincente (1991) 8: "Mutu-Abikh, son of Halupimu, beloved of Addu and of the Bēlet-Apim."
A Mutu-Abikh is mentioned in ARM 5: 2 (collated by Durand [1987] 212) as a brother of a ruler who joined a coalition that threatened Mari, then governed by Yasmakh-Addu. We learn practically nothing about Mutu-Abikh's background, whether or not we equate the two references. As to his father Halupimu, most of the names from Mari documents that are of similar coinage, belong to menials. Moreover, none of the kings of Shekhna and the land of Apum known to us from the Mari texts had a name that is anything like it. Although warned not to make too much from the absence of evidence, we may nevertheless be justified to assume that Mutiya was not to the manor born. Rather, like many leaders in the Khabur region of the Mari age, he rose to the throne on the corpses of previous holders.

13 This observation is consistent with the fact that in the ancient Near East, vows were most often formulated in proximity of a deity; Cartledge (1991) 134.

that were originally composed in first person mode (singular or plural) and those that were attributed to petitioners even when the vow they utter is quoted as if delivered in first person mode. The first category includes many formulaic and rhetorical sentiments that easily transport from one psalm, one petitionary prayer, to another.[14] Once such declarations are set aside, there remains in this category a few votive expressions that are carved on monuments and (letter-)prayers crafted under extraordinary circumstances. In such formulations, pledges, even when modest in amount, tend to be itemized and are often tailored to suit the occasion.[15] Two examples will suffice: If Nintinugga would restore Inannakam to full health, Inannakam would serve the goddess forever; if Lelwanis revitalizes her husband Khattushili III, Pudu-Khepa, queen of the Hittites, would donate a life-size statue of the king in silver and gold.[16]

Vows that are attributed to petitioners, however, are almost uniformly set in literary texts or in texts that partake of literary. To this second category belongs the handful of vows embedded in biblical narratives and, for that matter, in classical literature, although I do not report on them here. What makes these vows differ from those of the preceding category is not that they diverge in vocabulary or structure—in fact, there is much that they do share—but that the discharge or neglect of a vow itself becomes a plot element for new moves in a larger narrative. This is obvious when Jacob vows allegiance to the god who would protect his sojourn in Aram Naharaim (Genesis 28: 20-22), when Jephtha makes an unnecessary and seemingly irrevocable pledge (Judges 11: 30-40), when Hannah promises her son

---

14 On the issues, see Cartledge (1991) 150-61.

15 Compare with the many Roman inscriptions with the formulaic VSLM (*votum solvit libens merito*, "he gladly and duly paid his vow.")

16 For bibliography, see Cartledge (1991) 75, 105-7. Pudu-Khepa has left us many vows, some of which are cited in texts translated in Goetze (1969). Whether they are culled from dreams and whether they follow Kizzuwatna practices are not of immediate concern here. Fuller studies are in Otten (1975) and Otten and Souček (1965). See also de Roos (1987).

Beckman (1996) 12 reports the presence of an as yet unpublished "vow" among documents from Emar.

to God (1 Samuel 1: 11), and when Absalom invokes a vow as reason for setting off for Hebron (2 Samuel 15: 7-8).[17]

Plot design, however, is not at stake when, to quote Numbers 21: 1-3, "Israel made a vow to the Lord and said, 'If you deliver [the Canaanites of Arad] into our hand, we will proscribe their towns'." Beyond providing us with one of two etymologies for the place name Hormah (see also Judges 1: 17), this particular episode hardly advances the story line, which remains jagged and episodic in these chapters. Rather, the incident becomes emblematic and foretelling of what could be achieved when the Hebrews, acting as the corporate unit "Israel," commit themselves to God and thereby earn his favor. In this sense, it matches the moralistic and pedagogic goals of Ea-Malik's letter. Not surprisingly, the two share a directness in framing the protasis (condition). It might be said also that both contain rather "generic" formulations in the apodosis (promise) for, its generosity notwithstanding, Mutiya's pledge nevertheless lacks the enumerative realism or contextual particularism that we find, for example, in the many vows of Pudu-Khepa's. Whether we should ascribe this stereotyping to Mutiya himself or to Ea-Malik's willful reshaping of the original pledge cannot be easily solved; but the linkage among Mutiya, the neglect of his vow, and an implied sordid fate, will permit me to revisit one of the more famous extra-biblical vows that archeologists have recovered from the ancient Near East.

Ugarit was a great Mediterranean seaport, lying right across the sea from Cyprus's jutting accusing finger. Until its destruction around 1200 B.C.E., Ugarit hosted an international community of merchants. Its bards used alphabetic cuneiform to write a number of imaginative poems in a language closer to Hebrew than to any of the other living semitic languages. One of them features King Keret who, when his story opens, is bereft of family and therefore of hope for the future. The god El instructs him on

---

17 Classical texts are also full of narratives in which vows and their (non-)fulfillment were featured in narrative. Spectacular is the devotion of Publius Decius Meus who, in 340 B.C.E., paid the ultimate sacrifice as consequence of a vow (Livy 8.9.9). A similar story is told about his son, of the same name (Livy 10.28). For a fine introduction to the topic, see the fourth chapter of Hickson (1993).

mounting a military expedition to another kingdom from which to secure the bride with whom he will rebuild his dynasty. But on his way there, Keret meets Asherah as she makes her rounds and he delivers before her a most gratuitous pledge: "If I take Hurraya into my home, bring the maid into my court," he promises her, "I will give her double in silver, her triple in gold." A memory slip, a forgotten vow, almost brings Keret and his dynasty to a precarious end.

Over 20 years ago, Michael Astour examined the personal, place and ethnic names that are mentioned in the Keret Epic (*ḫbr, udm, ṣrm, ṣdyn, dtn,* and *ilḥu*). He found parallels for them not in the documents of Late Bronze Age Ugarit, but in the Middle Bronze archives of Mari, especially those concerned with Northern Mesopotamia. He therefore proposed that, whatever modern scholars may think of the story's historical roots, the poets of Ugarit themselves set their tale in the Khabur triangle rather than nearer the Mediterranean coastline.[18] Working in 1972, Astour could cite well-known Mari texts that demonstrated strong ties between Mari, Halab and Ugarit. But now, thanks to the Leilan archives, which had not been excavated when Astour wrote, we have come to realize how tight were these bonds; for these archives show that during the century-and-a-half interval between the collapse of Mari and the Hittite raid on Babylon (that is between 1760 and 1600 B.C.E.) Halab dominated the politics, if not also the intellectual life, of a vast area, from the Mediterranean coast to the Upper Khabur valley. Even more relevant is the recovery of the moral or ethical temper of the Middle Bronze Age, delivered to us in letters exchanged among the leaders of the time. Thus, from these letters,

---

18 Astour (1993). In that study, Astour also directed our attention to lines 197-99 [=KTU 1.14 IV.34-36]) of Keret which tell us how Keret delivered his vow: *ym*[*ġy.*] *lqdš aṯ*[*r*]*t*[.]*ṣrm wlilt ṣd*[*y*]*nm*. Because of the preposition *l* attached to *qdš*, Astour did not agree with the usual translations that would have Keret reach a shrine of Asherah before making his pledge. Rather, he proposed that *lqdš aṯ*[*r*]*t* was but another way of saying *lilt* and suggested a parallelism between "her holiness Asherah," and "goddess." Keret uttered his fateful vow, therefore, when Asherah met him as he made his way to Udm. At most, recent translations simply footnote Astour's suggestion; but in light of the letters I have cited above, with their information about access to peripatetic divinities, I think that Astour is surely correct here.

– we read about a king who openly admits that arrogance and repudiation of solemn oaths led to his own father's early demise;[19]
– we recover a prophet's admonition that God prefers the love of justice over the fulfillment of pious deeds;[20]
– we follow inspiring anecdotes about the miserable fate awaiting evildoers;[21]
– we are made privy to a nomadic chieftain's meditations on the futility of war and the allure of peace.[22]

---

19 The quotation is from A.4251, a text from which fragments have been cited in the literature. I have pieced it together from the following: [α] lines 3-23 (Durand [1993] 55); [β] lines 25-29 [*ibid.*, 60n93]; [γ] lines 36-46 (*sub* Sasson [1985] 254. Darish-Libur writes Zimri-Lim,

> [α] I have heard the tablet meant for Yarim-Lim that my lord sent me. I gave precise account of what my lord's position, as was written on the tablet, before Yarim-Lim and Aplakhanda [of Carkemish]. My lord should listen ... to his reactions. Once I gave Yarim-Lim a detailed account, he answered me,
>
> > Zimri-Lim has ousted his enemy, but now his requests are hard. Sumu-Epukh, my father, respected Shamshi-Addu but reached [his goals?]. [But when he came close] to the kingdom that Addu had given Shamshi-Addu, Sumu-Epukh, my father, did not live until old age: because [he attacked] the land that Addu had given Shamshi-Addu, Addu killed him. Until now, Addu has had no cause to be angry with me... .
> > [β] Zimri-Lim has forgotten the matter of Addu (*ṭēm* ᵈIM, Durand: "la volonté d'Addu"). It is evident that in Addu's territory, escapees must not be handed over (to anyone). Does Zimri-Lim not know (this)?...
> > [γ] Had these men been in my land and I denied them to Zimri-Lim, Zimri-Lim should be immediately resentful. From now on—be it one, two or, even ten years—should these men plan to enter my land and my kingdom, I shall bind them and have them brought to Zimri-Lim. Should I not fulfill this promise to Zimri-Lim, may Addu of Halab bring Yarim-Lim to account.

20 For discussion (and previous bibliography), see Sasson (1994) 314-16.

21 See my forthcoming comments to A.350+A.616, in which are reported three versions of the death of Susu (Zuzu), king of Apum. The original text is published in Durand (1992).

22 The following passage (ARM 26: 39: 32-42) is extracted from a letter Nakhimum, an Ubrabu leader, sent to Asqudum, one of the king's closest advisors,

> Is it normal/just, that all of you have set your mind to make trouble? that upon news of peace you plan to despoil your colleagues, (thinking) "Peace is distant,

Of course, I cannot claim that Mutiya's egregious lapse directly influenced what was told about Keret. I could, however, suggest that these two accounts of misbegotten vows, one embedded in an epic and the other conveyed in a letter, are exploiting two themes that readily combine in popular belief: the first develops from the commonplace that achievers too often neglect benefactors who had once boosted their rise; the second depends on the conventional crediting to wrathful gods any exceptional or precipitous collapse of power. To the pious, therefore, neglected vows give fine opportunity not only to reflect on the fall of the mighty, but also to delve into some of the less mysterious facets of theodicy.

Still, Ea-Malik's letter notwithstanding, we do not know what really happened to Mutiya. That he ruled but briefly there is no doubt, given the time brackets we have for him: a couple of years on either side of 1750, just when in Babylon Samsu-iluna was succeeding his father Hammurabi. That in his days, Mutiya was a significant, albeit regional, power-player is also beyond doubt thanks to the letters Eidem has cited in diverse publications, but especially in light of the administrative archives C. Vincente published in a Yale Dissertation (Vincente [1991]). Although datable to the better portion of just one eponymal year, these archives tell how Mutiya and Ashtamar-Addu [II] of Kurda formed an alliance to attack Khazip-Teshub of Razama and Buriya of Andarig. Naturally the victims counter-attacked, and they had success because Hammurabi of Halab dispatched *ḫabbātū*-mercenaries to their aid. Mutiya eventually sued for a separate peace with

---

> and we must constantly be concerned about war." Don't you know that when disturbances break out, they will never go away, and the future becomes worse than the past? Indeed, because of these conditions, will the bad—never the good—not triumph?

Mari documents occasionally deliver gnomic statements. I cite only two rather pungent examples. In ARM 26: 392: 45-48, Hammurabi of Babylon is quoted to say, "If a house has solid foundations while its upper storey has collapsed [...] of the house [...] remains solid. But if its foundations have collapsed, even when its upper storey is solid there is nothing its builder can do: it will fall." In ARM 26: 171: 14-15, tribal leaders embed the following rhetorical verity, "Does a man who dies of thirst come back to life when thrown in a river? Once (the gods) set up his score card, a dead man can never come back to life."

each of his adversaries, a solution brokered by Ben-Dammu, Hammurabi of Halab's own marshall. So much for what we more or less know.

The documents do not tell us how the change on the throne of Shekhna took place. But for the Ea-Malik lesson to work, Mutiya could not have ended his reign normally. Of course, he could have been unseated by Til-Abnu, who until then had been in charge of a minor locale in the region, and it would not have been the first time in those brutal days that such "not-so-musical chairs" were being played. If that is what happened, I fail to see the logic in Ea-Malik rehearsing Mutiya's fall to someone in a better position to know it. I rather think, therefore, that Mutiya died suddenly and unexpectedly, perhaps from a stroke or a heart attack, and the rumor mills quickly gave his inconstancy toward the goddess as reason for his fate.

What about Til-Abnu? Did he learn anything from Ea-Malik's letter? Did he load the priest up with gifts for Bēlet-Nagar? I have no answers here either; but I rather doubt it, for Til-Abnu's successor to the throne of Shekhna was his own brother, Yakun-Ashar and the transition seems to have been peaceful. Yet, Yakun-Ashar ruled that city but briefly. Within a couple of years of Yakun-Ashar's own rise to power, Samsu-Iluna of Babylon raided Shekhna and forced it into his own empire. Afterwards, we never hear anything more of either of Dari-Epukh's two sons. The moral to draw should be evident to any scholar, such as Michael C. Astour, whose command of near eastern lore includes that in biblical literature: As is told in Exodus 34: 7, some gods may skip a generation or two before exacting their full revenge.

TABLE 1: Tell Leilan L87-1317

obv. *[a]-na ti-la-ab-nu-ú qí-bí-ma*
um-ma ^{d}*é-a-ma-lik-ma*
pa-na-nu-um ^{1}*mu-ti-ia la-ma a-na* ^{giš}gu-za-*šu*
i-ir-ru-bu ki-a-am ik-ta-ar-ra-ab
um-ma šu-ma šum-ma a-na ^{giš}gu-za-*ia*
e-te-ru-ub kù-babbar kù-gi *ka-sa-at* kù-babbar
ka-sa-at kù-gi *ù* mí-tur-meš *it-p[u-ša-tim]*
a-na ^{d}nin-*na-ga-ar be-el-ti-ia l[u-ud-di-in]*
an-ni-tam ik-ta-ar-ra-ab
ki-ma lú *šu-ú a-na* ^{giš}gu-za-*šu i-ru-b[u]*
da-ḫa-at ^{d}*il-tim ú-ul i-ša-al*
ù pa-an ^{d}*il-tim a-ma-ru-um-ma*
ú-ul i-mu-ur

l.e. *i-na-an-na ka-ta* ^{d}*i[l]-/t[um]*
[i]-na ú-ba-nim il-pu-ut-ma
rev. *a-na* ^{giš}gu-za é *a-bi-ka te-ru-ub*
iš-tu u$_4$*-mi-im an-ni-im a-na* u$_4$-14-kam
^{d}*il-tum iš-tu* é-*ša uṣ-ṣe-em-ma*
pu-ul-lu-uk-ka-tum iš-ša-ak-ka-na
ù pa-an ^{d}*il-tim a-na* uru *a-la-a*^{ki}
iš-ša-ak-ka-na ḫi-še-eḫ-ti ^{d}*i[l]-tim*
i-di-in la ta-ka-al-la
as-sú-ur-ri te-qí-tam ta-ra-[aš-ši]
um-ma-a-mi ṣa-bu-um ú-ba-az-z[i]/-ḫa-an-né-t[i]
šu-ul-pu-ta-nu an-ni-tam la ta-[qa-ab]-bi
i-na ša i-ba-aš-šu-ma ^{d}*il-tam*
šu-ul-li-im-ma ^{d}*il-tum ši-i*
li-ba-al-li-iṭ-ka

u.e. *a-nu-um-ma* lú *ša-an-ga*
[š]a ^{d}nin-*na-ga-ar*
be-el-ti-ka
l.e. *[a]ṭ-ṭar-da-ak-kum an-ni-tam la an-ni-tam*
[ṭ]e$_4$*-em-ka ga-am-ra-am šu-uk-na-aš-šu-ma*
ṭúr-da-aš-šu

TRANSLATION

In the past, before he could ascend his throne, Mutiya kept on making the following vow, "If I were to ascend my throne, I shall donate silver, gold, cups of silver, cups of gold, and skillful maids to Bēlet-Nagar, my Lady!" This is what he kept on vowing. (Yet) when this man did ascend his throne, he totally ignored the goddess and did not even visit her once!

Now it is you whom the goddess has touched with her finger, and you have ascended the throne of your father's house. Within 14 days, the goddess plans to leave her temple so that boundary markers could be set in place. (*They should be set as the goddess heads to Alā.*) You must grant, and not withhold, whatever is the need of the goddess. You may wish to offer an excuse such as, "Troops are badgering us!" or "We are destitute!" But you must not think it! Satisfy the goddess with what is at your disposal, and this goddess will keep you healthy.

Now then, I am (also) sending to you the priest of Bēlet-Nagar, your lady. Send him back to me after you have advised him of your full intent, whatever it is.

Bibliography

Astour, M. C. (1973) A North Mesopotamian Locale of the Keret Epic. *Ugarit Forschung* 5: 29-39. **Bachelot, L.** (1990) *Tell Mohammed Diyab. Campagnes 1987 et 1988.* Nouvelles Assyriologiques Brèves et Utilitaires Cahiers 1. Paris. **Beckman, G.** (1996) Emar and Its Archives. In Chavalas 1996: 1-12. **Cartledge, T. W.** (1991) *Vows in the Hebrew Bible and the Ancient Near East.* Journal for the Study of the Old Testament Supplement Series 147. Sheffield. **Charpin, D.** (1990a) A Contribution to the Geography and History of the Kingdom of Kahat. In Eichler 1990: 67-85. (1990b) La région de Kahat et de Shoubat-Enlil d'après les Archives Royales de Mari. *Les Dossiers d'Archéologie* 155: 64-71. (1990c) Recherches philologiques et archéologie: Le cas du médaillon <<GUR$_7$-ME>>. *Mari. Annales de Recherches Interdisciplinaires* 6: 159-60. (1990d) Tell Mohammed Diyab, une ville du Pays d'Apum. In Bachelot 1990: 117-22. **Charpin, D., and J.-M. Durand**, eds. (1994) *Florilegium marianum, II. Recueil d'études à la mémoire de Maurice Birot.* Mémoires de Nouvelles Assyriologiques Brèves et Utilitaires 3. Paris. **Chavalas, M. W.**, ed. (1996) *Emar: the History, Religion, and Culture of a Syrian Town in the Late Bronze Age.* Bethesda, Md. **Classen, W.**, ed. (1970) *Text and Context. Old Testament and Semitic Studies for C. F. C.*

Fensham. Journal for the Study of the Old Testament Supplement Series 48. Sheffield. **Durand, J.-M.** (1987) Villes fantômes de Syrie et autres lieux. *Mari. Annales de Recherches Interdisciplinaires* 5: 199-234. (1988) *Archives Épistolaires de Mari*, I/1. Archives Royales de Mari 26. Paris. (1992) Ed. *Florilegium marianum. Recueil d'études en l'honneur de Michel Fleury.* Mémoires de Nouvelles Assyriologiques Brèves et Utilitaires 1. Paris. (1993) Le combat entre le Dieu de l'orage et la Mer. *Mari. Annales de Recherches Interdisciplinaires* 7: 41-70. (1995) La religión en Siria durante la época de los reinos amorreos según la documentación de Mari. In Mander and Durand 1995: 127-533. (forth.) *Mari, Ebla, et les Hourrites: dix ans de travaux.* **Durand, J.-M., and J.-R. Kupper**, eds. (1985) *Miscellania Babylonia. Mélanges Offerts à Maurice Birot.* Paris. **Eichler, S., *et al.***, eds. (1990) *Tall al-Ḥamīdīya, 2. Symposion: Recent Excavations in the Upper Khabur Region, Berne, December 9-11, 1986.* Orbus Biblicus et Orientalis, Series Archaeologica, 6. **Eidem, J.** (1987-88) Tell Leilan Tablets 1987. A Preliminary Report. *Les Annales archéologiques arabes syriennes*, 37-38: 110-27. (1991) The Tell Leilan Archives 1987. *Revue d'assyriologie et d'archéologie orientale* 85: 109-35. (1992a) *The Shemshāra Archives, 2. The Administrative Texts.* Royal Danish Academy of Sciences and Letters. Historisk-filisofiske Skrifter 15. Copenhagen. (1992b) Un 'Present honorifique.' In Durand 1992: 53-60. (1994) Raiders of the Lost Treasure of Samsī-Addu. In Charpin and Durand 1994: 201-8. (forth.) The Northern Ğazīra in the 18th Century B.C. To appear in Rouault and Wäfler, forthcoming. **Frankena, R.** (1966) *Briefe aus dem British Museum (LIH and CT 2 - 33).* Altbabylonische Briefe in Umschrift und Übersetzung 2. Leiden. **Goetze, A.** (1969) Prayers of Pudu-hepas to the Sun-Goddess of Arinna and Her Circle. In Pritchard 1969: 393-94. **Guichard, M.** (1994) Au pays de la Dame de Nagar. In Charpin and Durand 1994: 235-75. **Hickson, F. V.** (1993) *Roman Prayer Language: Livy and the Aneid of Vergil.* Beiträge zur Altertumskunde 30. Stuttgart. **Ismail, F.** (1991) *Altbabylonische Wirtschafturkunden aus Tall Leilān (Syrien).* Ph.D. dissertation, Eberhard-Karls-Universität. Tübingen. **Mander, P., and J.-M. Durand** (1995) *Mitología y Religión del Oriente Antiguo,* II/1. Semitas Occidentales (Ebla, Mari). Colección: Estudios Orientales 8. Sabadell. **Matthews, D. and J. Eidem** (1993) Tell Brak and Nagar. *Iraq* 55: 201-7. **Mieroop, M. van de** (1994) The Tell Leilan Tablets 1991. A Preliminary Report. *Orientalia* 63: 305-44. **Miller, P. D.** (1970) Prayer and Sacrifices in Ugarit and Israel. In Classen 1970: 139-55. **Otten, H.** (1975) *Puduḫepa. Eine hethitische königin in ihren Textzeugnissen.* Abhandlungen der Akademie der Wissenschaften und der Literatur: Geistes- und Sozialwissenschaftliche Klasse, 1975, Nr. 1. Wiesbaden. **Otten, H., and V. Souček** (1965) *Das Gelübde der Königin Puduhepa an die Göttin Lelwani.* Studien zu den Bogazköy-Texten 1. Wiesbaden. **Parker, S. B.** (1989) *The Pre-Biblical Narrative Tradition.* Society of Biblical Literature Resources for Biblical Studies 24. Atlanta. **Pritchard, J. B.** (1969) *Ancient Near Eastern Texts Relating to the Old Testament.* 3rd Edition. Princeton. **de Roos, J.** (1987) Gott und Mensch in den hethitischen Gelübdetexten. *Anatolica* 14: 101-6. **Rouault, O., and M. Wäfler** (forth.) *La Ğazīra et l'Euphrate Syriens. Tendances dans l'interprétation historique des données nouvelles de la protohistoire à la fin du second millénaire av. J.-C.* Actes du colloque international: Paris, 21-24 juin 1993. Paris. **Sasson, J. M.** (1985) Yarim-Lim's War Declaration. In Durand and Kupper 1985: 237-55. (1994) The Posting of Letters with Divine Messages. In Charpin and Durand 1994: 299-316. (forth.) On Reading the Diplomatic Letters in the Mari Archives. In J.-M. Durand, forthcoming. **Veenhof, K. R.** (1989) Mari A. 450: 9f. (ARM 26/1, p. 378 n. 13). *Nouvelles Assyriologiques Brèves et Utilitaires* 1989/40, p. 27. **Vincente, C. A.** (1991) *The 1987 Tell Leilan Tablets Dated by the Limmu of Habil-kinu (Volumes I and II)*. Ph.D. dissertation, Yale University. New Haven.

Neo-Assyrian Battle Tactics*

JoAnn Scurlock
Elmhurst College

Neo-Assyrian kings (934–612 B.C.) were proud of their military achievements and celebrated them both in their royal inscriptions and in a series of carved orthostats with which they decorated their palaces. From these, and from the surviving military-administrative records and letters, it is possible to reconstruct a relatively detailed, if somewhat sketchy, picture of Neo-Assyrian battle tactics.[1]

The original ninth-century three-horse chariot, with its small, six-spoked wheels, was only barely large enough to hold three men: the chariot fighter *per se* (^{lú}A/DUMU SIG/SIG$_5$), armed with bow and arrow, a driver (^{lú}DIB ^{kuš}PA.MEŠ = *mukīl appāti*), and what the Assyrians called the "third man" (^{lú}3.U$_5$ = *tašlīšu*),[2] whose job it was to ensure that the other two did not fall out of the springless cab.[3] All wore swords and were protected by conical helmets supplemented by leather halberks and ankle-length leather coats sewn with rows of bronze or iron scales.[4] By the seventh century, the

---

* This paper is a version of one originally read at the 1994 meeting of the Association of Ancient Historians in Dayton, Ohio.

Abbreviation list: RIMA 2 *Assyrian Rulers of the Early First Millennium BC I (1114-859 BC)*. Royal Inscriptions of Mesopotamia Assyrian Periods 2. Grayson (1991).

1 On this subject, see also Gabriel and Metz (1991) 31-32; Stillman and Tallis (1984) 60-62, 86-89, 154-74; Yadin (1963) 293-304, 382-463.

2 For references, see AHw 1339 s.v. *tašlīšu*.

3 Budge (1914) pls. 14/1, 16/2, 18/1; King (1915) pls. 9, 22, 52, 55, 69, 74.

chariot had grown considerably. Its eight-spoked wheels were equipped with studs for improved traction, and four horses were required to pull it; it could now accommodate four passengers armored with helmets and more practical, waist-length scale-metal jackets. The crew consisted of a fighter, driver, and a "first" and "second" third man (*tašlīšu šanû*) armed with target shields to provide extra cover.[5] Thus, there were four men in the chariot.

Chariotry requires a flat, hard surface and plenty of room to maneuver.[6] This limited its usefulness, but when it could be used, it usually was.[7] This was probably, at least in part, due to the fact that military men have always had a fascination with "high-tech" weaponry. It should, however, be remembered that chariots were not only the obvious answer to enemy chariots,[8] but also, being better armored and able to carry more ammunition, bow chariotry was very useful against enemy cavalry.[9] They also, like cavalry horses, raised their riders above the battlefield[10] and could be used quite

---

4 This is best seen when the chariotry is shown dismounted as in Budge (1914) pl. 18/2 but note Barnett and Falkner (1962) pl. 116; King (1915) pls. 22-23, 53, 66-68, 69, 71, 72, 75-76.

5 See, for example, Paterson (1907) pls. 9-10.

6 Needless to say, they were not at their best in winter weather: "I abandoned one chariot which was coming with me in Bit-Hamban because of the snow" (*ABL* 242: 8-11 [see Postgate (1974) 268]).

7 Note the efforts expended to get chariots across rivers and mountains as depicted on the reliefs of Aššurnaṣirpal II (Budge [1914] pls. 21-22) and the bronze gates of Shalmaneser III (King [1915] pls. 3, 61-62). Compare the Middle Assyrian king Tiglath-pileser I, who got his chariots across a mountain range literally on the necks of his soldiers (*RIMA* 2 18 iii 40-47; for the technique, see Botta and Flandin [1846–50] pl. 20).

8 See, for example Budge (1914) pls. 17/2, 18/1; Barnett and Falkner (1962) pl. 117; King (1915) pls. 72-73.

9 Budge (1914) pl. 24/2; Botta and Flandin (1846–50) pls. 57-59, bis. They could also be used against camels: Barnett and Falkner (1962) pl. 16; Barnett (1976) pls. 32-33.

10 Notice the height of the chariot as against the groom in Hall (1928) pl. 29 and Barnett (1976) pls. 16, 21, 68.

effectively to break up a line of enemy infantry,[11] provided that the field of battle had not been prepared against them with stakes, ditches, or flooding[12] (caltrops had not yet been invented) and provided that the infantry were bowmen and/or panicked at the sight of the line of chariots[13] bearing down on them.[14]

Assyrian chariots were really no more than mobile firing platforms[15]; they were not armed with scythes like the later Seleucid chariots and could thus not even hope to chew their way through a determined mass of spear infantry.[16] They could, of course, fire at the spearmen from a safe distance, but cavalry could perform this function just as well and much more cheaply.

---

11 For this use of chariotry, see Budge (1914) pls. 14, 15/2; Barnett and Falkner (1962) pls. 116-17; King (1915) pls. 8-9, 18, 41-42, 49, 51-53, 66, 69-72, 74-76; Botta and Flandin (1846–50) pls. 56, 58, 59 bis, 65, 67, 76, 92-94, 96, 100; Barnett (1976) pl. 32.

12 See below, under the Battle of Dur-Yakin.

13 See, for example, Budge (1914) pls. 14/2, 17/2; Barnett and Falkner (1962) pls. 116-17; King (1915) pls. 8-9, 41-42, 52, 69-76; Botta and Flandin (1846–50) pls. 57-59 bis, 92-100.

14 Note that Malbrun-Labat's contention that: "la charrerie disparaît come élément de rupture et sert principalement au transport rapide des troupes de combat" ([1982] 60) is directly contradicted by the evidence. The reliefs of Aššurbanipal, under whom, allegedly, "ses unités sont désormais, en quelque sort, une 'infanterie montée'" ([1982] 61) show the chariotry charging against enemy infantry and camel divisions at full gallop (Barnett [1976] pls. 32-33). There is, moreover, no reason to believe that chariots were ever used to transport troops to the field of battle. This notion of chariots as transport vehicles is probably based on the occasional representation of an empty and waiting chariot on the earlier reliefs, combined with Homer's semi-legendary account of chariot warfare in the Iliad. However, the empty chariots in question are only shown in connection with sieges and may be related with the practice (abandoned by the reign of Aššurbanipal) of having the chariotry (and also the cavalry) dismount to assist in what was basically infantry work. In any case, given the fact that the Assyrian chariot could carry no more than four men (or one man per horse), it was hardly the most efficient means of transport.

15 For the results of actual experiments to determine how effective ancient chariots might have been from this point of view, see Gabriel and Metz (1991) 78.

16 Note the representation of Assyrian spearmen combatting Elamite chariots in Hall (1928) pl. 41/A. Trying to run a chariot through properly trained infantry is not easy even with scythed chariots, as the Persians found to their cost. Presumably, this is one

Some of the defects of chariotry, particularly the less-experienced levied chariotry, could be ameliorated by including specially trained cavalry and infantry in chariotry units,[17] but as the Assyrians pushed their empire to its farthest reaches, they increasingly ran into the sort of mountainous or marshy terrain which made the use of chariots impossible, making them depend more and more heavily on cavalry and infantry.[18]

Ninth-century Assyrian cavalrymen (*ša pitḫalli*) were a curious sight indeed. They rode out in pairs; one of them shot at the enemy with his bow and arrow and carried a quiver on his back.[19] The other, who seems to have been a sort of assistant, carried a shield or lance to protect his partner, and held the reins of both horses in his hands.[20] Fortunately, by the eighth century the invention of the martingale (a rein holder designed to keep the horse on track while the bowman was shooting)[21] had rendered this extremely awkward arrangement unnecessary.

Eighth- and seventh-century Assyrian cavalrymen were of two types: lancers and bowmen. Both carried swords and wore helmets and scale armor jackets. The lancers made the best attack troops. They could be used against other cavalry, whose horses they downed by driving their lances into

reason why Greek phalangist mercenaries were so much in demand during the Achaemenid period.

17 Note Budge (1914) pls. 12, 17, 18/1; King (1915) pls. 8-9, 41-42, 48-49, 53, 66-68, 72; Botta and Flandin (1846–50) pls. 64-67, 92-100; Barnett (1976) pls. 16, 32-33.

18 Note the comments of Aššurnaṣirpal II on mountains "unsuitable for chariotry" (*ARI* II §§ 544, 562, 565, 568; compare *ARI* II §§ 16, 21, 216, 222, 468; Fuchs [1993] 172: 386c; Sg. 8 18-22; Sn. 36: 3-5, 58: 21).

19 Salonen's contention ([1955] 158 n. 2) that the Assyrian cavalry could not use the bow on horseback(!) is amply refuted by the evidence of the reliefs (on this point, see also Saggs [1963] 152).

20 Budge (1914) pl. 15/1 (*cf.* 12/1, 17/1, 25/2; Barnett and Falkner [1962] pl. 115); King (1915) pls. 7, 38-39, 48-49, 53, 72 (*cf.* 15, 17-18, 54-55, 57, 60, 74). Awkward as it seems, this method of employing the cavalry is also shown among Assyrian enemies (as in Budge [1914] pl. 24/2).

21 For illustrations of this device, see Botta and Flandin (1846–50) pls. 64, 66-67, 143.

their backs,[22] or against enemy bowmen and slingers.[23] All types of cavalry were, however, at a disadvantage when faced with a determined mass of infantry spearmen.[24] Bow cavalry are best used as skirmishers—bow and arrow are not of much use at close quarters, and the lack of stirrups would have made it difficult to use their swords which were, in any case, not designed to mow down foot soldiers from horseback.[25]

One would do well, however, not to underestimate the military effectiveness of ancient bow cavalry. The absence of stirrups did not in the least prevent them from turning backwards on their horses to shoot at a pursuing enemy; the so-called Parthian shot is actually first attested on Neo-Assyrian reliefs.[26] Bow cavalry could be used very effectively against enemy spearmen whom they could slaughter from a safe distance without fear of retaliation. They could also be used against enemy archers and stingers, enemy cavalry, and enemy chariotry, if necessary.[27] They were sometimes also given spears in addition to their bows to better suit them for attacks into enemy lines.[28] Cavalry of both types were also ideally suited for prebattle reconnaissance and for pursuing a defeated enemy.

---

22 Barnett and Falkner (1962) pls. 65, 67; Paterson (1907) pls. 108-9; Akurgal (1966) pls. 9-11. The same tactic was effective with camels (Barnett and Falkner [1962] pl. 14; Barnett [1976] pls. 32-33).

23 Layard (1853) pls. 37-38; Paterson (1907) pls. 108-9; Akurgal (1966) pls. 9-11; Barnett (1976) pl. 32. One of the comments made by Assyrian generals about terrain is to remark as to whether it was suitable for letting the cavalry gallop (Sg. 8 22).

24 Note the success of Swiss pikemen against the heavily armed medieval knight—see Oman (1953) chap. 5 and compare the representation of Assyrian spearman tackling camel-mounted Arabs in Barnett (1976) pls. 32-33 and Kaldean horsemen in Gadd (1938) pl. 37.

25 Assyrian swords were little more than daggers. To fight infantry properly from horseback, a cavalryman needs a scimitar.

26 Budge (1914) pl. 24/2; *cf.* Barnett (1976) pls. 32-33 (from camel back).

27 Layard (1853) pls. 37-38; Akurgal (1966) pls. 9-11; Paterson (1907) pls. 108-9; Barnett (1976) pl. 33.

28 Botta and Flandin (1846–50) pls. 64, 66-67, 99; Gadd (1938) pls. 39, 43, 45-46, 57; *cf.* Budge (1914) pl. 15/1; King (1915) pls. 7, 38-39, 48-49, 53, 72; Botta and Flandin (1846-50) pls. 53, 62, 142.

The original ninth-century Assyrian infantry consisted exclusively of bowmen (*ṣāb qašti*) equipped with composite bows and quivers full of iron-headed arrows.[29] Bowmen are not good attack troops—they are virtually helpless at close quarters, as ninth-century Assyrian monarchs discovered to their cost,[30] and could not withstand an attack by enemy spearmen, chariotry, or cavalry. They were, however, very effective at a distance,[31] especially since the Assyrians, like the Romans, had no scruples about crippling enemy cavalry and chariotry by pelting the horses with a hail of arrows.[32]

By the eighth century, Assyrian monarchs had made a first step towards remedying their over-reliance on infantry archers by introducing corps of spearmen (*nāš azmarê*) and slingers (*nāš kabābi*).[33] Assyrian bowmen and stingers as shown on the reliefs were armed in the same fashion as Assyrian chariot-fighters and cavalrymen.[34] The spearmen, on the other hand, first appear wearing such odd and un-Assyrian looking costumes that it has become conventional to refer to them as "auxiliaries" or even "mercenaries."[35] The texts, however, do not indicate that these spearmen were in any essential way different either in method of recruitment or in place of origin from the more conventionally dressed troops. We have reason to believe that the spear corps was specifically inspired by Assyria's Urartian neighbors[36]; we can only speculate that the crested helmets, chest plates, and

---

29 See, for example, Budge (1914) pl. 13/2.

30 Note the attempts to use bowmen against Urartian infantry spearmen in King (1915) pls. 37-38, 41-42.

31 One might think the stingers a harmless nuisance; on the contrary, "soldiers, notwithstanding their defensive armor, are often more annoyed by the round stones from the sling than by all the arrows of the enemy. Stones kill without mangling the body, and the contusion is mortal without loss of blood" (Vegetius [1944] 23).

32 Fuchs (1993) 161: 345-46; Sg. 8 139; *cf.* Michel (1952) no. 31 iii 31-32; Sn. 45: 80-82; ARI II §§ 424, 579.

33 These first appear on the reliefs of Tiglath-pileser III; see below.

34 See, for example, Barnett and Falkner (1962) pls. 28, 94.

35 See, for example, Reade (1972) 105-6; Stillman and Tallis (1984) 164-65.

36 Compare Barnett and Falkner (1962) pls. 34, 36, 38, 42, 51, 61-62, 73, 91 and Botta and Flandin (1846–50) pls. 55, 61, 68, 70, 77 with King (1915) pls. 37-38, 41-42.

upturned leather shoes came from the same source. It would certainly not be the first time in military history that a unit adopted from a foreign army continued to dress in the style of the country from which it was adopted, the case of Omanis parading about in western military uniforms to the music of Scottish bagpipes springs immediately to mind.

Spearmen were best used as attack troops and, if tightly packed and well disciplined, could be used even against enemy chariotry and cavalry. Their main drawback was that they were vulnerable to attack from a distance by archers and stingers if they were unable to close with them. By the seventh century, the Assyrians had realized that they could simultaneously remedy the defects of both spearmen and archers if they used the one to provide the other with cover. This use of the different types of infantry in combination was particularly important in the case of the Aramean Itua and Gurra-tribesmen, who went into battle wearing very little in the way even of clothing to protect themselves, and it is thus hardly surprising that these appear on seventh-century Assyrian reliefs paired with infantry spearmen carrying large D-shaped shields especially designed for this purpose.[37] Another, more mundane yet not insignificant innovation in equipment was the gradual replacement of sandals with proper military boots.[38]

The use which the Assyrians made of these various different types of troops may best be seen by reconstructing four actual Assyrian battles about which we have a fair amount of information: Mt. Uauš, Dur-Yakin, Til-Tuba, and Ḫalule.[39]

---

37 See, for example, Barnett (1976) pl. 33; Hall (1928) pl. 41/A.

38 See, for example, Botta and Flandin (1846–50) pls. 99-100, 143. These were probably adopted from Assyria's neighbors (compare Botta and Flandin [1846–50] pls. 125-36).

39 It should be noted that the reconstruction of the arrangement of god's divisions on the battle charts is not purely hypothetical. It is, however, far beyond the scope of this paper, and will have to be discussed in a future work.

The Battle of Mt. Uauš (714 B.C.)

When Rusa I of Urarṭu determined to meet Sargon II at Mt. Uauš, "he called up his numerous army together with his allies and, in order to [a]venge [Mitati of Zik]irtu (against whom Sargon was directing a campaign), he assembled his warriors, experienced in battle in whom [his] ar[my] put their trust. He detached their [bowmen and spearmen?] and [readied?] their riding horses and [a]rmed them with weapons."[40] Meanwhile, Mitati of Zikirtu was sent to bring in the troops of other tributary kings in the neighborhood.[41] When all were present, Rusa set up his battle line in the pass and sent Sargon a formal challenge to battle (fig. 1).[42]

Fig. 1: *The Battle of Mt. Uauš as Rusa of Urarṭu Planned It*

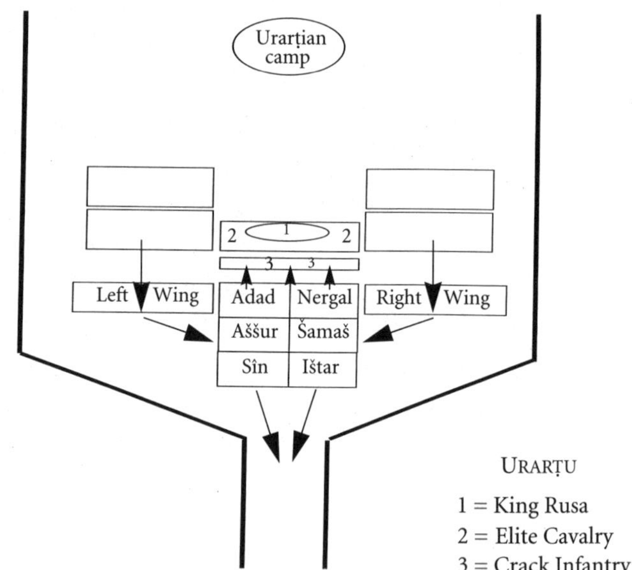

[40] Sg. 8 103-5. The restoration of Sg. 8 104 is based on Sg. 8 136; see below.

[41] These activities are described in Sg. 8 106-8.

[42] Sg. 8 111.

From Sargon II's description, it is possible to reconstruct what happened in some detail.[43] According to Sargon, the Assyrians did not bother to form up the wings or wait for the rear division.[44] Instead, Sargon immediately took the front and center divisions (that is, the forces led by himself and by the grand *sukallu*, Sîn-aḫa-uṣur) and attacked Rusa's center "like a fierce arrow and so defeated him" (figs. 2 and 3).[45] The brunt of Sargon's

FIG. 2 : *The Battle of Mt. Uauš — The Actual Battle I*

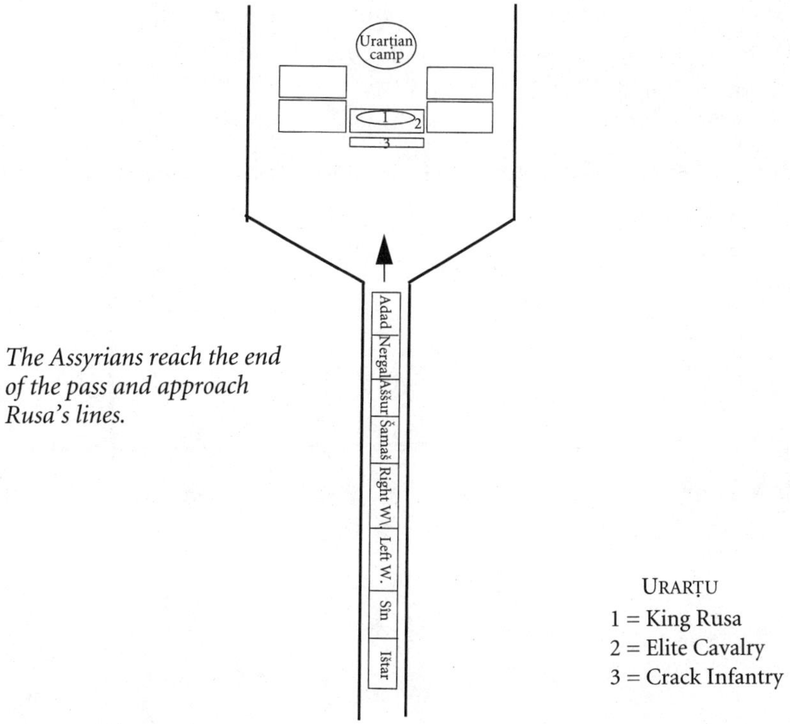

43 See also Saggs (1963) 151-54. Note, however, that, *contra* Saggs, the front line infantry troops did not "serve as scouts or snipers, spreading out over the hills above both wings to give security to a wide area." Neither is it the case that "the type of weapon was often a national characteristic."

44 Sg. 8 13.

45 Sg. 8 132-33. The following lines (Sg. 8 134-35) emphasize the totality of the victory by dwelling on the large numbers of corpses and copious amount of blood produced by the fighting.

attack was felt by a section of crack infantry archers and spearmen which seems to have been stationed immediately in front of Rusa's center: "His warriors in whom his army trusted, carrying bows and spears, I slaughtered before his feet like lambs and cut off their heads."[46] These unfortunates having been disposed of, Sargon succeeded in capturing some two hundred and sixty odd royal princes, high officials, and crack cavalry which resulted in the "loosening of the battle," *i.e.*, the collapse of the Urartian center.[47] Rusa fell back on his battle camp and tried to make a stand there, but Sargon "destroyed his chariot horses under him with arrows" (fig. 4).[48] Ultimately, Rusa "to save his life, abandoned his chariot, mounted on a mare, and led his army in flight."[49]

Fig. 3: *The Battle of Mt. Uauš — The Actual Battle II*

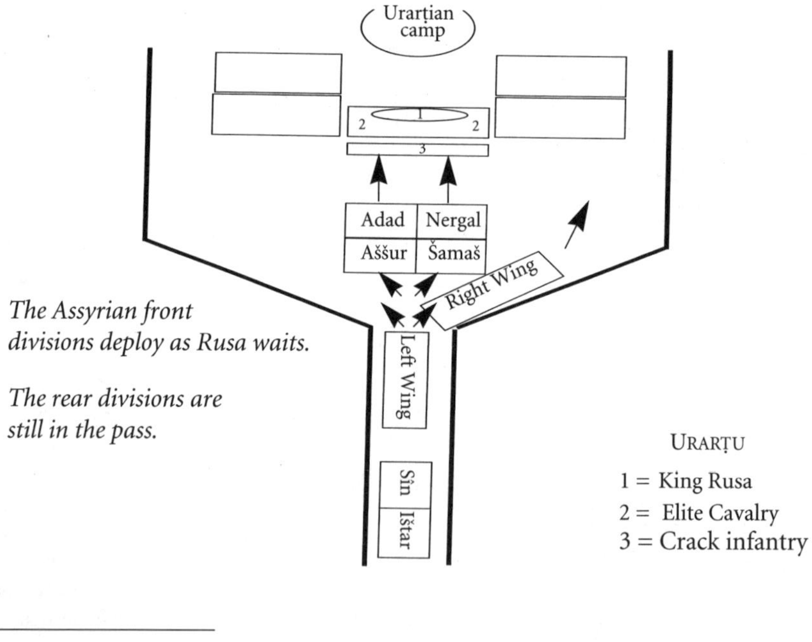

Urarṭian camp

Adad | Nergal
Aššur | Šamaš
Right Wing
Left Wing
Sîn
Ištar

The Assyrian front divisions deploy as Rusa waits.

The rear divisions are still in the pass.

URARṬU
1 = King Rusa
2 = Elite Cavalry
3 = Crack infantry

46 Sg. 8 136.

47 Sg. 8 137-38.

48 Sg. 8 139.

49 Sg. 8 140.

Fig. 4: *The Battle of Mt. Uauš — The Actual Battle III*

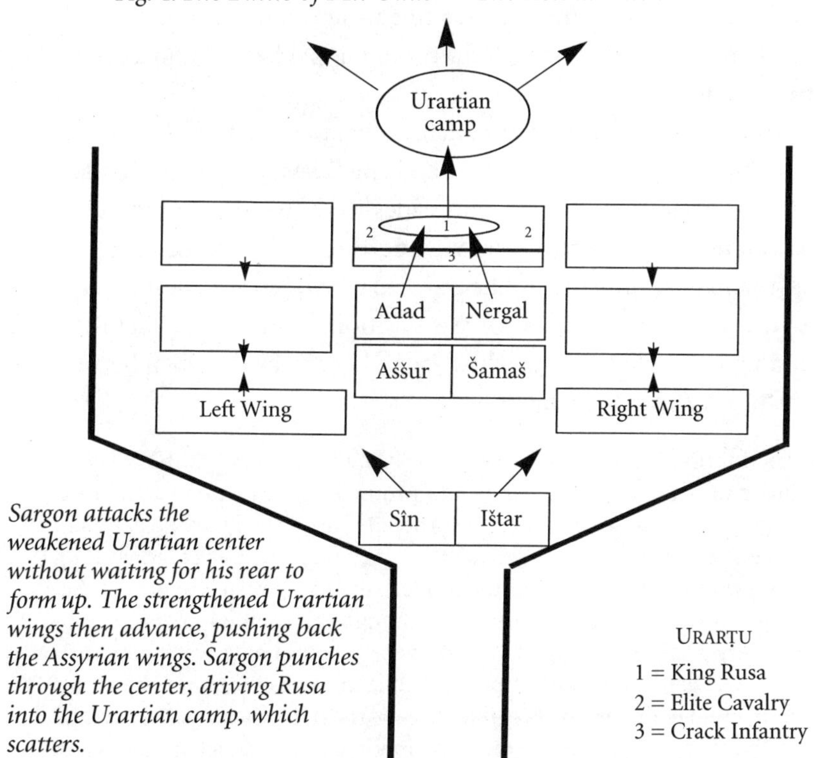

Sargon attacks the weakened Urartian center without waiting for his rear to form up. The strengthened Urartian wings then advance, pushing back the Assyrian wings. Sargon punches through the center, driving Rusa into the Urartian camp, which scatters.

URARṬU
1 = King Rusa
2 = Elite Cavalry
3 = Crack Infantry

Although Sargon also takes the credit for "boring through" (*purruru*) the forces of Mitati and other neighboring kings,[50] this feat of arms is mentioned last, almost as an afterthought, just before the description of the flight of the enemy army.[51] What this presumably means is that the defeat of the allies was the work of the rear division and wings which Sargon II had not paused to form up before attacking Rusa's center,[52] but which would have been given time to arrive and form up by the king's bold and unex-

50 Sg. 8 141.

51 Sg. 8 142-43; see below.

52 Sg. 8 130; see above.

pected action.[53] In any event, what was left of the army of Rusa and his allies turned tail and ran—"their horses filled the mountain ravines and they opened difficult roads (through the mountains) like an ant in a place (too) narrow for him."[54]

From this account, we may conclude that the Urartian king took up the center, surrounded by royal princes and crack cavalry, with the battle camp at his rear.[55] Flanking him on both sides were the forces of the tributary kings. Stationed in front of the line and directly before the center was a detachment of veteran foot soldiers armed with bows and spears.[56] To judge from the presence of infantry in this position, it is probable that Rusa was intending to employ a tactic which came later to be classified by Vegetius as his fourth and fifth formations:

> The fourth formation is this: As your army is marching to the attack in order of battle and you come within four or five hundred paces of the enemy, both your wings must be ordered unexpectedly to quicken their pace and advance with celerity. When they find themselves attacked on both wings at the same time, the sudden surprise may so disconcert them as to give you an easy victory. But although this method, if your troops are very resolute and expert, may ruin the enemy at once, yet it is hazardous. The general who attempts it is obliged to abandon and expose his center and to divide his army into three parts. If the enemy are not routed at the first charge, they have a fair opportunity of attacking the wings which are separated from each other and the center which is destitute of assistance. The fifth formation resembles the fourth but with this addition: the light infantry and the archers are formed before the center to

---

53 The fact that Mitati's defeat is recounted in the first person is not significant. As king and general, Sargon II was entitled to take personal credit for all the accomplishments of his troops.

54 Sg. 8 142-43.

55 We know that Rusa had surrounded himself with royal princes and crack cavalry, because these were captured when Sargon "fell in his midst" (Sg. 8 133, 137-38; see above). The battle camp had to have been behind the lines, or Rusa could not have retreated to it and tried to make a stand there (Sg. 8 139; see above).

56 The position of the detachment of foot soldiers is shown by the fact that Sargon mentions their demise first (Sg. 8 136; see above).

> cover it from the attempts of the enemy. With this precaution the general may safely follow the above mentioned method and attack the enemy's left wing with his right, and their right with his left.[57]

In the event, Rusa never had a chance to "disconcert" his enemy. Sargon, whose military intelligence system had given him advance warning of Rusa's intention to meet him there,[58] was ready with a plan of his own. He did not pause to construct a battle camp, rest his troops, or even to draw them up into regular formation. Instead, he took the fore and center divisions of his army directly into battle and charged at Rusa's center, leaving the wings and rear to form into position behind him and to engage Rusa's wings when the rest of the troops reached the scene of battle.[59] This counter move was not as foolhardy as it sounds; in a confined space such as that presented by a mountain pass, it is the larger of the two armies which is at a disadvantage,[60] and a bold attack has also the benefit of surprise. The small detachment of foot soldiers guarding the line were not enough to protect the exposed Urartian center from the full force of the Assyrian attack and it broke up under the pressure, despite a valiant effort by Rusa to use the battle camp as a rallying point.[61] With the flight of the Urartian king, the battle culminated in an Assyrian victory.[62]

The Battle of Dur-Yakin (709 B.C.)

When Marduk-apla-iddina, sheikh of the Kaldean Bit-Yakin tribe and self-proclaimed king of Babylon, determined to meet Sargon II outside of his tribal seat at Dur-Yakin, he made very careful preparations. He gathered his forces into the city and strengthened its fortifications in order to hold off

---

57 Vegetius (1944) 102-3.

58 For an account of this system, see Malbrun-Labat (1982) 41-57.

59 Sg. 8 127-41; see above.

60 Sun Tzu (1963) 164-66.

61 Sg. 8 136-40; see above.

62 Sg. 8 140, 142-43; see above.

an Assyrian siege.[63] Next, "he cut a breach from the Euphrates (and) made (the water) flow down to it; he filled the meadows of the city, where there was a battleground, with water and cut through the bridges.[64] He, together with his allies (and) battle troops, set up his royal tent and organized his camp between the rivers like a crane."[65] The purpose of this was, quite obviously, to ensure that the Assyrians would not be able to use their chariotry, a branch in which Marduk-apla-iddina's forces were comparatively deficient.

Sargon responded by making his veteran soldiers "fly over the rivers like eagles,"[66] or as a more prosaic source puts it: "I had a ramp packed down over his rivers" so that the army could pass across.[67] Having come up to Marduk-apla-iddina's forces by this means, Sargon proceeded to surround, literally "besiege,"[68] him or, as he puts it: "him together with his warriors I caught in a net like an eagle in flight."[69] The result of this maneuver was that Sargon "filled the environs of his city with the corpses of his wing soldiers and the Arameans, soldiers of the steppe, who went at his sides, as if they were sheep."[70] Sargon also pressed Marduk-apla-iddina from the front, slaughtering his best troops before his feet and killing his chariot horses with arrows.[71] In other words, the Assyrian forces kept up a steady pressure on Marduk-apla-iddina's center, while simultaneously outflanking and rolling

---

63 Gadd (1954) 186 vi 27-34; Fuchs (1993) 159f.: 333-35.

64 Gadd (1954) 186 vi 35-38; Fuchs (1993) 160: 336-38. For a discussion of the man-hours of labor which these measures would have required, see Powell (1982) 59-61.

65 Gadd (1954) 186 vi 39-42; Fuchs (1993) 160: 338-40.

66 Fuchs (1993) 160f.: 341-43.

67 Gadd (1954) 186 vi 44.

68 *nītu lamû* (Fuchs [1993] 161: 343-44).

69 Gadd (1954) 186 vi 45-46. Vegetius recommends trying this maneuver only on flat and level ground where one's forces are better and more numerous than those of the enemy (Vegetius [1944] 99 [1st formation]). The terrain in question is described as a battleground (see above) and was therefore presumably flat and level, and Sargon says that he sent his best infantry to encircle Marduk-apla-iddina (Fuchs [1993] 160f.: 341-45).

70 Gadd (1954) 186 vi 47-49.

71 Fuchs (1993) 161: 344-46.

up both of his wings. The Kaldean, wounded in the hand by an arrow, retreated into the city leaving his Puqudean, Marrsanean, and Sutean allies to be cut down before the gate (fig. 5).[72]

Fig. 5: *The Battle of Dur-Yakin*

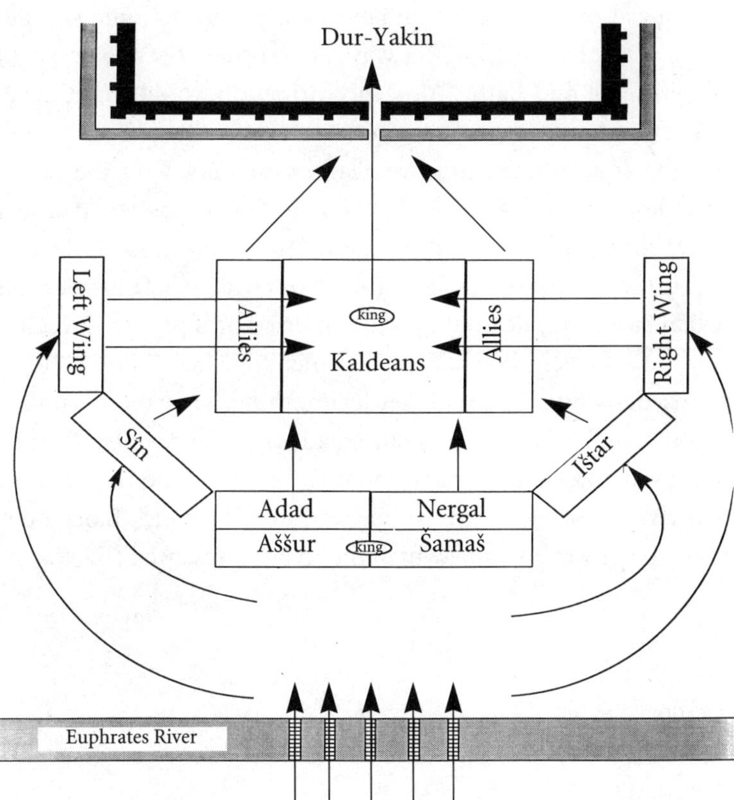

[72] Fuchs (1993) 161f.: 346-49.

The Battle of Til-Tuba (664 B.C.)

When the Elamite king, Teuman, determined to meet the forces of Aššurbanipal at the river Ulai near Til-Tuba, he also made careful preparations; as usual, we must read between the lines of the Assyrian account. "To save his life, he (Teuman) divided silver and gold among the people of his land,"[73] that is, he hired extra soldiers to add to the troops he had already called up.[74] Next, "he returned his allies, who go at his sides, to before him and so concentrated his forces before me."[75] This slightly peculiar description refers to the fact that, in normal formations, allied troops fought on the wings of an army, as we have seen the Aramean allies of Marduk-apla-iddina doing at Dur-Yakin.[76] Teuman's objective in stationing his allies in front of the rest of his army in this way can only have been to prevent them from deserting in mid-battle. Also, this formation would tempt the Assyrians into trying to surround Teuman's army, rather then chewing their way through the concentrated mass of Elamite soldiers, with the result that Teuman's less than trustworthy allies and hireling troops would be inspired by desperation to fight their best. To quote Sun Tzu, who advocates this very tactic: "Throw the troops into a position from which there is no escape and even when faced with death they will not flee. For if prepared to die, what can they not achieve? Then officers and men together put up their utmost efforts. In a desperate situation, they fear nothing; when there is no way out they stand firm."[77] Finally, Teuman "made the Ulai river his fortress and seized the way to drinking water," that is, he placed the river at his back, thus further "encouraging" his troops, and simultaneously blocking Assyrian access to the water supply which the river represented (fig. 6).[78]

---

73 Piepkorn (1933) 68 v 87-88.

74 Piepkorn (1933) 64 v 41-42.

75 Piepkorn (1933) 68 v 89-90.

76 Gadd (1954) 186: 47-48; *cf.* Sn. 47: 24-26.

77 Sun Tzu (1963) 134 (no. 33).

78 Piepkorn (1933) 68 v 91-92.

Fig. 6: *The Battle of Til-Tuba, as Teuman, King of Elam, Planned It*

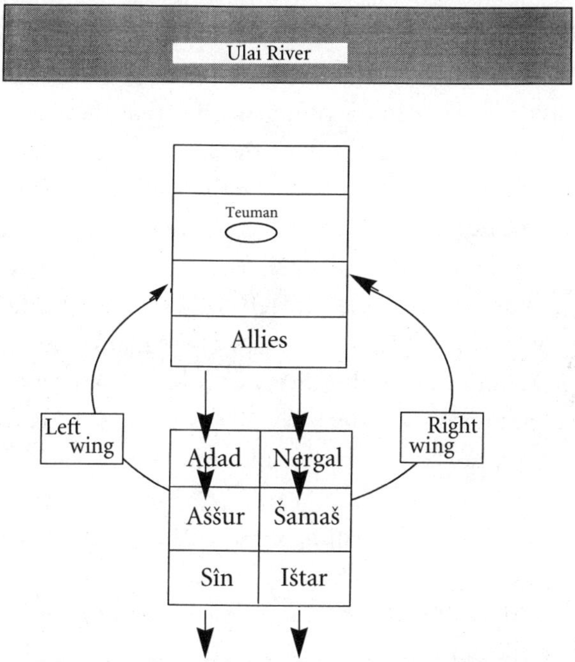

Ulai River
Teuman
Allies
Left wing
Right wing
Adad
Nergal
Aššur
Šamaš
Sîn
Ištar

Aššurbanipal does not say exactly what happened next; his description is purely conventional and could have been applied to any battle in which the Assyrians claimed decisive victory.[79] The reliefs, however, allow us to reconstruct the battle. The Assyrians seem to have left their chariotry behind them when they marched to Elam. They could do this with reasonable safety since, assuming Assyrian representations are accurate, Elamite chariots were comparatively primitive, lacking even a proper cab for the attachment of quivers. The Assyrians did, however, have both infantry and

---

79 Piepkorn (1933) 68 v 96-99 has: "In the midst of Til-Tuba I defeated them. I blocked the river Ulai with their bodies. I filled the district of Susa with their bodies like *baltu-* and *ašāgu*-thornbushes" to which Streck (1916) 26 iii 42-43 adds: "I made their blood run down to the river Ulai; I dyed its waters the color of red wool."

cavalry at their disposal. The former was used to engage the massed Elamite forces and to push them steadily towards the river.

Aššurbanipal's generals did not, however, succumb to the temptation to cut off all means of retreat.[80] Again in the words of Sun Tzu: "To a surrounded enemy you must leave a way of escape. Show him there is a road to safety, and so create in his mind the idea that there is an alternative to death."[81] More interesting still, from the point of view of the history of tactical warfare, is the fact that the brunt of the Assyrian attack was designed to fall on the Elamite left wing, as later recommended by Vegetius (his second or sixth formations).[82] Aššurbanipal's cavalry was stationed on the Assyrian right wing to outflank the Elamite left wing and roll it into the center, but an avenue of escape was left to the right of the Elamite lines.[83] Teuman and his son tried to get away in this direction and might have succeeded if their chariot had not had an accident (fig. 7). As it was, the Elamite king and his son were sent sprawling to the ground, where they were soon surrounded by a number of Assyrian infantry soldiers of no very exalted rank. After a brief struggle, in which the young man tried to defend his wounded father with bow and arrows, the two were killed; the soldiers cut off their heads and hurried to carry them to Aššurbanipal in an Elamite chariot requisitioned from the battlefield.[84]

---

80 *Contra* Yadin (1963) 303; see below.

81 Sun Tzu (1963) 109-10 (nos. 31-32); *cf.* pp. 132-33 (nos. 22-23); compare Vegetius (1944) 105-6.

82 Vegetius (1944) 100-1, 103-4. Vegetius was of the opinion that this arrangement was the best, because ancient armies tended to be stronger on the right wing than on the left and hence this mode of attack pitted one's own best side against the enemy's weakest (Vegetius [1944] 100-1).

83 Note the complete absence of Assyrian cavalrymen in this part of the field (see especially the drawing in Yadin [1963] 442-43).

84 Akurgal (1966) pls. 9-11; Paterson (1907) pls. 84-85, 104-5; Hall (1928) pl. 41/A; Barnett and Lorenzini (1975) pls. 138-54; *cf.* Weidner (1932–33) 178/180 nos. 4-10. A similar accident seems to have been fatal for the career of Suzubu, the king of Babylon who was captured in battle against Assyrian forces (Sn. 38f: 46-51, 87f: 34-35)—according to an epigraph, he fell from his horse (Sn. 156: 14-17).

Fig. 7: *The Battle of Til-Tuba as the Assyrians Fought It*

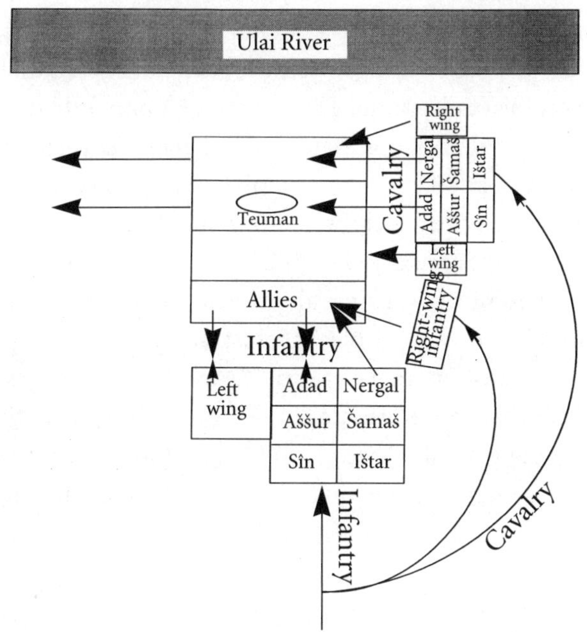

The Battle of Ḫalule (691 B.C.)

Perhaps the most colorfully described battle in Assyrian history was the battle of Ḫalule which pitted Sennacherib against Mušezib-Marduk, king of Babylon, and his Elamite allies. It is also one of those battles in which both sides, with some right as we shall see, could claim victory. From Sennacherib's account,[85] we may reconstruct the events as follows: Sennacherib made up his mind to march on Babylon and to dispose of

---

85 *In re* Grayson (1965) 337-42, suffice it to say that "explaining" the discrepancy between Sennacherib's account and the Babylonian Chronicle entry for the battle of Ḫalule by calling the Assyrian description of the battle "a prodigious falsehood" is not a very constructive way of dealing with an interesting problem. As we shall see, Sennacherib's account is quite serviceable, provided it is read carefully and with a grain of salt. On this point, see also Levine (1982) 49-51.

Mušezib-Marduk.[86] The Babylonian king responded by putting together a grand coalition including citizens of Babylon and Borsippa[87] together with Aramean and Kaldean tribesmen as well as Elamites, Persians, and Ellipans.[88] These forces, "came up against me together to make battle ... Before me in Ḫalule on the banks of the Tigris, they set up their battle line. They occupied my way to drinking water and sharpened their weapons."[89]

From this information and Sennacherib's description of what happened next, it is possible to reconstruct the enemy battle formation. Having made a prayer for victory, Sennacherib armed himself for battle[90] and, as he describes it, "I cried bitterly against all the evil enemy armies like an *ūmu*-demon; I roared like Adad ... I blew against the enemy on long and short sides like the attack of an angry storm."[91] Another source describes this maneuver, somewhat more prosaically, as "boring through" the enemies forces by scattering what they had assembled.[92] Ḫumban-undasi, "herald" (*i.e.*, the leading general) of the king of Elam and the Elamite nobles bore

---

86 "In my eighth campaign, I gave the command to march to Babylon" (Grayson [1963] 88: 11). The name of the Babylonian king is given by the Babylonian Chronicle (Grayson [1975] no. 1 iii 13).

87 Sn. 92: 11-12.

88 "They opened the treasury of Esagila and they took out the gold and silver of Bēl and Sarpanitu, property belonging to their temples and sent it as a bribe to Ḫumban-nimena, king of Elam who had neither sense nor judgment... he put together with him(self) a grand coalition of Parsuaš, Anzan, Pašeru, Ellipi, the Iazan, Lakabra, Ḫarzunu, Dummuqu, Sulai, Samuna, the son of Marduk-apla-iddina, Bīt-Adini, Bīt-Amukkana, Bīt-Ṣillana, Bīt-Sâla, Larak, Laḫiru, the Puqudu, Gambulu, Ḫalatu, Ruʾua, Ubulu, Malaḫu, Rapiqu, Ḫindaru, (and) Damunu. Massed together, they took the road to Ur and then came up to Babylon. They and Šūzubu the Kaldean greeted one another and joined their forces" (Sn. 42f: 31-34, 43-55).

89 Sn. 43f: 57, 60-62.

90 Sn. 44: 67-73.

91 Sn. 44f: 74-77.

92 Sn. 82: 37.

93 Sn. 45f: v 82-vi 16.

the brunt of the Assyrian attack,[93] and a number of the latter were captured, along with Nabû-šum-iškun, the commander of the Kaldean contingent.[94]

Now, assuming, as is probable, that Sennacherib was taking the most direct route to Babylon from Assyria, he would have been marching south, parallel to the right bank of the Tigris, when he encountered the allied army. If the allies were able to both bar his path and block his way to water,[95] they must have been facing north, with their right wing up against the river.[96] Anchoring one wing of the army in this way would have strengthened it sufficiently that it could safely be made up of the weakest or least trustworthy troops in the allied army, as, for example, the Aramean tribesmen (this is Vegetius's seventh formation).[97] Since Sennacherib attacked on the front *and* on the side,[98] he must have targeted the enemy's exposed left wing. The Elamite forces under the command of Ḫumbanundasi and the Kaldean troops under the leadership of Nabû-šum-iškun suffered the worst mauling from Sennacherib—presumably these two commanders were stationed on the allied left wing. This leaves the Babylonian and Elamite kings with their forces. Mušezib-Marduk was either in the center or to the right, but since the Babylonian Chronicle Series makes the Elamite king the leader of the allied forces,[99] it is likely that the Babylonian king "went at his side" as an ally.

In sum, it is likely that the arrangement of coalition forces was as follows: the Elamite and Kaldean generals were stationed in the left wing facing the Assyrian right; the Elamite king was in the center with the Baby-

---

94 Sn. 46: 16-19.

95 Sn. 43f: 57, 60-62; see above.

96 The swamp shown on the battle chart is purely hypothetical but something is needed to make sense of Sennacherib's claim to have been "blocked" from acccess to drinking water.

97 Vegetius (1944) 104-5.

98 Sn. 45: 76-77; see above.

99 "Ḫumban-nimena called up the troops of Elam (and) Akkad and they did battle against Assyria at Ḫalule and they forced Assyria to retreat" (Grayson [1975] no. 1 iii 16-18).

Fig. 8: *The Battle of Ḫalule I*

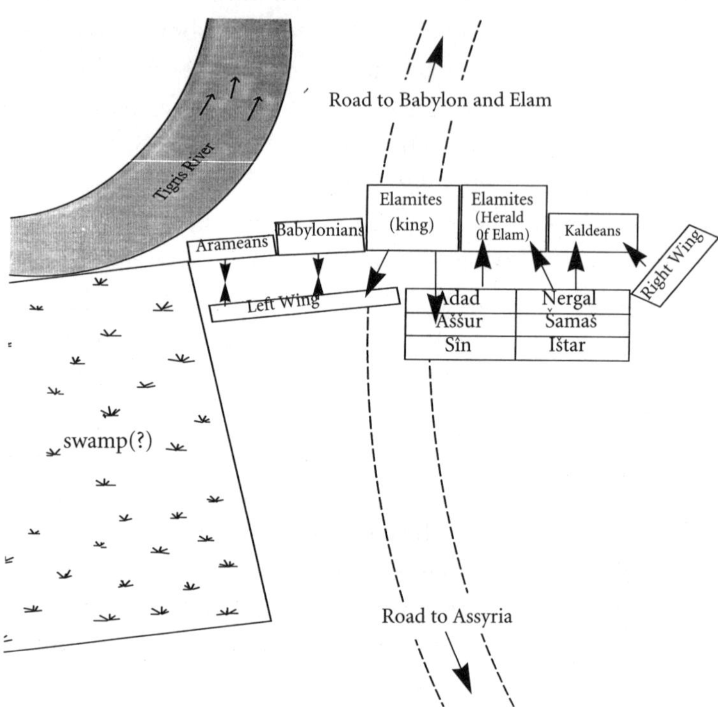

lonian king immediately to his right; the Aramean tribesmen and other less well equipped allied forces were stationed in the right wing facing the Assyrian left and anchored on the river Tigris. Sennacherib countered by attacking the allied center head on while the Assyrian right wing attempted to outflank and to roll up the exposed allied left wing (fig. 8).

To hear Sennacherib tell the tale, this left wing of the allied forces was very badly mauled indeed.[100] In addition, Sennacherib managed to capture a number of Elamite nobles and Nabû-šum-iškun, who surrendered to him

100 The gory details are given in Sn. 45f.: v 87-vi 16.

in the midst of the battle.[101] He did not, however, succeed in capturing or killing the leaders of the allied forces. By Sennacherib's account,

> Ḫumban-nimena, king of Elam, together with the king of Babylon and the sheikhs of Kaldea who went at his sides, were overcome by the fear (caused by) my demon-like battle. They abandoned their tents and, in order to save their lives, they trampled (and) passed over the corpses of their armies (in their eagerness to escape).[102]

It is, however, clear from Sennacherib's account that the Elamite and Babylonian kings did not just run away: "At my [fe]et, they beseeched my lordship: 'Allow us to live ... [you have won] your [vic]tory.' ... I (felt sorry for them) and let them get away with their lives."[103] We need not take this

Fig. 9: *The Battle of Ḫalule II*

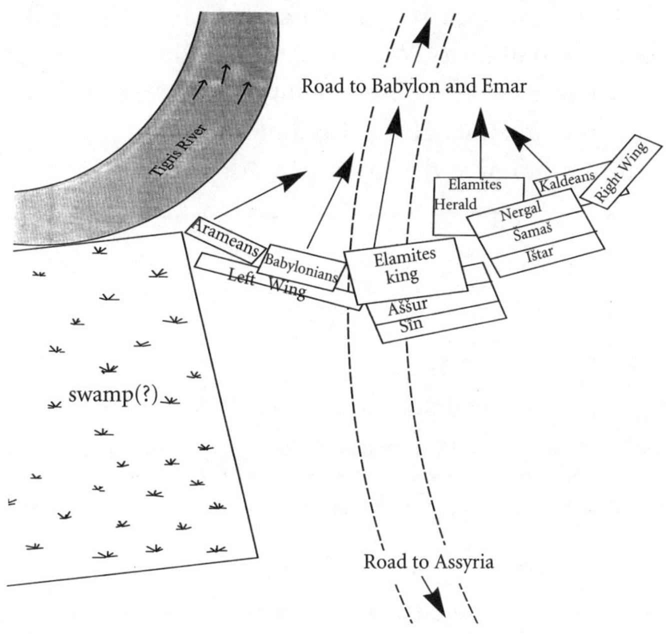

101 Sn. 46: 16-19; see above.

102 Sn. 47: 24-29.

103 Grayson (1963) 94: 99-101.

story of royal largesse too literally; it would appear that Sennacherib's attempt to roll up the allied left wing and push the enemy towards the river was not successful. Instead, the Elamite and Babylonian center seems to have advanced, badly mauling the opposing Assyrian forces until, finding themselves in serious danger of being outflanked by the Assyrian right wing, they quickly withdrew over the bodies of their comrades, leaving Sennacherib with no choice but to allow them to withdraw with most of their forces intact (fig. 9).[104]

Thus, the Assyrians were left in possession of the battlefield at the end of the battle[105] and, therefore, technically they were the victors. They were, however, in no condition to try to continue the advance against Babylon and left with little choice but to return home empty-handed or, as the Babylonian Chronicle puts it: "Ḫumban-nimena called up the troops of Elam (and) Akkad. In Ḫalule, he did battle against Assyria and forced Assyria to retreat."[106] By victories such as Sennacherib's, the British lost the South in the American Revolutionary War to Nathanael Greene.[107] Sennacherib, however much he may have boasted about his great "victory," was clearly aware of the true situation. He tarried long enough to erect a battlefield trophy,[108] then withdrew in the direction of Assyria.[109]

---

104 The Assyrians rarely admit to withdrawing themselves, but note: "(As for) my magnates, the attack of the enemy's battle became too strong for them so that they were not able to withstand him" (Sn. 50: 22).

105 The Assyrians erected a battlefield trophy (Grayson [1963] 94: 109-14; see below).

106 Grayson [1975] no. 1 iii 16-18. Note that the Chronicle tells us that the Elamites forced the Assyrians to retreat *(nabalkattu šakānu),* but it does not say that the Elamites defeated them *(dīktu dâku),* even though it is clear from the wording that the battle was engaged.

107 See Ward (1952) 793-94, 808, 834, 843.

108 "At the place where I had established the defeat of the king of Babylon and Ḫumban-nimena, king of Elam… (etc.) I harvested their skulls like shriveled grain and built them up like towers. I had a stela made and had written on it the victory over my enemies which I had achieved by trusting in the great gods my lords and set (it) up in the district of Ḫalule (Grayson [1963] 94: 109-14).

109 Grayson (1975) no. 1 iii 18; see above.

That he was less than pleased with the outcome of the battle of Ḫalule can be clearly read between the lines of his own account:

> They fled to their lands in order to save their lives and did not turn back (saying): 'Perhaps Sennacherib, king of Assyria, will become furiously angry and order a continual return to Elam.' Fear and terror were poured out over all the Elamites so that they abandoned their land and, to save their lives, took like eagles to difficult mountains; their breasts pounded like those of pursued birds. Until the day they died, they did not open a path to do battle (with me).[110]

It is obvious that the Assyrian king blamed the Elamites for his failure to advance beyond Ḫalule, and his "fury" is tacit recognition of the fact that, while Sennacherib could claim victory on technical grounds, it was Ḫumban-nimena and his Babylonian allies who had truly prevailed.

In sum, both Assyrian generals and their opponents sought to achieve their objectives in battle by means of a few, elegantly simple maneuvers. One was to use their lancer cavalry and infantry spearmen, assisted by the chariotry, bow cavalry and infantry archers to "bore through"[111] the enemy center with the object of killing or capturing the enemy leader or forcing him to flee, as Sargon II succeeded in doing at the battle of Mt.Uauš. An alternative strategy, and that attempted by Rusa I of Urarṭu in the same battle, was to hold the center, using a screen of infantry, and try to "bore through" the enemy's wings.[112] One could also try to collapse one of the enemy's wings by attacking it simultaneously from the front and side, as Sennacherib did at the battle of Ḫalule, although the precautions taken by the Babylonian-Elamite coalition in this case robbed him of all but a technical victory. Another, more difficult tactic, but one which took full advan-

---

110 Sn. 82f: 39-43.

111 The term is also used of hacking one's way through mountainsides with axes (Sg. 8 24), and of knocking holes in enemy walls with battering rams (Fuchs [1993] 91: 63-64; Ash. 57 v 5) or in lion's dens in order to capture the cubs (Bauer [1933] 88 r. 12).

112 "Boring through" enemy troops is also mentioned, inter alia, in Fuchs (1993) 76: 7; Sn. 35: 60-61, 39: 53, 51: 27-28, 82: 37-38; Ash. 65 ii 18-19, 105 ii 17; Piepkorn (1933) 10 i 8-9; Streck (1916) 164: 71; Weidner (1932–33) 198 no. 71; *cf.* ARI II § 554; ARAB I § 600 (ii 2). Compare *RIMA* 2 24 v 86-90.

tage of the presence of bow cavalry, was the partial encirclement and rolling up of one or both enemy wings, as in the battles of Til-Tuba and Dur-Yakin.

To conclude, we must not, like generations of British school boys, be carried away by "romantic" notions of the never changing "Orient." Neither are we to suppose that ancient Mesopotamia was characterized by "primitive" methods of conducting warfare of value to military historians only in so far as they enable us to recreate the long-lost world of Homeric heroes. Last, but by no means least, it should by now be apparent that, ancient and fragmentary though our sources may be, it is not at all impossible, by reading carefully and exercising a little common sense, to come up with perfectly reasonable reconstructions of the specific tactics used by the winners and losers of the some of the most ancient of ancient battles.

Bibliography

Akurgal, E. (1966) *The Art of Greece: Its Origins in the Mediterranean and Near East.* New York. **Barnett, R. D.** (1976) *Sculptures from the North Palace of Assurbanipal at Nineveh (568-627 B.C.).* London. **Barnett, R.D., and M. Falkner** (1962) *The Sculptures of Aššur-nasir-apli II (883–859 B.C.) Tiglath-Pileser III (745–727 B.C.) Esarhaddon (681–669 B.C.) from the Central and South-West Palaces at Nimrud.* London. Barnett, R. D., and A. Lorenzini (1975) *Assyrian Sculpture in the British Museum.* Toronto. **Bauer, T.** (1933) *Das Inschriftenwerk Assurbanipals.* Leipzig. **Botta, P. E., and E. Flandin** (1846–50) *Monuments de Ninive.* Paris. **Budge, E. A. W.** (1914) *Assyrian Sculptures in the British Museum.* London. **Fuchs, A.** (1993) *Die Inschriften Sargons II aus Khorsabad.* Göttingen. **Gabriel, R.A., and K. S. Metz** (1991) *From Sumer to Rome: The Military Capabilities of Ancient Armies.* Westport. **Gadd, C. J.** (1938) *Assyrian Sculptures in the British Museum from Shalmaneser III to Sennacherib.* London. (1954) Inscribed Prisms of Sargon II from Nimrud. *Iraq* 16: 173-201. **Grayson, A. K.** (1963) The Walters Art Gallery Sennacherib Inscription. *AfO* 20: 83-96. (1965) Problematical Battles in Mesopotamian History. In Güterbock and Jacobsen 1965: 337-42. (1975) *Assyrian and Babylonian Chronicles.* Texts from Cuneiform Sources 5. New York. **Güterbock, H. G., and T. Jacobsen**, eds. (1965) *Studies in Honor of Benno Landsberger on his Seventy-Fifth Birthday.* Assyriological Studies 16. Chicago. **Hall, H. R.** (1928) *Babylonian and Assyrian Sculpture in the British Museum.* Paris. **King, L. W.** (1915) *Bronze Reliefs from the Gates of Shalmaneser King of Assyria B.C. 860–825.* London. **Layard, A. H.** (1853) *A Second Series of Monuments from Nineveh.* London. **Levine, L. D.** (1982) Sennacherib's Southern Front: 704–689 B.C. *Journal of Cuneiform Studies* 34: 28-58. **Malbrun-Labat, F.** (1982) *L'armée et l'organisation militaire de l'Assyrie.* Hautes études orientales 19. Genéve. **Michel, E.** (1952) Ein neuentdeckter Annalen-Text Salmanassars III. *Welt des Orient* 1/6: 454-75. **Oman, C. W. C.** (1953) *The Art of War in the Middle Ages.* J. Beeler, ed. Ithaca. **Paterson, A.** (1907) *Assyrian Sculptures.* Haarlem. **Piepkorn, A. C.** (1933) *Historical Prism Inscriptions of Ashurbanipal.* Assyriological Studies 5. Chicago. **Postgate, J. N.** (1974) *Taxation and Conscription in the Assyrian Empire.* Studia Pohl: Series Maiar 3. Rome. **Powell, M.** (1982) Merodach-Baladan at Dur-Jakin: A Note on the Defense of Babylonian Cities. *Journal of Cuneiform Studies* 34: 59-61. **Reade, J. E.** (1972) The Neo-Assyrian Court and Army: Evidence from the Sculptures. *Iraq* 34: 87-112. **Saggs, H. W. F.** (1963) Assyrian Warfare in the Sargonid Period. *Iraq* 25: 145-54. **Salonen, A.** (1955) *Hippologica Accadica.* Annales Academiae Scientiarum Fennicae B-100. Helsinki. **Stillman, N., and N. Tallis** (1984) *Armies of the Ancient Near East.* Worthing. **Streck, M.** (1916) *Assurbanipal und die letzten assvrischen Könige bis zum Untergange Nineveh's.* Vorderasiatische Bibliothek 7. Leipzig. **Sun Tzu** (1963) *The Art of War.* S. B. Griffith, trans. Oxford. **Flavius Vegetius Renatus** (1944) *Military Institutions.of the Romans.* T. R. Phillips, trans. Harrisburg. **Ward, C.** (1952) *The War of the Revolution.* New York. **Weidner, E.** (1932–33) Assyrische Beschreibungen der Kriegs-Reliefs Aššurbanipals. *Archiv für Orientforschung* 8: 175-203. **Yadin, Y.** (1963) *The Art of Warfare in Biblical Lands.* New York.

Two Old Babylonian Contracts*

Ronald A. Veenker
Western Kentucky University

N198, an Old Babylonian tablet quite possibly from Kiš or Ur, is housed in the Nicol Collection of the Southern Baptist Theological Seminary in Louisville, Kentucky. This small black tablet, measuring 4.3 x 5.5 x 1.75 cm, is a record of a *ḫubuttatu*-loan (see Simmons [1978] 4). I thank Prof. Joel F. Drinkard, Jr., curator of the collection, for permission to publish this tablet .

* It is certainly an honor to contribute this small article for Michael Astour. His scholarship and erudition have been known to me since I was a graduate student. Michael is one of a very few "renaissance persons" to survive the explosion of data in Near Eastern studies since WW II. I am indebted to Michael for all of his helpful suggestions in my research through the years. Thanks are also due M. Stol, S. Greengus, P. Michalowski, A. Skaist, and T. Smothers who examined N198 and made suggestions. M. Stol and S. Greengus both offered suggestions on HUC 193. Errors in this article remain the responsibility of the author. Thanks also to E. Counts for providing excellent photographs of both tablets.

Abbreviation list: BE: *Babylonian Legal and Business Documents from the Time of the First Dynasty of Babylon, Chiefly from Sippar* (6/1 = Ranke [1906]; 6/2 = Poebel [1909]); CBS: Catalogue of the Babylonian Section, University Museum, University of Pennsylvania. *Siglum* for unpublished tablets in its collection; CT: *Cuneiform Texts from Babylonian Tablets … in the British Museum* (8 = Pinches [1899]; 33 = King [1912]; 47 = Figulla [1967]); OB: Old Babylonian; OLA: Orientalia Lovaniensia Analecta (21 = van Lerberghe [1986]); PSBA 33 *Proceedings of the Society of Biblical Archaeology* (33 = Langdon [1911]); RA 8: *Revue d'assyriologie et d'archéologie orientale* (8 = Johns [1911]); UET 5: *Ur Excavation Texts* (5 = Figulla [1953]).

N 198

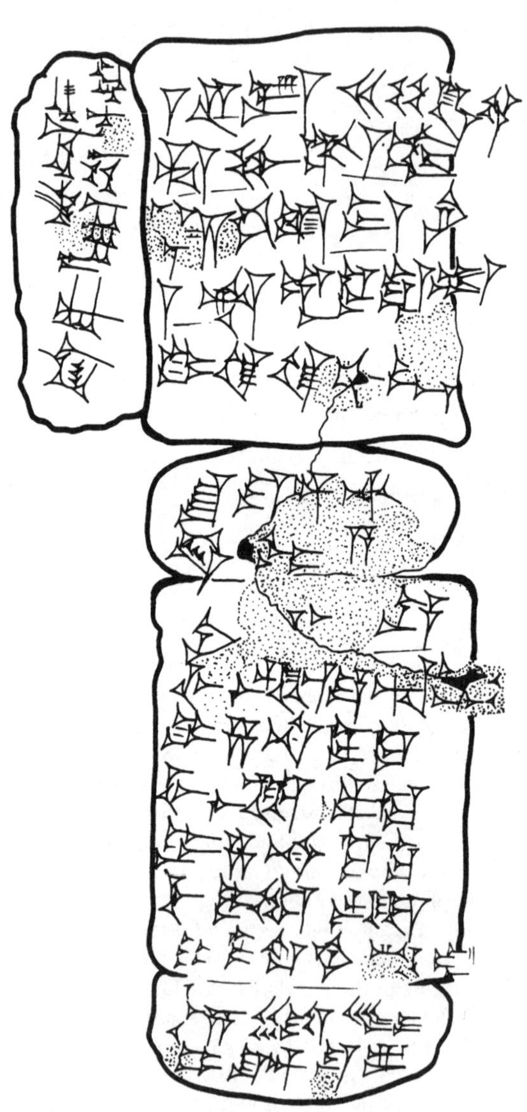

N 198

	1⅔ gín 20 še kù.babbar	1⅔ shekel 20 grain silver
	ḫu-bu-ta-tum	(for) a *ḫubuttatu*-loan
	⸢ki⸣ *A-ḫi-iš-ib*(?)*-ni*	from Aḫiš-ibni
	^{m}*Ìr-ra-qú-ra-ad*	Irra-qurād
	dumu *Ki-ki-nu-um*	the son of Kikinum
lo.e.	šu.ba.an.ti	has borrowed.
	itu.⸢sig$_4$⸣.a	In the month of *Simanu*
rev.	ì.⸢lá⸣.e	he will repay (the silver).
	igi ^{d}EN.ZU-*e-*⸢*ri-ba-am*⸣	Witnesses: Sîn-erībam
	dumu *Sà-na-ku*!*-ku*	son of Sanakuku,
	igi ^{d}EN.ZU-sipad	Sîn-rēꜥī
	dumu *Sà-na-ku-ku*	son of Sanakuku,
	igi *I-šar-*^{d}EN.ZU	Išar-Sîn
	dumu *Ku-ru-ub-Ìr-ra*	son of Kurub-Irra,
u.e.	igi! *Ṣa-li-lum*	Ṣālilum
	dumu *Šu-*^{d}*Ba-ú*	son of Šu-Baꜣu.
le.e	itu.zíz.a mu.ús.sa	Month of *Šabaṭu,* the year following
	bàd! ká.dingir.ra$^{⸢ki⸣}$	the “Wall of Babylon.”

Commentary

3 Perhaps the name *A-ḫi-iš-ma-ni* contains the *-išmeanni* element in OB personal names.

5 Although the provenience of this text remains ambiguous, there may be information available with regard to the family of Kikinum. See van Lerberghe (1982) 252-53.

15 Ṣa-li-lum: this personal name occurs eleven times in OB texts from Ur (see UET 5 p. 59).

17-18 mu.ús.sa bàd ká.dingir.ra, Sumu-abum 2. Perhaps this text is from Kiš: *RA* 8 74: mu-ús-sa bàd-bābilim^{ki} ba-dù; *PSBA* 33 Kiš 5: mu-ús-sa bàd-bābilim^{ki} (Edzard [1957] 131 n. 696). Further, Simmons (1978) 149 31 ⸢bàd ká.dingir.ra^{ki}⸣ (also see pp. 10-11).

HUC 193

This tablet is housed in the collection of the Klau Library of the Hebrew Union College – Jewish Institute of Religion in Cincinnati, Ohio. It measures 4.75 x 7.6 x 2 cm and is composed of black clay. The tablet has been covered with a substance like shellac and has the large red number "193" painted on the reverse. Its provenience is clearly Sippar and deals with a field rental for tenant farming. I wish to thank Dr. David J. Gilner for permission to publish the text.

2 gán a.šà ab.sín
a.gàr *Bu-*⸢*ra-a*⸣
a.šà ^{md}⸢EN.ZU-*iš-me-a*⸣*-ni* dumu *Ta-*⸢*ri-bu*⸣
ki ^{md}EN.ZU-*iš-me-a-ni* dumu *Ta-ri -*⸢*bu*⸣
be-el a.šà
^{md}EN.ZU-*mu-ša-lim* dumu *Šu-pí-ša*
a.šà *a-na er-re-šu-tim*
a-na gun *a-na* mu.1.kam
⸢íb.ta⸣.è.a
u_4.$buru_{14}$.šè
a.šà <*a-na*> ⸢*pí-i*⸣ *šu-ul-pí-šu*
lo.e *i-*⸢*ša-ad-da*⸣*-du-ma*
[x g]án.e 6 še.gur GIŠ.BAN ^{d}[utu]
rev. gun a.šà ì.ág.e
⸢igi⸣ *Šu-mu-um-li-ib-ši* dumu *I-na-pa-lé-e-šu*
⸢igi⸣ *Šu-mu-um-li-ṣi* dumu.é.dub.ba.a
⸢itu.du_6.kù⸣ u_4.21.kam
mu *Am-*[*mi*]*-ṣá-du-ga* lugal.e
u.e. ⸢sipa zi še⸣.ga ^{d}⸢utu ^{d}marduk⸣
bi.da.a.ke_4
⸢ur_5.ra⸣ kalam.ma.⸢an⸣.ni

SEAL 1.
^{d}EN.ZU-*i*[*š-me-a-ni*]
dumu *Ta-*[*ri-bu*]
arad X-[ ]

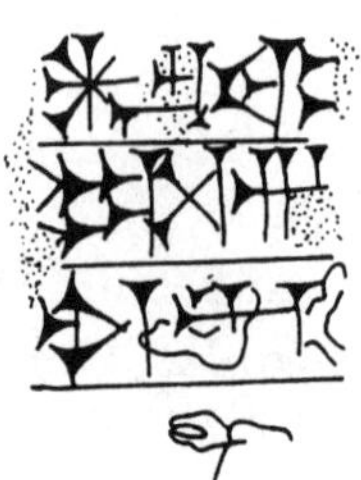

SEAL 2. (illegible)

HUC 193

Translation

A two-acre field, ready for sowing,
in the irrigation district of *Burâ,*
belonging to Sîn-išmeanni the son of Taribu.
From Sîn-išmeanni the son of Taribu,
owner of the field,
Sîn-mušallim the son of Šupiša
said field, for tenant farming,
for a period of one year
has rented.
At harvest time,
the field, according <to> its stubble,
they shall measure and
[for each] acre of harvested land, six kor,
according to the seah of Šamaš,
as field rental he will pay.
Witnesses:
Šumum-libši the son of Ina-palêšu
Šumum-liṣi the archivist
month 7, day 21, Ammiṣaduqa year 2.
The year Ammiṣaduqa, the king, the true shepherd,
obedient to Šamaš and Marduk,
released the debts of the land.

Commentary

2 For the village Burâ^{ki} and the organization of the *ugārum*, see Stol (1982) 351-55. The a.gàr *Burâ*^{ki} is well known in the Sippar archives: *Cf.* Harris (1975) 110; Waterman (1916) 41, 61; CT 33 36; CT 47 47 and 77; BE 6/1 119; BE 6/2 110; OLA 21 63.

16 *Šumum-libši* dumu *Ina-palêšu*: CT 8 10b 19 (AṢ 10); CT 8 14a 24 (AṢ 10); Meissner (1893) 107 37 (AṢ 16); CBS 134 6 seal.

17 *Šumum-līṣi* dumu.é.dub.ba.a: Harris (1975) 108; Stol (1976) 149b, 153a; OLA 21 46: 12 (AṢ 6).

Bibliography

Edzard, D. O. (1957) *Die "Zweite Zwischenseit" Babyloniens.* Wiesbaden. **Figulla, H. H.** (1953) *Letters and Documents of the Old Babylonian Period.* Ur Excavation Texts 5. London. (1967) *Old Babylonian* nadītu *Records.* Cuneiform Texts from Babylonian Tablets ... in the British Museum 47. London. **Harris, R.** (1975) *Ancient Sippar: A Demographic Study of an Old-Babylonian City (1894–1595).* Leiden. **Johns, C. H. W.** (1911) The Manan-Japium Dynasty of Kish. *Proceedings of the Society of Biblical Literature* 33: 98-103. **King, L. W.** (1912) *Cuneiform Texts from Babylonian Tablets ... in the British Museum* 33. London. **Langdon, S. H.** (1911) *Tablets from Kiš...* Proceedings of the Society of Biblical Archaeology 33: 185-96. London. **Meissner, B.** (1893) *Beiträge zum albabylonischen Privatrecht.* Assyriologische Bibliothek 11. Leipzig. **Pinches, T. G.** (1899) *Cuneiform Texts from Babylonian Tablets ... in the British Museum* 9. London. **Poebel, A.** (1909) *Babylonian Legal and Business Documents from the Time of the First Dynasty of Babylon, Chiefly from Sippar* 6/2. Philadelphia. **Ranke, H.** (1906) *Babylonian Legal and Business Documents from the Time of the First Dynasty of Babylon, Chiefly from Sippar* 6/1. Philadelphia. **Simmons, S. D.** (1978) *Early Old Babylonian Documents.* Yale Oriental Series 14. New Haven. **Stol, M.** (1976) On Ancient Sippar. *Bibliotheca Orientalis* 33: 146a-154a. (1982) A Cadastral Innovation by Hammurabi. In Veenhof, *et al.* 1982: 351-58. **van Lerberghe, K.** (1982) L'arrachement de l'emblème *šurinnum.* In Veenhof, *et al.* 1982: 245-57. (1986) *Old Babylonian Legal and Administrative Texts from Philadelphia.* Orientalia Lovaniensia Analecta 21. Leuven. **Veenhof, K., *et al.***, eds. (1982) *zikir šumim: Assyriological Studies Presented to F. R. Kraus.* Leiden. **Waterman, L.** (1916) *Business Documents of the Hammurapi Period from the British Museum.* London.

After Drinking (1 Sam 1:9)*

Stanley D. Walters
Toronto

Jacques Cartier, the discoverer of Canada and explorer of the great St. Lawrence basin, was at home in his village of St. Malo on the Brittany coast of northwestern France. His name is frequent in the archives of town and church, and the course of his career can be traced by the records of baptisms at which he had been an assistant or a sponsor. The record of one such event, in 1552, states that the written entry had been made in the presence of Captain Jacques Cartier "et autres bon biberons."[1] This cheerful note reminds us that liturgical events can be occasions of great celebration, and often bring people together around a festive board where eating and drinking are as prominent as priestly service and benediction.

Such was the case in ancient Israel, especially in Deuteronomy's description of the pilgrim feasts. One of its provisions concerns people who live too far from the sanctuary to carry with them their victuals and drink. In that case,

> ... you may convert them into money. Wrap up the money and take it with you to the place that the LORD your God has chosen, and spend the money on anything you want—cattle, sheep, wine, or other intoxicant, or anything you may desire. And you shall feast there, in the presence of the LORD your God, and rejoice with your household. (Deut 14:25-26 JPS)

---

* Abbreviation list: GK: *Gesenius' Hebrew Grammar.* Second Edition. ed. E. Kautzsch. transl. A. E. Cowley (1910); JPS: Jewish Publication Society; LXX: Septuagint; MT: Masoretic Text; NRSV: New Revised Standard Version; OG: Old Greek.

1 Dawson (1905) 212.

"Rejoice with your household." The words are suitable for the pilgrim festivals, but they comport ill with the opening events of the story of Samuel's birth in 1 Samuel 1. The occasion is the annual pilgrimage to Shiloh. It is a family event, and Elkanah is there with both wives—Hannah and Peninnah—and with Peninnah's several sons and daughters. In the Masoretic story, the scene is full of tension, as Peninnah taunts Hannah, hoping to provoke an outburst.[2] It had been like this year after year, but this time[3] Hannah bursts into tears and refuses to eat. Elkanah's words of comfort—"Am I not as good to you as ten sons would be?"—are as recognizable for their nonplussed earnestness as for their failure to comprehend Hannah's situation. Her further response is described in verse 9a:

ותקם חנה אחרי אָכְלָה בְשִׁלֹה וְאַחֲרֵי שָׁתֹה
Hanna arose after her eating[4] in Shiloh, and after drinking ...

The next clause (v 9b) is parenthetical and describes Eli sitting on his bench in the "temple," after which we hear of Hannah's earnest prayer (vs 10-11).

The words "and after drinking" in v 9 (let us call them the "drinking words") began to attract critical attention in the mid-nineteenth century. There were several reasons.

1. GRAMMAR

Above all, there is the anomaly that שָׁתֹה is the infinitive absolute, while the object of a preposition should be the infinitive construct.[5]

Already in 1863, Friedrich Böttcher had called it the only example of an infinitive absolute following a preposition,[6] and suggested that it entered

---

2 הרעמה "to make her thunder" (v 6).

3 The preterite ותבכה (v 7) resumes the narrative sequence of ויזבח and thus returns to the present occasion, after the frequentative verbs ונתן, וכעסתה, יעשׂה, and תכעסנה in vs 4-7 have described the customary events of the festival, year after year. See Driver (1913) 11.

4 The form אָכְלָה seems to be the infinitive construct with the feminine suffix "her" (so GK §91e, Driver [1913] 11-12).

5 The expected form would be similar to I Kgs 13:23, וְאַחֲרֵי שְׁתוֹתוֹ.

6 Böttcher (1863) 89-90.

the text as a gloss in a time when knowledge of the language had already decayed, so that an incorrect form could have been used. Thenius immediately agreed,[7] citing Ewald as well. Gesenius-Kautzsch call it "impossible Hebrew," shown by the LXX to be "a late addition" (§113e n 3). Driver gives the fullest discussion, calling it "very anomalous" and suggesting that it has entered the text through analogy with other passages in which שָׁתֹה follows אכל, mentioning Gen 24:54.[8] Waltke-O'Connor (1990) allow it, but it is their only clear example (p. 591). I will return to this below.

2. POSITION IN THE SENTENCE

The drinking-words also sound very much like an afterthought. For one thing, they stand after the words "in Shiloh," instead of beside the words "after eating,"[9] and for another, in the semantically parallel phrases "after eating and after drinking," the drinking-words are grammatically unparallel; after using the correct form of the infinitive for "eating," the MT uses an incorrect form for "drinking."

3. INTRA-NARRATIVE TENSION

In v 15 Hannah assures Eli that she had drunk nothing, a claim which appears to be in conflict with v 9.

This is not just a modern cavil. The Targum reads,

וקמת חנה בתר דאכלת בשילו ובתר דאשתיאו[10]

And Hannah got up after she had eaten in Shiloh, and after they had drunk.

---

7 In the second edition of his commentary, Thenius (1864) 5.

8 Driver (1913) 12.

9 Thenius seems to be the first to be bothered by the add-on appearance of the words, already in the first edition (Thenius [1842] 4).

10 This is Sperber's text, but the Bomberg Rabbinic Bible (Venice: 1515/17) reads דשתיאת "she had drunk," as does the מקראות גדולות in that tradition.

That is, Jonathan allows Hannah to eat, but uses "they" for the drinking in order to except her from that activity. This careful distinction suggests that MT's wording very early proved worrisome.

The mediaeval Greek mss c and x are even more bold:

> καὶ ἀνέστη Αννα πρὸ τοῦ φαγεῖν καὶ πιεῖν,
> καὶ ἔστη ἐνώπιον Κυρίου εἰς Σηλωμ.
>
> And Anna got up before eating and drinking,
> and stood before the Lord in Shiloh.

In this telling of the story, the hunger strike began just as Elkanah distributed the portions of food, and Hannah left the table before anyone took a bite.

The narrative dissonance has been productive of textual variants and of commentary because Hannah's character is on the line. After all, v 9 says that she ate, even though v 7 says that, in her distress, she always refused. Might she not also have drunk, even though she later said she didn't?

The older English commentators—who are still worth reading because they take the text so seriously—believed that she did drink. "The kind words of Elkanah seem to have persuaded her to eat and drink chearfully [sic]."[11] "Elkanah had gently reproved Hannah for her inordinate grief, and ... she eat [sic] and drank."[12] Gill, following the Targum that he knew (see note 10), says that she both ate and drank, but drank only water.[13] As to the tension with v 15, Henry, defending drinking in moderation, says that she drank but was not drunk.

4. THE SEPTUAGINT

Finally, the Old Greek[14] tells the story without including the drinking-words.

---

11 Patrick (1732) 187.

12 Henry (1758) 143.

13 Gill (1764) 385.

14 This term denotes the presumed oldest form of the Septuagint, recognizing that the Greek text changed over the years more or less in line with the developing Hebrew text, which had not yet stabilized. Precise dates are not possible, but, for convenience,

καὶ ἀνέστη μετὰ τὸ φαγεῖν αὐτοὺς ἐν Σηλω,[15]
καὶ κατέστη ἐνώπιον Κυρίου.

And she got up after they had eaten in Shiloh,
and presented herself before the Lord.

This telling of the story does not offer any internal difficulty, since the drinking-words are not present to cause conflict with Anna's statement to Eli in v 15. The "they" who ate (against MT's "she") would not include Anna. We also note that the LXX contains a clause lacking in the MT, "she presented herself before the Lord." Let us call them the "presenting-words."

Brief Review

On the strength of these considerations, most scholars from Thenius on have dropped or replaced the drinking-words and have added the presenting-words.

Thenius assumes that the drinking-words have been dislodged from their original position in v 18. Here is the reasoning: verse 18 originally reported that, following Eli's promise that God would give her what she asks, Hannah both ate *and drank* (as is still the case in the OG), but the drinking-words somehow came loose and ended up in v 9. Thenius accordingly drops them from the Hebrew text of v 9, and adds the presenting-words, retroverted as ותתיצב לפני יהוה (without saying that they are found in the LXX). His text thus becomes:

ותקם חנה אחרי אכלה בשלה ותתיצב לפני יהוה

Hannah arose after eating in Shiloh, and presented herself before the LORD.

The words of the second clause, he says, form a smooth transition to the parenthetical sentence in v 10 about Eli sitting on his bench. The new read-

---

we may put the OG in the second or third century before the common era. The Hebrew text shows stabilization only towards the end of the first century C.E. In this part of Samuel, the OG is more or less the text found in Codex Vaticanus, see Brooke-McLean (1927).

15 The drinking-words καὶ μετὰ τὸ πιεῖν are found as a plus in Codex A, in the Antiochene MSS, and in Chrysostom, and represent a Greek text conformed to the developing Hebrew text.

ing is *völlig sachgemäss* "entirely suitable," and allows us to restore through conjecture a passage which has otherwise become quite unreadable.[16] He repeats these suggestions in 1864, and Wellhausen concurred in 1871: "Thenius rightly decides for the LXX against the MT."[17]

The omission of the drinking-words and the addition of the presenting-words have proven "entirely suitable" to most subsequent commentators as well. Thenius's rewritten text virtually takes the place of the MT.

Budde says that we must first of all purify the text "nach LXX." The drinking-words must be struck out as an addition which arose "on the basis of many parallels." He does not ask why the addition should have been made, but his "nach manchen Mustern" suggests that he simply thinks the scribe believed every feast should have some drinking.[18]

Driver's celebrated *Notes* first appeared in 1890 and in an enlarged edition in 1913. In 1890 he notes that the presenting-words are found in the LXX, and says that they provide "an excellent introduction to what follows" and that they are preferred to MT by Thenius, Wellhausen, and Klostermann.[19] In 1913 he adds that these words are "indeed required for the sequel."[20] Smith simply adopts the LXX's reading, rightly rejecting Klostermann's conjecture. He inserts the presenting-words because "it seems necessary."[21] One notes in these justifications how powerful a role is played

---

16 Thenius (1842) 4.

17 Wellhausen (1871) p 38.

18 Budde (1902) 7.

19 Klostermann's originality makes him always interesting to read, and he is really the first to offer a history of transmissional events which might account for the MT. He proposes a typically-involved and -implausible process of corruption. The original text read, he suggests, וַתַּנַּח אַחֲרֶיהָ אָכְלָה בְּלִשְׁכָּה ותתיצב לפני יהוה "Sie liess hinter sich ihr Essen in der Zelle und stellte sich hin vor Jahve." The process of deterioration which led to the MT's form of the text included the following steps. First of all, the verb ותתיצב was lost; then יהוה was misunderstood to be שׁתה under the influence of אכלה; then לפני was corrected to אחרי in order to complete the parallelism. Further changes, such as the corruption of וַתַּנַּח into חָנָּה he leaves to the reader's epigraphic imagination to infer. Klostermann (1887) 2.

20 Driver (1913) 12.

21 Smith (1899) 8-10.

by the commentator's assumptions about what is "necessary" and "suitable" in a narrative. Both Thenius and Böttcher use the word *sachgemäss* "appropriate." The question is, "To whom?"

In 1973 Stoebe can say that the drinking-words are impossible because of the infinitive absolute, that they are wanting in the LXX, are in conflict with Hannah's claim in v 15 that she had not drunk anything, and are a later addition perhaps based on passages like Gen 24:54 and others.[22] McCarter, who knows that the drinking-words are, in fact, found in a few MSS of the LXX, similarly holds that they were added "subsequently." He omits them and adds the presenting words. Klein 1983 drops the drinking-words because they are contradicted by v 15, and accepts the LXX plus.[23]

That is, on the drinking-words, there is nothing new to say.

Unasked Questions

Let us grant that the above are cogent reasons. The words are probably an addition, inserted in order to make the Shiloh occasion a proper festive meal. End of discussion.

But there are unasked questions lurking nearby. First of all, Why would anyone tell this story in such a way that the pilgrim feast was not a proper meal? Was this just an oversight by the narrator? Or (more likely) was there not a reason for telling it like that in the first place? What would be the meaning of the story told just that way?

And then, granted that such a story might have its own meaning, Why would anyone disrupt it by adding words whose absence were important to its meaning? Was it because the old meaning was unrecognized? forgotten? Is there perhaps a new context in which circumstances require the story to have a different effect? What would those new interests be?

Our answers to these questions may not be coercive, but the questions themselves are very interesting, for they have to do with the meaning of scripture and how its tradents and users found God speaking to them

---

22 Stoebe (1973) 91.

23 McCarter (1980) 53; Klein (1983) 3.

through it. Those of us who are now interested in such things may wish to allow the unasked questions at least to come to center stage and be heard. That is what this paper is about.

Telling Stories

Assuming the drinking-words to be an addition, we enquire what understanding of the story would have been served by their inclusion. To put forth this question raises at once the fact that people usually tell a story to make a point, and that the same clutch of events can be reported in different ways—to make different points.

Of course, people may tell stories primarily for entertainment and diversion. But with the biblical material, we do not have isolated or free-standing narratives, but a sustained and reflective narrative of communal religious significance. In such a case, instruction is surely the purpose, even when the narratives are made as diverting as possible. Scripture openly acknowledges this by designating the first five books of the Bible—including the rich narrative traditions of Genesis, Exodus, and Numbers—as תורה "Instruction, Guidance," and the second major division—including all that modern scholarship has come to call the "Deuteronomistic History"—as נביאים "Prophets."

The fact that there is more than one form of the story—we have at least the OG and the MT—requires us to distinguish the basic set of events, the "fabula,"[24] from any particular telling of those events, the "story." The point to be emphasized here is that small changes in wording take on disproportionate importance. Large differences between two tellings would imply a somewhat different set of events, a different fabula. The story reveals its distinct slant in the subtleties of its telling.

---

24 This word, the Latin for "narrative, story," is Mieke Bal's term. Her definitions are: *fabula*, "a series of logically and chronologically related events that are caused or experienced by actors"; *story*, "a fabula that is presented in a certain manner" (Bal [1985] 5).

Each telling of the fabula is a story in its own right, to be considered in its own distinctiveness. The Greek Bible (Old Testament) often gives us a story which differs somewhat from the Hebrew (Masoretic) telling of the same fabula, and, in its various recensions and manuscripts, may further offer multiple tellings of the same fabula. Each of these manuscripts was somebody's Bible, and was read to hear what the divine voice was saying. These diverse tellings belong to the history of interpretation and must be read for themselves and their own distinctive meaning.

We therefore need whole narratives in order to descry their distinctive features. The OG and MT stories differ from one another in many ways, most of them small in themselves. A fragment from Qumran with a few words from this story (see p. 537) leaves us in the dark about possible variations elsewhere in its telling. We would like to know, for example: In the Qumran story, is Hannah depressed as she goes into her prayer and vow (as she is in the OG but is not in the MT)? Was there drinking at the feast before Hannah prayed (as there is in the MT but not in the OG)? Did Hannah drink after she prayed (as she does in the OG but not in the MT)? Besides the MT, there is no full story in Hebrew of the events at Shiloh and Samuel's birth.

The Story Without the Drinking-Words

The first question, then, is, Why would the Hannah/Anna story ever have been told *without* a reference to drinking in v 9? Eating and drinking frequently occur together in the Bible as activities which are part of daily life and certainly of any festivity.[25] It is the absence of these words which really requires explanation. Note that at this point we are interpreting the Old Greek story rather than the Masoretic Hebrew, or—assuming that

---

25 Among many examples, note: 1 Kgs 4: 20, 2 Kgs 6: 22-23, Judg 19: 4, 21, Ruth 3: 3, Prov 23: 7, Eccl 2: 24, 3: 13, 5: 17, 8: 15, Isa 21: 5, 22: 13; not to do so is to fast, Exod 34: 28, Deut 9: 9, Esth 4: 16, Ezra 10: 6. Note, in the New Testament, that when Jesus was criticized for not observing table purity, the charge in Matthew and Mark is, "Why does he eat with tax collectors and sinners?" (Matt 9: 11, Mark 2: 16), but in Luke—where Levi has thrown a δοχὴ μεγάλη "a great feast"—the charge is, "Why do you *eat and drink* with tax collectors and sinners?" (Luke 5: 30).

there was once a Hebrew story of which the OG is a faithful translation—a different form of the Hebrew story. There is no extant Hebrew story in which no one drinks in 1 Sam 1:9.

1. IT PROTECTS ANNA'S PRAYER AND VOW

The omission absolutely avoids any chance that Eli's suspicion of Anna was correct. Not only can she say (in v 15) that she had drunk nothing, but the story would expressly omit any reference to drinking at the table by anyone. Anna's sobriety is important to the story, given Eli's suspicions, for it protects Shiloh from a reputation for rowdyism such as Judges 21:19-25 might imply. The story is not particularly interested in Hannah's abstemiousness as such, but in the integrity of her prayer and vow.

It is true that she prays out of deep depression, as the OG story indicates three times by the words ἀθυμία "depression" (v 6) and ἠθύμει "she was in depression" (vs 6, 7). It is this fact that allows Elkanah to suspect that Anna will not really keep her promise; for, when she declines to take Samuel up to Shiloh at the next pilgrimage, he says, "May the Lord confirm what went forth from your mouth" (v 23). In the MT Hannah is vexed and distressed, but not depressed, and Elkanah's reply in v 23 does not doubt her.[26]

But the absence of drinking at the sacrificial meal at least means that her promise to give up the longed-for son was not made in an alcoholic muddle, but deliberately and knowingly. It would not do for the priestly blotter to show that she had been charged with PUI! Indeed, a talmudic saying prohibits praying while under the influence of wine (Erubin 64a), thus extending to everyone the biblical regulations for priests (Lev 10:8-11, Ezek 44:21). This ancient reserve about mixing drink with spirituality shows that the Apostle Paul's injunction rests on a very long tradition:

> καὶ μὴ μεθύσκεσθε οἴνῳ, ἐν ᾧ ἐστιν ἀσωτία,
> ἀλλὰ πληροῦσθε ἐν πνεύματι.
>
> Do not be intoxicated with wine, in which is dissoluteness,
> but be filled with the Spirit. (Eph 5:18)

---

26 For these matters, see Walters (1988) 385-412.

2. IT AGREES WITH SAMUEL'S DISCIPLINED LIFE

The story's reserve in not reporting drinking at the festive board is also in keeping with the promises Anna makes on behalf of Samuel. In both the OG and the MT she promises that he will not have his hair cut, but, in words found only in the OG, she says,

> καὶ οἶνον καὶ μέθυσμα οὐ πίεται
> And wine and strong drink he shall not drink. (v 11)

This is one of the prohibitions that the "nazirite" observes (Num 6:1-4). Although the OG does not use that word of Samuel, the inclusion of this promise certainly slants the portrayal of Samuel towards the disciplined sub-group in Israel described in Numbers 6. Samuel is called a nazirite in the Hebrew text of Sirach 46:13, and the historian Josephus also knows this tradition, saying that Samuel's "drink was water" (*Antiquities* 5:347).

Insofar as it associates Samuel with nazirite disciplines, the OG story is more ascetic in character. Anna is not herself abstemious, for she does drink after praying and talking with Eli in the temple (v 18); but Samuel is.

A fragment from Qumran Cave 4, 4QSam[a], identified as Hannah's presentation of the lad to Eli in 1 Sam 1:22, actually contains the word נזיר "nazirite."[27] We thus have a spectrum: on the one end, 4QSam[a] actually uses the term "nazirite"; then there is the OG, which does not use the word but stipulates that Samuel will observe prohibitions against having his hair cut and drinking alcohol; then there is the MT, which neither uses the word "nazirite" nor prohibits Samuel from drinking; and finally there is Targum Jonathan, in which Hannah promises only that Samuel will minister (משמיש) before the Lord, mentioning no specific prohibitions at all. The movement across this spectrum is from Samuel in a private, monastic (and, if Samson be compared, trivial) vocation, towards Samuel in a public, priestly and prophetic vocation. MT is closer to the Targum than to the OG.

On the strength of the single occurrence in 4QSam[a], the NRSV has inserted the word "nazirite" into its translation in both v 11 and v 22; the insertion in v 11 is based only on the reconstruction of a lacuna in another

---

27 See McCarter (1980) 56.

Qumran fragment.[28] The NRSV has also added to its text the promise against drinking found in the LXX of v 11. It has thus contaminated the masoretic story with ascetic emphases not proper to it, and skewed the figure of Samuel away from his open prophetic vocation.

Incidentally, the New Testament figure of John the Baptizer, whose birth and abstemiousness were announced ahead of time by an angel (Luke 1:15), recalls the OG story rather than the MT story. The prohibition in Luke reads, οἶνον καὶ σίκερα οὐ μὴ πίῃ "wine and strong drink he shall not drink." The MT does not require Samuel to abstain from alcohol, and of the several texts in Numbers, Judges, and Samuel to which this might be an allusion, 1 Reigns (= 1 Samuel) 1:11 is closest. Judges 13:14, which uses σίκερα instead of μέθυσμα, concerns the mother and not the son.

3. IT EVOKES DISTANT RESONANCE WITH SAMSON

The pre-natal promise of Samuel's birth has sometimes been compared to the similar promise of Samson's birth. Although Samson was designated a nazirite by the divine messenger (Judg 13:5, 7), it is the mother who receives the prohibition against drinking wine (Judg 13:4, 7, 14). We suppose that Samson's naziritism encompasses all that Numbers 6 mentions, but in the messenger's direct speech, uncut hair is the only restriction. By contrast, his mother cannot drink wine or other intoxicant. It is as if, prior to Samson's conception and during her pregnancy, she must observe that nazirite discipline herself. By withholding wine before Anna's vow, the OG story brings her alongside Samson's mother, and, tacitly, Samuel alongside Samson. However, the story's freedom to allow Anna to drink once she has received the promise from Eli undercuts the parallel.

28 McCarter (1980) 52. The reconstruction also assumes that δοτός in the Septuagint (1 Reigns 1: 11) is a translation of נזיר; this may be so, but cannot be shown, since δοτός does not occur anywhere else in the Septuagint, although נזיר occurs some sixteen times.

The Story With the Drinking-Words

Why, then, would someone feel the need to add these two words? The starting point is surely to say that a feast without drink is a disadvantaged festival, one "spirits-ually" (sic) challenged, we might say. With drink a regular accompaniment of food, it is really the omission of drink which requires explanation, and the addition supplies what was customary. There is the further fact that Deuteronomy recognizes wine as normal fare at religious festivals; recall Deut 14:25-26, cited at the beginning of this paper.

The addition of the drinking-words, therefore, makes Elkanah's meal a proper festive occasion. But the references to rejoicing in the Deuteronomy passage already cited points us still farther. The great pilgrim festivals are to be observed with joy. The LORD's people are not to worship as do the nations they will dispossess, but are to go to the place which God chooses.

> Together with your households, you shall feast (אכל) there before the LORD your God, happy in all the undertakings in which the LORD your God has blessed you.... You must bring everything that I command you to the site where the LORD your God will choose to establish His name ... and you shall rejoice before the LORD your God with your sons and daughters .... (12:7, 11-12, *cf.* 17-18)

It is especially the Feast of Booths which shall be marked by rejoicing.

> You shall rejoice in your festival, with your son and daughter, your male and female slave, the Levite, the stranger, the fatherless, and the widow in your communities. You shall hold festival for the LORD your God seven days, in the place that the LORD will choose; for the LORD your God will bless all your crops and all your undertakings, and you shall have nothing but joy (16:14-15).

"Nothing but joy." We sense again the shortfall of joy in Elkanah's household, especially at the annual pilgrim feast. 1 Samuel 1 does not identify its festival with one of the great pilgrim festivals, saying only that it was the yearly festival (1 Sam 1:3, 21). But Judges 21:19 speaks of a yearly feast (חַג) at Shiloh, and goes on to describe a robust vintage festival. If Elkanah's annual pilgrimage is to be understood as the same, the contrast is all the worse. At the festive board, Hannah burst into tears, and presently fled the table in desperation.

We should return to the "manche Mustern" to which Budde referred, to consider whether the addition of the drinking-words was intended to trigger an allusion. Only two are religious festivities. One of them is the ineffable vision of Exod 24:9-11 in which Moses and the seventy elders ascended the mount. "They saw the God of Israel, … and they ate and drank." The passage and the experience are both *sui generis*; it does not seem likely a late tradent of the Samuel story wished to claim this kind of spiritual intimacy for Elkanah and Hannah. Much more likely, our story has been brought alongside the festivities of Nehemiah 8. That account celebrates the reading of scripture, and the dispelling of grief by "the joy of the LORD" (Neh 8:10). Not only so, but it turns out to be the first observance of the Feast of Booths since the days of Joshua, "and there was very great rejoicing" (Neh 8:17).

With this nudge, we may note a number of features in Nehemiah 8 which we recognize also from 1 Sam 1 (MT).

1. There is both eating and drinking (vs 10, 12).
2. Weeping is prominent. In Nehemiah the people wept when they heard scripture read, and Nehemiah remonstrated with them for it (vs 9-10). In Samuel Hannah's weeping receives special stress: it signals that this year is going to be different (v 7), Elkanah remonstrated with her for it (v 8), and she continued it in the sanctuary as she prayed (v 10).
3. There are "portions" (מנות) of food. In Nehemiah they must be sent to people who have nothing ready (vs 10, 12); in Samuel Elkanah gives them to Peninnah and her children (v 4)
4. Women are specifically part of the gathering. Nehemiah mentions them along with men as part of the gathering (vs 2-3); Samuel's story (MT) is distinctly favorable to women, especially when viewed alongside the Greek version.
5. The expression "to bow to the LORD" occurs in both stories (Neh 8:6, 1 Sam 1:3, 19), although these words are otherwise common enough as to be only supportive to the present argument.
6. The weeping comes to an end, replaced by a proper festivity. "Then all the people went to eat and drink and send portions and

> make great merriment, for they understood the things they were told" (Neh 8:12). "The woman went her way and ate, and her face showed the difference" (1 Sam 1:18).

The redaction and compilation of the biblical materials were carried out by people who looked and listened to them for a divine word. It lies near at hand to suggest that a late tradent of the Samuel story, probably a preacher, noted the connection between 1 Sam 1 and Neh 8, especially as suggested by the weeping and by the "portions." He added the words "and after drinking" to the Samuel story to trigger a cross-reference to Neh 8, so that the two stories might be interpreted together. He was aware of the possible conflict with v 15, and added precisely that form of the infinitive which cannot be suffixed, so that the text might not be taken to assert that Hannah drank after she ate. If Hannah said she had drunk nothing, she had not, and even Eli had believed her. And anyway, this tradent is not as much interested in the person as in the festival.

The Stories Together

The simple juxtaposition of material is a frequent technique of the Hebrew Bible, and to be expected in the growth of a collection of written materials, where new materials take their place beside text that is already there. The editor does not usually explain; simple placement is enough. Position is hermeneutic, and the meaning of both stories will be affected.

Neh 8 is, of course, about the celebration of the Feast of Booths in Ezra's time, but the prominence which it gives to the reading and interpreting of scripture has always linked it with the later synagogue service as well.[29] What gains accrue to the interpreter from juxtaposing the two stories?

[1]. To start with, the vexed grief of the Shiloh sacrificial occasion comes alongside—and in some sense becomes—the Bible's most joyous festival, the Feast of Booths. The language of joy does not occur in 1 Sam 1, but to convert (as it were) the Shiloh festival into a celebration of Booths

---

29 See most recently Levine (1996) 425-48, especially 432.

is tacitly to make it an occasion of great joy. While it is the OG story that stresses Anna's depression, the Hannah of MT suffers vexation enough from the bitchy Peninnah (whose provocations are not mentioned in the OG story). Hannah will now be the person to hear the priest's words,

> This day is holy to the LORD your God; do not mourn or weep...; and do not be grieved, for the joy of the LORD is your strength. (Neh 8:9-10 NRSV).[30]

Hannah's mood does not turn until v 18, and the stories differ in their report of it. The Old Greek allows Anna to drink once she has left the sanctuary precincts.

> εἰσῆλθεν εἰς τὸ κατάλυμα αὐτῆς,
> καὶ ἔφαγεν μετὰ τοῦ ἀνδρὸς αὐτῆς καὶ ἔπιεν,
> καὶ τὸ πρόσωπον αὐτῆς οὐ συνέπεσεν ἔτι.
>
> She entered her chamber,
> and ate with her husband and drank,
> and her face was no longer fallen.

Here she gives up the hunger strike, and both eats and drinks. That she drinks "with her husband" is part of Elkanah's generally patronizing attitude towards his wife in the OG story. More important, one wonders how much the turning of her mood owes to Eli's promise and how much to the festivities that followed. Compare MT's story:

וַתֹּ֔אכַל וּפָנֶ֥יהָ לֹא־הָֽיוּ־לָ֖הּ

She ate, and her face showed the difference.

The second clause differs from the Greek in the way it describes Hannah's change of mood, and the Hebrew expression is unusual, literally, "she no longer had her face." But the omission of any reference to drinking makes it impossible to think that her new happiness was caused by alcohol. It was

---

30 The important words "the joy of the LORD" are found only in the MT and a few Greek cursive mss (namely, bcejnwe$_2$). The majority Greek reading is, "he is our strength" or "the Lord is our strength."

a truly spiritual victory which God had given to her, and the note of joy enters the story by virtue of its new proximity to the Feast of Booths.

It is possible that, in his explanation of a difficult word in 1 Sam 1:5, Rashi has this juxtaposition in mind, for he speaks of a "joyful face." In the biblical text, Elkanah gave portions to Peninnah and all her children, but, because Hannah was childless, he gave her מנה אחת אפים "one portion ᵓ*appayim*." Rashi explains, "dividing one choice portion worthy to be received with hope for a joyful face."[31]

[2]. And then, the transformation of grief to joy takes place in the context of public worship and of the reading and interpreting of scripture. Hannah's was a solitary struggle, carried on year by year with dignity and restraint, until finally ... And even then, her prayer was solitary, and the turning of her mood the result of an oracle by the red-faced priest who had so badly misread her situation. The post-exilic interpreter has no wish to discard this vignette of heroic personal piety, but believes it well to enlarge its reference and extend its force: God's people also have the Torah, they have interpreters, they have preaching. Neh 8 serves to draw the isolated struggler into a capacious collectivity of proclamation and understanding (vs 2-3, 8-9, 12). Take your distress to the believing community (it says), gathered around its scripture. There the opening of sacred words can bring divine help near in a way even the salvation oracle of the priest cannot.

[3]. Neh 8 is curiously vague about the cause of the people's sorrow:

> Ezra ... said to all the people, "This day is holy to the LORD your God: you must not mourn or weep," for all the people were weeping as they listened to the words of the Teaching. (v 9)

We might presume that they lament their sins, but the vocabulary of wrong-doing is conspicuously absent. The juxtaposition of the two stories supplies Neh 8 with a concrete instance, of the grief that people carry and of weeping and despair dispelled through worship, just as the people's grief was dispelled in Neh 8. The Nehemiah story may even have been left deliberately

---

31 חולק חד בחיר הראוי להתקבל בסבר פנים יפות., rendering more idiomatically, "to be received with joy," see Goldman (1951) 3.

a little vague, in order to suggest that any and all grief can be dispelled in the gathering for worship and instruction. This is a notable hermeneutic move: Hannah is thus more than an example, she becomes a type of all who bring their distress to the LORD.

[4]. One of the features of Hannah's distress is that Peninnah's hostility took place at the central sanctuary, and individuals who might identify themselves with Hannah and her needs must do so within the general framework of the pilgrim festival. The story does, after all, even use the word היכל "temple" of the Shiloh sanctuary. This imaging places the suffering individual amongst people otherwise unknown to her or at least encountered only once a year. Since the Nehemiah story is the prototype of the synagogue service, to bring the Hannah story along side of it is to invite sufferers to envisage their deliverance in a different context. As the local service of reading and interpreting scripture displaced pilgrimages to Jerusalem, God's people could find their needs met within the familiar and comfortable group they know so well.

[5]. Finally, to bring these two stories together is to leave Samuel's similarities to Samson far behind. After all, Samson's life's work was a series of pranks; he exercised no leadership and left Israel worse than he found it. This may be why MT omits any reference to Samuel's abstinence from wine. Samuel's followers prefer him to be paired with Jeremiah, each of them a נער called by God.[32] There may even be lurking in the background a tacit denigration of any form of solar Yahwism, since the personal name שמשון is obviously connected with שמש "sun." As Psalm 19 compares Torah very favorably with the sun, so the person Samuel signals the power of the prophetic word over against the effete and unproductive veneration of the sun symbolized by Samson's ineffectiveness.

---

32 1 Sam 1: 22, 24, 25, 27; 2: 11, 21, 26; 3: 1; Jer 1: 6-7.

Summary

This paper suggests that the words "and after drinking" in the MT (followed by a few LXX manuscripts) of 1 Sam 1:9 incorporate into the text a homiletic gloss whose purpose was to bring the Shiloh story alongside the Feast of Booths in Nehemiah 8. The story, told *without* those words, protects Anna's prayer and vow from the suspicion of intoxication, and acquires a somewhat ascetic character consistent with its depiction of Samuel as a nazirite. It also sets up more distant resonances with Samson. The story, told *with* those words, effects a cross-reference to Nehemiah 8 and brings the two feasts into juxtaposition. Both stories sustain some enlargement of force as a result. The vagueness of Neh 8's distress receives a concrete particular, and Hannah can be seen not as an *example* to God's people, but as a type or *figure* of any and all grief transformed into joy. The individual is subsumed into the communal, the priestly into the prophetic, the oracular into the scriptural. Hannah's distress at Shiloh is matched with the rich joy of the Feast of Booths, and especially by the transformation of grief into joy in the festivities under Ezra.

Hannah, we remember, does not drink at all in the masoretic story. Nevertheless, by virtue of a preacher's homiletic gloss, arising out of meticulous reading of Tanakh, she has been drawn into the joyful circle of *autres bons biberons* who hearken to the reading of scripture and discover the joy of the LORD to be their strength.

Bibliography

Bal, M. (1985) *Narratology*. Toronto. **Böttcher, F.** (1863) *Neue Exegetisch-kritische Aehrenlese zum Alten Testament, Erste Abteilung, Genesis-2 Samuel.* Leipzig. **Brooke, A., and N. McLean** (1927) *I and II Samuel.* In *The Old Testament in Greek.* London. **Budde, K.** (1902) *Die Bücher Samuel.* Tübingen. **Dawson, S. E.** (1905) *The Saint Lawrence.* New York. **Driver, S. R.** (1913) *Notes on the Hebrew Text and the Topography of the Books of Samuel.* Oxford. **Gill, J.** (1764) *An Exposition of the Old Testament, Vol II.* London. **Goldman, S.** (1951) *Samuel.* Soncino Books of the Bible. London. **Henry, M.** (1758) <1708> *An Exposition of the Old Testament.* 5th edition. Edinburgh. **Klein, R. W.** (1983) *1 Samuel.* In *Word Biblical Commentary.* Waco, Tx. **Klostermann, A.** (1887) *Die Bücher Samuelis und der Könige.* Kurzgefasster Kommentar zu den heiligen Schriften Alten und Neuen Testaments. Nördlingen. **Levine, L. I.** (1996) The Nature and Origin of the Palestinian Synagogue Reconsidered. *Journal of Biblical Literature* 115: 425-48. **McCarter, P. K.** (1980) *I Samuel.* Anchor Bible. Garden City, N.Y. **Patrick, S.** (1732) <1694> *A Commentary upon the Historical Books of the Old Testament.* 4th edition London. **Smith, H. P.** (1951) <1899> *A Critical and Exegetical Commentary on the Books of Samuel.* International Critical Commentary. Edinburgh. **Sperber, A.** (1959) The Former Prophets according to Targum Jonathan. In *The Bible in Aramaic.* Leiden. **Stoebe, H. J.** (1973) *Das Erste Buch Samuelis.* Kommentar zum Alten Testament. Gütersloh. **Thenius, O.** (1842) *Die Bücher Samuelis.* Kurzgefasstes exegetisches Handbuch zum Alten Testament. Leipzig. (1864) *Die Bücher Samuels.* Kurzgefasstes exegetisches Handbuch zum Alten Testament. Leipzig. **Walters, S. D.** (1988) Hannah and Anna: The Hebrew and Greek Texts of I Samuel 1. *Journal of Biblical Literature* 107: 385-412. **Waltke, B., and M. O'Connor** (1990) *An Introduction to Biblical Hebrew Syntax.* Winona Lake, Ind. **Wellhausen, J.** (1871) *Der Text der Bücher Samuelis.* Göttingen.

Polytheism and Politics: Some Comments on Nabonidus' Foreign Policy*

David B. Weisberg
Hebrew Union College - Jewish Institute of Religion, Cincinnati

The Neo-Babylonian period affords an excellent vantage point from which to examine the issue of politics and polytheism, especially during the reign of Nabonidus. In his time, factionalism between the followers of different deities in southern Mesopotamian cities influenced the course of events in the Chaldean state, and contributed ultimately to its downfall.

Due to his promotion of the worship of Sîn at the expense of Marduk, Nabonidus has been labeled unpopular and the king's reign has been characterized as one of misrule. However, we want to view Nabonidus' strategy as part of a complex politico-religious doctrine—a political agenda couched in a struggle for religious ideologies of two different deities in a polytheistic system that we might formulate in today's terms as nation-state imperialism versus globalism.

---

* This paper is dedicated to Michael C. Astour on the occasion of his 80th birthday and was delivered at the Midwest Region SBL/AOS/ASOR annual joint meeting in LaGrange, Illinois, on February 12, 1996. It is a pleasure to thank Richard E. Averbeck for his gracious help, and J. Kenneth Duvall, Sara Fudge and Brian A. Smith for their research assistance for this paper. I am grateful to my colleagues Herbert C. Brichto and Ellis Rivkin, who have generously given me the benefit of their wisdom in several areas. The origins of this paper lie in two recent seminars taught on "The Harran Inscriptions of Nabonidus" (Gadd [1958]) in which I had the chance to discuss many of my ideas with the students in these seminars. I appreciate the chance to hear their reactions and suggestions.

In introducing the theme of polytheism and politics, we would like to underscore that we do not believe that the existence of polytheistic groups within Babylonia unquestionably *caused* strife. Rather, the different religious groupings served as a convenient conduit, providing a *pretext and justification* for power-grabbing. It is our position that the interaction of the polytheistic parties in the Babylon of Nabonidus' time exacerbated the clashes within the society but were not their primary cause, which was rather political ambition for state power.

There is perennial interest in the figure of Nabonidus, and especially his motivations. Opinions have been wide-ranging, from the assessment of him as a religious fanatic,[1] learned antiquarian,[2] one who sought economic advantage in Teima,[3] etc. Another view holds that any attempt to arrive at an opinion would be too optimistic, given the limitations of the knowledge now at our disposal.[4]

In our examination of the problems of the reign of Nabonidus, we can build upon the work of many scholars, such as S. Langdon (1912), R. P. Dougherty (1929), E. Dhorme (1947), H. Tadmor (1965), P. R. Berger (1973), and P.-A. Beaulieu (1989). We shall mention others as well.

Is there reliable evidence bearing on the life of Nabonidus before his assumption of kingship, whether from Herodotus,[5] Josephus,[6] or Neo-Babylonian administrative records?[7] We should be cautious in examining

---

1 Beaulieu (1989) xiii cites a general view that holds Nabonidus to be "a single-minded religious fanatic obsessed with establishing the supremacy of the moon god in his realm, or a cynical and manipulative usurper whose inept policies brought his kingdom to an undistinguished end."

2 Campbell-Thompson (1925) 218: "He [Nabonidus] was a scholar with a most conservative respect for old records and customs, and was never happier than when he could excavate some ancient foundation-stone."

3 Dougherty (1929) 158 n 528.

4 See below for Ephᶜal's view.

5 On Herodotus and Babylon, see Drews (1973) 79-80 with nn 122 and 123 on p. 181 and Röllig (1983) 15-18.

6 On Josephus, see Röllig (1980) 282-83.

7 See, *e.g.*, Beaulieu (1989) 14-17.

texts that purport to shed light on this period. There is in reality nothing from extant records upon which to build any substantive theory.

Evidence from nineteen Royal Inscriptions, with attention to their chronological sequence, is assessed by Berger,[8] Tadmor[9] and Beaulieu.[10] Additionally we note the study of archival texts and other materials bearing upon the building works undertaken by Nabonidus at sundry points during his reign.

During Nabonidus' early years, we have indications of his historical and alleged "antiquarian" interests in Babylon,[11] as well as military campaigns to Northern Arabia, the Eastern Mediterranean, and Cilicia.[12]

The Teima period, a unique time in Mesopotamian history, is shrouded in mystery. Issues raised by this period include the exact beginning and end dates of this ten-year period and the reasons for a Babylonian king to take up residence in a distant Arabian desert town. Beaulieu holds that Nabonidus was absent from the capital from his third through his thirteenth years;[13] but Nabonidus' motivation, though thoughtfully explored by scholars, remains unknown.

One scholar holding a skeptical viewpoint is Israel Ephᶜal, who does not cite Nabonidus in his chapter on warfare in ancient empires.[14] The ostensible reason Ephᶜal does not cite Nabonidus becomes clear if one examines a chapter in another work by Ephᶜal, *The Ancient Arabs.*[15] In that work, Ephᶜal explicitly eschews speculating on Nabonidus' motivation regarding Teima with the following words:

---

8 Berger (1973) *passim*, especially 108ff.

9 Tadmor (1965) 358-63.

10 Beaulieu (1989) 20-42. See Weisberg (1991) 103-5.

11 See the unpublished manuscript, "The Antiquarian Interests of the Neo-Babylonian Kings," read at the Bible Lands Museum Jerusalem Symposium on May 28, 1996 by D. Weisberg.

12 Beaulieu (1989) 143-47.

13 Beaulieu (1989) 149-69, esp. 165-66.

14 Ephᶜal (1983) 88-106.

15 Ephᶜal (1982) 179-91.

> It is rare for a king to abandon his country and remain for many years in a remote place, as Nabonidus did when he quitted Babylon for Temaᵓ, leaving imperial matters to his son Belshazzar....[A]vailable data...are too meager to define Nabonidus' behaviour reasonably.[16]

What were Crown Prince Belshazzar's duties in Babylon as stand-in for his absent father? He functioned in an official capacity (although without assuming an official title) as a partner in the "double kingship" set up by the king.

The exaltation of the moon-god Sîn, as opposed to the national deity of the Babylonians, Marduk, was certainly a feature of Nabonidus' personal, as well as royal, conduct.[17] But what was the role of this in his regime? Was this feature a constant of the king's reign, or can changes be discerned as time went on? Studies of Nabonidus' inscriptions have brought varying responses to this question.

Whereas Tadmor 1965 sees evidence for a steadily increasing devotion to Sîn by Nabonidus, particularly during the last years of his reign, Beaulieu notes a *decrease* in the moon-god's glorification during the second period, Nabonidus' absence in Teima. Beaulieu holds that "the primary factor which determined the relative position of Sîn and Marduk in the inscriptions was not fluctuations in the king's religious policy, but simply his presence in, or absence from, the capital."[18]

Beaulieu perceives a split as having occurred between Nabonidus and his son, Belshazzar, who fostered the worship of Marduk in Babylon during his father's absence. According to Beaulieu, Nabonidus eventually resolved this problem by removing his son from power when he returned from Teima.[19]

Another debated issue is the role of "La Mère de Nabonide." E. Dhorme formulated a widely-accepted view on the fabled mother of Nabonidus,

---

16 Ephᶜal (1982) 179.

17 According to Lewy (1946) 426-27, Landsberger (1947) 92 and Beaulieu (1989) 76, this was not the Sîn of the Babylonians, but Ilteri of the Arameans.

18 Beaulieu (1989) 63.

19 Beaulieu (1989) 63-65.

Adad-Guppi.[20] Dhorme saw her as a priestess of Sîn at Harran.[21] In contrast, Beaulieu is of the opinion that she was a layperson, not a priestess, who spent her life not at Harran, but at the court in Babylon. Texts that would seem to indicate the contrary may be merely reflections of the usual "concern for cultic matters typical of Neo-Babylonian building inscriptions."[22]

Paul Garelli[23] offers a view of Nabonidus' acts as having been motivated by strong psychological drives relating to Nabonidus' mother. Garelli notes: "Un psychanalyste ne manqeurait probablement pas de relever une étonnante fixation sur sa mère."[24]

Amélie Kuhrt,[25] in assessing the texts at our disposal for evaluating the reign of Nabonidus, has presented a view conspicuously at variance with many ancient texts. She holds that

> It has proved extraordinarily difficult to demonstrate that there was any effective priestly opposition to the policies of Nabonidus. Apart from some understandable disturbances at the beginning of his reign, due to the mode of his accession, and some hostile judgments passed on him *after* Cyrus' conquest, nothing in the evidence as it stands allows one to accept the traditional explanation for his defeat by the Persians.

Moreover, the temples did not suffer a diminution of resources, and warfare between Persians and Babylonians was intermittent, rather than the sudden surrender depicted by Cyrus.

Tadmor and Machinist have criticized Kuhrt as a revisionist, a term that is defined as "a reevaluation of the past based on newly acquired standards."[26] In noting "the sophistication and sharpness of the intellectual reli-

---

20 Scholars are far from unanimous in their attempts to explain her name. I prefer the Aramaic, "Adad is my support" (= lit. גַּף "wing"). Of the two worshippers of Sîn, the mother's name was compounded with that of Adad and the son's with that of Nabû.

21 Dhorme (1947) 1-21.

22 Beaulieu (1989) 74.

23 Garelli (1958) columns 268-86.

24 Garelli (1958) column 280.

25 Kuhrt (1990) 117-55.

26 Stein (1967).

gious conflict," Tadmor and Machinist remark that "we [must] not ignore that conflict in writing the history of Nabonidus' reign." They continue in a footnote: "This last remark would not be necessary, given the general scholarly agreement with it, were it not for a 'revisionist' argument recently put forward by A. Kuhrt."[27]

We would be on altogether safe ground to take the position that the entire religious argument is diversionary. When dealing with state power, the issue comes down to what measures are necessary in order to hold that power, or, from the opposition's perspective, what measures are necessary to take power away from others.

The arguments on religion are interesting and necessary for understanding this issue, but they miss the point. We will demonstrate that our purposes may be accomplished without entering the religious debate. We may thus avoid taking up the cudgels on behalf of Kuhrt and against the criticism leveled against her by Tadmor and Machinist.

For example, Tadmor and Machinist raise the same issue as to what kind of text it was that Lambert cited.[28] To me this is a valid question, but it is not the point. The key question is rather, what kind of information is being conveyed in the text Lambert edited? The question is not "what kind of slander is being used?" but "why are they slandering?"

The texts cited by Tadmor and Machinist are propagandistic in character. They are, therefore, tendentious. Why take them as our starting point? Does it not make more sense to start from the perspective of Realpolitik?

Nabonidus has been compared to other ancient rulers. Two figures have been recently proposed: Akhenaton and Josiah. Reed suggests Akhenaton, in that he was a "reformer" (rather than a "renegade").[29] Tadmor and Machinist find a parallel in Nabonidus' behavior with Josiah.[30]

---

27 Machinist and Tadmor (1993) 150 n. 34.

28 Lambert (1968/9) 4-6; and Machinist and Tadmor (1993) Appendix.

29 Reed (1977) 24.

30 Machinist and Tadmor (1993) 151 n. 44.

We propose an altogether different figure: Nebuchadnezzar II, Nabonidus' predecessor. Both were interested in political gains. Oppenheim seems to agree with this comparison. See, for example, "Another Dream of Nabonidus,"[31] where Nebuchadnezzar appears to, and encourages, Nabonidus in a dream concerning heavenly portents that Nabonidus has seen in another dream. Note also Oppenheim's assessment that "Nebukadnezzar II, however, appears in the dream of Nabonidus not for necromantic, but for political reasons...."[32]

Nabonidus was ruler of one of the largest empires ever seen in antiquity. He did not reach that position except by convincing the power elites in his country that he would faithfully represent their interests, which were to expand economically and defend the boundaries politically. These were precisely the goals of his predecessor, Nebuchadnezzar II. Nabonidus was simply continuing in a direct manner the policies of Nebuchadnezzar II.

Let us put aside for a moment the accounts that have come down to us from Nabonidus' enemies, Cyrus and the Babylonian Marduk priests.[33] In addition, let us put aside the propaganda issued by Nabonidus' own chancery that was addressed to the masses. It appears to us that von Soden has grasped this aspect of our problem most successfully. He urges us to explore the propaganda angle in greater depth.

> Es ging hier um Argumente und Wirkung von politischer und religiöser Propaganda in einer Zeit, die unter diesem Gesichtspunkt bisher noch nicht intensiv genug erforscht wurde. Wir werden künftig auch bei der Betrachtung anderer Perioden der Geschichte des alten Orients die Auswirkungen von Propaganda-Aktionen stärker in Rechnung stellen müssen als bisher. Auch für die Jahrhunderte vor Kyros II. und Nabonid, z.B. für die Sargonidenzeit, geben unsere Quellen mehr dafür her, als gemeinhin angenommen wird.[34]

---

31 Oppenheim (1956) 250.

32 Oppenheim (1956) 204.

33 Oppenheim (1956) 312-15.

34 von Soden (1983) 68.

If, during his ten-years' absence from the capital, Nabonidus had been perceived by the power elites of his country as not serving their interests, his reign would have been brought to an unceremonious close then and there. We can assume that under normal circumstances, there would be court intrigue. We may also assume the presence of enemies of anyone at all who held power. If a ruler held court at his capital, at least under normal circumstances, he would have a natural advantage over his enemies. But a ruler who had headquarters away from the capital city of his empire would court additional disaster. His absence would encourage opposition on the theory "while the cat's away the mice will play." Consequently, the mere fact that Nabonidus survived the ten years of his absence from the capital city, with his son in charge at home, is clear evidence that he was well-accepted by the people whose opinions really mattered in the power-politics of his day. If the priests of Marduk of Babylon were involved in state power games, as we must assume they were, then we would have to evaluate their actions on the basis of how anyone would act to achieve state power.

Let us illustrate this with some points from Miles Copeland's, *The Game of Nations: The Amorality of Power Politics*, a book about the modern Middle East which emphasizes the universality of the "Game of Nations."[35] Copeland notes that national leaders achieve their positions *not* as the "Pollyannas they try to appear in their published accounts of themselves."[36] Rather, he observes, "Our statesmen...would not be where they are if they were not fully aware of what a generally amoral world we live in; they get daily confirmation of this as they read the secret intelligence summaries."[37]

Copeland emphasizes that "a national leader's first objective is to stay in power..."[38] and he calls our otherwise diverted attention to "the use of bluff, deliberate misinformation, and all the other game-type stratagems" by the national leader.[39]

---

35 Copeland (1969).

36 Copeland (1969) 10.

37 Copeland (1969) 10.

38 Copeland (1969) 22.

39 Copeland (1969) 32.

Nabonidus' actions are not related to religion, psychology, or antiquarianism. Discussions about the worship of the moon-god Sîn are entirely beside the point. However, we should not rule out that Nabonidus used his belief in Sîn for political gain. He undoubtedly saw Sîn as the chief god who would unify the world, just as the Assyrians had earlier seen Ishtar as the goddess under whom their rule would extend to all boundaries.[40] Nabonidus' actions were driven solely by political motivation. Any literature that comes down to us from antiquity to the contrary is propagandistic and tendentious.

Nabonidus' actions in Teima[41] are related to his position at Harran and Ur. His presence there was for a military purpose: to bypass the party of Babylonians who were against him and thereby minimize their clout, and then to outflank the Persians. The three cities Teima, Harran and Ur form a triangle which enabled Nabonidus to control the entire Babylonian empire and to extend its reach.

The view proposed here is far from revisionism; one might call it Realpolitik. On the contrary, this view is actually realism. The other views that have been proposed are unrealistic and impractical, overlooking as they do the basic realities of political life.

Bibliography

Beard, M., and J. North, eds. (1990) *Pagan Priests.* London. **Beaulieu, P. A.** (1989*) The Reign of Nabonidus, King of Babylon 556-539 B.C.* London. **Berger, P. R.** (1973*) Die neubaby-lonischen Königsinschriften.* Alter Orient und Altes Testament 4/1. Neukirchen-Vluyn. **Campbell-Thompson, R.** (1925) Decay and Fall of Babylonia Under Nabonidus.

40 For example, ^{d}30 LUGAL *šá* DINGER.MEŠ *a-šib* A[N-*e* (GAL.MEŠ) LUGAL LUGAL.LUGAL EN EN.EN]. Cited in G. F. Dole and W. L. Moran (1991) 268-73.

41 Nabonidus might have ruled for ten years from Teima, but clearly he did not spend all of that time in the city without traveling to other places. No king remains stationary during his reign, and this includes Nabonidus. He certainly repositioned at other places too, trying to build defenses against Persia. *Cp.* Eph^{c}al (1983) 180f: "He went about (various sites)..."

Cambridge Ancient History 1st ed., 3: 218-25. **Cohen, M., D. Snell, and D. Weisberg**, eds. (1993) *The Tablet and the Scroll, Near Eastern Studies, in Honor of W. W. Hallo.* Bethesda, Md. **Copeland, M.** (1969) *The Game of Nations: The Amorality of Power Politics.* New York. **Drews, R.** (1973) *The Greek Accounts of Eastern History.* Cambridge, Mass. **Dhorme, E.** (1947) La Mère de Nabonide. *Revue d'Assyriologie* 41: 1-21. **Dole, G. F., and W. L. Moran** (1991) A Bowl of Alallu-Stone. *Zeitschrift für Assyriologie* 81: 268-73. **Dougherty, R. P.** (1929) *Nabonidus and Belshazzar.* Yale Oriental Researches XV. New Haven. **Eph^c^al, I.** (1982) *The Ancient Arabs.* Jerusalem-Leiden. (1983) On Warfare and Military Control in the Ancient Near Eastern Empires: A Research Outline. In Tadmor and Weinfeld 1983: 88-106. **Gadd, C. J.** (1958) The Harran Inscriptions of Nabonidus. *Anatolian Studies* 8: 35-92. **Garelli, P.** (1958) Nabonide. Cols. 268-86 in *Supplément au dictionnaire de la Bible*, fasc. 31. **Güterbock, H. G., and T. Jacobsen**, eds. (1965) *Studies in Honor of Benno Landsberger on His Seventy-Fifth Birthday.* Assyriological Studies 16. Chicago. **Kuhrt, A.** (1990) Nabonidus and the Babylonian Priesthood. In Beard and North 1990: 117-55. **Lambert, W. G.** (1968/9) A New Source for the Reign of Nabonidus. *Archiv für Orientforschung* 22: 1-8. **Landsberger, B.** (1947) Die Basaltstele Nabonids von Eski-Harran. *Halil Edhem Hatira Kitabi* I: 115-51. Ankara. **Langdon, S.** (1912) *Die Neubabylonischen Königsinschriften.* Vorderasiatische Bibliothek IV. Leipzig. **Lewy, J.** (1946) The Late Assyro-Babylonian Cult of the Moon and Its Culmination at the Time of Nabonidus. *Hebrew Union College Annual* 19: 405-89. **Machinist, P., and H. Tadmor** (1993) Heavenly Wisdom. In Cohen *et al.* 1993: 146-51. **Oppenheim, A. L.** (1956) The Interpretation of Dreams in the Ancient Near East. *Transactions of the American Philosophical Society, New Series*, 46, Part 3: 179-373. (1969) Nabonidus and the Clergy of Babylon (The Verse Account of Nabonidus). In Pritchard 1969: 312-15. **Pritchard, J.**, ed. (1969) *Ancient Near East Texts Relating to the Old Testament.* 3rd edition. Princeton. **Reed, W. L.** (1977) Nabonidus, Babylonian Reformer or Renegade? *Lexington Theological Quarterly* 12: 23-31. **Röllig, W.** (1980) Josephus Flavius. *Reallexikon der Assyriologie*) 5: 282-83. (1983) Klassische Autoren. *Reallexikon der Assyriologie* 6: 15-18. **Stein, J.** (1967) *Random House Dictionary of the English Language.* New York. **Tadmor, H.** (1965) The Inscriptions of Nabunaid: Historical Arrangement. In Güterbock and Jacobsen 1965: 315-63. **Tadmor, H., and M. Weinfeld**, eds. (1983) *History, Historiography and Interpretation. Studies in Biblical and Cuneiform Literatures.* Jerusalem. **von Soden, W.** (1983) Kyros und Nabonid. Propaganda und Gegenpropaganda. *Archaeologische Mitteilungen aus Iran*, Ergänzungsband 10: 61-68. **Weisberg, D.** (1991) Review of Beaulieu (1989). (1996) The Antiquarian Interests of the Neo-Babylonian Kings. Unpublished paper presented at the International Symposium May 27-29, 1996. The Bible Lands Museum Jerusalem. Capital Cities: Urban Planning and Spiritual Dimensions.

The History of the Lake of Antioch
A Preliminary Note

T. J. Wilkinson
The Oriental Institute
The University of Chicago

Michael Astour's wide-ranging interests include the ancient history of the Amuq plain, and he has made informed contributions on ancient Alalakh and its geography to both the *Journal of Near Eastern Studies* (1963) and the *Anchor Bible Dictionary.*[1] Here I employ a range of information to provide a preliminary reconstruction of the history of the Lake of Antioch which, until recently, formed the most conspicuous geographical feature of the Amuq plain near Atchana/Alalakh. The following results derive largely from the 1995 field season of the Oriental Institute Amuq Project[2] that was initiated by Dr. Aslihan Yener, to build upon earlier surveys and excavations also undertaken by the Oriental Institute.

The Lake of Antioch must have played a major role in the ancient geography of the region first by considerably altering the resource base of the

---

1 Astour (1963) 220-40, and Astour (1992) 142-45.

2 I wish to thank the director of the project, Dr. Aslihan Yener for permission to publish this contribution, and members of the field survey team, Scott Branting and Jerry Lyon, for assistance in the field. Funding was provided by the Oriental Institute, and several private donors, to whom we are very grateful. I also wish to thank Professor Engin Özgen of the General Directorate of Monuments and Museums in Ankara and Kenan Yurttagül, Antakya for permission and general guidance during field work. Thanks also go to David Reece and Ghida al-Osman for additional references.

nearby communities, and second by constraining traffic to the north or the south of the plain, thus influencing the development of communications throughout the basin. Therefore, if at one time there was no lake, as has been suggested,[3] its subsequent growth might have entailed both a shift in communications and a re-orientation of the settlement pattern. Here archaeological sites are given the same numbers as allocated by Braidwood, but are prefixed by AS (for Amuq Survey); newly discovered sites are given numbers from AS 180 and on.

Historical Context

Being astride a major route from Upper Mesopotamia to the Mediterranean, the plain of the Amuq has received frequent mention in early texts. Tablets from the level VII palace of Alalakh provide toponyms that, when combined with epigraphic evidence from the reign of Thutmose III, can be used to sketch a historical geography of the region for the third quarter of the 2nd millennium BC.[4] Such a picture can be further elaborated by reference to the Alalakh texts, which provide hints concerning the distribution of settlements as well as the movement of goods between centers and villages.[5] However, the texts are silent regarding the presence or size of a lake during the 2nd millennium BC.

By late Assyrian times the picture is supplemented further by the annals of Shalmaneser III and Tiglath-Pileser III, who campaigned in the Amuq (the land of Unqi), exacted tribute, and even resettled populations in the area.[6] Although no explicit references are made in these annals to a lake or marsh, we are fortunate to have a visual record from the gates of Balawat in northern Iraq which provides a tantalizing, but somewhat ambiguous impression of the area (see below). Because of these various lacunae it is

---

3 For discussion, see the original survey volume undertaken by Robert Braidwood (1937).

4 Astour (1963) 220-40.

5 Wiseman (1953); Magness-Gardner (1994) 37-47.

6 Hawkins (1995) 94-95; Luckenbill (1926 [1968]) 276.

therefore necessary to combine the results of archaeological survey and geomorphological studies with historical records to provide a preliminary sketch of the changing geography of the lake.

Geomorphology

The deceptively featureless Amuq plain incorporates a range of geomorphological sub-units which reflect the operation of both natural and human agencies in the past (fig. 1). It is now possible to give a general description of the main geomorphological features as well as to provide some preliminary insights into the evolution of the terrain.

The Amuq plain, located at 80–100 m above mean sea level, is framed by mountains on all sides except where the Kara Su (from the north) and the Nahr al-ᶜAfrin (from the east) debouch via broad valleys. In the SW of the plain the combined flow of these rivers, now conducted along large drainage canals, meets the flow of the Orontes (Nahr al-ᶜAsi) to flow along a narrow gorge via Antakya (ancient Antioch) to the Mediterranean Sea. The high Amanus mountains to the west comprise basic and ultra basic intrusive igneous formations (to the south), and predominantly Eocene and Miocene sedimentary rock (to the north). In contrast, the southern and eastern sides are fringed by the high denuded limestone massifs of the Jebels Simᶜan, Barisha, and related uplands, well known for their dense spread of Late Roman and Early Byzantine villages and monastic complexes.[7] To the NE, and sufficiently convenient to provide a key resource for the inhabitants of the plain, are extensive outcrops of extrusive vesicular basalt ideal for manufacturing quern stones. Rainfall, at around 600–700 mm per annum, although sufficient for rain-fed cultivation, can be enhanced by irrigation to produce increased crop yields.

The Amanus mountains nurture active high-energy ephemeral streams that discharge onto the plain via a conspicuous series of gravel and alluvial fans of Pleistocene and Holocene date (fig. 1). Important for the development of settlement is the presence of a line of springs along the lower fringes

---

7 Tchalenko (1953), and Tate (1992). Geological data is from Tolun and Pamir (1975).

of the fans, where they overlap onto the impervious or waterlogged sediments of the plain. Alluvial fan development is attenuated to the south and east, however, where the limestone bedrock has mainly been denuded by chemical action.

The Lake of Antioch, which until the 1950s formed the most conspicuous feature of the Amuq, has now been drained. As a result, the only traces of its former extent are pale-colored lacustrine clays, scatters of freshwater molluscs, and low sand ridges, the last-named being the remains of beaches and associated dunes developed alongside the former lakeshore. Because drainage was effected by means of a small number of major drains, it is possible to get an impression of the sedimentary history of this lake by means of occasional exposed sections.

Surrounding the former lake is an indeterminate zone of low, flat silt clay terrain. Today soils of this zone are mainly gray, with red-hued and more oxidized soils becoming more common away from the lake. Although today virtually indistinguishable from the lake and the plain beyond, this unit was mapped on the French maps of the 1930s as marsh (fig. 1). During the surveys of Robert Braidwood in 1936, the marsh and interspersed pools rendered many archaeological sites inaccessible, but now it is possible to record some sites for the first time. In places the former marsh soils are framed by slightly raised silt/clay terrain (stipple fig. 1) that variously has been deposited by the Orontes, the Nahr al-ᶜAfrin, or by possible canal systems that once issued from them. The ᶜAfrin, which has its headwaters to the NE in both Syria and Turkey, is today dry for part of the year, but formerly it must have provided sufficient flow for irrigation. Gravel of early phases of this channel are aligned axially through the center of the former Lake Antioch, thus suggesting that earlier courses of this river flowed through the plain rather than terminating in a lake. In contrast, the Orontes still manages a sluggish flow, which, in the past, must have provided flow for a limited number of canals. Interestingly, the Orontes (the Nahr al-ᶜAsi [in Arabic "the Rebel River"]) has a reputation for its unruly flow. This results in episodic floods that inundate the lower ground, particularly the plain to the north. Such behavior must have significantly influenced the development of the lake basin in the past.

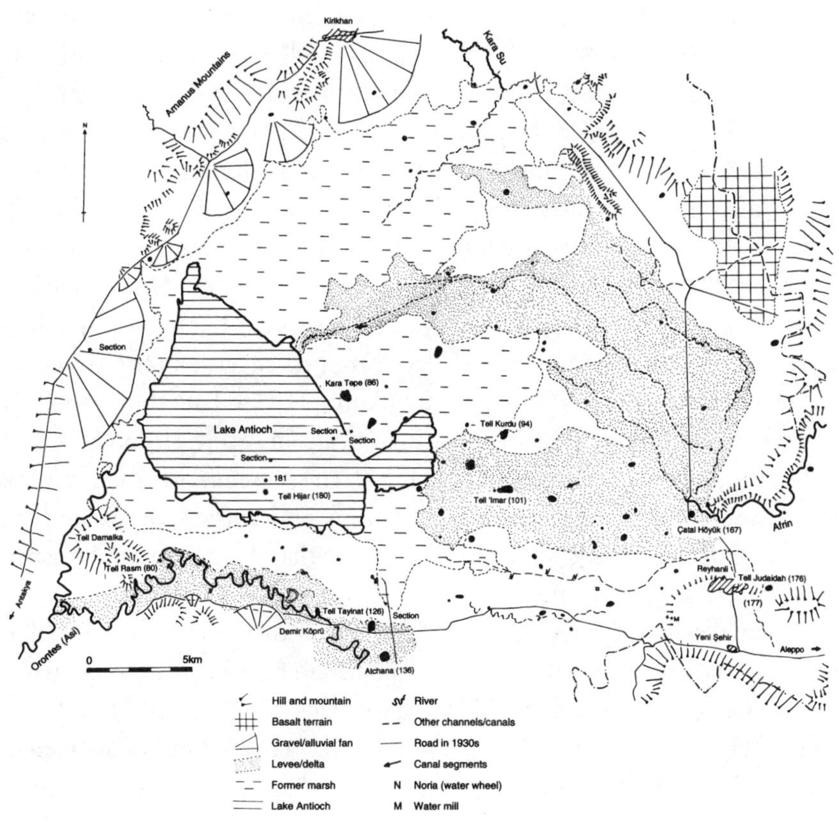

Fig. 1

Preliminary geomorphological map of the Amuq based on French series 1: 50,000 maps and limited field control.

Archaeological Sites beneath the Former Lake

Two archaeological sites were located within the former lake bed 1 km and 1.5 km respectively NNE of the village of Tell ed-Diss (AS 180 and 181 on fig. 1). Their presence in an area that had originally been covered by 1.3 m and 1.8 m of water (in the case of AS 180 and 181 respectively) suggests that when they were occupied, water levels were at least 1.5–2.0 m lower, unless of course both sites were deliberately constructed as islands within the lake. The main site, Khirbet (or Tell) al-Hijar, which today rises to ca. 1 m above the former lake floor, is recognizable as a scatter of limestone and basalt blocks, potsherds and other artifacts across ca. 220 m N-S by 150 m E-W (*i.e.*, covering some 3 ha). Surface ceramics suggest a range of occupations from mid-late 3rd millennium (Amuq H/I) to Late Roman—early Islamic, with occupation being most significant in Amuq H/I and the first half of the 2nd millennium BC (Amuq L/M). The presence of buried cultural layers, as well as eroded stone foundations and surface mounding, all demonstrate that this is an *in situ* site, rather than being material washed into the lake from elsewhere.

A smaller flat site (AS 181), some 0.5 km north of Khirbet al-Hajar, although flat and inconspicuous, also appears to have been an *in situ* habitation site. The pottery exposed in shallow lake-floor drains, spread over some 200 m N-S by 100 m E-W, appears to have eroded out of an ancient soil which occupies a gentle rise in the old land surface. Surface pottery is slightly earlier than at AS 180, being primarily of Amuq phases F, G and H,[8] with perhaps one Neolithic sherd belonging to Amuq A or B. This suggests that AS 181 was occupied at a time when water levels were reduced and it was therefore possible to occupy somewhat lower ground than became the case during later periods.

Assuming that habitation occurred originally on dry land, the presence of these two sites implies that during the 3rd and early 2nd millennia BC lake levels were 1.5 to 2.0 m below those that prevailed in the early 20th century

---

[8] Amuq ceramic phases are according to Braidwood and Braidwood (1960). Amuq F, G and H are dated to between the 4th and the mid-3rd millennia BC.

AD. However, later occupations on Khirbet al-Hijar implies a continuation of habitation as late as Hellenistic, Roman, and Byzantine times, at which time it is probable that Khirbet al-Hijar did form an island within the lake.

Stratigraphy through the Lake Floor

Sections exposed in the floor of the former lake indicate that in most places some 125-150 cm of pale gray silt lake marl overlies a brown clay which appears to represent an ancient, partially oxidized soil horizon, albeit one that has subsequently experienced localized waterlogging. Tentatively this brown subsoil horizon can be interpreted as a stratum that existed prior to the full development of the lake, but the presence within it of occasional fragments of small freshwater gastropod shells suggests that it was not entirely dry, perhaps having been deposited within a marshy environment. A layer of broken shells occasionally present at the interface between this soil and the lake marl may result from the encroachment of the lake over the pre-existing land surface. Occasionally present is an uppermost horizon of brown oxidized clay loam which possibly accumulated as a result of major sediment-laden flood events during the final stages of the lake, or immediately after it had dried up.

The Site of Kara Tepe and Its Environment in the 2nd Millennium BC

Today the site of Kara Tepe (AS 86) occurs within a flat silt and clay plain to the NE of the former lake (fig. 1). At the time of the original survey, in the spring of 1936, it was "in the deepest part of the marsh, where it meets the lake" and furthermore, dry arable land was entirely absent[9]; today however, the site is surrounded by cotton fields. Occupation commenced at least as early as the mid-3rd millennium BC, and an extensive lower town spread to the NE and east in the early 2nd millennium. Cuts within this lower area reveal one major occupation level of mud brick buildings and associated fills of Amuq L/M date (early-mid-2nd millennium BC). At least

---

9 Braidwood (1937) 29-30.

two of these walls were primarily comprised of brown mud brick that was apparently dug from oxidized soils typical of the well-drained parts of the plain. In addition, however, occasional mud bricks of gray silt contained small freshwater gastropod shells characteristic of a marsh or lacustrine environment. Although it is feasible that the mud brick was excavated at a distance from the site and was imported specially, it is much more likely that it was excavated from nearby pits.[10] If so, soils in the vicinity of the site can be inferred to have formed a mosaic of brown (oxidized) and gray (marsh/lake) deposits. Therefore, in contrast to the totally waterlogged environment that existed in the early 20th century, it seems that better drained

Fig. 2.

Panel from the Balawat gates showing depictions of Unkians bearing tribute. From L. W. King 1915: Plate XXVII.

10 Usually adjacent to or even within the mounded area; for discussion, see Wilkinson and Tucker (1995) 29-35.

(brown) soils suitable for cultivation were more common (for landscape reconstruction, see fig. 4).

The Neo-Assyrian Period

From the Neo-Assyrian period the development of the lake can be inferred from a range of textual sources and reliefs, the earlier of which relate to the land of Unqi (Hellenistic Amykes or Amyke). Although no direct reference to the presence of a lake in the pre-Seleucid period is known, Olmstead has suggested that during the reign of Shalmaneser III (mid-9th century BC) the inhabitants of Unqi lived on island settlements within the swamp or lake.[11] The evidence cited by Olmstead comprised decorations of the bronze gates at Balawat, executed in repoussé technique, which illustrate a number of fortified settlements apparently in areas of lake or marsh within the land of Unqi. The interpretation of such depictions presents certain problems, because it is not entirely certain that they are accurate.[12] Nevertheless, it is clear from the accompanying inscription that the reliefs do refer to the land of Unqi, *i.e.*, the Amuq plain,[13] being entitled:

"Tribute of the Unkians"

However, when scrutinized we see that the settlements depicted, rather than being surrounded by a lake, appear to be within limited bodies of water, the wave pattern of which diminishes in scale as a result of the water receding as it turns away from the eye (fig. 2). This contrasts to illustrations, on the same gates, of extensive bodies of water; for example the waves of the Mediterranean Sea at Tyre, which show no such foreshortening affect (fig. 3). Consequently, the reliefs of the Unqian settlements suggest the presence of a surrounding moat rather than a lake. Such a moated settlement may be represented by a site like Yer Köy/Tell Hassan Üçaği (AS 99) which in the

---

11 Olmstead (1921) 355-56.

12 Jacoby (1991) 130 maintains that details of fortifications *etc.* were of merely secondary importance to the Assyrian artists. For an opposing view, see Tucker (1994).

13 King (1915) pl. XXVII; Luckenbill (1926 [1968]) 25.

recent past was surrounded by a moat. Although now dry, at the time of Braidwood's visit this showed evidence of having held water during the rainy season,[14] an observation confirmed by the contained sediments, which indicates that water must have been present throughout much of the year. Therefore, by the time of Shalmanesar III's campaign the water table in the lower plain was probably at least sufficiently high to nourish moats, and in the lowest areas was probably swampy or lacustrine. However, the absence of a continuous sheet of water around the settlements of the Unqians makes Olmstead's assertion difficult to reconcile either with the gate reliefs or the absence of a record of such lakes in the campaigns of Shalmaneser III.

Fig. 3

Panel from the Balawat gates showing tribute being brought by boat from Tyre to the mainland. From L. W. King 1915: Plate XIII.

14 Braidwood (1937) 30.

The Hellenistic-Roman and Byzantine Periods

In contrast to the ambiguous record of the Neo-Assyrian period, during Antioch's heyday in Hellenistic-Roman time, the Amuq was clearly occupied by an extensive lake which even supplied Antioch with a varied and abundant supply of fish and shellfish.[15]

By the time of Libanius, writing in the later 4th century AD, hillsides near Antioch and even perhaps parts of the plain itself were sufficiently well-wooded to supply both building timbers and domestic fuel.[16] Furthermore, if the animals represented on mosaics from Antioch can be taken as having actually lived in the area, the region comprised a wide range of habitats with bear (*Ursus syriacus*), tiger (*Panthea tigris*), and fallow deer (*Dama mesopotamica*) representing woodland species, and ostrich (*Strathio syriacus*) and ibex (*Capra nubiana*) open ground.[17] The above, when combined with the fish and birds illustrated, implies a rich and verdant local environment.

However, a pristine environment should not be assumed, and human interference in the form of construction of major canals in the vicinity of Antioch must have resulted in significant changes in the natural environment. Of these, the dual canalization of the Orontes (and Kara Su?) noted on a cylindrical milestone(?) found to the NE of Antioch may have been either for drainage or to improve transport into, and potentially across the lake. Similarly, the cutting of a canal between Antioch and the sea to improve communications[18] may have also improved drainage away from the lake. If it did, however, as yet we have no real evidence in the form of lowered lake levels.

---

15 Downey (1961) 22-23 and n 47; see also Downey (1959) 652-86.

16 Libanius Or. 11.19 26-31; Dio Cassius quoted in Downey (1961) 150.

17 Bate (1959), based on mosaic originally from Antioch and now in the Honolulu Academy of Arts.

18 Pausanias: VIII 29, 3 (Frazer [1965]); discussed in Miller (1993) 86-87.

The Islamic Period

Medieval Islamic sources supply even more specific details about the regional environment and the lake. Not only were eel and catfish plentiful, but there were also marshes suitable for raising water buffalo. Again reference is made to woodland on the plain itself.[19] Yakut (died AD 1229) describes the lake as being of sweet water, in length about 20 miles and of width 7 miles,[20] while Abu-l Fida (1273–1331) is even more specific and provides vital clues about the channel system that both supplied and drained the lake[21]:

> Buhairah Antakiyyah lies between Antakiyyah, Baghras and Harim, and occupies the plain country called al-'Amk. It belongs to the district of Halab (Aleppo), and is situated about twelve days journey to the west thereof. Into this lake flows three rivers coming from the north. The easternmost of these is called the Nahr 'Ifrin; the westernmost, which runs under the Darbassak, is called the Nahr al-Aswad [the modern Kara Su], the Black River; and the third which flows between the first two, is called the Nahr Yaghra. Yaghra is the name of a village on its banks, the population of which is Christian. The circumference of the lake is about a days journey. It is covered with reeds, and there are fish and birds here the like to which we have mentioned in describing the Lake of Afamiyyah. The three rivers aforesaid—namely the Nahr al Aswad, the Yaghra, and the 'Ifrin—*come together to form a single stream before they fall into the lake on its northern shore* [emphasis mine]. And from the southern end a river flows out which joins the Orontes below the Jisr al-Hadid (the Iron Bridge), which lies about a mile above Antakiyya.

It is noteworthy that Abu-l Fida clearly describes the coming together of the three rivers before they enter the lake, a situation (also noted by Le Strange) that has not prevailed in recent times. This suggests that the ᶜAfrin was flowing along its northerly course (that which bifurcates on the map) before joining the other two rivers, all three of which then entered the lake.

---

19 Referred to in Abu al-Fida (1959) 41-42; al-Baladhuri (1957) 161-62; Yaqut (1965) 316; and Ibn Battuta (1871) 83.

20 Yakut 1: 524, in Le Strange (1890) 71.

21 Abu-l Fida: 41, quoted from Le Strange (1890) 71-72.

Rather than being a natural river, however, this appears to have been a canal system that irrigated an enclave of settlements which extended to the north in later periods.[22]

Sedimentary Aggradation: Channel Levees and Fans

The archaeological evidence noted above suggests that the lake was probably of diminished size, or even non-existent, in the 3rd millennium BC. Textual references indicate that the lake existed in the late first millennium BC, after which it probably attained its maximum extent in the Islamic period. References to a lake in classical sources disproves Woolley's suggestion that it was formed as a result of the damming of the Orontes by the 6th century AD Antioch earthquake.[23] Rather, the limited evidence available suggests that an earlier marshy flood basin became gradually transformed into a full lake sometime between the 3rd and 1st millennia BC.

Such a gradual growth may be the result of sedimentation by rivers and related channels that progressively raised water levels until a full, albeit shallow, lake was formed. A low-lying plain such as the Amuq would not be expected to have a stable surface over long periods of time, and sedimentary accumulations appear to have raised the terrain so as to potentially obscure archaeological features and sites. Aggradation has clearly been pervasive along the west side of the plain, where the gravel/alluvial fans have accumulated at least 2-3 m of silt, sand, and gravel (more or less depending upon the locality) over the past 10,000 years.

Extensive areas of the southern margins of the plain have aggraded as levees as a result of overbank sedimentation from the Orontes. This is best illustrated from a long cut exposed in a drain immediately east of Tell Atchana (ancient Alalakh: AS 136), where 3.5-4.0 m of alternating layers of silt and clay containing occasional freshwater mollusc shells (gastropods) accumulated as a result of overbank sedimentation from the Orontes. These sediments contained abundant pottery sherds, often large and un-abraded,

---

22 Braidwood (1937) 45-47.

23 Woolley (1953) 17-19.

at 3.5 to 4.0 m below the present ground surface on what appears to be horizontal beds (*i.e.*, not in an infilled channel) in the vicinity of Tell Atchana. The similarity of the pottery to simple bowls from Tabara al-Akrad levels VII and VI suggests a Chalcolithic date.[24] It is, however, unclear whether this material represents earlier phases of Atchana or simply belongs to an outlying scatter of occupation. Nevertheless, its presence suggests that at least 3.5 m of sedimentation has occurred since the sherds accumulated, probably in the 5th or 4th millennia BC. This depth of accumulation over the last 7,000 to 6,000 years supports Woolley's data from Atchana, and confirms that considerable sedimentation has indeed taken place. This would certainly have masked the terrain along the sinuous raised levee alongside the Orontes (stipple on fig. 1), and as Woolley remarked, such aggradation could almost certainly have obscured a number of smaller settlements.[25]

Further north this distinctive succession of levee-floodplain sediments merges laterally and downslopes into gray clay that presumably accumulated in waterlogged, perhaps marshy or lacustrine conditions. This clay overlays, in turn, brown or reddish-brown silt and clay that owes its distinctive coloration to having been washed from the limestone massifs to the south as well as having accumulated in a less waterlogged environment (*cf.* those describe above at sections within the former lake; fig. 1). It appears, therefore, that the lake extended over a land surface that probably fringed the basin on the southern side and was probably better-drained than the deposits that accumulated later. However, alternations of waterlogged and oxidized sediments in lower parts of the basin suggest that localized waterlogging prevailed for extended periods of time.

The Contribution of Canals.

Other areas of sedimentation (indicated by stipple on fig. 1) show (a) an early levee or fan delta of the Nahr al-ᶜAfrin (extending around Tell

---

24 Hood (1951) fig. 6: 3 and 3a.

25 Woolley (1955) 5.

ᶜImar on fig. 1); (b) a second fan which spreads to the north of Çatal Höyük. Three segments of undated channel (broken lines) follow the contours and are clearly relict features within this area of sedimentary aggradation. Support for their identification as canals comes from the presence of upcast deposits alongside the two channels north of Kara Tepe (AS 86), their straight and forked pattern, and their relationship parallel to the contours of the fan. The last named tendency is more characteristic of canals than of distributary channels of alluvial fans that normally follow a course perpendicular to the contours. Two channel sections were noted within this northern area of aggradation, and a third was recorded on the main relict ᶜAfrin fan to the east of Tell ᶜImar (arrowed, fig. 1). The channel to the NW lacked diagnostic features of a canal (except for its plan-form and the presence of upcast), but the feature arrowed near Çatal Höyük, which measures 180 cm deep by 170 cm wide, was clearly a rock-cut canal. Although undated, this apparently conducted water away from the Nahr al-ᶜAfrin, around the perimeter of a small group of hills towards the NW, where it probably functioned in the Hellenistic to Islamic periods distributing water into the NW area of aggradation.

Discussion

The above observations on the history of the lake, the sedimentary deposits of the plain, and on the canals can now be assembled to infer the process of development of the lake. If the above reconstruction of the evolution of Lake Antioch is approximately correct, settlements adjacent to the lake can be inferred to have originally been surrounded by greater areas of dry land than during recent times. If during the first half of the 3rd millennium BC the lake was no higher than site AS 181, then its elevation must have been approximately 78.5 m above mean sea level, that is 1.5 to 2.0 m below the level in the 1930s. Calculated sustaining areas[26] for sites adjacent to the lake suggest that during the 3rd millennium BC all known sites were

[26] In other words, the calculated area that would have been required to grow food to sustain the estimated population of the site.

sufficiently far from the lake to have comprised mainly dry land territories. Thus, according to this reconstruction, Khirbet al-Hijar (AS 180) would have fallen several 100s of meters from the lake, with most of its potential agricultural sustaining area being on dry land (fig. 4). Similarly, Kara Tepe, which was surrounded by marsh in the 1930s, would have been well clear of the lake, as would have been its surrounding territory. However, from the evidence of the mud bricks at this site, it can be suggested that water-logged soils were already present by the mid-2nd millennium. Ground water levels were probably even higher in the 1st millennium when even sites some distance from the eventual lake were surrounded by water (*cf.*

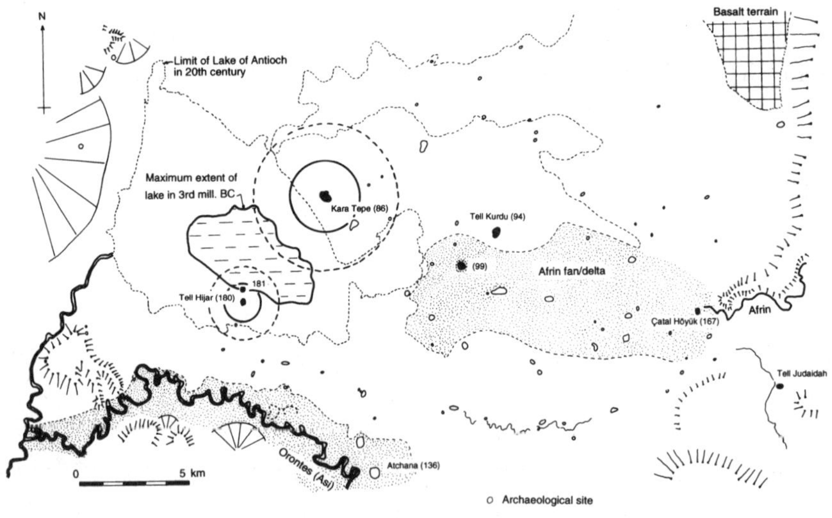

Fig. 4

Reconstruction of maximum level of the Lake of Antioch assuming a level no high than that of site AS 181. Concentric circles indicate approximate sustaining areas calculated from the maximum size of key sites AS 86 and 180 (see text).

Yer Koy [AS 99]). Certainly by Hellenistic times a lake was present, a situation which continued until the mid-20th century AD.

Present evidence suggests that the Lake of Antioch evolved gradually through time rather than resulting from the blockage of Orontes flow by a single tectonic event in the 6th century AD.[27] The above evidence accords reasonably well with the illustrations of the land of Unqi given on the gates of Shalmaneser III at Balawat, but this must be tempered by a certain caution when dealing with the representation of cities on Assyrian reliefs. In this context the historical specificity of the earlier reliefs employed here may not be as precise as those of, for example, the reign of Sennacherib[28]; nevertheless, the depictions on the Balawat gates seem to be fairly accurate.[29] In fact, reversing the argument, in the Amuq it may be possible to demonstrate the veracity of the depictions on the gates by reference to specific sites that still exist.

Regarding the growth of the lake, strata within the Atchana drain section suggest that the aggradation of the Orontes levees could have progressively resulted in the blockage of drainage out of the basin. Thus the 3.5 to 4 m of levee buildup along the Orontes may have progressively restricted outflow from the flood basin to the north, thus depriving floods and overflow of a convenient outlet towards the sea. Such blockage of natural river flow could have been complicated by additional natural and human-induced agencies. During floods, excess flow spills over the banks of the Orontes, accumulating in the low-lying flood basin to the north. Such floods may have been exacerbated by increased run-off that would have resulted from the progressive removal of vegetation from within the tributary river basins. This is best illustrated by pollen analysis conducted in the

---

27 *Contra* Woolley (1953) 19. It should, however, be pointed out that the location of the Amuq plain within the down-faulted valley of the Hatay-Kara Su graben makes it very susceptible to tectonic movements. These could contribute to changes in alluvial geomorphology. At present, however, we have no direct data on the operation of Holocene faults systems in the area. Note that the site of Khirbet al-Hijar appears to have been occupied both before and after the 6th century AD.

28 See Marcus (1995) 199, and references in notes 46 and 47.

29 See also Tucker (1994) 107-16 for a similar argument.

Ghab area of the Orontes valley some 65 km to the south of the Turkish border. In the Ghab III core, the pollen record shows a substantial decline in oak (*cerris*-type) and pistachio pollen after 4460–3560 BP, which very probably can be ascribed to the clearance of forest.[30] This, together with the increase in pollen of olea, vitus and juglans pollen (olive, vine and walnut), suggests an increase in domestic trees and bushes at the expense of natural woodland during the ensuing 2nd and 1st millennia BC, as well as for the remainder of the record. Such an impression of increased human interference with the landscape must, according to van Zeist and Woldring, have effectively suppressed any climatic signal that may be represented in the pollen record. Slightly later in the sequence, the arrival of a red-brown clay in the upper part of the core may have resulted from increased erosion of the characteristic reddish terra rossa soil that formerly capped hillslopes in this part of Syria. Taken together, we tentatively suggest that deforestation, after approximately 2000 BC, combined with increased human activity on slopes, probably increased runoff into river valleys, thereby increasing the severity of riverine floods. The tremendously increased settlement that took place in the Jebels Simᶜan, Zawiya, and related massifs between the 3rd and 6th centuries AD[31] must have resulted also in significant changes in natural vegetation, slope conditions, and hydrology that could have contributed to increased flooding in the region.

In addition to increased flow from the Orontes, the construction of canals away from the Nahr ᶜAfrin would entail water being diverted along a circuitous route, rather than along a direct course towards the sea. Surplus water would then accumulate at the end of canals, where it could eventually form marshes. In lower Mesopotamia similar swamps have formed as a result of overbank floods from rivers, overflow from canals, and related

---

30 Van Zeist and Woldring (1980) 115; 120-21. On the subject of deforestation, however, it is necessary to distinguish among those areas. The Amanus mountains were heavily wooded in antiquity and continued to be heavily forested even until recent times (Rowton [1967] 265). On the other hand, the limestone massifs of the Jebels Siman and Zawiya clearly lost much or all of their woodland prior to the Roman-Byzantine period, but when this occurred is not known.

31 Tate (1992) 238.

causes.[32] Particularly problematic in this regard is the process of avulsion, whereby a river on a levee breaches its bank to flood along a new course, usually through the adjacent topographically lower flood basin. In the Amuq the location of the Orontes upon such a levee represents a potential instability, but whether or not the river ever shifted into the area subsequently occupied by the lake is not known.

In conclusion, it appears that the level of the Lake of Antioch, unlike many lakes in the Near East and Africa, may not have been determined primarily by climate, but rather by the interaction of geomorphological processes such as levee aggradation, combined with changes of runoff from tributary catchments, flood discharge, and canal overflow—all of which are partly a result of human activity. This is not to exclude climatic change from the equation. It is possible that increased rainfall and/or decreased evaporation may have resulted in increased flow into the lake, thereby raising water levels. However, the apparent evidence of a gradually rising lake level over the past 5000 years is opposite to the progressive shrinking of Lake Konya on the Anatolian plateau.[33] Consequently, in the Amuq, climatic influence on lake-level fluctuations may have been overridden by human-induced and geomorphological factors.

Bibliography

Adams, R., McC. (1981) *Heartland of Cities.* Chicago. **Astour, M. C.** (1963) Place-Names from the Kingdom of Alalaḫ in the North Syrian List of Thutmose III: A Study in Historical Topography. *Journal of Near Eastern Studies* 22: 220-40. (1992) Alalakh. In Freedman 1992: 142-45. **al-Baladhuri** (d. 892) (1957) *Futuh al-Buldan.* Beirut. **Bate, D. M. A.** (1959) Note on an Animal Mosaic from Antioch-on-the-Orontes. *Honolulu Academy of Arts, Annual Bulletin* 1: 26-31. **Braidwood, R. J.** (1937) *Mounds in the Plain of Antioch: An Archaeological Survey.* Oriental Institute Publications 48. Chicago. **Braidwood, R. J., and L. S. Braidwood** (1960) *Excavations in the Plain of Antioch I: The Earlier Assemblages Phases A-J.* Oriental Institute Publications 61. Chicago. **Cole, S.** (1994) Marsh Formation in the Borsippa Region. *Journal of Near Eastern Studies* 53: 81-109. **Downey, G.** (1959) Libanius, Antiochikos.

---

32 Adams (1981) 205; Cole (1994) 81-109.

33 Roberts (1993) figs. 9 and 10.

Proceedings of the American Philosopohical Society 103. (1961) *A History of Antioch in Syria from Seleucus to the Arab Conquest.* Princeton. **Abu al-Fida** (1273–1331) (1959) *Taqwim al-Buldan.* Paris. **Frazer, J. G.** (1965) *Descripto Graeciae: Description of Greece.* New York. **Freedman, D. N.**, ed. (1992) *The Anchor Bible Dictionary.* New York. **Hawkins, J. D.** (1995) The Political Geography of North Syria and South-East Anatolia in the Neo-Assyrian Period. In Liverani 1995: 69-85. **Hood, S.** (1951) Excavations at Tabara el Akrad, 1948–49. *Anatolian Studies* 1: 113-36. **Ibn Battuta** (1304–1377) (1871) *Tuhfat al-Nithar wa Ghara'ib al-Amsar wa 'Aja'ib al'Asfar.* Cairo. **Jacoby, R.** (1991) The Representation and Identification of Cities on Assyrian Reliefs. *Israel Exploration Journal* 41: 112-31. **King, L. W.** (1915) *Bronze Reliefs from the Gates of Shalmaneser III, King of Assyria BC 860-825.* London. **Le Strange, G.** (1890) *Palestine Under the Moslems.* Boston. **Liverani, M.**, ed. (1995) *Neo-Assyrian Geography.* Quarderni di Geografia Storica. Rome. **Luckenbill, D. D.** (1926(68)) *Ancient Records of Assyria and Babylonia,* Vol.1. New York. **Magness-Gardiner, B.** (1994) Urban-Rural Relations in Bronze Age Syria: Evidence from Alalah Level VII Palace Archives. In Schwartz and Falconer 1994: 37-47. **Marcus, M. I.** (1995) Geography as Visual Ideology: Landscape, Knowledge, and Power in Assyrian Art. In Liverani 1995: 193-202. **Miller, F.** (1993) *The Roman Near East, 31 BC – AD 337.* Cambridge, Mass. **Olmstead, A. T.** (1921) Shalmaneser III and the Establishment of Assyrian Power. *Journal of the American Oriental Society* 41: 345-82. **Roberts, N., and H. E. Wright** (1993) Vegetational, Lake-level, and Climatic History of the Near East and South-west Asia. In Wright *et al.* 1993: 194-220. **Rowton, M. B.** (1967) The Woodlands of Ancient Western Asia. *Journal of Near Eastern Studies* 26: 261-77. **Schwartz, G., and S. E. Falconer**, eds. (1994) *Archaeological Views from the Countryside. Village Communities in Early Complex Societies.* **Tate, G.** (1992) *Les Campagnes de la Syrie du Nord, Tome 1.* Paris. **Tchalenko, G.** (1953) *Villages Antiques de la Syrie du Nord. Le Massif du Belus a l'Epoque Romaine.* Paris. **Tolun, N., and H. N. Pamir** (1975) *Explanatory Text of the Geological Map of Turkey.* Maden Tetkik ve Arama Enstitüsü Vayinlarindan. Ankara. **Tucker, D. J.** (1994) Representations of Imgur-Enlil on the Balawat Gates. *Iraq* 56: 107-16. **Van Zeist, W., and H. Woldring** (1980) Holocene Vegetation and Climate of Northwestern Syria. *Palaeohistoria* 22: 111-25. **Wilkinson, T. J., and D. J. Tucker** (1995) *Settlement Development in the North Jazira, Iraq. A Study of the Archaeological Landscape.* Iraq Archaeological Reports 3. Warminster, United Kingdom. **Wiseman, D. J.** (1953) *The Alalakh Tablets.* Occasional Papers of the British Institute of Archaeology at Ankara, No. 2. London. **Woolley, L.** (1953) *A Forgotten Kingdom.* London. (1955) *Alalakh. An Account of the Excavations at Tell Atchana in the Hatay, 1937–1949.* London. **Wright, H. E., J. E. Kutzbach, T. Webb III, W. F. Ruddiman, F. A. Street-Perrot, and P. J. Bartlein**, eds. (1993) *Global Climates since the Last Glacial Maximum.* Minneapolis, Minn. **Yaqut, Ibn ᶜAbdullah** (1179–1229) (1965) *Muᵓjam al-Buldan.* Tehran.

The Play of Ritual in the ʾAqhat Narrative

David P. Wright
Brandeis University

The ʾAqhat story displays numerous cases of ritual performance.[1] These are often quite formulaic. Many of them either reflect patterns known from other texts or they are repetitive within the story of ʾAqhat itself. This may make the ritual scenes appear negligible or relatively unimportant, mere embellishments around a more significant nonritual narrative core. But closer study demonstrates that they are in fact central to the story. Of its approximately 650 extant poetic lines, about 530 deal with ritual performances or their contexts, *i.e.*, 82%. Moreover, they are a chief means of structuring the plot. The main tensions and resolutions in the story occur in ritual contexts and even are the result of ritual activities or "misactivities," as we will see. Furthermore, the various ritual scenes do not appear randomly, but have a certain logic and interdependence. Later cases gain significance in relationship to earlier cases, especially as they build incrementally upon or develop contrasts with earlier cases. This paper, warmly dedicated to Michael Astour, outlines how this is the case with the two main types of ritual found in the story: (a) feasting and sacrifice and (b) mourning and recovery rites.[2] Study of these particular cases will

---

1 I follow Bell (1992) 74 in her definition of ritual, or more precisely "ritualization" as "a way of acting that is designed and orchestrated to distinguish and privilege what is being done in comparison to other, usually more quotidian, activities."

2 This study grows out of a larger study of ritual in ʾAqhat to be published by Eisenbrauns.

give an account of the majority of examples of ritual in the story and consequently describe the dynamics of much of the narrative.[3]

Feasting and Sacrifice

The theme of feasting dominates much of the story, either in the specific context of sacrifice to the gods or as more general banqueting.[4] These examples, however, are not all of the same "ethical" type. In some cases performance proceeds without difficulty while in others it is beset with problems. One could call the one type of ritual successful and the other failed. A less functionalist categorization, and one that can include all sorts of problems within ritual, as we will see below, is that proposed by Ronald Grimes.[5] Adopting the terms that J. L. Austin used to describe the effectiveness of speech acts,[6] Grimes labels the one type felicitous and the other infelicitous. In the ᵓAqhat story cases of infelicitous feasting constitute the main dramatic pivot: the reason and occasion for ᶜAnat's murder of ᵓAqhat. The story makes these visible and their effect keenly felt by initially setting up a paradigm of properly operating ritual. The infelicitous examples thus stand out in stark contrast against the model. The initial cases of felicitous and infelicitous ritual as a group, in turn, give definition to the two feast situations at the end of the story, each of which has a different ethical character.

The paradigm of felicitous ritual is presented at the beginning of the story[7] through a triad of feasts: Daniᵓil's six-plus-one-day feast of the gods, mainly Baᶜl and ᵓIl (1.17 I 1-43,[8] and see the following lines); his six-plus-

---

3 Interest in ritual in Ugaritic texts is the motivation for this study, but since ritual in narrative is the object of study, it has results that pertain to the literary study of the text. For this approach, *cf.* Parker (1989) and Aitken (1989).

4 On feasting in Ugaritic narrative texts, see Lloyd (1990).

5 See Grimes (1990) 191-209.

6 See Austin (1975) 12-24 and the following chapters.

7 It is reasonable to think that the story begins with tablet 1.17. The ten or so missing lines at the beginning could quickly set up the situation for the story in general and Daniᵓil's sacrifice in particular.

8 Text references throughout are to Dietrich, Loretz, and Sanmartín (1995).

one-day feast of the Kotharat (II 26-42); and the one-day feast of Kothar-wa-Hasis (V 15-33).

The first takes place as Daniᵓil is mourning the lack of a son. He gives the gods *uzr*-offerings to eat and drink.[9] These are offered in a state of ritual girding, *i.e.*, while wearing a *mizrt* and *ṣt*, mourning clothing, and so presumably come by the name *uzr*.[10] At night Daniᵓil can remove (*yd* < *ndy*)[11] this garb, perhaps to use it for bedding. The description of the rite itself (1.17 I 1-15) contains an outline of actions only, but Baᶜl's response (I 16-24) says that Daniᵓil has been moaning (*anḫ*), thus indicating that the offerings are to be thought of as having been accompanied by words. The type of thing that Daniᵓil might say can be seen in Baᶜl's words, spoken all or for the most part to ᵓIl. They contain elements of classic lament: a complaint, a rationale for divine aid, and a petition of ᵓIl to remedy Daniᵓil's situation.[12] Baᶜl thus prays *for* Daniᵓil in two senses: he recommends that the man be blessed and, at the same time, as a mediator carries Daniᵓil's words to ᵓIl. ᵓIl complies and blesses Daniᵓil.

---

9 Tropper (1990) 139-40, 165-70 has recently argued again for interpreting the verbs *ylḥm* and *yšqy* as G-stems with the simple meaning "eat" and "drink" (*cf.* Caquot and Sznycer [1974] 419-21 and note c.). This remains doubtful since *šqy* in the G-stem appears to have only the meaning "to give drink" not simply "to drink" (*cf.* de Moor [1971] 72; Dijkstra and de Moor [1975] 172-73 and n. 9; note the G in both Arab. *saqā(y)* and Akk. *šaqû* means "to give drink"). Thus *ylḥm* should be understood, if not as an internal causative, as a D-stem. *Cf.* the solution of Tsevat (1986).

10 On the *mizrt* in mourning, *cf.* 1.5 VI 17. *mizrt* and *uzr* appear to have the same root and thus a semantic-conceptual connection between the two may be attempted. An alternative explanation is to take *uzr* as an adjective meaning "girded" describing Daniᵓil's clothing (for the vocalization, *cf.* Huehnergard [1987] 105). One might, however, expect a passive participle /*ʼazīr-*/ (*cf.* Segert [1984] §54.28) which would be manifested alphabetically as *azr.*

11 See Tropper (1988) 340.

12 Complaint: "[Da]niᵓil, the Rapian, is miserable, the hero, the Harnamiyyan, is moaning, who has no son like his brothers, or scion like his kinspeople..." (the difficult *at* at the end of line 16 is omitted in this translation; de Moor [1987] 227; de Moor and Spronk [1987] 102). Rationale: "He fed the gods girded-offerings, he gave the holy ones girded-offerings to drink." Petition: "Please bless him, O Bull, ᵓIl, my father, / strengthen him, O creator of creatures!"

Judging a rite to be felicitous often requires distinguishing the views of the different agents. What proceeds properly for one may be a debacle to another. In the present case, however, it is clear that both Daniʾil and the gods are satisfied with the outcome of the petition sacrifice. Daniʾil gets what he seeks and the gods have not been forced against their will. The sense that this ritual succeeds also appears in how the offering and its consequences are described. Daniʾil's actions are delineated in detail. This creates the perception that Daniʾil performs the rite with precision; nothing is amiss. In their response, the gods recite the relatively long list of filial duties three times (1.17 I 26-33, 44-47, II 1-8), and Daniʾil repeats it once again in joyous response (II 16-23). This repetition conveys further the impression that the divine promise is certain and gladly given.

Of the three initial feasts that make up the paradigm of proper ritual, this first is the most elaborate. Though the offering to the Kotharat lasts six-plus-one days as this one does (see below), the present offering is more elaborately outlined. It includes lines separately devoted to describing the feeding and drinking, a description of clothing which serves as an envelope around the account of the six-day offering, and the detailed description of the gods' response on the seventh day. The third sacrificial meal, to Kothar-wa-Hasis, does not compete with the first in complexity, since it lasts only one day.

The extensive description in the first ceremony is perhaps necessary in order to overcome the inertia of Daniʾil's unfortunate situation. Once he has the promise of a son, the energy spent on offerings to sustain motion does not need to be as great. The contextual need for a complex initial feast carries with it a peripheral benefit. Up front it imprints clearly upon the mind of the reader or hearer the basic dynamics of proper ritual. Thus, while the triad of felicitous feasts as a whole is a paradigm for the infelicitous feasts that follow, the story's first feast is a paradigm for the rest of the triad.

The next feast, given to the Kotharat, lasts, as already noted, six days with their departure on the seventh. Daniʾil slaughters an ox for them and gives them drink. It may be that we are to think he slaughters a new ox each day rather than making one animal last for the week. If so, this is still a substantial affair, albeit not as elaborate as the one before.

This feast has a tone and purpose that are broader in scope than the first feast. Certainly solicitation continues in the second feast. The Kotharat are conception and birth goddesses.[13] Daniʾil is securing their services to ensure the fulfillment of the promise made to him. Yet, in contrast with the first feast, no sorrow is present. The former transformed Daniʾil's mourning into joy (*cf.* his delight in 1.17 II 8-12). This new temper pervades the whole of the second meal. Coming on the heals of receiving the gods' promise, the second feast also bears an element of thanksgiving. Moreover, Daniʾil is now at home, on his own turf. He no longer seeks the gods out; they come to him. As an offering given at home to visitors it is also an act of hospitality.

The new and varied motivations for this successful performance augment the model of felicitous ritual. The first rite was conceived in the gloom of lament and had the specific purpose of obtaining a son. Now, even though the ritual performance is less elaborate, the goals have multiplied and a new mood prevails. As the triad of rites unfolds we are introduced to a rainbow of ritual possibilities, a color at a time.

The third proper feast completes the spectrum. ʾAqhat has been born. The gods have, for some reason, decided to give him a bow and arrows.[14] Kothar-wa-Hasis fabricates these and brings them to Daniʾil, again at his home. The father now includes in the ritual preparations his wife, Danatay, who did not appear in the first two feasts. He has her prepare a lamb for the god to eat, with accompanying drink. This, which recalls Abraham's and Sarah's meal in Genesis 18, is primarily a hospitality offering, but to some extent also a thank offering for the gift that was brought. It, however, carries no element of request. All Daniʾil's desires were fulfilled previously. The

---

13 *Cf.* 1.24.

14 1.10 II 6-7 which has *qṣʿt* carried in the right hand may be an indication that these are arrows since most iconic representations in the ancient Near East have the bow itself carried or shot in the left hand (*cf.* Pritchard [1954] 3, 12, 25, 172, 183 [Ras Shamra], 190, 309, 318, 321, 327, 344, 358, 368, 369, 372, 373, 390, 519, 536, 626, 821). For bows in the left hand and arrows in the right hand, *cf.* Pritchard 1954 12 (?), 184, 185, 351, 371, and esp. 791 and 179. For the few cases of a bow in the right hand, *cf.* 12, 362, 365.

bow, which apparently is unsolicited, is icing on the cake. The extra gift confirms the sense that, from the beginning, feasting has been successful.

Now, ritual is activity that does not merely reflect or image social structures, nor is its primary goal the inculcation of cultural concerns in participants and observers. Rather, it is mainly a means by which social goals, such as the establishment of relationships between individuals and/or groups, are constructed. As such it is often concerned with the negotiation of power between individuals or groups.[15] This bargaining is undertaken by agents who, to a greater or lesser extent, have differing interests. This may therefore look, at least analytically, more as a struggle than as a smooth working toward a common goal and may make the dichotomy of felicitous and infelicitous ritual appear to be invalid. Infelicity would appear to be integral to what ritual is. But infelicity need not be construed to include these characteristic inherent conflicts. It may be reserved for other uncharacteristic anomalies, including cases where a negotiation of power relationship fails.

Judged against this canon the first three rites are immeasurably happy. They have succeeded in creating a series of interconnected superior-inferior relationships. The resulting hierarchy places the gods Baᶜl and ᵓIl at the top with the latter in the supreme position. The Kotharat and Kothar-wa-Hasis, because they supplement the initial and primary promise of ᵓIl, are subordinate to the high gods. The rites as a group indicate that humans are subject to all the deities. In the family the father is chief, with the wife his dependent, as shown in Danatay's ritual preparations for Kothar-wa-Hasis. The son, as the list of filial duties indicates, is also subordinate to the father.

This pattern of relationships is not striking. One could have guessed it on the basis of intuition and common knowledge about social/theological patterns in the ancient Near East and traditional societies at large before reading about the feasts in the ᵓAqhat story. What should be kept in mind, however, is that the story is a self-contained world. What is true for other texts or society outside the text is not necessarily true for this specific story. Therefore, it takes care to set out clearly at the beginning the relationships

---

15 For this analytic perspective, see Bell (1992) 182-223 and throughout.

that will play an important part in that world. Notably, it creates these through ritual, much the same way as they are created for the real world by actual ritual practice.

The expectations that the initial triad creates are completely upset in the following pair of feasts, which lead to and provide the context for ʾAqhat's death. In the first feast ʿAnat seeks to barter for the bow (1.17 VI 2-45). The feast's purpose is not clear because of damage at the beginning of the column. It may be the continuation of the occasion when Daniʾil gave the bow to ʾAqhat (V 33-39),[16] or it may be a celebration of the results of ʾAqhat's hunt, alluded to in Daniʾil's blessing uttered when he gives the bow to Daniʾil. In any case, there is plenty of wine and meat present. Their disposition and use are described in terms similar to those found in feasts in the Baʿl cycle.[17] Presumably, too, ʾAqhat's family is present and perhaps other gods besides ʿAnat.

This rite goes well by all appearances until ʿAnat spies the bow. She admires it so that she pours her cup out on the ground. This is ominous inasmuch as ʾIl had promised Daniʾil a son by the reverse gesture of taking up his cup in blessing.[18] ʿAnat's act is a signal that the promises are about to be undone. ʿAnat first offers ʾAqhat riches for the bow. ʾAqhat responds, apparently with respect, telling her what materials to obtain in order to have her own weapon built. ʿAnat makes another attempt to obtain the bow by offering the lad eternal life. ʾAqhat becomes contemptuous at this point, calling her offer a phlegmy lie and telling her that women do not need bows. She angrily responds, saying that if she finds him rebellious again she will kill him. She then abruptly leaves, to complain to Il.

---

16 Margalit (1989) 299-300 with good reason connects the feast with bestowing the bow on ʾAqhat and sees it as a "coming-of-age" party for the boy.

17 To 1.17 VI 3-8 compare 1.3 I 2-17; 1.4 III 40-44; IV 35-38; VI 40-59; 1.5 IV 10-21. Also compare 1.17 VI 2-3 to 1.23: 6.

18 1.17 I 34-36, emended according to the gesture in Kirta 1.15 II 16-20 (*cf.* Pardee [1977]). For possible iconographic attestations of the gesture, see Caquot and Sznycer (1980) plates VII (=Pritchard [1954] 493), VIII (=Pritchard [1954] 826), XXII (*cf.* Dijkstra and de Moor [1975] 178 and n. 66; de Moor [1987] 205 n. 49).

This is clearly a case of infelicity, and can be judged so on several counts. Grimes' full typology of infelicitous ritual is helpful in analyzing just what has gone wrong here. He posits nine categories, which build on Austin's preliminary typology of infelicity in speech acts: [19] (1) *misfire* (an illegitimate, void, or incomplete act), (2) *abuse* (absence of proper attitude, atmosphere, and follow through), (3) *ineffectuality* (lack of expected empirical results), (4) *violation* (a demeaning act), (5) *contagion* (where effects go beyond those expected), (6) *opacity* (lack of intelligibility), (7) *defeat* (invalidation of another's act), (8) *omission* (an act unperformed), (9) *misframe* (misconstruing of genre). The feast where ᶜAnat and ᵓAqhat argue includes the categories of misfire, abuse, and violation.

Misfire is evident in two ways. First, ᶜAnat's request seems out of the ordinary. Grimes would specifically call this a "nonplay," *i.e.*, an unconventional procedure. It is true that ritual in general and feasting in particular, which involves the transfer of food gifts, are often concerned with giving and receiving. But ᶜAnat's request for the bow goes beyond the template provided in the first feasts. In those feasts, the gods as good guests receive what is given them and do not ask for more. Misfire is also evident in the abruptness with which the feast ends. It remains unfinished. There is no mention of the party breaking up and anyone going home. Grimes calls such misfires "hitches."

Abuse is evident in the animosity that arises between ᶜAnat and ᵓAqhat in bargaining for the bow. ᵓAqhat's disdain and ᶜAnat's consequent threat are cases of "insincerity," a subcategory of abuse. Another subcategory, a "flop," where the ritual fails to produce the proper mood, accompanies this insincerity.

Violation is one of the more difficult categories to apply in ritual analysis because it is often a matter of impassioned external criticism. A ritual clitoridectomy, for example, can be judged a violation. But this will not necessarily be the view of those performing it or even those suffering it. Nevertheless, sometimes violation is evident within the context of a perfor-

---

19 *Cf.* Austin (1975) 12-24. See Grimes (1990) 174-209 for a complete description of these categories with examples.

mance when it contradicts internal cultural expectations. This is the case in the story where ᶜAnat threatens ᵓAqhat's life.

The next feast is, as it were, a conceptual extension of the foregoing. It is where ᶜAnat makes good on her threat and kills ᵓAqhat (1.18 IV 16-37). The context for the feast is unclear owing to damage to the tablet at the beginning of column IV and the apparent total absence of columns II and III. In addition, in describing the murder the story is more interested in what ᶜAnat is doing than in what ᵓAqhat is doing. It is doubtful that the feast is connected with celebrating a marriage that ᶜAnat deceitfully contracted with ᵓAqhat so as to lure him into a situation of vulnerability.[20] ᶜAnat is hiding and not a participant in the feast as one might expect if she were to be the bride. Perhaps the feast celebrates a successful hunt, as 1.18 I 27-29 may suggest. At any rate, ᵓAqhat holds the banquet in or near the city 'Abilum, having apparently been directed there by ᶜAnat earlier. If the specific purpose is not clear, it is at least to be viewed as an elaborate affair, since vultures are circling overhead, anxious perhaps to scavenge the remains of slaughtered animals.[21] ᶜAnat uses the vultures in her attack against ᵓAqhat: she hides among them and dispatches thence Yaṭupan, her mercenary, to strike him on the head.

The infelicity here is different from that in the previous feast. ᶜAnat employs *deceit*, a category that should be added to Grimes' list, perhaps alongside *violation* or *insincerity*, unless it is to be proposed as a category in its own right. An agent may use deceit within a ritual situation to achieve a certain end. For example, Jacob, disguised as his brother Esau, receives the blessing of his father (Genesis 27). Below, we will see Daniᵓil's daughter Pughat using deceit in a similar way, as a participant in a rite. The case of ᶜAnat is different. She is not a feigning agent *within* the feast, but stands *outside* the rite, hiding, waiting for an opportunity to invade. Her use of deceit is then more like that which Jacob's sons used against Hamor's people (Genesis 34). The latter performed a ritual (circumcision) and Jacob's sons

20 De Moor (1987) 242-43, 245; *cf.* Dijkstra and de Moor (1975) 194-95.

21 It is more than a "lunch break" as Margalit (1989) 336 has described it.

took advantage of the occasion—specifically, the recuperative aftermath—to stage an attack.[22]

In neither of these unhappy rites do ᶜAnat and ᵓAqhat successfully construct a relationship of power. To do this ritual requires give-and-take on the part of both parties. Both the superior and inferior need to make concessions, despite their individual interests, to make ritual work. In the feast where ᶜAnat and ᵓAqhat vie for possession of the bow, neither party yields and thus the performance breaks off without resolution. The contract is left unsigned. The failure to establish a relationship of power in the last feast has a different character. In it ᶜAnat avoids negotiation altogether and imposes complete domination on ᵓAqhat by killing him. Though power has been exercised, it ceases to exist as soon as it is deployed. Indeed, for true power to exist, as Bell, following Foucault, has noted,[23] it must grant some freedom to the subordinate so that the latter can acknowledge the power of the superior. Destroying the subordinate—and this destruction need not be mortal: banishment, harsh treatment, or even less may be sufficient—prevents or impedes the recognition of power. Thus the failure involved in both of these feasts stands at opposite ends of a continuum. The first did not go far enough in successfully constructing a relationship between ᶜAnat and ᵓAqhat; the latter went too far in murdering ᵓAqhat. Effective ritual stands somewhere between the two poles.

The dramatic effect of these last rites lies not just in their contrast with the initial three; they quite directly undo all that the earlier feasts accomplished. The promised son is killed. The bow, the gift of the god, is broken just after the murder. Tensions too arise between humans and the gods, as we have just seen. And tensions also arise among the gods themselves. ᶜAnat visits ᵓIl after the first botched feast and seeks his nod to go after ᵓAqhat (1.17 VI 46-1.18 I 19). To receive his permission she threatens him. Though in and around these last rites not every human and god are in conflict with

22 Perhaps a clearer form of external deceit (ambush) in ritual is found in the case of the Benjamites capturing maidens who are dancing at the annual feast at Shiloh (Judg 21: 15-25).

23 See Bell (1992) 199-202.

one another, and though there is not an all out general conflict among the gods themselves, the friction that does exist symbolically upsets the order that the first rites established.

An indication of the strain between the human and divine world is found in the long section of the text containing the rites of mourning (1.18 IV 38-1.19 IV 17; these are analyzed below in more detail). It does not describe any feasts or sacrifices taking place, only rites of healing and retaliation. Occasionally Daniᵓil refers to or addresses Baᶜl, in wonder about the drought that follows ᵓAqhat's death (1.19 I 42-46), in a request to fell the vultures from the sky so that Daniᵓil can find the remains of his son (III 2, 12, etc.), and in passing reference in a curse, along with the mention of ᵓIl (III 47; IV 5). But these prayers, curses, and accompanying performances do not develop the relationship between the bereaved father and the god as feasts do.

Feasting does not appear again until seven years of mourning are complete. At this point we find two feasts, though perhaps there were others in the story's missing conclusion.[24] The first of these, Daniᵓil's recovery sacrifice (1.19 IV 22-40), is performed in propriety; the second, Pughat's serving wine to Yaṭupan (IV 41-60), involves deception.

Daniᵓil's recovery sacrifice has several parts. The first mentioned component, the primary act if not the initial act, is presenting a *dbḥ* to the gods. What this entails is not described, but from other examples of *dbḥ* in narrative as well as ritual texts it is probably to be imagined as including the presentation of food to the gods.[25] Consequently it is a feast. A *dǵṯ*-offering accompanies the *dbḥ*. Since this is made to rise among the celestial beings/stars (*yšᶜly ... bšmym/bkbkbm*), it appears it is an offering, or part thereof, that is burnt, or perhaps incense.[26] If the latter, it may be a sign of the rela-

[24] I doubt that 1.20-22 should be read as part of the sequel. These tablets contain ritual performances which might be analyzed from a narrative point of view.

[25] On *dbḥ*, see de Tarragon (1980) 56-58.

[26] *dǵṯ* is usually seen as a Hittite borrowing, and may even be connected with the word *tuḫḫuessar*, perhaps some sort of purifying material and/or incense. See Hoffner (1964), de Moor (1965) 355-56, and Alp (1983) for some of the basic issues.

tively joyful nature of the occasion.[27] Joy is certainly to be seen in the accompanying music made by cymbals (*mṣltm*) and ivory dance-instruments (*mrqdm dšn*).[28]

The happiness comprehended in this feast is, of course, not of the same degree as that which Daniʾil experienced when he received the gods' blessing or when the Kotharat and then Kothar-wa-Hasis visited him. This may explain in part why the description is brief. Its brevity may also be due to a development within the feast situation itself. Pughat uses it to ask her father to bless her so that she can avenge ʾAqhat's death. The purpose of the feast is thus altered. The reminder that the balances of justice have not been evened out qualifies the joyous atmosphere. Complete satisfaction still awaits.

This sacrifice has parallels with the first feast in the story. That one begins with mourning and turns to cheer. The present feast similarly provides a passage from mourning to relative joy. In both feasts blessings follow, which are formulated in a similar way and set the stage for happier developments. The rites are also free of infelicity. This resemblance creates the impression that we have a new beginning at this point in the story.

One difference between the feasts, however, cannot be ignored. The first has the gods appearing on the scene as active participants, speaking to Daniʾil and blessing him. Here, however, they are not given a role. This is felt most keenly when Daniʾil blesses Pughat. One might expect the gods to do this, to help Daniʾil right the wrong he has suffered. As the story continues the gods do not appear. The sphere of action is now only the human world. This creates the impression that even though Daniʾil has returned to sacrifice, there is still some strain between the human and the divine.

As the *dbḥ* parallels the initial petition feast, the ensuing wine service to Yaṭupan parallels the feast situations in which ʿAnat kills ʾAqhat: Pughat uses deceit as ʿAnat did to rid herself of a foe. This ironic tactic entails

---

27 On incense as a sign of joy in the Bible, *cf.* Leviticus 5: 11; Numbers 5: 15.

28 *Cf.* these instruments (and others) in 1.108: 4-5. This hymn presupposes a feasting context (drinking, 1, 6, 10, 13; eating, 9). The instruments are played by a god. The context is a joyous celebration.

Pughat's dressing up as ʿAnat in order to gain access to Yaṭupan. As part of her preparations and disguise, Pughat rouges herself,[29] and she puts on a male garment and a dagger, over which she places a female garment. Her costume is not detected, and she is received as Yaṭupan's employer (*agrt*). The deceit here is internal, rather than external as in the case of ʿAnat, as noted above. Pughat becomes a participant in the rite in order carry out her design. When the two strategies are compared, it appears that Pughat's is the more daring. She subjects herself to detection and danger for a sustained period until she finds her opportunity. Once committed she cannot turn back. ʿAnat, in contrast, could have withdrawn at the last minute.

The ritual situation in this last case is serving wine to Yaṭupan.[30] This is the least elaborate of the feasts we have encountered, but it still involves ritualized action. The drinking occurs in two rounds (1.19 IV 54-56, 60), and it is unusual in that it has, at least according to Yaṭupan's point of view, a deity serving an underling. Perhaps this is part of the deal that ʿAnat worked out with Yaṭupan for his service. If so, it is another indication, in addition to the promise of eternal life to ʾAqhat, that the goddess is willing to advance the status of humans in one way or another when they comply with her wishes.

The tablet ends before we know what happens in this wine fest, but it is reasonable to think that, in view of stories such as Ehud and Eglon (Judges 3), Jael and Sisera (Judges 4-5), and especially Judith and Holofernes, Pughat dispatches Yaṭupan with the hidden dagger while he is incapacitated by drunkenness. One can only imagine how she makes her escape, how she keeps her act from being detected before she gets away, how she verifies her success to her father and family, and how he and the gods react.

The last two extant feasts gain particular significance against the triad of felicitous and the dyad of infelicitous rituals at the beginning of the story. It has already been noted that the *dbḥ* parallels the first rite in the initial triad and that the wine service to Yaṭupan parallels the second feast

---

29 This may be equally part of preparing for battle or other hostilities. *Cf.* 1.3 II 38-III 2; IV 42-46; 1.14 II 9-11; III 52-54.

30 On the meaning of the verb *šqy* in this passage, see note 9, above.

in the infelicitous dyad. By pointing to the first and last feasts in the triad-dyad group, the last feasts symbolically echo the entire inaugural pentad. But in doing this they stand in significant contrast. The movement from felicitous to infelicitous ritual at the beginning of the story leads to catastrophe; the movement from felicitous to infelicitous ritual at the end leads to consolation.

Mourning and Recovery

As noted above, a large portion of the story's middle deals with responses to the loss of ᵓAqhat (1.18 IV 38-1.19 IV 17). This does not include feasts, only mourning activities, prayers for recovery, and curses. ᶜAnat is the first to mourn and does so, surprisingly, immediately after ᵓAqhat dies (1.18 IV 38-1.19 I 19). Since this specific section is the most problematic of the existing text, I will postpone discussing it until after inspecting the responses by Daniᵓil and Pughat, which immediately follow ᶜAnat's response and which form a definable unit (1.19 I 19-IV 17). The father's and daughter's reactions display a coherent logic and structure. As they gain knowledge about ᵓAqhat's death, their ritual responses change in purpose and increase in formal complexity.

When the story turns back to Daniᵓil after ᶜAnat killed ᵓAqhat, it finds him tending to judicial duties, as he was doing when Kothar-wa-Hasis came with the bow (1.19 I 19-25). Pughat comes on the scene and observes that there is a drought, that plants are failing, and that vultures are flying over her father's house (I 26-33). This is all the result of ᵓAqhat's death, but neither she nor Daniᵓil knows of this event. She weeps (*tbky, tdmᶜ*), but only "in the heart" (I 34-35). Mourning on the part of Daniᵓil's family thus begins with the most minimal of responses.

It is Daniᵓil's turn next. He utters a prayer (1.19 I 36-48) in which he hopes for precipitation and dew and expresses the fear that Baᶜl—his effects—might be absent for a long time.[31] Daniᵓil apparently offers this

31 See Dietrich and Loretz (1986) 99-100 on interpreting *šbʿ šnt yṣrk bʿl etc.* as an expression of fear.

prayer, for lack of an indication otherwise, at the gate where he performs his judicial duties. Therefore, he is essentially at home. This, however, is not the first mourning activity undertaken by Daniᵓil. Enveloping his prayer are statements that he had rent his clothing.[32] He presumably did this when or even before Pughat came. Nevertheless, in the sequence of narration, if not in the actual chronology of the story, it is only now, after Pughat's silent mourning is described, that the rending of clothing is mentioned. Thus more vivid external responses are perceived to follow simpler internal response.

Daniᵓil's reaction is compounded further in what follows.[33] Instead of uttering a single prayer near home, he takes to the road with the help of Pughat to perform a rite which has two prayers (1.19 II 10-25). He stops at two places in his field(s) where plant shoots are emerging. He embraces and kisses each of them. One must imagine Daniᵓil doing this while kneeling or lying on the ground so as not to destroy the plants. For each plant he prays that it will flourish and that ᵓAqhat will harvest it. The mention of ᵓAqhat just here, in addition to the more elaborate actions, adds to the feeling of heightened description. ᵓAqhat has been ignored by the father and daughter until now—and just before they find out that ᵓAqhat is dead.

After messengers arrive with the sad news, Daniᵓil performs rites of greater scope, all with verbal components. He first conjures the vultures to fall from the sky so that he can rip them open and find his son's remains and bury them (1.19 II 56-III 41). These birds are no doubt to be understood as those flying about Daniᵓil's house when Pughat comes on the scene and also those who earlier fly over ᵓAqhat during the feast in which he was killed. Daniᵓil must conjure the birds thrice before succeeding in finding the remains. In these performances his concern is no longer for remedying nature, but for discovery. This turns to reprisal when, on the third occasion, he does not have Baᶜl restore the vulture as he did in the earlier cases. He

---

32 The interpretation of *tmzʿ* as a passive and connected with the Arabic *mazaʿa* "run, bound,...tear, rip" is still the best option. See, however, the objections and alternative interpretation of Margalit (1989) 359-60.

33 Pughat may be mourning outwardly in II 8-9 if *bkm* is from the root *bky*.

leaves her disemboweled, apparently as punishment for ingesting ᵓAqhat. The new theme of punishment continues when he next utters a capstone curse on all vultures who would disturb ᵓAqhat's remains.

Another threefold ritual and recitation (1.19 III 46-IV 6) follows the threefold conjuration of the vultures and its accentuating curse. In this one, however, Daniᵓil is itinerant, as he was in the earlier two-part prayer for the plants in the field. He goes to various places near which ᵓAqhat was killed, finally ending at ᵓAbilum, the town where, or near which, ᵓAqhat was killed. These curses continue the theme of punishment inaugurated in the conjuration of the vultures.

The structural intensification in this section can be represented schematically as: a → b1b → 2 | → 3 + 1 → 3, where "a" refers to Pughat's inward mourning, "b1b" to Daniᵓil's single prayer for rain and the surrounding statements that he had ripped his clothing, "2 " to his dual prayer for the shoots in the field, "3 + 1" to his threefold conjuration of vultures plus the capping curse, and the last "3" to the curses on the three locales. Over the course of the whole section there is a movement from the simple to the complex. But it also breaks down into two parallel subsections, as marked by the dividing line |, each having a similar pattern of development. The subsections begin with stationary rites and end with those performed itinerantly. In this way each subsection conveys a sense of intensification by having ritual apply to a larger domain.[34]

The overall structural intensification correlates with the evolution of the performances' goals and purposes. The rites performed before finding out about the death of ᵓAqhat are rather diffuse and externally oriented, toward nature. Though they seek healing for Daniᵓil's own fields, a cure will benefit a larger geographical area. When Daniᵓil learns of ᵓAqhat's death his goals become more personal and focused, certainly much more heated emotionally. He first wants to find ᵓAqhat's body or what is left of it. Then he begins to retaliate, and this grows in the precision of its scope. He first

---

[34] One can also note that each section begins with rites that have vertical reference, to something above (rain/Baᶜl and vultures), and end in rituals that have horizontal reference, to the worldly plane (plants in the field and various locales).

attacks the vultures, who did not kill ᵓAqhat, but only mopped up afterwards. Next, he curses the locales, who, again did not directly kill ᵓAqhat, but in the context of Ugaritic and Near Eastern legal and religious perspective might be considered responsible for those killed in their proximity or jurisdiction.[35] The focus of retaliation becomes even more precise when we look beyond this main block of mourning and recovery rites to include Pughat's assault on Yaṭupan. This takes care of the instrument of ᵓAqhat's death. It is interesting, however, that neither Daniᵓil nor Pughat, as far as we know, makes any move against ᶜAnat, the ultimate cause of ᵓAqhat's death. They are too pious—or too smart.

The rites of mourning in the middle of the story, along with the following briefly described seven-year mourning (1.19 IV 9-22), and the concluding *dbḥ* lead the players—and readers—out of the disaster. They are rites of crisis which are similar in their dynamics to *rites de passage.*[36] The main difference between the two is that, in the former, separation—movement into a liminal situation—is imposed by accident, not through ritual plan and means.[37] The two types are similar, however, in having rites that pertain to the marginal or liminal period and rites that have the purpose of aggregation and reintegration. The conflict between ᶜAnat and ᵓAqhat led to an upset in structure, to use Victor Turner's analytical term: the web of relationships between humans and the gods has been torn and damaged.[38] The rites for agricultural healing, recovering ᵓAqhat's body, and curse of the vultures and locales redefine the disturbed world. The *dbḥ* at the end of the liminal period restores feasting, the ritual activity that, in our story, is a primary means of creating structure.

---

35 *Cf.* Heltzer (1976) 65; Wright (1987) and Hammurabi's Laws §§23-24; Hittite Law §IV.

36 Van Gennep (1960) 10-11 (and *passim*) set out the basic pattern in *rites de passage.* They are composite rituals with three main phases: rites of separation, rites of transition (= liminal/marginal rites), and rites of incorporation (reintegration, aggregation).

37 As, for example, in the *rites de passage* for the consecration of priests in Leviticus 8-9. See Leach (1976) 89-91 (*cf.* 77-79) for an analysis. Impurity and recovery therefrom involve rites of crisis which are comparable to *rites de passage* (see Wright [1991] 173-74).

38 Turner (1969) 94-130 and *passim.*

The difficult passage describing ᶜAnat's mourning, which comes immediately after the death of ᵓAqhat (1.18 IV 38-1.19 I 19), appears to parallel to some degree the pattern of intensification found in Daniᵓil's and Pughat's responses. She seems to respond with two laments, the second of which is much more complex than the first.

The first lament is rather easy to delineate. The text says that she weeps (*tbk*, 1.18 IV 39). This is followed by lines with first person verbs and pronouns referring to ᶜAnat and second person pronouns referring to ᵓAqhat (IV 40-41). ᶜAnat is speaking to ᵓAqhat and regrets his loss. The text then exits citation and speaks about ᶜAnat again in the third person (1.19 I 2-3): she grieves (*tkrb*?) and falls (*tql*). At this point the bow is broken (*tṯbr qšt*, I 3-4).

The second speech is more difficult to demarcate. De Moor's solution that has ᶜAnat speaking from *ša tlm* (1.19 I 6) to the end of the scene just before returning to Daniᵓil (I 19 through *bǵlph*) is reasonable.[39] Understood this way, the speech breaks down into two parallel parts (I 6 *ša*-10 || 11-19 *bǵlph*). Each begins with a cry of mourning which other beings or entities recite: *kmr kmr(m)* "How utterly bitter!" (I 6 *ša*-7 *kmr* [*kmr*] || 11-12). In the first, the cry is what the "Furrow" (*tlm*) is to call out.[40] In the second it is what the *gprm* persons/beings are saying. ᶜAnat's own laments follow each of these parts. In the first (I 7 *ydh*-10) she may be lamenting the warrior potential that was forfeited by ᵓAqhat's death.[41] In the second (I 13-19) she reiterates her part in his death, her failure to obtain the bow, and the deleterious effects ᵓAqhat's death has had upon agricultural concerns. By mentioning agricultural concerns she ends with the same topic with which

39 De Moor (1987) 247-48.

40 See also Dietrich and Loretz (1979) 196.

41 I provisionally translate 1.19 I 7b-10:

> His arms were like a flash(?),
> like a flame, his fingers,
> like a cutter, his mouthstones.
> His teeth would lay hold and consume,
> among/against the enemies they would set a/the cutter,
> (like?) a divine/chthonic dog.

she started (cf. the *tlm* "Furrow" in line 7) and provides a transition to Pughat's and Daniʾil's responses to agricultural failure which directly follow.

If this understanding is correct, then ʿAnat's responses increase in complexity. First comes a short lament and then, when the bow breaks, a longer complex lament with two parts, each of which are further subdividable into two parts. This intensification correlates roughly with what is found in the following responses by Pughat and Daniʾil. Especially noteworthy is that in ʿAnat's series an event occurs after the first recitation—the breaking of the bow—which gives rise to the exacerbated second recitation. A similar event occurs in Daniʾil's series of responses. After his agricultural rites he is informed of ʾAqhat's death. This leads to the more intensive reactions of thrice conjuring the vultures and thrice cursing the locales. Thus ʿAnat's mourning establishes a pattern that is replicated in Daniʾil's.

Conclusion

The foregoing shows that the various types of ritual (felicitous and infelicitous, joyous and sorrow-filled), as well as the patterned groups of ritual (blocks of similar types or evolutionary concatenations), contribute significantly to the articulation of the plot, the creation of different moods, and the description and portrayal of characters in the ʾAqhat story. Ritual is particularly suited for this task in narrative because of its expressive nature.[42] While it is not a form of communication of the same sort as language, the actions and objects involved are symbolic, in various ways and at different levels. Ritual as symbol in real life defines the status of individuals, marks transitions, celebrates joy, makes the endurance of misfortune possible, and otherwise creates reality for participants. These functions persist in ritual within narrative. The main difference is that, instead of being participants in the rites, readers and hearers are observers. Nevertheless, story may act such as to draw them in so that they become virtual participants through sympathetic identification with characters.

---

42 *Cf.* Leach (1976).

A question that naturally grows out of the preceding study is why ritual is so prevalent and important in the text. One might imagine that the text had a cultic use, which has left an imprint on the story. But this is doubtful. Even if we grant that the story had a cultic use, a questionable thesis in the first place, the nature of ritual in the text does not match the interests of such a context. The ritual elements that appear are not solely cultic (*i.e.*, dealing with temple, priesthood, sacrifice, and/or purity). Many operate outside of a cultic milieu, especially the mourning and recovery rites. The performances in the story also have a private or domestic rather than communal, official, and high-liturgical orientation. Lastly, the story seems very much interested in dealing with what can be called "dark ritual," *i.e.*, infelicitous performances or those that involve negative emotions and situations. This does not coordinate well with a cultic use in which ritual is expected to be proper and celebrative.

Other factors are probably responsible for the concentration of ritual in the story. The story is primarily about the interaction of humans and deities. In the real life cultural world of the ancient Near East such interactions were largely viewed as occurring in and facilitated by ritual contexts. Thus it would be natural for an author to employ these contexts to describe how gods and humans interact in narrative. This hypothesis is supported by the similar preponderance of ritual in the Kirta tale, which also treats dealings between the human and divine sphere, versus the relatively more limited occurrence in the Baᶜl cycle, which deals with matters only on the divine plane. Another factor may have been the symbolic force ritual has, as noted above. With an economy of words it communicates much to readers and hearers. Ritual may play a large role too because of the power dark ritual has in a narrative context. Positive ideal ritual is relatively static; it brings about an equilibrium. It is therefore not very stimulating. Dark ritual, in contrast, has a dynamic character. It either undoes ideal ritual or it embodies a struggle to return to an ideal situation. Doing so, it engages the imagination.

Bibliography

Aitken, K. T. (1989) Oral Formulaic Composition and Theme in the Aqhat Narrative. *Ugarit Forschungen* 21: 1-16. **Alp, S.** (1983) Zum Wesen der kultischen Reinigungssubstanz *tuḫḫueššar* und die Verbalform *tuḫša. Orientalia* n.s. 52: 14-19. **Anderson, G. A., and S. M. Olyan**, eds. (1991) *Priesthood and Cult in Ancient Israel. Journal for the Study of the Old Testament.* Supplement 125. Sheffield, England. **Austin, J. L.** (1975) *How to Do Things with Words.* 2nd ed. Ed. J. O. Urmson and M. Sbisà. Cambridge, Mass. **Bell, C.** (1992) *Ritual Theory, Ritual Practice.* New York. **Caquot, A., and M. Sznycer** (1974) *Textes ougaritiques: Tome I: mythes et légendes.* Paris. (1980) *Ugaritic Religion.* Iconography of Religions 15/8. Leiden. **Dietrich, M., and O. Loretz** (1979) Einzelfragen zu Wörtern aus den ugaritischen Mythen und Wirtschaftstexten: zur ugaritischen Lexikographie (XV). *Ugarit Forschungen* 11: 189-98. (1986) *ṣrk* im Kontext der Rede Danils in KTU 1.19 I 38-46. *Ugarit Forschungen* 18: 97-100. **Dietrich, M., O. Loretz, and J. Sanmartín** (1995) *The Cuneiform Alphabetic Texts from Ugarit, Ras Ibn Hani and Other Places* (KTU; second, enlarged edition). Münster **Dijkstra, M., and J. G. de Moor** (1975) Problematical Passages in the Legend of Aqhâtu. *Ugarit Forschungen* 7: 171-215. **van Gennep, A.** (1960) *The Rites of Passage.* Chicago. [Original 1908.] **Grimes, R. L.** (1990) *Ritual Criticism: Case Studies in Its Practice, Essays on Its Theory.* Columbia, S.C. **Heltzer, M.** (1976) *The Rural Community in Ancient Ugarit.* Wiesbaden. **Hoffner, H. A.** (1964) An Anatolian Cult Term in Ugaritic. *Journal of Near Eastern Studies* 23: 66-68. **Huehnergard, J.** (1987) *Ugaritic Vocabulary in Syllabic Transcription.* Harvard Semitic Series 32. Atlanta. **Leach, E.** (1976) *Culture and Communication: The Logic by which Symbols are Connected.* Themes in the Social Sciences. Cambridge. **Lloyd, J. B.** (1990) The Banquet Theme in Ugaritic Narrative. *Ugarit Forschungen* 22: 169-93. **Margalit, B.** (1989) *The Ugaritic Poem of AQHT.* Beiheft zur Zeitschrift für die alttestamentliche Wissenschaft 182. Berlin. **de Moor, J. C.** (1965) Frustula Ugaritica. *Journal of Near Eastern Studies* 24: 355-64. (1971) *The Seasonal Pattern in the Ugaritic Myth of* Baᶜlu *According to the Version of Ilimilku.* Alter Orient und altes Testament 16. Neukirchen-Vluyn. (1987) *An Anthology of Religious Texts from Ugarit.* Nisaba 16. Leiden. **de Moor, J. C., and K. Spronk** (1987) *A Cuneiform Anthology of Religious Texts from Ugarit.* Semitic Study Series 6. Leiden. **Pardee, D.** (1977) An Emendation in the Ugaritic Aqhat Text. *Journal of Near Eastern Studies* 36: 53-56. **Parker, S. B.** (1989) *The Pre-Biblical Narrative Tradition: Essays on the Ugaritic Poems* Keret *and* Aqhat. Society of Biblical Literature Resources for Biblical Study 24. Atlanta. **Pritchard, J. B.** (1954) *The Ancient Near East in Pictures.* Princeton. **Segert, S.** (1984) *Basic Grammar of the Ugaritic Language.* **de Tarragon, J.-M.** (1980) *Le culte à Ugarit.* Cahiers de la Revue Biblique 19. Paris. **Tropper, J.** (1988) Ugaritisch *ndy, ydy, hdy, ndd* und *d(w)d. Ugarit Forschungen* 20: 339-50. (1990) *Der ugaritische Kausativstamm und die Kausativbildungen des Semitischen: Eine morphologisch-semantische Untersuchung zum Š-Stamm und zu den umstrittenen nichtsibilantischen Kausativstämmen des Ugaritischen.* Abhandlungen zur Literatur Alt-Syrien-Palästinas 2. Münster. **Tsevat, M.** (1986) Eating and Drinking, Hosting and Sacrificing in the Epic of

Aqht. *Ugarit Forschungen* 18: 345-50. **Turner, V.** (1969) *The Ritual Process: Structure and Anti-Structure.* Ithaca, N.Y. **Wright, D. P.** (1987) Deuteronomy 21: 1-9 as a Rite of Elimination. *Catholic B iblical Quarterly* 49: 387-403. (1991) The Spectrum of Priestly Impurity. In Anderson and Olyan 1991: 150-81.

Herodotus—Historian or Liar?

Edwin M. Yamauchi
Miami University, Oxford, Ohio

It is a privilege to honor a great scholar, Michael Astour, whose erudition even as a graduate student at Brandeis awed those of us who were studying with him under Cyrus H. Gordon. In his magisterial work, *Hellenosemitica*, based on his dissertation, Astour brilliantly analyzes the authentic core of Phoenician tradition contained in Herodotus' account (4.147) of the settlement of the island of Thera.[1] He concludes, "Our analysis established an important precedent as to the trustworthiness of Herodotus' information on Phoenicians inside his own Greek world."[2] Elsewhere in identifying the Semitic elements in the cult of Dionysos, Astour notes: "This close connection of the timbrel, sparagmos and omophagia in just five short lines of the Ugaritic fragment shows that Herodotus (2.49) was on the right track in presuming that the Greeks 'learned about the cult of Dionysos mostly from the Tyrian Cadmos and from those who came together with him from Phoenicia into the land which is now called Boeotia'."[3]

I would like to review recent assessments of Herodotus' work in the light of what we now know about the Egyptians, Babylonians, Medes, Scythians, and Persians.

1 Astour (1965) 113-14.

2 *Ibid.*, 127.

3 *Ibid.*, 181.

A. Herodotus[4]

Herodotus was born in Halicarnassus in southwestern Turkey about 484 BCE. After the Peace of Callias in 449 ended hostilities between Greece and Persia, he traveled to Egypt and Babylonia and also visited Scythia (the Ukraine).[5] Herodotus lived in Athens in the 440s and 430s. At the end of his life, he participated in the colonization of Thurii in southern Italy, where he died about 420 BCE.

Herodotus published his famous *History of the Persian Wars* at Athens c. 445. Though he came from a Dorian area, he wrote in the Ionic dialect. He wished to describe the Great Event of the 5th century, Greece's amazing defeat of the enormous army and navy of the Persian king, Xerxes. For his readers to fully appreciate the enormity of that achievement, he described Persia's prior expansion over Babylonia, Lydia, Scythia, and Egypt.

Herodotus was an indefatigable investigator, but he was dependent at times upon dubious sources, especially in his travels abroad. He did try to check his sources, and often acknowledged that information was lacking. He loved to tell a good story, even when he himself did not believe it to be true,[6] such as the circumnavigation of Africa (4.42).[7] He recorded with wonder, but with respect, customs of foreigners which seemed bizarre to Greeks. Just as the contemporaries of Marco Polo did not believe the account of his travels in the Far East in the 13th century, many of Herodotus' contemporaries did not believe he was telling the truth.

Herodotus was the first great prose writer of Classical Greece. He was called "The Father of History" by Cicero.[8] But Manetho, an Egyptian priest, objected to Herodotus' description of Egypt. Moreover Ctesias, who was a

---

4 See Drews (1973); Hart (1982); DeWald and Marincola (1987) 9-40; see also Yamauchi (1992a).

5 See Redfield (1985) 97-118. For a sceptical view of Herodotus' travels to Scythia, see Armayor (1978a) 45-62.

6 Waters (1985) 155.

7 Lloyd (1977) 148-55, questions this account, but its truth has been accepted by Cary and Warmington (1963) ch. 5.

8 But it should be noted that Cicero, in the same sentence (*De Legibus* I.1.5), links him

Greek physician at the Persian court, denounced Herodotus' account of the Persians as inaccurate, and Herodotus' generous treatment of the Persians earned the scorn of Plutarch, who in his *On the Malice of Herodotus* accused Herodotus of being a *philobarbaros*, "a lover of barbarians." Debate as to whether Herodotus should be viewed as the "Father of History" or the "Father of Lies" has persisted to the present day.[9] The latter reputation prevailed from the Middle Ages to the Renaissance. It was the discovery of the New World which, in revealing customs as unbelievable as those reported by Herodotus, revived interest in Herodotus' accounts. In the 16th century Henri Estienne (Henricus Stephanus) came to Herodotus' defense.

But later Herodotus was severely attacked in the 18th century by J.-B. Bonnaud and in the 19th century by A. H. Sayce.[10] His severest critics today are D. Fehling and O. K. Armayor. Fehling accuses Herodotus of making up his sources.[11] Defenders of Herodotus, such as W. Kendrick Pritchett, have responded to such criticisms in detail.[12]

Archaeology and inscriptions have confirmed the existence of such legendary figures in Herodotus as Midas (Her. 1.14,35), the Phrygian king who lived at the end of the 8th century BCE, the Lydian Gyges (Her. 1.8-15), who is credited with the invention of coinage, and the fabulously wealthy Croesus of Sardis (Her. 1.29-33, 70; 6.125). Midas is attested as *Mita* in the records of the Assyrian king, Sargon II.[13] Excavations directed by Rodney Young at his capital city, Gordium, have uncovered rich furniture which illustrates Herodotus' (1.14) remarks about a throne dedicated by Midas at Delphi.[14] A skeleton in a royal tumulus has even been identified by some as

---

with Theompompus as follows: *et apud Herodotum, patrem historiae, et apud Theopompum sunt innumerabiles fabulae* "in the works of Herodotus, the Father of History, and in those of Theopompus, one finds innumerable fabulous tales."

9 Evans (1986) 11-17.

10 Sayce (1883).

11 Fehling (1989).

12 Pritchett (1993).

13 Olmstead (1951) 221-22; Yamauchi (1982) 26-27.

14 DeVries (1980b) observes: "While gold is lacking and ivory scanty, fine furniture is

that of the famous Midas.[15] Gyges is mentioned in Assyrian texts as *Gugu.*[16] The tomb of Gyges has been found at Sardis,[17] though there is still controversy over whether coinage was invented at such an early date.[18] Croesus was said to have derived his wealth from the gold extracted from the sands of the Pactolus River, which flowed past Sardis.[19] In 1924 T. L. Shear denied that the ancient Lydians were able to exploit the gold of the Pactolus. But in 1968 excavations conducted under G. Hanfmann at Sardis uncovered installations for the purification of gold dating from the time of Croesus.[20]

B. EGYPT[21]

Armayor claims that Herodotus' description of the Labyrinth and Lake Moeris was not based on his observations in Egypt but was patterned after literary models from Homer.[22] Though no one doubts that Herodotus visited the Delta region, some scholars still question whether he visited Upper Egypt because of his failure to say much about the great hypostyle

---

abundant, and the dazzlingly complete state in which some pieces were found, especially in MM, reveals just what luxurious items they could be, with extensive inlays of contrasting wood."

15 Mellink (1959) 100-9; Akurgal (1970) 279-83; and Scurr (1989) 36-41.

16 Cogan and Tadmor (1977) 65-85; Spalinger (1978) 400-9; and Yamauchi (1982) 23-24.

17 Hanfmann (1980) 100 proposes this identification: "As to the strange sign … I read it as a gamma of Greek form plus Lydian upsilon and as a monogram for GuGu or King Gyges. The identification as the mound of Gyges is, in any case, made probable by a poem of the archaic Ephesian poet Hipponax. The wall and the monogram would then date around 645 B.C., the year King Gyges fell battling the Kimmerian invaders in front of Sardis." See also Hanfmann (1972) 153-59.

18 In favor of the tradition, see Yamauchi (1980a) 269-92; Kagan (1982) 1-18.

19 Pedley (1969).

20 Hanfmann (1972) 230-34; Hanfmann and Waldbaum (1970) 311; Yamauchi (1980b) ch. 5.

21 For the refutation of the charge that Herodotus invented his account of Egypt, see Spiegelberg (1927). For a detailed analysis of Herodotus' account of Egypt, see Lloyd (1975). See also Lloyd (1976) and(1988a).

22 Armayor (1985). See also Armayor (1978b) 59-74.

hall at Karnak. A. B. Lloyd, however, believes that Herodotus' errors and omissions can be explained. He affirms, "We can therefore accept that Herodotus traversed the entire length of Upper Egypt calling at Moeris, the Labyrinth, Chemmis, Thebes, and Elephantine at the very least."[23]

His account of early Egyptian history (2.99-142) is a grab-bag of folklore, though he correctly identified the first pharaoh as Min (Menes), and the builders of the three great pyramids at Giza as Cheops (Khufu), Chephren (Khafre), and Mycerinus (Menkaure).[24] His account of the Saite era (26th Dynasty), that is of the 7th to 6th centuries, is quite accurate.[25]

In some cases, observations made by Herodotus thought to be erroneous by scholars, have later been corroborated. John Wilson comments:

> Let us take the pig. Herodotus tells us (II, 14) that, after the farmer had sown his grain, he drove pigs into the fields to tread the grain into the soil. For a time modern scholars said that the pig was an unclean animal and there were no pigs in ancient Egypt. Then they found pictures in the Egyptian tombs, showing pigs following a man who was sowing grain, in order that their sharp little hoofs would tread in the grain. Herodotus had been right.[26]

A great deal of controversy has raged over Herodotus' account of the Persian conquest of Egypt by Cambyses in 525 BCE.[27] Among the most acute problems is Herodotus' account (3.27) which describes the Persian king in a rage stabbing the Apis bull. We have monumental evidence of two Apis bulls in the reign of Cambyses, though there are complicated chronological problems involved.[28] As one of the sarcophagi was dedicated by Cambyses

---

23 Lloyd (1975) 75.

24 Lloyd (1988b) 22-53.

25 According to Lloyd (1975) 194 "The details of his Egyptian Chronology are surprisingly accurate. Most of the main periods are mentioned and the Saite chronology is only seriously out in the case of Apries. Herodotus giving him a reign of 25 years instead of 19."

26 Wilson (1970) 2.

27 See T. S. Brown (1982) 387-403; Lloyd (1988c) 55-66.

28 Depuyt (1995a) 201-2.

himself, this seems to be a clear case where archaeological evidence contradicts Herodotus.[29] Wilson declares, "The story about the Persian king Cambyses stabbing the Apis bull and thus incurring the anger of the gods for his impiety does not bear historical scrutiny, because Cambyses is recorded as having piously dedicated an Apis bull to the temple."[30] But a recent study by Leo Depuydt has raised the possibility that we may not be certain that even in this case Herodotus was wrong.[31]

More decisive in supporting the view that Herodotus was misinformed by anti-Persian Egyptian sources is the evidence of the Egyptian collaborator, Udjahorresnet, who wrote of Cambyses in a positive fashion during the reign of Darius,[32] as opposed to Herodotus' description of his highly erratic behavior.

C. Babylon[33]

A. H. Sayce in 1883 had questioned whether Herodotus had ever gone to Babylon. But the excavations of Robert Koldewey there from 1899 to 1913 vindicated Herodotus, though he had greatly exaggerated the length and the height of the walls.[34] Herodotus noted that the Euphrates River bisected the city, and that the two halves were connected by a bridge. Koldewey discovered the foundations of the bridge. Herodotus' account (1.199) of prostitution in the temple of Aphrodite (Ishtar) is problematic. The clearest texts that deal with a *hieros gamos* come from the Sumerian period, rather than the Neo-Babylonian era.[35] His description of the auctioning off of brides in

---

29 Yamauchi (1990) 121-22.

30 Wilson (1970) 8.

31 Depuydt (1995b) 119-26.

32 Yamauchi (1990) 105-9; Lloyd (1982) 166-80. On the bearing of this important text on Ezra and Nehemiah, see Blenkinsopp (1987) 409-21.

33 For a detailed commentary, see McNeal (1986).

34 See Ravn (1942); Parrot (1956); LaRue (1969); Yamauchi (1985); Oates (1986); Wiseman (1985).

35 *Cf.* Yamauchi (1973) 214-16.

Babylon (1.196) appears to be closer to certain Greek customs than to Babylonian ones.[36]

Herodotus provides us with very little useful information about Babylonian history.[37] He promised a separate Assyrian account, which was never written. His Semiramis was probably the Assyrian Sammuramat, the mother of Adad-nirari III (811–784 BCE).[38] His other famous queen, Nitocris, may have been Naqi'a, one of the wives of Sennacherib, which would accord with the five generation interval between them (Her. 1.184).[39] Herodotus fails to mention the most famous Neo-Babylonian king, Nebuchadnezzar; his Labynetus is probably a reference to Nabonidus, the last Neo-Babylonian king.[40]

In a recent assessment of Herodotus' description of Babylon, J. MacGinnis cites as additionally erroneous elements Herodotus' identification of Assyria and Babylonia, and his account of date fertilization. He also lists as obscure or uncertain such items as 3- or 4-roofed Houses, Burial in Honey, Stairway of the Ziggurat, the Ardericca, and Fish-Eaters. On the other hand, he believes that Herodotus is correct in his account of the following: General Geography, Rainfall, Hit, Canals, Shadouf, Main Crops, Date-Palm, Boats, Double Walls, Quay Wall, Gates, Brick-making, Ziggurat Tower, Upper Temple, Lower Temple, Worship of Bel, Streets, the "Median Wall," and Seals.[41]

D. MEDES

Earlier scholars such as A. T. Olmstead had identified Herodotus' Deioces, the chieftain who united the Medes (Her. 1.96-99), with an individual named *Daiaukku* in the Assyrian texts.[42] But there are cogent reasons to

36 McNeal (1988) 54-71.

37 Baumgartner (1950); reprinted in Baumgartner(1959).

38 Thompson (1937).

39 Lewy (1951).

40 See Yamauchi (1986); Beaulieu (1989).

41 MacGinnis (1986) 81.

42 Olmstead (1908) 109.

doubt this identification.[43] The Median king called Phraortes has been identified by scholars with an individual named *Kashtariti*, but this identification has also been questioned.[44]

The value of Herodotus' account of the Medes, his *Medikos Logos*, has been disputed especially by P. R. Helm, who regards it as a mélange of oral accounts that have been artfully stitched together by Herodotus.[45] The lack of sufficient correlations with Neo-Assyrian texts causes H. Sancisi-Weerdenburg to doubt whether there ever was a Median Empire as described by Herodotus.[46]

Though Stuart C. Brown agrees in rejecting the proposed identifications of Deioces and Phraortes with individuals named in the cuneiform sources, and though he laments the lack of correlation with Neo-Assyrian texts, he believes that there still remains a considerable core of accurate traditions transmitted by Herodotus in his *Medikos Logos*.[47] In particular, he points to the accuracy of Herodotus' account of Astyages' reign. Following the lead of Louis Levine's geographical studies of the Zagros,[48] Brown argues that one should differentiate between the western Medes, who were in contact with the Assyrians, and those east of the Alvand range.[49] This could explain the lack of direct correlation between Herodotus and Assyrian sources. Brown concludes: "If, at a remove of some two centuries, they (i.e., refugee Persians in Greece) were correct in those details about the last two kings of Media, it is a reasonable working assumption that their oral tradition may also have preserved some reliable information about the first two kings of Media."[50]

---

43 Yamauchi (1990) 49.

44 *Ibid.* 51-52.

45 Helm (1981) 85-90.

46 Sancisi-Weerdenburg (1988) 197-212.

47 S. C. Brown (1988) 71-86.

48 Levine (1972) 39-45.

49 Brown (1988) 83-84.

50 Brown (1988) 86.

E. Scythians

Herodotus also provides us with invaluable information about the Scythians, a tribe of nomads who invaded the Near East from the Russian steppes.[51] He reports that the Scythians were pursuing the Cimmerians, another tribe, whose presence on the northern Assyrian frontier is well attested in cuneiform sources.[52] He reports that the Scythians dominated Asia for 28 years, during the Median era. Though some scholars have discounted Herodotus' account altogether,[53] there is archaeological evidence, such as the Ziwiyeh treasure[54] and the distribution of distinctive arrowheads which support his report.[55] J. Harmatta declares, "Historical research recognized long ago that Herodotus' comments on the Scythian rule over 'Upper Asia' and the operations of the Scythians in Transcaucasia and Northern Mesopotamia as well as on their raid into Palestine and Egypt are based on reliable sources and can be confirmed by other evidences."[56] However, his description of Darius' attack against the European Scythians has been severely questioned.[57] An extreme critic is F. Hartog, who analyzes Herodotus' account as a rhetorical discourse on the imaginary world of the Scythians.[58]

His account of the savage Scythian customs such as scalping and inhaling hemp fumes has been dramatically confirmed by the frozen burials of Pazyryk.[59] Further discoveries of frozen Scythian corpses include the so-

---

51 See Sulimirski and Taylor (1991) 547-90.

52 Sulimirski (1959) 45-64; Kristensen (1988); Ivantchik (1993).

53 Brown (1988) 82. On the problem, see Vaggione (1973) 523-30. On a possible solution, see Millard (1979) 119-22.

54 Sulimirski (1978) 7-33; Ghirshman (1979).

55 See Yamauchi (1982) ch. 4.

56 Harmatta (1990) 123.

57 Rybakov (1979); Nowak (1988); Harmatta (1990) 128; Yamauchi (1990) 160-61.

58 See Hartog (1988).

59 Artamonov (1965); Rudenko (1970); Rubinson (1975); Yamauchi (1982) ch. 6; Yamauchi (1983) 90-99.

called "Princess," discovered in 1993, and the "Horseman," discovered in 1995.[60]

F. Persians

Herodotus accurately describes the overthrow of the Medes in 550 by the first great Persian king, Cyrus, an account confirmed by a Babylonian chronicle. He most impressively renders correctly six of the seven names of Darius' co-conspirators as recorded in the Behistun inscription, as opposed to Ctesias, who gets only one of the names correct. There are, however, some scholars, who think that Darius made up the story of the murder of the usurper Gaumata (Smerdis), and that Herodotus was gullible in accepting the royal propaganda.[61] But despite some difficulties, others believe that the official version remains more credible than revisionist theories.[62]

One of the most suspect passages in Herodotus is the famed constitutional debate (3.80-88) before the accession of Darius, during which Otanes argued for democracy, Megabyzus for oligarchy, and Darius for monarchy. Almost all classicists have viewed this discussion as an artificial projection of Greek ideas into the mouths of Persian spokesmen.[63] But some Iranologists have argued that there may be elements in the passage that go back to Persian traditions.[64] Muhammed Dandamayev believes that the debate may reflect some of the motifs found in Darius' inscriptions.[65] Impressed by the accuracy of Herodotus' knowledge of Persian names, Rudiger Schmitt also argues that the passage contains authentic material and should not be dismissed as entirely fabricated.[66] A classicist, P. T. Brannan, noting coin-

---

60 Bahn (1994); Bahn (1996).

61 See especially Balcer (1987).

62 *E.g.*, Frye (1984) 99. See Yamauchi (1990) 143-45.

63 See Bringmann (1976) 266-79.

64 Gschnitzer (1977) 3l, calls attention to similar discussions in Judges 9:7-15 and 1 Samuel 8: 11-18.

65 Dandamayev (1976) 145, 163.

66 Schmitt (1977) 243-44.

cidences between Ctesias and Herodotus in the passage, has also concluded that the debate "May be prudently considered substantially historical."[67]

Herodotus remains our chief source for the Persian invasions of Greece in 490 and in 480–479. His work is indispensable for any historical account of the Persian and Greek conflict.[68] There are, to be sure, significant problems in attempts to correlate Herodotus' lists of the peoples of the Persian Empire with the cuneiform lists.[69] Despite his exaggeration of the Persian numbers, archaeology and topographical surveys have confirmed the general credibility of his accounts.[70]

In fact, when it became apparent that the important inscription discovered by Michael Jameson, the Themistocles' Decree,[71] contradicted Herodotus, not a few scholars have preferred to believe Herodotus' version in preference to that of the inscription.[72] M. Chambers concludes:

> The credibility of Herodotus has been upheld time and again in the recent studies of Greek topography by Professor Pritchett and in the microscopically thorough study of the second Persian War by Mr. Hignett. So far as concerns the general course of the war and the unfolding of the campaigns, Herodotus is largely unshakable.[73]

The partial publication of the Elamite Fortification and Treasury tablets from Persepolis, which date from the reigns of Darius and Xerxes, have provided a rich source for the testing of Herodotus.[74] Earlier scholars were

---

67 Brannan (1963) 438.

68 See Burn (1962) 1-17; Hignett (1963) 25-74.

69 See Armayor (1978c) 1-9; Yamauchi (1990) 178-80.

70 See especially the numerous articles of W. Kendrick Pritchett such as Pritchett (1957); (1959); (1961); (1963); and his monograph series (1969–82), and (1971–91).

71 Jameson (1960) and (1962).

72 On the considerable scholarly debate over the inscription's authenticity and implications, see Yamauchi (1990) 211-13.

73 Chambers (1967) 160.

74 On these tablets, see Yamauchi (1990) 189-90. For the bearing of these texts on biblical works such as Esther, Ezra, and Nehemiah, see Williamson (1991); Yamauchi (1992b).

certain that Herodotus had good Persian sources.[75] His account certainly features genuine Medo-Persian names.[76] Studies of these Elamite tablets by D. M. Lewis have provided evidence for the attestation of key leaders such as Datis, the commander of the Persian forces at Marathon in 490 BCE,[77] and many other individuals in positions of authority.[78] This includes some incidental references to royal women, who are otherwise absent from royal inscriptions and the reliefs of Persepolis.[79]

G. Conclusions

Though Herodotus has been attacked by critics ancient and modern for his flaws, few writers in antiquity observed as widely and as dispassionately as he did, or wrote in such an arresting manner. Lloyd concludes: "It is extremely doubtful whether any historian before modern times could have significantly improved on Herodotus' performance when faced with similar material and well-nigh certain that none would have made of it so consummate a literary masterpiece."[80] Arnaldo Momigliano observes:

> In other words Herodotus managed to produce a very respectable history mainly on the basis of sightseeing and oral tradition. He succeeded in putting together a trustworthy account of events he was too young to have witnessed and of countries whose languages he did not understood. … Herodotus' success in touring the world and handling oral traditions is something exceptional by any standard … .[81]

---

75 T. S. Brown (1987); see Yamauchi (1990) 137-38.

76 Schmitt (1976).

77 Lewis (1980).

78 Lewis (1985).

79 Sancisi-Weerdenburg (1983) 20-33 argues that Herodotus' depiction of Persian women belongs to literature rather than to history. Also see now M. Brosius, *Women in Ancient Persia* (Oxford, 1995) who spends a great deal of work criticizing Herodotus' account of Persian women.

80 Lloyd (1988b) 53.

81 Momigliano (1966) 129.

Donald Lateiner concludes that Herodotus does indeed deserve the title, "Father of History"—"Historiography as we know it was then created at one time and by one man, Herodotus."[82]

Bibliography

Adams, C. J., ed. (1972) *Iranian Civilization and Culture.* Montreal. **Akurgal, E.** (1970) *Ancient Civilizations and Ruins of Turkey.* Istanbul. **Armayor, O. K.** (1978a) Did Herodotus Ever Go to the Black Sea? *Harvard Studies in Classical Philology* 82: 45-62. (1978b) Did Herodotus Ever Go to Egypt? *Journal of the American Research Center in Egypt* 15: 59-74. (1978c) Herodotus' Catalogues of the Persian Empire in the Light of the Monuments and the Greek Literary Tradition. *Transactions of the American Philological Association* 108: 1-9. (1985) *Herodotus' Autopsy of the Fayoum: Lake Moeris and the Labyrinth of Egypt.* Amsterdam. **Artamonov, M. I.** (1965) Frozen Tombs of the Scythians. *Scientific American* 212.5: 101-9. **Astour, M. C.** (1965) *Hellenosemitica.* Leiden. **Bahn, P. G.** (1994) Scythian Burial. *Archaeology* 27.5: 27. (1996) Siberian Mummy Flap. *Archaeology* 33.1: 33. **Balcer, J. M.** (1987) *Herodotus and Bisitun.* Stuttgart. **Baumgartner, W.** (1950) Herodots babylonische und assyrische Nachrichten. *Archiv Orientální* 18: 69-106. (1959) *Zum Alten Testament und seiner Umwelt.* Leiden. **Beaulieu, P.-A.** (1989) *The Reign of Nabonidus King of Babylon 556-539 B.C.* New Haven. **Blenkinsopp, J.** (1987) The Mission of Udjahorresnet and Those of Ezra and Nehemiah. *Journal of Biblical Literature* 106: 409-21. **Boardman, J., *et al.***, eds. (1991) *The Cambridge Ancient History* III, pt. 2. Cambridge. **Brannan, P. T.** (1963) Herodotus and History: The Constitutional Debate Preceding Darius' Accession. *Traditio* 19: 427-38. **Bringmann, K.** (1976) Die Verfassungsdebatte bei Herodot 3, 80-82 und Dareios' Aufstieg zur Königsherrschaft. *Hermes* 104: 266-79. **Bromiley, G. W.**, ed. (1986) *The International Standard Bible Encyclopedia,* III. Grand Rapids. **Brown, S. C.** (1988) The Mêdikos Logos of Herodotus and the Evolution of the Median State. In Kuhrt, and Sancisi-Weerdenburg 1988: 71-86. **Brown, T. S.** (1982) Herodotus' Portrait of Cambyses. *Historia* 31: 387-403. **Burkert, W., *et al.***, eds. (1990) *Hérodote et les peuples non-Grecs.* Geneva. **Burn, A. R.** (1962) *Persia and the Greeks.* New York. **Cameron, A., and A. Kuhrt**, eds. (1983) *Images of Women in Antiquity.* London. **Cary, M., and E. H. Warmington** (1963) *The Ancient Explorers.* Baltimore. **Chambers, M.** (1967) The Significance of the Themistocles Decree. *Philologus* 111: 159-69. **Cogan, M., and H. Tadmor** (1977) Gyges and Assurbanipal. *Orientalia* 40: 65-85. **Dandamayev, M.** (1976) *Persien unter den ersten*

82 Lateiner (1989) 227.

Achämeniden. Wiesbaden. **Depuyt, L.** (1995a) Evidence for Accession Dating under the Achaemenids. *Journal of the American Oriental Society* 115: 193-204. (1995b) Murder in Memphis: The Story of Cambyses' Mortal Wounding of the Apis Bull (ca. 523 B.C.E.). *Journal of Near Eastern Studies* 54: 119-26. **DeVries, K.** (1980a) ed., *From Athens to Gordion.* Philadelphia. (1980b) Greeks and Phrygians in the Early Iron Age. In DeVries 1980a: 33-49. **DeWald, C., and J. Marincola** (1987) A Selective Introduction to Herodotean Studies. *Arethusa* 20: 9-40. **Drews, R.** (1973) *The Greek Accounts of Eastern History.* Washington, D.C. **Evans, J.** (1986) Father of History or Father of Lies: The Reputation of Herodotus. *Classical Journal* 64: 11-17. **Fehling, D.** (1989) *Herodotus and His "Sources."* Leeds. **Freedman, D. N.**, ed. (1992) *The Anchor Bible Dictionary* III. **Frye, R.N.** (1984) *The History of Ancient Iran.* Munich. **Ghirshman, R.** (1979) *Tombe Princière de Ziwiyé et le début de l'art animalier Scythe.* Leiden. **Gschnitzer, F.** (1977) *Die sieben Perser und das Königtum des Dareios.* **Hanfmann, G. M. A.** (1972) *Letters from Sardis.* Cambridge. (1980) On Lydian Sardis. In DeVries 1980: 99-131. **Hanfmann, G. M. A., and J. C. Waldbaum** (1970) New Excavations at Sardis. In Sanders 1970: 307-26. **Harmatta, J.** (1990) Herodotus, Historian of the Cimmerans and the Scythians. In Burkert 1990: 115-30. **Harrison, R. K.**, ed. (1985) *Major Cities of the Biblical World.* Nashville. **Hart, J.** (1982) *Herodotus and Greek History.* London. **Hartog, F.** (1988) *The Mirror of Herodotus.* **Helm, P. R.** (1981) Herodotus Mêdikos Logos and Median History. *Iran* 19: 85-90. **Hignett, C.** (1963) *Xerxes' Invasion of Greece.* Oxford. **Hoffner, H. A. Jr.**, ed. (1973) *Orient and Occident.* Alter Orient und Altes Testament 22. Kevelaer and Neukirchen-Vluyn. **Ivantchik, A.** (1993) *Les Cimmériens au Proche-Orient.* Göttingen. **Jameson, M. H.** (1960) A Decree of Themistokles from Troizen. *Hesperia* 29: 198-223. (1962) A Revised Text of the Decree of Themistokles from Troizen. *Hesperia* 31: 310-15. **Kagan, D.** (1982) The Dates of the Earliest Coins. *American Journal of Archaeology* 86: 1-18. **Kristensen, A. K. G.** (1988) *Who Were the Cimmerians and Where Did They Come from?* Copenhagen. **Kuhrt, A., and H. Sancisi-Weerdenburg**, eds. (1988) *Achamenid History III: Method and Theory.* Leiden. **LaRue, G. A.** (1969) *Babylon and the Bible.* Grand Rapids, Mich. **Lateiner, D.** (1989) *The Historical Method of Herodotus.* Toronto. **Levine, L. D.** (1972) Prelude to Monarchy: Iran and the Neo-Assyrian Empire. In Adams 1972: 39-45. **Lewis, D. M.** (1980) Datis the Mede. *Journal of Hellenic Studies.* 100: 194-95. (1985) Persians in Herodotus. In *The Greek Historians: Literature and History,* 101-17. Palo Alto, Calif. **Lewy, H.** (1951) Nitokris-Naqî-a. *Journal of Near Eastern Studies* 10: 264-86. **Lloyd, A. B.** (1975) *Herodotus Book II: Introduction.* Leiden. (1976) *Herodotus Book II, Commentary 1-98.* Leiden. (1977) Necho and the Red Sea. *Journal of Egyptian Archaeology* 63: 148-55. (1982) The Inscription of Udjahorresnet: A Collaborator's Testament. *Journal of Egyptian Archaeology* 68: 166-80. (1988a) *Herodotus Book II, Commentary 99-182.* Leiden. (1988b) Herodotus' Account of Pharaonic History. *Historia* 37: 22-53. (1988c) Herodotus on Cambyses, Some Thoughts on Recent Work. In Kuhrt and Sancisi-Weerdenburg 1988: 55-66. **MacGinnis, J.** (1986) Herodotus' Description of Babylon. *Bulletin of the Institute of Classical Studies* 33: 67-86. **McNeal, R. A.**, ed. (1986) *Herodotus: Book I.* Lanham, Md. (1988) The Brides of Babylon: Herodotus 1.196. *Historia* 37: 54-71. **Mellink, M.** (1959)

The City of Midas. *Scientific American* 201.1: 100-9. **Millard, A. R.** (1979) The Scythian Problem. In Ruffle 1979: 119-22. **Momigliano, A.** (1966) *Studies in Historiography.* London. **Nowak, T.** (1988) Darius' Invasion into Scythia: Geographical and Logistic Perspectives. Unpublished M.A. thesis, Miami University, Oxford, Ohio. **Oates, J.** (1986) *Babylon.* London. **Olmstead, A. T.** (1908) *Western Asia in the Days of Sargon of Assyria, 722-705 B.C.* New York. (1951) *History of Assyria.* Chicago. **Parrot, A.** (1942) *Babylon and the Old Testament.* New York. **Pedley, J. G.** (1969) *Sardis in the Age of Croesus.* Norman. **Pritchett, W. K.** (1957) New Light on Plataia. *American Journal of Archaeology* 61: 9-28. (1959) Towards a Restudy of the Battle of Salamis. *American Journal of Archaeology* 63: 251-62. (1961) Xerxes' Fleet at the "Ovens." *American Journal of Archaeology* 67: 1-6. (1969–82) *Studies in Ancient Greek Topography I-VI.* Berkeley. (1971–91) *The Greek State at War I-V.* Berkeley. (1993) *The Liar School of Herodotos.* **Ravn, O. E.** (1942) *Herodotus' Description of Babylon.* Copenhagen. **Redfield, J.** (1985) Herodotus the Tourist. *Classical Philology* 80: 97-118. **Rendsburg, G., R. Adler, M. Arfa, and N. H. Winter**, eds. (1980) *The Bible World: Essays in Honor of Cyrus H. Gordon.* New York. **Rubinson, K. S.** (1975) Herodotus and the Scythians. *Expedition* 17: 16-20. **Rudenko, S. I.** (1970) *Frozen Tombs of Siberia: The Pazyryk Burials of Iron Age Horsemen.* Berkeley. **Ruffle, J., *et al.***, eds. (1979) *Glimpses of Ancient Egypt.* Warminster. **Rybakov, B. A.** (1979) *Gerodotova Skifiia.* Moscow. **Sancisi-Weerdenburg, H.** (1983) Exit Atossa: Images of Women in Greek Historiography on Persia. In Cameron and Kuhrt 1983: 20-33. (1988) Was There Ever a Median Empire? In Kuhrt and Sancisi-Weerdenburg 1988: 197-212. **Sanders, J. A.**, ed. (1970) *Near Eastern Archaeology in the Twentieth Century.* Garden City, N.J. **Sayce, A. H.** (1883) *The Ancient Empires of the East: Herodotus I-III.* London. **Schmitt, R.** (1976) The Medo-Persian Names of Herodotus in the Light of the New Evidence from Persepolis. *Acta Antiqua Academiae Scientiarum Hungaricae* 24: 25-35. (1977) Die Verfassungsdebatte bei Herodot 3,80-82 und die Etymologie des Dareios-Namens. *Historia* 26: 243-44. **Scurr, D.** (1989) The Mask of Midas. *Aramco World Magazine* 40.5: 36-41. **Spalinger, A.** (1978) The Date of the Death of Gyges and Its Historical Implications. *Journal of the American Oriental Society* 98: 400-9. **Spiegelberg, W.** (1927) *The Credibility of Herdotus' Account of Egypt in the Light of the Egyptian Monuments.* Oxford. **Sulimirski, T.** (1959) The Cimmerian Problem. *Bulletin of the Institute of Archaeology* 2: 45-64. (1978) The Background of the Ziuwiye Find and Its Significance in the Development of Scythian Art. *Bulletin of the Institute of Art* 15: 7-33. **Sulimirski, T., and T. Taylor** (1991) The Scythians. In Boardman 1991: 547-90. **Thompson, R. C.** (1937) An Assyrian Parallel to an Incident in the Story of Semiramis. *Iraq* 4: 35-43. **Vaggione, R. P.** (1973) "Over All Asia?" The Extent of the Scythian Domination in Herodotus. *Journal of Biblical Literature* 92: 523-30. **Waters, K. H.** (1985) *Herodotos the Historian.* London. **Williamson, H. G. M.** (1991) Ezra and Nehemiah in the Light of the Texts from Persepolis. *Bulletin of the Institute for Biblical Research* 1: 41-62. **Wilson, J. A.** (1970) *Herodotus in Egypt.* Leiden. **Wiseman, D. J.** (1985) *Nebuchadrezzar and Babylon.* London. **Yamauchi, E.** (1973) Cultic Prostitution. In Hoffner 1973: 213-22. (1980a) Two Reformers Compared: Solon of Athens and Nehemiah of Jerusalem. In Rendsburg, *et al.* 1980: 269-92. (1980b) *New*

Testament Cities in Western Asia Minor. Grand Rapids, Mich. (1982) *Foes from the Northern Frontier.* Grand Rapids, Mich. (1983) The Scythians: Invading Hordes from the Russian Steppes. *Biblical Archaeology* 46: 90-99. (1985) Babylon. In Harrison 1985: 32-48. (1986) Nabonidus. In Bromiley 1986: 468-70. (1990) *Persia and the Bible.* Grand Rapids, Mich. (1992a) Herodotus. In Freedman 1992: 180-81. (1992b) Mordecai, the Persepolis Tablets and the Susa Excavations. *Vetus Testamentum* 42: 272-75.

Persia and Dhofar: Aspects of Iron Age International Politics and Trade

Juris Zarins
Southwest Missouri State University

Our knowledge of the Iron Age/Classical Period incense trade is largely derived from western historical sources. According to them, this trade emanated from the South Arabia or north Somalia source areas either by land or sea with ultimate destinations in the Levant, Eastern Mediterranean or points further north and west.[1] Less known is the relationship the producing areas had with Persia and India. This paper will seek to examine the relationship Achaemenid-Parthian and to a lesser extent, early Sasanian Persia had with one specific source area: Dhofar in the Southern Arabian region. As is known, by 572 C.E., the Sasanians exercised direct political and military control over the region. We hope that we have shed some light on this relationship as the result of archaeological work carried out in Dhofar, between the years 1992–1995. As such, we would like to thank our principal sponsors for the project, the Government of the Sultanate of Oman.

The Ecology of Dhofar

Dhofar, as a geographical entity today is difficult to define due to modern political conditions which place the region into two distinct countries: Oman and Yemen. One portion of what geologists call the Hadramaut

1 See for example, Whitehouse (1991) 216 and Begley (1991) 3-4.

Plateau (fig. 1) is found in the southernmost part of the Sultanate of Oman and the other part is in the eastern most district of Yemen (fig. 2). However, it is a distinctive geological and ecological study area inhabited by a unique group of people. It forms a part of the larger Indian Ocean Subtropical Zone encompassing sections of East Africa, the Arabian peninsula littoral and western India. This larger area is sometimes referred to as the "Eritreo-Arabian Province"[2] (fig. 3). Within this southern Arabian region, due to unique climatological and landform factors, an interesting flora has originated.[3] In addition, both archaeologists and botanists working within the

Fig.1: *Some Major Geological Provinces of Arabia including the Hadramaut Plateau*
(after USGS Professional Paper 560-D)

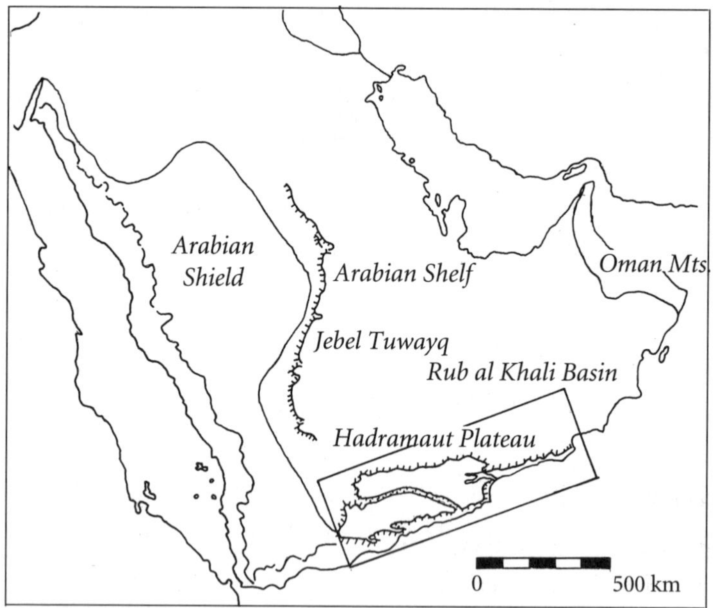

2 For various definitions of this province, see Al Hubaishi and Müller-Hohenstein (1984) fig. 1; Zohary (1973); Takhtajan (1986); Zarins (1992b) 470; Ghazanfar (1991) figs. 1 and 4 224; (1992) 191.

3 Miller and Morris (1988) xi, xv; Sale (1980); Radcliffe-Smith (1980).

last decade in this region, have begun to analyze the origins of such Indian Ocean cultigens as sorghum, the millets, indigo, and cotton among others.[4]

Within our study area in the Omani part of Dhofar, we have noted the presence of at least four major ecological zones critical to our understanding of the region (fig. 2).

1. The Coastal Plain (*including foothills, up to the 300 m contour*)

This zone in Omani Dhofar is centered on modern Salalah and is about fifty km in length and stretches to a maximum width of 15 km. From sea level to the 300 m scarp face there is a gradual slope. The entire plain from Raysut to Taqa is composed of Quaternary river deposits consisting of older travertine deposits to younger river terraces and alluvial fans. From Taqa to Mirbat, these ancient river systems cut through older Tertiary deposits. In turn, today these ancient plain river systems (wadis) produce small lagoons (khors) at the Ocean interface, creating a unique feature on the lower alluvial plain.

Similar coastal configurations can be seen in Yemen (fig. 2) although the only geomorphological study has been carried out in the vicinity of Qana.[5] Large-scale lagoonal systems promise to hold valuable information in the Wadi Jiz system as well as smaller complexes around Ash-Shihr, Mukalla, and Sayhut.

2. The Dhofar Hills (*escarpment*)

The scarp and hills rise up abruptly at an elevation of between 300-400 m above the plain and reach a peak elevation of 800 m. They form a plateau some 40 km wide dissected by a number of northward-flowing ancient rivers. This limestone karst plain has numerous caves and sinks. The vegetation of the southern portion of the plateau, consisting of trees and dense shrubs, gives way to a grassland and eventually a more barren scrub.[6]

---

4 For the latest summary, see Zarins (1992b) 469.

5 Chepaliga and Shilik (1995). The work carried out in Dhofar on which this summary is based, was done by B. Marcolongo at the Istituto di Ricerca per la Protezione Idrogeologica as part of the Consiglio Nazionale delle Ricerche at the University of Padua.

6 Miller and Morris (1988) xiii-xiv; Sale (1980) 35-38.

Fig.2: *The Geographical Homeland of the MSA Speakers in Oman and Yemen*

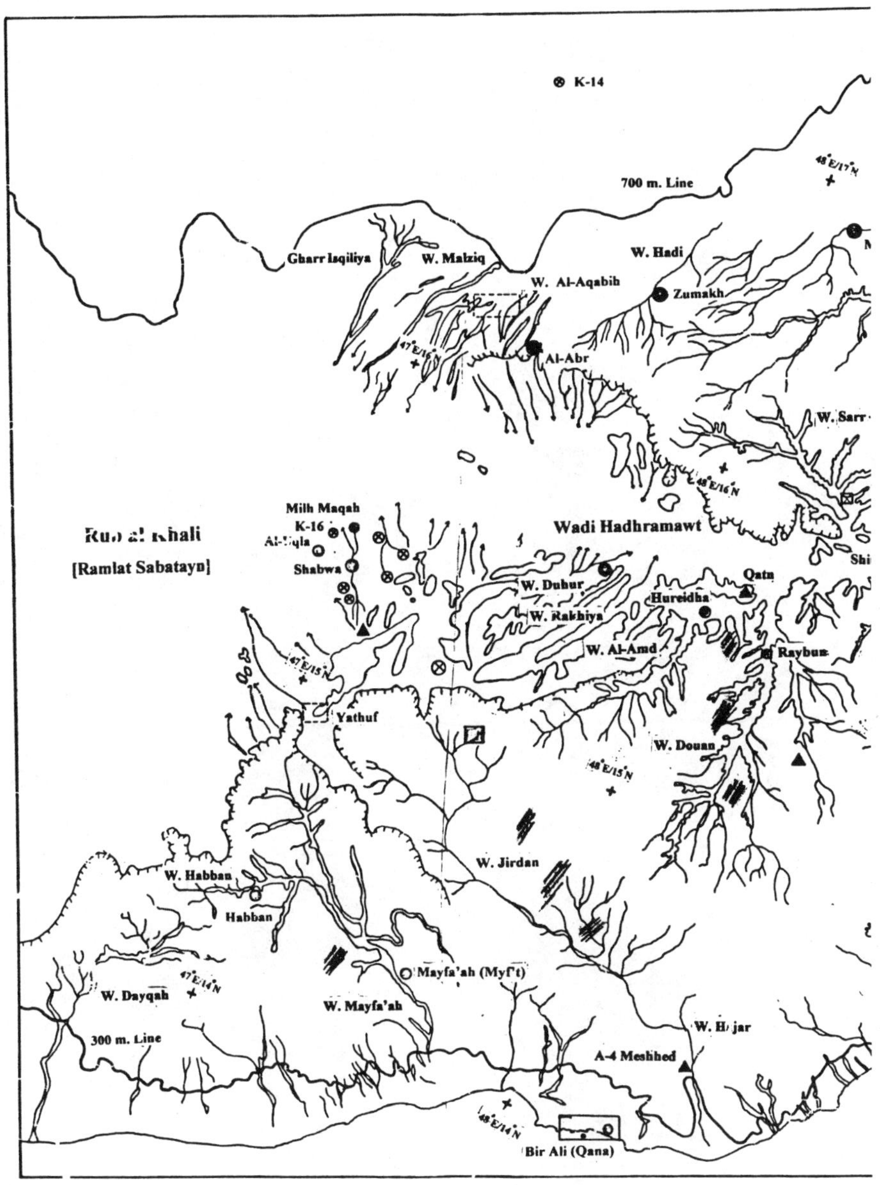
K-14
700 m. Line
Gharr Isqiliya
W. Malziq
W. Hadi
W. Al-Aqabih
Zumakh
Al-Abr
W. Sarr
Milh Maqah
K-16
Shabwa
[Ramlat Sabatayn]
Wadi Hadhramawt
W. Duhur
W. Rakhiya
Qatn
Hureidha
W. Al-Amd
Raybun
Yathuf
W. Douan
W. Jirdan
W. Habban
Habban
Mayfa'ah (Myf't)
W. Dayqah
W. Mayfa'ah
300 m. Line
A-4 Meshhed
Bir Ali (Qana)

Fig. 2A

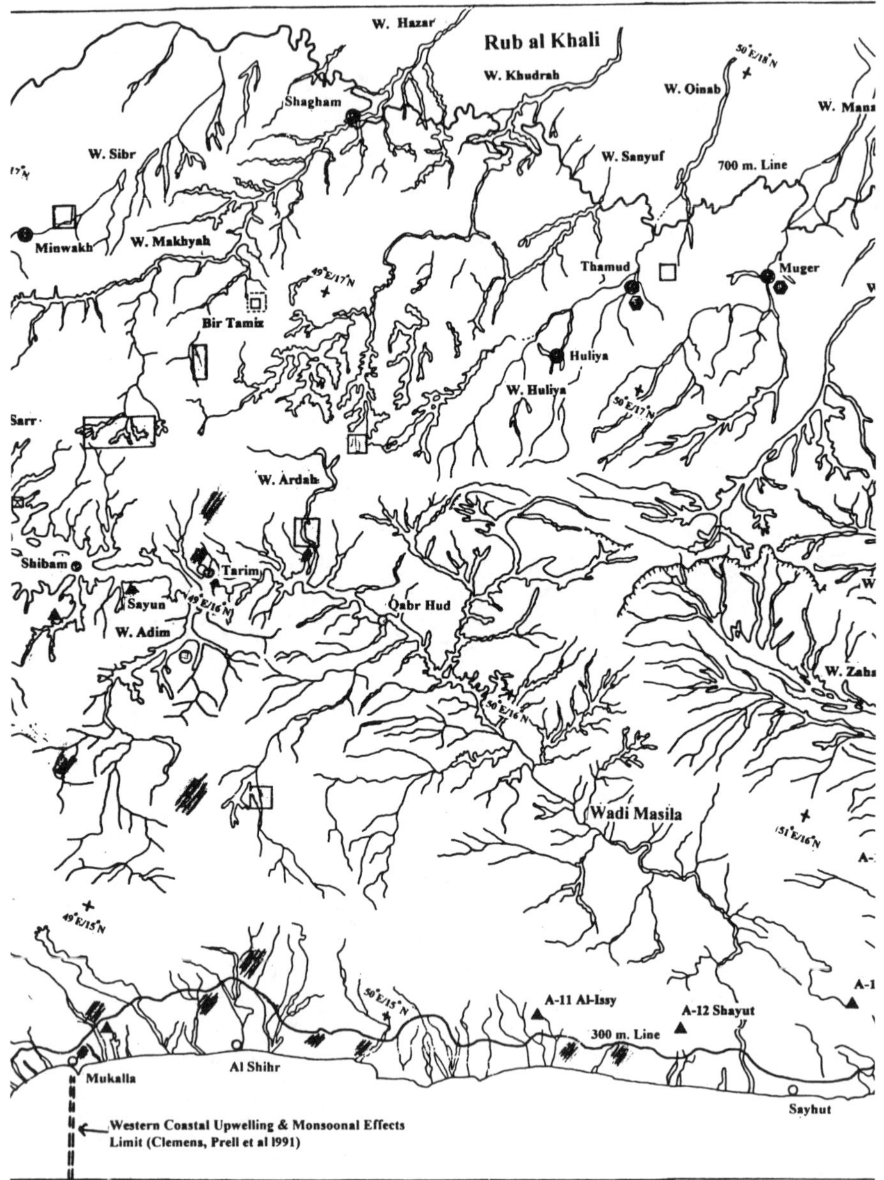
W. Hazar
Rub al Khali
W. Khudrah
W. Oinab
Shagham
W. Sibr
W. Sanyuf
700 m. Line
Minwakh
W. Makhyah
Thamud
Muger
Bir Tamiz
Huliya
W. Huliya
Sarr
W. Ardah
Shibam
Tarim
Sayun
W. Adim
Qabr Hud
W. Zahs
Wadi Masila
A-11 Al-Issy
A-12 Shayut
300 m. Line
Mukalla
Al Shihr
Sayhut
Western Coastal Upwelling & Monsoonal Effects Limit (Clemens, Prell et al 1991)

Fig. 2B

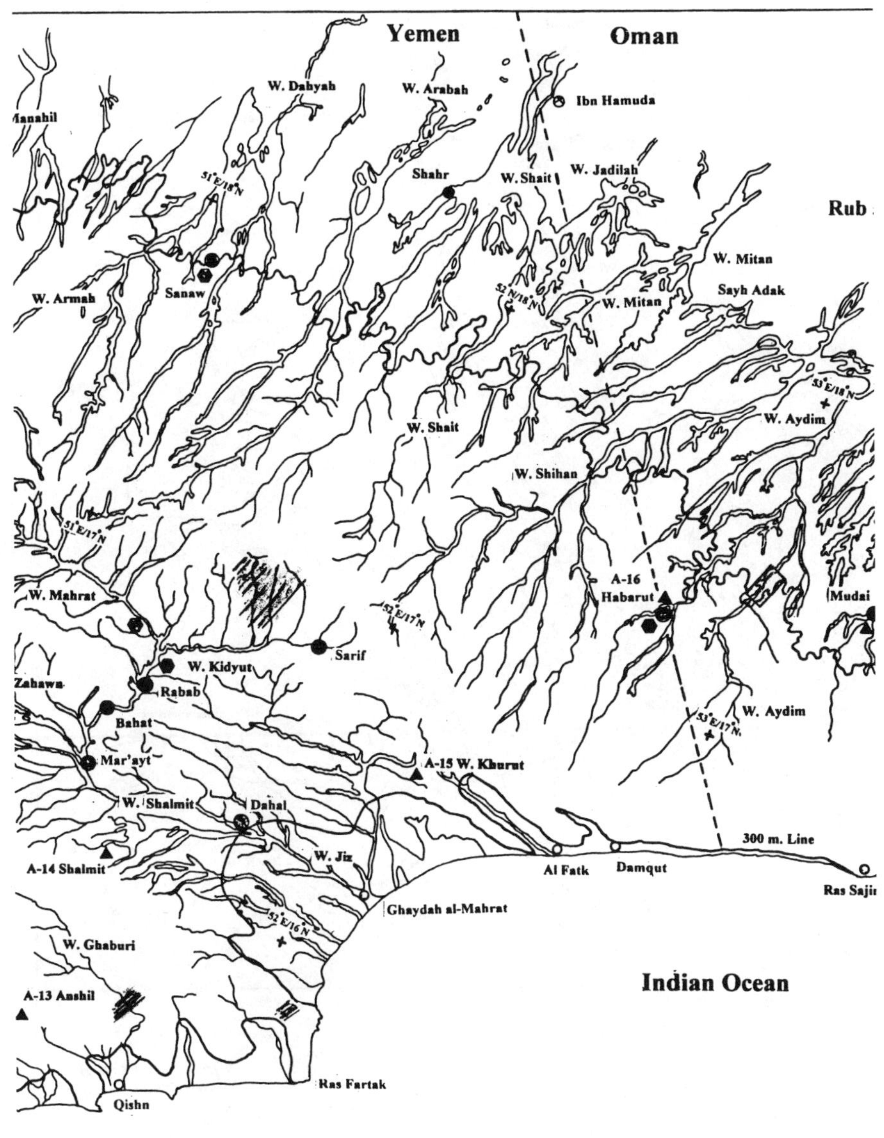
Yemen
Oman
W. Dahyah
W. Arabah
Ibn Hamuda
Shahr
W. Shait
W. Jadilah
Rub
W. Mitan
Sayh Adak
W. Mitan
W. Armah
Sanaw
W. Shait
W. Aydim
W. Shihan
W. Mahrat
A-16
Habarut
Mudai
Sarif
W. Kidyut
Rabab
Zahawn
Bahat
W. Aydim
Mar'ayt
A-15 W. Khurut
W. Shalmit
Dahal
300 m. Line
A-14 Shalmit
W. Jiz
Al Fatk
Damqut
Ghaydah al-Mahrat
W. Ghaburi
Indian Ocean
A-13 Anshil
Ras Fartak
Qishn

Fig. 2C

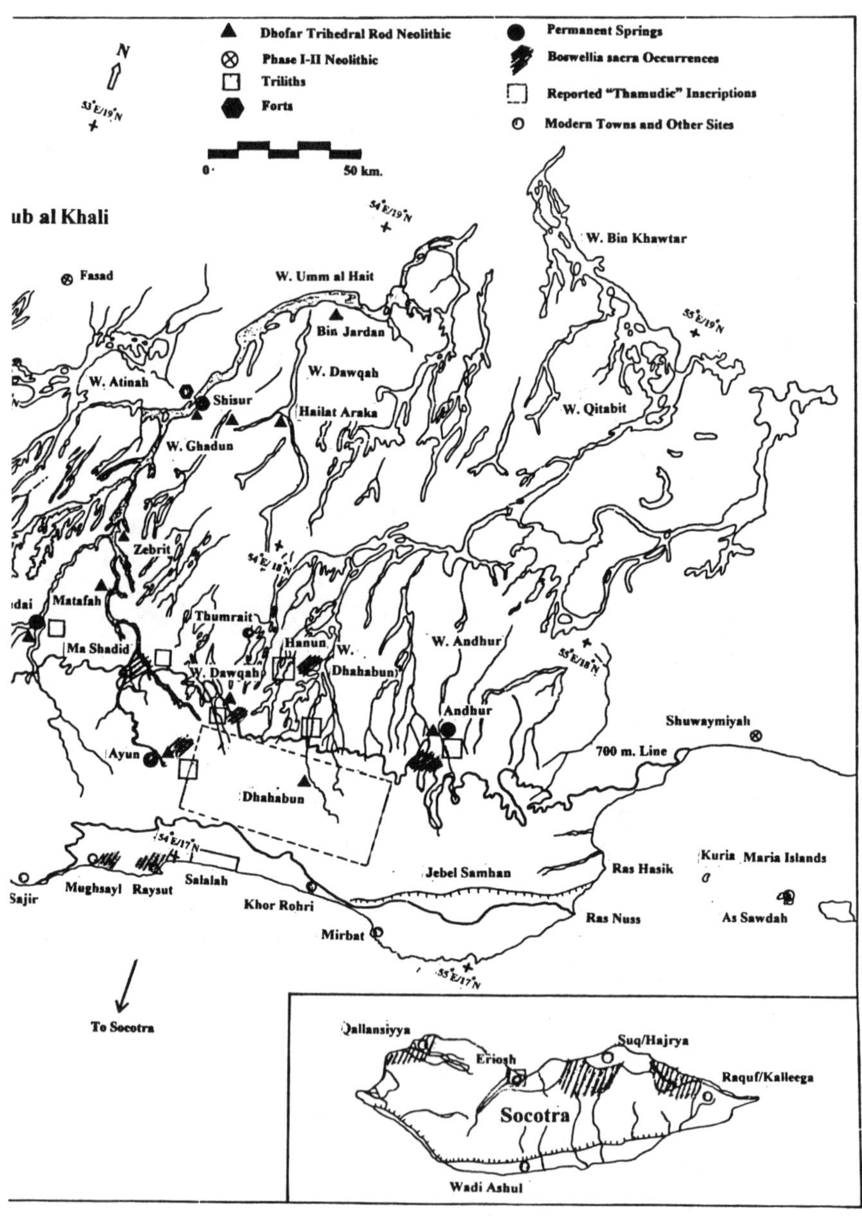

Dhofar Trihedral Rod Neolithic
Phase I-II Neolithic
Triliths
Forts
Permanent Springs
Boswellia sacra Occurrences
Reported "Thamudic" Inscriptions
Modern Towns and Other Sites
N
0
50 km.
ub al Khali
Fasad
W. Umm al Hait
W. Bin Khawtar
Bin Jardan
W. Dawqah
W. Atinah
Shisur
Hailat Araka
W. Qitabit
W. Ghadun
Zebrit
Matafah
Ma Shadid
Thumrait
Hanun
W. Dawqah
W. Dhahabun
W. Andhur
Andhur
Ayun
Dhahabun
Shuwaymiyah
700 m. Line
Sajir
Mughsayl
Raysut
Salalah
Khor Rohri
Mirbat
Jebel Samhan
Ras Hasik
Ras Nuss
Kuria Maria Islands
As Sawdah
To Socotra
Qallansiyya
Eriosh
Suq/Hajrya
Raquf/Kalleega
Socotra
Wadi Ashul

Fig. 2D

The hills themselves, a mix of several ranges, begin east of Hasik (Jebel Samhan), and stretch to the end of the Jebel Qamr range in Yemen west of the Wadi Jiz. The uplands between Wadi Dayqah and Ras Fartak are not part of this category.

3. The Nejd (*north-facing cliffs and dry plateau*)

This region is composed of dissected foothills forming a deeply-dissected tableland gradually giving away in the north to a gentle undulating plain. The major wadis which begin here, Dawqah, Ribkhut, Aydim, Dhahabun, and Ghadun, originated as Pleistocene rivers with at least three recognizable terrace systems spanning two million years. They drained northward into the Rub al Khali edge and currently, as non-active systems, merge north of Dawqah into the Wadi Umm al Khait leading to Mughshin and beyond. Remote sensing pictures indicate that at some time in the late Pleistocene, minor folding occurred which created faults in the Shisur region, opened up springs, and diverted stream flow substantially. Vegetation becomes moisture-stressed from a south to north direction and in the northern Nejd it is composed of xerophytic shrubs and grasses. [7]

The dry plateau in adjoining Yemen, is divided into two parts separated by the Wadi Jiz and the Hadramaut system (fig. 2).[8] The Nejd plateau of Oman described above continues across the frontier as far west as al-Abr. Numerous north-draining wadis, *e.g.*, W. Makhiyah, Manahil, Arabah, and Shait, produce permanent springs.

North of the Yemen coast between Ras Fartak, W. Dayqah and the Hadramaut, the Nejd is called the "Jol." This region is quite barren and lacking in permanent springs. It is dissected by either south-flowing fossil streams or north-flowing tributaries of the Hadramaut, *e.g.*, Douan, Amd, and Adim.

---

7 Sale (1980) 33; Miller and Morris (1988) xiv.

8 It is now clear that the Hadramaut-Wadi Masila is in fact a much larger river system originating in the highlands of western Yemen as the Wadi Jowf and draining across the Ramlat Sabatayn into the Indian Ocean through the Hadramaut system, see Cleuziou *et al.* (1992).

4. RUB AL KHALI (*sand desert*)

This large sand desert stretches from the northern fringes of the Nejd well into central Arabia. The large dunes represent the arid reworking of Late Pleistocene river systems draining into the Arabian Gulf.[9] Remote sensing images and geologic mapping clearly define interdunal deposits which in many cases are tied to river overflow and re-channelization. This sand desert fronts our study area from the W. Umm al Khait westward to W. Malziq in Yemen where the Rub al Khali plunges well south as part of the Ramlat Sabatyn.

These four major ecological zones define an integrated system for Dhofar in both Oman and Yemen. In the east, they are today extremely compacted microzones. In the west, The Wadis Jiz and Hadramaut dissect the region opening up greater north-south distances. Linking the zones described above is the climatic phenomenon known as the summer monsoon (fig. 3). Today, the effects are felt in the summer months (June-September) only on the coastal plain, the Escarpment Hills, and to a lesser extent in the Nejd from Jebel Samhan to Jebel al Qamr. Assessing the effects of the current monsoon and its actions in the past are directly relevant in understanding ancient settlement patterns of southern Arabia as well as the earlier distribution of the subtropical flora of the region, particularly frankincense and myrrh.

Frankincense and Myrrh

The modern distribution of *Boswellia sacra* in Arabia has come under some dispute (fig. 4).[10] In terms of habitat, *Boswellia* has been reported in Dhofar from three distinct ecological zones. First, a coastal variety has been found stretching westward from the Wadi Adonhib system. Many authorities

9 McClure (1978, 1984, 1988).

10 Compare Müller (1976) 124; Van Beek (1969) 46 and fig. 11; Casson (1989) 162, fig. 6; Groom (1981) 89; Monod (1979); Thulin and Warfa (1987); Hepper (1969) 66. Miller and Morris suggest a range extending from Hasik to Habban, (1988) 78; *cf.* Breton (1990) 114.

Fig. 3: *The Southwest Monsoon and Its Relationship to the Distribution of Frankincense and Myrrh*

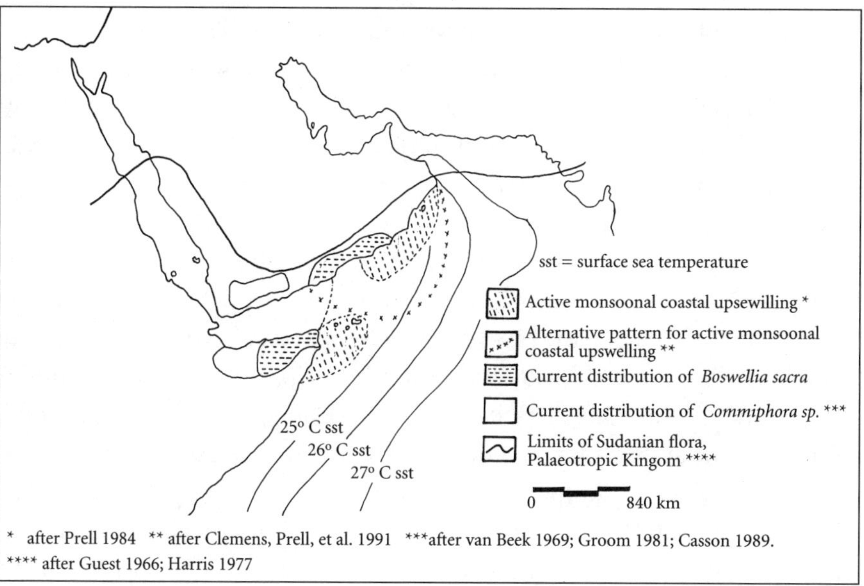

Fig. 4: *The Current and Past Projected Range of MSA Speakers in Relationship to Trilith Distribution*

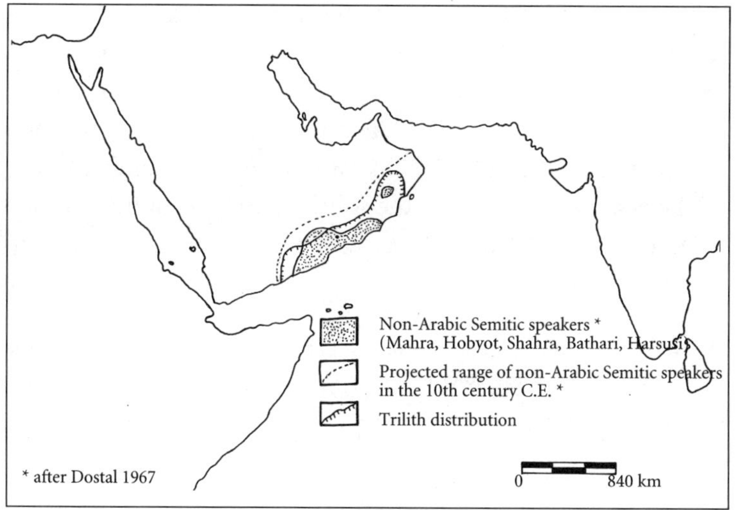

however feel that the plants are a late human introduction. The second zone has been labelled the "mountain escarpment." Here *B. sacra* grows with *D. serrulata* and *C. foliaceae* in a forest environment up to elevations of 900 m.[11] The occurrence of *B. sacra* on such scarps near the Indian Ocean provides enough moisture during the dry season. Local tradition however states that the best frankincense comes from trees growing in a belt in the arid zone behind the monsoon mountains "beyond the reach of the monsoon rain, but within reach of the cool winds which blow steadily during this [monsoon] season."[12] Based on temperature gradient studies and the existing range of *Boswellia*, we can conclude that in Dhofar the plant grows in the arid zone within a narrow (30-40 km wide) belt just beyond the northern Dhofar Hills scarp within summer, wind-borne precipitation in a temperature range of 20°-25° C. Based on LANDSAT images, we have noted that this tripartite system of adaptation exists as far west as Al Fatk on the east side of the Wadi Jiz complex.

The westward limits of the current summer monsoon along the Yemen coast have not been absolutely defined.[13] The effect appears to be very strong as far west as Mukalla and perhaps beyond to Bir Ali (figs. 2-3).[14] Coastal *Boswellia* specimens, as on the Salalah plain, have been reported below the 300 m contour line between Mukalla and Ras Fartak.[15] Specimens from higher coastal elevations above 300 m have also been reported at Mukalla, Ash Shihr, and Al Qishn, although the elevations represent gradual hill slope rises and not scarps as seen in Dhofar (fig. 2). Finally, in Yemen, *Boswellia* is also reported in the drier Nejd (Jol) primarily south of the Hadramaut. The plant is found in wadi tributaries running to the sea (*e.g.*, W. Mayfa'ah, W. Jirdan), or the south tributaries of the Hadramaut (*e.g.*, W. Douan and W. Adim). It has also been reported from the upper

---

11 The latest collection and systematic study of plant associations in coastal Dhofar was conducted in 1995 by N. Martinez (1997).

12 Miller and Morris (1988) 78.

13 Clemens, Prell *et al.* (1991).

14 First noted in modern terms by Wellsted (1840) 138, 140.

15 Monod (1979).

reaches of the W. Kidyut. Wellsted, in 1836,[16] also noted that in Yemen a primary and inferior type of frankincense were collected which presumably reflects on the excellent variety found in the interior and the lower quality form found on the coastal hills.

In sum, frankincense is to be found as far west as Habban (W. Mayfa'ah) and eastward to Jebel Samhan, near Hasik. The plant's current distribution is controlled by summer monsoonal conditions which in turn also involves topography, soil conditions, and landforms. The Rub al Khali is an effective current barrier on the west and along the northern edge of the Hadramaut plateau. The arid effects of the Rub al Khali also curtail the spread of *Boswellia* eastward beyond Hasik as no scarp is present to create a rain shadow.

The Modern South Arab Populations (MSA)

The present-day distribution of the six-subgroups of the modern South Arabic languages includes people living in both Yemen and Oman (fig. 4). The bulk of the population is to be found within the "Hadramaut Plateau" region described above well within the range of *Boswellia.* [17] Their eastward extent today is defined by the Harasis who came from Dhofar in the past.[18] Today, they are cut off from the bulk of MSA speakers located to the west. Westward, the boundary appears to be W. Masila (W. Hadramaut).[19] To the north, the bulk of MSA speakers skirt Thamud and range northward perhaps as far as the fringes of the Rub al Khali.[20]

The importance of identifying the MSA speakers as unique linguistically and culturally in turn hinges on the correct evaluation of historical and archaeological data assigned to the Iron Age. The MSA languages were first identified as being different from Arabic by Wellsted in 1836 and Fresnel

16 Wellsted (1840) 173-75.

17 Simeone-Senelle (1991) 337; Müller (1991) 80.

18 Chatty (1983) 152, (1990) 339.

19 Johnstone (1987) xi.

20 Lonnet (1985) 50.

in 1838.[21] Modern linguists group them as distinctive languages derived from classical South Arabian perhaps as early as 1000 B.C.E.[22] Their distribution on the mainland is complemented by an extended occupational history on the Islands of Socotra,[23] the Kuria Marias[24] and perhaps Masirah.[25]

The question of ethnic and linguistic identification is made more complicated by the lack of MSA recognition by explorers and travellers and the influence Arabic has had on these speakers. Johnstone[26] states that "in Mukalla itself, the Mehris lost their native language and speak only Arabic." For example, Wellsted remarked in 1836[27] that Mirbat was "completely under the control of the Bedowins." Describing Mukalla, he states that "Bedowins" not infrequently attack it, and also noted that "Bedowins" came to Ash Shihr from the interior. [28] On his comments concerning the Socotra inhabitants, he states that "Bedowins" inhabited the island but that older people living in the interior were called "aborigines."[29] He does, however, recognize the term "Mahara Arabs" in describing people of the southern mainland coast.[30] Miles noted in an 1883 visit to Hallaniya that

---

21 For a summary of the linguistic developments and particularly the linguistic work done at the turn of the century, see Leslau (1946) 3-5.

22 Zohar (1992) 167 and fig. 1 suggests the MSA languages developed into separate entities somewhere after 1000 B.C.E.

23 Wellsted (1840), (1840), *cf.* Naumkin (1993).

24 Leslau (1946), Hay (1947), Lorimer (1908) 1043-45, Miles (1919) 548.

25 Only the Jennebeh and Hikman, as Arab tribes, are reported as being the inhabitants of Masirah by Lorimer (1908), but now see note 67 below. Lorimer (1915) 13 goes on to say, however, that Masirah contained "Djibouti graves" and "Somali boats."

26 (1987) xi.

27 (1840) 129-30.

28 *Ibid.* 151.

29 *Ibid.* 301.

30 *Ibid.* 326; similar comments were made by Balfour later (1888) xxviii. Botting, as late as 1958, still referred to the upland inhabitants of Socotra as "aboriginal bedouin" (1958) 200.

only the headman spoke Arabic, the rest spoke Mahra.[31] Hay notes on his 1947 visit to Hallaniya in the Kuria Marias that when he landed "They talked Arabic but explained that their real language is Shihri...spoken by the people of Mirbat."[32]

Ecologically and culturally, the Shahra who specifically live in Omani Dhofar are transhumant, which involves at least two distinct periods of annual movement. As noted in 1992, we can define two settlement types based primarily on herding *Bos taurus.* First, a *fixed main settlement* (*mikifod*) occupied from June through September and November through March[33] These sites are usually found on protected rises on the edge of wadis or formal plateaus. These settlements, organized communally, incorporate both cattle and human houses. Placement and location of individual houses within the settlement follow designated subtribe lineage groupings. Individual circular houses up to 4 m in diameter usually have a constructed stone base wall and a superstructure of organic materials. The entire communal settlement is surrounded by stone and/or brush banks to prevent animals straying. The *temporary camps* (*musto*) occupied in April through June and September through November, are very lightly constructed. They consist of small poles rammed into the ground with their tops tied together. Twigs and grass cover the exterior. Cooking in hearth areas takes place outside the structure. In these locations, cattle wander freely and are herded together only at night.[34]

---

31 (1919) 548.

32 Hay (1947) 280. Haines in 1845 already had begun to use the term "Mahra" (1845) 109, 111-12 as a quote from Fresnel and recognized the people to the west as the "Gharrah" (= Qara), *ibid.* 116-20. Thomas noted in 1929 that "This region forms the habitat of a group of five tribes, which it would appear, are racially distinct from the Semitic Arab... Judging from their appearance, traditions, and customs,...they constitute a block of non-Arab tribes of great local antiquity" ([1929]) 98). Note also that the use of the term "Mahra Arab" by Wellsted, and "Mahri Arabs" by Balfour (1888) xxviii, confuses the two groups in a inextricable sense.

33 Janzen (1986) is the only source for the detailed description of the physical layout of MSA settlements. I adapted his material for consideration in a larger archaeological context, see Zarins (1992b) 220-25.

34 For photographs taken in 1929 of what I gather to be *musto* encampments at Taqa

Other aspects of Shahra life are also directly relevant to our inquiry. Hereditary headmen lead subtribes formed in lineage segments which occupy the local settlement groups described above. The dead are buried in formal, well-marked and constructed cemeteries. Animal sacrifice involving bulls and goats is still practiced. Supernatural beliefs incorporate aspects of a defined spirit world characterized by the presence of demons, wizards, spirits and witches who are influenced by people possessing shamanic powers.[35]

Agriculture is practiced during the summer monsoon period when large, irregular areas are walled off by stone fences. Using a digging stick, the Shahra plant primarily sorghum and millet. Cattle, as a primary source of wealth today, provide the mainstay of Shahra existence. Basketry and ceramic production are carried out by women. The outstanding activity of the area in the past, still practiced today, is the collection of frankincense.[36] Specific incense-producing trees are owned by wealthier lineage segments, although due to decreased prices today, the groves are rented out to Arab bedouin.[37] The tapping is done in the summer, and the crystallized resin is sold in the winter to Salalah marketplaces.

"Arabs": A Historical Perspective

During the Greco-Roman period in the Middle East, the southern portion of Arabia came under increasing scrutiny due to the monopoly of frankincense (*B. sacra*) as well as myrrh (*Commiphora sp.*). The accounts of the western classical historians seemingly localized the natural range of the plants producing the incense.[38] In addition, they gave us brief accounts of

---

and Shikait, see Thomas (1929) figs. 1-2; Peyton (1983) 69, 72. Other temporary enclosures are associated with rock shelters in the Qara mountains themselves, see Thomas (1932) photo between 50-51.

35 See summaries of the salient aspects of MSA lives in Lorimer (1908) 1478-81; Thomas (1929) 98-104, 110; Dostal (1975) 34-37; Johnstone (1974) 8-22.

36 An exhaustive treatment of this activity is provided by M. Morris (1995).

37 Thomas (1932) 123.

38 See the summaries in Van Beek (1958) 142, (1960) 72-73; Groom (1981) 55-115.

the city/regional states in the area (fig. 5) which controlled the products and described the dominant north-south trade routes (fig. 6).[39]

Herodotus, in c. 450 B.C.E., writes a description of the early Achaemenid empire and comments that "Arabians" (*Arabioi*) were not subject to tribute as other peoples.[40] Later, he states that the "Arabians" (*Arabioi*) contributed annual gifts (*dora*) of 1000 talents of frankincense to the Achaemenid kings.[41] Finally, Herodotus describes "Arabia" (*Arabie*) as "furthest to the south of all the world." This area grows myrrh, frankincense and laudanum, and is erroneously associated with cassia, cinnamon and storax. Spices and perfumes, then, are associated with the land of "Arabia," inhabited by "Arabians," who produce frankincense.[42]

In Herodotus, what does "Arabian/Arabia" mean? The original use of the term appeared in Neo-Assyrian context in the mid-ninth century B.C.E. and came to mean pastoral nomads living in tents found principally in North Arabia and on the Levantine fringe. It has no satisfactory etymology, and came to mean any pastoral group encountered by the Assyrians. The term was unknown in the South Arab city states and occurs only in the third century C.E. in the Hadramaut (*ᵓrb*, *ᵓrbn*) as a reference to encroaching bedouin who presumably were used as mercenaries and auxiliaries in warfare by the South Arab states (in this sense it parallels the term Mahra, see below). Ephᶜal, in his summary, notes that the term has no "linguistic meaning."[43]

Graf provides the latest summary for defining the term in Achaemenid context. In general, the Persians followed the use of the intended original term. To them, Arabia was a very vague concept which meant any pastoral

---

39 Doe (1971) 51, fig. 2; Zarins, *et al.* (1979) 35-37; Potts 1988a.

40 Herodotus 3.88. Grene (1987) 251 translates the relevant passage as "guest-friends." Godley (1938) 114-15 prefers the longer phrase "united to them by friendship."

41 Herodotus 3.97. One thousand talents has variously been interpreted as 25 to 30 tons of incense.

42 Herodotus 3.307, 3.113, 3.110.

43 See Ephᶜal (1982) 6-9.

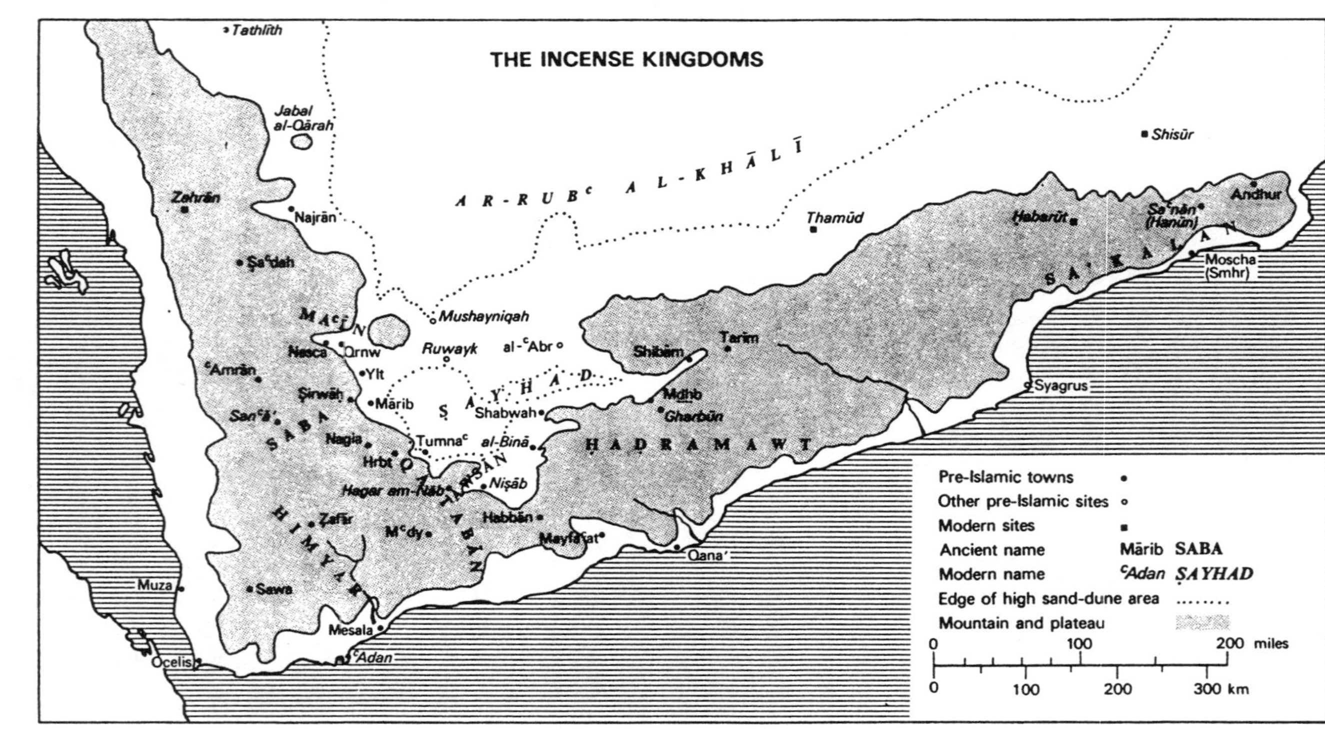

Fig. 5: *The Iron Age and Classical Periods Location of the South Arabian City States (after Groom [1981] 56)*

nomadic group from Iran to Egypt spanning all of northern Arabia.[44] Graf, however, based on more recent historical and archaeological evidence, distinguishes two groups of Arabs from the Persian perspective. First, he sees the independent Arabs (the clients of Persia) as primarily the Qedarite confederation occupying E. Egypt, Sinai/South Palestine, and Northwest Arabia. These were the "guest-friends" of Herodotus who helped the Persians conquer Egypt.[45] In contrast, the Arabs of Herodotus 3.97, are the HGR arabs who occupied East Arabia from Qatar to Mesopotamia.[46]

Who are the Arabs mentioned as producing myrrh and frankincense in Herodotus 3.107? Based on modern geography, they can only refer to the South Arab city states (fig. 5), or the ancestors of the modern South Arabic speakers described above (fig. 4). Eph^{c}al also noted that the 1000 annual talents of frankincense given to the Persians by the (presumably) HGR Arabs was really a tremendous and onerous levied tax.[47] Was the "lucrative incense trade" identified with East Arabia sufficient to pay 30 tons of incense as tribute to the Persians alone? Or does the passage refer to the "Arabs" of the producing region mentioned in Herodotus 3.107?

Maka and the Myci

Herodotus says in 3.93 that the 14th satrapy was composed of several groups of people which also included the Myci "and those who live on islands in the Indian Ocean." They paid a portion of 600 silver talents to the king. The Myci are a people who lived in Persian Maka/Mag.[48] Scholars are divided on the location of Maka, some preferring the Iranian side of the Hormuz

44 See Graf (1990) 138; Briant (1982) 169; De Blois (1989) 159.

45 Herodotus 3.88; Graf (1990) 139-43.

46 Cf. Roaf (1974) 135-36; Salles (1990) 124 n. 5; Graf (1990) 143-46 and references. Note that the lost city of Gerrha is probably confused Greek for Ha+gerr according to Potts (1984) 89.

47 Eph^{c}al (1982) 206-10. For a slightly different view of Arabs in the Achaemenid empire, see Cook (1985) 262, 297.

48 See the summation of earlier arguments in Eilers (1983); Roaf (1974).

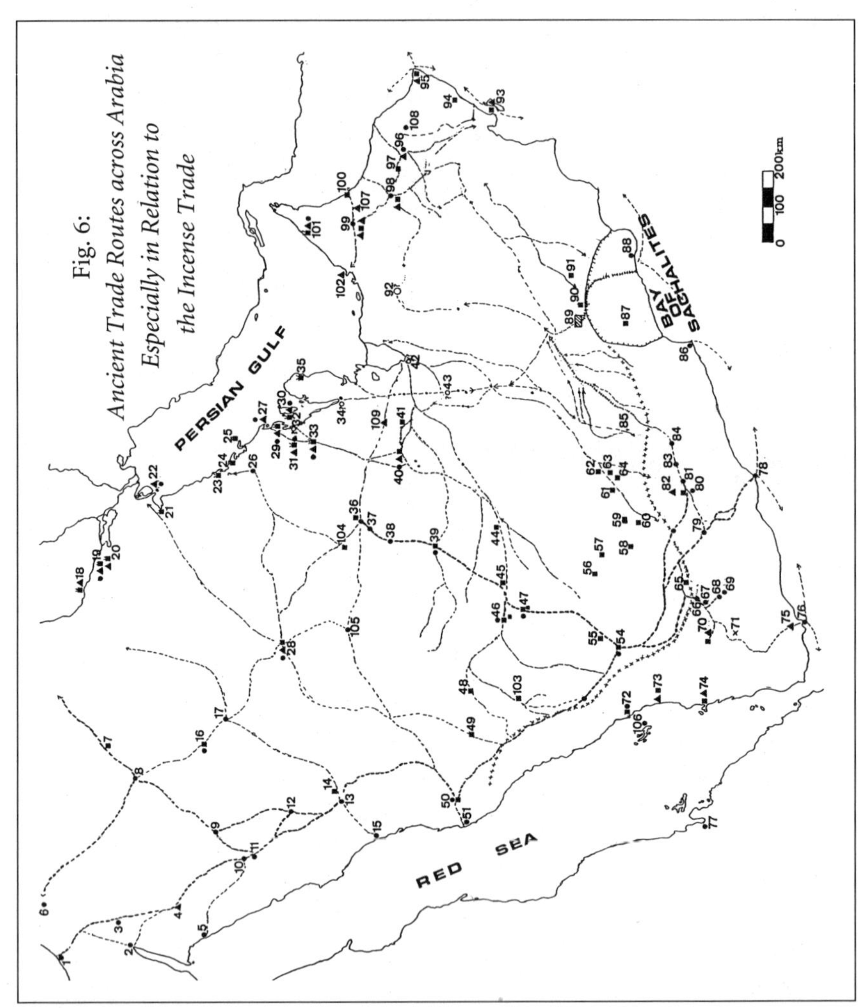

Fig. 6:
Ancient Trade Routes across Arabia Especially in Relation to the Incense Trade

Fig. 6

1	Gaza	40	Jabrin (Omana?) LABRIS
2	Ayla (Eilat/Aqaba)	41	Nadqan
3	Petra	42	Omana?
4	Qurayyah	43	Ubaylah (Omana?)
5	Leuce Come (Aynunah)	44	Rub al Khali neolithic
6	Amman	45	Sulayl
7	Wadi Ar'ar (201-42)	46	al Khamasin (Wadi Dawasir)
8	Duma/Tuwayr	47	al Fau
9	Taima	48	Ranyah neolithic
10	Hegra (Medain Saleh)	49	Turabahneolithic
11	Dedan (al Ula)	50	Makkah
12	Khaybar	51	al Shai'ba
13	Tathrib (Medina)	52	Bisha neolithic
14	Hannakiya	53	Jarash
15	Al Jar	54	Najran
16	Jubbah	55	al Qara (Bir Hima)
17	Hail	56	Jilada
18	Uruk (Warka)	57	Janub al Manbatihat
19	Ur	58	Rub al Khali neolithic
20	Eridu	59	Sharorah
21	Kuwait Ubaid Site	60-65	Rub al Khali neolithic
22	Icaros (Failaka)	66	Marib
23	Abu Khamis	67	Yala
24	Dowsariyah	68	Timna
25	Abu Ali	69	Hajar Bin Humeid
26	Thaj	70	Wadi Yana'i, al Massanah, al Raqlah, Wadi Nagid al-Abyad
27	Tarut	71	Dhamar / Reda
28	Unayzah / Buraydah (al Gasim)	72	Aththar (Ras al Tarfa)
29	Dhahran	73	Sihi
30	Bahrain States (including Qala'at al Bahrain, Barbar temple, tumuli fields)	74	Salif
		75	Subr
31	Abqaiq(including settlement and tumuli fields)	76	Eudomon Arabia (Aden)
		77	Adulis
32	Gerrha?	78	Qana
33	Hofuf (al Hasa)	79	Shabwa
34	Gerrha?	80	Hureidha
35	al Khor	81	Shibam
36	Yamama (al Kharj)	82	Wadi Sarr
37	Dilam	83	Tarim
38	Hawtah	84	Qabr Hud
39	Layla / Aflaj (al Ayun)	85	Thamud

86	Syagrus (Ras al Fartak)	98	Ibri
87	Habarut	99	Hili / Buraimi
88	Moscha / Sumhuram (Khor Rori)	100	Sohar
89	Wabar / Ubar?	101	Ed-Dur (Mleiha)
90	Fasad	102	Umm-an-Nar
91	Mugshin	103	Bisha
92	Omana? (Liwa Oasis)	104	Thumama
93	Organa (Masirah Island)	105	Dawadmi
94	Wahiba Sands neolithic	106	Farasan Islands
95	Ras al Hadd / Junayz	107	Hafit
96	Nizwa	108	Maysar
97	Bat	109	Jebel As Sahban

Straits, others the Arabian side, or a combination.[49] Potts and De Blois noted on the Darius Trilingual that Persian Maka was Elamite Maciya and Akkadian Qadu.[50] Both of them thought that Maka most likely referred to the Oman/UAE in light of the Neo-Assyrian inscription of Assurbanipal II (dated 640 B.C.E.) which mentions Pade, King of Qade (=Maka), living in Iske (modern Izki) in North Oman.[51]

The Persepolis Fortification Texts are ration texts authorized for travel by individuals and groups coming and going to the capital or Susa.[52] In summarizing this data,[53] we note that Maka had a satrap and other assigned

---

49 For various opinions see the summaries by Grohmann (1928) 615; Herzfeld (1968) 61, 63 n. 3, 283, 300; Salles (1990) 115; Vallat (1993) 163-64, Frye (1984) 113. Kiepert (1892) places them only on the Arabian side, east of the Chatramitae, Sachalitae, and Omanitae respectively.

50 Already noted by 1911, see Hansman (1973) 557; Potts (1985) 81-82; De Blois (1989) 158.

51 Potts (1985), (1990) 393-94; Cook (1985) 251 and n. 2 suggests that Maka(kash) was most likely to be found in Oman since a wine ration from the Persepolis Fortification Texts mentions the port of Tamukkan, identified by Hallock with modern Taoke on the Persian Gulf. The term Qade is retained as late as Pliny's Cadaei/Cadei.

52 Abbreviated PFT and PFa, these texts are dated to 509-496 B.C.E.; see Hallock (1969), (1978) 122 *vide* Makkash/Maziya. For the context of the texts, see Lewis (1990) 1-6; Vogelsang (1990) 101.

53 Potts (1990) 397-400.

Persian officials. However, some if not all of the people inhabiting Maka were "Arabs" since in several texts the Persians use the phrase Arabaya in this context.[54]

In sum then, both Herodotus and the Achaemenid kings saw the Arabian peninsula divided into certain regions. Northwest Arabia (Qedar), Northeast Arabia (HGR), Southwest Arabia (spice/perfume Arabia), and southeast Arabia (Maka). How does the evidence from later sources elucidate this picture?

Maka, Frankincense and the Arabs: Later Classical Sources

Agatharchides of Cnidus, writing in the second century B.C.E., describes Socotra briefly and mentions that merchant ships at anchor there included "not a few from Persia."[55] He fails to mention the ethnic or linguistic nature of the inhabitants other than the presence of Indians, Persians, and Greeks.

Strabo, in his Geography, in broad terms, refers to Chiefs of the Arabians occupying Eastern Arabia (Graf's HGR) as far as Mesopotamia, who play off both the Parthians and Romans.[56] He goes on to say that south of the Arabian desert inhabited by the Scenitae (tent dwellers) is Eudoman Arabia (Arabia Felix), defined as an area from the Persian Gulf to the Arabian Gulf along the Indian Ocean.[57] He also remarks on the area influenced by summer rains, but defines only the area of western Yemen as far

---

54 For example, Har-ba-a-be!, PFa 17, Hallock (1978) 122; De Blois (1989) 164. Historically, the term Maka gives way by A.D. 200 to a later term used in the Parthian and Sassanian periods. As modified by Arab usage, Maka becomes Mazun, (Parthian Mzw(n). The process is explained as Persian Mak/Mac changed by Arabic un to Macun or later Mazun; known since 1901, now summarized by Potts (1985) and De Blois (1989) 164 and n. 36. However, in Ptolemy, Geography, Book VI, Chapter vii, the Macae are listed as a people inhabiting the Persian Gulf area, Stevenson ed. (1932) 138.

55 Burstein (1989) 169 and n. 2.

56 Strabo contrasts "Arabs" (*Arabai*) to "Bedouin"(*Scenitae*) in this passage and suggests that politics between the Romans and Parthians was more intense near Arabia Eudamon (Strabo, Geography, 16.i.28) [Jones ed. (1930) 235-37].

57 *Ibid.*, 16.3.1 [Jones ed. (1930) 301].

as Shabwa.[58] As commented on by Van Beek and others, it appears that myrrh and frankincense were seen as separate production regions. Strabo does note that while Hadramaut produced frankincense (sic) and Qataban myrrh (sic), he states that the best frankincense was produced near Persis.[59] This may be a reference to Maka province, but Strabo makes no reference to specific groups of people in association with Dhofar.

Pliny, in his Geography, also uses the term encountered earlier by Herodotus. Both the Cadaei, Macae and Agraei are mentioned in the context of East and Southeast Arabia. Again the classical city states of Yemen are mentioned, this time in connection with the wealth of incense. "...They are the richest races in the world because vast wealth from Rome and Parthia accumulates in their hands, as they sell the products they obtain from the sea or the orchards...."[60] Royal perfumes used by the Kings of Parthia also incorporated myrrh.[61] As to the location of frankincense-producing country, he says that it is eight days journey from Shabwa, interpreted as going east or south (fig. 2). Other than some Mineans, Pliny says "Arabs" have not seen a frankincense tree.[62] He concludes that after the frankincense was collected it was taken to Shawba.

The Periplus notes from the perspective of maritime trade more details of the entire southern Arabian Indian Ocean coast than earlier writers. After Qana, (the seaport of Shabwa) a bay called Sachalites is found which has frankincense trees, a misty environment, and nearby a large promontory called Sygros.[63] Socotra (Dioscorides) is near it in the ocean. The next bay,

---

58 *Ibid.*, 16.4.2-4. Jones ed. (1930) 309-11.

59 *Ibid.*, 16.4.25 .Jones ed. (1930) 365.

60 Pliny, Natural History, VI.xxxii (Rackham ed. [1942] 461). The term *silvis* translated as forests by Rackham, is translated here as orchards.

61 *Ibid.*, XIII.ii, Rackham ed. (1942) 109.

62 *Ibid.*, XII. xxx, Rackham ed. (1942) 37-39. In fact, Pliny does not say that the frankincense-producing area is eight *days* journey from Shabwa. The term used is *a quo octo mansionibus distat*, perhaps translated as "eight stages" or "eight stopovers at (fortified) springs." As pointed out by J. Johnson (personal communication), the actual trip would have been nine days.

63 Periplus, sec. 29-30. Casson ed. (1989) 67-69.

called Omana, has a harbor called Moscha Limen, and the people living in the region are called "men who live in caves." Beyond Moscha Limen is Asichon (Hasik) and the Zenobian islands (Kuria Maria). "Beyond which stretches another country inhabited by indigenous people which is...already that in Persis." Beyond Kuria Maria is the island of Sarapis (Masirah) "populated by three villages of the fish-eaters. They use the Arabic tongue... merchants of Qane trade with it in small sailing vessels."[64] Schoff in his analysis of this passage, states that "the Arabian tongue" is in fact "Hadramatic" as represented by the modern Mahri.[65]

Ptolemy's Geography provides other additional details of the area (fig. 7).[66] The frankincense-producing region is identified with the term Sachalitae, below the Marithi mountains and amidst the Iobaritae. On his map, Sabbatha is Shabwa and the "outer myrrh producing region" is to the south of Shabwa. The placement of Cottabani in the east and Moscha and Ascitae in the west have probably been wrongly copied. Correctly placed are the Sygros promontory, the Zenobii islands, and Organa (Masirah). Thus, the last two sources provide the most detailed references to our study area.

The MSA Speakers and Their Historical Antecedents:

THE ISLAMIC PERIOD

What internal evidence of historical nature do we have suggesting that the ancestors of the MSA inhabitants lived in the region? The Medieval Arabic sources describe the MSA land in general terms corresponding to the territory they are now known to inhabit.[67] Tabari, writing around 900 C.E.,

---

64 *Ibid.*, sec. 32-33. Casson ed. (1989) 69-71.

65 Schoff (1912) 146. Casson (1989) 175 insists the language is "Arabic."

66 Ptolemy, Geography, Book Six, Chapter VII. Stevenson ed. (1932) 137-40 using the 1478 Codex Ebnerianus version of the text. For extant map versions of the text, see Dilke (1987) 177, n. 5, 267-74. For the map followed by Groom (1981) and Von Wissmann and Hofner (1952) fig. 10 322, see Sprenger (1875).

67 See the summary of relevant data by Tkatch (1913) 1188; (1936) 140-42; Müller (1991) 81. The only exception appears to be Masirah Island. Today inhabited by the

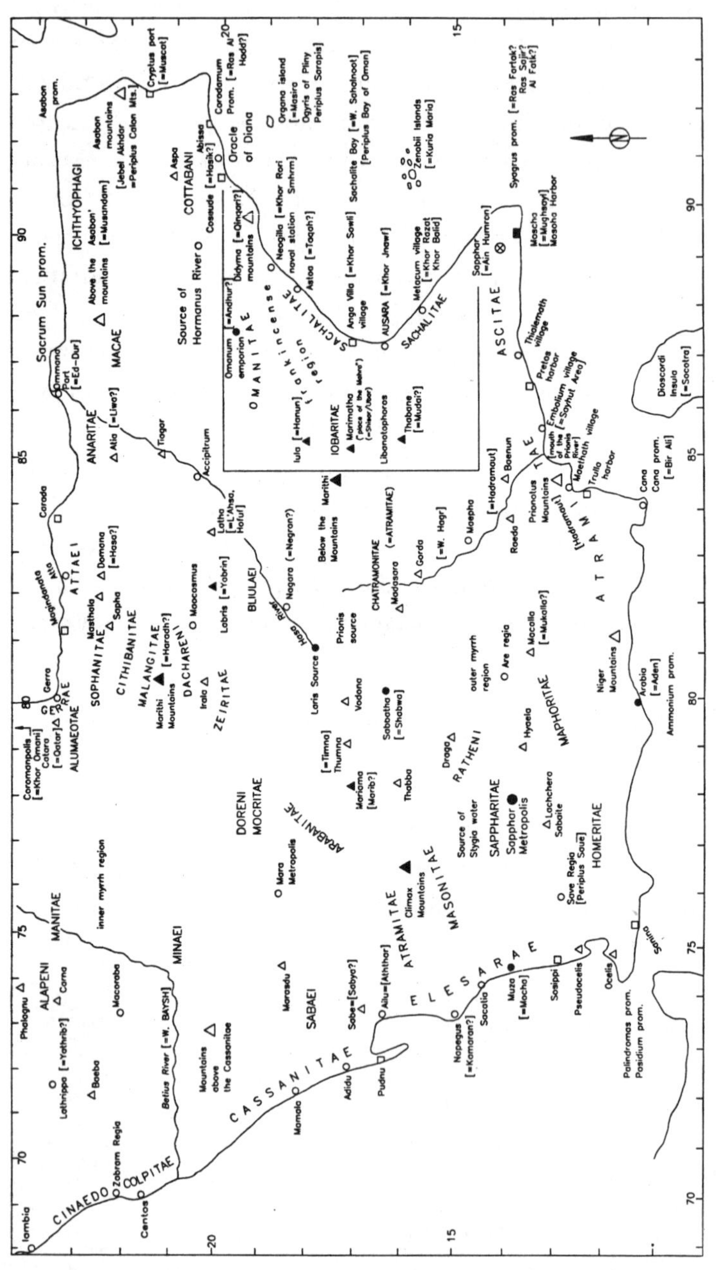

Fig. 7: *Annotated Map of Ptolemy*

(after Sprenger [1875], Von Wissman and Muller [1967] and Groom [1981])

recounts the Islamic conquest of the area in the mid-seventh century C.E. Abu Bakr gave orders for Arab armies to proceed from Oman through Mahra (MSA) to the Hadramaut and Yemen, perhaps in that geographical order.[68] In his text, the Mahra and Hadramaut areas are referred to as the "Lands of Myrrh and Frankincense."[69] Trimingham, describing the location of tribal lands in the sixth and seventh centuries C.E., places the Mahra in their modern geographical place.[70]

In 1959, Mathews suggested that based on a number of peculiar linguistic features still retained in topography, the broader geographical extent of MSA could be reconstructed.[71] In 1967, Dostal followed up this idea with a reconstruction of the former extent of MSA speakers by specifically identifying topographic settings with the endings *ut*/*-ot*/*-it* (fig. 4).[72] Müller more recently added other distinctive suffixes *-et*, *-oten*, *-uten*, and the prefixes *ya-* and *yi-*.[73] Both Dostal and Müller suggest that in the tenth century C.E. the range of MSA groups was much greater towards the east than at present (fig. 4).[74]

Arabic Jennebeh and Hikman tribes (Lorimer [1908] 1176-78; De Gaury [1957] 499-500; Schanfari [1988] 11 n. 26), Glaser suggests, based on Ibn Mudjawir (ca. 1220 C.E.), that Masirah was occupied by the Mahra (quoted in Tkatsch [1936]142). Even earlier, Hamdani (ca. 900 C.E.) stated that the Mahra of East Arabia occupied the islands of Socotra and Masirah (Sprenger [1874] 74; *cf.* the map and discussion by Dostal [1967]).

68 Donner (1993) 105.

69 *Ibid.* 157.

70 Trimingham (1979) 269.

71 Mathews (1959) 259-62.

72 Dostal (1967) 184-88.

73 Müller (1991) 82.

74 Dostal (1967) 133 and fig. 19; Müller (1991) 82. Wilkinson in his study of tribal settlement in northern Oman mentions that among the Qamr-Riyam and other groups associated with the Quda'a, the Mahra are strongly intertwined. Taken as a whole, the evidence does suggest that the MSA groups did extend in some fashion to the Sharqiya (Wilkinson [1977] 245-46; [1987] 75-76. (For the trilith evidence, see below.)

Müller's idea that particularly the interior Nejd was inhabited formerly by MSA speakers is supported by an earlier observation made by Philby. In his journey to Jabrin on the northern Rub al Khali, he noted that perhaps the people of Ad had extended their influence as far as Jabrin.[75] The al Murrah bedouin Ubar/Wabar legend centered on the meteorite strike in the northeast Rub al Khali not far from Jabrin, may be also an identification due to past Mahra control in the region.[76]

The Classical Sources

There is no agreement on the earliest attestation of the mention of MSA speakers, but some have suggested that the phoenix story in Herodotus (2.73) may refer to the Mahra.[77] The first reliable evidence comes from three terms found in later Classical sources.

Mahra

The term Mahra may be seen on the Ptolemy map. Tkatch suggests that the Greek term Mari/Mara conceals the Greek transcription for the Mahra.[78]

---

75 Philby (1933) 95-96, 163 notes the local Jabrin legend of the al-Murra that the original inhabitants of the oasis were driven into the desert by Ad ibn Kin'ad [Shadad] himself, the king of Wabar and thus the site set on fire, created the mound of ashes - Umm an Nussi. The attacks by the people of Ad presumably reflect on past incursions by the Mahra. We maintain that Ubar/Wabar is a reference to MSA speakers located south of the Rub al Khali. For the fourth and third millennia B.C.E. occupations of Umm an Nussi, see Piesinger (1983) 191ff. More significantly, the site continued to be occupied in the Hellenistic and Islamic periods as defined by fortresses (*Ibid.* 191 n. 65). Since the present territory of the Mahra extends into the Rub al Khali (Lonnet [1985] 50; Simeone Senelle [1991]), it would appear that medieval sources describing Mahra raiding into the Jabrin oasis can be important in reconstructing past territorial ranges as well as trading patterns. Yaqut (quoted by Guest [1937] 408) notes that Mahra coming from the south would meet up with bedouin coming from the Wadi Dawasir in locales in the Rub al Khali presumably in search of horse trade bargains.

76 For a description of the Ubar/Wabar crater, see Philby (1933) 157-80; more recently Bilkadi (1986).

77 Tkatch (1936) 139. Naumkin discusses the legend and adduces that Socotra was meant primarily based on the account of Diodorus of Sicily, see Naumkin (1993) 25-28.

78 Tkatch (1936)138.

This can be seen on the Ptolemy map in the term for the town of MARI + *matha*, MARI + *thi* and MARI + *thos* mountains, perhaps even the locality/town of MARA (fig. 7).[79] Independently of Ptolemy, but perhaps contemporary to him, the term Mahra appears in several ESA texts. At al-Uqla, an agricultural farm-hunting retreat west of Shabwa, favors were bestowed on clients of the Shabwa king. In RES 4877 dated to 200 C.E., Müller translates "Shahirum son of Wa'ilum, chief of the Mahra."[80] Another inscription from Wadi Abadan dated to 350 C.E. suggests military action against the Mahra (*qbl/ard/mhrt*).[81]

SAKALAN/SACHALITES

The term Sachalites is used both in the Periplus and Ptolemy (fig. 7). Both sources should be dated sometime in the early centuries C.E. Sprenger, already in 1865, noted "The Mahrites were called Sachalites by the Greeks."[82] The issue is somewhat more complex. In the two ESA gate inscriptions at Khor Rohri dated to the first centuries B.C.E./C.E., the invaders from Shabwa established a colony in the region which they called Sakalan (S'KLN or S'KLHN).[83] The text specifically says that the Shabwa colonists built and populated Sumhuram "in the country of Sakalhan." Sachalites is beyond all doubt the country of Sakalan in our Khor Rohri inscriptions.[84] But what does the term mean as either Sakalan, used by the Shabwa colonists, or

---

79 Ptolemy, Geography, Book VI, Chapter vii. (Stevenson ed. 1932:138-40).

80 Müller (1991) 80. Beeston (1938) 234 translates the phrase as "chief of the artificers." Jamme (1963) 50 states "leader of the specialized workers."

81 Pirenne (1981) 235. The term may also have come to be synonymous with "elite corps" or "contingent of bedouin mercenaries" in ESA, see Biella (1982) 268; Beeston, Ghul, Müller and Ryckmans (1982) 84.

82 Sprenger (1865) iii 437.

83 Albright (1982) 41-48 follows the original translations of Jamme who began to publish them in 1953. See the original citations of Jamme in Albright (1982) 41-48. (For the bronze inscriptions, see Albright (1982) 87-89). For other translations see Pirenne (1975), Beeston (1976), and Müller in Von Wissmann (1967).

84 Pirenne (1975) 95.

Sachalites as used by the Greeks? Lorimer stated in 1908[85] that the Qara people call themselves Hakli. Bertram Thomas reiterated in 1929 that the Qara populations of the region today call themselves "Hakalai" (Ehkli).[86] Müller in 1967 suggested that Sakalan is the term for Hakalai.[87] So Sakalan/Hakali is the term for the indigenous population of Dhofar, the Shahra, as Glaser suggested in 1865.

Iobaritae/Ubar/Ad

The last term used in Ptolemy is Iobaritae (fig. 7). As it stands, the term refers to a group of people inhabiting the incense growing region of Sachalites, or near it ("then near the Sachalita region are the Iobaritae").[88] Arab historians have suggested that the classical Iobaritae may have been the people and region of what later came to be known as Ubar (see below). In popular imagination and legend, it was even localized as the city of Ubar. The term may be retained by the modern spring and locale of Habarut, situated on the border between Yemen and Oman. According to Glaser, the Iobaritae of Ptolemy are the current Mahra hill people.[89]

Based on the account of Ibn Khaldun, the al-Shihr area (Mahra) had once been the land of Ad, the home of the ancestors of the Mahra who had come from the Hadramaut.[90] The Mahra themselves call the interior of their country Al-Akhaf where according to tradition, the home of Ad was located.[91] By inference, this locality may have been called Ubar, perhaps tied to the Iobaritae/Ubarites, the ancestors of today's MSA speakers.

---

85 Lorimer (1908) 1478.

86 Thomas (1932) 69.

87 Müller in von Wissmann (1967) 29 n. 75.

88 Ptolemy, Geography, Book Six, Chapter vii. Stevenson (1932) 139.

89 See the summary in Tkatch (1913).

90 Haines (1845) 112. The Mahra in the Wadi Masila referred to an archaeological site there as "Husn Ad" (see Ingrams [1936]).

91 See the summary by Tkatch (1936) 141.

The epigraphical material from the MSA region itself now confirms the tie of the region to the Classical period. Pecked inscriptions and drawings have been found in the southern Nejd[92] and within a small area of the central Dhofar mountains, a large number of painted inscriptions have been found.[93] This previously unattested South Semitic script (according to Beeston and MacDonald) is not related to ESA, but is "Thamudic," and may be thus of central Arabian origin.[94] The underlying language of the texts, while still not deciphered, is assumed to be Modern South Arabic.[95] Beeston noted that similar unpublished inscriptions have been found in Yemeni Mahra land, and perhaps further to the west at Bir Tamiz, Wadi al Aqabih, and Yathuf (fig. 2). Other inscriptions are known from Socotra.[96] Their specific age bracket has yet to be pinpointed, but in parallel to other scripts of this type, they should date to the Iron Age, ca. 500 B.C.E. to 600 C.E.

The Archaeology of Dhofar

The Sites

Past archaeological work in the Shahra/Dhofar area has shed virtually no light on these people except for the evidence of the so-called triliths reported by explorers (see below). Our more systematic work both on the coastal plain, the uplands, and the Nejd provides insight into the material past, and links our data to the historical and ethnographic data provided above.

---

92 Thomas (1932) 127-28.

93 Al-Shahri (1991a) 175-79; (1994) 61-165; King (1991) 19-20.

94 Beeston (1990) in a letter to the author. Cf. Thesiger (1946) 133 n. 2; (1984) 90; Al Shahri (1994) 254-55. The AFSM expedition in 1953 found a spiral inscription (JaT 77) on a stone in Wadi Adonhib in the area of our MSA sites. Jamme attributes it to "Thamudic," and translates it as such (Albright [1982] 89).

95 King (1991) 20.

96 Doe (1970) 5 and figs. 8-10; Naumkin (1993) 94-97; Naumkin and Sedov (1993) 582-83; Sedov in Naumkin (1988) 77-80. For similar inscriptions in red and white paint in the middle of the W. Masila (Hadramaut) at Sad, see Ingrams (1936) 546.

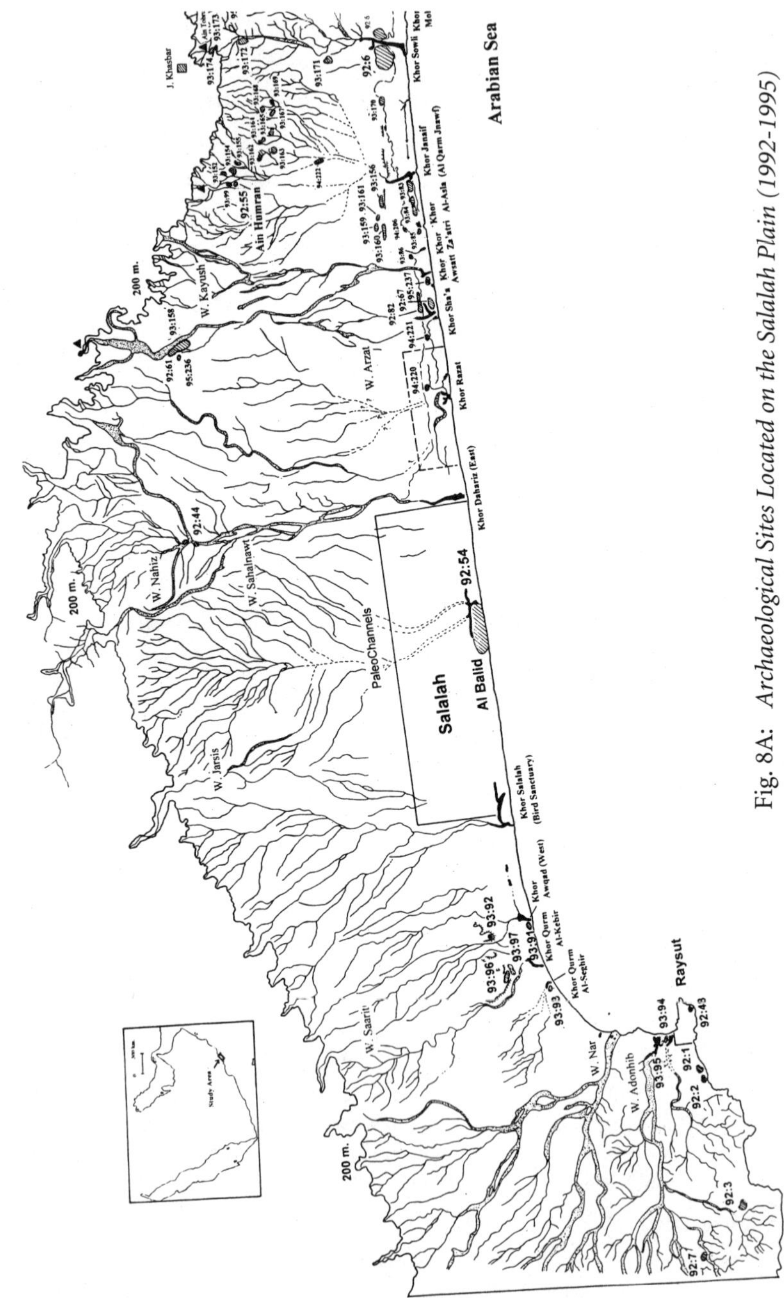

Fig. 8A: *Archaeological Sites Located on the Salalah Plain (1992-1995)*

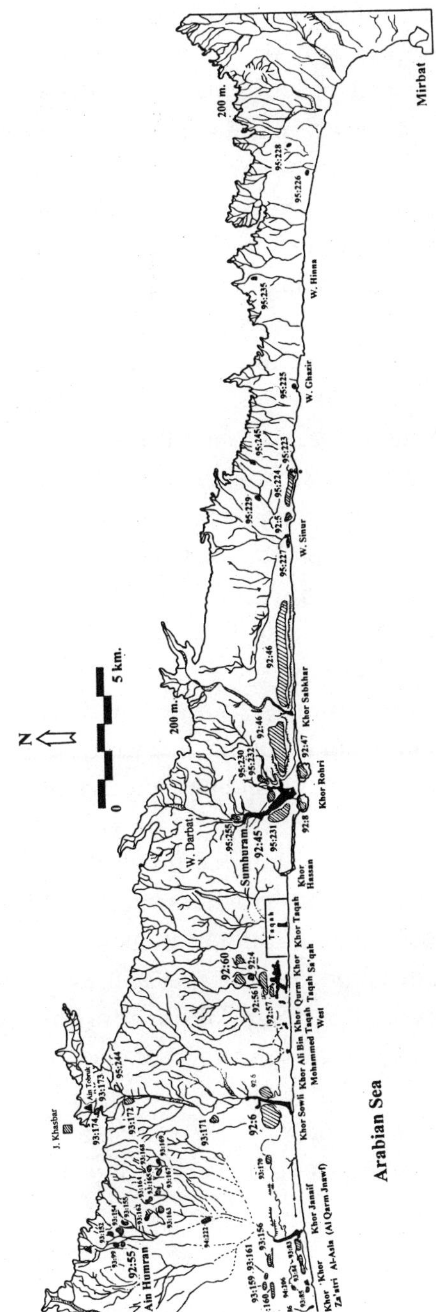

Fig. 8B: *Archaeological Sites Located on the Salalah Plain (1992-1995)*

Key sites can be found both on the Salalah Plain (fig. 8), the Qara plateau, and at oases such as Shisur and Ain Humran (fig. 9). On the plain, Taqa (93:60) is a key site. Situated on a high protected ridge-valley within the Salalah plain, it is approximately 2 km from the modern shoreline. This site was first established during the Bronze Age, but was re-used in the Iron Age. The latter period circular houses are defined by piled stone foundations about 1 m high. Clustered together, the over-all plan shows a settlement in a rectangular pattern surrounding a small depression (fig. 10). This settlement apparently was involved in agriculture since the alluvial soil in the depression has several small check dams crossing it. In many respects it resembles a ethnographic permanent settlement type described above. Excavations in two of the houses revealed a stratified deposit over 80 cm thick. Archaeological material recovered from these four levels consisted of lithics, some ceramics, animal remains, marine shells and fish material. In House 2, a C-14 date of 350 B.C.E. was obtained from level 4 (Beta 83797, 2340 ± 100 B.P.)and from level 1 in House 3 a date of 270 C.E.was recovered (Beta 83798, 1700 ± 60 B.P.), placing the Taqa 60 village complex well within the Iron Age as defined above.

Smaller-scale versions of this complex can be found on the upland terraces between Mirbat and Wadi Adonhib. Larger type homesteads consist of cattle biers, corrals, ancillary buildings, and agricultural fields. These complexes (TA 92:1-3, 7) are large in scale, covering thousands of meters. Smaller-scale versions are encountered on all terraces (*e.g.*, TA 93:94-95) without major structures, but have the same Iron Age material. Smaller versions of Taqa 60 including tumuli, homesteads, catchment dams, and animal pens were inventoried east of TA 93:60, *e.g.*, TA 92:4, and in the Wadi Nahiz (TA 92:44). Similar sites are known from Khor Rohri (TA 95:231) and again Iron Age buildings are superimposed over the Bronze Age site at 92:46 and extending over 25 km to the east. To the west of Salalah, a similar pattern was seen on the higher terraces overlooking the plain at TA 93:92 and 96. Almost identical site layouts have been reported from Socotra.[97]

---

97 Doe (1970) 4 and figs. 12, 14, 40 and pl. 67. (1983) 19. Naumkin and Sedov (1993)

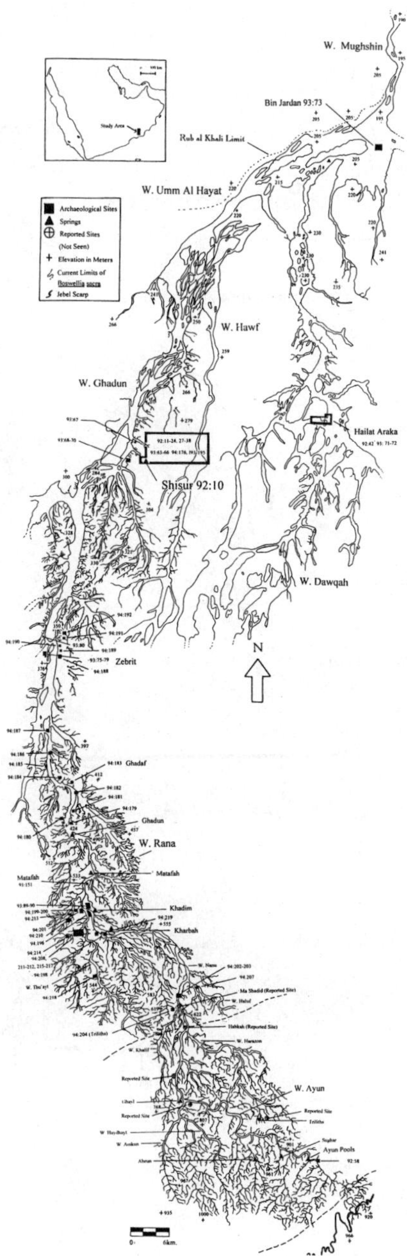

Fig. 9: *Archaeological Sites in the Wadi Ghadun System, especially in relation to Shisur (TA 92:10)*

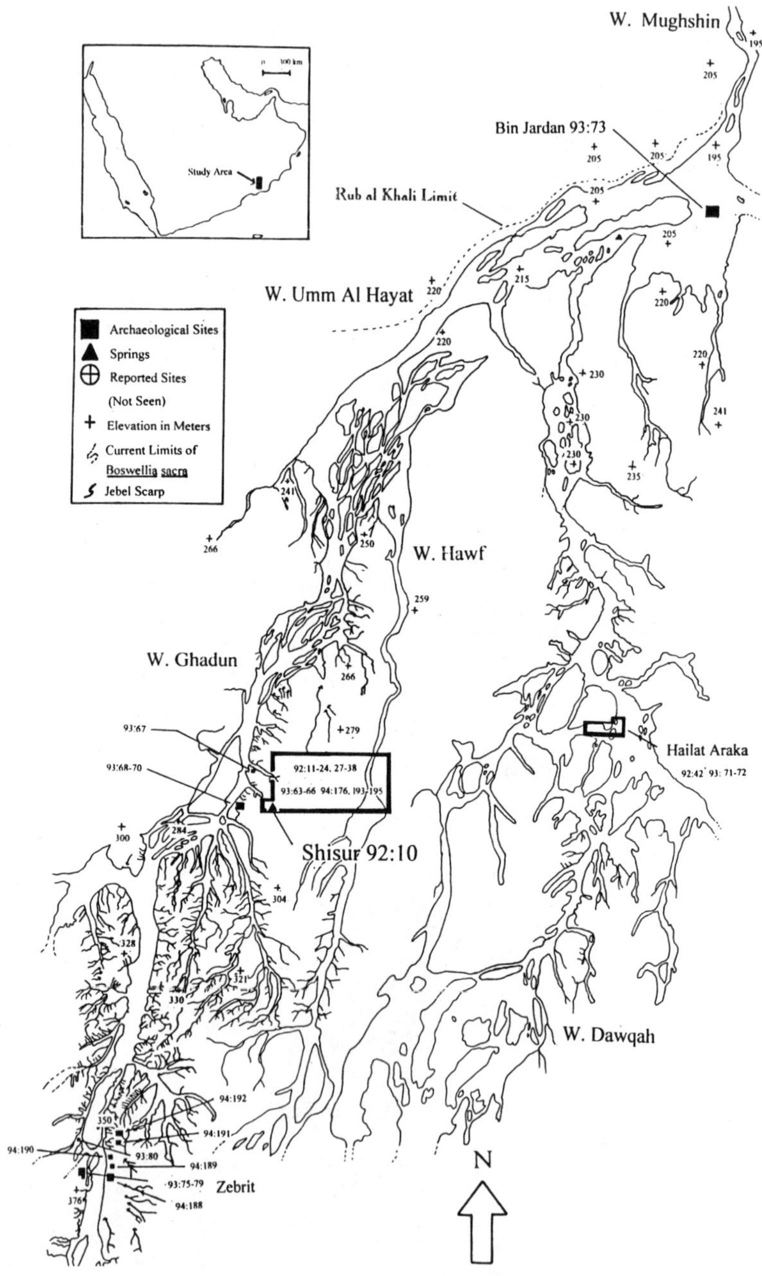

Fig. 9A: *Archaeological Sites in the Wadi Ghadun System*

Fig. 9B: *Archaeological Sites in the Wadi Ghadun System*

"Boat-shaped graves" constitute another feature of the Iron Age. At Ain Humran (TA94:209)., Khor Sowli (TA92:6), Khor Rohri (TA 92:46), Sinur (TA 95:5), Wadi Darbat (TA95:255) and Ain Razat (TA92:61), tomb-fields were located which consist of multiple graves constructed of large, often megalithic-sized stones. The ellipse-shaped plan suggests a boat or ship, hence the name. First noted by the Bents,[98] we have observed hundreds of such graves. They are always joined together creating the impression of rows or clusters. Excavation of several graves at Khor Sowli and Ain Humran suggests they were in place by the Iron Age as lithic and ceramic material was found scattered around them. The actual chamber dug as a shaft inside the grave revealed a single body laid extended in a simple pit. No grave goods were found inside.[99]

Turning to the Dhofari interior, we found a number of Iron Age sites. The most impressive are those at Hagif (TA95:241) within the Wadi Kharshit system. These sites follow the same pattern of re-occupation recognized on the coast. Original Bronze Age structures were re-used in the Iron Age. The use of small stone construction, as contrasted to the megalithic Bronze Age style, is found here as well. Bronze Age houses are on occasion linked together with larger Iron Age walls for stock care. To the south of Hagif we found smaller satellite sites or homesteads, such as TA 95:249, 250, and 252. At other sites further north into the Nejd, we saw little evidence of the Iron Age period.

The last sites to be examined are found on high terraces immediately overlooking the Nejd. They consist of circular houses, tumuli, boat graves and material culture on elevated terraces within the hills west of Jibjab (TA92:26). The oasis of Andhur (TA 92:41) may represent a similar Iron Age site.

---

584 support Doe's idea that the fields were used to grow incense, aloe, and cinnabar. Our examination of these fields yielded the typical local Iron Age ceramics, as well as isolated microliths and microcores.

98 Bent and Bent (1900), *passim.*

99 Naumkin describes almost identical graves from sites on Socotra (1993) 377-88; Naumkin and Sedov (1993) 577-611.

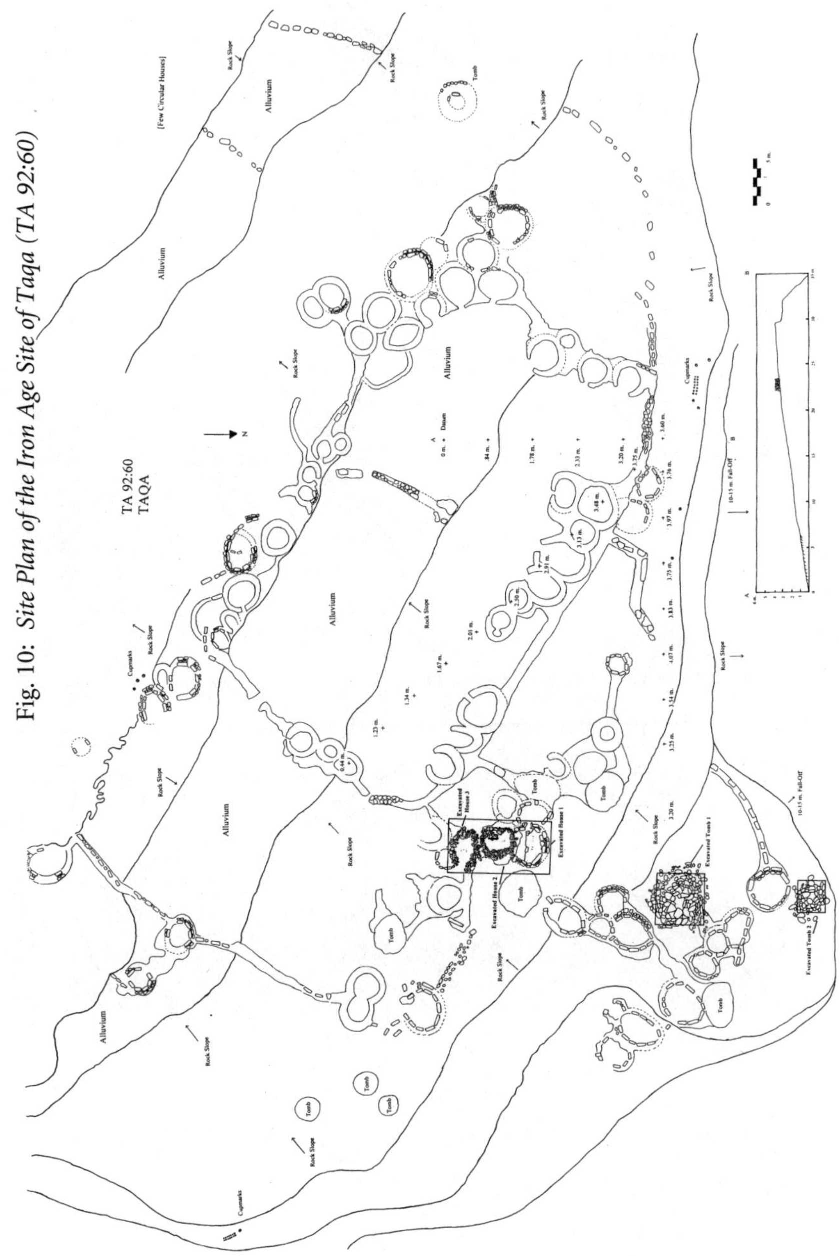

Fig. 10: *Site Plan of the Iron Age Site of Taqa (TA 92:60)*

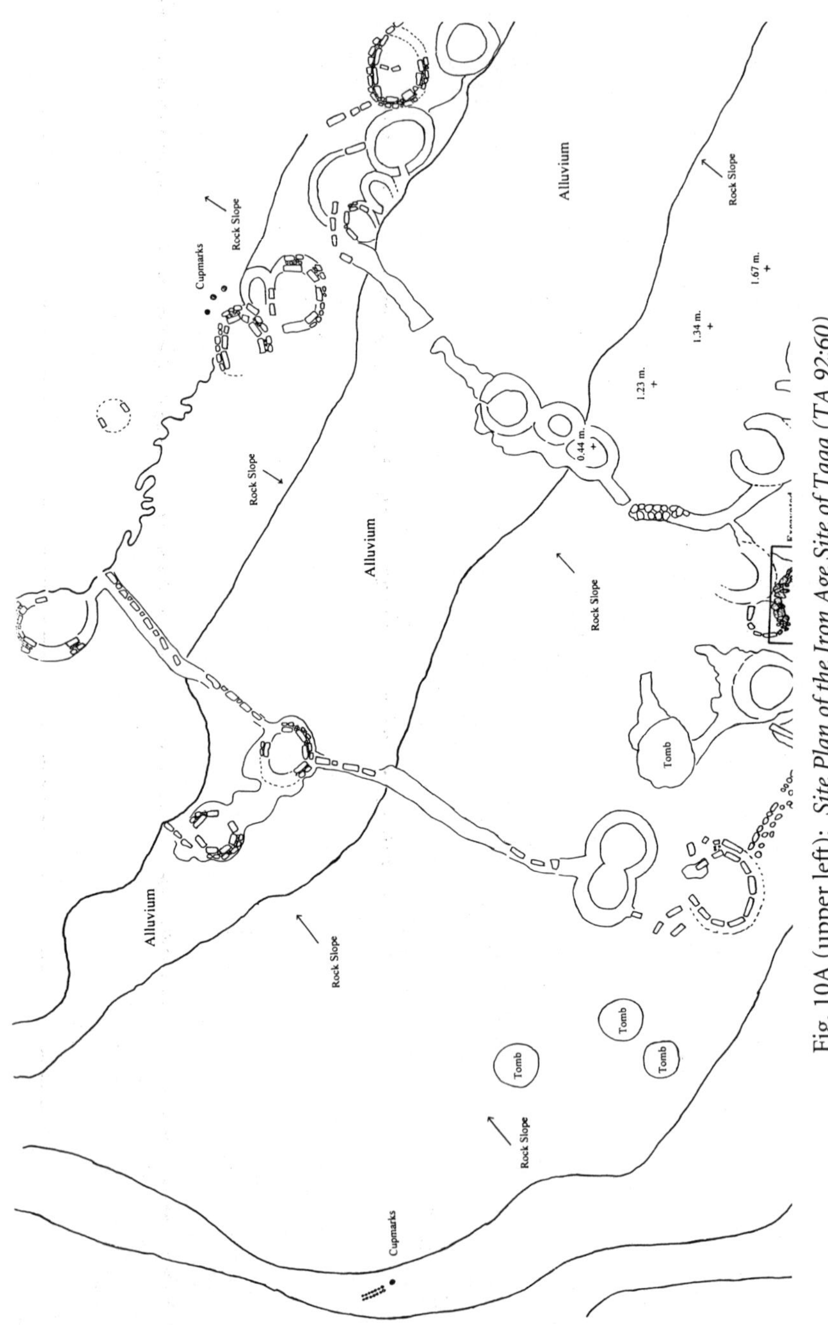

Fig. 10A (upper left): *Site Plan of the Iron Age Site of Taqa (TA 92:60)*

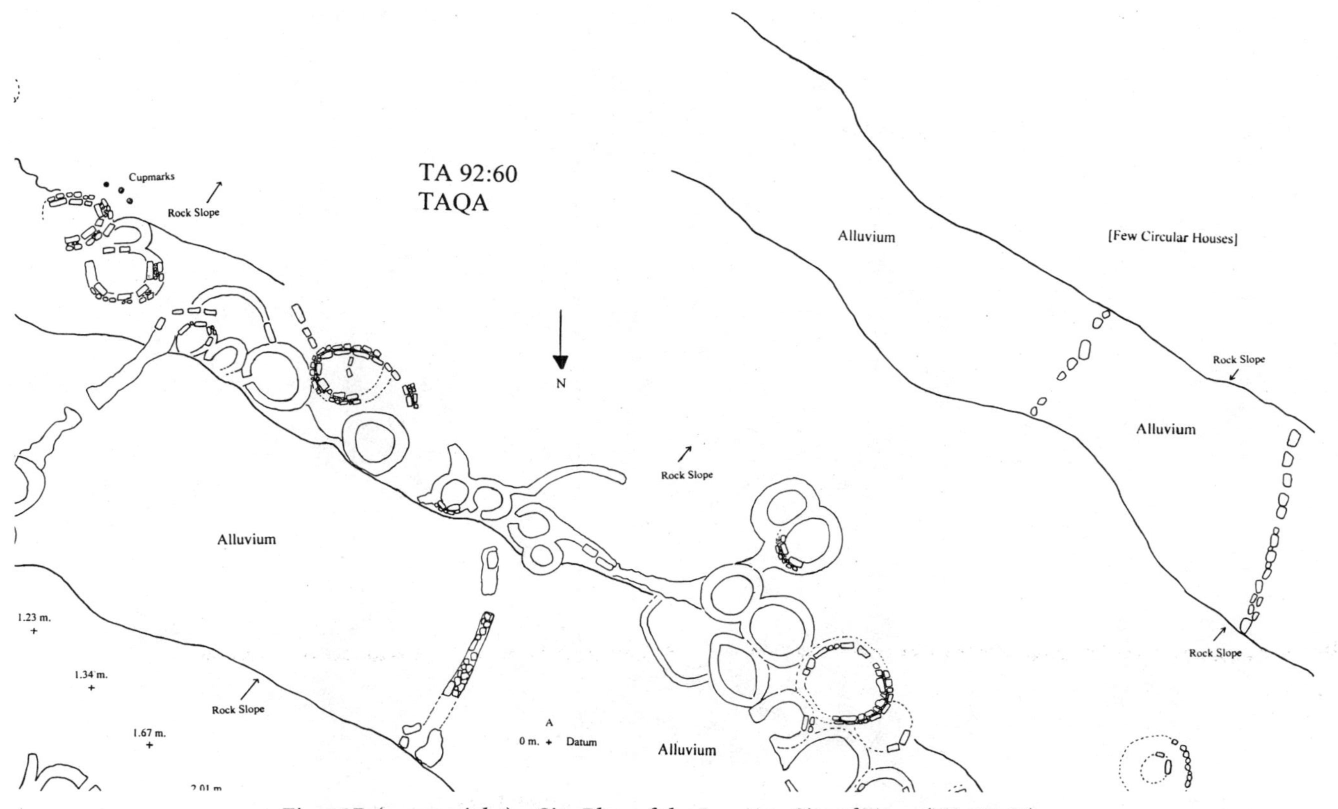

Fig. 10B (upper right): *Site Plan of the Iron Age Site of Taqa (TA 92:60)*

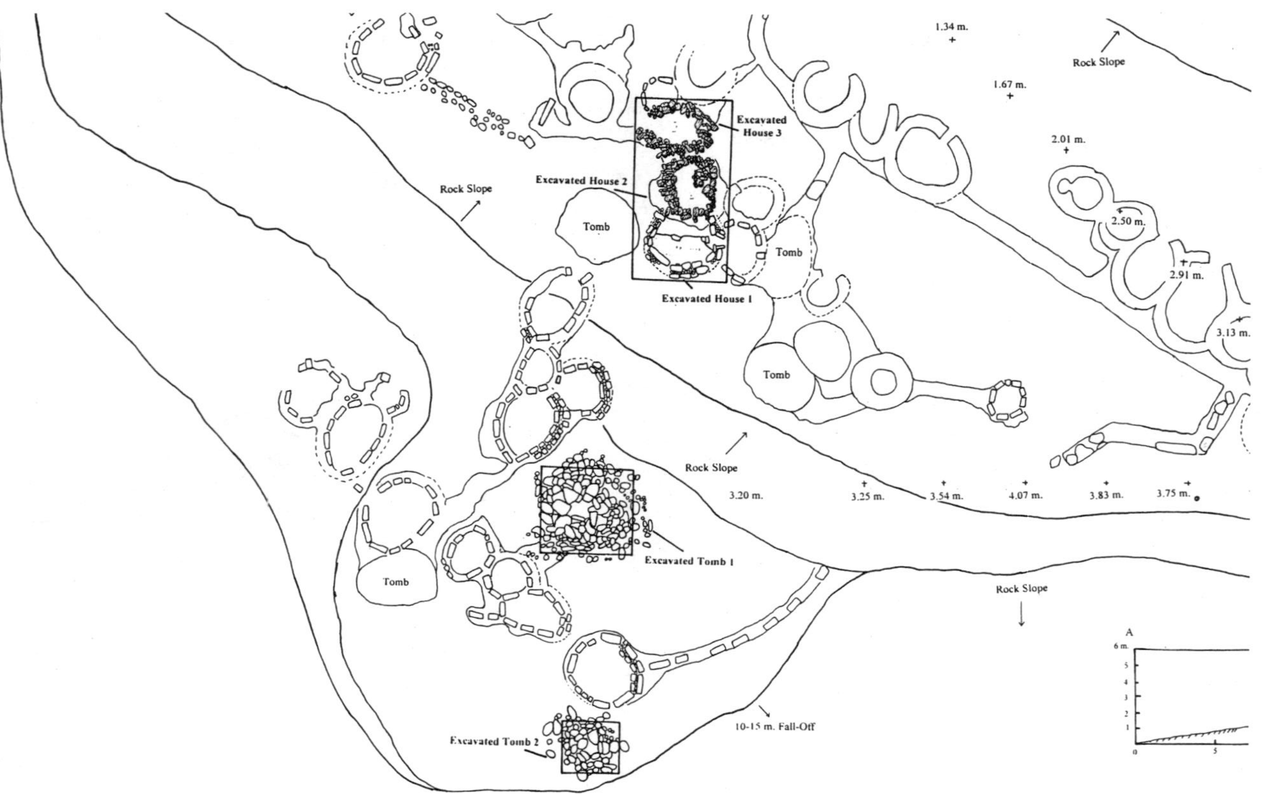

Fig. 10C (lower left): *Site Plan of the Iron Age Site of Taqa (TA 92:60)*

Fig. 10D (lower right): Site Plan of the Iron Age Site of Taqa (TA 92:60)

Impermanent settlements have also been found. For example, a Bronze Age tomb at site 95:224, on a high terrace east of Sinur, revealed a substantial Iron Age occupation. One-fourth of the structure was excavated and over 1 m of stratified material was found. Similar impermanent sites are known from other locales on the Salalah plain scarps and in the Qara Hills.

It appears that the MSA speakers also controlled territory by constructed fortresses in key oases areas (*e.g.*, even in the Wadi Masila, Husn Ad, Qara, Maqrat). The small settlement of Shisur, located 150 km northwest of Salalah, became a focal point of archaeological interest as the result of its association with localities on the Ptolemy map. Situated well within the interior Nejd on the edge of the Rub al Khali, it sits on a collapsed limestone dome from whose base emanates a permanent aquifer spring. Three years of excavation revealed that a central fortress complex dominated the site for over two millennia, from the mid-first millennium B.C.E. to ca. 1500 C.E., when MSA influence was broken by European intervention. The architecture (fig. 11) suggests parallels with other fortress complexes further to the east, notably in the Gulf (*cf.* Hili 14,[100] Jumeirah,[101] Qalat Bahrain,[102] and to the west Aqaba[103]). The standard partition walls within the interior part of the fortress were used for a variety of human activities in the past, and we discovered that different partitions had different occupational histories. Some were empty, others had been reused by bedouin, some were entirely Islamic in date, and others had Iron Age/Classical materials. No two adjoining partitions could be counted on to reveal the same sequence. The richest area proved to be the western wall area adjacent to the central citadel.

From Ain Humran, a large coastal fortress (TA 92:55 [fig. 12]), strikingly similar to Shisur, was brought to our attention. It sits on a small promontory about 1 km south of the hills proper at the head of a series of springs leading eventually to Khor Jnaif. The inner partitions of the main wall here

---

100 Boucherlat and Gorczynski (1985).

101 Potts (1990) 299.

102 Kervran (1993).

103 Whitcomb (1988).

Fig. 11: *Site Plan of the Shisur Fort* (TA 92:10)

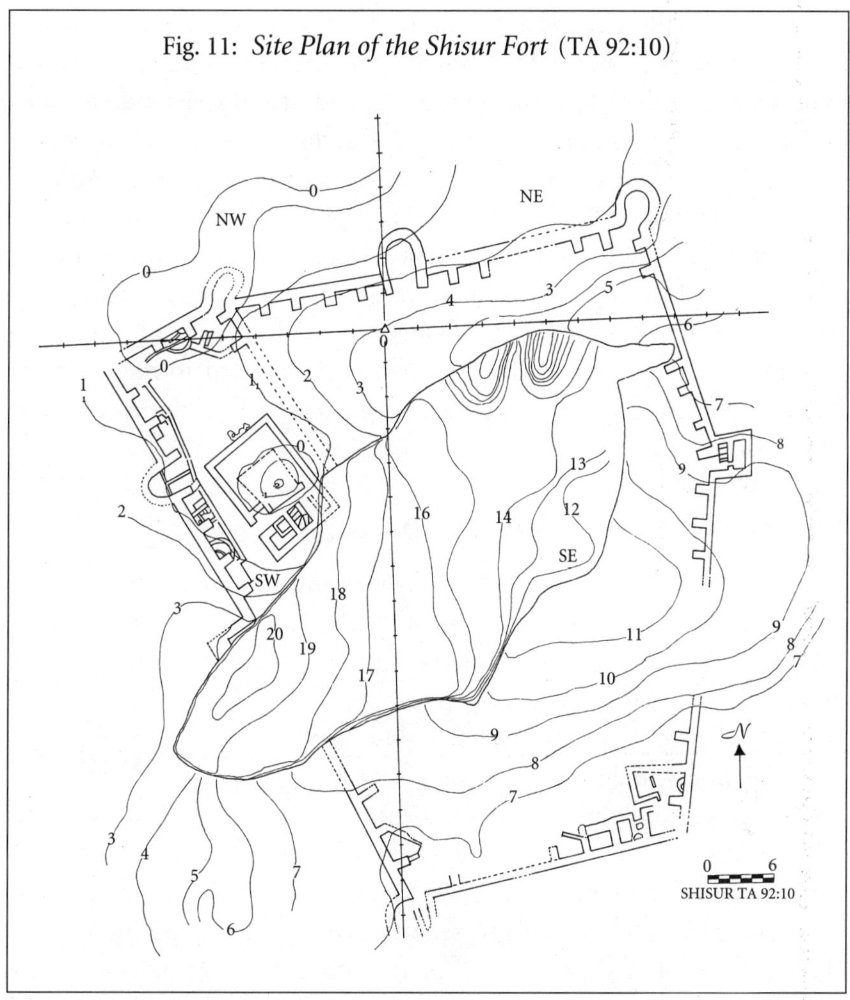

are identical to those found at Shisur. In contrast to Shisur, we found here numerous rectangular, fired clay bricks strewn over the site. Many retained mould marks. Since Dhofar is in limestone country and we found no kilns in the area, the presence of fired brick is highly unusual and suggests a northern Oman origin. Similar brickwork has been reported from Parthian, Sasanian and Islamic levels at Sohar.[104] In contrast to Shisur, the complex at Ain Humran, has been rebuilt and heavily disturbed over the centuries.

Below the fortress to the north and situated on a lower terrace is the Ain Humran village (TA 95:99). The layout of the walls, the size of rooms and general appearance of the village suggest close parallels to the village of Hajrya on Socotra (fig. 13).[105] Both are to be dated to the early centuries C.E. (see below).

Material Culture

The definition of the Dhofar Iron Age as contemporaneous in part with the "Arabs" of the classical writers, and their mention as Mahra, Hakali/ Sakalan or the Iobaritae, rests largely on lithic and ceramic definitions tied to settlement remains and C-14 dating.

Unfortunately, until 1992, our only relevant body of evidence came from the poorly understood excavations at Khor Rohri carried out by the AFSM [American Foundation for the Study of Man] in the mid-twentieth century. Khor Rohri was the Shabwa colony identified as SMHRM (see above). Other than the ESA [Epigraphic South Arabian] inscriptions mentioning the country of SKLN (see above), the evidence suggests that the Hadramis established an outpost for the collection of frankincense in a country already inhabited by ancestral MSA [Modern South Arabian] speakers.

Based on the continuing study of Roman and East Mediterranean imports, coinage and inscriptions, authorities have suggested the site was

---

104 Kervran and Hiebert (1991) 339-43.

105 Naumkin and Sedov (1993) 601.

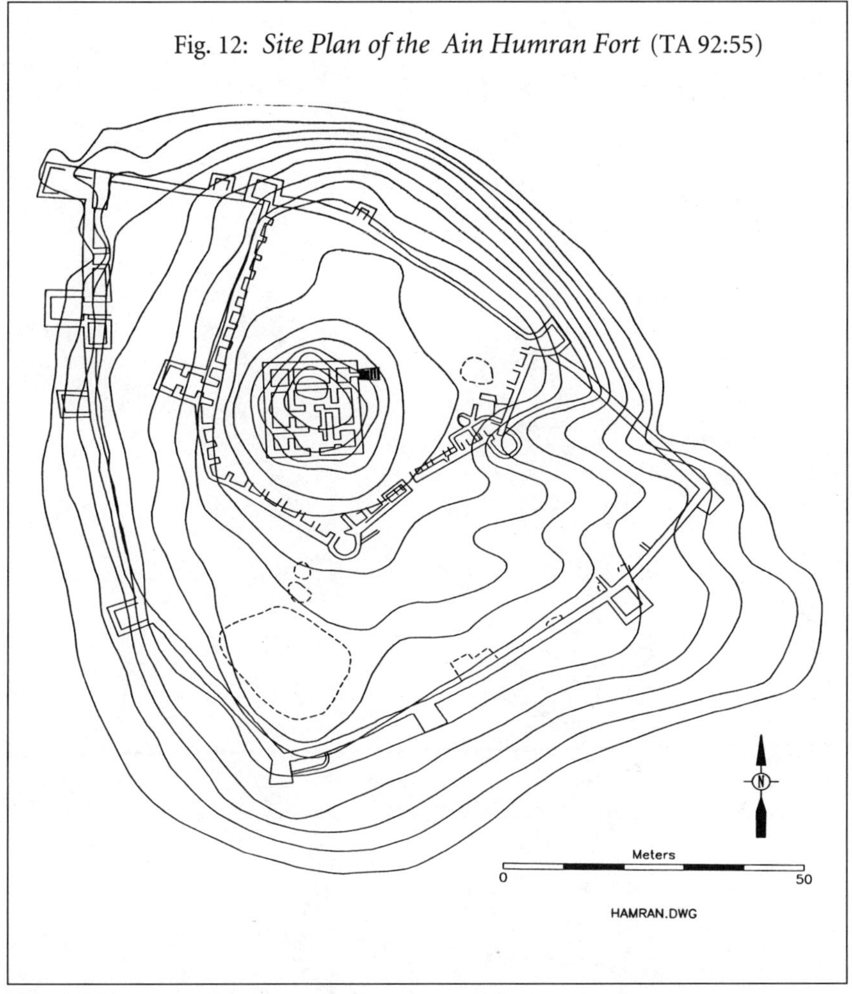

Fig. 12: *Site Plan of the Ain Humran Fort* (TA 92:55)

Fig. 13: *The Ain Humran Village Site* (TA 95:99)

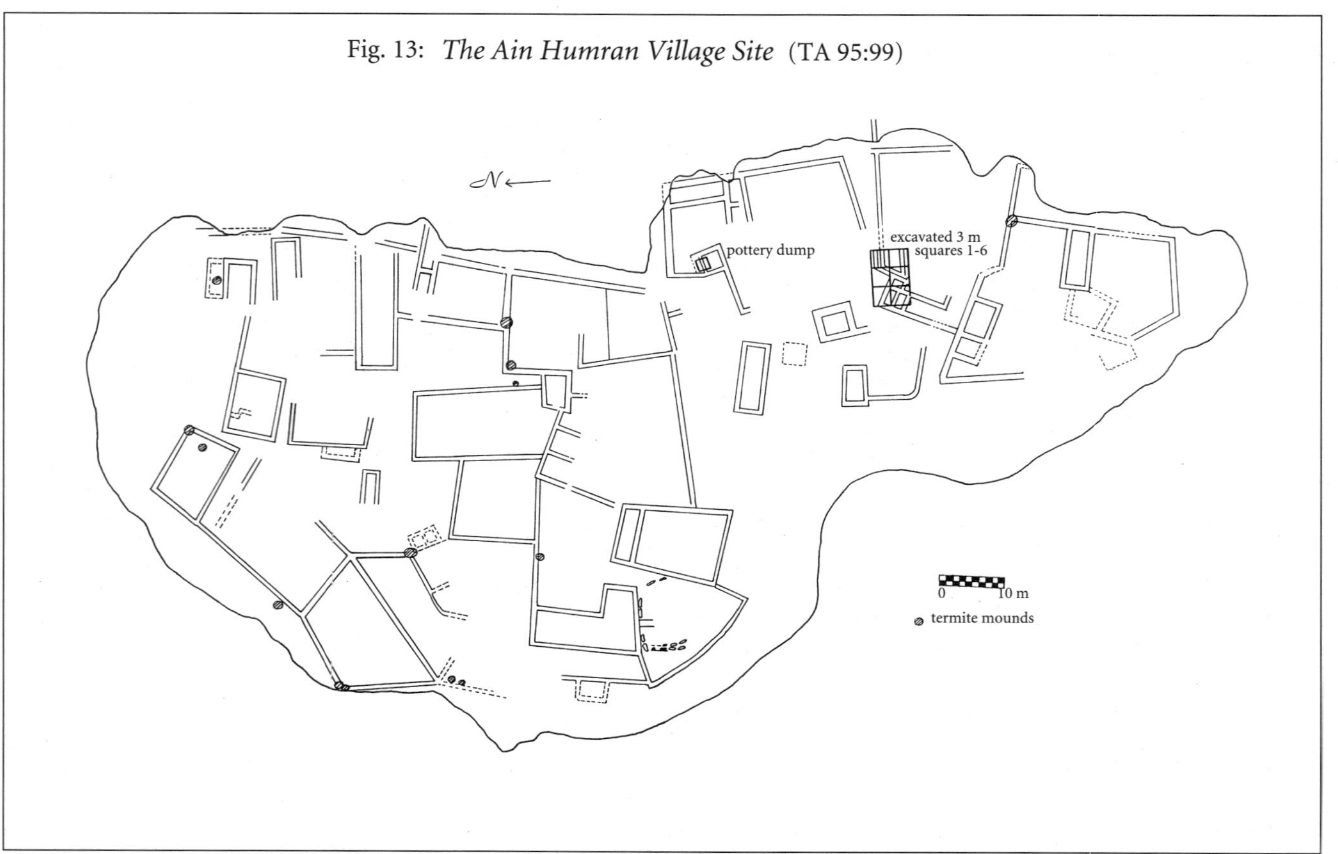

occupied from the first through fourth centuries C.E.[106] Since Khor Rohri remained the only Iron Age site reported by the AFSM expedition along the Dhofar coast, and the ESA inscriptions mentioned specifically the SAKALAN region, numerous subsequent authorities have reasoned that Khor Rohri and Sumhuram must be the Moscha Limen in the Periplus.[107]

The Ceramic Assemblages

Fortunately, despite the lack of work in the region until 1992, Yule and Kervran undertook an investigation of a large number of unpublished ceramics excavated at Khor Rohri.[108] They describe twenty-one sherds[109] which are of vital interest for chronological and geographical purposes. A number of red-slipped vessels are labelled as being imported, and described as Indian Red Polished Ware (RPW).[110] Similar to Roman sigillata pottery, the type is generally recognized on western Indian sites as belonging to the early centuries C.E.[111] This ware has been recognized at Ed-Dur and Sohar as well as other sites in the Gulf, and more recently from Iranian sites and Hajra on Socotra.[112] A distinctive variant, a polished black ware, has also

---

106 Albright, as the principal excavator of the site, provides this date bracket; see also Comfort 1960, Sedov (1992) 124-25; Sedov and Aydrus (1995) 19, 44-45.

107 Schoff (1912) is based on the opinions of Bent and Bent (1890, 1895). Many others have followed with a similar opinion, *e.g.*, Doe (1971) 16, 49; Pirenne (1975) 95; Müller (1977); Groom (1981) 110; Albright (1982) 7; Casson (1989) 172; Sedov and Aydrus (1995) 19.

108 For the study of seventeen sherds from the site by the excavator, see Albright (1982) 92-94. In spite of his disclaimer that only 73 sherds were worth noting, (*ibid.* 92), a very large corpus of material was in fact collected and stored. W. Glanzman is now in the process of studying this corpus.

109 Yule and Kervran (1993) figs. 3-4.

110 Yule and Kervran (1993) 91 and fig. 3/1-5; Yule (1993) 257. For a full discussion of the RPW in India, see Begley (1991) 189 n. 5; Orton (1991) and for a map showing the Indian distribution, see Begley (1991) map 10.1. In India, the consensus is that the ware represents a range from the middle of the first century B.C.E. to the fifth century C.E.

111 Yule and Kervan (1993) 93; Yule (1993) 257.

112 Naumkin and Sedov (1993) 600-5; Sedov (1988) 91.

been reported from Qana (lower phase), Socotra (Naumkin and Sedov 1993:605) and Arikamedu as well as ed-Dur in the Gulf.[113]

Other sherds illustrated by Yule and Kervran from Khor Rohri[114] are called "local ware," but based on collections from Yemen and our own collections from Khor Rohri, are, in fact, typical of South Arabic or Hadrami vessels.[115]

Of critical interest here is the vessel illustrated in Yule and Kervran.[116] They call the bowl fragment with rouletting and dot/circle motif "a pseudo-terra sigillata sherd of local origin from Khor Rohri." They add that it shows Indian influence in the use of burnishing and a chattered frieze. The row of dotted circles is a purely local addition. This vessel type then is defined as a local product merging Roman, Indian, and *native* taste.[117] They date this vessel type to the first-second centuries C.E. In fact, this type becomes a hallmark for the Dhofar region.[118]

Before we tackle the question of "imports" in Dhofar however, we must establish what the local ceramic assemblages from the Classical period really are. Local Iron Age material appears to be primarily either grit or shell tempered. Open jars and bowls are often plain and highly burnished. The most distinctive vessels are marked with incised decorations. Most often, the pattern consists of rosettes, chevrons, or pendant triangles. The rims are often incised with slashes or chevrons (fig. 14). Representative material is best known from the pottery dump at Ain Humran where distinctive pieces

---

113 Sedov 1992; Naumkin and Sedov (1993) 605. Two Nabatean painted sherds from Khor Rohri are assigned to the early first century C.E., see Yule and Kevran (1993) 93; Yule (1993) 258.

114 (1993), fig. 4.

115 Standard South Arabic ceramic assemblages are known from a number of sources, *e.g.*, Caton-Thompson (1944); Van Beek (1969); Glanzman (1987); Zarins *et al.* (1983); Vinogradov and Bamakhrama (1995); Sedov (1995) 106-12.

116 Yule and Kervran (1993) fig. 3/6; Yule (1993) fig. 6/19.

117 Yule and Kervran (1993) 93, (my emphasis).

118 Two other finds from Khor Rohri of Indian origin include a small bronze Salabhanjika dated to the beginning of the third century C.E. (see Albright [1982] 101 no. 137; Goetz [1963] 189) and a Kushan coin of Kanishka I and similarly dated (Sedov [1992] 126).

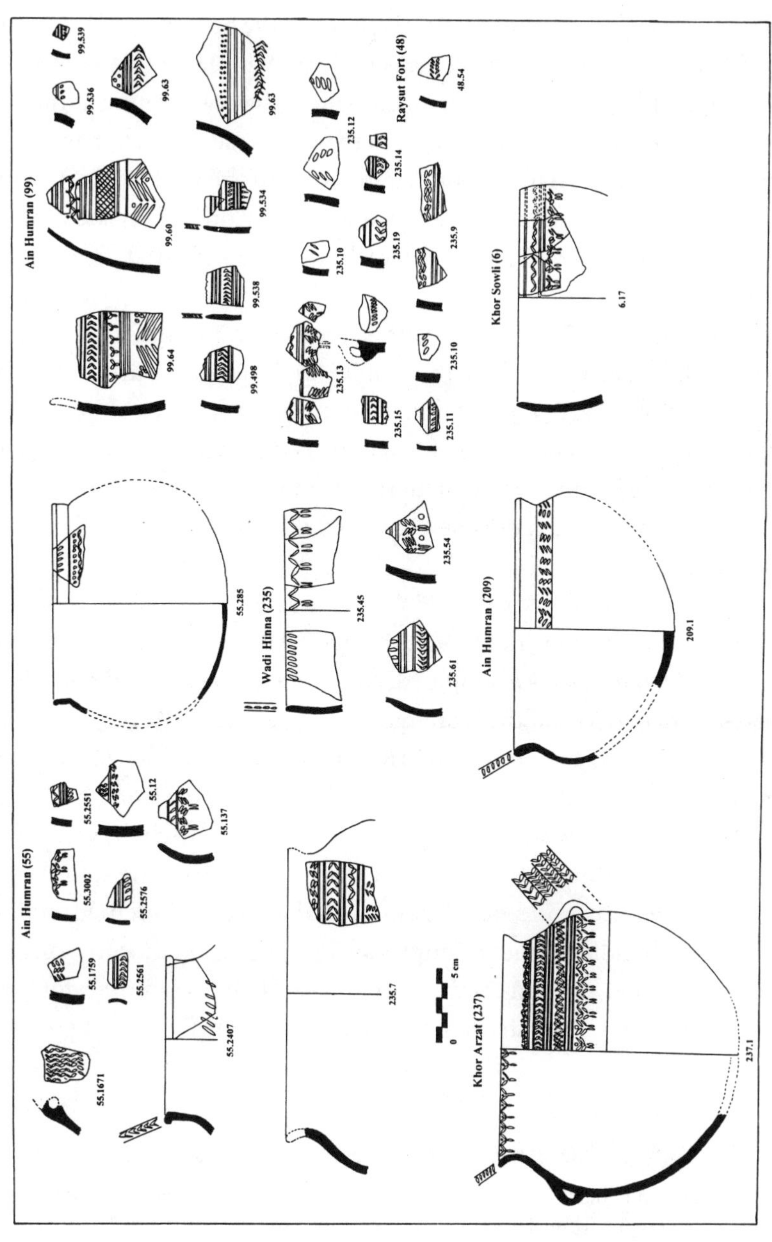

Fig. 14: *Iron Age Local Wares from Selected Dhofari Sites*

have several motifs integrated together. Other important sites are to be found on the paleo-lagoons (TA92:67, 237), at the boat-shaped burial areas (TA92:6) and the upper spring areas such as Wadi Hina (TA 95:235). On the Dhofar Hills and the Nejd, similar material has been found at the Hagif area sites. The ceramics, in contrast to the lithics (see below), have little in common with the classical South Arabic sites to the west or North Oman to the east. The closest parallels excavated to date come from Socotra.[119] Of course, no sites of comparable date have been reported from eastern Yemen.

Our greatest collection of material comes from Shisur. The earliest ceramics here are most likely the simple, typically red, burnished bowls. They are well known from the South Arabic tradition and can be considered to date the earliest phase of the formal fortress sometime prior to the first century B.C.E. The bulk of the material from the first century B.C.E. to the fourth century C.E. includes the types already discussed above from other Iron Age sites.

The Red Polished Wares (RPW), often with complex incised rim and upper body decoration, identified as Indian RPW, are well attested at Shisur (figs. 15-16). Numerous examples occur in lower levels throughout the site where *in situ* material of the Iron Age is present. The RPW ware from Khor Rohri and other coastal sites such as Ras Jinjali and Al Balid is virtually identical. Our excavated RPW wares have parallels to material from Sohar which are attributed to the early Parthian period.[120] The dot-in-circle ware is probably the most common type at Shisur (figs. 17-18). Here we found vessels with restricted necks and ticked rims, a double row of dot/circle and often attached lug handles. Other examples are open bowls often with a ring base. Another distinctive feature is the use of incised lines to multiple dot-circles located on the base. The chattered, rouletting varies from carefully executed

119 Naumkin and Sedov (1993) 595, 606-7; Naumkin (1993) 103, 121-23.

120 Kervran and Hibert (1991) 339-41 describe the lowest levels at Sohar as "Parthe?" and datable perhaps from the first century B.C.E. to third centuries C.E. The RPW wares, fig. 4/16-19, are described as imported from India, with parallels from Banbhore and Arikamedu.

Fig. 15: *Iron Age Imported Wares (RPW, Gray Wares) principally from Shisur*

rocker stamp (early) to degenerate rectangular impressions (late). Often polished, the ware as we suggested earlier is indigenous to Dhofar. The large amounts of this ware at Shisur and allied sites in the Qara Hills, and the coastal plain, suggest a Dhofari tradition belonging to the early MSA speakers (figs. 20-21). As indicated earlier, only one piece of dot-in-circle ware was reported from Khor Rohri.

Contemporary to the dot-in-circle and RPW wares from Shisur is a smaller category of carinate black shiny wares again paralleled at Socotra and Qana as well as Sohar (figs. 15-16).[121] Even more intriguing is a distinctive category at Shisur of large, open bowls with applique and incised rims (fig. 15). This type recalls Hellenistic or Seleucid types found in Eastern Arabia. The last category of ceramics at Shisur consists of a brown ware with mica temper and punctate decoration along the upper neck, again suggesting a local coastal connection.

The Shisur site continued to be occupied in the post-fourth century C.E. Two C-14 dates, one at 495 C.E. and the other at 595 C.E. come from levels defined by well-burnished brown ware bowls and jars. Purple paint was applied to the neck and interior of the vessel often in small triangles. Contemporary amphorae are known from the coast at Raysut, paralleling the finds from Masirah Island.[122]

At Ain Humran, excavations from the fortress produced few examples of RPW, black polished, dot-circle or rocker stamp wares. However, the 1995 excavations at the village site below the fortress (see above) produced a rich picture of the Iron Age. Over 2500 sherds were found in a pottery dump sondage 1 x 3 m less than 60 cm deep. Eighty percent of the finds were

---

121 The finds from Sohar are again attributed to the Early Parthian phase (Kervran and Hibert [1991] fig. 4/14-15; from Socotra, the type was found at the settlement of Hajrya, Naumkin and Sedov (1993) 605; Naumkin [1988] 91-92; Naumkin [1993] 120. At Qana, similar wares are reported, Sedov (1992) 126-27 and imply again, trade with India in the early centuries C.E.

122 Shanfari (1987) fig. 24; site 58; Sedov (1992) 113. Late Iron Age sites from the sixth to eighth centuries C.E. were also reported from Socotra (Naumkin and Sedov (1993) 582 n. 14, 608, 611. Similar material has also been reported from Aqaba, see Whitcomb (1988) 18.

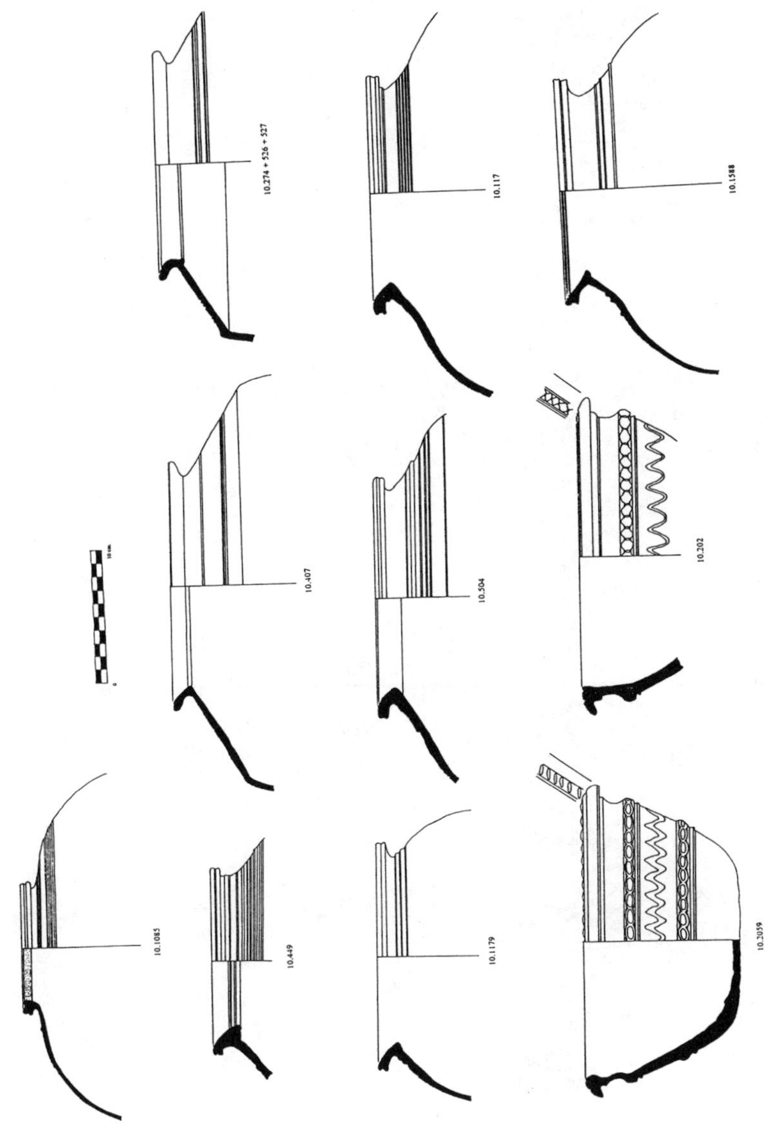

Fig. 16: *Iron Age Imported Wares from Shisur (RPW) and Applique Wares*

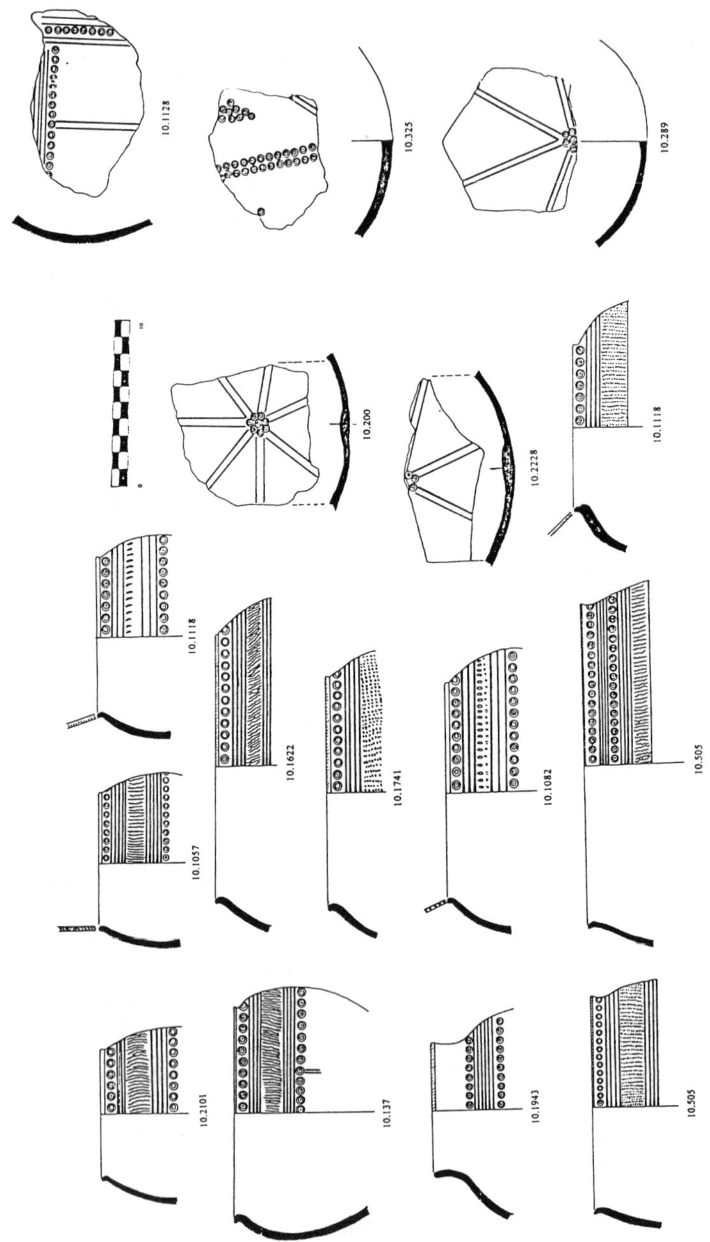

Fig. 17: *Dot and Circle Rouletted Wares from Shisur*

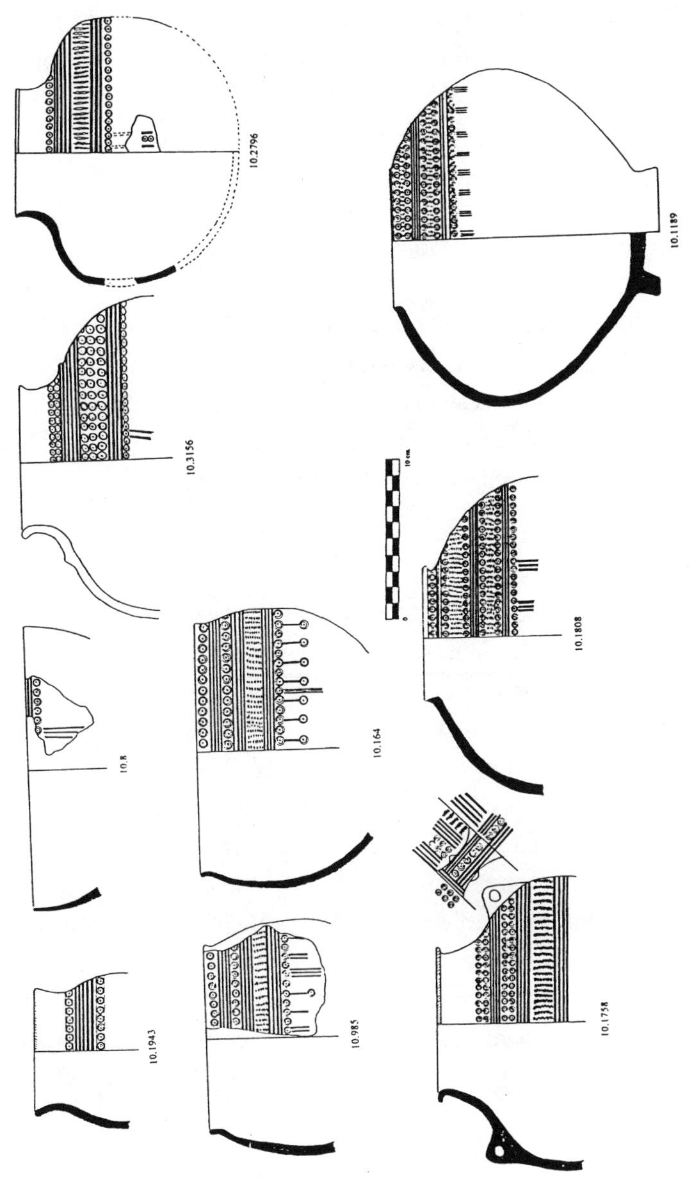

Fig. 18: *Dot and Circled Rouletted Wares from Shisur*

plain simple burnished bowls with grit temper. Another 15% were carinate high-necked vessels. But we also found numerous examples of both RPW and black polished wares. Also common were dot-circle vessels as well as examples with punctate shoulders and rolled rims. A new category was the impressed, not incised chevron design. Finally, a number of vessels had a combination of design motifs such as chevrons and pendant triangles. Others combined an impressed, chattered design with the dot-circle and punctate decoration.

In sum, the ceramic evidence links Dhofar as an integral whole with regions to the west (Hadramaut/Qana), Socotra as well as to the east (Sohar, Arikamedu, ed-Dur). Based on the commentary supplied by the Periplus, the Indo-Parthians/Scythians who controlled Iran and northern India participated in a large-scale trade network involving most of the northern rim of the western Indian Ocean. These ties not only involved the Dhofar coast, but also sites well into the interior, *e.g.*, Shisur.[123]

Lithics

Prior to our work, nothing was known of Iron Age period lithics. We quickly learned that Iron Age sites are characterized by microlithic technique (fig. 19). At most sites we found small flakes, scrapers, bladelets, and, particularly, microliths as well as evidence of microlith production such as wasted microcores, core-trimming elements and bladelets with lateral snaps. The microliths themselves take the form of trapezoids, rectangles, and crescents (lunates) with retouch on the lateral edge. At a particularly rich site, TA 95:224, the entire manufacturing process has been documented. Fashioned in chert/flint, these microliths have been found on Iron Age sites from Wadi Adhonib to Mirbat and from the coastal terraces to the interior Nejd.

The nearest parallels for this industry come from the Hadramaut itself, since no sites of this age have been examined in eastern Yemen. At four Hadramaut locations, microliths have been reported: Sune, Shibam,

---

123 Periplus, sec. 36-39. Casson ed. (1989) 73-75; for a summary of this historical data, see Frye (1984) 177-247.

Gheibun and Hureidha.[124] Caton-Thompson dated the microliths from Hureidha to the seventh-fifth centuries B.C.E. based on the style of seals from the same tombs (A5 and A6).[125]

From the highlands of western Yemen, Rahimi identified a similar collection of microliths and processing system. He dates the levels from Wadi Jubbah to the sixth and fifth centuries B.C.E. based on C-14 dates.[126] It is very interesting to note that in this regard the Dhofari and Hadramaut sites have a connection to the Iron Age of western Yemen, a feature not shared by the ceramic materials. Finally, our excavations at Taqa and Wadi Sinur suggest that the tradition of microlith use may have persisted well into the early centuries C.E. in Dhofar itself.

Triliths

Another feature of interest here are the triliths. These monuments are a long alignment of three-stone groupings with elliptical circles surrounding them as a collar. They are usually found on wadi terrace banks with no discernible single orientation preference. The full row in length varies from a few meters to over 25 m. Spaces between the triliths are filled with smaller stones. To the side, small boulders forming a rough square are usually present. Large firepits now filled with ash and lined with stones are always present to the side as well.[127]

It has been shown that a fourth, inscribed stone in local South Semitic script was placed on top of the trilith stones.[128] This would suggest that, in part, the triliths are to be identified with the MSA speakers since Al-Shahri has shown that "Thamudic" type inscriptions are known from the region

---

124 Caton-Thompson and Gardiner (1939) 31 and n. 2; Caton-Thompson (1944) 134-35 and figs. 58 and 60.

125 Caton-Thompson (1944) 93, 134.

126 Rahimi (1987) 139-43, fig. 8.2 and tables 8.1-8.4.

127 For basic descriptions by travellers and explorers, see Thomas (1932) 126-28; Thesiger (1946) 133; Dostal (1968); Von Wissmann and Hofner (1952) 320-21.

128 Thomas (1932)126-29; Al Shahri (1991a) 189-91.

both in Dhofar and Yemen (see above). C-14 dates from excavations of the firepits place the triliths firmly in the Iron Age (150 B.C.E. to 100 C.E.)[129] and thus contemporary to the Iron Age inhabitants of Dhofar.

Triliths have been found throughout the modern range of the Mahra (figs. 3-4) from the western-most examples near Habban to finds throughout both sides of the Hadramaut. They may have been present on Socotra[130] and on Abd al Kuri near Socotra.[131] The largest concentrations have been reported in the Dhofar region, prompting scholars to suggest that they are somehow to be associated with the MSA speakers.[132] We had suggested earlier that linguistic work hinted at a greater expansion of MSA speakers eastward than previously thought. This can be supported by the trilith argument, since they have been found as far east as the Omani Sharqiya.[133]

Excavations of the firepits noted that they were backfilled and contain no domestic refuse. This suggests a ritual rather than domestic function sometimes attributed to Indian connections.[134] The function of the triliths has caused continuing controversy, but it would appear that based on the description of construction and ritual, they could be linked to Zoroastrian practices.[135] These practices revolve around purification from exposure to

---

129 DeCardi, *et al.* (1977) 28; Al Shahri (1991b) 193.

130 Wellsted as cited by Dostal (1968) 58-59; Doe (1970) 9, pls. 5-6, 30-33. figs. 8-10.

131 Doe (1970) 116 and pl. 93.

132 Dostal (1967) 57; De Cardi *et al.* (1977) 29 and fig. 7; Doe (1983) 77.

133 De Cardi *et al.* (1977) 31.

134 DeCardi *et al.* (1977) 25-28, 32.

135 For direct evidence of Zoroastrian practices in Arabia, specifically at the port of ed-Dur, during the Parthian period, see Potts (1990) 274-85. Note especially the stone platforms, the ostotheques, and the strainer with bull's head and ladles. The Belgian work at Ed-Dur turned up additional items associated with Zoroastrian practices, as well as a fire altar dedicated to Shamash (see Haerinck [1992] 197-99; Haerinck *et al.* [1991] esp. fig. 6, 37-38; Haerick *et al.* [1992] figs. 1-4; *cf.* a Parthian shrine at Hatra dedicated to Shamash, Colledge [1967] 100, 132; Ed-Dur is one of the candidates [along with Sohar] for classical Omana, see a summary in Potts [1990] 306-9). Similar ladles, strainers, and other items have also turned up at Sumail and Rostaq in north Oman, (see Haerick [1992] 197-99).

the evil spirits emanating from death.[136] In a description of the Bareshnum ritual, we note the digging of pits and the use of stones set in clearly defined rectangles. The number of stone sets most often mentioned is three, five or nine.[137] Other rites (*e.g.*, Bui, Aesma-bui) involve fire purification which requires the use of frankincense.[138]The ritual use of ashes from the firepit may be a Hindu modification.[139] Ritual meals are also closely associated with these rituals.

In our survey of trilith data, we note that both Thomas and Thesiger noted that the trilith numbers invariably were three, five, seven, nine, twelve, or fifteen. In one case twenty-five were noted.[140] Thesiger notes that five was the most common number.[141] The number of triliths which consistently can be divided by three or five, the presence of boulders for seats or steps and non-reusable fire pits all may adequately explain the Zoroastrian rituals mentioned above. Given the nature of Indo/Scythian and Persian involvement in Dhofar in the Iron Age and the desire to collect incense from Dhofar for ritual practices in Persia/Northwest India, it could be argued that these triliths are not commemorative for people who have died, or just for ritual meals, but for ritual purity for living people warding off evil spirits.[142]

---

136 For a basic description of these rituals, see Boyce (1977) 110-16. Note the use of the phrase "went on the stones." For a more complete analysis of the rituals, see Modi (1922) 102-66.

137 Modi (1922) 122-25. For a shortened version of this ritual called Riman, see *ibid.* 153-57. For more recent descriptions and discussions of these rituals, see Choksy (1989) 23-40, 71-77.

138 Modi (1922) 238, 429; Boyce (1977) 75, 81, 157 n. 41, 217. In the Avesta, as part of the Yacna liturgical services, frankincense is also used on the fire, (Modi [1922] 320-21.

139 Duchesne-Guillemin (1966) 75.

140 Thomas (1932) 126; Thesiger (1946) 133, (1984) 90.

141 Thesiger (1946) 133.

142 Thesiger (1946) 133: "commemorate men of importance"; Thomas (1932) 126-28: "grilling flesh on heated stones...sacrificial significance."

Fig. 19: *Iron Age Dhofari Microlithic Technique Flint Tools*

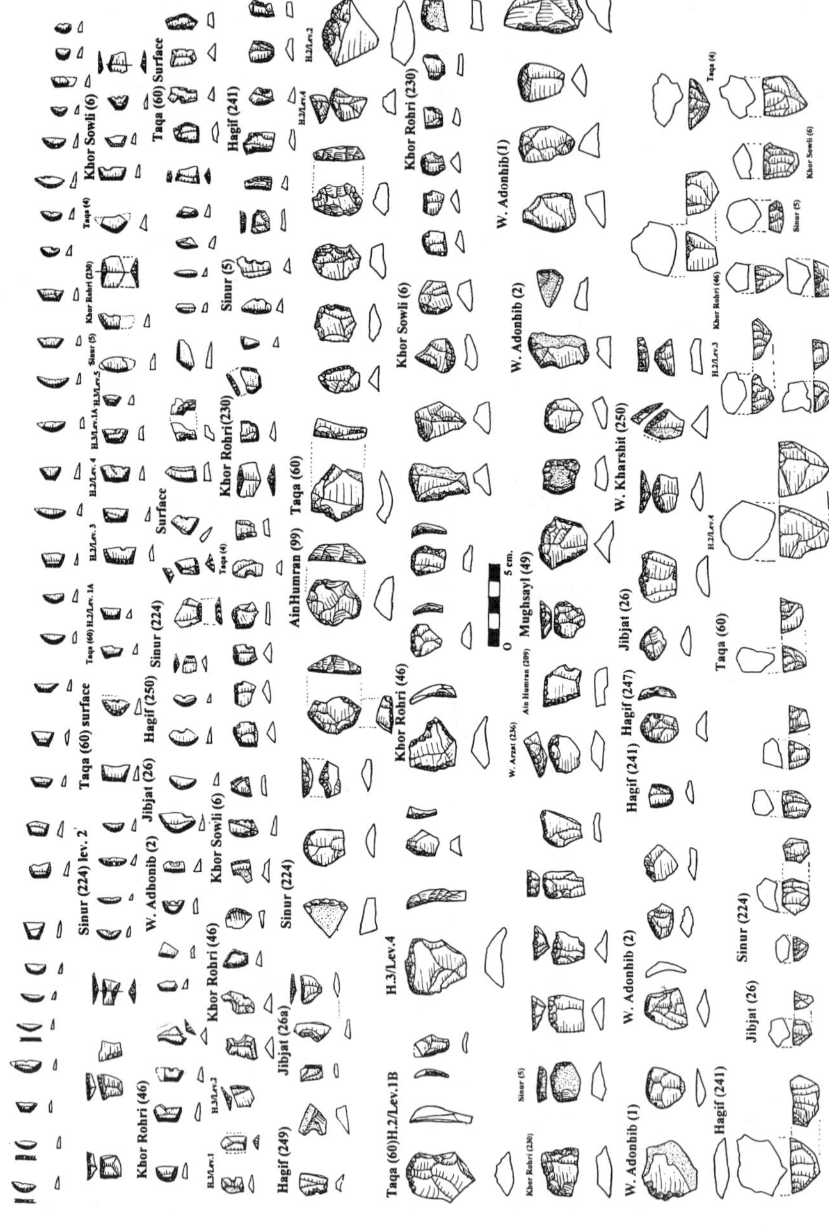

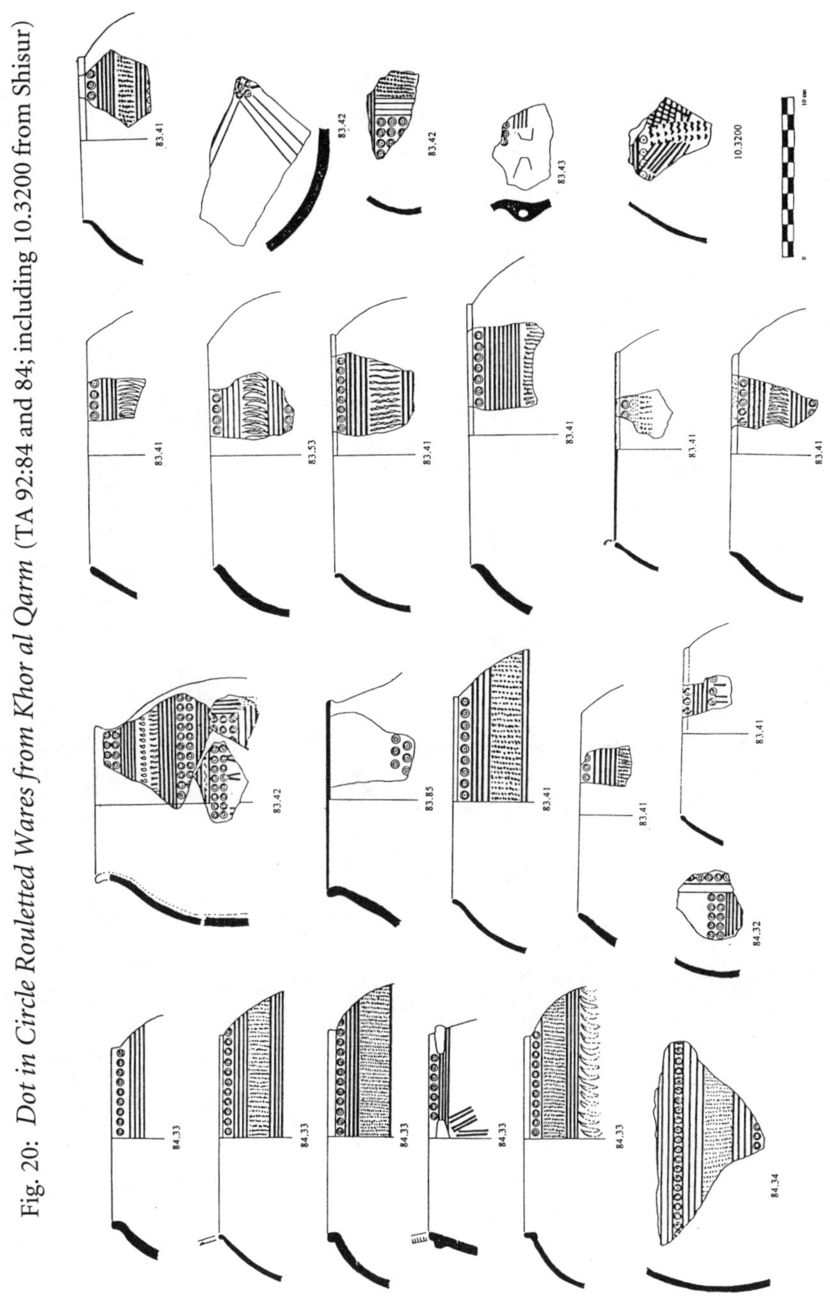

Fig. 20: *Dot in Circle Rouletted Wares from Khor al Qarm* (TA 92:84 and 84; including 10.3200 from Shisur)

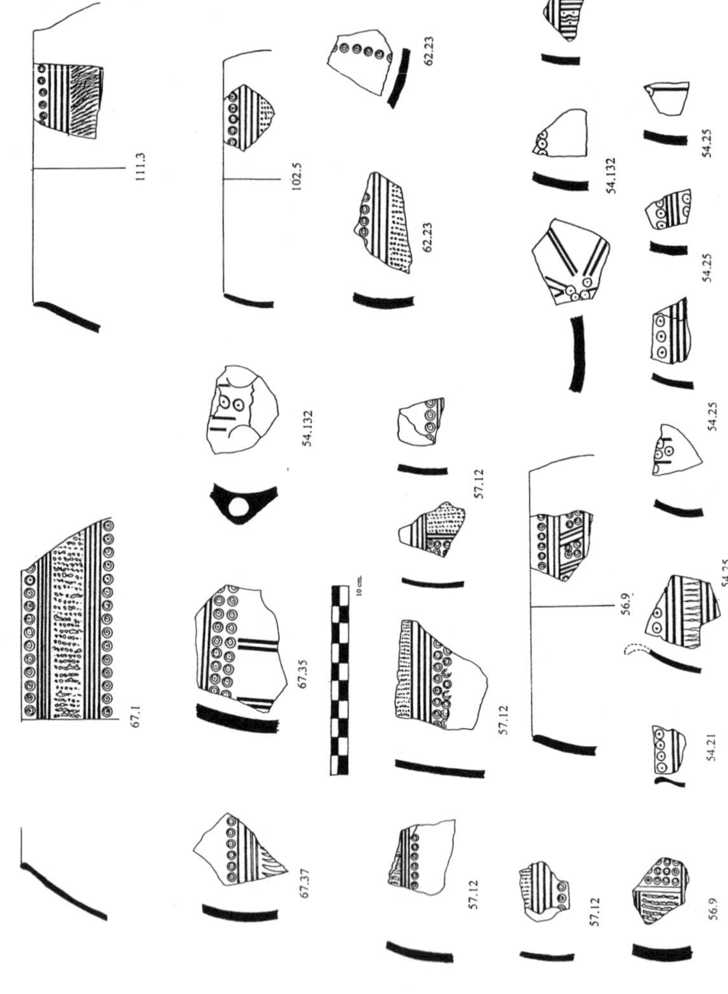

Fig, 21: *Dot in Circle Rouletted Wares from Assorted Dhofari Coastal Site)*

Seafaring

We know that the MSA people were known as seafarers. Settlements of MSA speakers are known not only from the islands mentioned above such as Masirah, the Kuria Marias, Socotra, and Abd al Kuri, but also from Somalia, the Comoro Islands, and possibly East Africa. Both Ibn Majid, who guided Vasco de Gama from East Africa to India, and Sulayman Mahri were Mahra who left behind nautical texts.[143] In our survey work along the Dhofari coast, we found numerous sites which produced the Iron Age Dhofar repertoire (Table 1). Many of the Iron Age Dhofari sites were found not only on lagoons, but usable anchorages.

In addition to the archaeological data, we have the artistic evidence found in Dhofari shelters high in the Qara Hills. Many locales depict fairly accurate renditions of ships. All are sailing ships, several of which resemble sewn boats of standard ancient construction, or inflated types (fig. 22).[144] They most likely demonstrate that MSA populations participated in sea trade from the many lagoons and anchorages found along the coast. Some of the depictions should be contemporary to the archaeological data already recounted above belonging to the Iron Age.[145]

Maka, Arabs and Dhofar

From the above discussion, perhaps several final salient points can be entertained. First, Herodotus and classical writers were aware of the populations who produced frankincense (and myrrh), and referred to them as Arabs (as did the modern explorers). We know that the Iron Age populations as a distinctive group existed in Dhofar and, perhaps due to the trade, extended

---

143 For the summary of data and references, see Müller (1991) 82.

144 Al Shahri (1994) 185-92; for detailed studies of Omani boats, see Vosmer *et al.* (1993); Vosmer (1994). For recent comments on the local sewn boats called the madarate mentioned in the Periplus, sec. 36, see Casson (1989) 181. For an assessment of ships and sailing in the Indian Ocean, see Casson (1991) 8-11.

145 For a preliminary assessment of Iron Age seafaring along the Dhofari coast, see Owen (1995).

TABLE 1
Coastal Sites with Reported Iron Age Dhofar Ceramics

	RPW	Dot/ Circle	Inc/ Imp	Punct	Blk Brn
Taqa (92:56)		✓			
Khor Sowli (92:6)			✓	✓	
Khor Jnawf (92:67; 93:83-84; 95:237)	✓	✓	✓	✓	
Al Balid (92:54)	✓			✓	✓
K. Awqad (93:91)	✓				
Mughsayl (92:49)	✓	✓	✓	✓	
Setima (93:101)	✓			✓	
Hoon & Alto (92:62; 93:102, 111)	✓	✓	✓	✓	
Hasik (94:117)	✓	✓		✓	
Ras Janjali (95:121)	✓		✓	✓	

their influence and connections as far north as the Sharqiyah which was in part influenced or controlled by the Persians (Maka). The population of Maka in Achaemenid and Parthian times may have included ancestral MSA speakers referred to by Persians authorities as "Arabs." The trade in incense certainly existed in Iron Age times and, more specifically, we know that Persian influence by Parthian times even penetrated inland as far as Shisur. The Persian drive to obtain incense may have been motivated both by economic, ritual and religious reasons. As Herodotus suggested, Parthian kings used incense for coronation rites. In Zoroastrian fire use, frankincense was commonly utilized and, perhaps by Parthian times, came to be required. This might explain the "gift" of 1000 talents of incense given to the Achaemenids as reported by Herodotus. The buffer zone linking west-

Fig. 22: *Iron Age Ships Depicted in Dhofari Shelters*
(after Al-Shahri [1994])

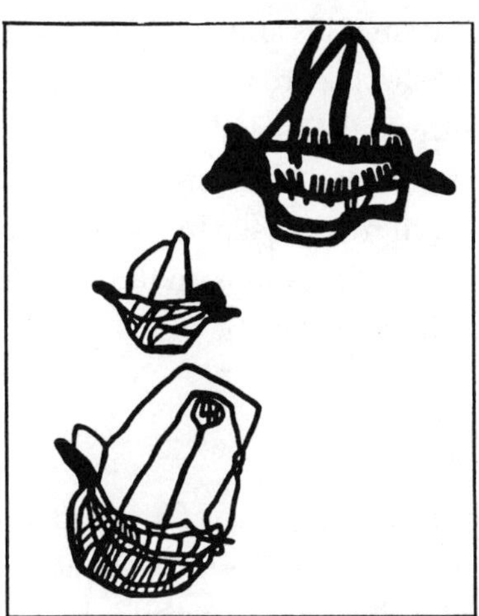

ern Arabia to Roman and South Arab influence was offset by Persian influence through Maka to Dhofar and the Gulf area. Thus, Parthian (Persian) influence mentioned in the account of the Periplus, probably in reality extended even west of Masirah island and, perhaps, substantially westward. Traditionally, while Achaemenids and Parthians were not considered seafarers (perhaps due to strict Zoroastrian practices), it appears that in concert with local MSA populations, the Persians had access to products along the coast as far as Socotra. Alternatively, land routes from Sanaw or Adam extended southward from Maka to Dhofar and penetrated as far as Shisur or beyond to other trade stations on the southern Rub al-Khali such as Sanaw, Muger, and Thamud (fig. 2).

Maka=Mag=Magoi?

Of final interest here is the relationship of Maka to incense, and the Magoi of the New Testament account.[146] Glaser suggested that Old Persian Maka was rendered in Greek by changing k to g and thus *mag*.[147] Therefore, the Persian Gulf, originally Kolpos Maka, became known as Kolpos Magon.[148] If Mag is Greek for Mak(a), and the land of Arabia was controlled or influenced by the Persians, Mag and the Greek plural of forming *magoi* could have meant "Arabs" coming from Oman in the Mathew account. Thus, a confusion may have originated between people of Maka (*macae/myci*) with "magush," Persian "priest," which later became irrevocably fused.[149] Chronologically, the correct time frame is also indicated, since Maka only becomes Parthian Mzw(n) at the time of Shapur I (241–72 C.E.).[150] Additionally, since frankincense and myrrh came from Dhofar, the connection

---

146 Mathew 2:1, 7, 11.

147 Glaser (1890) 215; Grohmann (1928) 615; Potts (1985) 85.

148 Eilers (1983) 107.

149 For the term "magi" meaning all Zoroastrians, see Potts (1990) 341.

150 Grohmann (1928) 615; Potts (1985) 88.

could be a logical one.[151] Justin Martyr in 160 C.E. asserted that the Magi came from Arabia. In this belief he was followed by Tertullian in 210 C.E. Others believed they came from Persia.[152] We would suggest that both points of view are correct. The "Arabs" (MSA speakers) obtained incense from Dhofar and passed via Maka, then under Persian control, on their way northward to the Levant, or proceeded directly westward from Dhofar.

Later sixth and seventh century traditions began to define the number, age, and names of the Magi. Growing crystallization of the account suggested that one came from Persia, one from Arabia and one from India.[153] From a Byzantine and later European Church tradition, relics, tombs, and even bodies became associated with the Magi. Again, a double tradition originated. One supported a Persian origin; another grew up around a western tradition that the relics of the Magi were taken from the Hadramaut in Yemen by the Byzantine emperor Zeno in 490 C.E.[154] Based on this interesting fact, it would appear that the tradition that the Magi came from MSA territory has as much validity as any.

---

151 For *gold* in the Mathew account being *golden frankincense*, see G. Ryckmans (1951), and a comment by Yamauchi (1990) 485 n. 108. Müller suggests that balsam was meant [ESA *bsm*, Arabic *basam*], (1995).

152 Justin Martyr, Dialogue with Trypho, sec. 78; Tertullian, Adversus Marcionem iii/13; see Evans (1972) 209; Brown (1993) 169; for other viewpoints, see the summaries in Duchesne-Guillemin (1965) and Yamauchi (1990) 485.

153 See a summary of the various accounts in Yamauchi (1990) 486.

154 Duchesne-Guillemin (1985) 157; *cf.* Yamauchi (1990) 491. For a history of Zeno(n), see Lippold (1894) 149-213. Salibi notes a legend that the tomb of the three Magi is to be found in south Yemen (1980) 46 note *. Shahid (1979) 83-84 notes that church legends state that the Magi returned to the Hadramaut after their visit to the baby Jesus and that their bones were removed from "the settlements of the Hadramis" by the fourth century C.E. More specifically, legend has it that one of the Magi came from the village of Azzan, in the vicinity of the classical South Arabic capital of the lower Hadramaut, see Doe (1971) 98. Mayfa'at is located within the frankincense zone and well within the western end of MSA territory. That legend attributes the recovery of the magi remains to Zeno in 490 C.E. is plausible in that Monophysite Christianity was strong in the area. For Christian remains from MSA territory, see the observations on Socotra, Naumkin and Sedov (1993) 615-18; Doe (1970) 45-46; Naumkin (1993) 29-34; from Qana, see Sedov (1992) 136-37. From Dhofar itself, the main fortress build-

Bibliography

Agatharchides of Cnidus. See Burstein (1989). **Albright, F. P.** (1982) *The American Archaeological Expedition in Dhofar, Oman. 1952-1953.* The American Foundation for the Study of Man. Vol. VI. Washington, D.C. **Balfour, I. B.** (1888) *Botany of Socotra.* Edinburgh. **Bar-Yosef, O. and A. Khazanov**, eds. (1992) *Pastoralism in the Levant.* Madison, Wisc. **Beeston, A. F. L.** (1938) The Philby Collection of Old South Arabian Inscriptions. *Le Museon* 51:234-39. (1976) The Settlement at Khor Rohri. *The Journal of Oman Studies* 2:39-42. **Beeston, A.F.L., M. Ghul, W. Müller, and J. Ryckmans** (1982) *Sabaic Dictionary.* Louvain. **Begley, V.** (1991) Introduction and Ceramic Evidence for Pre-Periplus Trade on the Indian Coasts. In Begley and De Puma 1991:3-7, 157-96. **Begley, V., and R. De Puma**, eds. (1991) *Rome and India, The Ancient Sea Trade.* Madison:3-7, 157-96. **Bent, J. T.** (1895) Exploration of the Frankincense Country, Southern Arabia. *The Geographical Journal* 6:109-34. **Bent, J. T., and M. Bent** (1900) *Southern Arabia.* London. **Bidez, J.** (1981) *Philostorgius Kirchengeschichte.* Berlin. **Biella, J.** (1982) *Dictionary of Old South Arabic.* Chico, Calif. **Bilkadi, Z.** (1986) The Wabar Meteorite. *Aramco World Magazine* 37/6:26-33. **Bivar, A., and J. Hinnels** (1985) *Papers in Honour of Mary Boyce.* Leiden. **Botting, D.** (1958) The Oxford University Expedition to Socotra. *The Geographical Journal* 124:200-9. **Boucherlat, R., and P. Gorczynski** (1985) First Survey at Hili 14. *Archaeology in the United Arab Emirates* 4:62-64. **Boucherlat, R., and J.-F. Salles**, eds. (1984) *Arabie Orientale, Mesopotamie et Iran Meridional de l'Age du Fer au Debut de la Periode Islamique.* Paris. **Boyce, M.** (1977) *A Persian Stronghold of Zoroastrianism.* Oxford. **Breton, J.-F.** (1990) Ancient Shabwa, The Capital of the Hadramawt. In Daum 1990:111-15. **Briant, P.** (1982) *Etat et pasteurs au Moyen-Orient ancien.* Cambridge. **Brown, R. E.** (1993) *The Birth of the Messiah.* New York. **Burstein, S. M.** (1989) *Agatharchides of Cnidus on the Erythraean Sea.* London. **Casson, L.** (1989) *The Periplus Maris Erythraei.* Princeton. (1991) Ancient Naval Technology and the Route to India. In Begley and De Puma 1991:8-11. **Caton-Thompson, G.** (1944) *The Tombs and Moon Temple of Hureidha (Hadramaut).* Oxford. Caton-**Thompson, G., and E. W. Gardner** (1939) Climate, Irrigation, and Early Man in the Hadramaut. *The Geographical Journal* 93:18-38. **Chatty, D.** (1983) The Bedouin of Central Oman. *The Journal of Oman Studies* 6/1:149-62. (1990) Tradition and Change among the Pastoral Harasiis in Oman. In Salem-Murdock, *et al.* 1990:336-49. **Chepalyga, A.L., and K. K. Shilik** (1995) The Reconstruction of the Ancient Coast Line in the Vicinity of Qana. In Griaznevich and Sedov 1995:302-13. **Choksy, J. K.** (1989) *Purity and Pollution*

---

ing at Ain Humran yielded a clay Christian chalice in the 1993 excavations. (For the location of Christian churches built by Theophilus in the Dhofar region, see Shahid [1984] 87-89 and nn. 47, 57-59; for the Greek account of Philostorgius, see Bidez (1981) 33-34). These examples cited above are dated to the fourth century C.E. at the earliest.

in Zoroastrianism. Austin. **Clemens, S., W. Prell, D. Murray, G. Shimmield, and G. Weedon** (1991) Forcing Mechanisms of the Indian Ocean Monsoon. *Nature* 353: 720-25. **Cleuziou, S., M.-L. Inizan, and B. Marcolongo** (1992) Le Peuplement pre- et Protohistorique du Systeme Fluviatile Fossile du Jawf-Hadramawt au Yemen. *Paléorient* 18/2: 5-29. **Colledge, M.** (1967) *The Parthians.* New York. **Comfort, H.** (1960) Some Imported Pottery at Khor Rori (Dhofar). *Bulletin of the American Schools of Oriental Research* 160:15-20. **Cook, J. M.** (1985) Chapter 5. The Rise of the Achaemenids and Establishment of Their Empire. In Gershevitch 1985:200- 91. **Daum, W.**, ed. (1990) *Yemen 3000 Years of Art and Civilization in Arabia Felix.* Frankfurt/Main. **De Blois, F.** (1989) Maka and Mazun. *Studia Iranica* 18:157-67. **De Cardi, B., D. B. Doe, and S. P. Roskams** (1977) Excavation and Survey in the Sharqiyah, Oman, 1976. *The Journal of Oman Studies* 3/1:17-33. **De Gaury, G.** (1957) A Note on Masirah Island. *The Geographical Journal* 123:499-502. **Dilke, O.** (1987) The Culmination of Greek Cartography in Ptolemy and Cartography in the Byzantine Empire. In Harley and Woodward 1987:177-200, 258-75. **Doe, B.** (1970) *Socotra: An Archaeological Reconnaissance in 1967.* Miami, Fla. (1971) *Southern Arabia.* London. (1983) *Monuments of South Arabia.* Naples. **Donner, F.** (1993) *The History of al-Tabari.* vol. X. The Conquest of Arabia. The Riddah Wars. Albany, N.Y. **Dostal, W.** (1967) *Die Beduinen in Sudarabien.* Vienna. (1968) Zur Megalith Frage in Sudarabien. In *Festschrift Werner Caskel.* Leiden: 53-62. (1975) Two South Arabian Tribes: Al-Qara and al-Harasis. In Serjeant and Bidwell 1975:33-41. **Duchesne-Guillemin, J.** (1965) Die Drei Weisen aus dem Morgenlande. *Antaios*: 234-53. (1966) *Symbols and Values in Zoroastrianism.* New York. (1985) The Wise Men from the East in the Western Tradition. In Bivar and Hinnels 1985:149-57. **Eilers, W.** (1983) Das Volk der Maka vor und nach den Achameniden. In Koch and Mackenzie 1983:101-19. **Eph^cal, I.** (1982) *The Ancient Arabs. Nomads on the Border of the Fertile Crescent, Ninth-Fifth Centuries B.C.* Jerusalem. **Evans, E.** (1972) *Tertullian. Adversus Marcionem.* Oxford. **Finkbeiner, U.**, ed. (1993) *Materialen zur Archäologie der Seleukiden- und Partherzeit im Südlichen Babylonien und im Golf-Gebiet.* Tübingen. **Franke, H.**, ed. (1959) *Akten 24sten Internationalen Orientalischer Kongress, Munchen.* [Sektion V: Semitisk]. Wiesbaden. **Frye, R.** (1984) *The History of Ancient Iran.* Munich. **Gershevitch, I.**, ed. (1985) *The Cambridge History of Iran.* vol. 2. *The Median and Achaemenian Periods.* Cambridge. **Ghazanfar, S. A.** (1991) Floristic Composition and the Analysis of Vegetation of the Sultanate of Oman. *Flora et Vegetatio Mundi* 9:215-27. (1992) Quantitative and Biogeographic Analysis of the Flora of Oman. *Global Ecology and Biogeography Letters* 2: 189-95. **Glanzman, W. D.** (1987) Ceramics. In Glanzman and Ghaleb 1987:67-126. **Glanzman, W. D., and A. Ghaleb**, eds. (1987) *The Stratigraphic Probe at Hajar ar-Rayhani.* The Wadi al Jubah Archaeological Project, Vol. 3. Washington D.C. **Glaser, E.** (1890) *Skizze der Geschichte und Geographie Arabiens.* 2 Vols. Berlin. **Godley, A. D.** (1938) *Herodotus* Books III-IV. Cambridge. **Goetz, H.** (1963) An Indian Bronze From South Arabia. *Archaeology* 16/3:187-89. **Graf, D. F.** (1990) Arabia During Achaemenid Times. In Sancisi-Weerdenburg and Kuhrt 1990:131-48. **Grene, D.** (1987) *Herodotus. The History.* Chicago. **Griaznevich, P., and A. Sedov**, eds. (1995) *Hadramawt. Preliminary Reports of the Soviet-Yemeni Joint*

Complex Expedition, Vol. 1. Moscow. **Grohmann, A.** (1928) Makai. In Wissova 1928: 614-15. **Groom, N.** (1981) *Frankincense and Myrrh.* London. (1994) Oman and the Emirates in Ptolemy's Map. *Arabian Archaeology and Epigraphy* 5:198-214. **Guest, R.** (1937) Zufar in the Middle Ages. *Islamic Culture, The Hyderabad Quarterly Review* n.v.:402-10. **Haerinck, E.** (1992) Excavations at ed-Dur (Umm al-Qaiwain, U.A.E.) Preliminary Report on the Fourth Belgian Season (1990). *Arabian Archaeology and Epigraphy* 3:190-208. **Haerinck, E., C. Metdepenninghen, and K. G. Stevens** (1991) Excavations at ed-Dur (Umm al-Qaiwain, U.A.E.) — Preliminary Report on the Second Belgian Season (1988). *Arabian Archaeology and Epigraphy* 2/1:31-60. (1992) Excavations at ed-Dur (Umm al-Qaiwain, U.A.E.) — Preliminary Report on the Third Belgian Season (1989). *Arabian Archaeology and Epigraphy* 3/1:44-60. **Haines, S. B.** (1845) Memoir of the South and East Coasts of Arabia. *Royal Geographical Society Journal* 15:104-60. **Hallock, R. T.** (1969) *Persepolis Fortification Tablets.* Oriental Institute Publication 92. Chicago. (1978) Selected Fortification Texts. *Cahiers de la Delegation Archeologique Francaise en Iran* 8:109-36. **Hansman, J.** (1973) A Periplus of Magan and Meluhha. *Bulletin of the Schools of Oriental and African Studies* 36:554-87. **Harley, J., and D. Woodward**, eds. (1987) *The History of Cartography. Vol. 1. Cartography in Prehistoric, Ancient, and Medieval Europe and the Mediterranean.* Chicago. **Hay, R.** (1947) The Kuria Muria Islands. *The Geographical Journal* 109:279-81. **Hepper, F. N.** (1969) Arabian and African Frankincense Trees. *Journal of Egyptian Archaeology* 55:66-72. Herodotus See Godley 1938; Grene 1987. **Herzfeld, E.** (1968) *The Persian Empire. Studies in Geography and Ethnography in the Ancient Near East.* Wiesbaden. **al-Hubaishi, A., and K. Müller-Hohenstein** (1984) *An Introduction to the Vegetation of Yemen.* Eschborn. **Ingrams, W. H.** (1936) Hadhramaut: A Journey to the Sei'ar Country and through the Wadi Maseila. *The Geographical Journal* 88:524-51. **Jamme, A.** (1963) *The Al-Uqlah Texts.* Documentation Sud-Arabe III. Washington D.C. **Janzen, J.** (1986) *Nomads in the Sultanate of Oman: Tradition and Development in Dhofar.* Boulder, Co. **Jarrige, C.**, ed. (1992) *South Asian Archaeology 1989.* Madison, Wisc. **Johnstone, T. M.** (1975a) Folklore and Folk Literature in Oman and Socotra. In Serjeant and Bidwell 1975:7-23. (1975b) *The Modern South Arabian Languages.* Malibu, Calif. (1987) *The Mehri Lexicon.* London. **Jones, H. L.** (1930) *The Geography of Strabo.* London. **Kervran, M.** (1984) A La Recherche de Suhar: Etat de la Question. In Boucherlat and Salles 1984:285-98. (1993) Qalat Bahrain. In Finkbeiner 1993:65-78. **Kervran, M., and F. Hiebert** (1991) Sohar Pre-Islamique, Note Stratigraphique. In Schippmann 1991:337-48. **Kiepert, H.** (1892) *Atlas Antiquus.* Berlin. **King, G.** (1991) Cave Talk. *Petroleum Development Oman News* 3:18-20. **Koch, H., and D. Mackenzie**, eds. (1983) Kunst, Kultur...und ihr Fortleben. *Archäologische Mitteilungen aus Iran (N.F.)* 10. **Leslau, W.** (1946) *Modern South Arabic Languages. A Bibliography.* New York. **Lewis, D. M.** (1990) The Persepolis Fortification Texts. In Sancisi-Weerdenburg and Kuhrt 1990:1-6. **Lippold, A.** (1894) Zenon (Kaiser). In Wissowa 1894:149-213. **Lonnet, A.** (1985) The Modern South Arabian Languages in the P.D.R. of Yemen. *Proceedings of the Seminar for Arabian Studies* 15: 49-55. **Lorimer, J. G.** (1908–) *Gazetteer of the Persian Gulf, Oman, and Central Arabia.* 1915, Vol. IIb. Geographical and Statistical. Calcutta. **Martinez,**

N. (1997) Succulents of Dhofar, the Land of Frankincense. *Cactus and Succulent Journal* 69:132-38. Mathew, St. See May and Metzger 1973. **Mathews, C. D.** (1959) Non-Arabic Place Names in Central South Arabia. In Franke 1959: 259-62. **May, H. G., and B. Metzger**, eds. (1973) *The New Oxford Annotated Bible with the Apocrypha.* New York. **McClure, H. A.** (1978) 2.6 Ar Rub al-Khali. In al-Sayari and Zotl 1978:252-63. (1984) Late Quaternary Palaeoenvironments of the Rub al Khali. Ph.D. dissertation. London. (1988) Late Quaternary Palaeogeography and Landscape Evolution of the Rub al Khali. In Potts 1988:9-13. **Miles, S. B.** (1919) *The Countries and Tribes of the Persian Gulf.* London. **Miller, A. G., and M. Morris** (1988) *The Plants of Dhofar.* Muscat. **Modi, J. J.** (1922) *The Religious Ceremonies and the Customs of the Parsees.* Bombay. **Monod, T.** (1979) Les arbres a encens [*Boswellia sacra* Fluckinger 1867] dans le Hadramaout (Yemen du Sud). *Bulletin de L'Museum Nationale de Histoire Naturelle, Paris.* 4ème serie. Section B/3:131-69. **Morris, M.** (1995) The Harvesting of Frankincense in Dhofar. Paper presented at the Conference *Profumi d'Arabia* 20 October, 1995. Pisa. **Mukarousky, H. G.**, ed. (1991) *Proceedings of the Fifth International Hamito-Semitic Congress, Band 2.* Vienna. **Müller, W.** (1976) Notes on the Use of Frankincense in South Arabia. *Proceedings of the Seminar for Arabian Studies* 6:124-36. (1977) Die Inschriften Khor Rori 1 bis 4. In von Wissmann 1977:53-56. (1991) Mahra. *The Encyclopedia of Islam.* Vol. 6:80-84. (1995) Names of Aromata in Ancient South Arabia. Paper presented at the Conference *Profumi d'Arabia* 20 October 1995. Pisa. **Naumkin, V. V.** (1988) *Sokotriitsy. Istoriko-Etnografichiskii Ocherk.* Moscow. (1993) Island of the Phoenix. Reading, UK. **Naumkin, V., and A. Sedov** (1993) Monuments of Socotra. *Topoi* 3/2:569-623. **Orton, N. P.** (1991) Red Polished Ware in Gujarat: A Catalogue of Twelve Sites. In Begley and De Puma 1991:46-81. **Owen, J.** (1995) Evidence for Maritime Trade in the Northern Indian Ocean. Paper presented at the Conference *Profumi d'Arabia* 20 October 1995. Pisa. Periplus Maris Erythraei. See Casson 1989; Schoff 1912. **Peyton, W. D.** (1983) *Old Oman. A Photographic Record.* London. **Philby, H. St. J.** (1933) *The Empty Quarter.* London. **Piesinger, C. M.** (1983) Legacy of Dilmun: The Roots of Ancient Maritime Trade in Eastern Coastal Arabia in the Fourth/Third Millennium B.C. Ph.D. dissertation. Madison, Wisc. **Pirenne, J.** (1975) The Incense Port of Moscha (Khor Rori) in Dhofar. *The Journal of Oman Studies* 1:81-96. (1981) Deux prospections historiques au Sud-Yemen. *Raydan* 4:235. Pliny the Elder See Rackham 1942. **Potts, D. T.** (1984) Northeastern Arabia in the Later Pre-Islamic Era. In Boucherlat and Salles 1984:85-144. (1985) From Qade to Mazun: Four Notes on Oman, c. 700 BC to 700 AD. *The Journal of Oman Studies* 8:81-95. (1988a) Transarabian Routes of the Pre-Islamic Period. In Salles 1988:127-62. (1988b) *Araby the Blest.* Copenhagen. (1990) *The Arabian Gulf in Antiquity.* 2 Vols. Oxford. Ptolemy, Claudius. See Stevenson 1932. **Rackham, H.** (1942) Pliny. *Natural History.* Cambridge. **Radcliffe-Smith, A.** (1980) The Vegetation of Dhofar. *The Journal of Oman Studies. Special Report* No. 2:59-86. **Rahimi, D.** (1987) Lithics. In Glanzman and Ghaleb 1987:139-43. **Roaf, M.** (1974) The Subject Peoples on the Base of the Statue of Darius. *Cahiers de la Delegation Archeologique Francaise en Iran* 4:73-159. **Roberts, P.** (1995) *In Search of the Birth of Jesus.* New York. **Ryckmans, G.** (1951) De L'Or(?), De

L'Encens et de la Myrrhe. *Revue Biblique* 58: 372-76. **Sale, J. B.** (1980) The Environment of the Mountain Region of Dhofar and the Ecology of the Mountain Region of Dhofar. *The Journal of Oman Studies, Special Report* No. 2:17-54. **Salibi, K.** (1980) *A History of Arabia.* Delmar, N.Y. **Salem-Murdock, M., M. Horowitz, and M. Sella**, eds. (1990) *Anthropology and Development in North Africa and the Middle East.* Boulder. **Salles, J.-F.** (1988) Ed., *L'Arabie et Ses Mers Bordieres.* Paris. (1990) Les Achemenides dans le Golfe Arabo-Persique. In Sancisi-Weerdenburg and Kuhrt 1990:111-30. **Sancisi-Weerdenburg, H., and A. Kuhrt**, eds. (1990) *Achaemenid History* IV. *Centre and Periphery.* Leiden. al-**Sayari, S., and J. Zotl**, eds. (1978) *Quaternary Period in Saudi Arabia.* Vienna. **Schippmann, K., A. Herling, and J.-F. Salles**, eds. (1991) *Internationale Archaologie 6. Golf-Archaologie.* Buch am Erlbach. **Schoff, W.** (1912) *The Periplus of the Erythraean Sea.* London. **Sedov, A. V.** (1988) Arkheologicheski Pamyatniki. In Naumkin 1988:72-94. (1992) New Archaeological and Epigraphical Material from Qana (South Arabia). *Arabian Archaeology and Epigraphy* 3/2:110-37. (1995) Bi'r Hamad: A Pre-Islamic Settlement in the Western Wadi Hadramawt. *Arabian Archaeology and Epigraphy* 6:103-15. **Sedov, A. V., and O. Aydrus** (1995) The Coinage of Ancient Hadramawt, The Pre-Islamic Coins in the Al-Mukalla Museum, *Arabian Archaeology and Epigraphy* 6:15-60. **Serjeant, R. B., and R. Bidwell**, eds. (1975) *Arabian Studies* II. London. **Shahid, I.** (1979) Byzantium in South Arabia. *Dumbarton Oaks Papers* 33:23-94. (1984) *Byzantium and the Arabs in the Fourth Century.* Washington D.C. **al-Shahri, A. A. M.** (1991) Recent Epigraphical Discoveries in Dhofar. *Proceedings of the Seminar for Arabian Studies* 21:173-91. (1991a) Grave Types and Triliths in Dhofar. *Arabian Archaeology and Epigraphy* 2:182-95. (1994) *Origins and Development of Civilization in the Arabian Peninsula. Dhofar: Ancient Texts and Scripts.* Dubai. **al-Shanfari, A. A. B.** (1987) The Archaeology of Masirah Island, Sultanate of Oman. Ph.D. dissertation. Naples. **Simeone-Senelle, M.-C.** (1991) Recents Developpements des Recherches sur les Langues Sudarabiques Modernes. In Mukarousky 1991:321-37. **Sprenger, A.** (1865) *Die Post- und Reiserouten des Orients.* Leipzig. (1875) *Die Alte Geographie Arabiens.* Bern. **Stevenson, E. L.** (1932) *Geography of Claudius Ptolemy.* New York. Strabo See Jones 1930. **Takhtajan, A. L.** (1986) *Floristic Regions of the World.* Berkeley. Tertullian See Evans 1972. **Thesiger, W.** (1946) A New Journey in Southern Arabia. *The Geographical Journal* 108: 129-45. (1984) *Arabian Sands.* [original 1948]. London. **Thomas, B.** (1929) Among Some Unknown Tribes of South Arabia. *Journal of the Royal Anthropological Institute* 59:97-111. (1932) *Arabia Felix. Across the Empty Quarter of Arabia.* New York. (1937) Four Strange Tongues from Central South Arabia — The Hadara Group. *Proceedings of the British Academy* 23:231-329. **Thulin, M., and A. Warfa** (1987) The Frankincense Trees (Boswellia spp.) in North Somalia and South Arabia. *Kew Bulletin* 42:487-500. **Tkatch, J.** (1897) Iobaritae. In Wissowa 1897:1831-37. (1913) Zafar and Wabar. *Encyclopedia of Islam.* First Edition. Leiden:1187-90, 1073-74. (1936) Mahra. *Encyclopedia of Islam.* First Edition. Leiden:138-44. **Trimingham, J. S.** (1979) *Christianity among the Arabs in Pre-Islamic Times.* London. **Vallat, F.** (1993) *Les Noms Geographiques des Sources Suso-Elamites.* Repertoire Geographique des Textes Cuneiformes, Band 11. Wiesbaden. **Van Beek, G.** (1958) Frankincense and Myrrh in Ancient South Arabia. *Journal of the American Oriental Society* 78:141-52. (1960) Frankincense and Myrrh. *Biblical Archaeologist* 23:70-95. (1969) *Hajar Bin Humeid.* Baltimore. Vinogradov, J. A., and M. Bamakhrama (1995) A Comparative Study of Pottery from Building VI and Area I, The Raybun I Settlement. In *Hadramawt, Archaeological Ethnological and Historical Studies.* Moscow:103-11. **Vogelsang, W.** (1990) The Achaemenids and India. In H. Sancisi-Weerdenburg and Kuhrt 1990:93-110. **Vosmer, T.** (1994) Traditional Boats of Oman, Links Past and Present. *Proceedings of the Conference on Techno-Archaeological Perspectives on Shipbuilding in the Indian Ocean.* Delhi. **Vosmer, T., R. Margariti, A. Tilley, and I. Godfrey** (1993) *The Omani Dhow Research Project, Final Report Field Work 1992.* Western Australian Maritime Museum Report No. 69. Fremantle. **von Wissmann, H.** (1977) *Das Weihrauchland Sa'kalan, Samarum und Moscha.* Vienna. **von Wissman, H., and M. Hofner** (1952) *Beitrage zur historischen Geographie des vorislamischen Südarabien.* Akademie der Wissenschaften und der Literatur. Abhandlungen der Geistes- und Sozialwissenschaftlichen Klasse Jahrgang 1952 Nr. 4. Wiesbaden. **Wellsted, R. J.** (*1840) *Travels to the City of the Caliphs.* London. **Whitcomb, D.** (1988) *Aqaba, Port of Palestine on the China Sea.* Amman. **Whitehouse, D.** (1991) Epilogue: Roman Trade in Perspective. In Begley and De Puma 1991:216-18. **Wilkinson, J. C.** (1977) *Water and Tribal Settlement in South-East Arabia. A Study of the Aflaj of Oman.* Oxford. (1987) *The Imamate Tradition of Oman.* Cambridge. **Wissova, G.**, ed. (1928) *Pauly's Realencyclopedie der classischen Altertumswissenschaft.* Stuttgart. **Yamauchi, E. M.** (1990) *Persia and the Bible.* Grand Rapids, Mich. **Yule, P.** (1993) Toward a Chronology of the Late Iron Age in the Sultanate of Oman. In Finkbeiner 1993: 251-76. **Yule, P., and M. Kervran** (1993) More Than Samad in Oman: Iron Age Pottery from Suhar and Khor Rohri. *Arabian Archaeology and Epigraphy.* 4/2:69-106. **Yule, P., and G. Weisgerber** (1988) *Samad ash-Shan. Preliminary Report 1988.* Bochum. **Zarins, J.** (1992a) The Early Utilization of Indigo along the Northern Indian Ocean Rim. In Jarrige 1992:469-83. (1992b) Pastoral Nomadism in Arabia: Ethnoarchaeology and the Archaeological Record — A Case Study. In Bar-Yosef and Khazanov 1992:219-40. **Zarins, J., M. Ibrahim, D. Potts, and C. Edens** (1979) Saudi Arabian Archaeological Reconnaissance 1978, The Preliminary Report on the Third Phase of the Comprehensive Archaeological Survey Program — The Central Province. *Atlal* 3:9-42. **Zarins, J., A. Kabawi, and A. Murad** (1983) Preliminary Report on the Najran/Ukhdud Survey and Excavations (1402/1982). *Atlal* 7:22-40. **Zohar, M.** (1992) Pastoralism and the Spread of the Semitic Languages. In Bar-Yosef and Khazanov 1992:165-80. **Zohary, D.** (1973) *Geobotanical Foundations of the Near East.* Stuttgart.